THE TECHNIQUE

OF FEMINIST

PSYCHOANALYTIC

PSYCHOTHERAPY

THE TECHNIQUE
OF FEMINIST
PSYCHOANALYTIC
PSYCHOTHERAPY

CHARLOTTE KRAUSE PROZAN

JASON ARONSON INC.
Northvale, New Jersey
London

Production Editor: Judith D. Cohen

This book was set in 10 point Garamond by Lind Graphics of Upper Saddle River, New Jersey, and printed and bound by Haddon Craftsmen of Scranton, Pennsylvania.

Library of Congress Cataloging-in-Publication Data

Prozan, Charlotte Krause.
  The technique of feminist psychoanalytic psychotherapy / Charlotte
Krause Prozan.
    p. cm.
  Includes bibliographical references and index.
  ISBN 0-87668-268-9
  1. Women and psychoanalysis. 2. Feminist therapy.   I. Title.
  [DNLM: 1. Psychoanalytic Interpretation. 2. Psychoanalytic
Therapy. 3. Women—psychology. WM 460.5.W6 P969t 1993]
RC451.4.W6P738   1993
616.89'17'082—dc20
DNLM/DLC
for Library of Congress   93-20278

Manufactured in the United States of America. Jason Aronson Inc. offers books and cassettes. For information and catalog write to Jason Aronson Inc., 230 Livingston Street, Northvale, New Jersey 07647.

To all my Patients

CONTENTS

ACKNOWLEDGMENT

The support, encouragement, and enthusiasm of my family and friends have been very important to me in undertaking and completing this project. My children, Jeff Krause and Karen Krause Andresen, my son-in-law, Eric Andresen, and my husband, Guy Smyth, have all stood by me with their interest, patience, faith in my ability, and a recognition of the importance of the task.

Over the past twenty-three years, friends and colleagues too numerous to mention have given me articles on this subject, knowing of my interest. My files were full of these papers when I began this project. My appreciation goes to all of you who contributed to this library of resources.

Friends have read several chapters and made helpful suggestions: Gloria Gold, Chapter 4; Diane Le Roi, Chapter 5; Sandra Butler, Chapter 7; and Joan Dunkel, Chapter 8.

The enthusiasm and helpfulness of my publisher, Jason Aronson, and my editors, Anne Patota and Judy Cohen, are much appreciated. It was their idea to have me write these books, and I am grateful for their trusting me with such an important responsibility. I was surprised when they proposed the idea of a book on feminist psychoanalytic psychotherapy and am pleased that they appreciate the results.

INTRODUCTION

I myself have never been able to find out precisely what feminism is. I only know that people call me a feminist when I express sentiments that differentiate me from a doormat or a prostitute.

—Dame Rebecca West

The Equal Rights Amendment encourages women to leave their husbands, kill their children, practice witchcraft, destroy capitalism and become lesbians.

—Reverend Pat Robertson
Republican Presidential Candidate

In my first book, *Feminist Psychoanalytic Psychotherapy,* I reviewed the literature and some research on the psychology of women and presented my views on the best of psychoanalytic and feminist theory that can be used in psychotherapy and psychoanalysis with women today. I described the multiple influences on the writings of Sigmund Freud and Helene Deutsch from their personal lives as well as the religious, political, cultural, and medical attitudes toward women that I believe affected their ability to be objective about female psychology. It was more than just Victorian attitudes that created the errors of the early analysts.

I then reviewed the early feminist writers, starting with Betty Friedan in 1963, and described the consciousness-raising groups that emerged across the country in the early seventies. Modern psychoanalysts such as Karen Horney, Melanie Klein, and Ethel Person, and the collections of Jean Baker-Miller, Jean Strouse, Janine Chasseguet-Smirgel, and Harold Blum were discussed; next, the work of the psychoanalytic feminists Dorothy Dinnerstein, Jean Baker-Miller, Nancy Chodorow, Carol Gilligan, Jessica Benjamin, Theresa Bernardez, and others was described and analyzed. I offered a critique of some of the published work with women patients by several psychoanalysts and then proposed an integration of feminist and psychoanalytic values.

A review of the research on the female orgasm and female homosexuality was presented, and both psychoanalytic and feminist theories were found to be inadequate when viewed alone.

My thesis throughout the book was that the times call for an integration of the best of both psychoanalytic and feminist theory in order that today's analysts and therapists can offer the best possible help to our patients. I concluded that both win when they learn from each other, and both lose if they ignore, reject, or discredit each other. I looked at both theories with a critical eye to see what was valuable in each, what needs to be rejected from each, and what needs further research and debate.

In this book, I will focus on clinical examples to illustrate the kinds of questions I ask and interpretations I make when working with women incorporating a feminist analysis to achieve an integration of feminist and psychoanalytic theory. The basic techniques of the analytic method are well established: the absence of personal revelations on the part of the analyst; the time, fee, and place; the structure of the treatment setting; confidentiality; neutrality; dream interpretation; free association; analysis of the transference; and attention to the countertransference. In my approach, these do not change. I employ these time-honored methods in my work and bring feminist values and theory to my diagnosis and treatment of the problems. Beginning therapists may be well read but need much help in supervision to know what to say. In incorporating a feminist analysis into treatment, even experienced therapists may need help in what to say and what not to say.

A feminist approach still requires differential diagnosis, a weakness in much feminist writing. Such a diagnosis is just as basic to feminist psychotherapy as it is to traditional psychoanalysis and psychotherapy. Not all patients are alike, and not all women patients are alike. Some patients may need help in letting down barriers and making a connection to the therapist, whereas others need help in constructing ego boundaries and not merging with the therapist. Some need help in recognizing anger and expressing it, whereas others are filled with undifferentiated rage and need help in clarifying, understanding, and controlling anger so that it can become a constructive tool rather than a destructive "crazy" identity.

Some need help to learn to cry, and some need help to stop crying and make changes.

Clinical experience is not research, and so it cannot prove or disprove any theory. What it can do is provide a depth and richness of detail from individual accounts that research never can. In this way it can illustrate theory, help to confirm and build theory, and make theory more meaningful to professionals and nonprofessionals alike. These are the goals of this book.

The importance of confidentiality poses certain problems when using extensive clinical examples. Each patient is disguised so as not to be identifiable, while maintaining enough accuracy to make the example meaningful. In certain cases, where there is the possibility that a patient may recognize herself, permission has been obtained for use of the material. I am grateful to all my patients for their intelligence, hard work, and dedication to their own growth. It is they who have constantly inspired me to keep working to understand their conflicts and desires, their suffering and their hopes. There have been many discouraging times, and it has been their courage to keep trying in spite of the often painful effort involved that has impressed me repeatedly and given me strength. Their progress and change has brought me much pleasure and gratification. Even small victories can bring rejoicing.

It is my hope that their efforts and mine these past thirty years can, through this book, stimulate and encourage psychotherapists who read these pages, and thereby bring help and hope to the many women who turn to psychotherapy in times of psychic need.

1

THE MOTHER–DAUGHTER RELATIONSHIP: DIFFERENTIATING FROM MOTHER YET STAYING CONNECTED

A mother is only brought unlimited satisfaction by her relation to a son; this is altogether the most perfect, the most free from ambivalence of all human relationships.

—Sigmund Freud

Mothers and daughters share a gender identity, a social role, and social expectations. They are both second-class citizens within a patriarchal culture and the family.

—Luise Eichenbaum and Susie Orbach

Freud recognized the ambivalence in all human relationships. I believe that the most ambivalent relationship is that between mothers and daughters. The splitting of good and bad qualities of mothers can be easily recognized in the many tales that children love to hear and adults choose to read, in which there is a wicked witch or wicked stepmother, and a good fairy or fairy godmother. A close second in ambivalent ties may be that between husbands and wives, but upon closer examination it is common to find that this ambivalence is rooted in the ambivalence felt by each partner toward his or her mother. Feminists have explored the mother–daughter relationship from both perspectives, how mothers feel about their daughters and how daughters feel about their mothers. Greenspan (1984) writes about the enduring hostility between mothers and daughters that she considers characteristic of our times:

Women learn through their mothers how to be the kind of female persons that the society needs: persons skilled in what (Jean Baker) Miller calls "subservient affiliation." It is almost uncanny how many times I have heard women utter virtually the same sentence: "I'm afraid of being like my mother." Alternatively, one hears heated denunciations such as "I hope I'm never like my mother," or "Thank God, I'm not like my mother." Apart from the vivid and heart rending display of the misogyny women have inherited from the culture—the conviction that the worst, craziest, stupidest or most evil lot that could befall a woman is to be like mom—these statements reveal a profound bond of identification that exists between mothers and daughters. More often than not, this bond is characterized by an apparently endless hostility—a phenomenon which psychologists dub "hostile dependence." [p. 107]

Freud's psychology has been father centered. Roy Schafer (1977) states:

That Freud was not prepared to think about mothers very far is . . . evident from how little he said directly about them and about relationships with them, and, correspondingly, how little he said about how they appear in the transference, the resistance, and the formation of the ego and superego systems. Additionally, in his writings he showed virtually no sustained interest in their subjective experience—except for their negative feelings about their own femininity and worth. [p. 357]

Blum (1977) agrees: "The mother is in relative eclipse in Freud's great case histories" (p. 184).

What Freud (1914) did observe about women as mothers was: "In the child which they bear, a part of their own body confronts them like an object to which, starting out from their narcissism, they can then give complete object love" (pp. 89–90).

MOTHERHOOD—HELENE DEUTSCH

Helene Deutsch has explored motherhood thoroughly. Volume 2 of her book *The Psychology of Women* (1945) is entirely on motherhood, including chapters on unmarried mothers, adoptive mothers, and stepmothers. She writes of motherhood in general and makes some observations about mothers and daughters, but most of her attention goes to the relationship between mothers and sons, such as her description of Tolstoy's Anna Karenina. About motherhood she does have some positive things to say. "In motherhood woman is given the wonderful opportunity of directly experiencing this sense of immortality" (p. 1). Deutsch distinguishes between *motherhood,*

> the relationship of the mother to her child as a sociologic, physiologic and emotional whole. This relationship begins with the conception of the child and extends throughout the further physiologic processes of pregnancy, birth, feeding and care. All these functions are accompanied by emotional reactions that are to some extent typical of or common to the species but for the most part vary individually, for they are inseparably connected, in each woman, with the total personality. The intensity of these reactions, and the new obligations and emotional relationships, mobilize fears and displace the existing boundaries both in the individual psyche and in its relations to the environment. [p. 17]

and *motherliness,*

> (1) a definite quality of character that stamps the woman's whole personality; (2) emotional phenomena that seem to be related to the child's helplessness and need for care. . . . I have defined as characteristic of the feminine woman a harmonious interplay between narcissistic tendencies and masochistic readiness for painful giving and loving. In the motherly woman, the narcissistic wish to be loved, so typical of the feminine woman, is metamorphosed; it is transferred from the ego to the child or his substitute. . . . despite this altruistic transformation the narcissistic elements are preserved. For instance, the mother's love for the child is often associated with the fact that she considers herself absolutely and exclusively indispensable to him. In the strongly narcissistic woman, the intensity of maternal love decreases when her children outgrow their need of her. [pp. 17–18]

In my first book, I said that Deutsch saw a woman's life as filled with conflicts, losses, and pain. She sees motherliness in conflict with sexuality. She states that the chief characteristic of maternal love is tenderness.

> All the aggression and sexual sensuality in the woman's personality are suppressed and diverted by this central emotional expression of motherliness. . . . [A]s for the sexual ingredient, there is sufficient room for it in the physical contact with the child, in caresses, and in many actions connected with care of him. [p. 19]

Yet only a few pages further she goes on to write:

> Sexuality and motherliness are sometimes in close harmony, yet at other times they appear completely separate. . . . There are women

who are both unerotic and unmotherly, and others who combine
extraordinary erotic intensity with the warmest motherliness. The split
between sexuality and motherliness can assume innumerable forms. [p.
24]

Deutsch sees motherliness and eroticism as the two aspects of femininity
and believes narcissism protects a woman from the masochism of motherhood. Yet again, in seeming contradiction, she states: "Erotic women,
perhaps even those who have certain qualities of the prostitute, often bring
more warmth into their maternal feelings than ascetic women; masculine
components may supply a useful addition to maternal activity" (p. 331).
Clearly the strong focus of Freud on female sexuality protects Deutsch's
view of femininity from excluding eroticism, as in the Victorian view of
femininity. Yet Deutsch still focuses on the tragic in women's lives by
defining the "tragedy of motherhood" as the mastery of the painful cutting
of the psychic umbilical cord that ties the mother to the child, in order to
allow the child to develop into a free adult by breaking the intimate relation
to the mother. This view has some truth, but the truth extends to fathers as
well, and grandchildren are often a joyful compensation for both parents,
as well as a replacement gift from the emancipated child to the parents.

Deutsch recognizes a difference in the separation process between
mother and daughter and between mother and son. The fear of incest and
of making her son passive and feminine forces the mother to let go of her
son, but she is not so aware or fearful of homosexual components, and so
"her attempts to seduce and tie the daughter are much more active, free,
and direct" (p. 307). In addition, identification with the mother is necessary for the daughter. When the daughter does gradually seek independence, hostility develops during puberty, strengthened by rivalry for the
father's love. There is often a compulsive repetition of the mother's own
unmastered tie to her mother. The ambivalence can create a very strong tie
as the mother tries to avoid the separation trauma by being overprotective,
and the daughter, owing to her long established intimacy and identification
with her mother, fails to pull away. She cites several examples of mothers
who slept in their daughters' beds until the daughters married.

Blum (1977) disputes Deutsch's view of motherhood as masochistic.

Motherhood need not represent masochistic renunciation, but loving
perseverance and the fostering of development in the service of the
maternal ego ideal. Commitment to children, despite frustration or
deprivation, is not equivalent to masochism or self-punishment. Maternal devotion should not be confused with masochistic enslavement
or preservation of the object from aggression. Masochism may actually
interfere with feminine empathy and predispose toward malformations

and pathogenic mother–child conflicts. . . . Maternal self-sacrifice out of consideration and care for the child is not masochism. . . . Mature mothering requires remarkable sublimation. . . . It is impossible to derive maternal devotion and empathy from masochism, narcissism and penis envy. [pp. 183–184]

MOTHERHOOD—FEMINIST VIEWS

Ironically, there are "radical feminists" who reject motherhood owing to the very confusion and misunderstanding that Blum so clearly describes. In a collection entitled *Mothering: Essays in Feminist Theory* (1983), Jeffner Allen describes motherhood as "the annihilation of women." She believes that feminists should reject motherhood on the grounds that it is dangerous to women. "Motherhood is dangerous to women because it continues the structure within which females must be women and mothers and, conversely, because it denies to females the creation of a subjectivity and world that is open and free" (p. 315). She believes that men impose motherhood on women and that women must "evacuate" themselves from all forms of motherhood. This is similar to the views of Shulamith Firestone (1970), who believes that women's biological role of childbearing is the source of all women's oppression. Firestone promotes the idea that the total sexual liberation of women requires freedom from their reproductive role, as motherhood and sexuality are incompatible.

"The Fantasy of the Perfect Mother"—Nancy Chodorow and Susan Contratto

In a 1976 essay, "The Fantasy of the Perfect Mother," Chodorow and Contratto give an excellent review of the feminist literature on motherhood and see four major themes:

1. blaming and idealizing the mother, assuming that mothers are or can be all-powerful and perfect and that mothering either destroys the world or generates world perfection;

2. extreme expectations of maternal sexuality, asserting the incompatibility of motherhood and sexuality or romanticizing maternal sexuality;

3. a link between motherhood and aggression or death;

4. an emphasis on the isolation of mother and child.

All these themes share common characteristics: their continuity with dominant cultural understandings of mothering and their rootedness in unprocessed, infantile fantasies about mothers. [1989, p. 88]

In Category 1 they place Nancy Friday, author of the popular *My Mother, My Self* (1977), who blames mothers for all their daughters' failings and unhappiness. Friday believes that mothers constrain and control their daughters intentionally to keep them from separating and from becoming sexually involved with men. Mothers deny sexuality to their daughters as it was denied to them in the process of motherhood. "(Friday) speaks to the daughter in all women and tells them that their problems are not political, social, personal, or, heaven forbid, caused by men; their problems are caused solely by their mothers" (p. 92).

Friday and Firestone both, in my view, take the reactionary position that women must choose between motherhood and sexuality, an error also made by Deutsch, but Deutsch was in fact less absolute about this. It reminds one of the outmoded dilemma that confronted so many women in previous generations, that of having to choose between family and career, a choice that forced many women into taking only half of what they really wanted from life and left them feeling deprived and incomplete.

Judith Arcana (1979) proposes a similar thesis to that of Friday but blames patriarchy for such evil maternal behavior. Dinnerstein (1976) falls in the mother-blaming category as well because of how powerful she views the role of mother and how desperate she believes both sons and daughters are to escape the mother's influence. Her solution is shared parenting to reduce the mother's power and thereby the adversarial role between mother and child and the lifelong ambivalence that follows.

Adrienne Rich (1976) and Alice Rossi (1973, 1977, 1979), writing from the perspective of the mother rather than that of the daughter, believe in the possibility that we could have perfect mothers with the overthrow of patriarchy, which leaves mothers powerless to be what they naturally can be, all loving and protective of their children. They see motherhood and sexuality connected in the sexual pleasures of mothering and, in Rich's view, the sexual bonds between women. Rich sees two meanings of motherhood, one superimposed on the other:

> the potential relationship of any woman to her powers of reproduction and to children; and the institution, which aims at ensuring that that potential—and all women—shall remain under male control. . . . In the most fundamental and bewildering of contradictions, it has alienated women from our bodies by incarcerating us in them. At certain points in history, and in certain cultures, the idea of woman-as-mother has worked to endow all women with respect, even with awe, and to give women some say in the life of a people or a clan. But for most of what we know as the "mainstream" of recorded history, motherhood as institution has ghettoized and degraded female potentialities. . . . Under patriarchy, female possibility has been literally massacred on the site of motherhood. Most women in history have become mothers

without choice, and an even greater number have lost their lives bringing life into the world. [p. 13]

Chodorow and Contratto describe the third theme, the link between motherhood and aggression, violence and death as the notion that

> having a child is enough to kill a woman or make a woman into a murderer. Being a mother is a matter of life and death; having a child destroys the mother or the child. If anti-feminists have tended more than feminists to blame the mother, feminists tend to blame the child, or the having of children. [pp. 86–87]

In this category are Rich, Kate Millett's *The Basement* (1979), and Blau-DuPlessis in *Feminist Studies* (1978), who give examples of women who murdered their children; as well as Allen, cited above. In my view, there is certainly a contradiction between the freedom of women and motherhood. This dilemma of contradictory desires exists for us all in different aspects of our lives and must be resolved by us in each instance of conflict so that the ambivalence in our feelings does not cripple our ability to make decisions and move ahead with our choices. Conflict resolution is an ego function that serves us at such times, and the capacity to let go, to compromise, enables us to make these difficult choices. We may need to choose between taking a new job, with more responsibility and higher salary, or staying with a less ambitious position that gives us more free time to pursue other interests, such as music, athletics, or friendships. The conflict for both men and women between wanting the sexual freedom of being single and feeling the need for the intimacy and security of a permanent relationship is comparable to the decision as to whether to have children. Sadly, we can't have it both ways. Each woman must weigh the loss of freedom and perhaps of advancement in her career, against the pleasures and burdens of child rearing.

What is clear in the writings of some feminists is the *absence of pleasure* in children. The narcissistic fragility of the woman has prevented her from being able to balance her own identity with the task of caring for others, and thus the burdens of motherhood cannot be balanced for her by the enormous opportunities for exquisite joy and pleasure that children can afford one, as well as the multiple opportunities for reworking old issues of values, deprivations, and conflicts from one's own childhood and with one's own parents. Parenthood also provides an opportunity to expand one's relationship to the larger community through schools, scouting, sports, other parents, and so on. In my experience, some women reject motherhood for themselves because they recognize that they are not psychologically up to the demanding task. They have had very disturbed relationships with their own mothers and therefore do not want to reproduce that relationship. Further, they have no good role models for motherhood and need good mothering themselves. Sometimes, after working through issues in their relationship with their own mothers in therapy, women are then able to have children with a newfound maturity of vision about what motherhood could mean to them in present terms apart from their painful memories of childhood unhappiness. It has been quite wonderful to see the happiness of a woman who had believed that motherhood was not available to her, when she does have her first baby and thrills to both her biological and psychological achievement.

I once saw a woman in her thirties who was so convinced that she would never have children that she had had a tubal ligation at age 23. I was angered that such a permanent surgery had been performed on such a young woman without any prior counseling. I first saw her in her mid-thirties when she was very depressed, desperately having one surgery after another to try to reverse that procedure. We spent two years uncovering memories of her painful childhood. She was the only child of poor and passive parents who had focused their attention on her chances for success, but her high intelligence and greater opportunities created a chasm that could not be crossed, and she resented their limited life and the way she was limited by them. Her resentment had become translated into a rebellion in the sixties when she quit college, led a hippie life, and was determined never to have a child.

She and her husband were members of a group for infertile couples where the hopeful parents shared their pain and frustration as years of infertility accumulated and created stress and depression. She felt very guilty because she couldn't bear to reveal to the group the true source of her infertility problem. She went through the painful process of in vitro fertilization and was finally successful on the third try, much to her and her husband's rejoicing. She terminated therapy just before childbirth but sent me an announcement with a picture of a gorgeous baby.

Feminists who reject motherhood because they see it as masochistic submission to children, men, and patriarchy are women who have been deeply damaged psychically and suffer from a strong masochistic character disorder, perhaps due to identification with a masochistic mother. Their feelings about men border on paranoia, and they project their own anger and rage onto children who are then seen as aggressive and destructive and threatening to their psychic and bodily integrity. This is a distortion of reality based on rather severe borderline pathology.

The majority of feminists believe it is important for women to have control over their own bodies through contraception, abortion, and planned pregnancies. Following a decision to bear children, they believe it is important for fathers to be active participants and for mothers to have the options to pursue school or work with the advantage of high-standard day care or a shared parenting arrangement. Feminists respect women who choose not to bear children because they do not want to compromise their careers or their political or artistic activities, not because children damage women. Rather than needing support and encouragement not to have children, as Allen and another writer in the same collection, Martha E. Gimenez (1983), suggest, most women, in my experience, want very much to have children and are grief-stricken when in their forties they have not had the chance to have a family. Some adopt children at that juncture; others use artificial insemination. However, there may be childless women who are not so distressed, but they are not in therapy. Lesbian couples feel the desire for children as well. Other women believe that they cannot raise a child alone and therefore become depressed. Those in therapy realize the factors in their histories that have led them to such an unhappy point, and feel renewed anger and loss at how earlier traumatic experience has affected the course of their lives. Some women are involved with older men who have had children from a previous marriage and don't want any more. Contrary to Allen's idea that motherhood is imposed on women by men, I have more often seen cases where the woman wants a child but the man doesn't want to make the commitment.

DISTURBANCES IN THE MOTHER–DAUGHTER RELATIONSHIP

In my earlier book, *Feminist Psychoanalytic Psychotherapy* (1992), I reviewed much of the feminist writing on mothers, their omnipotence and their consequent belittlement. In this chapter I want to focus on the disturbances that occur in the mother–daughter relationship and the hostility sometimes found in this intimate connection. As a therapist my experience is with women who seek help, and therefore this is not an unbiased sample. What distinguishes a "normal" degree of ambivalence from pathological hostility? Certain facts indicate that mothers, in the course of preparing daughters for acceptance in a male supremacist society, do very destructive things to their daughters.

The first example is the elimination of daughters through the practice of female infanticide. Two other examples specifically related to girls are the practices of foot binding in prerevolutionary China, and female "circumcision" or clitoridectomy, still practiced widely in the Middle East and Africa. Unlike the burning of women as witches, these two practices are imposed on girls by their own mothers. I use them as examples because I think that although they are vivid and extreme, they actually are comparable to practices by mothers in so-called civilized societies, in which the mother is the instrument of restriction and suppression of her daughter in order to prepare her and make her desirable for marriage. Mind binding in Western cultures has included the practices of not teaching women to read, not educating them, and the notion that an intelligent woman is not feminine. Women's bodies and their freedom of movement have been restricted by the wearing of high heels with pointed toes, girdles and cinches for the waist, and in today's very unliberated America, promotion of the ideal of achieving and maintaining an unnatural degree of thinness, which has convinced the vast majority of women to be on diets most of their lives. I recently scanned the covers of magazines at a supermarket checkout counter, and all but one of a dozen magazines, *Time,* had a cover promoting a diet story within. The pointed-toe shoes do in fact permanently injure the feet of women who wear them regularly.

Chinese Foot Binding

In the case of foot binding, although the practice was designed and promulgated by men for their erotic pleasure and to assure control of women, it was the mother who actually inflicted the painful process, forcing her daughter to submit to a permanent crippling of her feet and thereby of her movement. This is a rare instance where being of the peasant class was an advantage to the girl, whose feet were bound less severely because she had to be able to work, whereas the highest class girls were the most severely crippled. They were unable to walk and remained an ornament, a testimony to the wealth of the man who could afford to keep them idle. They were allowed out of the house on rare occasions, but only in a sedan chair behind heavy curtains. The following account, given by an elderly Chinese woman in 1934, describes her childhood experience.

> Born into an old-fashioned family at P'ing-hsi, I was inflicted with the pain of footbinding when I was seven years old. I was an active child who liked to jump about but from then on my free and optimistic nature vanished. Elder Sister endured the process from six to eight years of age (this means it took Elder Sister two years to attain the 3-inch foot). It was in the first lunar month of my seventh year that my ears were pierced and fitted with gold earrings. I was told that a girl had to suffer twice, through ear piercing and footbinding. Binding started in the second lunar month; Mother consulted references in order to select an auspicious day for it. I wept and hid in a neighbor's home but Mother found me, scolded me, and dragged me home. She shut the bedroom door, boiled water, and from a box withdrew binding, shoes, knife, needle and thread. I begged for a one-day postponement, but Mother refused: "Today is a lucky day," she said. "If bound today, your feet

will never hurt; if bound tomorrow they will." She washed and placed alum on my feet and cut the toenails. She then bent my toes toward the plantar with a binding cloth ten feet long and two inches wide, doing the right foot first and then the left. She finished binding and ordered me to walk, but when I did the pain proved unbearable.

That night, Mother wouldn't let me remove the shoes. My feet felt on fire and I couldn't sleep; Mother struck me for crying. On the following days, I tried to hide but was forced to walk on my feet. Mother hit me on my hands and feet for resisting. Beatings and curses were my lot for covertly loosening the wrappings. The feet were washed and rebound after three or four days, with alum added. After several months, all toes but the big one were pressed against the inner surface. Whenever I ate fish or freshly killed meat, my feet would swell, and the pus would drip. Mother criticized me for placing pressure on the heel in walking, saying that my feet would never assume a pretty shape. Mother would remove the bindings and wipe the blood and pus which dripped from my feet. She told me that only with the removal of the flesh could my feet become slender. If I mistakenly punctured a sore, the blood gushed like a stream. My somewhat fleshy big toes were bound with small pieces of cloth and forced upwards, to assume a new-moon shape.

Every two weeks, I changed to new shoes. Each new pair was one- to two-tenths of an inch smaller than the previous one. The shoes were unyielding, and it took pressure to get into them. Though I wanted to sit passively by the K'ang, Mother forced me to move around. After changing more than ten pairs of shoes, my feet were reduced to a little over four inches. I had been in binding for a month when my younger sister started; when no one was around, we would weep together. In summer my feet smelled offensively because of pus and blood; in winter, my feet felt cold because of lack of circulation and hurt if they got too near the K'ang and were struck by warm air currents. Four of the toes were curled in like so many dead caterpillars; no outsider would ever have believed that they belonged to a human being. It took two years to achieve the three-inch model. My toenails pressed against the flesh like thin paper. The heavily creased plantar couldn't be scratched when it itched or soothed when it ached. My shanks were thin, my feet became humped, ugly and odiferous [sic]; how I envied the natural-footed! [Levy 1966, in Dworkin 1974, pp. 99–101]

Most Westerners are unaware of the actual crippling that occurs with foot binding. Before reading this account, I believed that the binding was simply to prevent the feet from growing. I was not aware that the toes were actually broken. As a visitor in China I learned that one of the few things that the government forbids you to take pictures of is women with bound feet. This is certainly correct to protect the sensitivity of the women, but it keeps Westerners ignorant of just how deformed these women are. Seeing the tiny feet is truly a horrendous sight.

Clitoridectomy

Another example of mothers enforcing a cruel and barbaric practice upon their daughters in order to prepare them for marriage is the practice of clitoridectomy. Between 90 million and 100 million women in Africa are victims of this surgery, in which the clitoris is partly or, more commonly, completely removed, without anesthesia, with crude cutting tools, and with little or no precaution against infection. A second operation usually follows, in which the labia are partly cut away and then sewn together, leaving the vulva almost completely sealed with only a pinhole opening, just large enough for urine to pass drop by drop. As reported by Konner (1990),

> the immediate consequences of this operation sometimes include hemorrhage, tetanus and other infection, excruciating pain and death. More common results include painful urination, backup of menstrual blood and severe pain during sexual intercourse. Two to 12 weeks are required for gradual penetration, which is essentially a process of repeated tearing; for convenience, the honeymoon hotel in the Sudanese city of Port Sudan is next to a hospital. Traditionally women are resewn after the birth of each child ("renewable virginity") only to experience the same effects again. [p. 5]

In spite of efforts by the World Health Organization, which has condemned these practices as mutilations disastrous to women's health, the practices have not stopped and in fact are believed to be spreading, with the laws that have been passed in most countries prohibiting clitoridectomies being ignored. It has been hypothesized that the old scarring has contributed to the spread of AIDS among women in Africa by making them more vulnerable to infection. In her ten-year study of these practices, Hanny Lightfoot-Klein (1990) reports that women themselves perform the mutilation and force their daughters and granddaughters to submit to them. The operation is designed to reduce women's sexual desire and assure her virginity for marriage. The term *female circumcision* is really a euphemism for what is in fact a mutilation having almost nothing in common with male circumcision.

What are we to make of these practices of mothers inflicting such pain on their daughters? What do they tell us about maternal love, the instinct we trust mothers have to protect their young? Although neither of these practices has ever occurred in the United States, I have used these examples to help us understand how the oppression of women as a group can lead to oppression by women of other women and particularly of their daughters, and how this can create hostility in the mother–daughter relationship as girls come to realize that they are treated differently from their brothers and restricted in ways that boys are not.

The Cult of Virginity

An example that does apply to this country and throughout the Christian world is the "cult of virginity." Clearly the ideal of virginity for girls is due to the authority of the male powers to determine female behavior and the male prerogative for experience and freedom that men have denied to women. This is surely to the advantage of the male, who will then never have his penis or performance unfavorably compared to another man's. How is it an advantage to women? Only in the sense of preventing pregnancy in an unwed situation. When fear of pregnancy is eliminated through the practice of birth control, it is to the advantage of a woman to allow herself the pleasures and experience of sexual relations and to have this be a factor in her decision about whom she will marry. It is largely the role of the mother to inhibit her daughter's sexuality and to train her from childhood to repress sexual feelings in order to make her the desirable virgin that the patriarchal system has demanded of girls. By enforcing this demand, the mother has, like the African and Chinese mothers, been the agent of the male value system in controlling her daughter's behavior to satisfy the self-centered preference of men for inexperienced girls to marry. As the girl becomes aware of this system and recognizes that not only is the prohibition not enforced against boys, but that in fact boys are encouraged to have sexual experience, she may direct her anger at these restrictions against her mother, who is the one imposing them on her and who therefore gets the blame. She may engage in sex in spite of her mother's restrictions and then have to cover up and be dishonest, living in fear of discovery.

This is not to say that oedipal bisexual triangle issues are irrelevant in mother–daughter difficulties. They contribute to competition for father's love and resentment of mother's attention to father. My point is that as long as women are financially dependent on men and must marry for economic survival, men can control women for their own selfish purposes and mothers will continue to do whatever it takes to make their daughters desirable marriage objects. This will instill hostility in their daughters, which in turn will be reenacted by turning passive into active with their own daughters. Mothers inhibit girls to make them marriageable for their own good and manageable for the mother's good, so mother doesn't have to fear illegitimate pregnancy and the dishonor it brings to the family. Furthermore, to avoid loneliness, mothers who are isolated and depressed manipulate daughters to keep them at home, in what is also likely to be a reenactment of the mother's having been bound to her own mother. As mothers age, the manipulation of daughters and daughters-in-law through guilt and anger can continue through illness, nursing-home care, and until death do them part.

THREE TYPES OF DAMAGING MOTHERS AND THE MISUNDERSTOOD MOTHER

In my experience, I have found three types of mothers who have damaged their daughters. I have also found examples of women who experienced their mother as rejecting when in fact the mother had simply not been the traditional, fully devoted mother but nevertheless was loving and responsible. I will call this category the misunderstood mother. These women are simply doing the best they can, either as homemakers or in combining career and motherhood, sometimes under very difficult external circumstances. In cases of poverty and/or abandonment by the father, mothers may have to work at tedious jobs that leave them exhausted and emotionally depleted. In some families where there are a great many children, the sibling relationships may assume more importance than the relationship between parent and child. Mothers can be resented by their daughters in any of these situations. If the mother was a housewife devoted to her family, the daughter resents her for not having been a good role model of an independent woman, and perhaps for being subservient to the father. One quality I have found particularly difficult for children to forgive in their parents is the lack of courage. In the case of the career mother, the daughter resents her for not having been more available, devoted, and nurturant. Unfortunately for all women, the expectations of mothers are so high that mothers can be blamed no matter what they do. We would all like our mothers to be the best of everything for us and to meet all our needs at all times. That this is a humanly impossible task is something an adult daughter can best appreciate as she works through her ambivalence toward her mother, and especially when she becomes a mother herself. In fact, all mothers are misunderstood in the sense that until the daughter can mature to the point where she fully appreciates the factors in her mother's life that resulted in the disturbance in her mothering capacity, her anger and blame will be unmodified by empathy for her mother's own tragic circumstances. This understanding can be one of the most therapeutic results of psychotherapy, in that it eases the guilt and blame felt by the patient and allows for some recognition of the positive aspects of the mother's caring and qualities of which the daughter can be proud. The same can be true of the daughter–father relationship.

All these considerations notwithstanding, some mothers are overtly destructive, and they are described below.

The Narcissistic, Masochistic, and Depressed Mother

Type 1 is the narcissistic, masochistic, and depressed mother who attempts to manipulate the daughter to live out the mother's own unfulfilled wishes and thus tries to live through her daughter vicariously. She is overinvolved with her daughter, intrusive and controlling, and fears separation, trying to prevent it by eliciting guilt and sometimes through hypochondriasis. She may be a very good homemaker and attempt to instill in her daughter the importance of homemaking skills for her future marriage. If she is not seriously depressed, she may be very giving to her daughter, sometimes making sacrifices for her and putting much effort into helping the daughter be attractive and popular. She may shop for her or sew her clothes. She may arrange socially desirable music and dancing lessons and attempt to get the daughter into the best clubs and circles. She wants her daughter to be upwardly mobile through marriage. The problem is that she never knows who her daughter is or what her daughter wants for herself. The daughter is an extension of her mother, and the mother neither asks nor listens to what the daughter's independent desires may be. The mother does not recognize a boundary between them. The daughter senses the enormous need she is expected to fulfill for her mother and feels duty-bound to make her mother happy because her mother is making such personal sacrifices for her. She may get a double message about men from her mother: Men are terribly important in that one must have a man to marry, which is the only acceptable path. On the other hand, the mother's lack of involvement with her father sends the girl another message, that men are not so important and perhaps, if the mother uses her daughter as a confidant to complain about the father, even contemptible. Mother hopes her daughter will make a better marriage than she has, thus devaluing the father at the same time that his status as the provider is the key to mother's and daughter's success. This mother is usually not sexual and does not convey to her daughter the pleasures of an erotic union with a man. Thus the girl learns that she must attract a husband but that her true intimate relationship is with her mother. This intimacy can be transferred to women friends in an effort to break the tight bond with mother. These daughters yearn for autonomy in their adult lives but fear that their autonomy will be resented and destructive to others, transferring the reality of their mother's dependency to later significant figures, including their husbands and children.

In some cases the repressed rage of the mother toward her own mother finds expression in hostility toward her daughter, with projection of evil motives onto the daughter and belittlement of her abilities.

The Narcissistic, Immature, and Neglectful Mother

The Type 2 mother is narcissistic, immature, and neglectful and may be cruel. She is very involved in her own physical appearance and desirability as a sexual object to men. She spends much time shopping for herself but may also decorate her daughter as an extension of herself. Her own needs for male admiration come before her children's needs for nurturance. She may not be much of a homemaker, being too involved in decorating herself and preserving her beauty. The intensity of the relationship with her husband, which may be highly ambivalent because he cannot possibly give her all the attention she wants and be the provider she needs to decorate herself and her home, often blinds her to her children's needs. She may be physically abusive to her children. The marital pair go out together a lot and the children are often left with baby-sitters. The daughter does get the impression that sexuality is a form of power for women, but she is daunted by her mother's mature good looks and success in manipulating men.

Another mother in this category is the talented mother who pursues a career that she does not combine with child rearing in a manner that gives enough consideration to her children's needs. Her gratification comes from her artistic or intellectual pursuits, and her children are left to housekeepers. In some cases the housekeeper serves as a good substitute mother. These mothers may be alluring to men and have multiple marriages. Hollywood actresses easily come to mind in this group, as does Margaret Mead. They are neglectful mothers but do serve as positive role models for daughters who may pursue success in a career if they have some talent. Mia Farrow and Liza Minnelli are examples of such daughters. This is also true of some well-to-do mothers who do not have careers but are involved full-time in their social clubs and activities. Their neglect of their daughters may be compensated in part by their active, successful social life, which serves as a model to the daughter of a nonsacrificing life-style, but this is not much compensation for a lack of maternal love and care. Much depends on the quality of substitute care provided. If it is good, then the prognosis is good, but there will be some residual loss for the daughter.

The daughters of mothers in this category are forced into a premature independence with an underlying emotional neediness that appears in love relationships and that the woman fears to admit because she expects rejection and resentment if she exposes her true needs. This may lead to a pattern of alcohol, food, or drug dependency. Hostility toward the mother may be open, but is combined with an ongoing longing for the mother's acceptance, caring, and love. The daughter continues to test the mother, hoping for love, but rarely gets positive results. She projects her anger, pessimism, and mistrust into love relationships and in an intense negative transference to the woman therapist. She desperately hopes the therapist can be the longed-for good mother but spoils the relationship with her envy and anger. She experiences the woman therapist's caring as sour milk.

The Psychotic or Seriously Depressed Mother

The mothers in the above two categories may be neurotic, or have a narcissistic personality disorder, or suffer from a borderline disturbance. Type 3 consists of mothers who are seriously depressed or truly psychotic. These women may have been cruel and violent towards their daughters, or so depressed as to have been incapable of providing much care at all. The girl soon learns that she must take care of herself and her mother in order to keep the household functioning minimally. If she is the oldest daughter in a large family, she takes over childcare responsibilities. The father often has absented himself from the family with his work, may have affairs with other women, or may be an alcoholic and/or physically violent. Incest by either the father or a brother is a possibility in these very disturbed families. Some of these mothers abuse alcohol to cover their psychosis or treat their depressions, or may have physical illnesses or severe hypochondriasis and be in the care of doctors and often in bed. Some have multiple surgeries. They may be self-destructive and attempt or threaten suicide, holding the family hostage through emotional blackmail. If the mother is hospitalized, the daughter assumes the housewife role, whereas the sons are not so confined. The daughter lives in fear of becoming mentally ill herself and has internalized some of her mother's pathology through identification. The psychotic mothers may have certain characteristics of Types 1 and 2 superimposed on their psychotic disturbance; that is, they may be sexual and relate seductively to men, or be asexual and be involved primarily with their children. In either case, the relationships are disturbed. Severe boundary diffusion results in massive projections onto the daughter, with an intrusiveness that creates a rage in the child from which there is little opportunity for release, because the mother is so fragile as to be unable to tolerate the daughter's anger without "going to pieces" (fragmenting). This frightens the daughter, so she bottles up her rage and develops a false self whereby she is obedient to the mother and protects herself through trying to protect the mother and keep her whole. There may be terrible fighting between the mother and father, which frightens the children and creates an atmosphere of tension and anxiety much of the time.

The following case examples draw from the above categories. As in all categories, there are overlaps and combinations that make the cases less easy to categorize, but nevertheless, these distinctions can be useful. There is always a problem in attempting a diagnosis of the mother of a patient because you only have the secondhand impression that you receive from the daughter's account, clearly not an impartial rendering of the facts. Yet reports over a long-term analysis or therapy combined with an analysis of the transference can lead the therapist to at least tentative conclusions as to the mother's diagnosis, although it is not always possible to distinguish when the mother was truly psychotic from when she was borderline, or when she was severely neurotic as distinguished from a borderline or narcissistic personality disorder. In each case example, my diagnosis of the mother suffers from this secondhand knowledge. I will start with a mother who was not overtly harmful to her daughter but whose career the daughter experienced as rejection.

Clinical Illustration—The Misunderstood Mother

About ten years ago, I saw Ruth, a Jewish woman in her early twenties. She was a college graduate who had developed into a successful musician, performing with a group in the San Francisco Bay Area. She had come to California from the East Coast, the daughter of parents who were both physicians. She was one of four children. Her parents were both actively involved in their children's lives, but a housekeeper was in the home during the days when the parents worked. Ruth could not really find fault with either of her parents and consciously believed they were both caring, attentive, and supportive of her musician's life although they had not initially encouraged it.

Her complaint had to do with her anxiety in her relationship with her boyfriend, also a musician. She could not believe that he really loved her, was fearful that he would be attracted to other women, and could not feel secure that their relationship would last. She kept looking for signs that he was seeking other women, although as far as I could tell from her accounts, this was not the case and he seemed to truly like and admire her. In exploring the cause of her anxiety I tried various interpretations having to do with oedipal jealousy and sibling rivalry, none of which bore any fruit. The therapy seemed to be stalemated until one day Ruth happened to relate a memory of going to a friend's house after school and seeing her friend's mother at home. The mother was attentive to both girls, and Ruth felt very welcomed. With this as my clue, I tried another interpretation of her fear of being abandoned by her lover. I suggested that Ruth may have experienced her mother's work as a physician as an indication that Ruth was not sufficient to win her mother's lasting attention, that as a child she had interpreted her mother's work away from home as a rejection of her and felt she was not as desirable in her mother's eyes as the patients who took her mother away. She had compared herself with the other girls whose mothers were at home for them when they returned from school. I said I thought she might be transferring to her boyfriend these ideas of her insufficiency to hold his love and attention and therefore anticipated his rejection of her for another woman. Ruth was surprised by this idea but considered it thoughtfully and accepted that these feelings could have been her interpretation of her mother's absence from home, a misunderstanding of mother's dual roles as physician and mother, uncommon among her friends in the '60s.

This interpretation proved to be accurate. Her anxiety decreased and she was able to terminate therapy. It was clear to her, as an adult woman, that her mother's work was not a rejection of her or an indication of any flaw in her attributes. These feelings had remained buried and asserted themselves when she was again in a love relationship where she felt dependent and thus insecure of her value. Connecting these feelings with her mother served to relieve her current anxiety by correcting a mistaken idea that her mother did not value her.

Clinical Illustrations—The Masochistic, Narcissistic, and Depressed Mother

Theresa was from a middle-class Catholic family with an Italian mother and Spanish-Mexican father. She had one brother, two years younger. Her mother was a full-time housewife who spent all her days cooking and cleaning. Theresa did very well in school, better than her brother, and went to college in spite of some resistance on the part of her parents. Throughout her childhood she remembers being very close to her mother. Unlike the other children, she and her brother returned home from school for lunch every day so their mother could cook and serve them. She remembers going to camp one summer and being very anxious at the separation from her mother. In adolescence this changed and she had friends and was attracted to boys. She had terrible fights with her mother, who tried to keep her at home and control her sexuality. After their fights her mother would complain of illness and high blood pressure, and her father would be angry at Theresa for upsetting Mother. When Theresa fixed her hair and put on make-up, her father said

"No daughter of mine in going to look like a whore," and made her remove it. Mother had household tasks for her to do and was always criticizing her performance: nothing was ever good enough. The mother complained of tiredness a lot and always went on about how hard she worked to keep the house clean. One line Theresa recalls was her mother repeating that she "walked 5 miles every day" through the house, keeping it clean. She complained of heart problems and in her sixties did in fact have bypass surgery.

Theresa moved to San Francisco and established an independent life. She was artistic and musical and identified herself as a hippie during the '70s. She tired of doing clerical work and during her therapy returned to graduate school for a master's degree, which enabled her to do professional work. Visits to see her parents or visits from them always produced intense friction, since they did not approve of her life-style. When she lived with a man, they were very critical of her for not marrying.

When she did marry, she and her husband continued to live a very unconventional life-style, but at least she won some recognition from her parents. What then emerged was her powerful identification with her mother. She spent most of her sessions complaining to me about how hard she worked cooking and cleaning house and how her husband didn't help her enough or earn enough money. I began to comment on how much she experienced her life as one of suffering and blaming her husband, and how similar that was to the way she had described her mother's complaints. She recalled that her mother had always complained about how much she missed her family on the East Coast because her husband had taken her away from them to bring her to California where he had been living. When Theresa repeatedly complained about how many miles she had to drive to work and to my office, I commented on the similarity to her mother's complaint of the many miles she walked through the house each day. Theresa's extreme ambivalence toward her mother emerged as she began defending her against my comments that it appeared to me that the mother was hostile to Theresa for living a life of freedom, compared with her own restricted, religious life. She praised her mother, saying how warm, loving, and nurturing her mother had been, whenever I would comment on how it appeared that her mother resented her and was very angry at her. I also said that her mother suffered from a life she had apparently chosen and was in fact well treated and provided for by her husband.

Theresa continually complained that her husband was not a good provider like her father and that she wished she didn't have to work so that she could spend more time doing the things she loved at home, keeping a clean and lovely house, cooking good meals, and pursuing her artistic interests. She was terribly envious of women she knew who were supported by their husbands. There was great resistance to recognizing the masochistic component in her mother's character and the hostility that her mother expressed to her at any sign of her being not like mother and not choosing a similar life. I commented many times that Theresa, in complaining to her husband about his inadequate performance and about how tired she was and how hard she was working, was doing to him what her mother had done to her. I reminded her that she was doing a lot of what she chose to do and that her life was not in my view the victimization that she experienced. They were poor, but she had opportunities to work in her chosen field, and because she worked part-time, she had free hours to pursue her artistic talents.

Her complaining about her husband continued in the sessions week after week. The issue of who did the dishes came up repeatedly. Since it was such a contentious issue, I suggested they use paper plates. When she continued to complain about it, I realized that there must be another factor besides the identification with her mother, one that I was missing. I asked about dishwashing in her family and learned that she had had to wash dishes but that her brother did not. His chore was mowing the lawn. He got to sit in the living room with Father after dinner while she was stuck in the kitchen with Mother, who found fault with whatever she did. She would have much preferred the contact with Father that her brother had. I suggested to the patient that her continuing squabbles with her husband were due to a transference to him of her resentment against her brother for avoiding her mother's criticism. She realized that at times she called her husband by her brother's name. This interpretation was more successful, and her complaints about the dishes stopped. Her deeply held internalization of her mother's masochistic style continues, though she tries to be aware of it and control it. She recognizes that she denies herself some simple pleasures and could ask for more help with cleaning without the angry victimized attitude that causes her husband to withdraw.

Her transference to me had the same features as her relationship to her mother and her husband. She was a long-term patient who felt very dependent on me yet frequently complained about the burden of the time it took to come to her sessions and the cost of the sessions. I interpreted the ambivalence in her feelings toward me as both dependent and acknowledging my helpfulness yet resentful at the loss of time, the long commute (after she moved out of San Francisco), and the fee. I pointed out the similarity in her difficulty resolving the ambivalent tie with her husband and mother. She often spoke of termination but was too anxious to separate. I hesitated recommending termination because of my concern that her frequent attacks on her husband would drive him away; she insisted on how much she loved him and wanted his closeness. Since she had no children, she did not have the chance to reenact the mother–child love–hate bond, and it remained centered on her husband. She often feared he would leave her for another woman. She was very nurturant toward him and possessive, becoming very jealous of any attention he showed to other women.

We can speculate that Theresa's anger was about what she felt was missing in her life, the husband/provider that her mother had. Her mother's anger was about what was missing for her, the freedom that Theresa had to be educated, to enjoy sexual freedom, and to live a life of opportunity that had never been available to the mother. The lives of these two women were worlds apart, and yet their connection was deep and they were psychologically inseparable. Theresa's fear of her own anger and its potential for damaging her mother, especially with her heart problems, continued for years to prevent her from breaking away from her mother's neurotic style, even though she broke away geographically and socially and led a liberated life on the surface. She has deep difficulty integrating her positive and negative feelings about her mother, caring about her and appreciating her nurturant qualities but rejecting and differentiating from the angry complainer who feels unappreciated and victimized. Her mother could never resolve her own ambivalence, and the daughter, like her, has not as yet completely repaired the splitting of ambivalent feelings and repeats this with her husband and with me. The reality of their financial problems continually serves to reinforce her sense of deprivation.

Another case example in this category is Penelope, a Protestant, middle-class, midwestern woman who came to San Francisco after college. When Penelope was 9, her father suddenly died of cancer that had gone undetected. Until then, her mother had been a housewife; upon her husband's death, she joined the work force. Mother waited until Penelope started college to remarry, to a man she had been seeing for several years. Penelope had many problems, which could be traced to two sources. One was the fact, uncovered in therapy, that she had been sexually molested as a child by a very close friend of the family who "took her father's place" after his death as the male authority figure whom her mother depended upon. The second major factor in her problems was her relationship with her mother, which I will focus on here. The molestation issue will be described in Chapter 5.

Penelope was the second daughter. Her sister, older by three years, was domineering, critical, competitive, and a fearful and powerful figure in her life. There appears to have been no warmth or closeness between them after childhood, but the patient remained dependent on her sister and fearful of her disapproval throughout many years of therapy. Her sister was, according to Penelope's reports, very beautiful and slender and had been a homecoming queen in high school. She married a wealthy man from a prominent family but had no children and divorced after many years when her husband's mental condition deteriorated and he became quite disturbed. The sister was prominent in early transference to me, likely because I am slender and older than the patient. I noticed a common same-sex sibling pattern in that the mother, in her misguided effort to prevent competition, had set up territories for them. Sister was the pretty, popular, social star who was "selfish," whereas Penelope was the bright student, the "good" one. Her mother thought she should marry a minister. I have been struck by the frequency with which daughters who assert their autonomy are labeled "selfish" and there is praise for the daughter who is fearful of angering Mother and becomes the "pleaser." In this way a mother can control and shape her daughter's personality and the character of her future relationships.

Penelope suffered from many addictive problems: overeating, smoking, and occasional alcohol abuse. She has a respected but not highly paid profession, typical of many women's professions. She never married and had poor relations with men. In the beginning of her therapy she would get involved with men she met at bars, always inappropriate men with whom she had sexual relations but not fully developed relationships. She often was involved with married men. As her treatment progressed and we analyzed this pattern, she stopped meeting men in bars, was engaged for a period, but when that relationship proved disappointing, she did not develop beyond the married-man syndrome.

In focusing on Penelope's relationship with her mother, it appears that her mother, like many women, was part of a three-generation phenomenon of a mother who is tied to her own mother in an undifferentiated dependency and reproduces that pattern with her daughter. Mother chose Penelope rather than her sister to make this historically determined connection with because she identified more with her than with the thin, beautiful older daughter. When her husband died, the mother "coupled off" with Penelope and allowed her no privacy. Yet she was very strict and non-nurturing with Penelope and could not tolerate any expression of feelings—anger, grief or sadness—and therefore could never be comforting to the patient. After the death of Penelope's father, there was no open mourning. She has one memory of her mother starting to cry and leaving the room. The first time in her therapy that Penelope started to cry in recalling her father's death, she got up and left the office, ending the session. When we were able to talk about this during the following session, and in later references to her fear of her strong feelings, she revealed that she had never cried in anyone's presence, and I commented on how she suppressed her need for caring and then attempted to take care of herself through overeating, drinking and smoking, which were in fact self-destructive. This became a frequent interpretation. Along with her fear of revealing her feelings to others, her defeating efforts at nurturing herself were interpreted when she refused my suggestion of groups for help with her various dependency problems. As she came to accept my interpretation that her mistrust of others was based on her rejecting mother and sister, and on her fear of condemnation because of blaming herself for her sexual abuse, she made the step toward groups and found them helpful. For more than a year she was in a group I led for sexually abused women. Through the group's sympathy and encouragement she gained a lot of confidence and support about her sexual abuse experience and her reactions to it. She then was able to tell several women friends and received additional support from them, which helped somewhat to offset her family's continual rejection of the subject.

Her mother's life involved much self-sacrifice. Early widowhood meant much responsibility, and Penelope remembers her mother coming home from work each evening and lying down, exhausted, before cooking dinner, yet she never asked either daughter for any help in cooking or other housework. This was part of her martyrdom, apparently, because it was surely no kindness to the patient, who did not learn to cook until recently, when she realized what a limitation not cooking was to her own eating habits, which were very poor, and to her confidence in having guests over for an improvement in her social life. I said that by not teaching her to cook, her mother kept her dependent, and that by cooking healthy meals for herself rather than eating pizza and cookies, she could actually nurture herself.

Additionally, her mother's self-sacrifice extended to spending many years caring for her own mother, who died in her nineties, and then in nursing her second husband through a protracted illness, from which he died a few years ago. He insisted that she be there to care for him at all times, and she acceded to these selfish demands. After his death she attempted to engage Penelope in a companion relationship, urging her to move back to their home city and planning several vacations together. At first Penelope was tempted by these invitations, until she realized how regressive they were. I interpreted her longing to be taken care of by Mother, but the sacrifice in terms of any possibilities of her goal of forming an attachment to a man. Before a trip to Hawaii with Penelope, Mother said they could buy muumuus when they got there. Penelope was horrified to realize that her mother was encouraging her to be fat and shapeless and therefore unattractive to men and wedded to Mother for the rest of her life. She recognized that some of her women friends were still attracted to men, and that others had given up on men and were more possessive of her. She got frightened of the latent homosexual implications of closeness with these women and steered away from them and toward the sexually active friends.

During Penelope's adolescence, her mother was very involved in controlling her and restricting her connections to boys. Just as she found fault with all her adolescent boyfriends, so in adult life she found fault with the men Penelope met, even those who were not obviously inappropriate. It appeared to me that Penelope's mother needed to feel an exclusive possession of her and could not share her with either women or men friends. At the time of the father's death, the mother apparently made a substitute dependency tie to Penelope and never could let go, even after her remarriage. She complained to Penelope about her new husband and would stop the telephone conversation if he entered the room. The sense I got was that Penelope's mother wanted her to believe that their tie was the most valuable one in her life, that the husband was a financially necessary interference, and that Mother's life continued to be one of suffering despite the comfortable life her well-to-do husband provided. This conveyed the message that Penelope and Mother were still the primary couple.

For her part, Penelope enjoyed the special attention from her mother, and their conversations were pleasurable to her as long as she didn't disagree with anything Mother said. Disagreement would bring icy coldness and withdrawal and create anxiety in Penelope over loss of Mother's love. She had a clear memory as a young child of crying and her mother ordering her out of the house until she stopped. She learned never to cry in her mother's presence. Mother could not tolerate fighting between the two sisters, saying "This is killing me." I said I thought this resulted in the sisters never having a normal life of siblings, fighting and resolving the differences, which contributed to the hostile coldness between them. She felt Mother preferred her to her "selfish" sister, and Penelope enjoyed their special closeness, which was a victory over her sister. In therapy she came to appreciate the price she had paid for this special attention. She had been very conforming on the surface and kept a secret life of "badness" hidden from Mother.

As therapy developed, it seemed to me that we should increase our sessions to twice weekly, but she was unable to do so. She also was unable to share an apartment with another woman and has never done so, in spite of loneliness and financial need. We analyzed her fear of domination and control by another woman, and her own readiness to capitulate out of fear of anger and rejection. I said it was clear that she saw other women as narcissistically exploiting her and unable to show genuine caring or consideration for her needs and feelings. After some months of this type of work, she was able to increase her sessions to twice weekly and later to three times a week.

Mother's character involved self-sacrifice but also a strong disdain for people of whom she disapproved. There was a sharp splitting between the desirable people and the undesirable, who were viewed with contempt. There was a strong racial and class bias in Mother's values. It is interesting that both daughters acted out anger toward their mother by relating to African-American men. Anyone who was openly sexual fell within the contemptible category. This frightened Penelope and brought about the phenomenon of a secret life that she kept from Mother, which included her smoking, drinking, and sexual relations. When her dreams led to my recognition of symptoms of sexual abuse, she was so filled with shame, guilt, and fear that it took many years before she could accept that she had in fact been victimized. She was sure that Mother's view would be that it was her fault, since her recollections involved being highly sexually stimulated by the perpetrator. When she finally did tell her mother and sister, she received absolutely no comfort, support, or help. They both denied it could have happened and encouraged her to forget about it and "go on with her life." Their lack of sympathy was appalling, especially considering that her sister had had many years of psychoanalysis.

I commented that her secret life, which was so self-destructive, also served a very protective purpose in that it gave her independence from her critical, intrusive, controlling mother and helped her to feel she had a life of her own with some privacy. Mother had even insisted on her telephone calls being held where Mother could listen. I said she felt she had only two choices, to be an obedient puppet of Mother or to rebel and do the things Mother would disapprove of, but some of which were in fact self-destructive, in order to feel separate from Mother. I recognized the healthy aspect of her rebellion but expressed my concern that with only these two choices, she lost either way. This was also a factor in the transference, and she acknowledged that at times her smoking, drinking, and over-eating were done with a sense of secret rebellion in relation to me and made her feel free and independent.

As she gradually came to see how destructive her mother's possessiveness had been to her life, and at the same time how dependent she was on her mother, she began to develop friendships with women in which she worked through her fears of being controlled and dominated. As she came to trust me she was able to transfer this trust to other women. As these friendships flourished, they enabled her to begin the gradual process of detaching from Mother. She began to take vacations with friends and spend Christmas with the family of a friend whose mother was very caring and understanding. At one point, she actually withdrew from Mother in anger, when Mother was critical of her for pursuing her investigation into her sexual molestation. Her attachment to me served well as an alternative to her dependence on Mother but created its own problem of dependence on me. She had too much anxiety about being alone to terminate, although she wanted the independence and the relief from the financial burden of therapy. I interpreted her ambivalence toward me, which was hard for her to accept at first because of her idealized transference, but gradually she became able to tolerate it and even occasionally could report feeling some anger toward me.

As she worked through her terrible guilt and shame about the sexual abuse and, with interpretations from me, could stop blaming herself for it, she was able to begin pleasurable activities in her life that helped her meet new friends and enjoy her evenings and weekends in a constructive and healthful way. These activities also gave her more confidence that she could have a rich enough life to allow her to terminate therapy. She gradually began to be free to disagree with me and to be less subservient and more assertive in other relationships as well. Her fear of expressing anger made work relationships fraught with tension and limited her advancement; she dreaded becoming a supervisor and assuming a dominant position in relation to subordinates. She began to recognize how her "good girl" role was a reenactment of her dutiful daughter role with me and her supervisor.

The death of this woman's father was a tremendous loss for which she will always grieve. In therapy, with my encouragement she was able to truly grieve this loss for the first time. Her father had been the more nurturing parent, and his loss accentuated the already pathologically undifferentiated tie to her mother. Mother's clinging to her met her needs as a child but became oppressive as she entered adolescence and needed to leave the nest. Geographic distance failed to bring about the psychological separation she needed. The combination of a long-suffering, nonempathic, rigid and disapproving mother; the early loss of her father; and sexual molestation for which she could receive no help as a child, resulting in guilt and total repression, combined to produce many self-destructive symptoms and prevent her from forming a healthy, trusting attachment to a man and creating her own family. The lack of her own husband and children reinforced her dependent tie to her mother and sister, her only family, and her sister's divorce eliminated the only man in the family. All these losses and conflicts necessitated long-term psychotherapy for the kinds of analytic exploration and deep changes required for a healthy life.

Because she felt too alone in the world to sever the tie with her mother, she worked hard to differentiate from Mother yet stay connected. This meant overcoming fear of Mother's rejecting and angry response to Penelope's disagreements with her. Her self-assertion could only take place when she could overcome the severe anxiety associated with Mother's disapproval and the implied threat that she could cause her mother physical harm (illness) in Mother's statement, ''I just want to be left in peace.'' Since her mother had high blood pressure, Penelope had to overcome the guilt and fear that assertion of difference or disagreement on her part could make Mother sick.

This kind of emotional blackmail is common and can be very restrictive of the effort to differentiate. It takes courage to stand up to the implied threat. Often, by the time a woman enters therapy she may be in her thirties, and her mother may be a widow or aging or both. Interpretations can be made in which the patient's own anger and the mother's controlling element are stressed:

> Your mother controls you by her implied threat that you can destroy her by disagreeing with her.

> You are afraid that you can destroy your mother by separating from her, as if your anger were so great as to be lethal.

> You can't say no to your mother without fearing that you will destroy her.

> Your mother seems to be saying "My way or the highway."

> It's hard for you to imagine being independent from your mother, yet staying connected.

On the fear of disapproval, the therapist may interpret as follows:

> Your mother's disapproval feels so threatening to you, as if you were still a little girl, completely dependent on her approval for your survival.

You have sacrificed your independence (or autonomy) in order to hold on to your mother's approval. That's quite a price to pay.

Simple questions exposing the source of the anxiety can often bring forth very perceptive reflections on the patient's part:

What if saying no does make your mother angry. What frightens you about that?

What if your worst fears are true, that you assert yourself and your mother gets sick, what would be so terrible about that?

What if your mother does stop sending you money, how bad would that really be?

At least your mother has married, has a home, and has children. You haven't, yet you feel you must protect her, as if you are the one with the advantages and the strength. Has her life really been so terrible?

Clinical Illustrations—The Narcissistic, Immature, and Neglectful Mother

Some mothers seem, from their daughters' descriptions, to be truly unsuited for motherhood owing to their narcissistic preoccupations. Although I do not agree that motherhood requires masochistic self-denial, it does require maturity, stability, and a capacity to postpone one's own gratifications in order to attend to the needs of the child. This does require empathy (a quality lacking in narcissistic people), patience, and the capacity to tolerate frustration and ambivalence in order to achieve what has aptly been termed "good enough mothering." In some women patients who are daughters of a narcissistic, immature, and neglectful mother I have found a common syndrome that includes problems with depression, narcissism and masochism. This fits with my description of Type 1 mother, and so it is tempting to propose a cyclical configuration of a Type 2 mother producing a Type 1 daughter who then becomes a Type 1 mother. To verify this hypothesis would take observations over several generations of many mother–daughter pairs, and we do not have this information.

Sandra was the older of two daughters of a Jewish professional father and housewife mother. She had moved to San Francisco with her new husband after college graduation. She loved and admired her father but was angry and mistrustful toward her mother. She first came to therapy when she and her husband were divorcing. She was in her late twenties and had a professional job and no children. During her years in therapy, a succession of love affairs with suitable men had each ended in her being deserted and deeply disappointed. I believe her anxiety and dependency were a source of the problems in these relationships. Toward the end of therapy she established a successful relationship, but the man was older, a widower with several grown children, who would not agree to having a baby with her. This was a source of much sadness and regret for Sandra, but after much ambivalence she chose to remain in this relationship. The stability it finally provided her enabled her to make strides in her career and to achieve a level of success that met at least some of her needs. She had bought her own home and enjoyed its comfort and the help her lover gave her in maintaining and improving it.

Establishing a relationship of trust with Sandra was very difficult and, even with long-term psychotherapy, was never fully achieved. She was always late to sessions, failed to show for some sessions, and battled bitterly over the bill. The transference was the best source of information about her mother and the effect her mother had had on her.

Sandra described her family situation as more like three sisters relating to her father. She felt her mother was so immature as to be more on her level and that of her sister than comparable to that of her father, who was older than the mother. Her mother had lost her own mother at age 15, and Sandra supposed this to be a source of her immaturity. Striking was her mother's narcissistic concentration on her appearance, her clothes, and her activities apart from parenting. Sandra and her sister were left alone for many hours while their mother was out shopping or at clubs, never knowing when she would return. In order to protect the girls, the house was locked in such a manner that they were actually locked inside, which caused Sandra much anxiety as to what would happen if there were a fire or some other need to get out. The mother showed obvious preference for the younger sister, which caused Sandra great distress. Mother would buy the sister new clothes and not get new clothes for Sandra. Her only solace was her closeness to her father, but he worked long hours and she was not to disturb him except in case of an emergency. She prevailed upon Father to give her money to buy clothes for herself, but had to try to keep it a secret from Mother, who would then rail at Father if she found out.

Sometimes Mother would take the girls along on her shopping trips but make them wait in the car. She provided bags of cookies to pacify them during the long waits. Sandra traces her serious weight problem to those experiences when she was taught to replace mother with sweets. Bags of cookies continued to be her undoing, but she ate a lot of all kinds of food and was always struggling to diet, losing weight and then regaining it.

Mother was very competitive with Sandra, perhaps because of Father's fondness for her. They had terrible fights and Mother would beat her. She would complain to Father, which would cause more problems, and Father was ineffective in controlling Mother's rages. When Mother wasn't shopping or out with her club activities, she spent her time in her bedroom reading romance magazines. She did promote Sandra's talents, taking her to various lessons, but seemed to be motivated by the fantasy that Sandra could become an actress and bring fame to Mother. Mother suffered from colitis and would blame Sandra for her attacks, accusing her of causing the attack because of their fighting. Sandra felt very guilty about this but got some gratification from the beatings because then she could complain to Father and show him her wounds.

Mother was also deceitful and manipulative, stealing money from Father to spend on herself and including Sandra in the deceit, showing her the hiding place for the money. After father's death, during the course of therapy, Mother was very manipulative about the estate, as well as about the estate of an uncle who had left Sandra some money. Mother claimed to be protecting and investing the money, but the circumstances seemed suspicious and it was not clear whether she was in fact cheating Sandra and her sister. Unfortunately, father left his entire estate to Mother, none of it directly to the daughters, so Mother had a lot of money to manipulate and was not at all generous about it. I often wondered why the father could not have forseen this, but there must have been much denial on his part all along to protect himself from the knowledge of his wife's deceitful behavior. Mother was good-looking and voluptuous, and perhaps he was seduced and flattered by her attention.

The family lived in a fourteen-room mansion. Every spare room was filled with Mother's possessions, strewn about so that one could not walk across the floor. Although Sandra struggled to get by on a woman's salary until she got the money from her uncle, Mother never helped. When Sandra asked for her furniture from her bedroom in the family home, Mother refused to ship it and Sandra had to travel to the East Coast to arrange shipment and, of course, pay for it. Bizarre transactions occurred that always left us wondering if Mother was actually stealing from her daughters under the guise of avoiding taxes. When Sandra and her new man visited, Mother was so manipulative about the use of the car that on the second visit he insisted on renting a car.

Sandra's major complaints were depression and anxiety. She began treatment at the time of her divorce and continued on and off for many years, with worries about her relationships, her career, and her struggles with her mother. The negative transference was persistent. She saw me as competitive, withholding, selfish, uncaring, and accused me of cheating her on the bill. She withheld payments, battled and broke off treatment over fee increases, and always experienced me as depriving. The projections, accusations, and hostility were so continuous as to constitute a diagnosis of paranoia at times. At other times she was tearful, dependent, fearful, and desperately sought help.

I consistently made interpretations linking her accusations against me to her mother's actual behavior toward her. She clung to the hope of getting some real love from her mother, which kept her connected and unable to have much perspective. This is a common pattern and prevents the woman from accepting her mother's limitations, lowering her expectations, and proceeding with a disappointing, limited, yet much less frustrating, less ambivalent connection that allows her some degree of emotional detachment and autonomy. It took Sandra many years to assert herself with her mother, demand some respect, and draw some boundaries. Having a stable relationship with a man helped her to achieve this. A stable relationship with a woman could serve the same function. Mother reacted with anger, predictably, to these boundaries, but Sandra held fast and the relationship continued in a manner that was less masochistic for Sandra as she achieved some emotional distance from Mother and reduced her fear of and dependency on her.

Her treatment of me was so abusive that I often made the interpretation that she treated me the way her mother treated her.

As with some other patients with similar symptom configurations, the therapist must keep clear boundaries and always attempt to delimit what degree of mistreatment can be tolerated for the sake of the treatment and for use in interpretations. Setting limits ensures that the therapist does not behave masochistically, repeating the role of the patient in the earlier mother–daughter relationship. Although it may seem ''ungiving'' to set limits, we don't do the patient any favor by accepting browbeating. We do better setting a model of self-respect that combines caring for the patient's welfare with protection of our own welfare. This is very similar to the balance that must be maintained in the mother–child relationship. In the psychotherapy relationship, this can be struggled with on several levels, often over the fee, which should not be lower than the patient can afford, considering the going rate in the area. Another source of struggle may be the time of the sessions and the changing of the time, including cancellations and rescheduling. The fee should never be an insult to the therapist, because if it is, the patient will identify with the devalued therapist and feel guilty beneath the angry accusations. The devaluing of the therapist through acceptance of a low fee is particularly serious with women therapists, since we are already devalued as women. My fee is flexible, based on the patient's ability, but that assumes a trustworthy patient who will not conceal her true ability to pay and attempt to take advantage of the therapist. In my view, it is better to stay firm as to the fee you believe you deserve, even if it means angry sessions and threats to quit, or actually quitting, than to submit to intimidation. The treatment of the manipulative, sadomasochistic component of the patient's character is not well served by a therapist who allows the patient to be too powerful, to the point of abusing the therapist. Here too, the model of the parent–child relationship is valid in terms of balancing the needs and legitimate interests of both. Like the parent in relation to the child, the therapist always favors the needs of the patient, but must set boundaries against sadistic and destructive behavior. This is how the roles of mother and female therapist are kept from being masochistic, and how in each case respect is taught for the needs and feelings of the other. These interactions in the therapy, although very trying for the therapist, are the only way to make progress in the treatment of the narcissistic and sadistic components of the masochistic patient.

Sandra was terribly envious of her sister, who was married to a successful professional man, had a successful career of her own, a beautiful home, and a son. Sandra was devastated by the comparison. I often reminded her that the difference was due to Mother's differential treatment and not due to some innate unworthiness of hers. This supportive statement was appropriate, I believe, because it was true and helped reduce the suffering the patient experienced through self-blaming. Furthermore, by locating the source of the injustice in the mother's disturbed transference to the patient and thus turning the anger away from her sister, I felt the patient might be enabled to preserve a relationship with the sister. They were not close, but there was some potential for a supportive connection, which did develop around the money issues of mother's possible cheating and in the course of planning family reunions, which Mother always manipulated to her utmost advantage.

The patient knew some personal things about me, and the fact that I was married, had children and a successful career put me in a similar position to that of her sister, representing what Sandra so desired and was unable to achieve. I interpreted her possible envy of me when envy issues came up, and she listened but could not fully accept this as a factor in her negative feelings toward me.

Envy by the female patient of her female therapist is an important issue that must be addressed. The difficulty is that it is often based on factual differences that do exist and therefore is not a fertile ground for analysis of projections. What can be analyzed is the patient's imaginative construction of the therapist's life as being perfect and of the therapist as being totally in control of her life. Interpreting the idealized transference can help reduce envy and the patient's self-depreciation, which is based on the mistaken belief that other women, such as the therapist, have perfect lives and are perfect people as compared with the patient who is so unhappy, feels so unsuccessful, and belittles herself even more severely through this fantasized comparison. The idealization of the therapist can coexist with the depreciation of the therapist as the envy generates hostility and the wish to destroy the therapist's success in order to reduce the painful envy. The spitefulness becomes a significant issue for interpretation as the patient proceeds to destroy the treatment in order to keep the therapist from chalking up yet another success. The interpretation of "cutting off your nose to spite your face" is useful here in an effort to show the self-destructive nature of this phenomenon:

> You can't let me help you because you don't want me to feel successful, so you destroy your own chances for success.

This interpretation can be applied to the mother as well:

> You can't let yourself be successful because you don't want your mother to take the credit and think she was a good mother. You'd rather sabotage yourself to punish her or them (if there is anger toward both parents).

Another possibility can occur when the roles are reversed and the therapist envies the patient. I have seen in consultations examples of therapists who are single and childless who envy a patient who marries and has children. I have also seen the envy of a married woman therapist toward a single patient who is having a free and active sexual life that appears to the therapist as much more exciting than her own stable but unexciting marital life. Another source of envy can be a woman patient who divorces and then starts a new life with romantic involvements and travel, while the female therapist remains in her own comfortable but ambivalent marital relationship, fearful of divorce because of the possibility of not having affairs or remarrying.

Sandra did terminate with some satisfaction that her life had improved. She had developed a good relationship with a man who she was able to trust after much anxiety, she was advancing in her career, and she loved her home. She had more control over the sadomasochistic elements in her relationship with her mother, and although she still struggled over weight problems, she had a better understanding of the meaning of her weight in relation to her mother and to me and thought she might be able to achieve some success in controlling it. I will discuss weight problems in therapy in a later chapter, using examples of several patients, including Sandra. She did end with some discrepancy in her bill, indicating that she had not mastered the stealing problem, which contained elements of a deep identification with her mother, an acting out of her envy of me, and a paranoid fear of my dishonesty.

A second example of a patient with a mother in this category is Barbara, the elder of two daughters of a Jewish businessman father and housewife mother. To call this mother a housewife is a misnomer; she was more like a mistress. According to Barbara, her mother did no cooking, she just opened cans, and had housekeepers to do the child care and cleaning. Mother insisted on being taken out to dinner by Father frequently, and the girls were left with the housekeeper, who stayed late on those nights. Mother went shopping for clothes every day and came home about 3 o'clock, at which time she took a bath, had a drink, and settled into her bedroom with the door closed, to read romance magazines. Mother was very beautiful and had been a model before marrying Father. She had already had several face lifts, and when she and Barbara were out together, people thought they were sisters. Barbara was Mother's favorite and therefore got more attention and approval than her sister, who turned out to be very disturbed, probably psychotic. Yet Barbara envied her sister because she was Father's favorite and got away with a lot more with both parents. Barbara described herself as the aggressive one, whereas her sister was passive and sweet, more appealing to Father, who always called Barbara a "BB," ball-breaker, a strange characterization of a young girl. Barbara is very intelligent, and we speculated that her father was threatened by her sharp mind. Mother was very much the "dumb blonde."

Another factor that was very important in Barbara's life, and which her sister missed, was that she was her maternal grandmother's favorite and spent time each week with Grandmother, wonderful quality time of walking, bicycling, going to the library, painting (grandmother was an artist), and generally feeling loved and special. When Barbara was 9, Grandmother remarried and moved out of town. They visited, but of course the move was a big loss for Barbara. When I interpreted this as a significant trauma, she was surprised, having repressed its real impact on her.

The quality of the relationship between Barbara and her mother was very poor. Mother was both neglectful and controlling. When Mother was in her bedroom, she kept the door closed, making Barbara feel lonely, sad, and abandoned. She comforted herself by drawing, a connection to Grandmother. Barbara, however, was not allowed to keep her bedroom door closed, and when Mother would catch her masturbating, she would beat her.

Mother insisted on being the center of attention in the family. Every night when Father returned from work, Mother would complain and make accusations against him. There was fighting each night at dinner. Father often withdrew with his work, unfortunately for Barbara. He never protected her from Mother's attacks, nor did Grandmother, who failed Barbara in that sense, an interpretation I made and Barbara reluctantly accepted. Grandmother and Mother were locked into a powerful hostile–dependent tie, which continued into old age.

Barbara had moved to San Francisco from the East Coast after college, but occasional visits to and from her parents were very trying for her. Mother always caused some disruption at dinner that focused the attention on herself, and Father would try to appease her and calm her. Barbara felt she had nothing in common with her mother and communication was very difficult. She was angry at Father for his rejection of her and protection of Mother, so there were no positive feelings for either parent.

In the course of therapy she decided to go to graduate school for professional training. Years of secretarial work were clearly much beneath her potential, but she was very ambivalent about asking her father for financial help. Father did show much ambivalence about helping her, but we persisted to work on this issue in therapy, trying to resolve her conflict between the short-term dependence on his help, which she felt to be regressive and was the cause of many arguments, versus the long-term gains in independence from professional training. I always encouraged her to try to work out some help from her parents, since it was clear she was in dead-end jobs that caused her much frustration and anger at having to take orders from people she felt vastly superior to intellectually. She was already in her mid-thirties, so going to school part-time and working was too lengthy a project. Upon returning to school, she began to act out less and feel more ambitious, and she increased her sessions to two and then three times per week.

Mother had some paranoid qualities, being suspicious and accusatory of family members, neighbors, and Barbara herself. She saw insults and slights where there were none. She had great resentment and feelings of competition toward her sister, Barbara's aunt, a healthier woman who was always kind to Barbara. Barbara could not develop a closeness to her aunt, however, because of her mother's jealousy. She had a great-aunt who was childless and adventuristic, whom she admired. Barbara had a persistent fantasy that I was unmarried, childless, and devoted myself exclusively to my work. She recognized that this was a role model she identified with because she had no hopes of a loving relationship with a man, owing to her aggressiveness. In fact she was physically small and attractive, and I believed it was hostility, not aggressiveness, that could be her impediment.

The transference to me was unclear for a long time. She was sure I was not Grandmother, because I was not warm or nurturing and all-approving as Grandmother was. Barbara could do no wrong in Grandmother's eyes. She knew I was not like Mother, who had no college education, little apparent intelligence, and was so superficial. Of course there were many instances of projections of mistrust and mistreatment onto me, and accusations of insensitivity and cruelty that were clearly the result of the maternal transference, but Barbara insisted that she had no strong feelings about me and never could personalize the relationship, a *resistance to the awareness of the transference.* It was always "this office" and "the therapy" rather than "you, my therapist." I often interpreted these verbal distancing mechanisms, and she would always repeat that she felt nothing personal in our relationship and had no strong feelings toward me. However, I could tell how Barbara was feeling from the moment I opened the waiting room door and saw her facial expression. My suggestions that perhaps she was avoiding a sexual attraction to me were consistently rejected, although she was a lesbian. I heard a clue to the source of this problem when Barbara spoke of going to visit Mother and Grandmother in Florida but said she wouldn't be able to visit her aunt who was also there, because Mother would be so insulted and angry if she took any time away from her, except for Grandmother. I suggested that perhaps she was unable to let herself develop strong feelings toward me because she feared Mother's anger and jealousy of any attachment to me, as with her aunt, who is also a psychiatric social worker. This seemed to be accurate, and in the following months Barbara exposed more feelings of dependence and appreciation, although the anger over my supposed insensitivities continued as well. This interpretation fit with an earlier one that Barbara's poor performance on examinations was due to anxiety about Mother's feelings, especially the way education would distance Barbara from her. Thus her resistance to the awareness of any positive transference to me was her way of protecting her mother from competitive anger toward me and protecting herself from alienating Mother and creating another battle. However, her decision to go to graduate school was a big step in breaking the protective alliance with Mother and identifying with me.

These two examples present similar mothers but different fathers, which may account for the difference in heterosexual and homosexual choices of the patients. Both mothers are severely narcissistic, competitive, and neglectful, but Sandra's mother was actually more cruel and neglectful. However, Sandra's father was much more attentive and loving than Barbara's father. The involvement of the grandmother in Barbara's case, I believe, made the therapy process more stable for Barbara, and there were fewer suspicions and accusations against the therapist. Significant adults besides the parents in the patient's early life are important factors and should not be neglected in the analysis. They can offer some relief from the pathological mother–daughter enmeshment.

I have seen many patients whose mothers fit this category and who can be diagnosed as depressed, masochistic and narcissistic, or borderline. The variations in their life course are determined by the kind of relationship they had with their fathers or other significant adults. One thing the fathers have in common is that they do not have the ability to control the mother's cruelty and do not protect the daughter from her neglect. At times they protect the mother and serve as a negative force by demanding that the patient not fight with the mother. This leaves the daughter abandoned by them both. The strong negative maternal transference makes these daughters very difficult to work with: as they become sufferers in the therapy, experiencing the therapist as cold, cruel, selfish, and critical. Transference interpretations are essential early in the therapy, and transference issues are the heart of the treatment. The patient's feminism and the therapist's feminism are insufficient as a basis for an alliance or understanding, insofar as the patient is unable to experience a positive connection to the therapist because she feels so deprived and envious. (Barbara continually repeated, "We have nothing in common.") The task of individuating from Mother yet staying connected is most difficult as the hostile-dependent tie keeps the daughter locked in and unable to marry, or stay married, which reinforces the dependency on both parents. The bisexual triangle continues to play itself out in adulthood.

Clinical Illustrations—The Psychotic Mother

In my clinical experience the number of psychotic mothers of my patients who have never been hospitalized or even treated as outpatients is astounding. This is sad for the mothers and traumatic for their daughters.

> Carolyn was the second child of a Jewish businessman father and housewife mother on the East Coast. Carolyn's mother died when she was 9, a death at least partially caused by excessive smoking. Following her mother's death, Carolyn was raised by a housekeeper who was very warm and loving and with whom she remained in contact for many years. This woman later helped care for Carolyn's daughter in a time of need. Father remarried numerous times, but the housekeeper stayed on. Carolyn suffered as a child from eczema so severe that she had to be kept out of school for one year. When her brother, who was four years older, had friends to the house, he made her hide in her room, saying she looked so ugly he didn't want his friends to see her. When she later married a non-Jewish man, her entire group of relatives—grandparents, aunts and uncles— rejected her completely.

Her memories of Mother were that she was always screaming at Father, her brother, and her. She also remembers that toward the end of her life Mother spent most of the time in bed. Carolyn's memories include trying to help Mother in the kitchen but her screaming at Carolyn no matter what she did. One day Mother shoved her brother down the laundry chute. There was a large extended family on both sides in the city, but apparently no one intervened. Before Mother's death, the brother began raping Carolyn and continued to do so for four years, until a stepsister (Father's new wife's daughter) complained to her mother when he tried to molest her. Then Carolyn felt free to tell her father for the first time, and the brother was sent to boarding school. Prior to that, the brother had threatened to kill Carolyn if she told; she believed him and was very fearful of him because he was violent. He had once set off a bomb in the synagogue. She submitted in terror to vaginal, anal, and oral rape.

Carolyn was told that her maternal grandfather was a violent man who had beaten his four daughters, including her mother. This gives us some sense of the three-generational picture. Carolyn had no positive memories of her mother at all. In adolescence she began using drugs and has continued to do so through her adult life, including during the period she worked with me. She also was a successful drug dealer for many years. Her life included many tragedies, such as the accidental death of her only daughter, and a bout with Hodgkin's disease for which she was receiving chemotherapy during our work together. She had unsuccessful relationships with men, which were patterned after the relationship with her brother.

The severe pathology of this mother had terrible consequences for her children, and neither family nor any community agency intervened. The brother took out the cruel treatment he had suffered as a consequence of the disturbed mother on Carolyn, who was dependent on him and vulnerable. The father absented himself through work and, she suspected, with other women, thereby neglecting his responsibility to protect his children. Fortunately, her good relationship with the housekeeper following Mother's death enabled Carolyn to have a positive transference to me and to have a warm, trusting relationship with me once she was assured that her communications to me were entirely confidential and that I would not report her drug activity. She remained in treatment for three years, working on the incest issue, on her current relationships with men, on memories of her mother, and on her current relationship with her father and brother.

She terminated with positive hopes for her future. Her chemotherapy treatments were over and her prognosis was good. She had assurances from her father that she would inherit all his estate and the brother would be left out. She decided to go back to school for training in a field that had long interested her, while continuing her job during the day. She felt good that the antidepressant medication she had obtained in consultation with a psychiatrist friend freed her not only from depression but also from the expense of illegal drugs and the constant fear of detection. She took some steps to improve her appearance by having plastic surgery on her nose and was pleased with the results. She decided to concentrate more on school and less on men for awhile, and this enhanced her feelings of independence and of good self-care, although she didn't rule out relationships with men.

I will describe the incestuous relationship in Chapter 5. It is evidence of community avoidance of facing family violence such as in Carolyn's family that no extended family members or officials of the Jewish temple or other agencies ever intervened to help this mother and protect the children. Carolyn endured multiple trauma in her life and yet managed to retain an alert and inquiring mind and a sense of humor. She is one of the most courageous people I have ever known.

Francine was brought to see me by her father when she was 14. Her father explained that he had just taken over care of Francine, after having been divorced from her mother for many years, because Francine was fighting so much with her mother that Mother had "kicked her out," as she had kicked him out and her second husband as well. Father was aware that Francine was being mistreated by her mother but had not intervened. Additionally, Francine was making suicide attempts, cutting herself with a razor.

When I saw Francine, she was very regressed, spoke primarily to the doll she carried in her purse, and was barely able to speak with me. She had started carrying the doll after the move to her father's house separated her from her dog, to whom she was deeply attached. The dog had been her closest friend and companion for years, and she used to talk to her and knew that the animal understood her. She replaced the dog with the doll and imbued her with human qualities of understanding and responsiveness. She was quite paranoid, believing that people in the street were following her and would knife her. She had the idea that I was hiding a knife in the office and might stab her as she left. She had fantasies of immolating herself as a protest against the war in Viet Nam. I interpreted her cutting herself as a kind of protest against the injustice of her mother's treatment of her. Many interpretations in which I connected her fearfulness and mistrust of me to the cruel treatment by her mother gradually led to verbal communication, and the therapy continued for seven years. She was able to reveal that she felt no love from her mother, had been kept locked in a closet for hours at a time, was very jealous of her younger sister (from a second marriage) whom Mother was good to, and was very disappointed in her father who, she discovered, was an alcoholic who drank himself into a stupor every night, essentially leaving her alone. I often attempted to talk about her feelings of anger, but she refused to acknowledge angry feelings, saying it didn't do any good to feel that way and it isn't nice. I told her that nice people could feel angry, too.

On the plus side, Francine was very intelligent and had many talents. She was a musician and a writer and had these resources for expressing her feelings. I often interpreted her communicating with her doll and not with me as her disbelief that anyone could care about her or want to understand her. I commented that she kept herself inside that closet. Sometimes, when she couldn't talk, she brought me letters she had written for me, expressing her inner turmoil as well as her strong feelings about my efforts to help her.

I focused much effort on her repeated cutting of herself on her arms, which was deep enough to cause bleeding, but not deep enough to require medical attention or be life threatening. Occasionally, however, she miscalculated and did need medical attention. I tried to understand, with her help, what function this cutting served for her and how it was connected to her disturbed relationship with her mother. Apparently one function was that at times when she was so dissociated that she could not otherwise feel anything, seeing her own blood helped her to feel real and alive. She gradually was able to talk about the many beatings by her mother, which included bleeding and scarring. It became clear that the beatings inflicted by her mother, and now by herself, were preferable to the total isolation of that closet. The sadomasochistic connection was an improvement over the virtual death of her forced confinement. I explained to Francine that by inflicting the wounds on herself, she attempted to turn passive into active and have some sense of control over the terrible abuse that Mother had inflicted upon her.

Francine was able to continue in school and do well in her studies. After some time she gave up carrying her doll. She was aware of political events and, not surprisingly, identified with the underdog and got involved in some of the political activity in the Bay Area in the '70s. This was helpful in that it brought her in working contact with many people. She identified as a feminist and was pleased with that connection with me, but as it emerged she felt she was a lesbian and was not comfortable talking with me about her attraction to women. She attended a local college and continued her therapy until age 21, when she decided to drop out of college and take a break from treatment.

I know very little about her mother, other than that she was a successful professional musician and pretty and attractive. Father told me that Francine was an unwanted pregnancy but that her mother had decided not to have an abortion after considering it. I have no information about her background other than that she was a strong Christian Scientist who had a very dependent relationship with her practitioner that, according to the father, included two visits weekly, daily phone calls, and calls at the time of any crisis. Francine was raised as a Christian Scientist but rejected it. When Francine entered adolescence, she and Mother fought about everything, and Mother could not tolerate being disobeyed. When Francine had her breakdown, Mother sought the advice of her practitioner, who said that Francine should listen to her mother and try to please her. When that failed she sent her to live with her father.

Her treatment of Francine was so extremely cruel that I concluded that Mother must be psychotic, yet she received no psychiatric treatment. The only other possibility is that Mother had an intense negative transference to Francine based on whatever disappointment had occurred in the marriage to Francine's father, plus a very disturbed relationship with her own mother or other significant female that was split off and then projected onto her first daughter, but not her second daughter, although I do not know if the second daughter was free of serious psychiatric disturbance. The relationship with the practitioner is hard to evaluate. It could have been an undifferentiated extension of her relationship to her mother in which both parties participated; a folie à deux. The extreme dependency indicates, at the very least, a high degree of anxiety.

The sad and horrifying aspect of both these cases is that such abuse of children goes undetected, that the children are unprotected by other family members, and that such disturbed mothers go untreated and are left free to nearly destroy the lives of their children. No doubt the mothers were victims as well, but since the daughters were my patients I was most aware of the effects of the mother's disturbance on the child. The following poem was written by Francine after two years in therapy:

in this closet
in this closet is darkness of the richest kind
and scratched on the door is a pale light carrying sounds
into the solitude
chaotic house-noises of birds jabbering, pots clanging and
other life, music
there is a vacuum cleaner, a faded carpet and assorted other
objects to thump into
it is distressing to be sighted but made blind

in this closet is a three year old pounding on the door,
waiting and questioning
an arrogant, selfish child screaming and sobbing
hating, as all youngsters do, injustice in any shape or form
little did she know, she would spend the rest of her stupid
life thrashing around in closets
she had never anticipated the shocking swerve of events
you see, one day in that ridiculous hall closet
the three year old swallowed deeply,
let out a chilled sign and with an insurmountable determination
locked her own door
from the inside

In Francine's case, feminist theory really played no role, although she considered herself a feminist. This illustrates an important point that needs to be stressed. *The more severely disturbed the patient, the less a feminist analysis is applicable.* Interpretations must be of the most basic kind, focusing on issues of trust, caring, dependability, and the danger of exposing feelings. The success of the work depends on the emotional capacity of the therapist to accept the patient's communications, no matter how "crazy," in a caring, nonjudgmental manner, and a willingness to enter into the world of bizarre thoughts and behavior and not be repelled or frightened by it. Help is offered, not through any cultural analysis of the role of women, but through an effort to repair the damage done by a hostile, psychotic mother to her innocent daughter. In Francine's case, perhaps an analysis of her mother would reveal some facts whereby we could point to the role of patriarchal discrimination, but considering her mother's successful career as an independent entertainer, there is no evidence that I know of to suggest such an interpretation. This points to the importance of an individual approach to each case and a readiness to use or not use feminist theory as it is appropriate depending on your diagnosis.

A surprising postscript occurred recently when I was astounded and most pleasantly surprised to see Francine in a public theatre performance where she appeared as one of several comedians and did a very creditable job. After twenty years I was tremendously relieved and gratified that she was functioning well. What a long way from a closet to the stage!

These illustrations of mother–daughter relationships are just a few examples of women damaged by a close identification with dependent, needy mothers or by the hostility of unloving mothers and the tacit collusion of withdrawn fathers. The intensity of this bond makes it very difficult for the daughters of disturbed women to emerge into adulthood with positive feelings about their mothers or themselves. In my first book, I wrote of the view of Luise Eichenbaum and Susie Orbach in their book, *Understanding Women* (1983), that women feel emotionally needy and neglected but are taught to hide and repress this neediness. Mother denies her daughter nurturance because she herself feels bereft and cannot nourish her daughter emotionally. As the daughter gets older, her mother may cling to her in the hope of getting some of the nurturing she missed from her own mother. When the daughter is small, the mother experiences her as making emotional demands that the mother cannot meet, but as she gets older, mother views daughter as containing emotional capacities that the mother wants for herself. We are describing the activity of mothering and being mothered in which it is not always clear who is the mother and who is the child. The implication here is that mothers are training and preparing their daughters for marriage, where they will be the nurturers of men and cannot and should not expect to receive caring themselves. Caplan (1981, 1983, 1986) shares a similar position:

> We are further discovering how extensively, how pervasively the traditional, sexist forces in society have emotionally blackmailed our mothers, and us as mothers, into repressing our daughters; for it is in that earliest, most intense of relationships—the mother–daughter one—that so many of the barriers between women have their roots. . . . females are supposed to be patiently, endlessly nurturant. This has often meant that mothers were so busy training their daughters to give

nurturance that the daughters did not receive as much as their brothers. [1983, pp. 51–52]

In that sense, we can see a connection between the Chinese and African mothers, preparing their daughters by imposing physical pain and suffering on them to make them desirable marriage objects, and the Western mother who unwittingly passes on to her daughter a life of emotional deprivation and limited horizons in which the daughter learns that her independence and expectations of personal fulfillment from life are a liability and will ill prepare her for marriage. The competitive factor with other women is part of the anxiety in this picture. Many years ago I led a group of women who were the wives of medical residents with long working hours, who talked about their loneliness and resentment at having to do all the child care and perform so much personal service for their husbands. One member of the group warned ominously: "If you don't, someone else will!" The room fell silent as the women heard the message of how vulnerable they were. I commented on the anxiety, and they proceeded to talk of their fears. I was struck at how young they were to be having such fears, which until then I had associated with women who were aging and feared the competition of younger women.

I think that the rearing of daughters contains some of these features throughout the girl's childhood but that there are some separate phases. Carol Gilligan and her co-workers reported on a great change that takes place in girls after the age of 11, in *Making Connections: The Relational Worlds of Adolescent Girls at Emma Willard School* (1990). At age 11, Gilligan says that the girl is confident, articulate, and "not for sale," but as she reaches adolescence she enters a crisis and seems aware that her "clearsightedness may be dangerous and seditious." She believes that girls learn to censor what they think and how they act in order to meet the demands of the culture. Our question is, How are the cultural demands transmitted and by whom? Surely the communications media in all forms are very influential, as are teachers and friends. A mother plays a major role in transmitting the culture to her daughter and indirectly to other girls through the conversations girls have with each other, such as in the women's group cited above. Where had she heard that line, "If you don't, someone else will"? From her mother? From a friend through her mother? The messages from the media, from Mother and Father, from boys and older sisters may all join forces to produce a retreat from independence at adolescence and a conformity to the values of the culture. The adolescent cultural values may actually be in conflict with parental values and cause stress, especially in times of political and social change such as the '60s, and in that sense may be part of the process of breaking away from Mother. However, the conformity, whether it is in the style of the parents or in some ostensibly rebellious style, seems to have the same effect, which is to turn the girl away from pleasures in her own independent development and to focus on her attractiveness and popularity with boys.

An example of this was brought to my attention in 1969 when my own daughter turned 12 and began to develop breasts. Until that time her two grandmothers had delighted in her brightness, her achievements, and her loveliness. In separate visits but within a few months of each other, each grandmother noticed her development and immediately began talking to her about whom she should or should not marry. I was stunned and distressed that she had suddenly become, in their eyes, not the charming, intelligent person that I viewed her to be but instead a marriage prospect, being groomed for what they apparently believed was the only important role she had in life. Multiply these clear messages by the many more subtle ones from other sources and we can see a bombardment of communications to girls putting them in their place as a future Mrs. Somebody, not as a separate individual with many meaningful roles and possibilities. That was 1968, and I wonder how different those messages might be now. Until adolescence, until the pubertal changes unfold, life is more open and girls are encouraged to do their best in school, to develop talents, and to express themselves freely. As soon as sexuality emerges, other components fade except as they are viewed as enhancements to her marital chances, such as going to college to meet the right man.

Here we can return to the Chinese and African mothers who relate to their daughters as marriage prospects. Foot binding and sewing of the labia are severe physical restrictions and humiliations the girl must suffer in those cultures. In our culture the binding and mutilation is more subtle because it has been a binding and mutilation of her *possibilities.* The mothers are doing what they believe is best for their daughter's future, by imposing the crushing force of culture on her as was done to them. Economic and social realities are powerful forces, yet I do not know how this can be a loving act, even though it may be experienced as such by the mother. The competitive component in their relationship makes it quite difficult for a mother to tolerate her daughter having freedoms that she was denied and from lack of which she has suffered. Turkel (1976) comments on this as follows:

> Many of the young women I have treated had "strong" mothers, not necessarily career women but active in the community. Others had mothers whose unfulfilled dreams are being vicariously gratified by their daughters' success. At the same time there is hostility expressed by mothers who see their daughters as competition, with so much more sexual freedom, and even achieving the same salaries as their fathers. This is often manifested by sarcastic comments about the daughter's inability to get married. [p. 123]

One hopes that the mother can bring her intelligence to bear on her job and not let her narcissistic investment in preserving the value of her own choices undermine her daughter's chances for a better life, or, later, her own gratification at her daughter's success, even if she is saddened and anxious that her daughter is not yet married.

THE FEMALE THERAPIST AND THE FEMALE PATIENT

Many reasons are offered for the high percentage of women in psychotherapy, especially the positive one that women are better able to explore their feelings. However, it could also be true that psychotherapy is one of the few opportunities that our culture offers to women to have their own emotional needs attended to and to receive some of the nurturing that their mothers and fathers denied them. Katha Pollitt (1986), in a column in *The New York Times,* asks the question, "Why are women psychotherapy's best customers?" She comments on her observation that most of her friends are patients in psychotherapy, even though they all have interesting jobs and lovers or spouses; some have babies; and all lead comfortable, even affluent lives. "Could it be that women are in therapy because men aren't?" she asks. Her answer is that women serve in a nurturing role to men, performing a variety of essentially therapeutic tasks, and that the men do not reciprocate, "so what a husband gets for free, his wife has to pay a professional for." In psychotherapy, Pollitt observes, as opposed to the male-dominated real world, women get to talk about themselves, they are the stars.

> That sense of being at the center of her life rather than at the periphery of the lives of others, is what therapy offers women. It's quite an intoxicating feeling, and quite a feminist one too. It would be better of course, if we got that feeling from simply living, and if the women's movement succeeds in transforming personal relations and social attitudes on a grand scale, perhaps we will. Until then, women will continue to be therapy's best customers. [p. c2]

The issue of gender in choice of a therapist has been researched by a number of writers. This is one aspect of the topic, but another one that is of great interest is what actually happens in the interaction process between two women when one is the therapist and the other the patient.

Impact of Therapist Gender

Enrico E. Jones and Christian L. Zoppel

Jones and Zoppel (1982) showed significant differences in therapy outcome and client's judgment of therapist's effectiveness in two studies carried out in the San Francisco area. Interestingly, Jones, an African-American, set out to see if there were racial differences depending on racial match or mix between therapist and patient. He found none but instead was surprised to discover gender differences between men and women therapists in abilities or behavioral skills and emotional capacities as well as in attitudes. Although women clients in same-gender pairings did tend to show greater change, male therapists did not prevent women clients from demonstrating significant improvement. Women patients were more likely to be described by women therapists in a more desirable fashion than by male therapists as "capable, emotional, healthy, shy, understanding, efficient, honest, confused, strong, and intelligent." Women patients were more likely to be described by male therapists as "wary, simple, affected, commonplace, superstitious, conventional, awkward, cautious, conceited, and temperamental" (Table 4, p. 264). Even in describing male patients, male therapists are more "severe and stringent" than female therapists.

In regard to therapy outcome, gender-matched dyads resulted in therapies of significantly longer duration. On a score called the "therapeutic alliance" factor, both men and women clients in treatment with women therapists achieved significantly higher scores than those treated by male therapists. Women patients with women therapists scored higher on a score of "emotional intensity," and clients in same-gender pairings were more likely to view their therapists as neutral or nondirective. Regardless of therapist gender, women clients were more likely than men to experience being depreciated by their therapists. Results show that female therapists are more effective with both male and female clients and that male therapists experience more countertransference problems with women patients than do women therapists. Women therapists were perceived by all patients as more accepting, attentive, and comprehensible, and in general the patients reported forming more effective therapeutic alliances, which promoted more successful outcomes.

One of our many great debts to Freud is his discovery of the transference, which he at first viewed as an obstacle to analysis, dubbing it the "transference neurosis." He focused on genetic material and genetic interpretations for reconstructing and resolving the transference. Modern analysts and psychotherapists recognize that the actual relationship between therapist and patient is the best source for analyzing the transference, because it is most reliable. It bears directly on the interactions in the psychotherapy and is influenced by the gender of the therapist, other known facts about the therapist, fantasies, and projections from the patient's history. This approach actually makes the therapy process much more personal, more intense, and fraught with ambivalent connections for both patient and therapist. It does not allow the distance imposed by the professional aura of the physician treating a patient.

Transferences can be positive or negative and can be eroticized. Lester (1982) believes that the four possible analyst–analysand dyads differ qualitatively in that resistance and identification in the transference may be enhanced or inhibited by the gender of the analyst and/or the homosexual or heterosexual nature of the dyad, with male patients more inhibited in their expression of erotic urges to the female analyst than the female patient toward her male analyst.

Clara Thompson

Thompson (1938) proposed that for many patients the belief that a male is more capable will determine their choice of therapist but that among those who are knowledgeable about analysis, patients choose therapists of the sex with which they feel the most capable of intimacy. "Women who fear competition with their own sex and have strong feelings of envy for a successful woman find it too great a humiliation to be analyzed by a woman" (p. 210). Shainess (1983) concludes that patients generally choose to avoid the therapist who reflects the sex of the most damaging parent and recommends asking at the outset of treatment how the patient feels about your being a woman. She discounts the significance of the role model element between female patient and therapist because the unconscious attitudes—the parental introjects—are more important and are in fact what you work with. However, she does conclude that, other things being equal, women patients are more likely to be helped to be autonomous and self-reliant with competent woman therapists who are alert to gender-role stereotypes.

Rebecca Goz

Goz (1973) states that a woman may request a woman analyst in allegiance to her feminist beliefs, but that in fact this request is a "disguised request . . . to duplicate, review, reinstate, reenact, repair, and recreate some powerful unresolved tensions in her relationship to her mother" (p. 299). Yet I would hold that even if this is so, her concern about and valuing of her relationship with her mother could have been prompted by her feminist beliefs. She does believe that a woman therapist may be an advantage to women in three areas: pregnancy, symbiosis, and homosexuality.

There has been a contradiction in psychoanalysis between the "proposition that an analyst of either sex can treat a patient of either sex and that transference, by definition, bears little relation to the reality of therapist attributes" and the traditional view that "pre-oedipal problems were best dealt with by women, who were believed more intuitive and empathic" (Person 1983, p. 193). The women's movement has brought about many changes in the world of psychoanalysis and psychotherapy, not the least of which is the tremendous influx of women into the field and the changes in the choice of therapist, with women showing a marked preference for women therapists since the 1970s.

Ann Ruth Turkel

Turkel (1976), a psychoanalyst in New York, writes that prior to the women's movement there was a preference on the part of women for male analysts because women had internalized the "male oriented, male-aggrandizing culture, with resultant lower self-esteem and respect for their own abilities or those of other women." Women analysts were stereotyped as

> quiet, patient, nurturant, practical persons endowed with natural warmth, empathy, intuition, sensitivity and understanding—a virtual earth mother. . . . The patient population has long been conditioned to look upon competent females with distrust and tends to avoid them even when they are highly regarded by their male peers. . . . Thus for many years, my referrals consisted primarily of adolescent girls (they need a good mother), homosexual males (they might develop homosexual panic with a male therapist), lesbians (they are too hostile or fearful of men), and those patients for whom I was a re-analyst (as long as they are changing analysts, they might as well try a woman). Now, however, many women actively seek out women analysts, and some of them are so determined to see a woman that they will choose an almost untrained woman over a highly competent and sympathetic man. They perceive men as hostile to women and as not wanting women to achieve. [p. 120]

We might become concerned that this new rush toward women therapists is the renewal of an old stereotype of the nurturing female, and as critics of Carol Gilligan have claimed, this is dangerous for women and a regression from the view of women and men as equals. However, in my view, this is not a regression but in fact a new appreciation of women's empathic advantage combined with a newfound recognition of her intellectual equality with men. Remember that the old stereotype included an either/or dichotomy that acknowledged male superiority in the rational world of ideas but proclaimed women's special gifts in the emotional realm. The current attraction to female therapists—and in fact to female physicians in other specialties, especially gynecology—includes a recognition of women's strength in both areas and the fear that male therapists and physicians share with all men an irrational fear and distrust of women's strength and independence and therefore cannot be trusted not to belittle and inhibit women's autonomous strivings. This may be true for some male therapists, but it may also be an unfair and inaccurate projection onto a therapist from the woman's experience of her own mother or father.

A number of writers have explored the issue of whether there is in fact an advantage to women in seeing women for their psychotherapeutic treatment. A factor mentioned by some women patients is their wish to avoid the common erotic transference to a male therapist, which they fear will be a diversion from the issues for which they are seeking help. Conversely, some writers report an apparent difficulty for men in achieving an erotic transference to women therapists, an observation I do not share since I have seen a number of male patients who did develop an erotic transference in their work with me.

Ethel S. Person

Person concludes that the erotic transference is seen more frequently in women in treatment with men than in the reverse. Citing Gill's (1979) distinction between "transference resistance" and "resistance to the awareness of the transference," she writes: "I propose that, in general, the erotic transference utilized as resistance is more common in women in analysis—and, more particularly, women in treatment with men—while resistance to the awareness of the erotic transference is more common among male patients" (1985, p. 3).

Person believes that there may be limitations and negative ramifications in the female patient–male analyst combination:

1. The single woman may use the analyst as a phantom lover and mate.
2. The married woman may use her idealization of the analyst to denigrate and belittle her husband.
3. It may perpetuate dependent or worshipful relationships with men.
4. They may fail to work through their self-identity as women, their loving or competitive feelings toward women, or their inhibitions against self-expression.
5. It may perpetuate a low-grade depression or a subjective sense of inauthenticity, owing to a persistent negative identification with the "bad" mother.

In the female patient–female analyst pair there may be an erotic transference that may not be explicitly sexual, according to Person, but rather a wish for intimacy, understanding, affection and caring. An eroticized homosexual transference may be extremely intense and appear as part of an idealizing transference, which may be a reaction against a competitive transference. Person finds that the most intense maternal transferences are not erotic but rather are filled with fury, envy, rivalry, and fear as part of the oedipal constellation. This is the transference I described above in response to having been mothered by a narcissistic, immature, and neglectful mother, and I believe it contains strong preoedipal components as well, owing to the intense, unconsciously driven anger about deprivation of warmth and loving attention.

Another factor given by women for seeking a female therapist is the wish for a female role model, because the mother did not serve as a positive model and the culture, until recently, has offered so few. However, Person points out that a woman does not have to be in therapy to find positive role models. She believes that improvement comes not primarily from identification, but from "the permission the patient gets from the therapist to compete, succeed, enjoy. Such permission may be explicit or implicit. . . . an impersonal role model cannot grant permission to achieve and 'promise' not to exact retribution" (1983b, p. 202).

Yet the woman patient's success in the course of therapy is often the source of transference reactions to the woman therapist in which the patient imagines that the therapist will resent her patient's success and envy her for it, resulting in imagined anger and retaliation, which can be very frightening for the patient. These fears occur in spite of the patient's conscious recognition of the therapist's career success, for two reasons: the transference occurs on an unconscious level, and in fact the patient most often does not know much about the therapist's private life. Interpretations can be as follows:

> You seem reluctant to tell me how good your relationship with Bill is. I wonder if you're afraid I'll be envious, and resent you?

> You haven't said anything about sex with Bill. I wonder if you're afraid that I'll envy you for having an enjoyable sexual life?

> Now that you are becoming successful, it means you might be able to terminate your therapy. You seem hesitant to report your success to me. I wonder if you fear that I'm afraid of your leaving me, that I need you?

> It seems that as you become more successful at work (with men, in your marriage, with your family, and so on) you are complaining more about other dissatisfactions. I wonder if you're afraid I will envy your success and so you are reassuring me that you are still unhappy and need me?

For master's-level therapists:

> Now that you are close to getting your Ph.D., you seem to be
> belittling your achievement. I wonder if you are afraid I will resent
> your surpassing me, since I only have a master's degree.

For therapists who hold a Ph.D:

> Now that you are close to finishing law school (or medical school)
> you are complaining more about your relationship with Bill. I wonder
> if you are trying to assure me that you are not more successful than I
> am?

> You say I look tired, (or I seem worried); you seem to be fearful that
> your success can destroy me.

The therapeutic relationship does not rule out competitive elements in
female relationships. As long as the patient is doing poorly, these feelings
may remain hidden, emerging only as improvement brings some success.
Person comments: "A woman's wish for a role model may be a component
of an idealizing transference which, in part, defends against competition
and homosexual themes" (1983b, p. 202).

Countertransference

Anger, Aggression, and Grief—Theresa Bernardez

Bernardez (1988) states that the term *countertransference* has not included
culturally determined reactions but rather individual or family conflicts of
the therapist. Those reactions of male or female therapists to female
patients that are a result of socialization have been more difficult to
separate out because the supervisors or training analysts of these therapists
have shared the same biases; in other words, they are culture syntonic.
Feminism has changed that by elaborating the cultural effects of being
raised in a patriarchal system on all those within it. The system is absorbed
like the air we breathe, and until questioned and attacked by feminist
scholars and clinicians it was an unexamined aspect of countertransference
toward women and men patients.

In my own work I realized after many years that when I examined my
own practice of handling situations in which the patient had had a financial
reversal during the course of therapy, I had referred two male patients to
male therapists who could see them on Medi-Cal payments, for which I was
not eligible; and yet there were several female patients I had kept on under
similar circumstances and seen at a much lower fee. My conclusion was

that I was better able to tolerate the dependency in the women than in the men.

Bernardez (1988) observes three reactions of therapists to women patients that constitute errors of commission or omission:

> 1. The discouragement and disapproval of behaviors that did not conform with traditional role prescriptions for the female, e.g., rejection of motherhood, role reversal in marriage, lesbianism and/or rejection of heterosexuality.
>
> 2. The disparagement and inhibition of expression of anger and other "negative" affects as well as a whole spectrum of aggressive behaviors not expected of women.
>
> 3. The absence of confrontation, interpretation and exploration of passive-submissive and compliant behavior in the patient within or without the therapeutic situation. [p. 26]

She concludes: "The male therapist may be more inclined to reproduce the dominant-subordinate position, by unconscious encouragement of the female's compliance, submissiveness and passivity" (p. 27).

Bernardez then turns her attention specifically to the reactions of female therapists and divides the topic into two parts, namely, reactions to the anger and aggression and reactions to grief, stating:

> It is the incapacity of the therapist to maintain a benevolent neutrality towards the patient at those times that alerts us to the existence of strong feelings about them. . . . the interventions of the therapist (including her silence) have the direct or indirect aim of suppressing, discouraging and inhibiting those communications and attitudes. . . . they communicate their distaste for the patient's behavior. The negative reaction of the therapist has the purpose of protecting the therapist from similar feelings in her of which she disapproves. . . . The female therapist needs to be free of the dread of "female" destructiveness and of the compulsion to expect in all women nurturing and maternal characteristics. [pp. 28–29]

Suggestions for Interpretation

Bernardez makes many valuable observations based on her years of supervision of female therapists. Here are some of her major points, with my suggestions for interpretations to counter the problem.

1. Women have an idealized image of an all-loving, nurturing, maternal woman alongside a fantasy of a vengeful, omnipotent, unloving mother. The angry, aggressive, nonmaternal female patient arouses anxiety in the female therapist of the vengeful mother.

You are very angry at him (her, them) and that is understandable, but I wonder if underneath that anger there are also feelings of hurt and pain and fear.

(In this way you are recognizing the legitimacy of the anger but interpreting the defense, that is, that anger is one side and pain is the other. This shows that the therapist recognizes the anger, is not frightened by it or critical of it, but also knows that anger is a response to pain or frustration.)

2. The self-centeredness of the female patient may arouse conflict within the female therapist because of her own expectation of other-directed, altruistic behavior on the part of women. She may be unable to encourage women patients in self-serving behaviors no matter how appropriate to their development and how desirable an improvement.

(I have found it important for a therapist to be able to differentiate for herself and then for her patients the differences between self-denial, self-caring, and selfish attitudes and behavior.)

3. Some women therapists have difficulty drawing firm limits so that the female patient can test the boundaries vigorously. The therapist must feel free to deny and frustrate demands for nurturance, support, and dependency without feeling guilty and placating the patient.

You wish I could meet all these needs for you that you missed as a child. I can't ever be the good mother you needed and deserved then.

It's hard to take good care of yourself now because nobody took good care of you when you were young, when you were so dependent.

You're angry at me for not being more available to you, as if you were a helpless child and I was your mother.

4. A patient's angry behavior toward men can cause the therapist considerable discomfort and conflict, and she may communicate disapproval or deflect the anger, out of fear of arousal of her own anger toward men. She may have her own loving affiliations with men threatened if underlying feelings of resentment are tapped. The need to protect men from female anger may be unconsciously operating in the female therapist.

(If the angry reactions seem appropriate, it is best to just hear them out and say nothing, giving the patient the freedom to express herself by your accepting, noncritical manner. Here, just being a listener is therapeutic. By being quiet and not feeling any pressure to respond, the therapist can take time to reflect on her own reactions and bring them into perspective. If there is projection in the anger, an interpretation of the projection would be appropriate.)

You're angry at your husband for showing interest in other women at the party, yet I recall that last week you were talking about being attracted to his friend, and having fantasies of having an affair. I wonder if attacking him for talking to other women is a way you relieve yourself from guilt about your recent fantasies.

5. If the patient splits off anger and can speak only of feeling hurt and depressed, the therapist can become the recipient of that anger and may act out by voicing it. This may gratify the patient who receives confirmation of her split-off anger, but it does not help her to acknowledge, explore, or express her own negative feelings. This problem presents the flip side of the example in (1). Now the patient shows one side of her experience, the sadness and pain, and needs to acknowledge the other side, her anger.

(This is an example of how an awareness of her own angry reaction can help the therapist to know that there must be anger in the patient that is being communicated to her in a disguised way. This can help her to make interpretations about anger with confidence.)

I notice you are not expressing any anger toward your father (mother, boyfriend, husband, etc.)

If this comment does not bring any recognition of anger, you can proceed with:

It seems to me it would be natural to feel anger about this.

And further:

You haven't expressed any anger. I wonder if you are afraid to let yourself know when you feel angry?

I think you are protecting yourself from knowing how angry you are because you think you have to protect your father (mother, husband) from your anger. It feels dangerous to you and you are afraid of his (her) retaliation.

6. Many women feel cheated because of being female, blame and resent their mothers for not valuing them, and may feel disappointed in their mother's behavior, position, and aspirations. Some women may seek identifications with males to attain a sense of value, but internally retain a devalued view of themselves and other women. This can appear in a negative countertransference to women patients. One way to work this

through is by a positive identification with a female supervisor. Bernardez observes an "identificatory hunger" with female role models.

7. Women therapists may have trouble tolerating the expression of deep grief and sorrow in their women patients, and so such expressions are discouraged and inhibited in subtle and consistent ways if the therapist feels overwhelmed. Sometimes, being in therapy will be the first chance a woman has had to express deep sorrow, and although at first this may evoke an empathic response in the therapist, if it leads to intense and uncontrollable weeping the therapist may get anxious and be frightened by it, and thus defend herself against the recognition that her patient's sorrow is part of her own and her mother's sorrow. As the patient comes to realize that the sacrifices made in the expectation of being compensated or valued for them have been useless and that the supposed gains are illusory, the female therapist may be forced to examine her own and her mother's life with this emotional awareness. The knowledge of the deep mutilation that social expectations cause women and mourning for these losses can be devastating as the recognition of a universal "hatred of the female" emerges. A reaction of great anger in the therapist is another possible reaction.

> It is this fear of a paranoid position towards the world, of a grave disappointment with and distrust of men, of a feared loss of relations of loving nature with men and of an equally feared rage against women for their complicity, helplessness and victimization, that the acknowledgment of the devastating effects on women of their socialization and compliance with their victimization cannot be allowed in consciousness except in small degrees and at controlled intervals. This defense against overwhelming despair or disorganizing rage is tampered with when the woman patient's deep sorrow is allowed to emerge. For the patient, however, the experience of integrating these losses into a pattern of awareness of the social determinants of suffering and inequality in women is deeply healing. [p. 38]

As with the expression by female patients of great anger, in my view there is not much that a therapist has to say when a patient expresses grief. I think much is offered by simply allowing the expression of sorrow and of crying *without interfering with it*. The common reaction of family and friends to crying is to try to talk the person out of it, or cheer her up with insensitive trite sayings ("Everything happens for the best," "You'll feel better tomorrow," "God works in many mysterious ways," "It doesn't do any good to cry about it," or "Get a hold of yourself"). The experience of being able to cry with someone who simply listens and accepts your grief calmly with no fear or saccharine reassurance is remarkably therapeutic. It is only if the patient herself expresses fear about her crying or grief that interpretations are called for.

> You're being apologetic for crying, as if it's something to be ashamed of.

> You seem afraid to let yourself cry, as if once you started you couldn't stop.

To elicit projections:

> You seem to think I'm feeling critical of you for crying. Why would I be critical?

Bernardez never mentions the issue of suicide, but I believe that the anxiety that the patient might attempt suicide if such feelings are allowed expression is part of the fear of the therapist and her impulse to sidetrack the grief. How can the therapist be helped to tolerate the grief and anger and contain it for the patient? Surely good supervision is helpful, but not all supervisors are sympathetic to female grief, and some may even propose medication as a solution to the patient's depression. If the therapist has had a male analyst, a male supervisor, and no consciousness-raising group for herself, she may not have the foundation for the awareness of the "cultural countertransference" issues Bernardez raises.

Groups for Women Therapists

This points to the essential nature of a women's group for women therapists at some point in their training so that they have an opportunity to explore the deep pain and anger in their own lives that they must resolve before they can be of help to women patients. Ordinary supervision and consultation are not sufficient because it is not appropriate to bring up serious personal concerns in these settings. In my experience, there is a significant difference in content and affect between the traditional male consultant, a male-led consultation group, a female leaderless consultation group, and a consciousness-raising group. All four, in addition to the traditional personal analysis or analytically oriented psychotherapy, are the basic ingredients of a well-trained and personally well-developed female psychotherapist. Of course a consultation group could be female led and a consultant could be a female, but this would not be a place for personal exploration.

As an example of how personal needs are unmet in the training and traditional psychotherapy of most women therapists, it was of great interest to me to hear the reactions of many women therapists in the audience at a meeting of the Women's Institute of the American Orthopsy-chiatric Association in San Francisco many years ago to the presentation given by my all-woman peer consultation group of how we organized and functioned. We had been meeting for about five years, and members of the audience were amazed at our success. We were told by a number of them following the presentation that they too had started all-female consultation groups but the groups had dissolved after a year or two because the women had spent all the group time talking about personal problems. In my group, we had laid down clear boundaries of how the group time was to be spent, and although there was always some personal news-telling informally at the start, the work began promptly after some announcements. We realized that our group membership criteria had included women who had the personal maturity to stick to the task and to receive help for their personal issues from other sources as they needed it.

Just as it has been an accepted fact as a psychotherapist one is expected to undertake a personal analysis or psychotherapy, so I believe it is also essential for women therapists to undertake consciousness raising in order to work through the issues of sexism, which could easily include self-loathing, low self-esteem, suppression of anger, pathological niceness, and a difficulty valuing women as intelligent and capable persons. We cannot help our patients with any of the great conflicts and challenges of life if we have not fully explored them in our own lives.

Eastwood, Spielvogel, and Wile (1990) report on their experiences with women inpatients at San Francisco General Hospital where they were part of a Women's Issues Consultation Team in the Department of Psychi-atry. The team had the goal of improving the treatment of women patients through treatment by women therapists, but they were surprised to find that "not only our problematic responses, but also our effective solutions, have often occurred unconsciously" (p. 273). They found they had particular difficulties with four types of female patients: extremely aggres-sive women; dependent women; sex-trade workers; and women viewed by themselves, others, and the therapists as "bad mothers." With the aggres-sive women the problem was being able to tolerate their own hatred for the patient without fearing that this hatred would kill her, the fear of becoming the "powerful witch." With the sex-trade women responses varied be-tween laughter, disgust, and embarrassment, and the therapists focused on reinforcing rules for behavior on the ward. The staff encouraged each other to read about prostitution, which did help to soften their moralistic condemnation but was later recognized as dealing intellectually with their fascination with the patients' sexual lives. An older depressed and depen-dent woman elicited fears of aging, giving in to dependency needs, and the possibility that after a life of service to others, a woman can end up alone, poor, unattractive, and unloved. This led to their distancing themselves from this patient. A cocaine-using pregnant woman also elicited moral condemnation and withdrawal. The group concludes:

> Our common assumption that shared gender would lead to successful treatment outcome was challenged by these particular patients. This led to individual and collective feelings of self-doubt and devaluation. . . . Women therapists who are devoted to providing sensitive and caring treatment to other women may then have special difficulties acknowledging their disapproval and dislike of certain female patients. . . . Having learned from these experiences, we believe that particularly in same-gender treatment an active search and discussion of feelings such as anger, avoidance, failure, envy, and disapproval must and can occur with the group. [pp. 279–280]

ADVANTAGES FOR WOMEN WITH A WOMAN THERAPIST—CLINICAL ILLUSTRATION

I agree with those who see possible advantages for women in seeing female therapists, but I do not rule out the possibilities of women having highly successful treatment with men and failed treatment with women. Over the years I have seen many women who have come to me after being disappointed with their treatment with both male and female analysts or therapists. Another clear advantage, often neglected, for a woman seeing a female analyst is the chance to work through inhibiting sexual attitudes and fears. Most of the literature I have reviewed on the issue of therapist gender has not cited this topic as an area of advantage for a woman with a female therapist. Lerner (1982) does include it in her list of advantages.

I have worked on the issue of sexual fears and inability to achieve orgasm with many women, and I wonder if the patient would have felt as comfortable with a male therapist. It usually was only after much resistance and reassurance on my part of my comfort with the subject that these women have revealed their difficulties to me. The following excerpt (Krause 1971) describes a specific case example where the former psychiatrist, who is male, had been unable to work effectively in the sexual area with a female patient I was seeing.

> I feel there might be real advantages for certain women in seeking out a female therapist. First let us consider the sexual area. Masters and Johnson (1970) state: "Certainly, controlled laboratory experimentation in human sexual physiology have supported unequivocally the initial investigative premise that no man will ever fully understand woman's sexual function or dysfunction. . . . For example, it helps immeasurably for a distressed, relatively inarticulate, or emotionally

unstable wife to have available a female co-therapist to interpret what she is saying and, far more important, even what she is attempting unsuccessfully to express to the uncomprehending husband and often to the male co-therapist as well'' (p. 4). Certainly the Masters and Johnson approach of direct education differs markedly from the analytic mode of therapy, yet for some women the initial exposure of intimate sexual feelings and desires may be less difficult with a woman whom she may hope will appreciate her torment.

I have been seeing a married woman for several years now, Mrs. J., who prior to seeing me had been in psychotherapy for five years, twice weekly, with a male psychiatrist of good reputation. It turned out after I had been seeing her for a while that she had never discussed her sexual feelings or experiences with him. When I attempted to include exploration of sexuality in our sessions, she became quite uncomfortable and revealed she had never talked about this in therapy before. In analyzing the fears behind this we discovered that it related to many experiences as a little girl when the group of boys in her neighborhood would chase her and try to catch her in order to pull down her pants. She had always been successful in evading them and escaping to the protection of her home. In dating, she had always felt that men were trying to ''get her in the sack,'' as she puts it. She realized that whenever her male therapist had attempted to explore sex with her it had felt as if he was trying to get her pants down and once again she successfully evaded a male pursuer.

The strength of this woman's sexual fantasies about her psychiatrist had never been explored either and this put the pressure on her to project her own sexual desires and fear of acting them out onto her therapist. Of course discussion of intimate sexual material with a female therapist could be threatening to repressed homosexual wishes, but for this woman there was less resistance to discussing sexual matters with a woman because a woman was seen by her as less threatening sexually. She was then able to reveal her shame and guilt about masturbation and as she felt more certain of my non-critical approach, she could describe her sexual attraction to other men and active fantasy life. I was able gradually to help her to see how she had been projecting this fear of sexual acting out onto her husband because these feelings had been so threatening to her. She had been accusing him of infidelity and actually provoking him by her suspicions and accusations.

What counter-transference problems of her previous therapist interfered with his treatment of this woman we have no way of knowing, but poor therapy was the result. It is unfortunate that he could not help her to re-evaluate her mistrustful attitude towards men but with me she could have the experience of relating to another woman who did not view bodily odors and desires as shameful and did not see men as predators and women as helpless victims.

A second advantage for a woman in seeing a woman therapist relates to the potential for identification with an understanding, capable female who is successfully employed outside of her home. For women with conflicts in the area of independence, the obvious example of the therapist herself functioning independently can be a source of strength to an ego which has always identified being female with being damaged, vulnerable, silly or helpless. No matter how much we conceal of our personal lives and personalities, the fact of our working as professional women is an obvious fact and a direct indication of what we think about "a woman's place." Potential for super-ego identifications with a less punitive woman is another positive feature. [pp. 481–482]

I have explored the relationship between mother and daughter and then extended it into the relationship between women in psychotherapy. As the relationship develops, the same issue of differentiating from the analyst yet staying connected applies to the woman patient. By the time she is ready to terminate treatment, the woman patient should be able to appreciate the help of her therapist and the strong qualities she communicated. The patient should also be able to know and accept that her therapist made some mistakes, has some weak spots, and that they may disagree on some matters, perhaps even on certain interpretations. The development of this independent stance toward the therapist should be reflected in relationships with other people, especially her parents and husband or lover; women and men in positions of authority, such as doctors and supervisors; and also with friends. She may not be able to successfully achieve a separate yet intimate tie to her mother because of her mother's limitations, but it is hoped that she can make peace with what her mother does, and does not, have to offer her in a relationship and maintain a connection to her mother that, if not close, can be cordial and preserves her autonomy. She will be able to say no to others to protect her own self-interest, without feeling fear and guilt. I feel optimistic that the new generation of women who grew up in the era of feminism will be more autonomous than their mothers were and will, when they become mothers, be more tolerant of their daughters' needs for separation. If their lives are fulfilling, there would not be the same reasons to resent their daughters' opportunities. Let us hope that we do not so frequently hear in the future those anguished fears of "being like my mother" and the corollary, "I hope I'm never like my mother." What a sad indictment of the state of women in the United States so far in this century.

2

THE FEARS OF WOMEN

Where the husband holds the wife in subjection, married happiness is impossible. It can exist only in an atmosphere of freedom. Women would make no demands if they were loved as they wished to be. As things are, they are ill-used. They are forced to live a life of imbecility, and are blamed for doing so. If they are ignorant, they are despised, if learned, mocked. In love they are reduced to the status of courtesans. As wives they are treated more as servants than as companions. Men do not love them: they make use of them, they exploit them, and expect, in that way, to make them subject to the law of fidelity.

—George Sand

It was once said that men did not marry women who showed too much intelligence. In my youth I knew women who hid their college degrees as if they were one of the seven deadly sins. But all this is passing, as so will pass many other prejudices that have their origin in the ancient tradition that women are a by-product of creation.

—Eleanor Roosevelt

Whether or not women are more fearful than men is hard to judge because men are taught from an early age that being fearful is being a "sissy," that is, being feminine, and so they learn to either master their fears or hide them. A British pilot interviewed after a return from a bombing mission over Iraq said that he was terrified at the enormous antiaircraft fire directed at him and so he had "tried to run away coura-geously." His candid comments revealed his honest emotions with the element of saving face. On the contrary, being fearful is considered feminine and appealing in women and has the secondary gain that showing weakness can make men feel strong and superior and thus can be flattering to men. Unfortunately, this ideal of femininity does not prepare a woman for adversity, such as divorce or widowhood. Having courage is required for life whether you are male or female, so women are at a disadvantage in the world if they are unable to overcome the female stereotype. Women need to be brave if they are going to be independent, and they are often called upon by life to be independent whether they want to be or not.

Closely related to the fears of women is the issue of female depen-dency. In my first book I compared female and male dependency. Here I want to point out how dependency is related to fear and fear adds to dependency so that the two are interconnected. As with fear, the sources of dependency lie in both internal dynamics and external realities for women. Often women will enter therapy at the time of divorce or when a relationship ends. I have found it common for therapists to define the problem as the poor judgment of the woman in picking the wrong man. The focus of the therapy then becomes an examination of her history, in the course of which they learn that there have been a lot of "wrong men" in her life, starting with her father. This conveys hope to the patient that with the therapist's help she will learn to recognize and weed out the wrong men and find Mr. Right. The patient stays in therapy with the goal of developing her psychological awareness of how her bad relationship with her father has determined her choice of men, while they both eagerly await the results of her newfound insight to produce a wonderful, caring, mature, healthy man. This is wonderful if it happens, but there is no guarantee that it will.

The problem with this approach is that the focus is on finding a better man rather than on the woman's extreme dependency on men and her failure at any point in her life to develop the capacity to live alone and explore her independent interests apart from men. These women usually go from one man to the next with almost no period for self-reflection and self-development in between. It is much more likely that a woman will attach herself to so-called wrong men if she cannot tolerate being alone long enough to wait for the right man. These women feel incomplete and ashamed to be without a man, as if having a man were what made them worthwhile, not any of their own attributes. This is not to be confused with the genuine pleasures of male companionship that most women miss when they are alone. I am describing a woman for whom life is practically unbearable without a man because her self-esteem is so low that she is entirely dependent on a man to confirm her as lovable and desirable, for social status, and to give her life meaning. Her childhood dependency gets transferred to a man because her autonomous development away from family was short-circuited by the anxieties of her parents and the societal pressures to have a boyfriend and then a husband. Periods without a man are filled with anxiety and depression.

THE FEAR OF NOT BEING LOVED: FEMALE DEPENDENCY

The all-encompassing fear of women is the fear of not being loved. A number of writers have recognized this. Most other fears follow under this general heading, such as the fear of being selfish, being blamed, being unfeminine, and being unattractive, all leading to the overriding fear of being abandoned and then finally to the fear of being alone and poor. To gain and keep love, women develop styles that include being ingratiating, submissive, placating, deferring to men, being servile, and concealing their success, intelligence, strength, anger, and opinions. They learn not to disagree. Very often these traits first develop in childhood in relation to mothers and fathers, or perhaps older siblings, but instead of women developing out of them, these fears are then transferred to relationships with men, bosses, and therapists, both male and female. Approval-seeking behavior can develop a false self that is appeasing while underneath there is anger at having to depreciate oneself in this way. Sometimes, the mask becomes ego syntonic, and the quest for pride is buried in manipulations and deceits to maintain the love and approval of a lover or husband upon whom the woman feels dependent for her survival. Person (1983b) identifies the common practice of "faking orgasm" as paradigmatic behavior for many women seeking to gain approval and needing to be loved. This exposes another aspect of this syndrome, the fear that making requests for her own satisfaction will be considered selfish, aggressive, and therefore unfeminine. Person cites the case of a woman patient, Mrs. C, who needed to appear to be a good patient and perform according to the therapist's expectations, and points out that this was analogous to her pretenses in sex, faking orgasms.

Ironically, this constellation of traits can at times be used quite manipulatively with men to attain power through helplessness and can be part of an only partially concealed contempt of men. The idea is that men are so fragile that they cannot tolerate equality and will be threatened by a challenging or confident woman, so they must be deceived into believing the woman is needy, delicate, and weak.

One of the ways that dependency is rewarded in women is through the practice of alimony, or spousal support. A woman who has not worked in her marriage is rewarded for her dependency by the provision of alimony at the time of divorce. A woman who has worked will not be entitled to alimony because she is seen as capable of supporting herself.

The fear of loss of love has often been described as a fear of *abandonment,* yet often the fear is even more intense and debilitating than that and upon close examination turns out to be a fear of *annihilation.* For men the fear is regression to identification with the mother, femininity, and the loss of male identity. For women the fear is regression to fusion with the mother, the loss of ego boundaries. It is in this regressed state of fusion that abandonment becomes annihilation. The gender difference protects the male from fusion.

Person (1985) states: "These fears are often expressed in oral, sometimes cannibalistic terms. The woman's fear is of loss of love, of starvation and annihilation. Most likely, competitive fears take these forms because the object of competition is also the source of nurturant and dependent gratification" (p. 23).

> Self preservation frequently becomes symbolically linked to pair-bonding, which emerges as the dominant motif in mental life. . . . in female development a prolonged erotic attachment becomes the pseudo-solution to so many problems whereas in male psychology the problem is in achieving a love relationship integrated with sex. [p. 32]

This points us to the Chodorow and Gilligan work on the importance of connection and bonding in female development and in the formation of a female identity, as opposed to the attainment of identity in men through achievement and autonomy.

> Men may have the same magnitude of dependency needs and affiliative yearnings but are less fearful that they will go unfulfilled. . . . the girl's erotic rival, her mother, is also the source of dependent gratification, a situation that intensifies the girl's fear of retaliation. [Person 1985, p. 32]

In what has been called the "change of object," the girl renounces her mother in favor of her father and may experience this as a betrayal of her mother for which mother will retaliate. This puts the girl in an anxious position of competing with mother to win father's love but appeasing mother at the same time, because she is still very dependent on mother for nurturing and has a close identificatory relationship with her. This fear of loss of love can be transferred to the husband with, in some cases, the reenactment of her own sense of betrayal if she is attracted to another man. This may be converted through the mechanism of projection to a fear of abandonment (retaliation) by the husband. This projective mechanism protects the woman from the aggression and guilt of her own fantasies of sexual affairs by imagining that that is what is on her husband's mind. She prefers the fear and suffering of that terrible imagined abandonment because the victim position is more acceptable to her than that of the angry betrayer. That was the case in the examples I gave in Chapter 1 of Mrs. J. and Theresa.

Thus we see once again the complications in love relationships that can result from the girl's ambivalent tie to her mother and her suppression of angry and aggressive feelings. The projective mechanism becomes a dangerous defense because the unfair accusations can in fact anger the husband and become a self-fulfilling prophecy.

External Realities—Feminist Views

So far I have focused on the internal sources for the fear of loss of love, the psychoanalytic approach. Shifting now to a feminist approach, feminists cite the external reality of the desirability in our culture of younger women, which results in frequent examples of the abandonment of a wife for a younger woman and/or the remarriage after divorce to a much younger woman. These statistics cannot be ignored as a source of genuine anxiety and anger for women who, as they get older, are placed in competition with younger women and therefore may resort to appeasing styles of behavior in order to avoid the psychological and financial trauma of divorce for themselves and their children.

Also common is the practice of men seeking out women of lesser education and knowledge, and more dependency, making the fear of success for women an example where internal dynamics based on old oedipal conflicts converge with the external reality of lowered value in the marriage market. A feminist-psychoanalytic approach to the fear of abandonment in women would include both the intrapsychic and the external reality sources in the therapeutic work, asking questions and making interpretations based on both possible sources of anxiety.

The Femininity Complex—Clinical Illustration

In 1971 I published a paper describing the "femininity complex," which focused on the fears of women if they did not conform to the prevailing view of what was the correct role for women. These values and roles had been so well internalized by women raised in the prefeminist era that changing these internalizations required much effort. I am including a long excerpt from that paper, which focuses on a case example of a woman devastated by a divorce because she had to completely revise her identity and goals in order to adjust to the reality of being a single woman.

My clinical experience plus my personal experience knowing many women have led me to be concerned about a particular kind of woman, one who is unable to integrate the traditional ideals of womanhood with the expanded experience and opportunities of a modern woman. The extensive education received by women today combined with more effective birth control methods and more relaxed sexual attitudes give women choices they never had before. Yet to many women these choices do not exist because they are bound by an internalized image of what is the "natural" role of a woman, that is, as a wife and mother serving her husband and children and always placing their needs first. On the other hand, some single women fear marriage and resist it due to the belief that marriage will spell the end of their individuality and freedom. It is this configuration—the binding of a woman's life to a man, the denial of her needs in favor of serving and pleasing a man and their children, the sense of abnormality if she does not marry and bear children combined with an internal prohibition against self-assertion and development outside the context of a family, that comprises the "femininity complex," an aspect to the functioning of many women which as therapists we must be aware of if we are to be ready to help women work through to creative solutions.

"What do women want?" is often heard now in response to cries for liberation. Freud, too, had difficulty with this question. In 1937 he emphasized that women come into analysis looking for a penis and leave unreconciled to the fact that they can't get one. In a recent paper Mildred Ash wonders: "Is it that women come into the analysis looking for an honorable identity which they think is a masculine identity and leave not having found a satisfactory feminine identity because for the male analyst too, the only honorable identity is a masculine one?" (unpublished). I wish to add to this the proposition that some women come into therapy in the hope of getting a man or for help in keeping the one they've got because the only honorable identity for all but the most extraordinary women in this society is to belong to a man in marriage. Belonging to a male therapist can substitute.

Freud defined mental health simply and succinctly: to love and to work, yet when it comes to women patients I wonder if we have tended to be too strongly influenced by traditional expectations that goals for a woman are to love and to work for the objects of her love, her husband and her children. In this way the work life is intrinsically bound with the love life so that women are dependent on men to fulfill them in both these vital areas. For the many women who work outside the home their work often does not have the meaning and therefore the satisfaction that it might and that it does for most men. Now you may say here, "Wait, most men work at jobs that do not provide them with satisfaction, jobs that are tedious and unfulfilling." Yes, certainly one hears complaints from men but I am not referring to the problem of boredom which may ensue after four to seven years of working at a particular skill or profession. I refer to the self-esteem to be gained by an adult from the challenge of a skill which can be learned, a job accomplished and done well, a job compensated by a fair salary and in which a real investment of self can be made in the task. Too many women withhold a real commitment to their work because they see it as temporary until they marry or until they have children, or as secondary to their so called truly feminine and natural work-role of wife and mother. If any of us can't take our work seriously, whether it be housewife, teacher or salesman, we can't take ourselves seriously. Many women feel a pressure to get to the "serious" work in their lives, marriage and children, minimizing other possibilities for gratification. Those women who for whatever reasons are unable to marry; those who marry but are unable to bear children; and those who marry, bear children, but feel a lack of satisfaction from this work are confronted with identity conflicts of great magnitude which sometimes land them in our offices. They have internalized the patriarchal ideal of woman-hood, of a woman longing only to love a man and be loved by him, to admire and serve him and to bear and rear his children. All else pales in significance because no other role is compatible with her feminine identity, that is, her introjects of society's expectation for a female. If she cannot fulfill this internalized image she fears she is not normal and may seek therapy in fear of this abnormality. Her femininity complex is blocking her from freely seeking out all possible solutions. All available paths cannot be explored if a pre-determined "right way" for women is held in the way.

In 1934 Karen Horney published a paper entitled "The Over-Valuation of Love, A Study of a Common Present-Day Feminine Type," to which I owe many of the ideas in this paper. In that paper she points out that the analyst's discernment of the importance of heterosexual experience can on occasion blind us to a neurotic over-valuation of and overemphasis upon this sphere. She describes a group of woman patients who think they can only find happiness through a love relationship with a man, yet because of their character they cannot be happy with a man. On the other hand, they minimize the value of their talents and abilities and thus deprive themselves of the satisfaction of achievement from work. "For although in the last analysis sex is a tremendously important, perhaps the most important, source of satis-faction, it is certainly not the only one, nor the most trustworthy" (p. 187).

I would like to describe a former patient of mine whom I saw for about two years twice weekly and whom I was able to help work through her femininity complex. This woman came to me at the age of 25, shortly after filing for divorce from her third-year law student husband. They had been married five years but had dated seriously since they were 16 and in high school together. My patient is a high school teacher and had been supporting her husband through law school. He had begun to feel quite unhappy in the marriage, had become attracted to other women and had begun to find fault with her. She was very hurt by all this but had made an effort to hold on to him by indulging his whims such as for the purchase of a sailboat and for frequent skiing vacations when in fact, she wanted to be saving money for a house. Nothing worked, and when he moved out she filed for divorce. It is important to note that this was just at the point in the marriage when she had been looking forward to getting pregnant, resigning from her teaching position and being supported by a promising young attorney, who she was convinced would be very successful, might go far in politics, and would bring them both into important social circles.

During the first year and a half of the treatment she continued to suffer from the rejection by her husband and to experience severe pain when she would hear through some mutual acquaintance that he was seen with a woman or at a party. She didn't date very much and when she did she managed to discourage the men and be fault finding with them. I should mention here that she is an extremely attractive looking young woman whose looks alone are outstanding enough to make her desired by men. She felt quite disillusioned about love, yet was lonely and anxious at the possibility of not marrying again. She didn't like going to parties without a date yet felt insecure at parties with a date, fearing he would find another woman more attractive. She refused to go to bars to meet men or even admit to anyone she wanted to meet men. She related stories to me of women she knew who wanted to marry and hadn't found anyone, and as she would go on I would find myself getting anxious at the prospect of her not finding a man she could marry. However, I was able to catch my own anxiety and focus on her pessimism, her criticism of men, her transfer of dependence back to her family and to me and to question why life could not be more satisfying without a husband.

One of the factors that made it difficult for her to take any other man seriously was that she still entertained the fantasy of an eventual re-uniting with her husband after he had had his fling and was ready to settle down. She searched for hidden messages in his communications and would be happy if she heard something positive and crushed if she felt coldness. Another factor had to do with her depreciating most of the men she knew because they were "only teachers." When I pointed out to her that she was in this way indicating how little she thought of herself, she was quite surprised. She had maintained the illusion of being very proud of herself for having done so well in college that she had been offered a job teaching high school in this area right out of school. She had often told me how proud her parents were of her and how they bragged about her to friends and relatives, yet she knew that they would not be satisfied that a teacher was good enough for her to marry. Here we can see the gender factor. Being a teacher was good for her because she is "only a woman" but when it comes to a man she had felt marriage to a man who is "only a teacher" to be impossible. She had clung to the hope of re-uniting with her husband because as an attorney he would bring her the status and esteem vicariously which she could not feel about herself through her own work.

It is interesting that since they did continue to have contact with each other, she was very conscious of how much anxiety he was experiencing in anticipation of taking the bar examinations. When in fact he did not pass the bar the first time she could no longer deny what she had always felt, that she in fact is brighter than he is, that she was never anxious about taking exams and that she would probably have been able to take the bar and pass it the first time. She could then recognize how in many subtle ways she had communicated this to him and how he really always felt that she was smarter and had been uncomfortable in their relationship because of this, in addition to the fact that she was supporting him. It had been necessary to her for all these years to see herself as inferior to him in order to fulfill the expectation she had of herself as a feminine woman, which means looking up to the man (how do we feel about a couple when the man is shorter?), catering to him and pleasing him in order to receive the benefits of his status in the community and the security of a prosperous home for herself and her children. She had denied her own competence because she feared that exposing it was an aggressive, hostile and unfeminine act.

Her major complaint was depression, which she responded to with overeating. When we first began to investigate her depression it became apparent to me that she was cutting off one potential source of gratification with her attitude that she didn't want to make teaching "her whole life." Of course this is a rationalization, which was destructive because in her effort to avoid future loneliness and dissatisfaction she was only adding to her current loneliness and lack of satisfaction. When she recognized how she was actually depriving herself in this way she began to involve herself with her students and with student activities. She took courses in advanced education for teachers, which culminated last year in her participation in a study abroad program which took her to Europe for the summer. She has found great satisfaction and stimulation from continuing her education, and she has enjoyed getting close to her students and participating in their activities. This involvement, plus our analysis of her depreciation of male teachers, combined to involve her in long-term dating relationships with first one and now a second male teacher. Unlike her counterparts in the first sixty years of this century, she could have these affairs without guilt and without fear of pregnancy. She has many friends and relatives in this area and is able to work out a happy balance of teaching, dating, visiting, entertaining and just being by herself, to read, grade papers and do her housework.

In the final six months of treatment she did a lot of reevaluating. She realized that she could have a satisfactory life being a single woman. She knew it helped a lot when she did have a boyfriend but she was able to anticipate periods without a boyfriend which would still contain enough satisfaction for her so that the depression would not return. She realized she very much enjoyed the freedom of not having to come home after school every day to cook dinner for her husband. She also liked the freedom to choose friends and activities to suit herself, rather than spending time with her husband's friends, whose wives she didn't enjoy, or feel she was dragging her husband to parties involving her relatives and friends, whom he didn't enjoy. She felt dubious about the likelihood of a marriage in which each partner cared equally for the other and felt in each of her relationships the men cared more for her than she for them, the reverse of her marital relationship. But the pressure to attach herself to a "superior" man was off and she enjoyed her current boyfriend's kindness and appreciation of her. She even had the children angle resolved. She stated at one of our last sessions that she has no strong desire for children but that if she didn't marry and did in the future feel a strong desire for a child, she had read that a single person could now adopt a child and that is what she would do. Considering her involvement with her students we might conjecture that her parenting needs are being met through her job. She stated that she loved her job, loved her apartment and enjoyed skiing and other vacations with friends. She had almost everything she wanted. A year before she had often repeated that she could not imagine ever stopping her appointments with me as she looked forward to them so much. In January 1971 she terminated with confidence, with the feeling she might even eventually want to marry her current boyfriend, but not for a while. How her life will develop we do not know, but at this point she is allowing herself some healthy doses of narcissism in contrast to her former masochism.

Now this story is successful partially because of the many strengths with which the patient entered therapy. She was bright and beautiful, she was young and had no children, she had a challenging and well-paying job, had loving parents and many friends. However, rather than focusing on how much easier that made the treatment, I'd like to ask the question why a woman with all these assets should experience serious depression and require psychiatric treatment? Certainly there were problems such as unresolved dependency struggles with her parents and other areas with which we worked that I have omitted in order to focus on the aspects of the case which illustrate her femininity complex. What I hope to have shown by way of this particular woman's example is the degree of dependence she felt on her husband's love for her and the degree of emptiness she experienced without it. She had defined her worth almost exclusively in relation to a particular man's love for her and had been dependent even for her will to live on the knowledge that this man loved her, found her desirable and allowed her to serve him and keep his house for him. This pathological state of mind made the experience of being a single woman fraught with anxiety and depression, relieved only by fantasies of not having really lost her husband, until therapy and experience combined to enable her to experience herself as a capable, independent woman with choices other than the traditional one of marriage and child rearing. [Krause 1971, pp. 476–480]

THE FEAR OF BEING SELFISH

I have often been struck by how many of my women patients live in fear of being accused of selfishness. This fear has its roots in their memory of their mother's accusations of selfishness against them in childhood and adolescence as well as the many cultural messages of condemnation of women who consider their own careers and own needs of equal importance to, or more important than, pleasing and caring for others. My conclusion has been that a mother's accusing her daughter of selfishness is a means of discrediting her strivings for autonomy. The mother controls her daughter's efforts toward independence by labeling them "selfish," in that way controlling her daughter to behave in ways that suit the mother's needs rather than her own. Since being "selfish" is so blameworthy, my patients usually tried to avoid the label by not asserting their own needs and thus falling into the trap of failing to differentiate their own legitimate needs from their mother's demands for conformity and obedience. This failure follows the woman into all relationships in adulthood, being reenacted with husbands, bosses, and her own children. Clashes with the mother can result in serious fighting, with further accusations of making the mother ill. If the father is brought in he often will tell the daughter to do what her mother tells her to do, without any awareness of how this may be reinforcing the mother's narcissistic exploitation of the daughter. Sometimes battles develop over who the girl chooses for friends or boyfriends, how she spends her leisure time, what clothes she wears, and how much she helps mother in household chores as opposed to pursuing outside interests. The mother may be truly dependent on the daughter, as she was on her own mother, and may in fact be made very anxious as the daughter starts to separate in adolescence, doing all she can to manipulate the girl into remaining attached to her and in her control.

Suggested Interpretations

It is not easy for many women to differentiate selfishness, a truly narcissistic orientation to the world, from healthy self-assertion and self-caring. Often the reaction against the accusation of selfishness is to be selfless, to serve and please others without expecting reciprocation. A typical inter-action in therapy around this issue with a single woman may be as follows:

Patient: My parents want me to come home for my birthday (or Thanksgiving or Christmas) and I really don't want to. I know just what it will be like, the same people, the same tension for me. My mother will tell me about all her friend's daughters who have gotten married and my relatives will ask me when I'm going to get married. I'll get depressed and it will take me a week to recover.

Therapist: Why go, then?

Patient: What, not go, how could I do that?

Therapist: Why not?

Patient: My mother would be so upset, she would call and complain and tell me I'm ruining everything, and what will she tell the family. It would be so awful, it wouldn't be worth it. It's easier to just go.

Therapist: So it's better for you to be depressed for a week than to upset your mother.

Patient: Well, I can handle it. I guess it's still easier than getting her all upset and feeling it's my fault.

Therapist: You're so afraid of feeling selfish that you can't act in your own self-interest, to protect yourself from an insulting and unhappy weekend. You're entitled to enjoy the holiday.

Patient: But what if she gets one of her high blood pressure attacks?

Therapist: What if she does?

Patient: It would be my fault, they would all blame me.

Therapist: If your asserting yourself in your own best interest makes your mother sick, that is your mother's responsibility. Allowing yourself to always be blackmailed into doing what's best for your mother and never putting your needs first, means you'll continue to be depressed.

As is obvious here, the daughter can simply rely on a character defense of masochistic suffering in order to avoid a confrontation with her parents. Her fear of exposing her own anger and being on the receiving end of angry retaliation from her family is enough to continue the pattern of parental control over her autonomy.

Acting in her own self-interest may feel unfeminine to a woman. Jean Baker Miller described this in *Toward a New Psychology of Women* (1976). Since traditionally a woman's sense of self-worth was based on her provision of care to others, it is hard for a woman to value herself for an activity that is not primarily for the benefit of others. An activity is experienced as more satisfying to many women if it takes place in the context of relating to another and leads to the pleasure or enhancement of others. A woman who will spend hours preparing an elaborate meal for a male guest will not take even five minutes to prepare a nourishing and tasty meal for herself. This problem is seen strikingly in marriage and child rearing. A woman will spend hours driving her children to various lessons and classes but not make time for a class for herself. She will plan her activities to accommodate her husband's interests and his schedule but will never expect that her husband should accommodate her. Here is an example of work on the fear of selfishness with a married woman:

Patient: I was so looking forward to taking that class I wanted on Wednesday night, and now my husband tells me he can't be home in time on Wednesdays for me to go. I feel so disappointed.

Therapist: Why can't you take the class anyway?

Patient: I can't, I don't have anyone to leave the children with.

Therapist: Don't you have a baby-sitter?

Patient: Yes, I use a neighbor girl sometimes when we go out at night.

Therapist: What about using her on Wednesday so you can take your class?

Patient: You mean pay a sitter just for myself?

Therapist: Yes, why not?

Patient: But it's so expensive, my husband will have a fit, and I don't like leaving the children with someone else to put them to bed.

Therapist: What could happen?

Patient: Well, they're used to my reading to them at bedtime.

Therapist: Can't the baby-sitter read to them?

Patient: I suppose, but I don't know, the money, my husband being angry, it's just too difficult.

Therapist: It sounds to me like you're saying you're not worth it. It's OK to hire a sitter for you and your husband to go out, but not OK to spend the money for you to take a class you've been looking forward to. It's hard for you to do it for yourself, as if you don't count.

Patient: It is hard for me not to put my husband and children first, and besides, I don't earn any money.

Therapist: You and John agreed it was better for you to give up your job to be home with the children. You denied yourself the independence of a job for the children's sake, now you seem to feel you don't deserve one night a week for yourself because you don't work. It seems like you don't think you can be a good mother and think of yourself once a week, too. That and your fear of John's anger is enough to turn you off course. What if he is angry?

Patient: I hate to fight with him, he sulks for days, is irritable with the children, it's just not worth it.

Therapist: He tries to control you by his sulking and he succeeds. You let his withdrawal stop you from pursuing your own needs. You try to appease his anger by giving in to him and giving up what you want. Then you live with the disappointment and grow to resent him for it.

In both these examples, first the mother and then the husband are able to control the woman by their manipulative behavior, yet have her convinced that she is selfish if she doesn't go along with their demands. The single patient in the first example could easily become the married woman in the second example, if therapy doesn't help her to see how her fear of anger and dependence on others' approval can result in her negating her own self-interest. The difficulty in making this change comes from her feelings of femininity when she caters to others' needs, and the aggressive unfeminine feelings when she asks that her own needs be considered.

When the last child leaves the home, the woman whose orientation has been toward serving others' needs can feel quite empty and even disoriented. There is no one to take care of, and she is at a loss to know what to do with herself. A patient of mine was working on this sense of confusion about her life when she had an idea. She came in one day and said she had solved her problem. She had realized that now she could do whatever she wanted to do! This was a totally new realization to her, and freed her to explore her own desires for the first time. She could now act on her own behalf.

A similar story was told by another patient, who had difficulty with her husband over the newspaper. He was in the habit of taking it with him to work each morning so that he could read it on the bus or at lunchtime. He brought it back home at night for her to read. Because she worked as well this hadn't bothered her, but then her schedule changed so that she had some time at home on Thursday, and she asked him to leave the paper with her one day a week. He complied at first but then began to take it again. She got very angry and discussed it in therapy. I suggested that she get her own subscription so that they could each have their own news-paper to read. She was stunned by my suggestion, yet she had to admit the price was easily affordable. She decided to do it and felt a tremendous release of a suppressed desire for separateness. She felt like a "real person," she said, with her own paper, not having to depend on her husband's permission to read it. It is worth adding that they had each paid for half the subscription price of the paper, so in fact the dependence was purely emotional, not financial, with the husband assuming the prerogative because of his sense of entitlement, a sense she lacked. When she told him that she had ordered her own paper he was stunned and critical, saying it was a waste of money. He withdrew for a few days as he dealt with what was a significant change in her, that she was able to detach herself from a small aspect of his controlling and self-centered way of relating to her.

In each of these examples the therapist makes a direct suggestion, to hire a baby-sitter and to order a newspaper. This is an interactive not an analytic intervention, yet it in fact served as an interpretation of a dependent attachment that infantilized the woman and from which she could easily break free. The suggestion served as a vehicle for insight into dependent patterns, which can serve the patient well in future instances where breaking a dependent bond can have a liberating effect.

A third clinical example took place in a group I led for wives of interns and residents. They all had small children and some brought the children to the group, which of course was very distracting. I asked them if they thought that their husbands would bring the children to a meeting at work, and they all agreed the husbands would not. This question stimulated them to think about their own needs for concentration at the meeting, and they subsequently joined together to hire a baby-sitter for the time of the group.

THE FEAR OF BEING BLAMED

The story of Adam and Eve is the prototype for the blaming of women and for women's self-blame. The frequency and the inappropriateness of women's saying "I'm sorry" is a constant reminder of how ingrained it is in women to feel responsible and to blame themselves for any misfortune or unpleasantness. In my view, one does not say "I'm sorry" unless one has actually caused the problem, but if you notice, women say it in all sorts of situations where they cannot possibly have been to blame. For example, an overworked waitress who is clearly rushing around doing her best to provide service will be apologetic when she comes to your table.

An example that seemed to have particular meaning to a patient of mine occurred on the occasion when she called to cancel an appointment because her grandmother had died and she was leaving town to attend the funeral. She had often spoken fondly of this grandmother, so when she gave me the news I said "That's too bad." At her next session she commented on my response and was pleased that I had not said "I'm sorry" as she had observed most of her friends to say. She said she was so glad I hadn't said it, because clearly the death was not my fault. She had realized that my not saying it meant that although I regretted the death, I did not feel to blame.

On the contrary, in my observation many men do not have this quality, the ingratiating style of those who are in the oppressed group. Rather than blaming themselves, many men seem quite adept at absolving themselves and blaming others or the object. A common example is in the functioning of some mechanical device. Any time something does not work I assume I am doing something wrong, that is, that I am to blame. I have noticed that men do not react in that manner but rather get angry at the object, saying it wasn't made right, it's made of cheap material, and thus avoid any sense of personal inadequacy.

This difference between the sexes in explaining life's difficulties to themselves could help account for women's higher incidence of seeking treatment for depression, since they see failure as the result of some personal inadequacy. If a man fails at work he might conclude that the challenge was impossible or that he didn't get enough support from the boss.

The usual psychoanalytic explanation for self-blame is guilt, yet there seems to me to be a gender issue here besides the obvious explanation of repressed guilt. Men who do engage in self-blame strike one as masochistic. I have wondered whether the female propensity for believing she has done something wrong and the man's sense of "I'm OK, so if there is something wrong, it must be outside of me" could be an extension of a body image difference whereby girls develop the idea that they are not OK the way they are (without a penis), and boys develop the idea that they are all right the way they are. I was driving with a male friend on a country road when another car honked and he realized he had driven through a stop sign. If I had been the driver I would have felt terrible, blamed myself for not being more observant, imagined the horrible accident I might have caused, and felt guilty and awful. My friend, to my amazement, got angry about the stop sign, saying that it was not there the last time he had been at that crossroads, and that if they were going to put in a new stop sign, they ought to warn you in advance. This is not unique but rather typical in my experience. If a man gets a traffic ticket, it is somehow an injustice to him, not his fault. How can we account for this difference? Surely being a member of the ruling class—white, male, and well educated—is a factor. Second, these men have usually been adored and pampered by their mothers, and so grew up believing they were quite special and superior. (I actually had one male friend whose mother truly believed he was the Messiah.) Third, having a penis meant to them and their families that they were in fact privileged and entitled to special treatment.

Their sisters, on the other hand, were not treated as special but rather as a potential burden if they should fail to marry. Their value was determined by the value of the man they could succeed in marrying. As girls, they observed their lack of a penis and believed that they were missing something valuable; therefore they were certainly not special and had no sense of entitlement. On the contrary, the sister may have believed that she was not good enough as she was and blamed herself for what she was lacking, thinking it was her punishment or her fate to be inferior. When this belief is reinforced by society in various ways, the girl develops a sense of inadequacy and incompetence, and an apologetic style, asking for forgiveness and trying to compensate for her lower status with a pretty face and a pleasing smile. (Jeanne Kirkpatrick, former U.S. representative to the United Nations, is the only woman I've ever seen who does not smile for the camera.) These factors combine to make her vulnerable to accepting blame and to blaming herself.

From a feminist viewpoint, male fantasies of female destructive power permeate society from Eve on down. From witches and wicked stepmothers to femmes fatales and castrating women, from the overprotective mother to the schizophrenogenic mother, from the mother-in-law jokes to the "take my wife" jokes, women are blamed for man's ills, internalize this societal message, and are ready to blame themselves.

Suggested Interpretations

A clinical example might be as follows:

Patient: I feel so stupid. I was in a car accident last night and John is furious with me. Now I have to get estimates and the car will be in the shop for repairs. What a mess.

Therapist: You feel stupid?

Patient: Yes, I saw a car starting to pull out of a parking space I wanted, so I signaled to stop and the car behind me rear-ended me.

Therapist: So the accident was not your fault.

Patient: Well it sort of was. I guess it was dumb to stop right there with a car behind me. John thinks I caused it.

Therapist: You stopped to let the driver out so you could take the space, and the driver behind you wasn't alert, or was going too fast, and hit you from the rear. He is responsible, yet you feel you are to blame.

Patient: Well, I know legally he was at fault, but it was a quick stop on my part and the other guy was really mad at me. His car was damaged too. He claims I didn't signal, but I know I did.

Therapist: This is another example of the trouble you have holding your own. Two men blame you, and even though you know you did nothing wrong, you give their opinion more credit than your own.

Patient: It's always hard for me to stand up for myself if someone is angry. I start to feel unsure.

Therapist: It's easier to feel unsure, to feel stupid, than to fight back and defend yourself. You're afraid to show your anger. You remain the lady.

Patient: Maybe. It wasn't until I got into bed last night and had a chance to think it through that I realized it was one of those unfortunate things that can happen, and that no one is really to blame. You know, my father always used to rail against "women drivers." Maybe I'm still affected by that. I don't know.

Therapist: Your father didn't think much of women's abilities, and your mother never protected herself from his attacks on her.

Patient: That's right, and I don't defend myself either.

Therapist: I wonder how the accident would be explained if your father had been in your place and a woman driver had hit him from the rear.

Patient: Oh God, he would have been furious. She would have been dumb, shouldn't be allowed to drive, you know, it would have been all her fault and he would have been completely innocent.

Therapist: You are still feeling inferior as a woman and still afraid of the anger of men if you assert yourself. You play dumb, take the blame to appease them and make them right, while you suffer in silent anger.

Patient: Maybe I was angry. I woke up with an awful headache.

THE FEAR OF BEING UNFEMININE

A few years ago I began noticing a dramatic change in the lingerie section at Macy's. I was shocked to see the mannequins decorated in the most overtly sexual underwear, styles that I had associated with the idea of a brothel, real Frederick's of Hollywood items from sleazy magazines. Who wears this stuff? I wondered, but clearly it was being bought and worn by a lot of women because it took up a good-sized section of the department. I then connected it with the Maidenform bra advertisements which show women poised for serious work, but in their underwear, and I began to get the point. The more seriously women were taking themselves in the work world, the more their fear of losing their femininity and thus their attraction to men. This fear was being exploited in the marketplace by an appeal to ultrafeminine, very sexy underwear to help the woman overcome her fear of losing her female allure. Under that business suit and behind that briefcase is a total sex slave, passive and passionate.

Femininity has so long been associated with weakness, passivity, suffering, and helplessness that a competent woman may in fact be viewed as unfeminine. How many heroines of operas and novels have died of consumption in a lover's arms to advance that message of woman as sickly and dependent? Men die courageously in battle, women die helplessly of consumption. The competence of a woman can be welcomed if it is in the service of her family, church, or charity, but when it is combined with an independent income, men's fears of dominating women emerge and women get anxious that they won't be considered feminine enough to attract a man.

During the 1992 Democratic presidential primary campaign, Hillary Clinton, the wife of Bill Clinton, emerged as a very impressive woman as she campaigned for her husband. A Yale law school graduate and successful lawyer, her intelligence and competence so impressed people that there were comments about Mrs. Clinton as a possible presidential candidate. According to the *San Francisco Chronicle* on 27 February 1992, Richard Nixon suggested in an interview that her forcefulness might make her husband appear a "wimp." That her aggressive campaigning was on her husband's behalf did not deter Mr. Nixon from attacking her femininity.

The So-Called Masculinity Complex

According to traditional psychoanalytic theory, an assertive, independent woman is suffering from a masculinity complex, the basis of which is penis envy and a failure to accept her damaged state. Her entrance into the career world is motivated by her competition with men rather than her own desires for personal development and satisfaction. The stereotype of the "bitch," the "castrator," the "battle-ax," the "shrill" woman or "pushy broad" is there in the background with its dreaded images, long ago established and then confirmed by the popularization of psychoanalytic theory in the mass media. Our gender identity is vital to our self-image and self-esteem, and an attack on it can be very threatening. This is well recognized among men, who fear losing their masculinity, and is just as true for women. The difference is that the loss of femininity for women marks the beginning of real, competent adulthood, a progression, whereas the loss of masculinity for men is a regression.

This dilemma puts women in a double bind: remain weak and ineffectual and be admired as feminine, or develop valued skills and be successful in the business or professional world and stand the risk of male hostility and rejection. I had a patient who held a management position at a bank and was advanced to the status of a vice president. She was the only woman at meetings of her peers. She was significantly overweight but believed that being overweight was an advantage in her position because she was then not considered sexual and could be accepted more easily by the men in the company. I found this hard to believe, but in *The New York Times* a few weeks later I found a lengthy article about women in management that made the same point. The extra weight took the form of a compromise. She could be accepted as an equal as long as she was not sexually appealing. Sexual appeal *and* power is too threatening. Older women sometimes have that advantage of being acceptable in a position of power because they are considered past the age of sexual desirability.

A similar story was told by my consultant. He treated a woman for an obesity problem who did succeed in losing considerable weight. She was the manager in an auto repair shop and in her previous condition had had no problem with customers. When she lost weight, people would approach her and ask to speak to the manager. She realized that she "carried more weight" when she was larger, a result I believe of the perception of a slimmer woman as feminine and the need of men and women to diminish the power of women who are sexually attractive.

The Brain as Phallic Symbol

A woman's fear of loss of love if she is successful has both internal and external roots. Applegarth and Ticho both describe this interaction in their articles in the Blum collection (1977). The fear of success in competition in the oedipal drama with mother, combined with the actual rejection from men that women who are successful in competing with men experience, result in many women fearing their brain power and concealing it to maintain a feminine image.

Some women doubt their capability and even believe that some essential feature necessary for success is missing, often specifically that something is lacking in their brain. This is not a very surprising notion in a society that refers to women as "empty-headed." Applegarth comments that these women, in spite of actual success, believe they have fooled people and feel like frauds. Apparently, an anxiety about the absence of a penis has been displaced to the brain. They admire men and are often contemptuous of women, yet they are also hostile toward, and contemptuously devalue, men because to worship them produces envy and results in rage.

I have given some thought to another aspect of the concept of the brain in our competitive, aggressive, and male-dominated society. Linguistically, it is interesting to note the way a good brain is pictured; that is, the brain as metaphor for the phallus. A good argument for an idea is frequently described as "penetrating," an answer or an individual will be called "sharp," an analysis may be "piercing" or "incisive," or the writer's thesis will be described as the "thrust" of his argument. One cannot help but be "struck" by the phallic nature of our language as it is used to apply to the brain, as if the brain were a masculine organ. This puts a smart woman in a highly conflicted position, for if she presents her views in a forthright manner, if her analysis is penetrating and incisive, she will be accused of being a "phallic woman," and if she engages with men in an argument and proves to be "sharp," she may well be accused of being "castrating." A man speaking similarly will not be castigated, and will be heard as presenting his ideas confidently or perhaps forcefully. Additionally, valuable information is "hard" data, whereas less valuable data is "soft," another example of a masculine bias in the language of knowledge and the sexualizing of the brain. In Ticho's case example, a female patient who did well in medical school was experienced as castrating because she succeeded in competition with men. She dissembled, and hid her brain. Keller (1985) wrote of the gender issue in science, but I believe her analysis can apply to any area of knowledge valued by society, especially an area that is traditionally male, wherein the brain functions as the tool or weapon of success. A "scatterbrained" woman is less threatening to men and has conveniently been defined as "feminine." The word *seminal* is defined as "pertaining to, containing or consisting of semen" but also as "highly original and influencing the development of future events." Graduate students meet in "seminars" and young men study for the priesthood at "seminaries." Ideas are "disseminated." Clearly the ovum is as latent with potential as the semen is, each is dormant without the other, yet nowhere in our patriarchal language can we find use of the word *ovum* other than in its strict biological sense. No ovumnars or ovumnaries. Is it any wonder that women have had serious conflicts about using their brains and behave in a "dissembling" manner around men? The fear of being accused of being unfeminine and losing something of great value to her personally and to her future if she wants to marry and have children has frightened all but the most unusual women. Katherine Hepburn played roles of smart women and Spencer Tracy admired her for her brains, but she always ended up happily and snugly just a bit beneath him. Today we have no actress comparable with Hepburn, but thanks to the women's movement we now have more role models of successful women in nontraditional roles.

THE FEAR OF BEING UNATTRACTIVE

This fear is so widespread that one might even say it was at the core of a female identity. Almost every woman is dissatisfied with her body, and here too the sources are both internal and unconscious *and* an accurate perception of the external reality in which women are judged so heavily by their physical appearance. Women complain of being too fat, too thin, hips too big, legs too heavy, hair too curly, hair too straight, breasts too flat, breasts too large, skin too dry, skin too oily, all trying to reach the current Hollywood ideal of the attractive woman. It seems to me such a shame to hear bright, articulate, pretty, and talented women spend so much of their energy in obsessing about their appearance and trying to change themselves to fit an ideal of height, weight, shape, and coloring. I had a friend who was a beautiful actress but was ashamed of her legs, which she believed were too heavy. She never wore a skirt or dress, except for a long costume in the theater, because she did not want to expose her legs.

Undoubtedly, this obsession with appearance is based on the compelling need to be attractive to men because of dependence on male approval. These women cannot believe that their intelligence, vitality, charm, and personality can possibly be enough to please a man if there is some flaw in their appearance. Upon examination in psychotherapy, this focus is some-times related to the mother's focus on her daughter's appearance and especially the mother's dissatisfaction with some particular aspect of her appearance: figure, hair, makeup, or clothes. The mother communicated that there was something not right, something less than satisfactory about her daughter and would try to help her conceal or correct the flaw. In some cases the mother was apparently trying to be helpful, but in fact her anxiety about her daughter's appearance was conveyed along with the suggestions and left the girl with the conviction that she was *not all right the way she was*. Mother's goals for her daughter were to catch a desirable man, and she only showed interest in those qualities she considered desirable for this end. This illustrates the multigenerational quality of the anxiety: as the grandmother critiqued the mother's appearance, so did the mother then critique the patient's appearance. In this way a demeaning of the girl as anything other than a potential sex object for a man is communicated. The role of the father in this process is one of omission more than commission. He does not relate in a really affectionate way to his daughter, so he never conveys to her that she is adored as a female nor does he praise her.

How widely accepted this overemphasis on physical appearance is and how "normal" our society considers it was illustrated in the early months of 1992, when the issue of the possible danger to women of silicone breast implants became a big news item. It was revealed that 80 percent of breast implants are done for purely cosmetic reasons. I sat in amazement watching and reading story after story on this topic with absolutely none of the speakers or writers ever raising the question of what is wrong with a society where so many women undergo serious surgery to give the appearance of having larger breasts. Did no one see the tragedy in the terrible sense of undesirability that these women must have felt, leading them to make this expensive and risky decision? The manufacturers of the implants were portrayed as the bad guys, but the women themselves sought out the implants, creating the market, which the manufacturers then gladly exploited for profit. The source of the problem, in my view, is that so many women are so easily exploited because women are judged so severely on their appearance, no matter what valuable qualities and talents they may have.

Clinical Illustrations

Jeanne's family fit this picture. She was the only girl, and her mother was strongly focused on Jeanne's appearance and prepared her for each party and dance. No matter how Jeanne dressed, Mother always found a flaw: the dress needed a pin somewhere, or her hair wasn't quite right. When I saw Jeanne she was in her thirties, unmarried and dissatisfied with her job. She did not date, and one of the major factors was her obsession with her large hips and thighs. She had a small waist and dressed very nicely in business suits with flared skirts, but she would not be seen in a bathing suit and was horrified of sex with a man because her large hips and thighs would be revealed. However, it also came out that her mother had repeatedly warned her against any sexually stimulating activity with boys, stating that she could lose control and "go too far." We worked on family-of-origin issues, such as her mentally ill brother and how he had affected Jeanne and the family; and her relationship with her parents. We also focused on her unhappiness at work. After about two years she was feeling much better and had made a job change that allowed her to work at home. She was delighted with this arrangement, which gave her much more freedom and independence. She terminated therapy quite pleased with her life although she still didn't date.

I heard from Jeanne again several years later. She was very depressed because she had injured her back, could not work, was in constant pain, and saw no promise of improvement. Her doctors did not recommend surgery. She resumed therapy, either lying on the floor of my office or standing up during the session. She had become quite slender, and she explained that she had joined a gym and begun working out and had restricted her food intake, which had resulted in her losing the fat on her hips and thighs. She had felt on top of the world until, most likely as a result of strenuous exercise, she had injured her back. She thought she had probably overdone it in her determination to lose weight. She was now financially dependent on her mother (her father had died when she was in college), which threw her back into the conflictual relationship with her. We worked on that, her relationship with her brother whom she felt responsible for, and her fears of being unattractive to men, now not because of overweight but owing to lack of sexual experience, hard to explain at age 40. I was struck by the fact that her dread that her hips were unattractive had caused her possibly permanent injury.

Nevertheless she pursued therapy in a dedicated manner and began to talk about her loneliness and the absence of sex in her life. She was advised to wear a brace for her back but was afraid to do so because she would then not be able to walk as much and was afraid of gaining weight. I made it clear that I thought the chance of improving her back condition was more important than the possibility of gaining a few pounds. Gradually she was able to loosen up on her rigid weight requirements and did wear the brace, which seemed to help her some after 6 months. She met a man in her neighborhood and began her first affair, very pleased at how much she enjoyed sex and having male companionship. She was thrilled that he was pleased with her body and she recovered from her depression as she felt attractive to him and had more periods without back pain.

Another patient, Melissa, came to me at age 22. She had just broken off a relationship with a man she had lived with for two years and was anxious about living alone. She was exceptionally pretty, with blond hair, blue eyes, and fair skin, so I was especially shocked when she announced in the first session that she had recently had liposuction surgery to remove fat from her hips but was still very distressed by her legs, which were too heavy. In fact they were heavy, but with her unusually pretty face it was hard to believe she would be so distressed about her hips and legs, or that anyone else would much care.

Melissa described a rather traumatic adolescence. Her mother, who had been a housewife, went back to college when Melissa was 12 and her older sister was 14. Then her mother started going to bars at night, picking up men, drinking too much, and using Melissa to cover her stories of where she was. Her father, a nice but nonassertive man, remained passive about it all, and her parents did not fight. Mother's drinking got heavy and she became more irresponsible, never shopping or cooking for the family. Father died very suddenly of a heart attack and Melissa was deprived of the only stable parent. She felt guilty that she had not spent more time with Father, who was often alone owing to Mother's dating and school activities. I told her it had not been her responsibility to take Mother's place, that being out with her friends was the normal thing for her to have done. Father was responsible for himself, for either demanding that Mother cut out her dating or telling her to leave. Her father's inaction became clear to her and she was able to blame herself less. She could also see a connection between her inability to stand up for herself with her boyfriend and her father's passivity in relation to her mother's disrespect for him. After Father's death, Mother's drinking got worse. She went into a 30-day hospital recovery program, where she met another alcoholic man, and then left the state with him, leaving Melissa on her own at age 19. She clung to her boyfriend, a drug addict, for protection. He was older, more worldly, and supported her. She had started attending a local college but owing to her father's death and mother's drinking had not been able to concentrate and had dropped out, thinking she was not college material. She worked as a legal secretary and earned a good salary, which gave her independence that she liked. She started to furnish her new apartment and we worked on her separation from her boyfriend, a narcissistic and angry man who had always treated her badly, but whom she felt responsible for. As his addiction got worse, he worked less and tried to get money from her. I told her I thought her guilt about her father was involved in her feeling responsible for this depressed young man. She was finally able to say no to his demands for her money and attention and move on to dating other men.

It was clear to me from observation of Melissa's vocabulary and thought processes that she was very intelligent and definitely college material. I helped her to understand how traumatic those college years had been for her and how unfair it was for her to judge her potential based on her performance when she was feeling so abandoned by both parents. She agreed that in looking back at it, those were hard years. I had also pointed out that when her mother went back to college she had not graduated and that Melissa was strongly identified with her mother. Her sister often said "You're just like Mom," not a compliment. I linked her lack of valuing her intelligence and musical talent to her intense focus on her physical appearance.

Patient: I had a date with my new boyfriend on Sunday and we went to the Monterey Aquarium. I wore shorts. I don't know how I could do that, my legs are so fat! I felt like people were staring at me, saying What fat legs, but of course they weren't. *(laughs)*

Therapist: You don't have anything that is of real interest to you, something that you love and that you work at. You used to have your music. You focus so much on your body because you don't count your mind and your talents.

Following session:

Patient: Look what I found in the paper *(waves a clipping at me and reads aloud):* "The Barbie doll is a scale model of a woman who tapes 39–23–33."

Therapist: Did you have a Barbie doll?

Patient: Yes, but only one. Well, I decided I want to end the relationship with my new boyfriend—I'm getting irritated by him. I wish I could be on my own and not need to be dating someone. I have friends, and I think I need to think of my future and going back to school, but I don't. If I didn't have a boyfriend, I would have to think about my future.

Therapist: Men think about a relationship and their future, but for you, with your mother a housewife and the Barbie doll, a boyfriend is the career—your future. It could be both.

Patient: Yes—if I had something I was involved in, I wouldn't be so preoccupied with my clothes and hair and figure.

Therapist: It's hard to imagine Barbie without Ken.

THE FEAR OF BEING ANGRY

A lady is many things, and there are many things she is not. One of them is angry. In my first book, I reviewed the feminist theory on the fear of women related to female power and thus to a fear of female anger. Men and women, including psychotherapists, are made uncomfortable by an angry woman because it destroys our beloved image of women as kind and considerate nurturers. Yet anger is essential in the process of differentiation, starting with the 2-year-old who says no. Women fear their own anger as dangerous and destructive because they think they will be unloved and perhaps even abandoned if they show anger. Their dependency on others is a big factor in keeping anger repressed. It is more acceptable to repress anger and have psychosomatic symptoms or suffer from depression than to express anger and be the "battle-ax."

Women in therapy differ. Some are very free in expressing anger—at parents, at bosses, at husbands, at previous therapists, at you, and at life in general. Others are fearful and do not even let themselves be aware of feelings of anger. It has seemed to me that those who do express anger freely are the ones with some paranoid features, and in fact this can be a diagnostic clue to the existence of paranoia in a female patient. Borderline patients often engender anger in the therapist through the process of projective identification, and this too can be diagnostically valuable information from the countertransference.

Suggested Interpretations

For those patients who are too fearful to express anger, one clue to the therapist of a patient's inability to express anger is her frequent use of the word *upset*. The patient often describes herself as very upset by some experience and readily complains about it. I have decided not to let that pass and always stop her, saying that I don't know what that means, and ask what is she really feeling when she describes herself as upset. It is most often a combination of being hurt and angry, but the angry part takes the most skill to elicit, as follows:

Patient: My husband was supposed to be home for dinner at six o'clock and he called at six to say he would be late. I had everything all planned and I really got upset about it. He does this a lot.

Therapist: You say you were upset; that could mean almost anything. Could you try to be more specific about what you actually felt?

Patient: I don't know, I just feel he is inconsiderate. He often keeps me waiting.

Therapist: Yes, but how do you feel when you think he is being inconsiderate?

Patient: Well, I always try to be considerate of him, and with other people too. I try not to keep people waiting. I try to be on time.

Therapist: Yes, that seems true, you are always on time for our sessions. But I wonder, since you make an effort to be on time, how it feels to you when people keep you waiting?

Patient: Well, I don't like it, and if it happens a lot, I get upset.

Therapist: I have found that the word *upset* is pretty meaningless, it doesn't really tell me what the person is feeling. It could be hurt, it could be anger, it could be jealousy or envy. Saying that you are upset really hides the true feelings. It's important that we know what they are.

Patient: When he's late it makes me feel that I'm not really important to him. That does hurt me. He is so important to me, I wouldn't treat him like that. Maybe I feel a little angry too.

Therapist: It's easier for you to feel hurt, or upset, as you say, then to let yourself know that you are angry. It's easier to suffer than to confront him with your feelings of anger and insist that he be more considerate of you.

Patient: If I did, I know he would insist that he couldn't help it, that some very important matter came up that simply had to be taken care of.

Therapist: That might be true, but if that happens often, it might be best not to schedule any specific time. He can call when he's ready to leave, and you can be free to go about your activities rather than wait for him.

Patient: But then I wouldn't have everything ready when he gets home.

Therapist: Then he might have to wait a bit, but that's not so bad considering he can't tell you when he'll be home. It's better than your waiting and resenting him and suppressing your anger.

Patient: I don't think he'll like it, but it would give me more freedom. I could just relax until I hear from him.

Therapist: Maybe he won't like it, but that way you'll be letting him know that your time is valuable too, and you won't be angry at his lateness.

Another example might go as follows:

Patient: My parents called to say that they want to visit the weekend after next. It's really not a good time for me because I've made some plans with friends already. Now I'm upset because I hate to cancel with my friends, but I can't tell them not to come.

Therapist: Why is it impossible for you to tell them not to come?

Patient: You know how they are, they think I should drop everything and entertain them at their convenience. They don't think I have a life of my own.

Therapist: You said you are upset because you don't want to cancel your plans. Saying that you are upset doesn't really tell me much. Could you be more specific in describing what you are feeling?

Patient: Well, I just don't feel that I'm important to them, like my brother is. They would never just announce their arrival in his home. For one thing, his wife wouldn't stand for it, and because they know he has an important job they kind of defer to him. You know what I mean? It's always Ben is doing this and Ben is doing that. With me they think they can just tell me what to do for their convenience.

Therapist: Not having a family of your own keeps you the daughter; you are not established as an independent unit the way your brother is. But what about these feelings of not being seen to be as important to your parents as your brother is. That is part of your resentment and what is making you, as you say, "upset" about this visit, but what are your feelings about this unequal treatment?

Patient: It's just not fair. He has always been the special child to them. No matter what I do, it never seems to please them as much as what Ben does. I never get recognition. Remember that time they visited my aunt just an hour away and didn't even bother to visit me?

Therapist: It seems to me that these incidents would make you angry, but I don't hear you saying that you feel anger.

Patient: Well, I don't know, I guess I have disappointed them because I'm overweight and haven't gotten married. My mother always says, "When are you going to lose weight?"

Therapist: Your over eating is a way in which you suppress your anger. Then you use your being overweight to excuse their treatment of you and suppress the anger again. You are afraid to demand equal treatment from them. You don't think you deserve it, but as long as you accept that it's OK to be treated like the second-class child, you'll be depressed, overeat, and not feel entitled to be angry.

THE FEAR OF BEING ALONE

This is a common fear among women and one that infantalizes them and keeps them dependent. Some women cannot sleep alone and therefore attach themselves to sometimes inappropriate men, just to avoid the anxiety of being alone at night. Some married women feel alone when their husbands are away and are anxious even if their children are in the house. Other married women feel anxious about being alone when their children are in school, and especially when they leave home as young adults. Psychoanalytic literature is replete with cases of school phobia where the child is reacting to the mother's fear of being alone. Greenspan (1983) believes that the psychoanalytic understanding of the fear of being alone, that the woman does not have firm ego boundaries and therefore is unable to feel whole when she is alone, is not a full explanation for this specific fear in women. She compares it with the male experience of being unemployed. This is a threat to his masculine selfhood in the same way that the deprivation of relationship is a threat to a sense of female selfhood. Man's work is to produce and achieve. Women's work is the labor of love, to love and care for others, so that when she is alone the woman feels a threat to her female identity in the way a man does who is out of work.

I believe this is a valuable addition to our understanding of this problem. To be comfortable in being alone requires a sense of separateness that allows the woman an alternative to her most valued role, caring for others. This necessitates a new self-concept whereby the woman is also able to value herself apart from her pleasing others and has developed a capacity for achieving satisfactions for her own sake. The earlier example of the patient who realized that she could do "whatever she liked" illustrates this new self-concept. I find it interesting that some women are able to begin to develop this capacity when they start to exercise, whether it be in a gym or through jogging or swimming. They are involved in an activity for their own health and welfare, and it feels legitimate and worthy.

Applegarth (1977) adds that women have a greater problem than men in being alone and especially in doing things alone.

> They feel incomplete, not in a libidinal sense, but a narcissistic one, having the feeling that they lack the essential connection which gives them status or simply a feeling of importance and meaning. They are

afraid to undertake tasks alone, assuming their incapacity and that unknown dangers will overtake them if the magic of the protective man is not present. For many such women, the shadow of the strong mother of early childhood can be easily seen in this invulnerable image of the man. The fear of venturing out alone physically is these days usually rationalized by invoking the real dangers on the streets, but a little investigation easily reveals that the problem is far more fundamental and basically of internal origin. Such an attitude toward being alone in a physical sense also has its reflections in the mental sphere, and produces a tendency to be quite circumscribed in the range of their minds, especially in permitting originality. [pp. 263–264]

These are valuable insights, but I would not limit the source of this fear to the old dependence on the mother alone, although this may well be the original source. Added to it is the daughter's observation of her mother's dependence on the father, which is sometimes considerable. One of the few rewards for women for their inferior status and submissive role in past generations has been the protection of the man. In fact the percentage of single women who are raped is very much higher than that of married women, and the increasing incidence of reported rape may be related to the greater numbers of women who are single or divorced and living alone.

Another way in which the father plays a significant role in the fear of being alone is in the profound sense of being unlovable by a man that often accompanies the state of being alone and turns it into a painful and anxious experience. Some women could tolerate solitude if they did not give it this additional meaning and interpret it as a sign that they will always be alone, that no man will ever love them. It would seem that many women never get enough love and positive attention from their father and thus they are left feeling anxious about ever obtaining a man's love. Many sons do not receive adequate love and attention from their father either, but the results of this would be different than for daughters. The effect would show more in the boy's development in the male competitive world of work and achievement. Many women never had the important experience as young girls of feeling that their father was simply delighted with them, adored them, and loved their company. The few women I know—and they are few—who did feel beloved by their father have had much less difficulty managing in relationships with men. The long hours of absence of fathers due to work away from home is well recognized. Yet there is opportunity to convey love if it is sincerely felt. Some fathers withdraw when their daughters begin to mature sexually, fearing their own impulse control, and this can be hurtful and confusing.

A different problem exists for girls who realized that their father loved them more than their mother and preferred their company to hers.

This arouses a confusion of feelings of triumph, guilt, and disloyalty. These women may find themselves repeating triangles in adult relationships, intrigued by the power to be the chosen one in a competition, but causing themselves and other women much unhappiness in the process. This is a possible outcome of father–daughter incest.

Another component that may exist as part of the fear of being alone relates to the daughter's knowledge or suspicion that her father had extramarital affairs. Children suffer when their parents engage in extramarital affairs, even when the parents succeed in keeping the affairs secret. Children sense that the parent is expending emotional energy outside the family and may become anxious, feel rejected, and think they must have done something wrong (Brooks 1989). Frank Pittman (1989) researched this topic and reports that an adult becomes so swept up in personal needs during an affair that he or she is incapable of focusing on the effect on the child. A girl who is aware of her father's behavior seems to grow up angry at men and unsure of her relationships with them. A married woman's fear when her husband is out of town or late in getting home is sometimes related to a fear of his having an affair. This fear can be related to her own father's affairs and also to her own desire to have an affair, which can be projected onto her husband. When the boundary of fidelity has been violated, there is never a feeling of safety that that boundary will be respected.

Clinical Illustrations

Mrs. D. was referred to me by a male psychiatrist after he heard me give my 1971 paper on the femininity complex and the value for some women in seeing a female therapist. He had been seeing Mrs. D. but felt stalemated in his work with her and thought she might do well working with me. Since he was recently divorced, he may have had some personal reactions to her transference to him that prevented him from clearing away his own needs in order to be able to focus on the pathological components of her dependency. In any event he was wise enough to turn her case over to another therapist.

When I first saw Mrs. D., she was married to her second husband and had two children. She was aware that her attraction to her male psychiatrist had been an obstacle to her chances of changing, and she welcomed the switch to a female therapist. She was unhappy in the second marriage because she had discovered many unsavory things about her husband, including that he was engaged in sadomasochistic affairs with women he met through advertisements in a local newspaper and that he was a fairly heavy drug user. Her chief complaint was anxiety, which she handled by keeping very busy and using illegal drugs, though not as much as her husband and not to the point where she was addicted. Her husband's income was such that she could afford full-time live-in help, which left her free to go out often and do a lot of clothes shopping for herself and her children. She started an affair and pursued it actively but then became disappointed in the man. Not long afterward she started another affair and this time decided to leave her husband to live with her lover, whom she eventually married. She moved out, and with the money from her divorce settlement she purchased a smaller house. This was a big adjustment because her new man did not earn much money and she had to give up her household help. A fear of being alone, which had never before emerged, began to assert itself; without live-in help, she was alone some evenings with her children when her husband either worked late or had to be out of town on business. Her fear was so intense that she barricaded the doors with furniture. We were both concerned about the effect of this irrational behavior on her children.

In exploring the source of her anxiety she focused on how dependent she felt on men. Although she had taught school before her first marriage, she did not work, so she felt financially dependent. She was used to being able to buy whatever she wanted. She couldn't tolerate the idea of being divorced and trying to support herself and live on a restricted budget. Her new husband was quite handsome, according to her, and about ten years younger than she was, so she developed the fear that he would leave her for a younger woman. We talked about this in relation to her having left her last husband for him, and whether guilt and retribution might be at work here, but this did not seem to help. I approached the issue of her financial dependence with the proposal that she return to work so that she did not feel so beholden to her current husband and ex-husband for support, especially since her former husband was dishonest and unreliable, and she was anxious about his anger against her for having left him for another man. She liked the idea but recognized that she could not earn much money teaching and decided to start her own business, instead. She formed a partnership with two other women and began to build the business. It succeeded nicely, they expanded it, and after a few years she was earning a decent income and had the advantage of freedom, so she could check on her children each day after school.

That her mother was a successful businesswoman made the patient's extreme dependency on men more perplexing. Yet she claimed that her mother was very emotionally dependent on men, and in her second marriage her mother was easily swayed by her husband's opinions and had made some very poor financial decisions based on his advice. In her parents' case, her mother had been very dependent on her father as well. They were in business together, and her mother had spent most of her time with the father and left the patient and her sister in the care of household help, particularly a man. It is interesting that Mrs. D's. help for her children had been a man also, a homosexual whom she felt very close to.

Her father had an organic brain disease that resulted in unprovoked and unpredictable temper outbursts, especially as his condition deteriorated. His mood was generally irritable, a side effect of the drugs he used, and his moods were disturbing to her and unexplainable until a friend let out the secret of her father's hereditary and fatal illness. She concluded in therapy that her mother had failed to protect her from him and was more devoted to him than to her and her sister. She began to experience anger at her mother for her current devotion to her second husband and the poor judgment she used in relation to him. She believed that she was good as a grandmother, always buying her grandchildren expensive gifts, but was not a good mother. My patient could never turn to her mother for help on any emotional matters, as her mother was critical rather than sympathetic about her divorces. As these family-of-origin stories emerged, she became more concerned about how her many relationships with men had affected her daughters, but she did feel she was a more devoted mother than her own mother had been. This understanding of her father's emotional lability helped explain her poor decisions in choosing men, especially men who used drugs. Her first husband had been quite unstable and had never supported his child.

As her self-knowledge progressed, she gradually became less anxious and was able to stop her use of drugs and her excessive clothes shopping, especially for very expensive items. She worked very hard at her business and used good judgment. She had many responsibilities supervising staff, relating to her clientele, and working out duties and finances with the partners. As the business expanded, new locations needed to be found and leases negotiated, all of which she handled capably. She developed from an apparently superficial "princess" into a mature woman. Her intelligence was always evident, but hitherto she had been too anxious to apply it constructively.

However, she grew dissatisfied with her marriage and again began an affair with a recently divorced man. Her current husband was chronically depressed and refused to seek psychotherapy, so she grew increasingly frustrated with him. She thought and agonized a long time about putting her children through yet another divorce but finally did leave him for the man who would later become her fourth husband, again moving out in order to move in with her new lover. He too was a man with some problems, but he had had extensive psychotherapy and was the most stable of all the men, as well as being successful financially. Her fear of being alone did not return, but she never really tested herself by living without a man. Nevertheless, she had a new respect for herself that gave her some pride and self-confidence. As would be expected, she had trouble with her children in adolescence, which she handled capably although she was saddened and discouraged by their problems, feeling responsible at times but also able to see where her children bore responsibility for their own lives.

This example shows a combination of a traditional analysis of childhood history along with a feminist analysis. I determined that the patient's financial dependence, which created so much anxiety for her, would best be approached by encouraging her to become financially independent in order to overcome the reality factors in her inordinate fear of abandonment, fear of poverty, and fear of being alone, which had left her pathologically dependent on men. Her awareness of my independence, of my having essentially my own business, along with her knowledge through the grapevine that I was divorced, added the element of her identification with a woman who was financially independent but, unlike her mother, could show understanding and caring about her many emotional conflicts. Her relationship with her previous therapist, a male psychiatrist, had naturally taken the direction of an erotic transference, and they had not been able to work it through to get to the sources of her dependency on men. It may have simply reinforced that dependency, thus resulting in the stalemate. Her superfemininity had some positive aspects in that she dressed and groomed herself very attractively and was flattering to men in ways that obviously drew much male admiration, but the negative components of her femininity—the helplessness, fearfulness, and lack of power in and control of her life—rendered her chronically anxious, dependent, and unproductive. The luxury of being pampered was paid for with the high price of surrendering autonomy and self-respect.

On the recommendation of a friend, Mrs. B. first consulted me on some problems with her oldest daughter, and we met for short-term work on this topic. She returned some years later in terrible marital conflict. She had started an affair with a younger man who worked with her husband, was deeply in love with him, but knew he would never marry her and felt unable to leave her husband. Mrs. B. was married to a successful and well-regarded physician and had four children, all the social status and economic freedom that his position offered her, and from outward appearances had everything a woman could want. She was active in community activities, traveled, and had a vacation home and an active social life. However, she complained that her husband was unemotional, unromantic (did not even believe in recognizing Valentine's Day), controlling, harsh, critical of her and the children, and sexually inept. As was typical of her generation, she was a virgin when she married him, and it was not until she had this affair that she realized how wonderful lovemaking could be. Her husband was controlled and routine when they had sex, and had premature ejaculation. Her lovemaking with her lover was so superior that she realized what she had been missing all these years. It was hard to talk to her husband about it because she couldn't reveal the source of her newfound sophistication, so she merely said she had been reading books on the subject and urged him to go for sex counseling. He went briefly but then rejected it and nothing changed.

In the meantime, Mrs. B. continued to be emotionally dependent on the young man, who varied in his attentions to her. At times, he would start dating another woman and she would hope for the relationship to end. When it did, she was relieved and again hoped for more of his attention. On the rational level she knew there was no future for her with him, but emotionally she was unable to break it off and remained willing to stay married and see this man in an affair for as long as it could possibly last, even if it meant periods of depression when he would not see her except platonically. When he did meet a woman whom he seemed really involved with, her depression deepened and she was quite miserable. Nothing else in life mattered to her. She went through the motions of caring for her children, doing her community work, going on vacations, yet her mind was always on him and she felt her heart was breaking. Although she had admired her husband when they met in college, she never had experienced this kind of falling in love with him, so this was like her first romance. In exploring her history it became clear that Mrs. B.'s mother was a self-centered and cold woman who had never given her real warmth and emotional nourishment. In her current observations of her mother she could see how emotionally detached her mother still was from her and even how little involvement she had with the grandchildren. Her second marriage, after Mrs. B.'s father died, was to a wealthy, self-centered man whose moods and needs came first. Mrs. B.'s memories of her father were of a warmer, more caring man, but her parents' constant fighting when she was a child took precedence over his involvement with her. I pointed out how her economically secure but emotionally empty childhood had been repeated in her marriage to Mr. B. and had enabled her to live relatively comfortably in this familiar, unaffectionate, but financially and socially privileged family until her love affair had opened to her a new realm of sensuality and warmth from which she could not go back. She recognized the truth in this but was still stuck in the dilemma and feeling hopeless about her husband's changing or of her ability to love him again.

As she gained self-understanding she began to experience real anger at her husband for the first time. In the past she had tended to keep him on a pedestal and blame herself for her unhappiness. She withdrew from sexual relations with him and occupied herself with running her home and a temporary job managing a friend's office. I urged her to find a real job doing similar work or to go back to school and get a degree in a field of her interest where she could eventually build a career, but she procrastinated and never did. She had been an elementary school teacher before her children were born but did not want to return to teaching. It seemed that it was too hard to give up the freedom she had to travel and be available for her children and pursue her love affair by committing herself to a career, and there was no financial incentive to make such sacrifices.

I told Mrs. B. that she had several choices. One was to leave her husband and hope to have a better life with the freedom to meet other men. She consistently rejected this, fearing that divorce would deprive her of the active social life she had with her husband and that such a course might not result in her meeting anyone better. This pessimistic outlook was based on her knowledge of several women who had left their husbands and had been very disappointed in the men they met, wondering later if they had made a mistake. She repeated that her husband was widely admired, very intelligent, and was recognized in the community, sitting on various boards of directors, and so on. She had serious doubts of her chance of meeting a man who could compare with him in his intelligence and achievements. I acknowledged that there was no guarantee of this, but that surely nothing would happen if she stayed in the marriage as it was, and being separated at least would give her some new opportunities.

Another option she had was to stay in the marriage and try to meet other men so that she could have an affair with someone else and at least be able to withdraw from the current affair, which left her feeling powerless and depressed most of the time. I suggested that school or a job might be a way to break out of her routines and meet some new people, but she did not make any such changes. She could not believe any other man could be as warm, caring, and wonderful as her lover was.

The other alternative was to press her husband to go into individual therapy and perhaps couple therapy as well. She was very doubtful whether she could accomplish this, but with her fearfulness about being alone it seemed like the best hope for her. I kept pressing her to make demands on her husband, and gradually she was able to develop the confidence to stand up to him, in spite of his superior and condescending stance with her, and eventually he did agree to accept a referral I gave her to consult with a male psychiatrist with whom I felt he might be able to work. Because of some serious problems with an older child who had dropped out of college, he agreed to go to family therapy including all the children, and that child entered individual treatment as well. At that point Mrs. B. stopped her treatment with me, believing she had done all she could do in understanding herself and that the rest would have to be up to her husband.

Mrs. D. and Mrs. B. are two of many women I have seen who are financially and emotionally dependent on their husband although not really in love with him. They come to therapy either depressed or anxious or both, because they are unhappy in the marriage but too frightened to leave it. Their financial dependency keeps them unable to negotiate terms in the marriage that better suit their current needs, because of fear of their husband's anger, disapproval, and rejection; yet they are unable to leave the marriage, because of their fear of being alone, that is, without a man. Without that connection to a man they feel worthless, without status in the community, and unprepared to face life without that protection and security. Mrs. D. could leave only when she had another man to go to. They are all intelligent and capable women, yet facing the world without a man seems grim and unpromising. The reality of life for a woman alone plays a significant part in their fears and reinforces dependency that existed prior to the marriage. The pattern of men choosing younger women haunts these women as they observe this pattern occurring among people they know. As therapists we cannot promise them anything other than help in understanding their choices.

THE FEAR OF BEING POOR

Many unmarried women have a fear of being poor, as visualized in the image of the "bag lady." Many have not been able to accumulate any savings or property because of the unfairly and discriminatorily low salaries they receive. The idea of being one month's paycheck away from being homeless is frightening. I know one such divorced psychologist who decided to leave the profession for this reason (she had worked for nonprofit agencies) and entered the field of real estate. She made much more money, started investing in property, and through hard work and good investments gained confidence in her future.

Clinical Illustration

> When I started seeing Linda she was in her early thirties. She had been in once-weekly psychotherapy with a colleague, and they had terminated with Linda having a much clearer picture of her mother's disturbing effect on her, but without much relief from her chronic depression and without any change in her life. About a year later I was recommended to her by a friend, and she began treatment again. Her former therapist told me she believed the mother was psychotic, and this was confirmed by the material that emerged over the next few years I worked with the patient. Linda remembers her mother repeatedly telling her and her sister that they would be lucky if they could get jobs selling in Woolworth's. She said she still cannot go into a Woolworth store without wondering behind which counter she would sell. The mother had not attended college and had done clerical work until she married. When Linda was graduated from a good eastern college with a degree in teaching, her mother insisted that she take a secretarial course at a business school, which she did.

She came to San Francisco and held various jobs, some part-time teaching but mostly of the administrative-assistant type. At times she did sales and once took a job doing telephone solicitation. All her jobs offered low pay and no benefits. She enrolled in a program for a master's degree in sociology and did all the course work but never completed her thesis. She was ambivalent about it because she didn't believe that a master's degree would get her a job. She may have been right, but having the degree would be better than not having one, so I thought her not completing it was another symptom of her self-defeating behavior by which she paid homage to her mother's hostility toward her as expressed in the form of dire predictions about her ruinous future.

In her love life, she maintained a long-standing affair with an older man who was married. She saw him several evenings a week; he apparently did not maintain much of a relationship with his wife. This too was self-defeating, since it clearly had no future and did not help her with her ongoing anxiety about her financial situation. She had internalized her mother's constant belittlement of her and had difficulty trusting that anyone could ever like her or value her. There was an element of paranoia in her expectation that people would think she was stupid and unworthy. We worked hard on connecting these feelings to her mother's mental illness as well as to her own negative and critical thoughts about people, an identification with her mother's hostility.

Her father was a moderately successful businessman but never gave Linda love, support, or praise. He rationalized the mother's disturbed behavior, and even when he could acknowledge her illness to Linda he did nothing about it and nothing to protect Linda and her sister. In the course of therapy Linda was able to get angry at him about his failure to protect her or help her. She did express this to him, but as she had predicted, he responded by agreeing but without any conviction, apology, or effort to change.

Linda did make some changes, however. When her parents visited, she spent very little time with them, and left the room whenever her mother began a tirade of abuse against her. One of mother's favorite predictions was that Linda would end up being a bag lady. Needless to say, this was not helpful and added to Linda's anxiety and depression, but she was able to recognize that her mother's characterizations of her were a product of a serious mental illness for which she had never been treated. Linda's mother is another example of a mother who truly seemed to hate her children and could not provide for their emotional needs. Linda often compared herself unfavorably with her sister, who had talked back to the mother and fought with her whereas Linda was always very timid and tried to keep on her mother's good side. She was very critical of herself for not having her sister's courage and for not being as successful as her sister was. I had to keep reminding her that there were two factors that were different. One was that the father had a closer relationship with her sister, and the other was that the sister was close to a paternal aunt who offered her attention and caring, giving her alternatives to her mother.

Although Linda's insight was showing improvement, she was still depressed and unable to make any significant external changes. After several years of individual therapy, I invited Linda into a women's group I had formed for battered women. As that group developed, it seemed clear to me that the women had all, in some way or another, been abused children, and that their battering relationship with a man in adulthood could be seen as a symptom of their family-of-origin mistreatment. I decided to expand the definition of the group to include any woman who had been an abused child, including sexual abuse, particularly borderline and severely depressed women; and as openings occurred, I included several of my own individual therapy patients in the group. Linda's self-revelation in the group was slow at first, but she did make supportive and insightful comments to the other women. Parenthetically, it was extremely pleasurable for me to observe the helpful participation of my own patients as they showed the results of their personal therapy in the comments they made to others. This is an opportunity we as therapists ordinarily never have.

When she did volunteer information about herself, she got very strong reactions from the group about her mother. The chorus of anger and dismay at the terrible way her mother treated her seemed to have a very profound effect on Linda. There is something quite powerful about a whole roomful of women who speak as one voice—much more meaningful, I believe, than the comments of a psychotherapist who restrains her emotions. Linda seemed to respond quite positively to what might generally be called "support" but in this particular setting I believe is more accurately described as *the power of the community to pass judgment* and to offer sympathy to a victimized member. To my surprise, Linda began to explore the possibility of going to law school, and with the group's encouragement she proceeded with her applications. She was admitted to a good school in San Francisco and obtained the necessary student loans so that she could attend. We were all curious as to what her parents would say. They offered no help, but neither did they say anything negative.

Once she began school, Linda became very busy and left the group. Her financial position had always been weak, but I had seen her for a low fee. Now even a low fee was not possible, so I urged her to inquire as to the possibility of free counseling through the university. She did and was able to obtain a counselor at school, so we terminated. She recently conveyed a message to me through a current patient whom she had met in the group that she would be graduating in June 1991 and would be sending me an announcement. Her bag-lady fears are probably over now, although it may be difficult to find a job. She will have to pass the bar examination, and that may be quite a hurdle, but at least she is on her way.

WOMEN'S FEAR OF BEING AGGRESSIVE—PENIS ENVY OR PRIVILEGE ENVY?

A not-so-funny thing happened to women in this country on the way to emancipation in the twentieth century. Just when the ideal of the Victorian Lady—the gracious, sweet, submissive, passive, pliable, loving, asexual, nurturing female who cared for all and demanded nothing for herself—was beginning to crumble in the "roaring '20s," the Freudian theory of the universal affliction of penis envy penetrated, so to speak, intellectual circles, the academic world, and the mass media in the United States and served to turn that emancipation backwards in favor of a new Victorianism: the supermom, superwife ideal of femininity whose total satisfaction was derived from serving her family. Even in the sexual area, satisfaction for the woman came from satisfying her husband, not from sexual pleasure of her own; and Helene Deutsch warned that orgasms were not good for women, who are too delicate for such a powerful experience. Any ambition for personal achievement, any competitive or aggressive goals or behavior on the part of women was interpreted as a symptom of envy of men and dissatisfaction with their own natural role in life, putting a pall of suspicion on any woman who was not happy in such a physically restricted and intellectually deadening definition of womanhood. It led many women to hide their natural active and aggressive desires for fear of being labeled "castrating" and "masculine."

Many feminist and psychoanalytic writers have dealt with this issue critically, and many revisions have been offered. I discuss this in *Feminist Psychoanalytic Psychotherapy* (1992), my first book. The damage that this theory has done to women's potential for achievement and the loss to society from this absence of contributions of the female mind and talent cannot be calculated. The anger directed against psychoanalysis and the dismissal of the entirety of the theory not only because of an inaccurate, but also because of an accurate, understanding of the concept is unfortunate and well known. The view that makes most sense from my perspective is that penis envy may indeed be a phase in a young girl's development, but it is a temporary misunderstanding on her part until she can be assured that she too has special body parts and sources of pleasure, and that when she grows up to be a woman she will have a valuable and admirable role to play in sharing with the male in the creation and nurturance of life. Like other mistaken ideas that children may have that give rise to fears and confusion, the mistaken idea that a girl is inferior because she lacks a penis can be easily corrected if her family and community do not reinforce the idea of male superiority.

Yet, as with other childhood fears and misconceptions, even an effective correcting of the idea and reassurance as to its invalidity may not completely erase anxiety, which can then continue to exist on an unconscious level and cause later problems. Men may continue to unconsciously fear castration and be very defensive about women having power. Women may continue to feel incomplete, punished, and inferior owing to the long-forgotten but still unconsciously operative primitive belief that they are deficient.

A Feminist Approach to Penis Envy

How might a feminist understand and use the concept of penis envy to help women? In one sense, I use it and call it *privilege envy*. This is very close to Lacan's definition of penis envy as a "socially specific jealousy" (Turkle 1981). Of course, we all envy those who are privileged: the poor envy the middle class, the middle class envy the rich, the plain-looking envy the beautiful and the handsome, the chubby and awkward envy the lithe and athletic. In America, this is an external reality, a cultural given that we each respond to with varying degrees of success in reconciling ourselves with who we are and what we have been given in life. In a patriarchal system in which women have been undervalued, underpaid, and sexually and economically exploited, there should be no surprise that envy of male privilege and advantage is common. Anger is common also and is a healthier response, albeit an unwelcome one.

The little girl may have envied the boy for his penis, and her lack of one may have made her feel damaged and inferior. She has these feelings repeatedly reinforced by the actuality of woman's inferior status in society and the promotion of her dependence on men. The little boy's feelings of envy toward women, around pregnancy for example, can be more easily sublimated as society keeps reinforcing his ego by telling him that he is superior and promotes his independence. Here we have an example of the dialectical interplay of internal and external reality, both of which operate to influence a woman's reactions to life experience. In a clinical situation it is important to bring to bear both the psychoanalytic theory, which enlightened us as to the young child's sexuality, and the feminist theory, which analyzed and challenged the long-held cultural, religious, and political beliefs in the inferiority of women. There are many examples of women who in therapy express feelings of inferiority, inadequacy, and worthlessness and in my view a complete analysis with such a patient includes the family history of her treatment as a child and adolescent; the views of women held by family members; the particular religion and culture in which the woman was raised, including the nationality or ethnic background; the position of women in society during the decade in which she was raised; and the history of women in her family. Often many valuable insights as to the patients feelings of self-depreciation emerge from this review and seem sufficient for her to proceed with making the changes she needs for improved mood and functioning.

Suggested Interpretations

When the feelings of inferiority persist, it is necessary to dig deeper for unconsciously held beliefs, and it is here that there is a place for an inquiry as to the patient's possible belief of anatomical inferiority. Rather than an accusation of penis envy, I pose the question as to her early thoughts and feelings:

> You know it is quite common for little girls to think they are inferior when they realize their body is missing a penis. I wonder if that could have been true for you?

Or:

> Your ideas that you are missing something that could enable you to be smart and successful make me wonder if when you were a little girl you had the idea that you were missing something important when you saw your brother's penis and realized you didn't have one.

Or:

> You know psychoanalytic theory believes that some girls grow up thinking they are damaged and inferior when they compare their bodies with boys' and realize they are missing a penis. You seem so uncertain of your abilities, almost as if you actually believed something was missing from your brain. Sometimes little girls get confused and think that because they don't have a penis, it means that their brain is missing something too. I wonder if that could have happened to you?

Or:

> You are so fearful of being without a man, as if you were incomplete without an attachment to a man. We've talked about your dependency on your mother and how that was transferred to men, but now I'm wondering if there is something else going on. Some little girls develop the mistaken idea that because they don't have a penis, it means they are incomplete, damaged, and inferior. You may feel so dependent on a man because you had those ideas as a little girl and they are still operating unconsciously to make you feel you must have a man to be OK.

The responses to these interpretations vary, and your work will follow from the kind of response you get. Most women have no recollection of these beliefs or feelings from childhood, but some show interest and are willing to consider the possibility that unconscious ideas are determining their belittlement of themselves. These women are helped by at least an intellectual recognition that this silly idea could be harming their self-confidence now. It opens up the whole notion of it all being a terrible mistake that they have been burdened with and could be free of. Sometimes they reject the notion flatly, but at least the seed has been planted that perhaps not all their feelings and behavior are within conscious control. If a woman does not want to pursue it, I will drop the topic for a while and raise it again if there is a clue in a dream or a slip of the tongue, if the self-image of being mutilated appears, or if an irrational conviction that her body is unattractive persists.

The important thing in all these exchanges is to convey the attitude that you think it is an unfortunate but clearly erroneous idea that was a fantasy of a child who did not understand, because she could not see, that she has female parts that are wonderful and valuable. This can then be incorporated into any earlier material that you have learned from the patient about sexist attitudes in her family, school, or community, or about belittled and dependent images of women she has absorbed from such media as songs, books, and films. These are an important part of the culture in which we are each reared; from them we form gender images and identification models that are very important during adolescence. As a music lover, I sometimes will recite a line from a well-known song, and it can be fun to recall how these songs shaped our views as we grew up—for example, "Can't Help Loving That Man." The lyrics convey the plight of what we can now recognize to be a totally dependent, masochistic female helplessly in love with a man who is unreliable, undeserving, and does not reciprocate her devotion. Of course, timing is very important, but a bit of recognition of how these cultural images of female dependency and suffering have shaped our views can be very helpful. Who can forget beautiful and desirable Ava Gardner singing that song in *Showboat*? Surely a belief that she is damaged (the absence of a penis) creates a sense of inadequacy that intensifies a woman's dependence on a man and leaves her vulnerable to tolerating mistreatment.

Women's Feeling of Being Damaged

Another way that our understanding of the concept of penis envy can be used by therapists to help women is in relation to a feeling of being damaged, an irrational idea that can unconsciously represent a childhood belief in castration. I am always impressed by how many women feel there is something wrong with their bodies. I described that problem earlier in this chapter (The Fear of Being Unattractive). Why have today's young women cooperated so willingly in the current fashion of being skinny—torturing themselves with diets, forced vomiting, and laxatives, and corseting themselves in tight pants? I have found it useful to ask some questions of women when the issue of their displeasure with their body comes up, especially in relation to shame at being seen naked by a man. The questions are designed to probe for unconscious feelings of missing a penis. I ask:

What do you think you're missing?

Or:

What is the secret that you think your clothes conceal?

Or:

> You do have breasts and female genitals; what would be disappointing about that to a man?

They are often taken by surprise when encouraged to contemplate their body from the point of view of the man they are consciously trying to please, rather than from the infantile, narcissistic perspective of injury or mutilation.

The feeling of something damaged or missing can also be displaced to the brain, with ideas about intellectual damage usually expressed as inadequacy or incapacity. Fortunately, this is less common than it used to be. The feeling of being a fraud can be interpreted as the woman's fear that she is passing herself off as a man, as if only men have what it takes to be able, smart, and successful. If the brain were located in the penis, this fear would have some basis.

The anxiety about body image occurs once again at midlife with the aging process, as women obsess about the appearance of wrinkles, grey hair, and changes in skin texture. They spend billions of dollars on cosmetics that promise irrational and scientifically impossible benefits for "younger looking" skin. Note the frequency of references in advertising to "damaged" hair and "damaged" skin, playing on women's unconscious fears. The creams and lotions are called "therapy" for a pseudomedical mystique. Women are told their faces can be "firm and smooth—unworried by lines, sags, puffs." Skin can be "vitalized," can be fed a "daily diet that offers unique refreshment, eye tech efficiency, a support system that keeps working on any skin, with no letdown, . . . all the nourishment it wants" (Clinique). Or how about "Marine Therapie Active-Sea Skincare releases its sea born benefits to your skin upon contact . . . high intensity formulas . . . derived from fresh living seaweeds, rapidly frozen to retain their sea born benefits" (Germaine Monteil). What terrible nonsense, yet women buy these products because they are convinced that they are not OK the way they are, aging. I believe this is another example where we can see both the effects of an early education as to the inferiority and dependency of women plus unconscious ideas about body damage combined with the harsh reality of the depreciation of older women because of the vulnerability of aging men to the flattery of attention from younger women. How unfortunate that this anxiety so pervades our society; how much money is made owing to the vulnerability of women who are desperate to hold on to a man for fear of losing him to a younger woman. It is important to keep in mind that this fear of being damaged is both fantasized and internally incorporated in the woman's youth and externally validated in her mature years.

In Chapter 8 I will be discussing women at midlife and older women, women who were raised in the '30s and '40s. What about younger women? Are they different? Have they benefited from the women's movement? Melissa, at age 22, had already had liposuction. Is she typical? In the next chapter I will look at the modern woman and see if her fears are less than or different from those of many of the women I described in this chapter.

3

THE NEW WOMAN:
HAVING IT ALL

Were our state a pure democracy there would still be excluded from our deliberations women, who, to prevent deprivation of morals and ambiguity of issues, should not mix promiscuously in gatherings of men.

—Thomas Jefferson

The surest guide to the correctness of the path that women take is JOY IN THE STRUGGLE. Revolution is the festival of the oppressed. For a long time there may be no perceptible reward for women other than their new sense of purpose and integrity. Joy does not mean riotous glee, but it does mean the purposive employment of energy in a self-chosen enterprise. It does mean pride and confidence. It does mean communication and cooperation with others based on delight in their company and your own. To be emancipated from helplessness and need, to walk freely upon the earth that is your birthright. To refuse hobbles and deformity and take possession of your body and glory in its power, accepting its own laws of loveliness. To have something to desire, something to make, something to achieve, and at last something genuine to give. To be freed from guilt and shame and the tireless self-discipline of women. To stop pretending and dissembling, cajoling and manipulating, and begin to control and sympathize. To claim the masculine virtues of magnanimity and generosity and courage.

—Germaine Greer

Certainly it is hard to generalize about the "new woman" because there are variations by class, race, geography, and ethnicity, and we never know if the attitudes presented by our own patients reflect trends in the general population. Statistics do tell us something concrete that can help us to follow the trends and evaluate how our patients fit or diverge from the norms. Surely one of the most significant—and rather amazing—statistics is that less than 13 percent of American families conform to the traditional male-breadwinner, female-homemaker ideal that those of us over age 40 were raised to expect and to view as normal and right.

We all have our personal impressions of the new woman, but to try to get an accurate picture I have used three informal means of research. The first approach was to review current women's magazines to attempt an analysis of the goals, values, and concerns expressed through articles, advertising, and fiction, a miniversion of what Betty Friedan did thirty years ago. The second was to interview two therapists who have worked at university counseling centers for many years, to ask them to assess changes in college women of today. The third approach was to conduct individual interviews in which I asked about personal lives and also about impressions of friends and co-workers. This includes one married woman of 26 who works full-time and has a 1-year-old child; one married woman of 33 who has two children and works part-time; a single man of 38, whom I asked about his impressions of the women he meets socially; a divorced woman of 39, with no children; and a never-married woman of 37. My goal is to attempt to assess how the women's movement has changed the lives of the generation of women who have grown up since 1970 and to examine both the positive and the negative aspects of these changes.

Many young women do not call themselves feminists; in fact are critical of feminism, although they live in a way, and have choices available to them, that would have been impossible were it not for the women's movement. I recently met a 32-year-old woman at a social function who asked me how I would define feminism. Trying to conceal my shock that she should need to ask the question, I gave her a three-sentence definition about women having equal opportunity, women not being inferior to men, and women having choices other than wife and mother. She said she agreed with that, but the radical feminists seemed to her to just hate men and blame men for everything. I said that had been a small part of the women's movement, but that this did not represent the majority view. I told her that the job she held, selling college textbooks and traveling alone to cover her territory, staying in hotels overnight, was a job that a woman could not have held twenty or thirty years ago; it would have been unacceptable for a woman to travel alone as she does. She said she understood this, since her father was always worried about her. Yet she apparently did not give credit to the women's movement for her freedom and opportunity. The fighters for her right to that job are viewed with disdain. She would have been 23 in 1982 when this phenomenon was noted in a *New York Times Magazine* article, "Voices from the Post-Feminist Generation," in which college women are quoted expressing similar views:

> Feminists are losing the second generation because of this incredible bitterness that we can't identify with.
>
> I don't label myself a feminist. Not for me, but for the guy next door that would mean that I'm a lesbian and that I hate men. It's very hard to get heard if you assume a label that's going to turn people off to you. And while it should not, of course, I am afraid that the lesbian connotation would affect my credibility with many of the people I want to reach.
>
> I feel badly for them, it's all right to be independent and strong, but a lot of those women are alone. They've set these goals for the ideal male, a male they've fabricated in their minds.
>
> The unhappy women are all feminists. You'll find very few happy, enthusiastic, relaxed people who are ardent supporters of feminism. Feminists are really tortured people.
>
> Feminists should try to be more . . . warm.
>
> They let themselves go physically . . . they have no sense of style.
>
> Feminism means equal rights so I'm a feminist. But I'm not a women's libber.
>
> The original . . . styles weren't ours, and the revolution wasn't ours. So we put together our own kind of feminism which has very little activism in it. I wish that I had had a revolution to go to, a cause to believe in. My life has been lacking in the kind of upheaval that allowed women to become feminists. [pp. 28–31 and 103–107]

The author, Susan Bolotin, concludes, "Younger women just call their beliefs moderate, while ten years ago we knew they were radical" (p. 117).

Gloria Steinem (1983), in her essay "Why Young Women Are More Conservative," reports on her observation that unlike men, who are most radical in their youth, women may grow more radical with age.

> As young women, whether students or not, we're still in the stage most valued by male-dominant cultures: we have our full potential as workers, wives, sex partners, and child bearers. That means we haven't yet experienced the life events that are most radicalizing for women; entering the paid-labor force and discovering how women are treated there; marrying and finding out that it is not yet an equal partnership; having children and discovering who is responsible for them and who is not; and aging, still a greater penalty for woman than for men. [p. 212]

WOMEN BY AGE GROUP

I propose drawing some fairly arbitrary lines to form age groupings based on age in 1970, six years after the appearance of Friedan's book *The Feminine Mystique,* when the book had been well disseminated (a male metaphor); consciousness-raising groups were spreading; books, articles, and demonstrations by feminists were appearing; and society was beginning to experience the power of the movement to change long-held stereotypes. Women who were born in 1970 or later are truly in the most advantageous position to benefit from the psychological, economic, and political changes brought about by the movement. Their mothers, born between 1940 and 1970, were influenced by feminist values and principles and may well have pursued careers, gone back to school, and been somewhat independent, serving as role models for their daughters as women who have children and work outside the home.

Women born between 1950 and 1970 are also in a good position to have benefited from the feminist influence on our society. Their mothers, born between 1920 and 1950, were most likely traditional housewives, and their daughters are often those who grew up thinking that they do not want to be like their mothers whose lives were dominated by serving husband and children. Now in their early twenties to early forties, they have had opportunities and social encouragement for alternative life choices. They may have married young, had children, and then returned to school; or perhaps have gotten their education first and married and had children later, in their thirties.

Women born between 1940 and 1950, now in their forties and fifties, were sometimes in the front lines of the movement, having been in college in the sixties. The birth of feminism took place in their teens and twenties and they may have been caught up in the antiestablishment experimentation of those years, which included the sexual revolution, radical politics, Vietnam war protests, the civil rights movement, and the rebirth of feminism. Theirs was the first generation of women to have abandoned the ideal of virginity and to have lived with their boyfriends. Those women who did not attend college most likely pursued more traditional lives, marrying young, having children, and then feeling the influence of feminism in their lives when their children went to school and economic and social pressures made them question continuing to stay home as full-time housewives. They often sought part-time work or returned to school for additional training.

Those of us born between 1930 and 1940 were raised with the expectation of becoming full-time wives and mothers, and most did so, whether they went to college or not. Some worked for a few years until they married or until they had children, but typically they married and had children in their twenties. In 1970, we had two to four children in school and were between ages 30 and 40. This is the group who had a second chance, if they wanted it, and many did make significant changes after some years of ambivalence and the need to work through old values and self-concepts. These women sometimes came to therapists for help in resolving conflicts about leaving their children in order to pursue independent goals. Some, who had graduated college, returned to graduate school. Others had to start from the beginning. Divorces sometimes followed. Among this group there were many angry debates during these years, as some women defended the traditional position and were defensive with other women who were becoming feminists and making changes. I observed several instances of acquaintances who seemed hostile toward me and then upon after returning to school several years later, were warm and friendly.

Women born before 1930 were over 40 when the new feminism exploded. If they were politically aware and acted fast, they too may have returned to school and developed careers, but if they were not feminists and stood by the traditional values of being a housewife, they most likely continued life as their mothers had, working in the PTA, doing volunteer work, or perhaps helping their husbands in business as the children grew and time was available. In some ways the women in this group were the ones most injured by the women's movement, because they saw their lives dismissed by a younger generation, including their own daughters, and yet they were not free to reverse the past nor to chart new trails for the future. This group, and some in the group born between 1930 and 1940, have borne the brunt of the criticism and have been the most resentful of and resistant to the changes brought about by the women's movement. Yet they were doing what they had been led to believe was the best thing for their children, and the natural and right thing for a woman.

WOMEN'S MAGAZINES

I surveyed ten magazines—one weekly, *Woman's World,* and nine monthly or bimonthlies: *Redbook, Complete Woman, Lears, Cosmopolitan, Ms., Woman's Day, Entrepreneurial Woman, Mademoiselle,* and *Working Woman.* All were on the magazine rack of a large chain drugstore in my middle-class residential neighborhood in San Francisco. Other magazines were clearly intended for women, having to do with home decorating, sewing, and other traditional crafts, but I did not include them. I also excluded *Vogue* because it is specifically a fashion magazine. The new *Ms.* has no advertising, a decision explained in an excellent article by Gloria Steinem in the premier issue (1990). She exposes how advertisers virtually dictate the content of women's magazines and had thereby put the former *Ms.* in difficulty, trying to maintain editorial independence while struggling to get the much-needed revenue from ads. Reading this article is essential for understanding the power of advertisers in the mass media.

Betty Friedan must be rather pleased when she looks at today's women's magazines. There is still a great deal of emphasis on beauty—clothes, makeup, hairstyles, weight loss—but the focus on health and fitness is a strong component of the usual "diet" articles. The ads having to do with appearance are still plentiful: hair coloring, nail polish, makeup, fashions, perfumes, and wrinkle creams. The Steinem article explains the connection between the ads and the accompanying articles. But the articles and stories are definitely not traditional, with a great deal of focus on work; indeed, two magazines are directed exclusively at working women. All the magazines have columns by psychiatrists or psychologists answering letters or giving advice on a particular topic.

Mademoiselle, March 1991, has four sections: Beauty and Health, Articles, Fashion, and Departments. The short story is about a man who falls in love with a powerful woman lawyer who is very busy and often keeps him waiting for dates. She is overweight, but he is smitten by her intelligence and sensuality and is hurt when she does not have time to return his calls. He is not a professional. He invites her for dinner, which he lovingly cooks and serves to her. It seems like an absolute role reversal and surely illustrates, on the fantasy level, that not all men are put off by successful women.

In the same issue, Nike has a six-page color advertisement for their different styles of running and exercise shoes that describes a girl growing up and ends with this statement:

> Sooner or later, you start taking yourself seriously.
> You know when you need a break. You know
> when you need a rest. You know what to get worked
> up about, and what to get rid of.
> And you know when it's time to take care
> of yourself, for yourself. To do something that makes
> you stronger, faster, more complete.
> Because you know it's never too late to have a life.
> And never too late to change one.
> Just do it. [pp. 81–88]

An article entitled "The New Sexy Is Strong" shows a beautiful model in a formal gown with clenched fists and an angry face.

> Femininity used to be thought of as soft, frilly and—all too often—
> ineffective. But nowadays, there's nothing weak about it. In fact, some

of the most admired women around are the ones who manage to combine qualities both tough and tender . . . women who can look like a pushover in the prettiest pale-pink cashmere—but fire you while wearing it. . . . women who are intent on squeezing in their weekly manicure between two corporate meetings. What makes these dichotomies work so well together is confidence—knowing that you can run with the boys, yet still be one of the girls. Today's twenty-somethings have high expectations. Thanks to the twin legacies of the '50s housewife and the '70s feminist, the assumption now is that women can do anything men can—without compromising their femininity. [pp. 106, 171]

Another article, "The Intelligent Woman's Guide to Sex," actually gives very sensible advice on the kind of men to stay away from, "bad men" who mistreat women. A two-page ad for a nonprescription vaginal cream for use with yeast infections has a full-page color photo of a lovely young woman gynecologist with a prominent wedding ring, recommending the product with a statement that, "From personal experience I know how maddening the symptoms of a vaginal yeast infection are." We have become our own experts! An article entitled "The Boss—How to Read Your Leader" describes different kinds of personalities, both male and female, and recommends ways for dealing with them.

Cosmopolitan magazine and the "Cosmo girl" have been the target of ridicule by feminists for years. The Cosmo girl's one goal in life has been her dedication to finding and capturing a man. Tips on how to succeed in this holy-grail mission have included getting up out of bed in the morning an hour before your overnight guest so that he doesn't see you without your makeup, and keeping a sandwich under the pillow because men get hungry after sex. I never could figure out how you were supposed to keep the sandwich from getting smashed. Women were advised to work because "The working world is where men are!" Open sexuality in dress and behavior has been the Cosmo image, all designed to lure the male. The February 1991 *Cosmopolitan* has its typical female model on the cover, looking like a high-class whore. It has plenty of beauty and fashion content but also recognizes the real importance of work in the modern woman's life. One article includes advice on how to get ahead at your job, and another asks "What is Corporate America Doing for Women?" It talks about gender bias, day care, parental leave, and lists Cosmo's Top 20 U.S. Corporations who accommodate women's changing needs. Criteria used include (1) promotion, mentoring, and sexual harassment policies; (2) pay equity; (3) family benefits; and (4) flexible work scheduling policies. Yes, *Cosmopolitan,* not *Ms.* Other articles include "Male Athletes and Sexual Assault," followed by "Marrying Up Is Marrying Smart." In the latter we find the following:

Being well-off isn't about diamonds and furs, insists Ellie. "Having money means that you don't have to do menial tasks," she says. "Instead, you can pay to have them done, which frees you up for the things you really enjoy. In my case, that's doing some of my own artwork and spending quality time with my husband. It also means having a home big enough so that we can get away from each other to do our own thing. And if I want to take a year off from my job to see if I can make it as an artist, I can do that too." [pp. 224–227]

The new Cosmo "girl" doesn't look for a rich husband so that she does not have to work, but rather so that she has a choice about working and can try her efforts at creative work that cannot guarantee an income.

Complete Woman touts on the cover a common theme ("What Men Want in Bed, 8-page Guide to Making Love") but also has regular columns called "Career Woman Advisor," "Auto Advisor," and "Health Briefs." An article entitled "Status Clash—When You Earn More Than Your Man" warns against marrying a man who is not status conscious and upwardly mobile if you are, and also warns against status-hungry, driven men. A story on divorce focuses on "how men really feel about it" and starts with the statistic that three-quarters of all divorces are initiated by women, although admittedly often for good reason. A story on "Feeling Fat" takes the position that being overweight is an emotional issue and will not be helped by dieting. "A Day in the Life of a Makeup Artist" focuses on a successful career woman, followed by "Is Your Relationship Going Any-where?" with some sensible advice on how to tell the men who are serious about you from the ones who do not want a commitment.

Redbook has sections on Health, Fashion, Beauty, Food and Nutrition, Decorating, Fiction, Articles (family oriented), Celebrities, and features regular columnists Benjamin Spock and Judith Viorst. It seems to be directed at young women with families. The same ad for a nonprescription vaginal cream for yeast infections appears with an attractive, more middle-aged woman gynecologist, again telling us that "From the vaginal yeast infections I've experienced myself, and from my work at St. Luke's Roosevelt Hospital . . . ." She holds her glasses in one hand as her arm rests on a desk, very much the expert but also very much a woman like the reader.

The fiction piece is a nicely done story by a woman, again from the point of view of a man, about an older, lonely widower who observes, and appears to fall in love with, a lonely housewife next door who is neglected by her husband. Romance never comes, but he is pleased at the end of the story when he observes her loading her car and leaving. Her husband arrives later to find her gone. The main character tells us the husband deserves it, but nevertheless sympathizes with him. Another short story by a man is mother and child oriented, but the mother does work and is described as busily rushing through her day trying to keep up with her household chores, get the children delivered and picked up, and get to her job.

A special section on raising preteens and teens in the '90s is a guide for parents. Another section is a special celebration of thirty years of young mother's stories in which seven women who were among the more than 300 women featured over the years are revisited for updates to their original stories: "Many of these women were among the first to speak out about issues that have since become the focus of wider public concern, issues that defined their times and charted the progress of women's—and men's—lives during three decades of phenomenal social change" (p. 101).

One writer, Mary Higgins Clark, was interviewed twenty-five years ago when she learned her husband was dying. She had five young children she would have to support. She has become a very successful writer of suspense novels, with an $11.4 million contract. She remarried once, after fourteen years, but divorced and says she does not wish to marry again.

The next, Harriette Robinet, an African-American woman, had purchased a home with her husband in an all-white neighborhood twenty-five years ago and had moved in under police protection, but later became close friends with many of her neighbors. Today she is an author of children's books.

Linda Hendrix wrote her story for *Redbook* in 1973 and again in 1976, about her dilemma as a feminist trying to pursue her career and be a mother. Eighteen years later, now a lawyer and remarried, she says it is still a very tough situation for women and recalls her own struggles, not seeing much improvement.

Mary Boyd was a mother of three children in 1969 when she and her husband sued a local rubber-goods manufacturer and the city of Dyersburg, Tennessee for environmental pollution and were successful. The illnesses and deaths in the community as a result of the burning of rubber were stopped. Boyd then went to law school and is now an assistant district attorney.

Jean Mufti wrote to *Redbook* in 1976 of the loss of her premature baby son due to a pregnancy during her use of the Dalkon Shield, which had been lodged in her uterus. When she became aware of the lawsuits, she wrote to A. H. Robins asking for compensation and received $30,000. Today, at 40 she is remarried, a housewife, and the mother of three, after leaving her job as a science editor when the family no longer needed her income. She says she needed years to recover from the grief of the loss of her baby and from eight years of an abusive marriage.

Marilyn Johnson became a surrogate mother in 1984 and again for the same couple in 1987. She now writes that she and her husband and three children are like "family," with regular visits and with all five of the children knowing they are brothers and sisters. She says, "Becoming a surrogate mother was one of the best decisions of my life; it has been nothing but positive." In 1988 she and her 18-year-old daughter testified against proposed legislation banning surrogate mothering in Michigan, but the ban became law.

Claudia Peterson's story appeared in January 1987. Her sister and 5-year-old daughter were both dying of cancer, the result of atmospheric testing by the U.S. government at the Nevada Nuclear Test Site between 1951 and 1963. Claudia lived in St. George, Utah, downwind of the fallout. Some townspeople filed suit, but Claudia and her husband did not because it went against their patriotic principles. They wanted an admission of guilt from the government. She became an antinuclear activist and now is pleased to report the passage of the Radiation Exposure Compensation Act in October 1990, which includes a trust fund of $100 million to compensate families for their suffering. It's not much, she reports, but she did get the apology she wanted.

What is striking about each of these women is that they are recognized for something they did outside their roles as wife and mother. What a contrast to the 1950s women's magazines as reported on by Friedan in 1964, when mothers were depicted as having no interest in anything outside of the immediate needs of their families. Each of these women is selected specifically because of her contribution in speaking out on public issues and making a contribution to society based on her active role on an issue that deeply affected her life.

Lear's is a new magazine targeted for the middle-class woman over 40. In the February 1991 issue there is an article on going back to school as an older woman, which tells us that by 1997, according to the Department Of Education, 28 percent (2.1 million) of all women in American colleges and universities will be 35 or older, up from less than half a million in 1972. The author attributes this rise to women's expanding economic expectations and the high divorce rate. There are columns on economic advice, including how to launch a new business, and an interview with Linda Wertheimer of National Public Radio's nightly show, "All Things Considered." Wertheimer, age 47, has been a political reporter for NPR for nineteen years and tells her interviewer that when, at age 12, she saw Pauline Frederick cover the Hungarian revolution on television she realized that she, as a woman, could become a reporter.

A beautifully illustrated story tells of a woman's journey down 2,300 miles of the Amazon with a group called Society Expeditions, designed for ecology-minded tourists. We learn about the indigenous peoples and the problems of preserving the rain forests.

"A Woman for *Lear's*," a monthly feature, contains an interview with a recently widowed woman, a former teacher who at 48 took over the management of 2,000 acres of crop land, learning a whole new world after years of being primarily a wife and mother: "What she lacked in first-hand farming knowledge she made up in spirit and determination. After Al's death Carol donned blue jeans and sweatshirts instead of mourning garb and distracted herself by learning what she needed to know about the nitty-gritty operational part of farming" (p. 126). We learn that she has been successful and is proud of herself, although at times she feels overwhelmed. She says that as a young woman she always liked adventure and muses that if she had not been born female with a "'50s mentality" of getting married and having kids, she would have spent a few years as a deckhand on a freighter.

Two notices tell us that *Lear's,* the New York Women's Bar Association, and Anne Klein II are sponsoring a benefit fashion show in support of a New York City shelter for victims of domestic violence, and that *Lear's* and Vanity Fair Lingerie are sponsoring a "Mothers Who Make a Difference" awards contest in which readers are invited to submit a 250 to 500-word essay about a mother who has made a meaningful and significant contribution to her family and community. But this is no tame mother: "Perhaps she is caring for children, the elderly or the homeless, cleaning up the environment, exploring ways to better the economy, making scientific discoveries, or working for global peace. Whatever the community concern—we want to hear about and recognize the mothers who are improving our world" (p. 36). This image of mothers surely holds out as admirable women who do more than care for their own children and homes; the mothers sought for awards are those whose world is large enough to encompass their children, the community, a career, or significant volunteer activity.

Woman's World is clearly a lowbrow magazine. The short story is a highly romantic tale of a young woman who falls in love with her neighbor through their contact with their cats. Although she is immediately sexually attracted to him, there is no sex at all as the relationship slowly develops into one of love and caring. Articles are short and somewhat sensationally oriented.

Woman's Day has a regular feature called "Money Facts," with a current advice article on what to do when you cannot pay your bills. There are many short columns with health and nutrition tips, beauty tips, shopping tips, money-saving tips, and sewing tips. Recipes, downplayed in the other magazines, are a focus in articles and ads. This is definitely targeted for the full-time homemaker, with no articles for working women.

Working Woman is clearly all about work, although many of the ads are for the usual cosmetics, perfumes, hair and skin care products. An article about a black woman promoted to vice president of marketing at Pillsbury says, "Pillsbury's Linda Keene tells how sales popped up when she went after the modern mom" (p. 29). Others focus on Japanese management styles, career strategies, estate planning, credit, bargaining with a car dealer, developing your own business, hiring a personal shopper, organizing your work, and changing your hair color for more business success. An interview with Valerie Salembier, fired as president of the *New York Post,* tells what it was like to manage men. She started as a secretary and worked her way up to be publisher of *TV Guide* and senior vice president of advertising at *USA Today.* She talks about the need to be tough, how to manage, how to deal with the owners, and how to handle stress.

Entrepreneurial Woman was launched in 1990. Articles include how to handle high-stress periods in your business, workplace hazards, how to buy a car and a computer, and how to apply for business loans. A role-model column focuses on a woman who founded a fresh produce business in 1962 that now does $20 million in annual sales. Other successful women entrepreneurs are featured, including two women who founded a sports-bra company that they then expanded to include a full line of exercise wear. In 1978 their profits were $3,000, and the very next year their sales totaled $500,000. It is now described as a multi-million-dollar company. Other business recommendations are featured, and there is a guide to 167 new businesses.

Ms. has the most political-legal focus. International news of feminist interest, a six-page regular feature, is followed by a long feature story on Women and AIDS. Gloria Steinem writes about the sexual abuse of well-known Hollywood actresses, such as Rita Hayworth. There are book, film, and record reviews focusing on women artists, a call by Ellie Smeal for a Feminist Party, and an article by Jane O'Reilly, a feminist essayist, on the harm done to the author by her Catholic upbringing. "I am only one of millions who suffer from the insults inflicted on our sacred dignity." A review of the election features the victories of Ann Richards as governor of Texas, and of Eleanor Holmes Norton and Maxine Waters, two African-American women elected to Congress. Actress Rita Moreno describes her illegal abortion at age 23, which landed her in the hospital because it was badly done. She tells of her fear and shame, but of feeling she must do it because the man would not marry her. She thinks she may have gotten pregnant "accidentally" in the hope he would marry her, which would have been a terrible mistake, she says in retrospect.

The world of women as shown in magazines for women now includes financial responsibilities, concern with social issues, college and career advancement, and business know-how, along with the traditional concern for physical appearance, getting a husband, and having children. There are choices among these magazines that reflect the actual choices in women's lives today. There is no one standard theme, no one right way for women to be. It is a reflection of the choices women now feel they have, as I learned in my interviews.

COLLEGE AND UNIVERSITY WOMEN

The entrance of women into previously all-male professions and trades has been obvious to all of us since 1970. To get some specific figures I called the University of California Medical School admissions office in San Francisco. I was told that 48 percent of entering students in the 1990 class are women, as compared with 34 percent in 1980, 15 percent in 1970, and 7 percent in 1960. The admissions office at Boalt Hall School of Law at the University of California at Berkeley reported that 46 percent of its 1990 class are women, compared with 40 percent in 1980, and 18 percent in 1970. They did not have the figures for 1960, but I can remember as the wife of a law student in the class that graduated from Boalt in 1957 that there were 2 women in a class of over 100.

The question that is of interest and concern for our purposes is whether, and in what ways, this increasing drive for achievement and financial independence has changed women's emotional dependence on men and marriage and women's feelings about themselves; their self-esteem, pride, incidence of depression, and general life satisfaction.

San Francisco State University

I spoke with Gloria Carr Gold, a clinical social worker at the Counseling Center at San Francisco State University for the past twenty-four years, and asked her if she has seen changes in the young women students there since 1966. "State," as it is called locally, is an urban school drawing from middle-class and working-class neighborhoods in San Francisco and the suburbs. It is a commuter school and has older students as well as recent high school graduates. With Stanford an hour to the south and Berkeley across the Bay, it tends to draw the less affluent, less scholastically outstanding students, but there is a wide range, and some departments have had outstanding reputations for years, such as Creative Writing, where many nationally known local writers and poets have taught.

Ms. Gold reports that the emotional need for an intimate relationship with a man is still present in the women she counsels, but there are clear changes. There is no longer the expectation that a man will support them and there is pressure to choose a career because it is not acceptable to be a housewife. This leaves a small group of women who truly want to be full-time wives and mothers feeling guilty and ashamed of these dependency wishes. They will often "make up" a career plan, just so as not to expose these wishes, which they fear will make them appear inadequate.

The majority of women students who do take their careers seriously expect to work for their entire life, and this does make for significant changes in relationships. They will not move to follow a man but will move for their own career opportunities. In some cases the men move to follow a career opportunity for the woman, and the men do not appear to feel guilty about not being the sole support for a family. Those students who are from blue-collar families often have a mother who worked at menial jobs; they may be the first member of their family to attend college. Some grew up not having a father who reliably supported the family, in some cases because the father was an alcoholic.

In response to my question as to whether this focus on career and economic independence has changed the emotional dependence on men, Ms. Gold stated that marriage and children are no longer the primary goals of women in their twenties. She believes that they are just as emotionally dependent on a love relationship as were women in the past, but because of their interest in getting an education and developing a career, they will not stay with men they are not really happy with. This means they are freer to leave a bad relationship. They used to have to marry for status but now achieve their own status and are freer to marry for love. There is no longer a stigma attached to being an unmarried woman; the derogatory term *spinster* is not a part of their vocabulary. Many women live together with their boyfriends without any shame or stigma. Both parties are monogamous and serious about these relationships. She compares this with twenty years ago when such a situation was seen to be degrading to the woman, with the presumption that the man was taking advantage of her.

I asked Ms. Gold to share her impressions of noncollege women on these issues of career and marriage. One observation is that there are not as many women available to do volunteer work as in previous generations because so many are back in school or working. Even upper-middle-class and upper-class women are much more likely to be doing something of their own, such as starting a small business or art gallery. It appears that although the college and noncollege single working women Gold knows in the real estate office where she works part-time as an agent are interested in marriage, they really do not feel any pressure about it until age 30. The pressure gets stronger at ages 35 to 40. Some may have a fantasy of marrying a rich man, but along with the fantasy is the reality that they need to have a career and be financially independent. They are sexually active and often unsure about whether they want children. For those who are divorced and already have a child, the pressure for marriage is much reduced. The theme of choice is very strong. There are a number of possible choices for them, and this allows them to be very selective. One agent is 40 and has never been married. She is attractive and would like to marry but is not desperate. The biological clock is the only determinant, as compared with earlier generations when marriage between 18 and 25 was all but mandatory.

Cooking is not as essential a part of a feminine identity as it once was. Some of the women agents, married and single, eat all their dinners out or order food to take home and in fact have neither time for nor interest in cooking. This is in sharp contrast with prefeminist generations for whom cooking was a major part of their work and role expectation.

The University of California at Berkeley

R. Bonnie Thompson Glaser, a psychologist, worked at the Counseling Center at the University of California at Berkeley from 1974 through 1990. She says the men are cooking and parenting now and are coming to couple sessions complaining that the women are too focused on their academic ambitions and have no time to talk or relax, or even for sexual foreplay. The men say they want more intimacy, a role reversal from earlier generations when similar complaints were generally heard from women. Dr. Glaser notes that some of the women students have conflicts about autonomy and achievement that interfere with both their academic performance and personal relationships. As with the students at State, the women expect to have a lifelong career, but some, if they are high achievers, do get anxious that they will be socially isolated. Women cannot boast about their good grades, whereas it is comfortable for men to do so. Sometimes, according to Glaser, psychological symptoms such as anorexia or bulimia are women students' ways of saying that they are not really strong and therefore are not a threat to men or other women. They all worry about being a threat if they stand out and therefore belittle themselves to reduce that imagined threat to others.

The sexual freedom of this generation has put pressure on young women to lose their virginity; those who are frightened of sex can no longer hide behind a strict moral code and therefore are anxious about their sexual inhibitions. In previous generations the girls who had trouble inhibiting their sex drive were those with a problem.

They expect that men will help with children and housework. However, they commonly delay marriage and children until they have established themselves in their chosen field. Many have mothers with careers, and many come from divorced families and have a fear of divorce. This element reinforces the concept of work in their lives and the postponement of marriage and children until the right person comes along. The pressure to marry is off, the focus is on a secure marriage that will not lead to divorce. As with the State students that Gold sees, the emotional dependence on men and the desire to marry is still there, but is on a par with a desire for a rewarding career. What comes across from both these therapists is the impression that love and marriage are no less important but that career is equally important, a major change in relative values and thus in the dependence on men as the only source of value and gratification in the lives of these young women. The valuing of work, together with the end of the taboo against premarital sex, decreases the pressure for early marriage and allows the woman many years to explore different relationships as well as her own interests.

Butte College

Oroville is a small farming community in North Central California. California has a system of community colleges, two-year colleges that feed into the university system at the junior level, serving the dual purpose of providing a two-year, employment-oriented training program for a part of the student body and a two-year university-level equivalent program for those who cannot enter the university directly from high school. Many who attend community colleges live at home, and many are older students, returning to school after several years of working or being housewives. A high school diploma is not a necessary prerequisite for entrance.

Jaime M. O'Neill teaches English at Butte College and, writing in a column in the *San Francisco Chronicle* (1990), says that at a college where he taught in Washington State, 66 percent of the students are women with a median age of 29.8 years. 'To be a man,' according to French writer Antoine de Saint-Exupéry, 'is, precisely, to be responsible.' By that definition, most of the men I come across these days are women,'' writes O'Neill.

He describes a typical woman community college student:

> She is 32 years old and has two children, ages 11 and 6. After a litigious divorce from a husband of 12 years, she finds herself only marginally employable because she has neither an education beyond high school nor a consequential employment history.
>
> She entered adulthood with the conventional dream: husband, children, picket fence. That dream has not entirely died, but one of the lessons life has taught her is that she cannot allow the realization of that dream to depend upon the man she married. . . .
>
> Upon her return to school, she is diffident. The process of registration alone nearly sends her packing. She feels herself hopelessly out of her depth and is fearful that the younger students will find her ignorant and foolish. Within weeks, however, her confidence grows. She is an excellent student, despite her other responsibilities—or because of them.

She is much more disciplined and focused than her younger class-mates. Though her skills may be rusty, she compensates with diligence, thoughtfulness and the wealth of experience that has come to her almost without her awareness. Her presence complements the class-room atmosphere; younger students behave with more maturity when she is there.

She supports herself and her children with a poorly paid clerical job or with a combination of financial aid and welfare benefits. Mornings are for school, afternoons for work. Evenings are reserved for cooking, cleaning, and the quest for elusive "quality time" with the kids. Once they are in bed, study begins.

She is nearly always tired, but she is indefatigable, and she loves school. She is happy to be using her mind again and she has met a number of women like herself. Their company is reassuring; it does much to disabuse her of her sense of personal failure. . . .

The entire enterprise is extremely fragile. All the resources of money, time and energy are allocated to the widest margins, leaving nothing for the unexpected. If something goes awry—as it always does—she is forced to think of quitting school. . . . But she doesn't quit. More often than not she finds a way to manage. The alternatives, after all, are bleak. . . . Families headed by women are six times more likely to be poor than families headed by men. Escaping that poverty . . . is seven times more likely if she completes college. Besides, she feels that her efforts and her hoped-for successes will serve as a model and an inspiration to her children.

O'Neill goes on to show us a typical piece of writing by one of his women students:

I am a single parent of two children. A boy who is 13 years and a girl who just turned 4. I'm sure I do not need to tell you just how hard it is to get a decent paying job with some sort of bennifits without an education. I am 30 years old now, and I need to start thinking of both mine and my children's future. It's an awful experience for parent and child to have so much time taken away from each other.

Up until Spring semester, I was a welefare parent, siting at home because I couldn't afford to work. It costs a minimum of $10 a day for child care. Then there's travel expences. I know many single parents who arn't even trying to get work anymore because they can't afford it, or it just isn't worth it.

I can't speak for everyone, but the thought of becoming indepentent thrills me like nothing else. My whole life has changed. I feel as if I am somebody—not just a welefare mother. My son is so very proud of me for putting my best foot forward and trying to make something of myself. After school I can't wait to share with him all I've learned. When he looks at me and says "ALL RIGHT, MOM" it's the happiest

times I have right now. And it makes all that extra work of studying
after being both a mother and a father each day worth it. (Please excuse
my spelling. It's one of the reasons I'm here!)

O'Neill concludes with this final compliment: "I have written letters of
recommendation for a great many of these women as they go on to seek
jobs or continued education. What I often say in those letters is that if all
my students were like these women, I would feel guilty about getting paid
for what I do" (p. 20).

Two Southern State Colleges, 1979–1987

By contrast, *Educated in Romance: Women, Achievement, and College
Culture* (1990), written by two anthropologists, is a study of twenty-three
women on two Southern campuses, one historically black, the other
predominantly white. The women were interviewed three times: in 1979,
their sophomore year; at graduation; and again in 1987. In an article in the
New York Times Book Review, J. J. Brumberg (1991) says the authors
conclude that in the college environment on these two campuses, "young
women's career aspirations evaporate, go underground or get derailed. By
default, most fall into reliance on men for marriage and economic support.
Both institutional practices and informal networks reinforce it" (p. 29).

These colleges are described as state-funded institutions attracting a
primarily regional, nonelite student body. Yet both San Francisco State and
the University of California at Berkeley are state funded and San Francisco
State is "nonelite," so the difference may lie in the region, the South
consistently being socially and politically behind the East Coast and West
Coast. The reviewer describes the book's conclusions:

Peer culture, it argues, is actually the most powerful force on campus;
its imperatives can transcend even the most persuasive pedagogy or
progressive curriculum. . . . The story is discouraging because of what
it suggests about the continuing power of a patriarchal system to shape
female aspiration and achievement despite influential educational de-
velopments such as women's studies. . . . Women students are subjected to the indignities of what the authors call a "sexual auction
block," run by peers. In short order, they come to accept the fact that
grades on sexual attractiveness are more important than their grade-
point average. A woman's real value in college will be determined by
attractiveness and proximity to high-status men; friendships with other
women will take a back seat to relationships with sympathetic
males. . . . Students scaled down their ambitions, so that most ended up
with the desired heterosexual romantic relationship but also a marginal
career and inferior preparation as a wage earner. [p. 29]

This sounds like an accurate description of college women in the 1950s. Even allowing for regional differences, it is unfortunate that these women were so unrealistic about their future, as shown in the statistics below. It also makes me wonder how typical are women in the San Francisco Bay Area, and whether it is appropriate to draw any conclusions about other parts of the country based on one's experience as a psychotherapist in this area. However, since the women who were sophomores in 1979 were born, generally, in 1960, perhaps a current study of Southern colleges would reveal some significant changes among the students in 1989, born in 1970. The young Southern women I know today have married young (in their early twenties) but are pursuing careers or returning to school.

FACT SHEET ON WORKING WOMEN

The Women's Bureau of the U.S. Department of Labor issued statistics on working women in September 1990, based on figures collected in 1989. A summary includes the following:

1. Fifty-six million women aged 16 and over were working or looking for work as compared with 44 million in 1979.

2. Sixty-nine percent of all women 18 to 64 were working as compared with 88 percent of men. Seventy-six percent of women aged 35 to 44 were working.

3. Fourteen million, or 26 percent, of all women workers held part-time jobs.

4. The average woman worker aged 16 between 1970 and 1980 could expect to spend 29.3 years of her life in the labor force, compared with 39.1 years for a man.

5. Women accounted for 45 percent of the civilian labor force.

6. Participation of women in the labor force is nearly equal for black, white, and Hispanic women.

7. Most women work because of economic need. The majority of women in the labor force (58.5 percent) in March 1988 were either single (25 percent), divorced (12 percent), widowed (4 percent), separated (4 percent), or had husbands whose annual earnings were less than $15,000 (13.5 percent).

8. Women who maintain families have the lowest median income, $15,346. The median income of married couples with a working wife was $42,709 compared with $27,220 for couples with a wife at home.

9. The more education a woman has, the greater the likelihood she will seek employment. Among women aged 25 to 54 with four or more years of college in March 1988, 81 percent were in the labor force. Among women of the same age group with less than four years of high school, only 51 percent were working.

10. Median earnings for women in 1988 was $17,606. For men it was $26,656.

11. Median income for a women with four years of college was $25,187. For men with a high school diploma it was $26,045.

12. The number of women-owned businesses rose from 2.5 million in 1980 to 4.1 million in 1986.

13. In March 1988, 65 percent of women with children under 18 were in the labor force; of women with children under age 6, 47.5 percent were in the labor force.

14. In March 1988, there were 3.6 million families maintained by women living below the poverty level. Of these 44.7 percent had children under 18.

15. Of all families, 16.9 percent are maintained by women; of black families, 45 percent; of Hispanic families, 23 percent; of white families, 13 percent. Between 1940 and 1960 only 8 percent of families were headed by women.

THE TWO GROUPS OF WORKING WOMEN: BY CHOICE OR BY NECESSITY

Some women work because they have to, others work because they want to, and still others work because they want to improve the standard of living of their family, perhaps to be able to buy a home. This group is in the gray area because a woman may describe herself as having to work but a co-worker may see her as working by choice. This division may create some tension between women in the workplace. Those working by choice are likely to be married, whereas those by necessity are single, widowed, or divorced.

Those in the gray area are most likely married, but a small number may be separated or divorced, receiving spousal and child support and working to supplement that inadequate income and to get out of the house and back into circulation. In previous generations, a man drew pride from supporting his family—being a "good provider." A woman felt it desirable to be married and "taken care of." Not working was a badge of her having attained her complementary position of pride in her dependent role. A married woman who worked was in effect telling the community that her husband was an inadequate provider. In a middle-class family, a wife working was aberrant behavior. In poor families, it was a tragedy. Married couples without children were rare. Psychoanalytic theory confirmed the belief that there was something wrong with a woman who chose to work. She was competing with her husband, castrating him, and could not accept her natural role as a dependent woman. A woman who did not work and complained that her husband didn't earn enough money was also diagnosed as castrating. A woman who did not have a financially successful husband was in a double bind: she couldn't work and she couldn't complain.

A Job by Necessity

Kathy, born in 1964, lives in San Francisco. She has been married five years, works full-time, and has a 1-year-old baby in full-time day care in a private home. She has worked as a secretary for the same firm since high school graduation, working two years before her marriage to her 33-year-old husband, who has his own house-painting business. Her husband does all the cooking, which he likes to do and which Kathy is not interested in doing. Her husband does his full share of the cleaning and laundry and food shopping. Kathy is very pleased with his participation. There are periods when he has no jobs and does more of the housework. Kathy helps him with the advertising for his business, but currently work is slow.

They are very satisfied with the day-care home. Her baby daughter is happy to see the day-care mother each morning and stretches out her arms to go to her. Kathy's feelings are hurt when this happens. She realizes that the baby spends more time in day care than at home and Kathy regrets that but says there is no alternative now because her income is the only stable income the family has. Kathy's mother went to work after her children were in school, and Kathy wishes she could stay home with her daughter while she is young. I said that since she has never done that, her wish is based on what she imagines it would be like. She agreed and said she might go "stir crazy," but if that were so, then she would like to work part-time.

They are planning to have another child but not until this one is in school, because they cannot afford the day care-costs ($360.00 per month) for two children.

I asked Kathy about the other young women who had graduated from high school with her. Of those she knows, all are unmarried except for one who just got married. They would like to marry but either have not found the right person, or the right person has not asked them. They are looking for a committed relationship but are willing to wait for the right one. As far as she knows, they are not anxious about it, and marriage is not a top priority for them now.

A Career by Choice

Anne is 33, married at age 27, and has two children, ages $2\frac{1}{2}$ and 6 months. She lives in a suburb of San Francisco. After high school she worked for a few years, then went to college and, before marriage, she got a master's degree and began her career. After her first child was born she was able to arrange a job-share and reduce her work to 20 hours per week. Her husband, also 33, works at home on computer software design and does the child care while Anne is at work. Anne likes to cook and does all the cooking, but she and her husband share the housework, laundry, and gardening. Anne believes that the earning capacity of a man does not become a significant issue for women until children are born, at which point the woman's choice to work or not depends on the man's income. She believes that before children are born it is socially unacceptable for the woman not to work; it will be seen as her taking advantage of the man. She has one married friend without children who does not work and is embarrassed about it. She knows two women with children who do not work and they both feel some social discomfort around men, fearing they have nothing to talk about, but feel comfortable talking with other mothers. Both make self-disparaging comments and feel lowered self-worth because of being "just a housewife."

Anne has observed that men share the child care in all the families she knows, and are eager to be active participants in raising their children. In the families where the wife works, the husband shares in the housework as well. She has never heard a woman complain about her husband not helping out enough, surely a big change from earlier generations of men. She does acknowledge that the woman is still responsible and the man is "helping" when it comes to the housework, but not so with the children. The fathers know all the details of the child's routine and the doctor's reports, and are very involved with all aspects of their child's life. She finds that all the women she knows cook and exchange recipes.

As to career and motherhood, Anne feels that the important issue for all the women she knows and for herself is choice: when to have children and when to return to work. The choice to have children has been made by all her friends, neighbors, and co-workers, often in their thirties, but then the focus is on having the choice to return to work or to take time out to be at home with the baby. The difference from previous generations appears to be that for these women motherhood is not their role in life, not a vocation or their sole identity. It is the product of a decision to be a mother as a temporary job until they feel ready to go back to work. Whereas women of earlier generations thought that something was wrong with them if they were dissatisfied being full-time housewives, the women's movement has allowed this generation the freedom to move in and out of the housewife role by choice, if at times the couple can afford to do without the wife's earnings.

On the other hand, Anne believes that today men better appreciate all the work involved in the maintenance of a home and in child care. The husband who is involved in housework when both partners are maintaining careers will be more appreciative when the woman then does choose to stay home and take over that job after a child is born.

Anne does not think there is a stigma to remaining single or divorcing. In the past, she recognizes, it meant to a woman that no one wanted her, but now it could mean that she would not compromise. She may be lonely but is not stigmatized. Again, the key element is that the woman has a choice.

I asked Anne about her sister-in-law, Carol, a midwestern woman living in a midwestern city, for a glimpse of middle America. Carol is 31, a college graduate, has been married for six years, and has two children, aged 3 and 1. Carol worked full-time before her children were born, and then half-time. She has recently decided to go back to school to get her master's degree in social work. She is enrolled part-time, takes classes at night, and studies on the weekend. Since she is not working and is home all day, she does the housework. Her husband takes responsibility for the children when Carol is in school and on the weekends, so that she can study. Anne thinks Carol has gone back to school partly to improve her earning capacity and partly because she does not want to be a full-time housewife. Both Carol and Anne fall in the aforementioned gray area of women who are working not because they absolutely have to but because their earnings do make a difference to the quality of life for the family. They have to work to help buy, furnish and maintain a home, to have money for vacations, or perhaps for private school and later college tuition.

Jim, a Single Man

To get a thirty-something man's perspective, I talked to Jim, a never-married 38-year-old teacher, and asked him his impressions of the women he has dated and of women friends and teachers he knows. He lives in San Francisco and works in a suburb. Jim would like to marry and have children, but so far the right person hasn't come along. He is not sure why, and is somewhat perplexed by it, but with the availability of interesting women to date, he does not seem to be under much pressure. The sexual revolution gives a man like Jim more choices as well.

Jim thinks that the traditional woman whose primary goal is to marry still exists, but the number of such women has declined. He knows a lot of women who have successful, rewarding careers in which they are very interested. Not that marriage is unimportant to them, he says, but careers are equally important. It's a matter of weight, he says, and each is equally weighted. I asked if he knew of any women for whom a career is more important and family is secondary. A few, he said. I asked if he could give a rough estimate, and he said 5 percent.

Before returning to teaching, Jim had tried being a salesman for a few years in a medium-sized, central California city. I asked him about the women he knew then, working for his company in office jobs and on the assembly line. His impression is that those women's primary interest was in having a family and that they worked out of economic necessity. This shows the striking class differences between women who work at "jobs" versus women who work at "careers." I asked if these women really thought they would be happy being full-time housewives, and he said they would probably pursue other activities of their choice as well as doing homemaking, but would like to have that choice and not have to work. This coincides with the wishes expressed by Kathy, my first example.

I asked Jim if he thought the importance of a career meant that women were less emotionally dependent on men. Again he saw the answer as relative, that compared with an earlier generation, they are less emotionally dependent. If a woman does not have a date on Saturday night, she won't stay home and mope, she'll make plans with family or friends, either female or male. These women do want children, but as with marriage, there is a lessened sense of urgency. They can contemplate life with and without marriage and can even buy their own home.

Jim has a younger sister, age 36, who was trained as a registered nurse but married, had three children, and never worked. Her children are now 13, 10, and 7, and she is taking a review course for returning nurses so that she can start working part-time. I asked if he knew why, and he said he thinks it is because she would like more than to be a housewife at this point. Jim's mother was an RN and also had three children, but never went back to work. His sister has followed her mother's role model so far, but her return to school and plans for work show the change between the lives of mother and daughter in this family as a result of the women's movement.

Divorced and Alone at Age 39

Linda was married for two years at age 28 and lived with her husband for two years before their marriage. She had expected to remarry and is perplexed and confused about why she has not. She would like to be married again and have children, but children are not a priority for her, probably because she helped raise three younger brothers and sisters. As to her failure to remarry, she wonders, "Is it because I come across as too independent? Do men need a woman who is dependent on them? Or am I doing something to push them away?" Linda lives in a small city about one hour north of San Francisco. Her life is very full and satisfying. She has a bachelor's degree and likes her job, a semiprofessional position in a hospital, and is very active in community affairs, serving on the board of directors of three organizations, on two commissions, on the board of trustees of her temple, and as president of another organization.

She talked a lot about her mother's life and her grandmother's and believes that her mother, who never worked and had four children, gave up a lot of autonomy and freedom of choice in being dependent on her father. Their roles were very clear, but it was not an egalitarian marriage. Linda says she could never have a marriage like her mother's. Her needs are different because she is not financially dependent on a man. "I'm self-sufficient," she said. "My mother and grandmothers never had that opportunity to be self-sufficient. I can do whatever I want." Single women aren't thought of as spinsters anymore, she says, although she notices that never-married women may wonder if there is something wrong with them. Linda has many friends and feels comfortable socializing with couples and singles. She helps married friends with their children, sometimes taking them for a weekend.

Linda has given much thought to this issue and wonders whether the down side of all this freedom is that it may be harmful, that maybe there are too many choices that allow you to postpone making decisions. It used to be that there was a fixed time for everything—going to school, having children—but now nothing is fixed. She wonders what her life would have been like if she had had to be married by age 25. She knows she does not need a mate as her mother did, but for more intangible things like emotional nurturing. For now, she gets a lot of nurturing from her friends. I ask if she worries about being single at age 50. "At 50?" she asked in surprise. "No, but at 70—I don't want to grow old alone. Sometimes I really wish I was in a healthy, committed relationship, but it eludes me. I have come to accept that this is the way it is for now, and that someday a man will come into my life. My life isn't empty without a relationship, but on Valentine's Day I felt a little blue. It would be nice to have someone to give a card to. I'm holding out for Mr. Right, but I know he'll have flaws, he won't be Mr. Perfect."

An Active Feminist and a Single Professional Woman

Janet moved to San Francisco three years ago from the East. She is 37 and received a B.A. degree in English Literature from Swarthmore. She dates her feminism from when she was 16, and between 1970 and 1974 she was an active feminist in college when feminism was very important on campus. She continued her involvement in the abortion field in her twenties, when she worked for six years in hospital administration. She had trouble choosing a career, and at 27 decided on a career in the health field and got her M.S. degree. She would like to marry and have a child and is beginning to get anxious about her possibilities. In her twenties she dated a number of men but did not worry or think about marriage and children. She knew she had time to think about it and felt no social or personal pressure to marry. She had other priorities: finding a career, travel, more experience with men, and more adventure. At present she is finding it hard to meet eligible men, and many of the single women she knows in their thirties and early forties have the same complaint. As they get older, more of the men their age are married or dating younger women. Janet realizes she no longer is a younger woman and is feeling some panic. She agreed with my suggestion that she sees 28 to 35 as the prime age to marry.

Janet had a two-and-a-half year relationship in her early twenties and a four-year relationship from age 30 to 34, which dissolved, she said, because of religious and political differences. She now wonders if that was a mistake, if she expected too much from a relationship. Now the "biological clock is madly ticking" and she feels the time pressure. Marriage and children are increasingly important to her. Some women she knows do not want children because of their own unhappy childhood and fear of their inability to mother. Some are afraid children will be too limiting.

Her mother was a traditional housewife with four children but Janet believes her mother suffered because of it. She was financially dependent on Janet's father, who was not financially stable, yet because she had no education to prepare her for work, she could not earn money and was too timid to go back to school and try something new.

Janet remembers how hopeful she and other feminists were when the movement was just beginning. They believed that with careers their futures could be wonderful, that "our lives would get better and better," and that when we did have children we would be better mothers than our mothers had been. They did not realize that feminism would create new problems, the kinds of conflicts between men and women that resulted when women were competing with men in careers, the problems for men in not having all the power. They expected too much of men. They were the vanguard. They lacked the role models the young women today have. Their only models were their mothers, who were all housewives. She thinks that younger women have it much easier: "They didn't have to fight for the changes and opportunities. They are much more self-confident because they have benefited from the battles fought by people like me. They take for granted parity with men, the chance to go to medical school. We went through more questioning about having children and careers. They are not as tormented about it, they take it for granted. They have abortion, access to careers, the battles have been fought. We were a transitional group."

I asked Janet if she feels any resentment about the women's movement. Did she feel misled by it?

"In some ways feminism was simplistic. It offered lots of promises: have your career and marry later. It underestimated two things; the impact of class on the ability of women to fulfill themselves and the impact of childhood, the past history of the woman limiting her possibilities. Feminism didn't take that into account. Some women feel they were fed a false bill of goods. I don't know if we are more or less happy than our mothers."

What about the possibility that you won't marry and have children, I asked. How does that feel to you?

"On a good day I can imagine being single. I would be more open to opportunities, not responsible to anyone else, my life would have more possibilities. But it would be sad to miss the experience of marriage and of having a child."

I asked what her impression was of her women friends who are divorced. She said there are a lot of bad examples of divorced women and she believes women now are more cautious about divorce. There is more awareness now of the difficulties of divorce, with or without children. Those who have children have less pressure to marry because they have a family, but they would like a man in their life, too. She thinks women are not divorcing as readily now because they do not want to trade the husband they've got for what they see the life of a single woman to be like. They are more likely to accept a husband's flaws. I asked if the AIDS epidemic had made being single less desirable and she agreed that it did, and that that was another reason for what she believes is a lower incidence of divorce now.

Janet made good points about the importance of class and childhood experiences on a woman's potential for happiness. This strengthens the thesis that it is only with an integration of feminist and psychoanalytic theory, and, let us add, sociological theory about the importance of class, that women will attain the best possible life for themselves and their children.

WOMEN IN THE MEDIA

The power of film and television stars to affect the image of women is well known and has both positive and negative potential. Comparing themselves with the current Hollywood sex symbol can shrivel the self-esteem of most women, who cannot possibly attain the physical perfection displayed on the screen. However, the role a woman plays on the screen can have a positive influence in presenting images to young women. Hollywood has been notoriously bad in this regard, with some notable exceptions: Katherine Hepburn was often cast in the role of a very strong woman who got her man without compromising her intelligence. The emphasis on romance and marriage has been the almost exclusive role model for women, except for prostitutes and an occasional evil woman character. Any job or career is tossed over as soon as Mr. Right comes along. This is evident to even a casual observer.

A surprising development since the women's movement has been a backlash in Hollywood against the "new woman." A report issued by the Screen Actors Guild disclosed that actresses earn half as much as actors and that their prominence in Hollywood has declined sharply over the last three years. Men were given more than twice as many roles as women in 1989 movies and received 65 percent of all parts in television. Actress Meryl Streep projected that if the Hollywood employment trend continues, by the year 2000 women will have 13 percent of roles. A growing number of movie roles going to women cast them as prostitutes, rape victims, and needy companions to domineering men. Women held leading roles in only 14 percent of films. Screen Actors Guild studies show that female commercial voice-over artists are equally effective as men in selling products, yet women receive only 17 percent of voice-over work, down from 20 percent in 1986. Hollywood is surely doing its part to keep women in their place.

Television has expanded its plots to include the wider variety of roles women play in society. It certainly has come a long way from "Father Knows Best," but women on the TV screen must be young, slim, and beautiful except for a few characters such as Roseanne, whereas many of the men look like normal average guys with hair loss, expanding waistline, and other signs of middle age. Women reporting the news are now commonplace. It may surprise young people to know that women rarely appeared as newscasters until 1970. Today women are regulars on most news shows and are also starting to appear more as experts in panel discussions. They are often the single token woman, but under pressure from feminism, that is changing too. On "MacNeil Lehrer NewsHour" on 21 February 1991, the panel of experts discussing the Soviet peace proposal to end the war with Iraq included three men and three women, a first in my experience. In the days immediately after the war began, we all watched the news and saw various former generals and Middle East experts interviewed. I was pleasantly surprised to see introduced as a chemical weapons expert Elisa Harris, a fellow at the Brookings Institute and the author of seven books on this subject.

A Role Model for Teenage Girls: Madonna

In the field of popular music, videos frequently portray women only in the context of sex and violence. At the same time that women are appearing as experts, they are still being shown as sex symbols. Judging by the dress and makeup of many adolescent girls, it would seem that Madonna is more of an idol than Judy Woodruff.

Speaking on the TV show "Nightline" as quoted in the *New York Times,* Madonna describes herself as a feminist: "I may be dressing like the traditional bimbo, whatever, but I'm in charge, and isn't that what feminism is all about, you know, equality for men and women. And aren't I in charge of my life, doing the things I want to do?" (James 1990, p. 38). As the world's highest paid woman entertainer, she certainly is in charge of a lot of money. The *Times* reviewer, Caryn James, writes:

> Those who judge Madonna by traditional standards miss the point. She is redefining feminism itself, and though her intellectual grasp of the subject is slippery, no one can discount the impact of her image. . . . Madonna is at the very heart of American pop culture, the woman who most astutely embodies how feminism has shifted in the last decade. To her, feminism means the freedom to be sexy as well as sexual, to be in control of one's image as well as one's life. Conveying these ideas through movie-star looks, glitzy videos, defiant lyrics and shrewdly calculated sound bites, she has become the quintessential feminist for the video age. [p. 38]

She does address one feminist issue with her answer to a question about where she would draw the line on what is acceptable on television. "Violence, humiliation, and degradation," she replied. MTV should have a "violence hour and degradation to women hour" (p. 38) instead of playing such videos 24 hours a day. According to James, her lyrics are a "feminist anthem." They urge women not to settle for second best and not to let men dominate them. She also proclaims that sex isn't enough in a relationship, that a man needs to respect a woman's mind as well as enjoy her body. Madonna urges women to have high standards for men and to "move on" if things aren't right in the relationship.

"No other pop heroine approaches this image of women's self-sufficient power. . . . Madonna, suggesting mastery of one's fate, can be as inspiring to 30-year-old women, who know it is wishful thinking, as she is to teen-age girls, who have yet to be disillusioned'' (p. 44).

Unlike Marilyn Monroe, Madonna never acts dumb. She is more of a throwback to Mae West, who "always got her man but never let him get her." It is no coincidence that Mae West appeared on screen as an independent, sexually powerful woman during the earlier phase of feminism, before the regression to the passive, impotent ideal of femininity. Monroe was the ideal for the '50s and '60s—beautiful, vulnerable, and dumb. The reviewer does see the problem with this portrayal of sexual freedom as the key to women's liberation, but seems not to take it too seriously. Perhaps she was not around in the 1970s when we experienced the limited value to women of such freedom.

Conflicts between mothers and their young daughters are heightened as 13-year-old girls use Madonna for their model. Each generation seems bent on flouting the values of their parents, so as mothers have gone back to school to develop their minds and their skills, daughters bleach their hair and wear low-cut blouses, revealing bosom. We can understand the need these girls have to separate and individuate, but for the mothers who rejected *their* mothers' role as housewife, it is nonetheless trying to see their daughters emulating a sex goddess. The example of the community-college women who go back to school at 30 may be the eventual role model for these young teens. If the message of financial independence, a direct result of the feminist movement, is taken as seriously as the message of sexual freedom, the combination may prove powerful. If the economic factor is ignored, it could herald a dangerous regression to dependency and depression for women when they realize that a woman's life can still be quite vulnerable, even if she does go to bed with a man whenever she pleases. If, as they mature, these girls heed the lessons of Janet and women like her, they will recognize that equal power in a relationship does not guarantee happiness: there must be a capacity to compromise and not have idealistic expectations of relationships just because the woman has more control.

THE FEMINIST CRITIQUE OF MARRIAGE

An issue of much debate in the women's movement was the effect on women of marriage and child rearing. Some feminists have seen the family as an instrument of patriarchy and as the institution most deeply implicated in the oppression of women. The question is, Can we have both closeness and independence, challenge and security, children and jobs? I believe that if we recognize the validity of the feminist critique of marriage but also recognize the value of marriage as the institution that meets our needs for intimacy, security, and child rearing, we can modernize marriage and make it viable for women by creating a new ideal for a relationship in which respect and autonomy are encouraged for both partners.

Murray Bowen's work on the family includes a description of the "differentiation of self" scale. As outlined in a 1972 paper, the greater the degree of undifferentiation, the greater the emotional fusion into a common self with others. The *basic self* is a definite quantity illustrated by such "I position" stances as "These are my beliefs and convictions. This is what I am, and who I am and what I will do, or not do." The basic self is not negotiable in the relationship system and is not changed by coercion or pressure to gain approval, as opposed to the *pseudo-self,* which is adaptive in order to enhance one's position in relationship to others. People choose spouses or close friends from those with equal levels of differentiation, and the degree of fusion depends on that basic level before the marriage. One of the selves in the common self becomes dominant and the other submissive or adaptive; thus the dominant one gains a higher level of functional self and appears "stronger" at the expense of the adaptive one who gave up self and who is functionally "weaker." It does not take much imagination in studying Bowen's work to see how in a traditional marriage the dominant partner, who would gain, would be the husband and the submissive or adaptive partner, who would regress, would be the wife. It is with Chodorow's, Gilligan's and Bowen's concepts in mind that I believe we can make sense out of the research on marriage that appeared in the '70s and identify quite precisely the danger of marriage to women, unless and until the woman rejects the role of wife as submissive and refuses to merge her identity with her husband and children. Of course similar dangers are inherent in marriage for a man who is passive and submissive, and we see men such as this in our practices as well. The difference is that the culture supports the fusion of the woman with the man, as illustrated by the practice of the wife taking the husband's name, whereas society is contemptuous of a man who adapts himself to his wife—he is referred to as henpecked.

For those women who do want marriage and children, which now appears to be the vast majority, parents and psychotherapists alike have been greatly influenced by the traditional psychoanalytic view that women are fulfilled by motherhood and that children require consistent mothering from a single caretaker, ideally the natural mother, for their psychological well-being. With the rise of divorce and single-parent child rearing, plus the economic necessity in many homes for two incomes, this so-called ideal seems to be going the way of the dinosaurs, and some mothers want to work for their own satisfaction and stimulation, finding full-time housewifery too limiting. The new feminism has clearly had an effect on the view that there is something abnormal about a woman who is not satisfied with staying home for her entire adult life, but there has been much conflict about possible negative effects on the children. As clinicians we are often in the position of working with women who are torn by the decision whether or not to have children, and then when they do, whether to work or not to work, if they have some choice. In consulting with these women, it is important for us to pursue the individual meaning of these conflicts for each woman, but we should also be familiar with research findings that bear on this important issue. The questions are:

What is best for the mother?

What is best for the children?

Do the two conflict?

THE VALUE OF WORK FOR WOMEN

I propose that a nonexclusive mother–child relationship in the first five years can be conducive to a healthy separation-individuation process for the child and the mother and can allow the mother to develop her identity and self-esteem from independent work and relationships in the adult world, or to continue at a job or career in which she had invested herself before having children.

Before industrialization, the nuclear family did not exist as we know it. Humans lived in tribes, and a variety of forms of the extended family existed throughout the world. The modern geographically mobile nuclear family is a form of child rearing never before known in history. It isolates young women and small children from the economy, from other mothers and children, from grandparents, fathers, aunts, uncles and cousins, and often even from neighborhood interactions. Even the small size of the nuclear family is very recent, with the accompanying loss of interaction and interdependence among siblings that was formerly a natural consequence of older children taking responsibility for the young. The isolation of the young mother and her young children can lead to the kinds of mental deterioration seen in sensory deprivation experiments. Yet we continue to idealize it in spite of its reputation as a hotbed of neurosis, and we continue to hope that young mothers and children will flourish in this arid climate. Because girls identify with the mother, they remain closer to her, more dependent, and have more of a risk of looser ego boundaries than do boys, who are forced to break the dependency tie and identify with the father in order to achieve a masculine identity. On the positive side, this process produces caring, nurturing adult women who are capable of intimate, warm relationships. However, girls, because they remain more dependent than boys, grow into women who have trouble successfully completing the process of separation-individuation owing to this very close tie to the mother. For many women this tie also includes an identification with the self-denial and dependency of the mother in her role as housewife.

When the daughter later becomes a wife and mother herself, if she does so without an intermediate period of independence and identity formation as an autonomous, self-sufficient, working adult, she may not be capable of successfully guiding her children, especially the girls, through this all-important phase. Her failure to attain autonomy is then transferred to a dependent, undifferentiated relationship to her husband and children, and the cycle is repeated. Her vulnerability to depression is very high. Her ability to meet her children's dependency needs might be very good, but the question is how well she can meet their needs for independence, because their need for autonomy conflicts with her dependency needs. Anxiety and depression in the mother as her children assert their independence creates guilt in the children. Crippling of the child's autonomy can be the result of the mother not releasing the child to protect herself from feelings of emptiness, meaninglessness, and depression.

I believe that work provides the crucial step in a woman's maturation that allows her the experience of functioning in the real adult world and developing her separate identity. As a high-school or college student you are not truly an adult insofar as your behavior is regulated by the school authorities, and most often you are not fully financially independent. Recent research has found that the high incidence of depression in women, which of course has consequences for their children, is linked only to married women and even more specifically to nonworking married women. I do not believe marriage inevitably leads to oppression and then depression, and surely I have seen many single women who were depressed, but there is a specific danger of marriage and child rearing to a woman that lies in the risk to her sense of self if she merges her identity with that of her husband and children and thus suppresses her needs for fulfillment apart from the gratification of her needs for intimacy within her family. Women need intimacy and achievement, no less or more than men do. Women do feel a sense of achievement in raising children, but it is not paid work, and if the children turn out not to be successful in the mother's terms, an eventuality over which she has very little control, she can feel her whole life was for nothing. This puts far too much weight on attainment of one's life satisfaction through another person.

In her article "The Paradox of the Happy Marriage" (1971), Jessie Bernard questions whether the qualities associated with marital happiness for women may not themselves be contrary to good mental health. Is it possible that many women are "happily married," she asks, because they have poor mental health? She reported that more married than single women are passive, phobic, and depressed. Based on such factors as alcoholism, suicide attempts, medical complaints, and reports of well-being, the group with the best mental health proved to be single women. The next healthiest group was married men, followed by married women, and least healthy of all were single men.

Erik Erikson, in his monograph "Identity and Life Cycle" (1959), has suggested that for women, the resolution of their identity crisis occurs after choice of a mate and the birth of children. D. J. Levinson's (1978) theory of states of development focuses on the world of work, which a man enters in his twenties and in which he matures through his thirties until becoming his own man at about 40. Neither of these authors related the role of work to identity formation in women. It has been clear to male authors that work is of central importance to the self-esteem and maturational growth of men. Surely women mature as they take on the responsibilities of parenthood and running a house, but this would also apply to men. Women, no less than men, need experience in the world outside the home to measure themselves, to test their skills, to feel competent, and to interact with adults in exchanges of social and productive value to society.

A woman who is totally dependent on her husband for financial support has a tough time feeling like an adult, is more fearful of displeasing him, and is thus more likely to compromise herself in order to hold on to her husband's favor. In the extreme case of battered women, these women often state that they cannot leave their husbands because they do not know how to support themselves and their children.

Judith Birnbaum (1975) studied satisfaction and self-esteem at midlife in comparable groups of married professionals with children, single professionals, and homemakers. Both groups of professional women were more satisfied and had higher self-esteem than did the women who had lived out the traditional role pattern. In Sears and Barbee's (1977) analysis of Terman's sample of gifted women, married women were less satisfied with their life patterns than were women who were single, divorced, or widowed. Satisfaction was highest among women who were both single and income producers. Of course the vast majority of working women, and men, do not work in professional jobs. However, we should not underestimate the psychological and social value that all people can get from work. In a study in London (Brown, Bhrolehain, and Harris 1975) it was found that for women who were both under stress and able to turn to a confidante, work served to prevent the development of psychiatric symptomatology; only 14 percent of such women who worked developed symptoms, compared with 79 percent of those who did not work. In 1980 Walter R. Gove concluded that higher rates of mental illness among women are largely due to societal and not biological factors because they generally appear to be specific to particular societies at particular times and, most importantly, appear to be limited to married women, with never-married, widowed, and divorced women having rates comparable to, if not lower than, men.

Grace Baruch, Rosalind Barnett, and Caryl Rivers

In a book published in 1983, researchers Baruch, Barnett, and Rivers reported similar findings in a study of 300 women between ages 35 and 55. All groups of employed women rate significantly higher in mastery and lower in depression and anxiety. A woman's level of well-being could not be predicted by whether or not she had children. Married, employed mothers were rated the highest in well-being. This research confirms my impression that it is not marriage per se that is dangerous to mental health for women, but rather undifferentiation and dependency that are dangerous, and which are less likely in a woman who works outside the home. Another important factor may be the opportunity to have close relationships with other women, which is afforded by many job situations where women work. In factories, offices, stores, or schools, women most often work around other women.

The Baruch, Barnett, and Rivers book *Life Prints: New Patterns of Love and Work for Today's Women* (1983), is a source of very valuable material on women's lives. They divide all their subjects into six groups based on three factors: marriage, children, and employment. The groups are (1) never-married, employed; (2) married, with children, at home; (3) married, without children, employed; (4) married, without children, at home; (5) married, with children, employed; and (6) divorced, with children, employed. As you see, certain groups are omitted, such as divorced, without children, either employed or at home; and widows. The purpose of the study was to compare these women's lives to discover the sources of well-being or lack of well-being. Well-being was divided into two factors, namely, mastery and pleasure, and women were rated on their responses to questions designed to determine their levels of a sense of mastery and a sense of pleasure in their lives. The result is depicted in a map in which the six groups are placed according to their relative position on these two scales. Pleasure is tied to areas of intimacy. The four groups of married women, whether employed or not, whether mothers or not, all have higher pleasure scores than the two groups of unmarried women. On the contrary, of the groups of working women, all four are in or near the top half of the mastery scale. Whether married or not, whether they have children or not, they all have higher scores than the groups of homemakers. Divorced women are the highest of all in a sense of mastery.

Since our concern is only the differences between the working mothers and the nonworking mothers, the high sense of mastery and pleasure in the working mothers compared with the low sense of mastery and high sense of pleasure in the nonworking mothers is the key to our inquiry. The danger to the mental health of the nonworking mothers is summed up in the folk saying "She's got all her eggs in one basket." The self-esteem of these women is very closely tied to their husband's approval and to his level of achievement. This is the danger: this vulnerability, the loss of self-esteem she can suffer if her husband withdraws his approval, places the woman in exactly the same emotionally vulnerable position as a child whose only source of love, security, and well-being is derived from the approval of its parents. Her "boss" and her romantic attachment are the same person. Is this woman truly an adult? And if there is some question about this—how can she, with her own dependency problems, allow her children, especially her daughters, the autonomy they need?

Another conclusion of this study is that, contrary to myth, the most powerful contributor to pleasure in a woman's life was sexual satisfaction. This research found a positive relationship between occupational prestige and sexual satisfaction. So much for the myth of the successful but cold and sexless career woman.

THE EFFECTS OF MATERNAL EMPLOYMENT ON CHILD DEVELOPMENT

What about the children? The source of fears about the effects on children of working mothers can at least in part be traced to John Bowlby's research of 1951 on infantile autism in nurseries for orphaned and abandoned babies and to Margaret Mahler's theory of object constancy (see below). Bowlby's concept of *maternal deprivation* posits a serious effect on infant development if that infant does not receive continuous care from the mother or permanent mother substitute. In my view, the mistake has been to equate maternal employment with maternal deprivation. Studies show that infants under age 2 are able to form attachments to nonmaternal stable caretakers paralleling their attachment to the biological mother. What happened to our sense of history? Have we totally forgotten that generations of grandparents, aunts, older siblings, nurses, and even fathers have throughout history been caretakers of infants along with the natural mother? How did we come to the irrational conclusion that mothers and infants must be isolated in two-bedroom apartments or suburban ranch houses for optimal psychological health? Should we suspect foul play—that this was a convenient rationale for keeping women in their place?

Object Constancy—Margaret Mahler

Object constancy, according to Mahler, depends on the gradual internalization of a constant, positively cathected inner image of the mother, and a unifying of the good and bad object in one whole representation. Mahler's work on the separation-individuation process, which she calls *The Psychological Birth of the Human Infant* (Mahler et al. 1975), begins with her positing the universality of the symbiotic origin of the human condition, which must be followed by the separation-individuation process beginning in the fourth or fifth month and progressing through the thirtieth to thirty-sixth month. Awareness of separateness is a precondition for a true sense of identity and object relations. Once the infant realizes it is separate from its mother and the world, separation anxiety occurs, which Mahler differentiates from fear of annihilation through abandonment during the symbiotic phase. The mother, as the primary love object, is used by the infant as a real external object and thus as a basis for developing a stable sense of separateness. The four subphases—differentiation, practicing, rapprochement, and consolidation of individuation—all lead to libidinal object constancy, with its sense of intrapsychic autonomy; perception and memory cognition; reality testing; boundary formation; and disengagement from the mother.

The important part to note is the crucial role assigned to the mother for the normal development of this process and the obvious implication that if the mother fails in this role, the child is permanently damaged. Mahler's work, like Bowlby's, was an effort to understand childhood psychosis. Both gave us invaluable material for understanding normal and pathological development, but I believe both have been incorrectly applied to the dangers to children of working mothers. Mahler talks of the "optimal emotional availability of the mother," (p. 77) the baby's fear of losing the love of the mother, but there is no evidence that object constancy requires a single adult. It can develop from continuous attentive, empathic, consistent caretaking from several warm, loving adults. In fact, Mahler does talk about the mother's "emotional willingness to let go of the toddler"—that giving a "gentle push, an encouragement towards independence" (p. 79) is very important and may even be a sine qua non of healthy individuation. As the child's shadowing of the mother gives way to some degree of object constancy at about age $2\frac{1}{2}$, there can be a problem because "some mothers by their protracted doting and intrusiveness rooted in their own anxieties and symbiotic-parasitic needs become themselves the shadowers of the child" (p. 80). Let's not put mothers in a double bind, the same double bind they experience when children leave home. We cannot expect mothers to devote exclusive attention to their families and neglect their own interests, talents, and opportunities for independent achievements, and then chastise them for being "doting" or overinvolved because they get depressed when their children need that very same freedom.

Research Findings

In 1984, I did library research on the children of working mothers, and was surprised to discover a thorough examination of the subject dating back to the '60s, yet I had never come across this work in psychiatric literature. My research of the literature that compares the children of nonworking and working mothers does not support the notion that a mother's employment will necessarily be harmful to the child. The adjustment of children of working mothers is a function of the mother's attitude toward her child, satisfaction with her work, and the psychological conditions within the family. Negative effects on children tend to be traced to a mother's dissatisfaction with her work or with her role as a housewife, a rejecting attitude on the part of the mother, poor quality of substitute care, or an unstable marriage. High-quality nonmaternal care has not been found to have negative effects on preschool children. Research proves what common sense should tell us: The important ingredient in the outcome of children's mental health is how the parents *feel* about their children. When parents love their children and express that love so that the children are aware of it, the children grow up with good levels of maturity. The only specific practice that seemed to harm children was parental rigidity. When parents could not tolerate noise, roughhousing, or spontaneous behavior, the child was negatively affected.

On the other hand, conflicts and problems with children have a greater negative impact on the working mother because of all her fear and guilt about working. She is more likely than the nonworking mother to see any problems with children as her fault because she is working. There are many interesting and subtle differences that are worth thinking about. For example, if the mothers are divided into middle class and lower class, the middle-class mother is more likely to have positive feelings about work and a more positive feeling toward her children than either the lower-class working mother or the nonworking mother. The working mother who likes her work shows more sympathy toward her children and less hostility than does the nonworking mother. The nonworking mother uses more severe discipline and is harder on children's performance of tasks. Neglect is more of a lower-class response with working mothers who may not only dislike their work, but be poorly paid, have financial problems and be overwhelmed by their responsibilities. Siegal et al. (1959) find no differences. In their study of dependence and independence among kindergarten children they say "We must conclude that, when the sexes are considered separately, no differences emerge between the children of working mothers and the children of nonworking mothers'' (p. 542).

Almost every childhood behavior characteristic and its opposite can be found among children of employed mothers. Almost no constant differences are found. In answer to our third question, Do the two conflict? the Child Study Association of America concluded, in a 1975 pamphlet, (Sally Olds) that mothers who resent staying home and mothers who resent working have unhappy, troubled children. What is best for the mother is best for the children.

Eleanor Maccoby (1958) concludes that the mother's employment is only one of several factors, and a small one at that, in children's development. She lists the three major factors as intellectual and physical capacity, kind of community, and emotional stability of parents.

At-home mothers are more likely to attribute their feelings of nervousness to their children. On the other hand, some positive effects on the children of working mothers have been noted. Part-time employment of the mother has been shown to have a positive effect on adolescents. It is more likely to encourage independence and autonomy because the nonworking mother stressed nurturance and security in her child-rearing practices. Children of working mothers showed greater admiration for their mothers. Girls especially had a positive role model in their mothers, an improved self-concept, and higher career aspirations (Hoffman and Nye 1963). In the lower class some negative effect on the sons is shown in some studies with the boys being more withdrawn and dependent. However, this is likely to be a reflection of the mother's employment representing a failure of the father as a stable provider and positive role model.

Another piece of research (Mering 1971) that reflects on our question about separation-individuation divides mothers into three groups: Group I, professionally active; Group II, previous professional experience; and Group III, no work experience. All groups are similar in the degree of democratic communication between mothers and children. However, Group I emphasized discipline and independence training as primary functions of the parent, whereas Groups II and III emphasized protective, empathic, and understanding functions of the parenting. Group I mothers saw their role as teaching the child to cope with the culture effectively. The child is defined as a potential adult who must learn to succeed in the adult world. Groups II and III stressed emotions and security and viewed the child not as a potential adult but as a unique social personality whose needs should be understood and allowed spontaneous expression. Note that all three groups are attempting to serve the child's best interests, whereas Group II is unique in that these mothers were found to professionalize the role of mother and adopt the role of clinician toward their children.

In his more recent work, Bowlby (1969) suggests that attachment may be more secure and intense in an infant who has a few attachment figures rather than only one. Child psychiatrist Michael Rutter (1972) and psychologist Rudolph Schaffer (1977) both summarize studies that evaluate variations in parenting.

Reviewing these studies, Nancy Chodorow (1978) states:

> When one major mothering person shares her duties with a small but stable number of mother-surrogates (when she goes out to work, for instance), when there is shared responsibility for infants with a high degree of continuity (as in the Israeli kibbutzim), when societies have extended households and share child care, there is no evidence that children suffer from such arrangements. Where children do suffer is in multiple parenting situations associated with sudden separation from their primary caretaker, major family crisis or disruption in their life, inadequate interaction with those caretakers they do have, or with so many caretakers that the child cannot form a growing and ongoing bond with a small number of people. In fact these are the settings in which the psychoanalytic argument was formed. Schaffer affirms, "There is, we must conclude, nothing to indicate any biological need for an exclusive primary bond; nothing to suggest that mothering cannot be shared by several people." [p. 75]

In 1983 a book appeared called *The Handbook for Latchkey Children and Their Parents,* by L. and T. Long, which asserted that such children were more lonely and fearful and showed more signs of emotional conflict and stress than other children. In my review, the few other studies of the issue completed since then, however, have failed to find any major differences between latchkey children and others. Studies of grade school children who go home to an empty house have shown that any potential ill effect on a child's social, emotional, and academic well-being can be offset if the child knows that a parent is monitoring his after-school time, if the parent is readily available by telephone, and if the parents come home and really care what the child did after school. The psychological connection is more important than the physical one.

Even in the area of nutrition, working mothers do better than at-home mothers according to *Nutrition Action* magazine. In 2,000 U.S. households surveyed by MRCA Information Services, a market survey firm, children whose mothers are at home consume 23 percent more presweetened cereal, 33 percent more cookies, 11 percent more pizza and salty snacks, and 25 percent more candy than do children whose mothers work. They did not find a significantly lower percentage of foods prepared from scratch among households with working mothers who in fact feed their family 7 percent more salad and vegetable dishes. With all those sweets being consumed, one can conjure up the picture of a mother just trying to keep her children quiet to give herself relief from constant child care. The higher educational level of working mothers may also be a significant factor.

CLINICAL ILLUSTRATIONS

This chapter has brought together a variety of material in an effort to arrive at a picture of the "new woman," the woman who has had choices that her mother did not, and who is living a life of independence, freedom, and responsibility in what was formerly a man's world. Here are some brief vignettes of patients who present conflicts around the issues of the new roles of women, and especially the integration of roles: sexual, maternal, and work related. Resolution enables her to develop her creative, intellectual, and nurturing potential in a manner which furthers self-esteem and gives her life meaning. There is often unconscious guilt toward parental figures, a feeling one is not supposed to have it all; after all, mother never did.

A Graduate Student at San Francisco State University

This case example was contributed by Gloria Carr Gold of the Counseling Center. Mrs. S., a 42-year-old African-American woman and twice-divorced mother of four, worked as a sales clerk while also working toward a graduate degree. She entered therapy because of intense conflict and a sense of inadequacy in her pursuit of graduate education that would lead to a professional career.

Her aptitude, talent, and motivation all seemed high for her chosen field. Although she was experiencing academic difficulty in specific aspects of her work, and although the stresses from her other life pressures would appear monumental for a less able and energetic person, none of these pressures nor minor deficits alone explained the severe paralysis and panic she was experiencing. The therapist had previously noted that her major educational gains had been accomplished during periods when she was not involved with men, either preceding an involvement or following a divorce. When the therapist interpreted this to her, Mrs. S. began crying uncontrollably. She felt the pressure of both school and a demanding relationship with a man were nearly incompatible when combined with the mother and breadwinner roles. As these feelings were explored and as the therapist clarified the very real demands placed upon Mrs.

S.'s time and energy, it became obvious that she experienced strong guilt feelings over her love relationship, feeling she was being selfish, wasting time, or neglecting her children. Despite these "unworthy" feelings, she acknowledged how important such a relationship was to her. This led to an important working through of her guilt feelings and to an acceptance of her emotional need for such a love relationship, which meant, among other things, differentiating from her mother and the whole social matrix in which she had been raised. Her life experiences growing up had not included an important male figure.

A Career Woman in Conflict about Having a Baby

I had been working with Mrs. R. for about a year in relation to her marital problems. She was feeling more positive about the marriage, when she raised a conflict about having a baby. She was in her late twenties, her husband was now well established in his profession, and it was time to start a family. Mrs. R. enjoyed her work very much, but it was not necessary for her to work, and so she had the choice of having a baby and staying home to raise it for as long as she would wish. She posed the conflict as one between her career and a child. If she left her job, she would be replaced, and she did not know if it would be possible to find a comparable one should she want to return to work. She feared that she would want to return to work, would not be able to find a good job, and would be stuck. Yet the economy was not in a recession, her field of work was an expanding one, so it seemed that she was exaggerating the difficulties. I wondered if there could be something else involved in her conflict.

Mrs. R. was an only child of a couple who divorced when she was just 5. Her father remarried a woman with a daughter of her own, and she enjoyed visits to her father and step mother and friendship with her stepsister. Her mother never remarried, however, and was always angry and resentful about her visits and tried to discourage them. Her mother was consistently bitter toward Mrs. R.'s father, and the father was always saddened and frustrated by the difficulties surrounding his daughter's visits. Throughout her childhood there were frequent visits by her maternal grandmother, whom Mrs. R. described as hostile and domineering.

One of her worst memories was of the preparations for her wedding. Her mother refused to attend a family dinner after the ceremony so Mrs. R. had to arrange for two dinners, one with her father and another with her mother. It seemed to me that the mother's narcissism was well illustrated by her inability to put aside her own feelings and place her daughter's happiness first, even on the day of her wedding. Much of her childhood was lonely and unhappy, with continued tension between her mother and herself.

I drew the connection between her helplessness over her parents' unhappiness, her own unhappy childhood, and her conflict about becoming a mother. Mrs. R. had not thought about this as a source of her feelings and was relieved to understand the connection. She felt certain that she would be able to provide a happier environment for her child and realized that her life did not have to be as empty as her mother's had been. The then current prominence of the feminist issue of the problems of career and motherhood had in fact masked the true meaning of her conflict about becoming a mother. She terminated her therapy during her pregnancy, and I received the following note with her birth announcement: "I enjoyed a healthy, happy pregnancy, and as you can see, am now the mother of a wonderful, not-so-little baby boy. I feel great as I settle into the new life-style of motherhood. Quite a challenge—and what a joy!"

A Desire for a Career and Ambivalence about Motherhood

Mrs. T., an African-American woman in her late twenties, was married to a man a few years older whom she had helped support through graduate school. He was just starting his career, with a good job and good prospects. He wanted a child, but she saw this time as an opportunity to complete her schooling, which had been interrupted many times, either for financial reasons or to pursue relationships with men. She was determined not to let that happen again. She felt entitled to have him support her in school now, was bothered by his pressure to get pregnant, and started to withdraw from sexual relations. Her fears were centered around the possibility of their marriage breaking up and her being left to raise the child alone. She had a number of friends in this position and knew what a hard time they were having being single mothers. I questioned the fear, because her husband seemed quite devoted and there were no major marital problems that did not get worked through with what seemed to me a sincere effort by both partners to maintain and improve the relationship.

What emerged as the key factor was that Mrs. T. had been left by her own mother and was raised by her grandparents. Her parents had never married, and her father's interest in her was never very strong. The fear of being left with a small child by her husband was actually related to what her own parents had done to her. After working through her feelings toward her mother, who had been a drug addict and very unreliable, she was able to plan to have a child in two or three years but to complete her academic work first, which was very important to her confidence in herself and her future. When her daughter was born, she and her husband shared in the baby care. She worked part-time evening shifts and he took over when he came home from work. He was not reliable with his share of the housework, which angered her, but he did provide good fathering.

A Single Professional Woman Who Wanted a Child

Dr. P., a woman in her mid-thirties, was depressed because she wanted to marry and have a child, yet her life was very disorganized and she had trouble attracting a man for long because her pathology was such that her ambivalence in any intimate relationship inevitably destroyed it. Yet her longing for a child was so intense that she often sobbed in my office at the thought of remaining childless. She met a somewhat younger professional man who fell in love with her, and she managed not to alienate him long enough to get pregnant at age 38. She was thrilled, and they planned to marry. After the child was born, the problems in the relationship went from bad to worse, and they separated before the child's first birthday. She frequently complained bitterly about how much trouble the father caused her by his demands for visits with the baby and his tightness about child support. She remained depressed and disorganized but she adored her child, whom she occasionally brought to sessions. He was beautiful and bright and active, and she expanded her social life by relating to other mothers. Although her underlying problems continued, the desperation was gone, and she got organized enough to arrange child care, continue to work, and develop a social life for her son. She wanted to marry again and have a second child. There was no guarantee of that, but at least her grief was gone and her life had purpose and focus.

An Aversion to Marriage

Melissa, a 22-year-old secretary, was discussed in Chapter 3 (Fear of Being Unattractive). She had had liposuction to reduce her hips. This is the young woman whose father had died when she was 17 and whose mother had become an alcoholic and left the state. In spite of Melissa's obsession with her looks, she was firmly convinced that she did not ever want to marry or have children. She liked her independence and never wanted to lose it. She did not trust in marriage, fearing that the man would leave. When in the company of her married friends, she thought they seemed bored with each other and was especially bothered by noticing how the husbands looked at other women. She never wanted to be in that position. Children would just make matters worse. Her friends who had babies were tied down, and Melissa thought their life was terrible in comparison with her freedom. She never wanted to be restricted by children. She loved to travel and to eat out and have her weekends to visit friends, read, shop for clothes, and date.

I pointed out to Melissa that in her family it was actually her mother who was unfaithful to her father, and I wondered if she feared being the unfaithful one. She agreed that that was also a fear and that she felt very bad about having dated other men during her last relationship of living with a man for two years. I also observed that in that last relationship she was like her father in some ways, and perhaps she feared that what had happened to her father would happen to her. She granted that these factors could be influential but was still quite firm in her aversion to marriage and children and spoke with contempt about "families." Her family life prior to her mother's alcoholism was quite dull. Her mother was very restrictive of the time she could spend with friends, and they battled over her going out with friends after school. They never had money to do much, and the only excitement was occasionally going out to dinner. They could not afford vacations, and weekends were spent doing laundry, house cleaning, and schoolwork. They watched television in the evening. She never wanted a life like that, and this is what she feared about marriage and children. The connections to her own family life did not change her views, and she terminated feeling much better about herself and having made plans to return to college, but still convinced that she would never want to marry. Her images were of boredom, dullness, and restriction. She wanted relationships with men but saw a serious relationship as too restrictive. I would be curious to know if she had changed her view ten or even twenty years from now.

THE BACKLASH AGAINST FEMINISM—SUSAN FALUDI

Susan Faludi, in her book *Backlash* (1991), argues that the new woman is being attacked by a backlash against women's rights and the gains in her self-confidence, independence, and freedom of choice. Besides the obvious struggle over abortion rights and the Equal Rights Amendment, Faludi argues that feminism is being blamed for multiple ills in our society, from the lonely single woman to infertility problems to overworked employed mothers.

Especially revealing is her investigation of the reporting of the famous 1986 so-called Harvard–Yale study on women that concluded single, college-educated women over 30 had only a 20 percent chance of marrying and by age 40 had only a 1.3 percent chance. These figures were given by telephone to an eager reporter writing a story for Valentine's Day and were reported as factual throughout the country. The study had not been published, and when it finally was, three years later, the flawed statistics on marriage were not even included. Faludi tells of the U.S. Census Bureau demographer Jeanne Moorman, whose figures disproved the "Harvard-–Yale" study but whose statistics never got the front-page media attention that had frightened so many unmarried women—and their parents. Other studies showed that men were facing a shortage of marriageable women owing to women's increasing independence and selectivity, but these reports also failed to receive attention in the media.

The thesis that successful career women are leading miserable lives, regretting not having married in their twenties, cannot be proven. Anecdotal reports are not scientific research. In effect, women are being warned by the press and right-wing political groups that they must compromise and raise families or they will be punished by loneliness and childlessness. Faludi says that the detractors of feminism stand logic on its head, blaming equality for women's woes. In fact, when women are asked, they rank their persistent inequality, especially the lack of economic opportunities, as one of their most urgent concerns, not marriage, and report that a major source of stress and resentment is not their independence but men's opposition to it. She describes the backlash as a relentless whittling-down process—much of it amounting to outright propaganda—that has served to stir women's private anxieties and break their political wills. Identifying feminism as women's enemy only furthers the ends of a backlash against women's equality, simultaneously deflecting attention from the backlash's central role and recruiting women to attack their own cause. [p. xviii]

She reports on a 1980 study, The Mills Longitudinal Study, that confirms earlier research showing that married women run a higher risk of developing mental and physical disorders than single women. In addition, she reports, a *Cosmopolitan* survey of 106,000 women found that single women make more money than married women, have better health, and are more likely to have regular sex (p. 37). In my experience, many single women patients do complain of loneliness and wish they could marry, but when they compare their lives with those of married friends, they often report they would not want to be married to those husbands.

CONCLUSION: A RANGE OF CHOICES AND POSSIBILITIES

The "new woman" may be married or single, a housewife or a career woman, may have a low-skilled job or be a mother in college, may be hoping for a child or be resigned to not having one. She may be combining work, motherhood, and marriage, or any combination of them. At age 30 she may already be divorced with young children and be back in school, or have a career and be starting to think seriously about marriage and motherhood. She may be a welfare mother. She may have a life like her mother never had, or be living her life very much like her mother's, but life may still be full of disappointments or of conflicting desires. Divorce has changed the life of women in profound ways that the feminists of the '60s never anticipated. The fear of divorce influences the decisions that young women now make.

The women's movement has not brought happiness to all, and it may have even contributed to unrealistic expectations for some. But it has brought possibilities that older women never dreamed of, and with these possibilities a variety of styles and experiences. With all its sadness, the choice of divorce is now available to women who can support themselves, whereas their mothers may have been stuck in demeaning and unhappy marriages.

Social class is a major determinant of choices, and childhood experience is a second major determinant of the degree of flexibility, emotional strength, and positive energy available for reaching challenging goals. A combination of high intelligence, good mental health, talent, and money means unlimited opportunity for a young woman today. For others of average intelligence, no special talent or beauty, and in circumstances of poverty and early pregnancy, the victories of the women's movement may be insignificant in their lives. The expanding roles of women in the professions, business, and the media touch the lives of all women and offer role models for a life of independence, but some women still chose the traditional roles of wife and mother and fight for those roles by joining anti-abortion and anti-ERA campaigns. They are fighting to preserve their chosen role and may fear that women's liberation will mean that men will no longer have to support women. Psychotherapy continues to be important to many women either because they have had a disturbed childhood, are experiencing marital or relationship problems or the aftermath of divorce, or are torn by conflicting desires and confused by the new roles available to them. An understanding of both psychoanalytic theory and feminist theory is important to understand and help the new woman.

Another important component of life for the new woman is her sexual fulfillment. A woman's capacity for orgasm has been enhanced by the knowledge obtained from the sex research of the '50s and '60s, and as this research became incorporated into our common knowledge by a multitude of books and articles in the popular press, liberation from the sexual ignorance and sexual inhibitions of their mothers became a birthright of the modern woman. My first book includes a chapter on the female orgasm, reviewing psychoanalytic and feminist writing and the work of sex researchers.

4

WOMEN WHO EAT
TOO MUCH

"I always wanted you to admire my fasting," said the hunger artist. "We do admire it," said the overseer, affably. "But you shouldn't admire it," said the hunger artist. "Well then we don't admire it," said the overseer, "but why shouldn't we admire it?" "Because I have to fast, I can't help it," said the hunger artist. "What a fellow you are," said the overseer, "and why can't you help it?" "Because," said the hunger artist, . . . "because I couldn't find the food I liked. If I had found it, believe me, I should have made no fuss and stuffed myself like you or anyone else."

—Franz Kafka, "A Hunger Artist"

Just as in most of the work done with alcoholics and drug users, the books written and groups led for women with "eating disorders" are most often done by reformed overeaters who have found a method that works for them, which they then attempt, with messianic zeal, to apply to helping other women. I must confess from the beginning of this chapter that I am not now nor have I ever been an overeater, anorexic, or bulimic. My interest in the subject comes from my recognition that the problem is widespread among my women patients and friends and, along with smoking, is one of the most difficult addictions to overcome. I do think compulsive eating or noneating is best considered an addiction and, as with other addictions, psychoanalysis and psychoanalytic psychotherapy alone have often been inadequate to help the many patients with this problem.

Psychotherapy along with a group focused on the issue of eating disorders does appear to be somewhat successful. The ongoing support of people who share the same problem augments the individual exploration of psychotherapy to lessen the associated isolation, guilt, and shame, as was so significant in the feminist consciousness-raising groups. The lack of "community" in the lives of so many of us, especially in urban areas, combined with the lack of family and the competitiveness of the market-place for both jobs and love relationships, makes for an unnatural alone-ness for many people, which cannot be changed by psychotherapy alone. The intensity of the relationship with the analyst is necessary and desirable for working through the transference, but it may not change the patient's social life or help her to feel connected, to feel a sense of being a part of something larger than herself, for many years, if ever. Belonging to a group provides some of the sense of community that is often lacking and can provide concrete help and healthier attachments as well.

OVERVIEW AND STATISTICS

According to a Nielson survey in 1978, 56 percent of all American women aged 25 to 54 were "dieting." In 1984, *Glamour* magazine conducted a survey of 33,000 women. Of those surveyed, 75 percent said they felt too fat even though only 25 percent actually were clinically obese. Forty-five percent of those who were actually underweight still felt too fat. When asked if their weight affected their feelings about themselves, 96 percent said it did.

My first realization of how intense was the preoccupation with eating among many women occurred at my first job as a social worker in 1962. At our agency, all the staff went out to coffee at 9:30 each morning. Every day the women discussed diets. I made several efforts to bring up items from the morning newspaper for discussion, but I was repeatedly met with complete silence and then the conversation would return to dieting. These were all women with master's degrees; I felt disappointed and perplexed. My full recognition of how widespread the problem is came in the early 1980s at a conference of the American Orthopsychiatric Association's Women's Institute in a session on weight problems. The speaker opened the session by asking the room of about 125 women how many had never been on a diet. I was one of five women in this audience of mental health professionals to raise my hand. It was shocking to us all. Perhaps the few of us without a food problem should be considered deviant and studied. In my own case I know there must be a biological factor because my two paternal aunts were both quite small-boned and thin. Because of my constitutionally determined petiteness, eating was always a struggle between me and my mother. She never believed I was eating enough and force-fed me as a small child, and for years afterward she pressured me to eat more. As with many other Europeans, for her being thin meant illness, weakness, and vulnerability, whereas being sturdy meant health, strength, and the ability to withstand disease and hard times such as war. I can still remember discovering that I could store the food in my mouth and then spit it out in the toilet after the meal, undetected. I know this had the effect of making food an unpleasant subject for me, with bad memories of being forced to eat when I was not hungry and felt full. For me, eating only when I feel the need and the desire to eat is an essential part of my sense of freedom and autonomy. This abnormality puts me in the small, fortunate category of women who do not overeat. I had to learn to undo the bad connections to food in order to be able to enjoy cooking.

In analyzing this problem from a psychoanalytic and feminist viewpoint, we must integrate the psychological, biological, and cultural perspectives. The fact that an overwhelming majority of people going to diet centers and buying diet books are women indicates that there must be something more to this addiction than the early oral experience of suckling and the symbolic nature of food, which apply to men and women alike. According to Chernin (1981), 95 percent of those enrolled in weight loss programs are women, 80 percent of those using surgical intervention for weight problems are women, and 90 percent of those suffering from anorexia are female. About half the adult women in the U.S. are dieting on any given day.

Something specifically to do with being a woman in the latter part of the twentieth century in a nation with no food shortages has made eating an obsession for most women and one of the most common complaints brought by women to psychotherapists. Virtually every woman's magazine contains an article on dieting. That is not the case with men's magazines, even though many men are overweight, showing that for men there is not the obsessive quality to their concern about weight that there is for women. Men do not consider weight a problem until they are 35 pounds overweight, whereas women regard themselves and are regarded as overweight if they are 15 to 20 pounds overweight. This may be because for men, concerns about size are focused on the penis, and no food intake or decrease can alter the size of the penis the way it can alter the shape of a woman. Also, for a man, not his physical appearance but his achievements in the world of business, sports, professions, and other skills are the standard by which he measures himself and others measure him. His financial shape is his attraction, not his body shape. In order to get her job as a wife and mother, a woman must sexually attract men. Imagine the reverse, that a man could not start his career without first having a wife. What a pressure to please a woman that would put on the male.

Clearly, many factors contribute to the agony of so many women about body size. It is also clear that around this agony has developed a multibillion dollar industry ($10 billion cited by Orbach in 1978, and Wardell in 1985, $33 billion by Roth in 1991) that encourages women to believe their addiction to food can be cured. In truth, all the diet programs have very little long-term success and about a 95 percent failure rate. This includes regaining the original weight plus adding more weight. Another source puts it this way: out of every 500 people who diet away as much weight as they want to lose, about 20 will keep it off for a year but only one will stay trim for two years. One program tells its new members that success after two years, that is, keeping off the weight that was lost, depends on three factors: keeping accurate records of eating and exercise, exercising a minimum of 20 miles per week, and staying in the maintenance program for at least one year. In my experience, some women deny that they overeat and cannot understand why they gain weight. When I ask them to recount what they have eaten, it is clear that they are eating more than they need, that is, there are more calories being taken in than the body is putting out.

According to a report in the *San Francisco Chronicle,* individual differences may well account for some people putting on weight more rapidly than others under similar conditions. This was shown in an experiment with men who were confined to a hospital, fed large amounts of food, and not permitted any exercise. With controlled conditions that were exactly the same, all the men gained weight but the range of weight gained was broad, most likely owing to individual differences in metabolism. It does appear to be true that some people must eat less and exercise more than others to maintain the same weight, but the source of these metabolic differences is still unknown.

A phenomenon I observed had to do with differences in soothing babies. When my babies got fussy, I always assumed they were bored and needed a bit of stimulation, so I would carry them about, play with them, give them new toys, and so on. I observed that a young Latin American woman whom I hired for child care when I was working would respond to the baby's fussing by giving it something to eat. The adult attempts to guess at the source of the baby's cry by projection, based on her style of soothing herself when she is dissatisfied. The response of the adult has great learning value to the baby. The baby is being taught to quiet its discomfort, from whatever source, either by eating or by relationship, possibly including a change of scene or a new source of stimulation. In the relationship/stimulation model, the attention of the mother or other caretaker becomes the source of relief, rather than food. In these early interactions the baby learns to turn for relief to people, to stimulating objects, or to eating.

PSYCHOANALYSIS: THE MOTHER–DAUGHTER
RELATIONSHIP

Typical of the psychoanalytic approach to food disorders is the following:

> The regression to pregenitality in puberty reactivates the preoedipal
> relation to the mother. In some girls, the regression takes the form of
> severe eating disturbances, which contain intense aggressive strivings
> against the mother.
>   In the severe forms of anorexia nervosa in adolescence, much more
> frequent in girls than in boys, the rage at the mother, which has been
> externalized and displaced onto food, has its roots in the repressed oral
> sadomasochistic conflicts with the mother. The symptoms frequently
> occur upon separation from the mother when the adolescent goes away
> from home. It is the introjected mother whom the adolescent is starving
> for and trying to control and punish. [Ritvo 1977, p. 132]

Chodorow (1978) focuses on the mother–daughter relationship as
well:

> During her prepubertal period, the central issue for the girl is a
> two-person issue—a struggle for psychological liberation from her
> mother. Her father—loved or rejected, experienced as powerful or
> weak—is emotionally in the background. It is not simply that a girl is
> preoccupied with her attachment to her mother, however. This attach-
> ment, as Deutsch and Blos describe it, reproduces its two-person
> preoedipal counterpart in its ambivalence, its binding quality, its
> nonresolution and often in its involvement with food and body issues
> (at this later time, this involvement is often around weight, clothes and
> so forth). A girl tends to retain elements of her preoedipal primary love
> and primary identification. This has been compounded through the
> years by reinforcement from a more conscious gender-role identifica-
> tion with her mother. The ease of this identification and the feeling of
> continuity with her mother conflict with a girl's felt need to separate
> from her and to overcome her ambivalent and dependent preoedipally-
> toned relationship. [p. 136]

AGE AND WEIGHT GAIN

People gain excessive weight at different points in life. There are some
women who are overweight from childhood, some who become overweight with the coming of puberty, and some who gain too much weight
with a pregnancy and then never can lose it all. Others maintain a fairly

normal weight until the mid-thirties, when the metabolism slows down. At about age 35 it becomes necessary to eat less or exercise more or do some of both to prevent weight gain, and those who are unwilling to make this adjustment are destined for the gradual addition of unwanted pounds. They are unable to deprive themselves of the pleasures of eating because they may already be feeling deprived in some other area of life and be mildly depressed.

It is important to differentiate between overweight and obesity. It seems likely that in those who are overweight from childhood there is a strong biological factor, although the example I gave of soothing a baby with food reflects the environmental component. A patient of mine weighed 300 pounds. Her family history included many obese members on her father's side. Her paternal grandmother weighed 500 pounds when she died. Her father reached 300 pounds as a young man. Of her five brothers, two weigh about 280 pounds. Her paternal aunt weighs 280 and had four children. Of the three sons, two are obese, weighing over 300 pounds, and one daughter weighs 250. My patient has five children, of whom two are already obese. Her daughter is not obese but has just gained 25 pounds owing to the stress of her first year in college. This patient traces a history of three points of weight gain in the family. Some, such as herself, gain weight between ages 5 and 7 and are obese for life. Some, such as her father and one of her sons, gain the weight between ages 13 and 15. Other family members, who have maintained normal weight, show a gain after age 35, a more normal pattern. Until age 5 there is no problem with overweight. With a family picture like this it seems likely that a genetic factor is operative. She claims that her weight can never be normal but can be controlled with strict diet and exercise. She complained that over the years, diet recommendations have changed from high protein no starch, to grains and vegetables.

For others, weight gain has a stronger psychological and cultural component, reflecting attitudes toward the body and methods of coping with conflicts around independence, disappointment, frustration, anger, sexuality, and depression. Sometimes weight gain follows a trauma, such as the death of a parent or a divorce. On the other hand, some people lose weight after a divorce, eager to look attractive again to the opposite sex. A common dilemma is that of the person who tries to stop smoking in midlife owing to a persistent cough, bronchitis, or some strong advice from a doctor, and then proceeds to gain weight, which can be so disturbing that the individual returns to smoking.

A factor revealed in recent years in weight gain for women is sexual abuse. In Overeaters Anonymous, the stories of incest and molestation began to emerge, and overeating is now recognized by all those working with such women as a common symptom. In fact, because of the many patients for whom these incidents are repressed, being overweight should be a signal to the therapist to search for sexual abuse in the woman's history. Psychoanalysts, in neglecting this area for so long, also neglected to see the connection with overweight, and, as in the quotations above by Ritvo and Chodorow, concentrated all their attention on problems in the mother–daughter relationship. Even when there is no overt seduction or molestation, the anxiety around oedipal wishes and fears with the father can result in overeating.

Weight Gain at Puberty—A Clinical Illustration

Dianna's parents were both alcoholics. They led an apparently successful life in a small community near San Francisco. Her mother was a nurse who worked the night shift, which meant that Dianna and her younger sister were left in their father's care in the evenings. He got drunk every night and fell asleep in his chair in the living room. Dianna was in her twenties when she came to see me for anxiety, depression, and sexual problems with her husband. She was a member of Overeaters Anonymous and managed to control her weight through careful attention, calls to her sponsor, and attendance at several meetings per week. She clearly remembered gaining 40 pounds in her first year in high school and was quite certain that it had to do with her extreme discomfort with her newly emerging woman's body. She consciously wanted to conceal her shape by putting a barrier of fat around it.

Dianna had herpes, which she had contracted from her husband. She had frequent serious episodes, which interfered significantly with their sex life together. She gratified her husband orally during these periods but could not bear to have him touch her. She could masturbate to orgasm, but felt terrible shame about her genitalia, believing herself to be smelly and disgusting. In the process of exploring her current sexual dysfunction, material about her father emerged. She remembered his wanting to hold her on his lap and how stimulating that had been to her. The absence of her mother during the evenings had created a situation that felt dangerous to her as a little girl, especially since it was clear to her that there was disharmony and much distance between her parents. She began to be able to put together the picture of her fear of her maturing female body in the context of her erotic attraction to her father, the absence of her mother, and his drinking, which made her feel unsafe with him because it was clear to her that he was not in control of his own behavior. The 40 pounds she gained was her protection from her own sexual feelings and from him.

She had had several poor relationships with men in her early twenties and was thrilled to have met and married her husband, a responsible and nice man her own age. They both smoked marijuana, which she later stopped using and which she pressured him to stop using. He gradually was able to stop. As the material about her father emerged, I connected her distancing herself sexually from her husband by both the repeated herpes episodes and her refusal to engage in manual or oral sex for her own gratification, with her distancing herself from her father through her weight gain. Her herpes attacks diminished significantly, and her phobic attitudes toward her genitalia were overcome. She began to enjoy regular sexual intercourse with her husband. Comments such as the following were used:

> Your husband isn't your father. What could be wrong with enjoying sex with him?

> You seem to believe there is something wrong with your female parts. What do you have to be ashamed of?

> Your shame about your genitals with your husband is strange. You imagine he finds your body unappealing, yet if he did, why would he have married you?

> You gained all that weight to make your body unattractive, and now that you are no longer fat we can see that the problem was your fear of your own sexuality.

These interpretations are psychoanalytic in character because they rely on an understanding of her weight problem as resulting from her poor oedipal resolution. Yet they are also feminist because they focus on her dislike of her genitalia as irrational, rather than as a reasonable, normal response to the absence of a penis. My attitude is that her female body is just fine and wonderful the way it is and that any fear or shame is the result of some erroneous ideas she developed along the way. This worked very well with Dianna, as it has with many other women patients. Sometimes I describe the misunderstanding some little girls have when they think they have been deprived of or lost a penis and they are not aware of all the pleasures awaiting them in sexual intercourse and in the wonders of pregnancy and the birth and nursing of a baby. We all get sad and angry when something is stolen from us. The expression "ripped off" is a significant slang expression for being robbed. What is being ripped off? The derivation of this idiom might be the unconscious fear of castration.

As her symptoms receded, her confidence increased and she began to confront her parents, now divorced, with their drinking problems. She was able to get each of them to join Alcoholics Anonymous, although it was a difficult struggle, especially with her mother, who denied she had a drinking problem. Dianna was aware of how distressing it was to her when she could tell over the phone that her mother was drunk. At my suggestion, she told her mother she would not speak to her when she was drinking, which led to her arranging to have lunch with her mother and to a direct confrontation with her mother about her drinking. As an adult she was finally in a position to take charge of her life and to make demands on her parents. As a 13-year-old girl, her only outlet for her anger, confusion, and fear was to protect herself by eating herself into an anesthetized state, as her parents did with alcohol.

Another observation I have made relies on only two examples, but illustrates the psychoanalytic approach to overweight, which focuses on the girl's undifferentiated relationship with her mother as the source of her overeating. There have been two occasions in my thirty years as a psychotherapist when I have opened the door to my waiting room to greet a new patient and have been surprised to find two women. In each case, the "patient" I had set the hour for introduced the other woman as her mother and then arose and followed me to the office after saying a few words of parting to her mother, who would wait there for her return. Who was the mother and who was the daughter? In one of these cases the patient was obese; in the other, she was overweight but I learned that she had had a stomach-stapling operation the previous year, had lost considerable weight, and was coming for help because she was having difficulty adjusting to her new body after years of obesity. In the latter case, when I commented on her mother accompanying her to her appointment with me, the story of her guilt-ridden attachment to her mother, a widow, emerged, and I commented that this was an area we would be exploring together. She canceled the next visit, and I never heard from her again.

FEMINIST APPROACHES TO WEIGHT GAIN

Fat Is a Feminist Issue—Susie Orbach

Much of the feminist work on weight problems stresses the oppressive nature of the forces of patriarchy that confine women to the roles of wife, mother, and sex object, and focus on the female body to cater to the needs of men. The earliest feminist work on weight was done by Susie Orbach in *Fat is a Feminist Issue* (1978). A later book, *Understanding Women—A Feminist Psychoanalytic Approach,* by Luise Eichenbaum and Susie Orbach (1983), describes these authors' approach to treating women and their understanding of the problems of women in terms of inadequate nurturing from their own mothers. This thesis was first developed in the 1978 book. Orbach's book is representative of a genre of books that encourage anti-diet approaches to weight loss, recognizing that diets are punitive and fail. These books promote instead a new attitude of self-acceptance and appreciation of food. Here, Orbach uses the formula that emerged from the consciousness-raising groups: each woman describes her failures with doctors and with dieting, how she feels about her body and about being attractive to men, and the painful experience of being a compulsive eater.

> We began asking new questions and coming up with new answers. We were a self-help group at the time when energy from the women's liberation movement prepared a fertile soil in which feminist ideas, nurtured and developed in countless consciousness-raising groups, in mass marches and demonstrations, in organized political campaigns, found new applications and usefulness. Compulsive eating was one such area. [1978, p. xiv]

Her approach is to see compulsive eating as both a symptom and a problem in itself. She uses "fat" and "thin" to represent mental states:

> We explore and demystify the symptom to find out what is being expressed in the desire to be "fat," in the fear of thinness and in the wish to fill and starve ourselves. At the same time we attempt to intervene directly so that the feelings and behavior around food can change. Underlying problems need to be exposed and separated, though not necessarily worked through. The perspective is always to see the social dimensions that have led women to choose compulsive eating as an adaptation to sexist pressure in contemporary society. [p. xvii]

Orbach goes on to state that psychoanalytic theory without a feminist perspective is inadequate, because the central issues of compulsive eating are rooted in the social inequality of women. "Fat" represents an attempt to "break free of society's sex stereotypes," (p. 5) a purposeful act consciously or unconsciously challenging sex-role stereotyping and culturally defined definitions of womanhood, a rebellion against the powerlessness of being a woman, and an avoidance of being marketed according to a prescribed image. " 'Fat' is a social disease, and 'fat' is a feminist issue. 'Fat' is not about lack of self-control or lack of will power. 'Fat' is about protection, sex, nurturance, strength, boundaries, mothering, substance, assertion and rage. It is a response to the inequality of the sexes'' (p. 6).

The most common benefit that the women in her groups saw in being "fat" was as sexual protection, as a way to desexualize themselves, to avoid sexual approaches from men and competitive situations with other women. This is clearly an avoidance of oedipal rivalry and success for neurotic women but can also be a result of actual sexual trauma, remembered or repressed, in childhood. On the other hand, being "fat" may be the way a woman controls her fear of being promiscuous. I have seen this factor in some of my patients, and Orbach gives such examples as well.

According to Orbach, the realization that being "fat" performs a positive function for them helps women to see it as an adaptation rather than a failure of self-control. "Fat" as a symptom of fear of success can be both the result of unconscious oedipal wishes and an anger at her recognition of the desirability of weakness and helplessness in women. Being overweight can be a way of being bigger and taken more seriously, like a man, especially in a work setting where it serves additionally to neutralize the woman's sexual identity. "Fat" can also serve to create a boundary and thus serve as a protection against nonsexual invasions of autonomy as well.

> The loss of fixed boundaries of the self produces another of the terrifying states women have associated with loss of weight. This terror a woman may feel is the fear of people invading her. The "fat" may have allowed her to keep a certain distance from people. She imagines that it all has to do with the "fat," that people themselves do not approach her and that she has little right to approach them. Thus, a woman will worry that while thin, people will encroach on her space in an active way and penetrate her. [p. 80]

By her attributing to the "fat" this protective function, the loss of the "fat" would, she imagines, expose her to the dangers of sexual or psychological invasion. Thus treatment needs to help the woman see that she has the potential for protecting herself as a "thin" person, that that power lies within her, not in the "fat". The power to say no is often a key to uncovering one's internal control, yet for many women saying no has been experienced as too aggressive, angry, and independent. Struggles around the issue of autonomy and separation from parents are dramatized by Orbach in the question, "How will I be who I wish to be if I look as I am supposed to look?" (p. 99).

Yet Orbach also focuses on the ambivalent, conflict-laden mother–

daughter relationship as a source of overeating. She lists four meanings of "fat" in relation to the mother:

1. I'm substantial. I can protect myself. I can go out into the world.
2. Look at me. I'm a mess; I don't know how to take care of myself. You can still be my mother.
3. I'm going out in the world, I can't take you with me but I can take a part of you that's connected to me. My body is from yours. My "fat" is connected to you. This way I can still have you with me.
4. I'm leaving you but I still need you. My "fat" lets you know I'm not really able to take care of myself. [p. 21]

These unconscious meanings are interesting not only in relation to the mother but also in relation to the analyst. In my experience, the mother transference is so strong in women with weight problems that their weight takes on all the ambivalence and dependency conflicts in the analysis that it had and still has with the mother, and can serve as an obstacle to termination. I have been both surprised and pleased to hear from some long-term overweight patients some time following termination, that they have been able to lose all the weight they wanted to since they last saw me. Apparently they needed to break the dependency tie with me before they could be successful in losing weight.

The goal of Orbach's approach is not primarily to lose weight but to break the addictive relationship toward food. She suggests the following steps:

1. Learn about your eating patterns, when you are particularly vulnerable to an attack, and become an observer of yourself.
2. Identify the difference between mouth hunger and stomach hunger. Learn how stomach hunger feels and what emotional reactions are aroused by it.
3. Eat out of stomach hunger only.
4. Try to locate precisely what food or liquid your body is hungry for.
5. Pamper yourself with food. Allow every eating experience to be a pleasurable one. Do not worry about regulation mealtimes or balanced meals. There are no good foods and bad foods. Eat as much as you want and exactly what you want. [pp. 118–122]

The Obsession—Kim Chernin

A second feminist approach to eating disorders is that of Kim Chernin, in her book *The Obsession: Reflections on the Tyranny of Slenderness* (1981). Her feminist analysis of weight problems is much more radical than that of

Orbach, but some of their underlying assumptions about the meaning of overweight for women are similar:

> The body holds meaning. A woman obsessed with the size of her body, wishing to make her breasts and thighs and hips and belly smaller and less apparent, may be expressing the fact that she feels uncomfortable being female in this culture.
>
> A woman obsessed with the size of her appetite, wishing to control her hungers and urges, may be expressing the fact that she has been taught to regard her emotional life, her passions and "appetites" as dangerous, requiring control and careful monitoring.
>
> A woman obsessed with the reduction of her flesh may be revealing the fact that she is alienated from a natural source of female power and has not been allowed to develop a reverential feeling for her body. [p. 2]

In describing her own obsession with food, starting at age 17, she recalls awakening one night feeling lonely, sad, and frightened. "What I wanted from food was companionship, comfort, reassurance, a sense of warmth and well-being that was hard for me to find in my own life, even in my own home" (p. 11).

Yet she describes eating as a "yearning for permission to enjoy sensual aspects of the self":

> Frequently, as I observed this conflict over food, I noticed that the permission to eat was closely linked to a delight in life, a sense of joy and abundance, an awareness of some unexpected meaning or beauty. . . . There was a state of mind and being in which food became a simple, uncomplicated sensual pleasure. [p. 17]

She decries that, as she observes, most women are alienated from and dissatisfied with their bodies and are then vulnerable to exploitation by doctors, writers of diet books, and diet clinics and programs. She wonders:

> It is possible then that we today worry about eating and weight the way our foremothers and their doctors worried about women's sexuality?
>
> There is a similar atmosphere—of desperation, of frantic struggle against natural appetite—apparent in the procedures employed at the hundreds of weight and diet clinics that have appeared all over the country. [p. 39]

She believes that there is a great exaggeration to the fear of fat, just as there has been, historically, to the fear of a woman's sensual attraction. The deeper, less rational fear is of the body itself, of not being in control of our natural urges, of the sins of indulgence of the flesh. She quotes Norman O. Brown (1959):

> For two thousand years or more man has been subjected to a systematic effort to transform him into an ascetic animal. He remains a pleasure seeking animal. Parental discipline, religious denunciation of bodily pleasure, and philosophic exaltation of the life of reason have all left man overtly docile, but secretly in his unconscious unconvinced. [p. 31]

Some women fear the roundness and fullness of a woman's body and are at war against it. Both the anorexic and the obese woman share this fear. Yet Chernin sees the pressure to be thin as a response emanating from the outside, from a society that fears the strength and power of women, that wants to keep women small and childlike, and that created the thin-woman ideal in response to the power of women that emerged from the women's liberation movement: "The image of women that appears in the advertisement of a daily newspaper has the power to damage a woman's health, destroy her sense of well-being, break her pride in herself, and subvert her ability to accept herself as a woman" (p. 87).

She remembers Marilyn Monroe in 1960, "grand and voluptuous," and insists that if Monroe were alive today her abundant body would be considered fat. Yet she considers Monroe a transitional figure—allowed large breasts, hips, and thighs but required to have an adolescent innocence, a pouting coyness, the smile of a little girl, the reassuring vulnerability of a child. She contrasts the large-bodied women of Renoir and the early film stars such as Mae West with a leading model of the early '80s, Christine Olman, who was featured in *Vogue* and *Bazaar* posing in the traditional seductive postures of a woman although she was only 12 years old. Her slender, undeveloped body was draped and made up as if she were a woman. Even more shocking, at a lecture I heard Robert J. Stoller, a psychoanalyst specializing in the treatment of transsexuals, state that half of the fashion models are in fact men, transsexuals posing as women. Chernin makes the analogy between the restricted body of women today and the bound feet of the Chinese woman: in each instance a restriction of size is also a restriction of power and development. She notices that during the '60s the feminist movement began to emerge, asserting women's right to authority, development, dignity, liberation, and above all, power. Also during the '60s, Weight Watchers, Overeaters Anonymous and other weight control groups emerged, as did the conditions of anorexia and bulimia in the late '60s and early '70s.

> I am suggesting that the changing awareness among women of our position in this society has divided itself into two divergent move-

ments, one of which is a movement toward feminine power, the other
a retreat from it, supported by the fashion and diet industries, which
share a fear of women's power. . . . In both, women are driven to
gather together and make confessions and find sisterly support for the
new resolutions they are taking. In both, women have created new
forms of social organization, apart from the established institutions of
the dominant culture.

There is, however, also a fundamental divergence here. . . . Thus in
the feminist groups the emphasis is significantly upon liberation—upon
release of power, the unfettering of long-suppressed ability, the freeing
of one's potential, a woman shaking off restraints and delivering herself
from limitation. But in the appetite control groups the emphasis is upon
restraint and prohibition, the keeping of watch over appetites and
urges, the confining of impulses, the control of the hungers of the
self. . . . [pp. 100–101]

To reinforce her thesis that male society prefers small, weak women,
Chernin turns to the issue of child pornography as a symptom of the male
fear of large, powerful women. She claims that in the same era of women's
development some 364 periodicals appear on the marketplace with child
pornography and quotes Florence Rush (1980b) in describing Martin
Scorsese's film *Taxi Driver,* which stars Jodie Foster as a 12-year-old
prostitute and then in her next film as a 13-year-old "bundle of budding
sexuality." In Woody Allen's film *Manhattan,* a man of 40 who is left by
his wife turns to a 17-year-old girl "for comfort and redemption," and a
cartoon character called "Chester the Molester" appears regularly in
Hustler magazine. Admittedly, she says, she cannot prove that the masculine preference for little girls is on the increase because grown women are
asserting their right to power, but she raises the question. One could also
extend that question to the meaning of middle-aged men of 40 to 50
remarrying women of 25 to 30—surely not children, but nevertheless not
comparable in maturity and wisdom to women their own age. The 15- to
20-year age difference means that when the man was 25, his new wife was
5 to 10.

For her discussion of the fear and envy of female power by both men
and women, she draws on the work of Wolfgang Lederer, *The Fear of
Women* (1968), and Dorothy Dinnerstein, *The Mermaid and the Minotaur* (1976), but fails to recognize that Karen Horney wrote about the envy
of women. She reminds us of the children's riddle, so meaningful in this
regard:

"What is the strongest thing in the world?"

"A brassiere, because it holds two huge mountains and a milk
factory."

She continues:

> When we attempt to determine the size and shape of a woman's body,
> instructing it to avoid its largeness and softness and roundness and
> girth, we are driven by the desire to expunge the memory of the
> primordial mother who ruled over our childhood with her inscrutable
> power over life and death. . . . We laugh at this (fat) woman to disguise
> our longing and our terror. . . . If we place pornography and the
> tyranny of slenderness alongside one another we have the two most
> significant obsessions of our culture, and both of them focused upon a
> woman's body. [pp. 143, 145]

She describes the dilemma of the adolescent girl,

> who is asked in this moment of her development to become what her
> mother is—not by nature, but in all the restrictions imposed upon her
> by culture. For the adolescent girl is being brought by nature to become
> a woman, when everything in her culture tells her that woman is to be
> despised and feared. [p. 161]

WHAT IS HEALTHY?

These arguments amount to somewhat of a conspiracy theory of the
current fashion of thinness and are fascinating. Certain weaknesses, however, are evident. For many women, being overweight is itself a restriction
of the freedom of movement and action. The freedom to go backpacking,
to play tennis, to dance, and to do so many of the joyful, pleasurable things
that the lithe body can do with ease becomes a burden when the body is
overweight. Another problem is that Chernin makes no attempt to differentiate between the 15-pound weight difference that distinguishes the
current thin fashion from the previous more comfortable and natural body
type, and serious overweight. If a woman who can comfortably weigh 130
pounds tries to keep herself at 115, she will be in a constant struggle. If a
woman who in 1950 was satisfied with a weight of 145 now tries to be 125,
she will probably be alternately on and off diets, making herself miserable.
What Chernin does not discuss with concern are women who are truly
heavy, such as a woman who is short and would look and feel fine at 115
and now weighs 160 or 170, or a taller woman who should weigh 145 and
weighs 190 or more. It is the woman in this group, in between the obese
examples of 300 pounds and the normal 115 to 145, depending on height
and bone structure—that is, the woman who is using food to meet
emotional needs—who gets merged in Chernin's book with the healthy,
full-bodied woman with a classic rounded shape. One gets the sense that fat

is beautiful and thin is oppression. In my view, any degree of overweight that limits activity is most likely not physically healthy, although some writers such as Chernin claim a degree of overweight is healthy. Of course it is healthier than binging and purging, but there is some disagreement among the experts on the issue of ideal weight. The truth is that some women want to stay thin because they feel more energetic and can participate in many desired sports when they are thin. The fabled Rubens woman looks seductive on a bed, but she might have trouble climbing the stairs without losing her breath.

Some recent research reported in the *New York Times* by Natalie Angier (1990) has suggested that our natural life span could be extended to as much as 170 years with a diet low in calories, keeping the mind supple and the body spry, preventing heart disease, diabetes, kidney failure, and greatly retarding all types of cancer. So far only rats, mice, fish, spiders, worms, water fleas, and protozoa have been studied and all have had their life spans greatly extended with a restricted diet containing all the necessary vitamins and other nutrients but only 60 to 65 percent of the calories of the animal's normal diet. What makes the possibility of the extension of this research to humans so intriguing is that the animals maintain the vigor and robustness of youth. Surprisingly, it does not matter whether the diet is composed largely of fat or of carbohydrates as long as the animal receives a minimum amount of protein and enough vitamins and minerals. The research will now be extended to primates—squirrel monkeys and rhesus monkeys. The physiologic difference between the two groups of experimental animals is that the animals fed a restricted diet burn as much glucose per gram of tissue as do the plumper control animals, but the low-calorie rats have a significantly lower concentration of glucose circulating in their bloodstream than do the controls.

> Free floating glucose can interact with many important enzymes and proteins in the body, distorting their shape and function. . . . Food metabolism creates so-called free radicals, highly reactive oxygen molecules that combine with and can damage many parts of the body, particularly the slippery, fat-studded membranes that surround cells. . . . [There is] far less oxygen damage to cell membranes in food-restricting animals . . . a liver enzyme designed to detoxify free radicals is 50 to 70 percent more active in the dieting animals than in the controls. . . . In the calorie-restricted animals the enzymes that repair damaged DNA are more robust. [p. B7]

The shocking story by Elizabeth Gleick (1990) that 80 percent of fourth-grade girls in San Francisco are on a diet (Jane Brody in 1988 quotes 50 percent) is certainly disturbing, but neither source tells us whether these girls are being encouraged to stop eating junk food or whether they were in fact at an unhealthy weight according to their pediatricians. The possibility that they have simply incorporated the cultural norm for women, that is, dieting, and are feeling grown up by being on a diet is a sad commentary indeed.

THE STONE CENTER—JANET L. SURREY

Janet L. Surrey of the Stone Center (1984) has written on eating patterns among women and, after noting the high percentages of women who are on diets, concludes that concern about weight is the norm, beginning in adolescence. She believes there is a tendency among mental health professionals to underestimate and invalidate patients' real concerns about their body size and shape through interpreting them as masking deeper psychological problems. She quotes Maj-Britt Rosenbaum, a psychiatrist, describing adolescent girls who are her patients: "Many of my female patients express anxiety and conflict in terms of concerns about their bodies. There is the preoccupation with various body parts and with asynchronous growth; there are many questions about normalcy and the innumerable concerns that come under the guise of weight control" (Rosenbaum 1979, p. 239).

Surrey believes that the current preoccupation with body image and size is a major cultural disturbance, or cultural "disease," and interprets it as a communication about the experience of growing up female in this society. In this regard her views are identical with those of Chernin and Orbach. She also stresses the mother–daughter relationship and its connection with food. She believes that disturbances in eating patterns reflect critical aspects of discontinuity for women between early childhood self-development and the demands and values of the current culture during adolescence.

The first of these discrepancies is between the comfortable mother–daughter relationship of childhood and the emergence of sexuality and the growth spurt responsible for weight gain in girls in adolescence, leading to conflicts around food and resulting in mutual blaming and severe discord. In her opinion, so called separation issues and sexuality are often less conflictual today than the conflicts around food.

The second cultural inconsistency she describes is between the pathways of relational self-development for young girls and the current values of self-development, academic self-sufficiency, autonomy, assertiveness, and competition. Surrey thinks the loss of the traditional female values of emotional openness, cooperation, and attention to and concern for the needs of others leaves women feeling unsupported:

The internalized mother–daughter relationship is disrupted, and food becomes an important arena for acting out this disruption. Eating becomes an attempt to reinstate the sense of connection. However, for many reasons, the surrender to these impulses is highly conflictual and tends to create progressive disturbance and disruption, especially in individuals who are physically or psychologically vulnerable to developing more serious disorders. [p. 6]

EATING IN RELATION TO SEXUALITY

Louise J. Kaplan

In her book *Female Perversions* (1991), Louise J. Kaplan views anorexia as a sexual perversion because it is a solution to the dilemma of becoming a woman.

The anorexic is not an infant struggling with issues of separation-individuation but an adolescent or adult woman struggling to come to terms with genitality and female gender identity. The deception that she is only an innocent child struggling with infantile conflicts, a saint lacking in all sexual desires or shameful lusts of the body, is central to the anorectic's perverse strategy. . . . Behind her caricature of an obedient, virtuous, clean, submissive, good little girl is a most defiant, ambitious, driven, dominating, controlling, virile caricature of masculinity. Although her mother consciously wanted a perfect good little girl, in her very determination to stamp out rebellion and active sexual striving, she was also communicating to her daughter her own repressed intellectual and sexual strivings, which throughout her own childhood and adolescence and adulthood she had been regarding as forbidden masculine wishes. And it is these unconscious wishes of her mother that the anorectic is now symbolically enacting and granting to her, with a vengeance. . . . With her sexless, gender-ambiguous body and with her ghastly, off-putting emaciation, the anorectic mocks the power of adult sexuality. [pp. 457–459]

According to Kaplan, the anorexic girl had maintained the "cherished, unconscious fantasy that there are no real differences between the sexes or the child and parent generations" (p. 462). This fantasy is perpetuated by the behavior of her parents. Her father is very involved in his professional ambitions and cares little about sex. The parents show no sign of sexual desire for each other. They obscure the differences between the child and the adults so that the child becomes a third party in their marital life.

Because of their terror of their forbidden and shameful cross-gender strivings, mother and father have been unable to enjoy any sexual life together or to resolve the sexual tensions between them. When this perfect little girl comes along, she is a solution to their sexual dilemmas. . . . As she arrives at adolescence, the sight, merely the thought of her budding breasts and her menstruation rekindles in her parents their erotic fantasies. That is, these fantasies would be stirred up if there was not something very dramatic going on in the family to distract them. . . . She comes to the rescue of her parents now by focusing her parents' attention on her eating problems. Now nobody in the family has to acknowledge her sexuality or theirs. Now that she is starving, every day, everyone is peeking at, staring at, scrutinizing her body and wondering whether . . . she will or will not succumb to desire. Though her parents deny any interest in bodies, they are always looking at her body. . . . The anorectic no longer envies the parents for their power over her. She no longer envies her therapist for having the power to cure. . . . It is they who envy her for her power to humiliate and defeat them. [pp. 462–465]

Kaplan's understanding of the sexual components in anorexia is insightful and compelling. Neither the Orbach nor Chernin books relate disorders with food to incest and other sexual abuse. This is largely because sexual abuse is one of the more recent issues exposed as a result of the woman's movement. Much has been liberated, especially the truth, and one of the most horrifying truths is that of the sexual abuse of children. It was not until about 1985 that the grim reality of this perversion came to the attention of most therapists and the general public.

Ellen Bass and Laura Davis

In their book *The Courage to Heal* (1988), Ellen Bass and Laura Davis state that eating disorders often result from incest and other sexual crimes against children. Here are quotes from some of their patients:

I've been overweight since I was nine. I remember exactly the day I started eating. It was the day my stepfather fingered me in front of other people. He took off my bathing suit and under the guise of drying me off, got his fingers inside of me. I felt completely exposed and I remember I started eating that day. And I really ballooned.

I frequently eat very consciously to gain weight to cover me, to protect me. When I lose weight, I feel totally exposed and naked. I can't stand it. There's a lot of heartache in being so overweight. It affects every part of your life, but I still need the protection. [p. 50]

And another: "I kept eating so I wouldn't have to talk about what had happened. I just made sure my mouth was always full" (p. 50).

They say that some women overeat to numb themselves from the painful feelings, as a way to nurture themselves, to feel sexually unattractive and to be large, because when they were small as children they were so vulnerable. A description of work with a bulimic patient is dramatic:

> After one survivor read her writing (in a workshop) some painful and humiliating memories began to surface. She felt a strong urge to vomit. . . . I encouraged her to get that penis out of her mouth another way. She was terrified and shaking, recoiling into a small childlike bundle. But with encouragement, she gradually sat up and began to say no. Bit by bit she got louder, until she was pounding the pillow in front of her with a passionate force, screaming "No! Get that out of me! You can't put anything in me that I don't want! NO! NO! NO!" She screamed and pounded to exhaustion and then leaned back. Sweating, trembling, and smiling, she looked at us and said, "That felt a lot better than throwing up." [p. 219]

Another example is that of a woman who was an incest victim. She met a wonderful man whom she loved, trusted, and married.

> I was uncomfortable having sex, but I never knew why. Every time Howard and I had sex in our marriage, I would wake him up and tell him I was sure someone was breaking into our house. And afterwards, I would get up out of bed, go the the kitchen and eat, and make like it had never happened: "Who, me? Have sex?" And the strange thing is I enjoyed the sex! It was hard to get started, but once I got into it, I really enjoyed it. There were parts of the incest I enjoyed too, and that has been a really heavy trip for me. I mean, my body responded. It had to. But I'm not so quick to forgive that part of me. [p. 361]

Sandra Butler (1978) quotes a woman who says:

> My weight still is the central physical manifestation of my incest experiences. All that extra flesh is the separation I need between myself and my sexual feelings . . . and if I can keep myself fat and unattractive, I don't need to deal with them at all. . . . My weight also is the source of my power and protection against feeling small and vulnerable, like I was as a skinny little kid of eleven [when the incest occurred]. [pp. 21–22]

OVEREATING—A CLINICAL ILLUSTRATION

Overeating as a Response to Boundary Diffusion with Mother and to Sexual Molestation

I described Penelope in Chapter 1, where I focused on her relationship with her mother, whom I categorized as the masochistic, narcissistic, depressed type of mother. Penelope had conformed to mother's need for her to be a "good girl" in order to avoid mother's angry disapproval and rejection and to nurture her fantasy of being preferred to her "selfish" older sister. Penelope's father suddenly died when she was 9. Her mother's dependency needs were transferred from her husband to her daughter, which was both reassuring and inhibiting to Penelope. Sexual molestation by a close family friend added to her trauma and led to many self-destructive symptoms, one of which was overeating. I interpreted her overeating as multidetermined: a way to suppress sexuality, anger, anxiety, and loneliness so that she could maintain a happy, good-girl outward appearance; a way to keep men away so that she would not betray mother by marriage; a way to keep out of her sister's territory of beauty and social success so as not to compete with her sister and incur her wrath; a way to stay connected to mother, who was an overeater; a way to stay connected to father, who had been an overeater; and a way to stay connected with me, since her weight problem kept her therapy from being successful and thereby kept us together.

Overeating as a Means of Suppressing Feelings

As described earlier, no strong feelings were tolerated in Penelope's household. The most natural responses of children were dealt with severely, leaving her frightened and alone with her emotions. Not only was there no open mourning for her father's death, but her mother's best friend told this 9-year-old child that now it was her job to look after her mother, since mother had had such a great loss, as if the loss were not great to her as a child. Mother was to be protected and Penelope had no place to turn for comfort in her terrible grief and fear. She can clearly remember her gym teacher at school, a man, offering her sympathy and her smiling and saying "Oh, that's all right," in a cheerful manner. (It is horrifying to realize how little was known at that time, the early 1950s, about the needs of children. My own early edition of Dr. Spock's *Baby and Child Care* makes no reference to the death of a parent.)

Mother could not tolerate anger either, and therefore anger between the two sisters was squelched, interfering with the possibilities of any normal relationship between them. Sexual needs were never acknowledged, and in fact sexuality was viewed as bad. Penelope knew when mother disapproved, whether by an act of rejection such as her leaving the room or by her body language, especially a very stern, critical face which filled Penelope with great fear. In the early years of therapy she began to be able to identify that face, recognize her fear of it, and begin the long journey involved in not being intimidated by this facial expression of disapproval that had always made her retreat from whatever assertion had brought it about.

I repeatedly connected her overeating to her mother's intolerance of any expression of strong feelings. This was the way she coped with both the feelings themselves and her mother's disapproval. Since she got rejection rather than sympathy or comfort from expressing them, eating was the way she gave herself the comfort she craved.

> You turn to food for comfort because you can't turn to people.

> You can't trust that people will accept your strong feelings, so you comfort yourself with food—anesthetizing yourself from your feelings and defending against the imagined disapproval.

> You hide your real feelings from people, remain good and cheerful, and then you overeat when you are home alone.

> Your mother was so afraid of strong emotions that you never had a chance to learn that they can be expressed without anyone being destroyed.

> You would rather destroy your body with overeating than risk the destruction you imagine if you said how you really feel.

> You protect yourself and other people from the strength of your feelings by eating yourself into a state where you are too stuffed to feel anything.

> You swallow your feelings with the food.

Swallowing her feelings was also related to her sexual molestation: by overeating she forced down the rage and fear—but again at her own expense—to protect the perpetrator, his family, her family, and herself. As she saw the connection between her fear of exposing her strong feelings and her smoking, eating, and drinking, she began to use the expression that she was "stuffing" down her feelings. In one incident where she could see the connection between anger and eating, she coined the expression "eating furiously."

Overeating to Stay Close to Mother

Food is always connected to the mother, but in some cases there is more of a connection through overeating if the mother is also an overeater. Following the death of Penelope's father, Mother had to work. She would return home tired, make dinner, and then get into bed to read a book and eat candy. Clearly Mother was mourning the loss of her husband by attempting to replace him with sweets. She often encouraged Penelope to share the candy with her. Food continued to be a way that Mother connected to Penelope as she got older and they would go on diets together. During therapy, she realized that Mother tried to remain joined with her through food by sending her diets from the newspaper and magazines and by urging that they diet together even when they were thousands of miles apart. She put a stop to the practice and told Mother not to send her any more diets. She suspected it was a ploy to get her to lose weight, and she recognized that it made her angry.

On the other hand, she felt that Mother wanted her to be fat and unattractive so that she would stay close to Mother. During high school, before Penelope gained weight, Mother had discouraged all her attachments to boys, finding fault with each of them. After Mother's second husband died, Penelope suspected Mother wanted her to be fat so that there would be no competition from men in their relationship. In Chapter 1 I mentioned their trip to Hawaii together, when Mother proposed they wear muumuus and Penelope was struck by the asexuality of the garment as well as the merging inherent in the proposal.

There were many other indications of Mother's attempt to merge with her, and as therapy progressed she was less and less pleased and increasingly angered at what now was obvious to her, and she attempted to resist it. Yet she was still drawn to the comforts and treats mother could offer, just as she had offered candy after father's death. Mother had money to spare, which was always seductive to Penelope, who had a responsible but poorly paid job in a traditional woman's profession. The following interpretations were made regularly:

"When you overeat you stay close to Mother; you reassure her you will always be there for her.

When you overeat you keep men away and keep yourself available to meet Mother's needs.

When you overeat you protect Mother from your anger and stay dependent on her, instead of starting a family of your own.

When you overeat you protect yourself from Mother's angry disapproval of your sexual involvement with men.

You are so concerned about your Mother, but after all, she has had two husbands and two children whereas you have never had a family of your own.

The food is always there. You can always count on it. It can't die and it won't disapprove of you. It will never leave you and it will always comfort you.

Overeating to Stay Connected to Father

Father was somewhat overweight and liked to cook breakfasts. She remembered Father making oatmeal for her and putting lots of brown sugar on top. She also remembered his cooking pancakes on the weekends and serving them with lots of butter and syrup. These were warm and happy memories of being with father.

Overeating to Avoid Competition with Sister

Her sister was thin, very pretty, and always popular with boys. Even as adults Penelope was sure that if they went anywhere together, the men would all desire her sister and nobody would show interest in her. She told me that when she introduced her sister to friends, people would comment later that they didn't look anything alike. She had a clear memory of a time in high school before she was overweight, when her sister had broken up with a boyfriend who then asked Penelope for a date. She went, thinking it was OK because her sister didn't want him, but when her sister found out, she went into a rage, cried, and went to her room. Penelope was very frightened by this, felt it was unfair, but nevertheless didn't go out with the boy again. After sister's divorce, they were both single and there was a period when Penelope was engaged. She returned to her home city with her fiancé and her mother gave a party for them. Her sister had no man in her life at the time and talked a lot about what she was going to wear, not being satisfied with anything she had. Penelope had lost a lot of weight at this point and had a lovely dress for the party. Her sister made a number of comments before and during the visit that made Penelope feel that her sister was jealous and couldn't handle not being in the spotlight. Her sister's narcissism and competitiveness was clear to us both as a result of this visit.

Later, Mother and both sisters went traveling together. Her sister had made all the arrangements for the itinerary and planned every detail of the trip. This was another point when sister had no boyfriend and Penelope was having a rather gratifying affair with a married man with whom she spent a lot of time and who was very nurturing to her. During the vacation she received several letters from this man; her sister's reaction was clearly one of envy and resentment. These two incidents led to my making interpretations of her fear of her sister's anger if she loses weight and is attractive to men. Since Penelope still was very intimidated by her sister and felt very dependent on her (sister paid for the entire vacation), the fear of alienating her sister was another factor in her continuing to overeat and remove herself from the competition, leaving the social scene in her sister's territory and fearing to enter it.

Overeating to Avoid the Painful Memories of Sexual Molestation

In Chapter 5, I will elaborate on our work on the issue of sexual molestation; here I will describe only the way it affected Penelope's eating. For many years I worked with her without knowing that she had been sexually molested. When material suggestive of molestation appeared in her dreams, I raised the question, but she had no memory of being molested. This was years before child molestation became an issue of media and psychiatric attention, and the possibility was shocking to me and unbearable to her. She avoided it consciously, but her mind worked on it unconsciously, and dreams continued to offer clues to the person and the events. The terrible shame she felt about her overweight body reflected the terrible shame she felt unconsciously about her participation in the sexual abuse, for which she had held herself responsible. Overeating served several functions in regard to the sexual abuse.

1. It masked the issue of sexual molestation. She thought about food instead of thinking about her past.

2. She anesthetized her feelings of rage, fear, humiliation, and suppressed her fantasies of revenge by stuffing herself with food.

3. It expressed the sexual molestation symbolically by keeping her feeling ashamed of her body and its appetites.

4. In her relationship to food, smoking, and alcohol, she reenacted the story of her seduction. The food (or alcohol or cigarettes) was always tempting her, she seduced herself into eating it, it provided immediate relief and gratification, but it left her with terrible regret, shame, physical discomfort, and feeling more depressed the next day.

5. It kept her feeling guilty and undeserving of the love of a man who could be her own, feelings that actually stemmed from the sexual abuse.

As the story of her sexual molestation became clearer and more convincing to her, she alternated periods of actively working on memories and denying that it could have happened. Overeating served during both times: the stronger was the realization of her abuse, the more frightened she was of revealing the truth and being blamed for it. Telling her mother and sister brought disbelief and rejection, which was so disheartening that she ate to deal with the frustration, pain, and rage at their total lack of support. Mother continued her close friendship with the man who was the perpetrator. One way to keep their approval and remain close to them was to deny that she had been molested, so as not to experience rage at both the perpetrator and her family for their failure to believe her. Periods of denial resulted in overeating to help her keep the truth from herself. Thus the cycle—revealing the truth, rejection, overeating, denial of the truth, more eating to suppress the truth, realization of the meaning of the overeating, return to work on the issue, anxiety about the repercussions, overeating again, and so forth—went on for several years.

Overeating as Resistance to Termination

Based on my understanding of one of the functions her weight served with her mother, I made many interpretations that Penelope was afraid I would be angry if she lost weight, was successful with men, and left me. At other times she expressed the wish for termination at points in the therapy when she still had considerable work to do on her molestation, saying she believed that if she left therapy she could lose weight. This idea was both an avoidance of the frightening subject of her sexual molestation and also a recognition that the dependency tie to me required, in her mind, that she remain overweight. This idea was rooted in her unconscious recognition of her mother's dependency needs and her conscious recognition of her own. The following are sample interpretations:

> You can lose weight and still stay connected to me to continue working on other issues and on the problems in relationships with men that may then arise.

> You have the idea that you can't be close to me if you lose weight.

> You are afraid I will be jealous and competitive with you if you are thin.

> Your sister got angry when you were successful with boys, so you had to get fat to appease her.

There was also resistance to termination because of her fear of being without my nurturing presence in her life.

> Being overweight means you are a good girl, not sexual. You are afraid of losing my approval if you lose weight and get involved with a man. You want to be my favorite patient.

> As long as you don't lose weight, you still have a problem for us to work on and you imagine you can't leave therapy. Your weight protects you from leaving me and protects me from losing you.

> You can stop therapy when you feel you have no more need for my help and still be overweight, or you can lose weight and still choose to continue in therapy to work on other issues.

Even though her weight was symptomatic, I believed it was important to try to separate the issue of her weight gain and loss from her dependency on me, so that it would be clear that her weight did not have the same meaning for our relationship that it did with her mother.

OTHER NONDIET APPROACHES TO WEIGHT CONTROL

When Food is Love—Geneen Roth

Two other important contributors to the field of eating disorders are Geneen Roth and Judy Wardell. Roth has written four books, *Feeding the Hungry Heart* (1982), *Breaking Free From Compulsive Eating* (1984), *Why Weight?* (1989), and *When Food is Love* (1991). In her group treatment program called "Breaking Free," Roth espouses a philosophy of "trusting yourself, nourishing yourself, accepting yourself." In *Breaking Free From Compulsive Eating,* she describes the process. Eat only when you are hungry, not in anticipation of getting hungry. To learn your actual pattern of eating, she recommends keeping a chart of what you ate, when you ate, and whether or not you were hungry before you ate. By noticing your eating when you are not hungry, you start to notice what needs the food is serving, that is, what you are feeling when you want to eat but are not hungry. At one point Roth seemingly contradicts herself in saying there is nothing wrong with eating when you are not hungry, as long as you eat what you want (p. 62). Perhaps the point is the self-awareness that you are eating out of some need other than hunger.

Her next recommendation is to choose the food you really want to eat. She says that most of the time people with food problems eat what they should eat but at other times eat forbidden food, rebelling against the "good" foods by eating "bad" foods. In her program there are no bad foods, only the foods you want to eat. She describes her own experiment with this approach:

> But I had promised myself to eat exactly what I wanted, believing that eventually my body's natural wisdom would surface. I didn't know how long it would take but I was willing to find out. After seventeen years of dieting and bingeing, seventeen years of losing and gaining weight, I figured that if it took another six months and another fifteen pounds to begin to trust myself, it would be well worth the wait. [p. 22]

She ate only chocolate chip cookies for two weeks but then wanted vegetables. She went through stages of eating only pizza, hot dogs, popcorn, ice cream and chocolate, the bad foods that she had deprived herself of for years. She gained 15 pounds, then her weight stabilized, and then over the next two years, eating only what she wanted when she was hungry, she lost 30 pounds. She believes that what is so wrong with diets is that they remove the factor of choice, of how you are feeling and what you want. Her other rules are to eat when you are sitting down, not to eat in the car, and not to eat in secrecy. Eat without distractions, like TV, radio, books, the newspaper, and eat in as lovely an environment as you can create. Avoid emotional conversations when eating. The third step is to learn when to stop eating—to know when you have had enough, when you feel satisfied. Yet many women fail using Roth's formula, as with all other approaches.

Perhaps the importance of choice does not work as well when a group member is essentially following Roth's advice about choice. It is not truly her own choice in the sense that it was for Roth when she created the concept. Perhaps a battle between mother and daughter is recreated on a psychological level for some women even when they are following her recommendations to eat only when they are hungry and only what they truly want to eat. They are still being dependent on someone telling them what and when to eat, even though the choice of what to eat is up to them. The potential for rebelling against this mother/teacher/therapist figure in order to assert autonomy and not feel controlled by the leader is a danger that could sabotage the effect of this or any "leader" method for weight loss. My recommendation, if this happens to a patient, is that she read the books, take the courses, and then create her own plan for eating sensibly, distilling what is best and most compatible from the different approaches she has studied. In this way she can avoid the reenactment of the hostile-dependent tie to earlier maternal figures.

Roth's theory is that weight protects the woman from reality. She describes her own injuries as a child subject to the mood swings of her mother, and refers to the many abused women in her groups, although she does not stress sexual abuse.

> Some of the women I see have been sexually abused, some have been raped, some have been abandoned by a father or a lover. Some are frightened of intimacy. Most are confused by what it means to be living in an adult woman's body with an adult woman's sexuality, and they use what is forever in the spotlight—their bodies—to express their confusion. They use their bodies as their battlegrounds; they know that in our culture, women's voices may not always be heard, but their bodies will still (and always) be noticed. [p. 213]

It appears to me that the abused child learns to create a false reality, a fantasy world, in order to survive; perhaps imagining having other parents, or imagining being truly loved and appreciated by the real parents, or fantasizing what it will be like when she grows up and is free of her family. Once she has become an adult, overeating allows her to continue to live in a fantasy world, one based on what life will be like when she is thin. In the meantime nothing can hurt or disappoint her, because the present reality is not her true reality; that will begin only when she is thin. She continues the pattern of living in a fantasy world that she began to protect herself from the cruelty inflicted upon her in childhood, in order to protect herself from the cruelty she imagines (projects) she will face in adulthood if she loses weight and tries to have a close relationship. This can be true for friendships as well as sexual relationships. Penelope was unable to have women friends for a long time, until she overcame her fears of disapproval and domination by other women. Roth says:

> When I weighed 145 pounds, I was in control. People couldn't reject me; I had already rejected myself. I knew I was too fat. I knew I was unattractive. They couldn't like me any less than I already liked myself. Each time I felt rejected, my secret self, the vision of who I was under all that fat, caught me. Like a net underneath a tightrope, it kept me from smashing to the ground. . . . If I were thin, they'd love me. [p. 140]

She describes a kind of split personality—the fat me and the thin me. There is a fear of the thin me because of a lack of protection that the layer of fat unconsciously provides. This was true for Penelope; she once had a dream in which a man was shooting at her with a gun and she covered herself with loaves of bread for protection. In another dream a threatening man came into her workplace and she hid behind a counter to protect herself—another barrier against dangerous attack. The thin me may not be able to say no to sexual advances or to other kinds of requests for time or attention. I believe Roth is actually describing what could be called a woman with boundary problems. The fear of being thin is a fear of having no boundaries, of being subject to the wishes and demands of others without a capacity to express her own needs, to say no or to get angry to protect herself from unwanted intrusions. Being fat makes her feel impenetrable. Being thin means being powerless. Being fat is the only way she knows to have the power to say no.

Roth instructs her clients to learn to say no by starting to say no once a day to something they do not want to do but would ordinarily agree to. She tells them to pick a safe person, someone who loves and respects them.

> Many of the women who come to me do not set limits. They feel they can't say no, or they wouldn't be loved. They feel that they give and give, do things they don't especially want to do, and then they have to eat to replenish themselves to get something back. They use their weight, not their voices, to say no. . . .
>
> Anger is a way of saying "I will take so much and I won't take any more. You've crossed the line and now I want you to stop." Anger is a way to set limits. Many compulsive eaters eat because they are angry and they don't know they are allowed to say so. [pp. 190–191]

This hearkens back to women's fear of anger, which I discussed in Chapter 2. It is very hard to break with the past and to feel safe expressing anger. In fact, expressing anger after years of not doing so can sometimes lead to divorce and to breaks with friends and family members. Some women cannot tolerate that risk of loss, and after a few instances of trying to express anger and seeing the results, they retreat to eating. Not only a great deal of support and help from a group but also individual therapy would be necessary to see this through. Indeed, Roth does encourage the women in her groups to seek individual therapy.

Roth never mentions feminism or describes herself as a feminist. Her only reference to the women's movement appears at the end of the book in a section entitled "On Powerful Women."

> Most of the women I work with are afraid that if they lost weight, they would be *too* powerful. One woman said "I would scare everyone away. I would mow them down." They are frightened that losing weight would make them perfect, since being fat, in their eyes, is their single most tragic flaw. And they are afraid that being perfect would threaten everyone around them. . . . We're afraid of being called bitchy and arrogant and aggressive and demanding. We're afraid of becoming ball breaking amazons. Those are fears. Those are myths. . . . Since the women's movement began in the sixties, many more successful, expressive women are becoming visible. We are no longer anomalies. There is support for women who refuse to deny their capabilities. . . . And there are men who are willing to be emotionally supportive of strong women while facing their fears about them. . . . We are trail blazers. [pp. 197–198]

This is another reflection of the boundary problems experienced by many overeaters. They are either being overwhelmed by others or are overwhelming, either frightened or frightening, either being invaded or invading. Being fat protects them and others from the terrors of closeness. Either dangerous or in danger, they are out of control except when the layer of fat that they create to surround themselves provides an imagined barrier from their own destructive wishes and the fears—partially projections—of others' destructive power. The internal pain and rage live on in the disguised form of fat.

In her new book, *When Food is Love: Exploring the Relationship between Eating and Intimacy* (1991), Roth is very self-revealing, both about her past in her family and about her own emotional struggles in her past relationships with men and in her current marriage. Unlike traditional psychotherapists, who keep their personal lives very private, Roth reveals all her own anxieties and depressions in the interest of helping others with similar conflicts, this time focusing on the problems for formerly over-weight women who lose weight and then get involved in love relation-ships. She says that the fantasy is that when you lose weight, all will be perfect, but the reality is that losing weight does not change any of the internal scars that hinder relationships and that originally led to the overeating. Keeping the weight off is only likely if you can work through the internal problems relating to trusting others in intimate relationships. "The wonderful thing about food is that it doesn't leave, talk back, or have a mind of its own. The difficult thing about people is that they do. Food was my lover for seventeen years and demanded nothing of me. Which was exactly the way I wanted it'' (p. 2).

In this recent book she states that half the women in her workshops were sexually abused as children, and more than half are adult children of alcoholics.

> Diets don't work because food and weight are the symptoms, not the problems. The focus on weight provides a convenient and culturally reinforced distraction from the reason why so many people use food when they are not hungry. These reasons are more complex than—and will never be solved with—will-power, counting calories, and exercise. They have to do with neglect, lack of trust, lack of love, sexual abuse, physical abuse, unexpressed rage, grief, being the object of discrimina-tion, protection from getting hurt again. People abuse themselves with food because they don't know they deserve better. People abuse themselves because they've been abused. They become self-loathing, unhappy adults not because they've experienced trauma but because they've repressed it. [p. 4]

The connection between eating disorders and sexual abuse is now clear, and the difference between Roth's 1984 and her 1991 book reflects the changes in society. The issue of sexual abuse was brought into the open by the women's movement, and when it finally received due attention in the media and from psychotherapists, more and more women began revealing the truth about their secret past. I am almost certain that half of her clients were survivors of sexual abuse at the time her earlier books were written, but the way had not yet been paved for them to have the courage to remember it and to reveal it. The same is true for other forms of physical abuse such as spanking or beating children for misbehavior, which had never been called child abuse in the past. Women with serious weight problems have been sexually, physically, or psychologically abused or neglected. Men who were abused or neglected may also have weight problems but are more likely to have alcohol and drug problems and/or to be lawbreakers and to be in jail and prison. The rage and pain that exist within women who have been abused and neglected are much more likely to be expressed in nonviolent, secretive ways like binging, purging, fasting and dieting, which are self-destructive, whereas men are much more likely to openly express their rage in antisocial acts and acts of violence perpetrated against others. According to some surveys, one out of four girls has been sexually molested, but one out of nine boys has been as well. Many of these boys become the aggressive perpetrators of sexual abuse against boys, girls, and women when they become adults, whereas the women are turning the rage against themselves by torturing their bodies. Many of the boys who become criminals have been physically abused. Sexual abuse is in fact physical abuse, as is rape. It is a crime of violence in the guise of a sexual act.

As of March 25, 1991 there were 61,225 prisoners in all federal prisons and an additional 6,750 in halfway homes or housed in local jails. As of March 24, 1991 there were 99,421 prisoners in the California State prison system. It is important for us to note that of the 747,991 in state prisons on 1 January 1991 nationwide, 94.4 percent were men and only 5.6 percent were women. Of the 61,225 in federal prisons, 7 percent were women.

Women who struggle to be thin but are not truly compulsive eaters may not have been abused, but they do not have enough confidence in themselves, their intelligence, their abilities, their independence, their sense of being worthwhile, without conforming to the current fashion of thinness. This is more truly a feminist issue than compulsive overeating is. These are the women who do not value themselves enough to believe that they are fine the way they are, at whatever weight is comfortable for them, because the focus on women's appearance and physical attraction continues to be the primary means for most women to achieve self-esteem, in spite of twenty years of the women's movement. This speaks to the powerful forces in society that still prevail to keep women dependent on men because they desire companionship, marriage, and children, for which they must attract a man. In this context, Chernin's (1981) argument of a women's reduction movement emerging to parallel the women's liberation movement makes sense. Why does fashion now dictate that women be smaller, when the political climate is one of expansion for women? Women's economic dependence on men in order to have children is at the heart of this dependence, and thus women's vulnerability to the dictates of the fashion of thinness.

Thin Within—Judy Wardell

Another writer and leader of weight loss groups without dieting is Judy Wardell, author of *Thin Within: How to Eat and Live like a Thin Person* (1985). Wardell's approach, developed with Joy Imboden Overstreet, is similar to the others in that she says diets do not work and that the change required to lose weight is a change in attitude toward yourself and your possibilities. As with Chernin, Orbach, and Roth, she herself suffered from years of being overweight, dieting, and regaining the weight. She is a psychiatric nurse who was bulimic for a year and even had her jaws wired shut. She differs from the others in that she neither has a feminist approach nor, apparently, is she favorably inclined toward psychotherapy, which she never once mentions in her book. Hers is more of a "power of positive thinking" approach. "Thin Within" is a 30-day group program that includes a follow-up group, and for which she claims a long-term success rate of over 60 percent. She quotes statistics that there are 79 million overweight Americans, 40 million of whom are seriously overweight, defined as 30 pounds or more. She, like Roth, claims the key to permanent weight loss is not what you eat but when you eat and how much. What Wardell calls the Keys to Weight Mastery are as follows:

1. Eat only when my body is hungry.
2. Reduce the number of distractions in order to eat in a calm environment.
3. Eat only when I'm sitting.
4. Eat only when my body and mind are relaxed.
5. Eat and drink only the food and beverages my body loves.
6. Pay attention only to my food when eating.
7. Eat slowly, savoring each bite.
8. Stop *before* my body is full! [pp. 6–8]

Determining when you are hungry and when you are full is a key tool in her approach. The Hunger Scale runs from 0, which means empty, to 10, which means stuffed. Number 5 is comfortable. Her prescription is to eat only when you are at 0 and to stop at 5. She believes that if all your eating is between 0 and 5 you can eat any food you like, lose weight, and remain slim. If you eat between 3 and 7, you will maintain your weight and not lose. If you eat between 5 and 10, you will gain. Learning to judge your degree of hunger and fullness is part of the exercises in her 30-day program. She asks that each group participant throw out her bathroom scale and tune in to her body instead, her hunger scale.

She tells the reader that he or she has a subtle but powerful belief inside herself, namely, "I don't deserve to be thin." In what she calls "My Fat Story," she lists seventeen reasons why people start to overeat, including items like a failed relationship, a death or divorce, a sexual trauma or, as in her case, an abortion. She then minimizes the significance of these events: "But what does the past have to do with the present or present-time eating? Absolutely nothing! Present-time eating is asking our body if it is hungry and eating from 0 to 5 or less, eating the foods we love. . . . Set yourself free from your Fat Machinery by forgiving yourself" (pp. 70–71). Wardell advises you to get rid of past failures and get rid of guilt, "the most fattening thing there is." She encourages her readers to love themselves and to create a supportive and nurturing environment for themselves. She tells them to buy beautiful new clothes. She suggests observing how thin people eat. She recommends forgivenesses, affirmations, visualizations, and daily acknowledgments. She is very practically oriented and is impatient with suffering. "Thin Within is a place for winners. The question we always ask each other is, 'What's working in your life?' Instead of sitting around telling each other our sad stories and all of our problems we focus on our successes rather than our failures" (p. 190).

In her chapter on forgiveness she writes about "staying stuck" and we sense that she is also impatient with anger:

> A lack of forgiveness is a fantastic way of staying stuck in the past and closing off our future. It's also a great way to torture other people and perpetuate their guilt feelings. A lack of forgiveness blocks receiving. How can we allow ourselves to receive the blessings of a radiantly slim body if we've blocked the way with hatred and resentments. When we give up our anger and our desire for revenge, we set ourselves free. [p. 146]

However, her examples of what should be forgiven are rather minor infractions. One member forgives her family for pushing food on her when she visits them. Wardell's own forgiveness is of her father, whom she had always resented for not having been a big business tycoon. Instead he owned and managed butcher shops. This is small potatoes compared with some of the truly nightmarish childhoods some people have had—children who were locked in closets for hours, beaten with sticks and straps, repeatedly raped, abandoned by one or both parents, left alone and without food for days, or subjected to the sadistic psychological abuse of parents who were mentally ill or alcoholic and were never really loved and cared for.

At times she leaves the world of the rational for magical thinking, such as in an example of a woman who privately committed to paper her forgiveness of her brother whom she had not heard from or spoken to in twelve years. The next morning she got a phone call from Australia from her brother. A similar "miracle" quality at certain points in the book gives it a quasi-religious tone at times.

She distinguishes between satisfaction and gratification:

What creates everlasting thinness is a harmony in our lives between satisfaction and gratification. This is because when we feel we're not producing enough satisfaction in our lives, we mistakenly look for it in food. So too, when we're overinvolved with satisfaction without enough gratification, we'll mistakenly look for our pleasure in food. If we enjoy sufficient satisfaction and schedule gratification along the way, our lives will be full enough that we won't feel the compulsion to "reward" ourselves with food. [p. 213]

Her no-nonsense approach includes her critical view of trying. She asks that you put her book down and then try to pick it up, illustrating her point that trying is not doing, that trying to lose weight is not making a positive commitment to losing weight. Other examples are similar in their positive-thinking approach, which I do not believe can be effective for truly depressed people. Wardell asks each participant to set up a "gameplan for life mastery" (p. 217) and writes of "achieving all that your heart desires" (p. 217). She wants you to "visualize the infinite possibilities for your life," (p. 216) stressing having fun, living life "in the fast lane" (p. 197) and "total success" (p. 208). Never once are financial limitations mentioned, or the responsibility of caring for children. My impression is that this is a person who came from a basically caring family but who had some complaints against her parents, as we all do. For her, extreme feelings of guilt following an abortion was what triggered overeating. She often stresses getting rid of guilt but apparently does not recognize rage. She equates having an abortion as an adult with childhood traumas of incest, physical violence, alcoholism, neglect, psychological and physical sadism, and expects her group members to overcome these severe early experiences as she overcame some disappointments in her own life, which include the abortion and not becoming a dancer. They are not comparable. For those with these early severe experiences of deprivation and cruelty, psychotherapy and group support would be a necessary accompaniment to her weight loss program.

OVEREATING AS A RESULT OF MATERNAL ABUSE AND NEGLECT—A CLINICAL ILLUSTRATION

The exotic disorders of anorexia nervosa and bulimia have gotten most of the attention in psychiatry and in the media in the last few years, but in fact the vast majority of women with food problems are simply overeaters.

Sandra, described in Chapter 1 in connection with her narcissistic and cruel mother and also in Chapter 6 of my first book as an orgasmic woman, is an example of an overeater for whom the analysis of her very hostile-dependent relationship with her mother, reenacted in the transference with her therapist, revealed many of the aggressive and masochistic meanings of her weight problem. You may recall that Sandra's mother was often neglectful and cruel to her. Sandra and her sister were left alone for long and indefinite periods while mother went shopping or to clubs. Sometimes they were left in the car with a bag of cookies. Sandra had only a slight weight problem when I first saw her in her late twenties, but, as is common, metabolism changes in her mid-thirties resulted in gradual weight gain; by her early forties she was seriously overweight, about 100 pounds.

As with other patients with overweight problems, I recommended to Sandra that in addition to our individual therapy sessions she exercise regularly and join a group for women with overeating problems. In my experience, individual therapy does not suffice to reverse the trend unless exercise and group support are also part of the program. Sandra's group experience was not good, and she struggled with diets and several diet programs. In each case some failure of the leader to prove that she loved Sandra sabotaged the program. Sandra would do provocative things such as come late or miss sessions, just as she did in her therapy, and then be hurt and angry if the leader failed to offer her another time or if she was criticized for her lateness.

She noticed a pattern that when she had reduced to 180 pounds, she sabotaged herself and began to gain weight again. We worked on what was frightening or otherwise conflictual for her about getting below 180 pounds. The answer lay in her still highly ambivalent and competitive relationship with her mother. Sandra's overeating was a response to her anger and sadness about being unloved as a child by her mother, and about not having a man who loved her so that she herself could have a child. After her father died, her depression had increased and eating was a frequent escape in her effort to ease her feelings of emptiness. She looked forward to meals and snacks, and saw them as just rewards for hard work and for the deprivations she experienced in her life. Just as her mother had substituted cookies for real care and attention, Sandra substituted cookies and other snacks for the love and care that was missing when a man she was involved with was away, when she had been rejected, or as compensation for a variety of disappointments on the job and with her family or friends.

However, her disturbed relationship with her mother still figured in her conflictual relationship to her body. When Sandra's mother became a widow and was seeking men, Sandra herself was looking for a man. This seemed to trigger competitive feelings similar to those that had occurred when Sandra and her mother had vied for her father's love and approval. Sandra believed that she was unable to lose weight because that would put her in direct competition with her mother for men. In fact, the man Sandra lived with toward the end of her therapy, a widower, was halfway in age between herself and her mother. She felt strongly that her mother was resentful that Sandra had a man and she did not.

This competitive factor with other women was prominent in her therapy as well. Because I had no weight problem, her weight gain transferentially kept her out of the competition with me, yet envying and resenting me. Being overweight completed the picture of masochism as she suffered shame at her increasing size, along with her other feelings of deprivation. Sandra experienced herself as overworked and underappreciated. This included her administrative job where she had a great deal of responsibility but was underpaid and repeatedly put off whenever she asked for a raise commensurate with her worth. This theme was repeated in relationships with men and with women friends, where she felt she did the work, the entertaining, the care giving, and did not get enough back. It was a repetitive theme in her therapy with me, in which she frequently complained of how much money therapy was costing her, how little I cared, and how little I gave her. She often accused me of not caring about anything but the money she paid, even though she never paid a full fee.

She never expressed anger in her relationships with men or toward her father. She stoically took their abandonments without standing up for herself, just as she had never allowed herself to blame her father or get angry at him for his failure to protect her from her mother's neglect or her rages. Her father, a physician, had been very involved with caring for his patients, and the patients came before his children. She recalled having dinner with Father one night when Mother was out, and his being called away for an emergency cardiac case. She was frightened of being alone and was unsure when, or even whether, he would be back. Mother was due home at 10 o'clock but in fact did not return until 2 A.M. When home alone with her younger sister and frightened, she knew she was not allowed to call Father unless it was an emergency. The only exception to this was that if a patient called for him at home, she was allowed to call to convey the message from the patient to her father's answering service. If she called out of fear, her father would be irritated with her. In therapy this transferred to her calling me and leaving messages with my answering service. She said she preferred to get the service because of a fear I would be angry with her for calling. I focused on her failure to hold men responsible for their weaknesses.

Therapist: It is so hard for you to feel anger toward your father, yet he failed to protect you from your mother's cruel treatment.

Patient: But he worked such long hours.

Therapist: Your father knew your mother was neglecting you and mistreating you, and he allowed it. By his inaction, your father did not protect you, yet you don't hold him responsible.

Patient: But my father really loved me and he took my side.

Therapist: But he didn't stop her. You protect him because you need so much to love him and feel loved by him.

Yet the nurturing she counted on from men often led to disappointments, and her need to protect men kept her from expressing her needs directly. By overeating she nurtured herself after his death and the breakup of a serious, long-term love relationship that occurred shortly afterward. Eating was a magical way of incorporating her father and her lover, Jim. Her sadness and loneliness were expressed by consuming large amounts of food to comfort herself during periods of anxiety and depression. In Sandra's case, her being overweight did not keep her from men or them from her, and she continued to have intimate relationships. Her attraction to men, no doubt related to the love she did get from her father and the closeness she felt with him, showed that for her the pathological component in her eating disorder was rooted in the abuse by her mother. That abuse, however, had left her anxious, insecure, and angry, and these problems affected her love relationships, making her vulnerable to any slight yet too eager to please the man to protect herself from feared abandonment.

Sandra recognized that her passive response to unhappy situations at work and in love relationships was connected with her eating patterns. The portion of a session that follows took place during the long-term relationship with Jim, which started when he was still married but planning to leave his wife, proceeded to their living together, and ended when he left and moved in with another woman. Her hope had been to marry Jim and have a baby with him.

Patient: Do you think there's a connection between waiting and my weight problem? I've been putting on weight and that's really discouraging to me. On the surface I'm happy and satisfied, I feel good being with Jim, but gaining weight means something. Could it be that I put on weight when I'm waiting?

Therapist: There certainly is a connection between anxiety and gaining weight. The fact that Jim has not been able to follow through with his divorce and has not asked you to marry him is serious.

Patient: Other times I've gained weight was when I was waiting—like waiting to hear about the Los Angeles job and waiting for my divorce. I lost weight when I was engaged.

Therapist: You lost weight when you first started living with Jim, too. You felt that was a sign that it was a good thing for you. We know how anxious it makes you to have to wait. You always arrive late for your sessions because you can't bear the thought that I will keep you waiting—so you keep me waiting to feel in control.

Patient: Yes. Maybe when he comes home tonight he'll have worked out the custody plan with his daughter.

Therapist: But that isn't the substance of what you need to know. You need to know if he plans to marry you.

Patient: You think I should just ask him that? I don't know if I can.

Therapist: It will be hard, but it will be hard whenever you do it, and the sooner the better. Pick the time when it will be easiest for you to handle a loss, knowing that if it means losing him it will be painful and sad.

Patient: But what if he says yes and then postpones it and doesn't really mean it.

Therapist: You're afraid you can't trust his answer. That is a way of postponing asking the question.

Patient: I'm afraid I'll be feeding right into what his wife said about me—that all I want is for him to get a divorce from her so I can marry him and have a baby with him.

Therapist: I don't see anything criminal about any of those wishes. It's not like all you're after is his money.

Patient: (smiling) That's true.

Therapist: You're stuck because you're afraid if you ask he'll say no, but if he says yes you're afraid you've forced him.

Sandra experienced the suggestion of asking as an aggressive, hostile act and therefore was frightened of it. Waiting and eating felt much safer and more acceptably feminine. She would not incur any anger but unconsciously she was stuffing down her anger and sabotaging herself. Her oedipal struggles with her mother were reawakened by getting involved with a married man and then having to fear the vengeance of his wife. Her guilt and shame over having the affair and then living with him before he obtained a divorce added to her conflicting feelings of wanting a commitment from him but not feeling she deserved it. As it turned out, she was a ''transitional object,'' common as a marriage is breaking up, and was crushed when the relationship ended.

Because I was working with Sandra on a number of important issues, I did not take a direct role in her weight problem. She brought it up at times and told me what she was doing about it. I believed that if we kept working on her psychological issues, the understanding of her food disorder and her ability to deal with it would follow. When she raised the issue, I responded by working on it with her, but I did not introduce it. I did not see it as my job to bring it up or to recommend remedies in the form of diets or books. I did recommend group work and exercise when she complained that she was feeling out of control and getting worried about the effect on her physical health. I was concerned that her weight not become another arena of struggle in what was already a difficult therapy, one in which she struggled over everything possible and was mistrustful of me on many levels. Control issues were so prominent that I was reluctant to introduce an issue that had such potential for becoming another control battle, and which might have even resulted in her sabotaging her own efforts to spite me in order to assert her autonomy. Other than recommending that she try a group, I remained neutral.

However, this may have been an error. Toward the end of her therapy, when she was seriously overweight, she went for a medical checkup and was warned of the danger to her health if she did not lose weight. She angrily accused me of neglecting her weight problem:

Patient: I could have killed myself and you did nothing. You are just like my mother. She didn't care and she didn't set limits. You should have loved and accepted me no matter what. My weight gain was a suicide effort.

Therapist: You bludgeon me with your weight the way your mother did to you with her colitis.

I used a transference interpretation; however, such an episode may be an indication that with overeating, as with other addictions that have serious self-destructive consequences, the "neutral" stance of the therapist is inadequate. Treating the addiction as a symptom is not enough, it must be treated with direct interventions as well, and then the therapist must interpret any accusations of criticism and disapproval on the therapist's part. It is one of those dilemmas where you can be damned either way. The feminist view propounded by Chernin that being large and curvaceous is truly womanly flies in the face of medical realities. After reading Chernin I had attempted to monitor my own feelings of disapproval of fat women and to develop a more generous attitude, which backfired in the case of Sandra. This again points to the need to differentiate between that 15-pound weight difference between fashionable thinness and a comfortable body weight, and the weight gains of 30 to 100 pounds that are truly a burden on all body systems and constitute a recipe for poor health.

When Sandra did decide to terminate therapy, she was very unsure of herself but decided to try it for six months. The next year I got a Christmas card from her telling me that her home life was going well, she had had an advance at work and undergone a major weight loss. She is another example of a woman patient who needs to sever the dependent tie with her therapist before losing weight. It is only when the fantasy of being totally loved and cared for by the mother/therapist has been analyzed and worked through that termination and weight loss can follow. The ambivalent bond is finally broken.

CONCLUSION: A MULTIPLE-LEVEL TREATMENT PLAN

The problem of overeating is both a symptom of underlying psychological problems and an immediate crisis for the woman suffering from compulsive eating and reaching an unhealthy level of weight. It must be treated at both levels, with a psychotherapeutic approach to get to the sources of the addiction and with a practical approach to reduce weight. The combination of individual psychotherapy, exercise, and a support group which promotes a sensible, nonpunitive approach to eating is a multiple-level treatment plan that can succeed.

Both psychoanalytic theory and feminist theory are valuable for any therapist working with women with eating disorders. For some women, the mother–daughter relationship is a source of both boundary diffusion and repressed hostility, often shown in a hostile-dependent relationship with both the mother and the therapist. For other women, sexual abuse by either a family member or other significant male can create a sense of shame of one's body, guilt, and a fear of sexual invasion, from which a layer of fat serves as her protection.

That a fashion of thinness emerged at the same time the feminist movement was developing a feeling of greater power among women raises questions about the underlying meaning of the weight of women for men. Small, fragile women may be less threatening and more flattering to the male ego, a modern form of foot binding that cripples the strength and freedom of the woman. In our work with women who complain about their weight, it is important to distinguish between the currently fashionable weight; a healthy, normal, rounded female body; and a truly unhealthy obese degree of overweight. In the first case, the issue is one of conformity to an idealized and unimposing body shape, truly a feminist issue. In the latter case, serious overweight may be symptomatic of childhood physical or sexual abuse (or both) or neglect. Here is where the skill of the psychotherapist is aided by an understanding of psychoanalytic theory and method employed in the service of uncovering repressed and split-off memories of painful and frightening events. An integration of feminist and psychoanalytic theory in the treatment of eating disorders, combined with practical help from a supportive group and a sensible food and exercise plan, can offer the troubled patient the best of all approaches.

5

VIOLENCE AGAINST WOMEN AND CHILDREN

A husband's fist leaves no bruise.

Beat your wife with the butt-end of an axe: if she falls to the floor and cries, she is fooling you—give her some more.

Girls, don't worry when you marry—when your husbands start beating you will be time enough.

Slap your woman before dinner and you'll have to beat her before supper.

A wife isn't a jug—she won't crack if you hit her a few.

—Russian proverbs

Child sexual abuse is an intensely controversial, deeply divisive subject. It splits children from parents, mothers from fathers, and families from their friends, neighbors, and relatives. It divides social workers against psychiatrists, therapists against investigators against prosecutors against judges against jurors, and every player against society itself. . . . Those who fight for power are courageous. Those who crusade for the underdog are called hysterical.

—Roland Summit, M.D.

Incest is not a topic that one embraces; one backs into it, fighting every step of the way.

—Judith Herman, M.D.

MEMORIES

When I was a child, I could not eat bananas. Upon the urging of my mother I would at times try to bite into a banana but would be filled with revulsion. Apparently, no one wondered about this, and it was not until I was in my twenties and began to read psychoanalytic theory that I suspected that the revulsion had something to do with forced oral copulation. With this connection in mind, I took a bite of a banana and it was just fine. Over the next twenty years I discovered bits of memories and became aware of sexual arousal in the presence of a certain swarthy type of man. I started filling in the picture of sexual molestation by a tenant who had rented a basement apartment in our house in New York. It was not until I was in my late forties and the sexual abuse of children had become a prominent issue in the women's movement and then among mental health professionals that I decided to approach the subject more seriously and focused on it in my own analysis. Dream after dream revealed more pieces of the puzzle until I felt certain who it was, what had happened, and how I had reacted. It was with great exaltation that I recalled a dream that went as follows:

> I am my current age in my office, which is in a psychotherapy suite with the usual two doors, for entry and exit. The door from the waiting room to the offices, which is always kept locked, has been opened and a man comes down the hall to my office and forces his way in. He carries a hypodermic needle and tries to force the needle into my mouth. I clench my teeth very tightly and he is unable to get it in.

I was thrilled with the dream because it meant to me that I fought back, that I did not allow the penetration of my mouth after the first successful attempt. I was clever enough as a 2- or 3-year-old to know that if I clenched my teeth shut, the abuser could not get his penis in my mouth again, just as my mother could not force in another spoonful of unwanted food. This fit with the other times in my life when I have fought back against unwanted sexual advances, and I was pleased with myself as a fighter rather than a victim, starting at age $2\frac{1}{2}$.

What is important about this story is how well repressed the memories were and that I have never been able to remember the actual moments of the abuse itself, only the man, the location, the symptoms that followed, and the long-term effects. I have utmost confidence in the knowledge of what happened, even without the actual memory, and this personal experience was a great help to me in my work with my own patients who struggled with memories of sexual abuse. The work is like putting together a huge jigsaw puzzle of 1,000 pieces. You start with one piece and, very gradually, other pieces fit. Starting from the outside, you build the frame and then fill in the picture. Years later you have assembled all but the final few pieces in the center, and those pieces are nowhere to be found. The other 995 pieces fit together, so the picture is quite clear except for that missing part at the center, the precise memory, which has been lost because it was so horrendous, such a brutal and terrifying attack, that in order to survive you dissociated yourself, psychically removed yourself from your body in order to preserve your sanity and wholeness. Those moments of terror and rage are gone forever, and perhaps it is best that they are, so that you are never forced to live them again in memory.

And yet some women do remember incest and other kinds of sexual molestation. What is the difference between those who remember and those who forget, and for whom it may take years of psychoanalysis or psychotherapy before the memories start to emerge? First, it appears that not all children dissociate the event when it occurs, and therefore the sexual abuse is not split off or repressed (depending on the developmental stage at which the abuse occurred). The difference between those who dissociate and those who do not would include the degree of fear, danger, pain, and humiliation involved. The more brutal, painful, and frightening the assault, the more likely it will be disassociated. How important the perpetrator is in the life of the child may be a factor in remembering but is not the primary factor. I believe the brutality is the major factor. In *DSM-III-R* (1987), the diagnosis "Dissociative Disorders or Hysterical Neurosis, Dissociative Type" refers to "Dissociative Disorder Not Otherwise Specified," 300.15. Category 3 is called "trance states": "altered states of consciousness with markedly diminished or selectively focused responsiveness to environmental stimuli. In children, this may occur following physical abuse or trauma" (p. 159).

Another factor may be age. Certainly abuse occurring in the preverbal stage could not be remembered verbally but perhaps only with feelings and images. A third factor may be the degree of guilt experienced by the child. A child who may have sought out or welcomed attention and affection from an adult and experienced pleasure with some genital fondling is more likely to believe herself or himself responsible for a sexual attack that follows. The sense of complicity can create so much guilt owing to an exaggerated sense of power vis-à-vis the adult that total repression or splitting off of both the event and the affect associated with it occurs as a defense against the shame, fear, and guilt. Many patients who do remember the event have repressed the affect, and so for them the task in therapy is to recall the affect and see how those feelings relate to current problems of trust, shame, guilt, and fear in relationships. A fourth factor would be the child's assessment of whether there is anyone he or she can tell about the molestation and whether the telling produces sympathetic and helpful listening and protection from further abuse. The child who does not tell anyone—friend, family, or teacher—may well have been threatened with dire consequences if she did, or may have no faith that she will be believed, comforted, or protected and is thus more likely in this actual or imagined hostile atmosphere to repress the memories of the events and the affect associated with them. The child who tries to tell but is ignored is also more likely to repress the memory because there is not only no relief from the anxiety but also an additional trauma of not being believed or taken seriously. One unusual form that the splitting off may take is in the creation of multiple personalities. Sexual abuse, physical abuse, and even ritualistic torture are common in the childhood of those with the multiple personality disorder.

In order for an adult to remember what has been repressed, conditions of safety and trust must be created that alter the sense of danger and shame. The therapist must be open to hearing about the abuse and may be tested by the patient several times to see if the clues are picked up and if there is a reaction of criticism, condemnation, anxiety, or disgust. The importance of the receptivity of the therapist is illustrated by the patients who do not tell several therapists and then find one who they feel safe to tell or safe to remember with.

THE CONTRIBUTIONS OF FEMINISM TO
PSYCHOANALYSIS AND PSYCHOTHERAPY

It may be hard for those younger than 35 to imagine what life was like in the United States before the women's movement. Prior to 1970, many of the subjects that are now commonly written about, discussed, and dramatized on television and in movies were secret—totally taboo to talk about, except perhaps to one's very closest friend or family, but sometimes to no one. This includes abortion; breast cancer; hysterectomy; premenstrual tension; rape; sexual molestation of children, physical abuse of children; wife battering; sexual harassment on the job; sex between therapist or physician and patient, lawyer and client, pastor and parishioner, teacher and student; as well as the more general negative effects on female development of being raised in a society riddled with patriarchal biases in all social institutions and fields of knowledge. In a parallel movement, alcoholism and its effects on the families of alcoholic mothers and fathers also was revealed and explored, and the connections between alcoholism and incest and other forms of physical abuse and neglect of children have emerged.

It was the courageous women of the women's movement who, breaking all taboos, exposed and explored these issues so that the public became aware and alert. Psychotherapists were forced to face the facts in order to be able to help their patients to reveal and work on their secrets. Many of those who were helped to recognize abuse in their own lives went to school and became psychotherapists and counselors to help others. As these dark and ugly stories were brought out of shame and secrecy into the daylight, the chance to recognize the symptoms and work through the traumatic effects gave psychotherapists new opportunities for helping our patients.

In this chapter and the next, I am going to focus on three major areas where feminists have crusaded and where psychoanalysis and psychotherapy have been influenced and have responded, although with some defensiveness and resistance: battered women, childhood sexual abuse, and therapist–patient sexual relations. There are similarities among all three topics because in each case the issue of who is to blame meets with highly emotionally charged debate. In the case of the battered woman, is she masochistic, unconsciously inviting brutal treatment in order to sustain her image as a martyr, or is she a woman of such low self-esteem that she does not believe she has the right to protect herself or protest? Is the molested child in fact the seducer, a "Lolita" who deserves no sympathy, or the innocent victim of a perverted male or, in some cases, female perpetrator? In the case of a woman who has sex with her therapist, is the therapist a victim of the woman's overpowering sexual seduction, or as some have claimed, is sex in some cases really for the patient's benefit? Or is the predominantly male therapist the exploiter of an already sexually damaged woman, using her for his own fantasy of power? The former explanation in each case is the traditional patriarchal rationalization, which unfortunately was taken up and made into theory by psychoanalysis, most well known in Freud's case of Dora. The latter explanation in each case is the feminist view, which does not explore the ambivalent and often unconscious forces at work propelling a child to seek out desperately needed attention and the adult to compulsively reenact earlier traumatic experience. The psychoanalytic view failed to appreciate the powerful cultural factors at work in the degree of power and control held by adult males and the economic and emotional dependency of women and children on men. The feminist view looked at the overt content and did not explore the many pulls in the mind of the victim, the factors of reenactment and of oedipal triumph.

In discussing each of these three subjects I will first review the available statistics to indicate how widespread the problem is, then review the literature on the psychology of the perpetrator and the psychology of the victim, explore the long-term effects on the victim, and deal with treatment approaches. Case histories will complete the discussion. It is with an integration of the best of psychoanalytic theory and practice and the best of feminist theory and practice that I believe we can get the fullest picture of the factors contributing to these tragic events and thus have the most up-to-date knowledge and understanding to help our patients who may be either victims or perpetrators of the sexual and aggressive exploitation of women and children.

BATTERED WOMEN

Psychoanalysis, Psychiatry, and Female Masochism

One area where psychoanalysis and feminism have clashed severely is in the understanding of the phenomenon of battered women. Battered wives or girlfriends, like women who are raped, have often been held in contempt by men with the view that they "deserved it," "liked it," "needed it," or "provoked it." Unfortunately, some of that contempt has contaminated the thinking and practice of psychotherapists. The work of Helene Deutsch and other analysts on the essential role of masochism in women's nature distorted the view of the profession so that women have been blamed for their own victimization. One study, published in *Archives of General Psychiatry,* concluded: "We see the husband's aggressive behavior as filling masochistic needs of the wife and necessary for the wife's (and the couple's) equilibrium" (Snell 1964, p. 110). One wonders what they think of the couple's equilibrium when the wife is dead. Another report, published in *Medical Aspects of Human Sexuality,* advises: "The masochist must be forced to bear responsibility for his plight. A woman who had been choked several times phoned me late one night to say that her husband was again choking her. I replied 'What right do you have to place your neck between his hands?' " (Kaunitz 1977, pp. 79–80).

In my view, both of these psychiatrists are having strong countertransference reactions to their women patients. I suggest that Dr. Kaunitz strongly dislikes his patient and that when she calls him at night in an emergency situation, he would like to choke her. He identifies completely with the husband and turns his hostility on her in a vicious and surely unprofessional manner. And since when do psychiatrists "force" their patients to "bear responsibility" or to do anything else other than pay the bill? One hopes his patient quit after that demeaning response, but more likely she did not and continued to reenact her most likely brutal childhood with her psychiatrist, like her husband, in the role of the brutalizer. What is amazing to me is that a medical journal accepted this article for publication! I certainly hope that someone called Dr. Kaunitz to task for acting out in the countertransference.

There are biological differences between men and women that play a role in the predominance of men among the perpetrators of domestic violence, and these factors are simple to recognize. The likelihood that the man is physically larger and more muscular than the woman is obvious, and the role of testosterone in aggression has been demonstrated in studies across species, but even the basic biological tendency for aggression is shaped by cultural norms. Women have heard these tales or been the victims of such abuse with a sigh of resignation and acceptance that this is the lot of woman, that "it's a man's world" and that "suffering is part of a woman's life." Wife beating has been such a traditional part of marriage that jokes and tales, such as these proverbs with which I introduced this chapter, have taken it for granted. Many people do not know the origin of the expression "the rule of thumb," which dates to medieval times when English law declared that a man could not beat his wife with a stick wider than his thumb. It is the task of a psychotherapist who sees a woman with such historically determined attitudes to question the wisdom of her acquiescence to such demeaning views of women and to such dangerous attacks. Her life may depend upon it. Wife beating exists in many cultures and across many centuries, but I do not know if it exists in all cultures and times. The common image of the cave man dragging away his woman by her hair with a club in his hand may be accurate or may be a male fantasy and projection, but in either case it is part of our common lore.

An article about Jordan by Milton Viorst (1991), published in *The New Yorker,* is illuminating about Islamic culture. In the context of writing about the Jordanian response to the Iraqi invasion of Kuwait, Viorst interviewed a Jordanian woman, Toujan Faisal, a university graduate who was an announcer on the national television station in 1988 and was assigned to cover women's affairs. She became the hostess of "Women's Issues," a series that covered different problems of special interest to women, which turned out to be the most controversial series in the history of Jordanian television. The show that stirred up "the most frenzy" was on wife beating. Faisal says:

> The fundamentalists tried to have that particular program banned before it went on the air. Afterward, the local newspapers received hundreds of letters of protest from outraged men. The letters were unbelievably sadistic. They maintained that it was a God-given right for men to beat women, and that my program was challenging God's order. [p. 50]

According to Faisal's description, the Muslim woman is kept powerless by her total economic dependency. Her husband often takes her property and income. He can have three or four wives and divorce and remarry at will. The divorced wife can be thrown out of her house, be left destitute, and lose her children. No woman, no matter what her social rank, is protected. Faisal became a student of the Koran and learned that the mistreatment of women was nowhere authorized in the scriptures. It was a tradition established and enforced by men in their own self-interest. She was then able to rebut the fundamentalists by quoting directly from the Koran, but she was called a heretic. After a year of threats, the Ministry of Information took the program off the air and Faisal decided to run for Parliament, campaigning on, among other things, a proposal to amend Jordanian family law to give women greater rights. Because of this the fanatics brought charges of apostasy against her in a religious court, for which she faced penalties including dissolution of her marriage and separation from her children. In addition, her accusers called for the lifting of punishment from any Muslim who might choose to assassinate her. She had to campaign for office and attend hearings with police protection and bodyguards, while her husband and family were constantly subjected to harassment and intimidation. Her husband, a gynecologist, eventually had to close his clinic and find work out of the country. In the election, she came in third in a field of six, but there was evidence of irregularities. Since the election she continues to be denounced as a heretic from the pulpits and is unable to find work. Unfortunately the abuse she suffered will, she believes, discourage other women from running for office for a long time.

The situation in Jordan is merely an exaggeration of the attitudes in the contemporary Christian world. Wife beating had been considered a husband's right and duty until women's activists challenged the police, the courts, and all of society's attitudes by coming to the defense of battered women. The right of a husband to beat his wife was part of the law in this country until 1974, and de facto until quite recently. Estimates vary, but a commonly quoted figure is that between 25 and 30 percent of all wives have been beaten at least once by their husbands.

Statistical Estimates and the Role of the Police

The fear of violence in American society focuses on the lack of safety in the streets, yet violence occurs in as many as 50 percent of American families. Violence between spouses is not limited to any particular social or ethnic group(s). Although the highest reported incidence is among the poor, this may reflect a reporting bias in that poor people are more likely to come to the attention of public agencies. However, the strains of poverty and unemployment may contribute to wife and child abuse. About 40 percent of female homicides are committed by husbands, whereas 10 of male victims are killed by wives. Wives are seven times more likely than husbands to have killed in self-defense. Police are called for domestic disputes more than for all other criminal incidents combined, and one-fifth of all police fatalities occur while intervening in family fights (Carmen,

1982). The *New York Times* reports 32 percent of assaults against officers and 16 percent of officers' deaths nationwide occur while responding to these disputes (Nix 1986, p. 12).

Another way to appreciate the breadth of the problem is with statistics that show that every 6 hours a woman is killed in the United States by someone who has been her husband or lover and that every 13 seconds in this country a woman is beaten (Salter 1990). This translates to 4 million American women beaten annually and 2,000 to 4,000 murdered. In San Francisco there are twice as many family violence as drug-related killings, and wife beating results in more injuries to women than auto accidents, rapes, and muggings combined. Brody (1992) uses a figure of 6 million women beaten each year by the men they live with.

A study by Levinger (1966) showed that among applicants for divorce who cited physical cruelty as grounds, 40.1 percent of the lower-class wives and 22.8 percent of the middle- and upper-class wives considered physical abuse a major factor in their decision to seek a divorce. Alcohol is a factor in some cases, with estimates ranging from 30 to 48 percent. One woman who helped bring to light that even professional, well-educated, successful men can be wife beaters was Charlotte Fedders, wife of John M. Fedders, the former chairman of the Securities and Exchange Commission who resigned when details of their divorce papers were publicized, revealing years of psychological and physical abuse. Her book *Shattered Dreams* (1987) recounts the years of their marriage. She was one of those testifying in December 1990 when Senator Joseph Biden, chairman of the Senate Judiciary Committee, held hearings to consider the first federal legislation dealing with domestic violence, which would triple federal spending for battered women's shelters and subject abusers to stringent penalties.

Edmund Stubbing, a retired police officer and former director of the Domestic Violence Prevention Project in Queens, New York, described the incidence of domestic violence as an "epidemic" (Nix 1986). In the 103rd Precinct, with 82,000 residents, 5,400 families called the police about domestic violence in 1985–1986, a number that officials said was "alarming." About 70 percent of the victims are women, which represents the nationwide average. Starting in the mid-1980s there has been a national trend in police departments away from seeing domestic disputes as a family affair and toward arresting men or women who seriously beat spouses or companions. An officer in the precinct reported that when the police arrive, many men don't think the situation serious and say, "You can't arrest me, this is my wife." In many cases the offenders are jailed, even if the victims do not file formal complaints. Detective Joseph F. Ryan stated: "In the 1960's and 1970's we practiced 'crisis intervention.' Officers would take the men out for a walk around the block or tell them to cool down. Now the message is getting across—domestic violence is no longer a family affair'' (Nix, 1986, p. 12).

What was responsible for bringing about the change in policy on the part of the New York City Police Department was that in 1984 a woman named Josephine Sorichetti, who had begged repeatedly for police protection after her husband attacked her with a butcher knife, won a $2 million damage award for New York City's failure to protect her. The Police Department changed its policy dramatically, and instead of trying to mediate disputes they began making arrests. The policy change, part of a national trend, resulted in an increase of 62 percent in arrests for assault in domestic violence cases. As a result of the fact that in other states as well, courts are making large damage awards to victims who are not properly protected by the police, seven states as of 1986 had laws that required arrests in domestic assault cases. This is a good example of how feminist political and legal activism can change policy, which can then protect women's lives.

Family History and Characteristics of Battered Women

"I always felt there was something wrong with me," Mrs. J. said. "I tried so hard to be a good wife and a good mother, and he was never happy. . . . To me, the most important thing in my life was to get married and have children and have a nice family. ["Holiday Appeal," 1986, p. 82]

These quotes are from a December 1986 *New York Times* article on psychotherapy for abused wives. Mrs. J., who had 2 children, had given up her job to be a full-time mother. As a result of individual therapy at Staten Island Family Service and after obtaining a part-time job, she separated from her husband, an alcoholic and cocaine user. She described her marriage as follows:

Dishes were smashed, food scattered around the kitchen, pictures flung from the walls, and freshly ironed laundry trampled underfoot. . . . [she] was called "every curse word under the sun" in front of her family and her friends. She was pushed and shoved and once, hurled against a wall. . . . For nearly a decade, she quietly swept up the broken china, nursed her injured feelings and ignored her bruises, making excuses to herself and others on behalf of her husband. She feared financial ruin if she left him. [p. 82]

Mrs. J. shows many of the common qualities of battered women. She is strongly identified as a traditional woman in a hyperfeminine way, wanting little more from life than to please her husband, be a good mother, and have a nice home and family. She had become financially dependent on her husband and could not imagine how she could care for herself and children without him. Her self-esteem was so low that she blamed herself for his violent, alcoholic rages against her.

Feminists took up the cause of the battered woman in the mid-1970s with a series of books: *Scream Quietly or the Neighbors Will Hear* by Erin Pizzey (1974, English edition), followed by *The Violent Home* by Richard Gelles (1974), *Violence in the Family* by Suzanne Steinmetz and Murray Straus (1974), *Battered Wives* by Del Martin (1976), *Battered Women* by Maria Roy (1977), *Conjugal Crime* by Terry Davidson (1978), and *The Battered Woman* by Lenore Walker (1979). Leidig (1981) gives a feminist analysis of violence against women:

> From a feminist perspective, the reasons for violence toward women involve a male-dominated culture in terms of power, economics, and control over women's bodies. A male-dominated culture needs and maintains anti-woman behaviors because it is to men's advantage in maintaining their position of power vis-à-vis women. . . . violence cannot occur where there is complete equality. From a feminist analysis sexism—not general "violence in America," external stress, alcohol, or psychological abnormality—is a major foundation if not the foundation for violence against women. . . . Instead of seeing these male behaviors as abnormal, deviant, or "sick," it seems far more parsimonious to theorize that these very behaviors on the part of men are to some extent socially accepted behaviors. . . . To the extent that males are reinforced for dominance, taking control of women, and the overt expression of strong anger, the man who displays violence against women . . . may well be the perfectly socialized male. [pp. 203–204]

Feminist influence even reached into the traditional women's magazines on this topic. The October 1986 issue of *Glamour* featured an article entitled "Would Your Man Ever Beat You? How to Recognize a Potential Batterer," by Helen Benedict, the author of *Recovery: How to Survive Sexual Assault* (1985). She cites the statistic that 20 to 25 percent of all American women are victims of serious assault by their mates and instructs the reader to search for warning signs, quoting Evan Stark, a sociologist who says "If he's hit you once, he'll do it again."

The Cycles of Violence

Lenore Walker's work (1979) introduced the theory of the "cycles of violence." If battering occurs more than twice in a relationship, a three-phase cycle appears to be established that varies in both time and intensity for the same couple and between different couples. The definition of a battered woman is a woman who stays in the relationship after two incidents of physical violence. Situational events will influence timing. The cycle can take place over years, months, or days, with some battering episodes occurring daily and in other cases separated by a year or two.

Phase 1: Tension Building

Minor incidents occur.

Woman tries to calm man, using whatever she thinks might work.

Woman denies feeling angry, denies terror: both increase.

She feels there is not much she can do.

He attempts to act out only in private.

He becomes fearful that she will leave him, because he knows his behavior is not appropriate.

He becomes more jealous and possessive.

There is a delicate balance between the two.

She withdraws more and more.

Minor incidents increase.

Tension becomes unbearable.

Phase 2: Acute Battering Incident

Uncontrollable discharge of tension has built up in Phase 1.

Man loses control over his behavior.

He starts out wanting to teach woman a lesson, not to hurt her.

He tries to justify his behavior with something she did.

Briefer phase than others: 2 to 24 hours.

Men do not remember much during incident; women do.

She tries to wait out the storm rather than fighting back, thinks she would be hurt more if she did.

Anticipation of this causes severe psychological stress for woman; inability to sleep, loss of appetite or overeating, constant fatigue, headaches, and so on.

Attack is usually followed by shock, denial and disbelief.

Both people try to rationalize.

Women do not seek help during Phase 2 unless badly hurt, and tend to return to partner from emergency room.

Phase 3: Kindness and Contrite Loving Behavior

Welcomed by both.

He knows he went too far and tries to make it up to her.

Victimization of woman becomes complete.

Period of unusual calm.

He is sorry, begs forgiveness, and promises never to do it again.

He is sincere and believes he can control himself.

She wants to believe him.

She sees how wonderful he can be.

Traditional notion that Love Conquers All prevails.

He reminds her of how much he needs her.

Each is dependent on the other, bonding occurs.

Hard to break bond in Phase 3.

Both want to make their relationship work. (See Walker, pp. 56–69.)

Walker lists the following as characteristic of the women:

Low self-esteem.

Believes myths about battering relationships.

Believes in family unity and prescribed stereotype of the female sex role; a traditionalist about the home.

Willing to accept responsibility for the batterer's actions.

Suffers from guilt while denying the anger and fear she feels.

Presents a passive personality but has strength to prevent further violence and to prevent her being killed.

Has severe stress reactions with psycho-physical complaints.

Uses sex to establish intimacy.

Believes no one can help her resolve her predicament.

Martyrlike behavior.

Emotionally and/or economically dependent on husband.

Family history of domestic violence.

Accepts violence in the hope that she will be able to help husband change; believes she provoked anger and violence.

Gives in to husband's demands in order to protect children and pets.

Was physically and/or sexually abused as a child or saw violence at home.

Often employed but not allowed to control finances.

Loses contact with her family due to embarrassment or forced isolation; may maintain contact with husband's mother.

Traditional expectations of husband as provider and of self as mother and wife. (See Walker, pp. 31–35.)

Why Does She Stay?

The question most often asked is Why does the abused woman remain in the relationship? Why does she not leave? The fact that so many women do stay, or leave and return, is used as evidence that she is masochistic and an active participant in the abuse, even the provoker of the abuse, and that she is getting something out of it, "enjoys it." But leaving, especially with children, is no simple matter, and often constitutes "escape" rather than just leaving, because some of the most brutal, and many fatal, attacks against women occur when they leave. As many as three-quarters of reported domestic assaults take place after the woman has left. The establishment of shelters for battered women and their children, also an outgrowth of the women's movement, has recognized this problem, and the location of the shelters remains hidden so that the man cannot track the woman down. There are about 1,200 shelters throughout the country now, many reporting they must turn away three out of four women who ask for help (Hoffman 1992, pp. 22–27, 65–72). Without shelters, men have gone to the homes of family and friends, found the woman and severely beaten and even murdered her for leaving. Thus the simple question of why she doesn't just leave reveals ignorance of the nature of the problem.

On March 9, 1992, Shirley Lowery, a 51-year-old grandmother of eleven, was murdered by a man she had just left. She was stabbed nineteen times in the hallway outside the hearing room in the courthouse in Milwaukee, Wisconsin, where she had gone to obtain a restraining order against Benjamin Franklin, her former live-in companion. Dr. Carole Warshaw, a psychiatrist who served in the emergency room at Cook County Hospital for eight years, reported in the *New York Times*, "The greatest risk of getting killed is when the woman attempts to leave, as we've just seen in Milwaukee" (Terry 1992, p. A7). This story also reports the latest available Federal Bureau of Investigation statistics, which show that in 1990, 30 percent of 4,399 women identified as murder victims in this country were killed by their boyfriends or husbands.

Walker lists the abused woman's roadblocks: lack of money, lack of job skills, threats to her children, loss of custody, fear of loneliness, fear of even more violence or death, and love and concern for the batterer. Most important, attempts to pacify the batterer fail repeatedly, depression follows, self-esteem and assertiveness diminish, and initiative crumbles. The condition of the battered woman has been compared with that of a hostage who has been brainwashed and tortured. Repeated verbal abuse gradually destroys her ego, so that when the physical abuse begins she is already psychologically stripped naked and is extremely vulnerable. Verbal abuse frequently involves being called a whore, ugly, fat, stupid, and being told that she can't do anything right and that no other man would ever want her.

Dutton and Painter (1981), using a behaviorist model, studied battered wives and introduced a theory of "traumatic bonding" to explain why the women do not leave. They point out that the beating leaves the women exhausted, emotionally and physically hurt and drained, and thus in more than usual need of some human warmth and comfort. It is just at this point that the men are feeling guilty and frightened by their loss of control, by having "gone too far," and move into what Walker described as Phase 3, "Kindness and contrite loving behavior." Thus, whatever warmth or affection these men offer tends to be accepted by the women because they are in such need. Their theory emphasizes that it is not the abusive side of their abusers to which these women bond, but rather to the warmer, affectionate side that meets their needs to be loved and cared for.

Workers in shelters and therapists in this field describe abused women as readily accepting blame projected toward them and often taking full responsibility for their marital problems. Battered women need to be needed. Their husbands seem to be utterly dependent on them, both for emotional support and as an outlet for tension. The wives care for their husbands as patiently as mothers care for their 2-year-old sons, regardless of incessant demands and frequent temper tantrums. In return, they believe their husbands cannot live without them, which gives them a certain sense of importance. It is this aspect that may answer the question of what the women get out of it.

The central issue is control. The husband is the head of the house, and his wife considers herself subordinate to him. Control is maintained by the husband through isolation, humiliation, economic deprivation, sexual abuse and starvation, in addition to the physical violence and threats of violence. The relationship can come to resemble one of prisoner and prison guard, with the woman living under house arrest. Symptoms of severe depression, disorganized and tangential thinking, and paranoia can result. It takes about four days of safety in a shelter for the worst of these symptoms to clear away.

Battered Women—A Clinical Sample

In reporting on research done with a clinical population, Elaine Hilberman Carmen (1982), an associate professor in the Department of Psychiatry at the School of Medicine in Chapel Hill, North Carolina, urges psychotherapists to ask women about violence. In her sample of sixty battered women, fifty-six were identified only because they were asked. As a checklist for therapists, she proposes the following constellation of symptoms and circumstances that are closely correlated with wife abuse:

1. Violence and/or child abuse in families of origin.
2. Suspected physical or sexual abuse of children in the family.
3. Multiple somatic, emotional, behavioral, and sleep problems in the children.
4. Aggressive and destructive behavior in teenage sons.
5. Alcoholism and pathological jealousy in the husband.
6. Multiple somatic complaints, frequent medical visits, and chronic use of tranquilizers and analgesics by the wife.
7. Severe agitation, anxiety, insomnia, and dreams with violent themes reported by the wife.
8. Chronic depressive symptoms and a history of repeated suicidal behavior. [p. 62]

The sample of women studied were forty black and twenty white women, ranging in age from 19 to 82, who were from rural mill and tenant-farm families with high unemployment rates and severe economic stress. They were referred by the medical staff of a small health clinic for psychiatric evaluation and were found to be victims of marital violence. In only four cases was the referring clinician aware of the violence, although the patients had received ongoing medical care at the clinic. As the psychiatric evaluation progressed, the clinicians were struck by the paralyzing anxiety among the patients, which they found was linked to physical abuse.

> Lifelong violence was the pattern for many of these women, who gave remarkably similar histories. Violence between their parents (usually the father assaulting the mother), paternal alcoholism, and physical and/or sexual abuse as children were described by half of the women. The men also were said to have had early exposure to emotional deprivation, alcoholism, lack of protection, and violence, both as witnesses and as abused children. Suicides and homicides among family members and neighborhood acquaintances were common occurrences and were usually committed with guns.
>
> Most of the women had left home at an early age to escape from violent, pathologically jealous, and seductive fathers, who kept their wives and daughters imprisoned at home. The usual age of marriage was 16 and many of the women had been pregnant or had had children prior to marriage. Once married . . . [they replicated] exactly their lives prior to marriage. Alcoholism was said to be a significant problem for all but four husbands in this sample. . . .

The violent relationship is one of extraordinary intensity. When not aggressive, the men were described as childlike, remorseful, and yearning for nurturance; this picture of fragility was confirmed by the occasional reports of the husband's suicidal or psychotic behavior when there was any threat to dissolve the relationship. The women, understandably, felt quite sorry for them because they often shared similar histories of deprivation and abuse. Since the men could never understand or acknowledge a termination without murderous rage, these marriages became life sentences for their wives. . . .

In this study, many women had left their marriages for brief periods, but they inevitably returned. Their return was related to economic dependence on their husbands and threats of further violence, from which they had no protection.

They felt drained, fatigued, and numb, and without energy to do more than minimal household chores and child care. There was a pervasive sense of hopelessness and despair about themselves and their lives. They saw themselves as incompetent, unworthy, and unlovable women and were ridden with guilt and shame. They felt that they deserved the abuse, had no vision that there was any other way to live, and were powerless to make changes. . . . [yet] at times they fought back with kitchen knives, broom handles, frying pans, hot grease and lye, hammers, screwdrivers, and, rarely, guns . . . the use of violence by the women was related to a direct threat of [sic] life and usually came as a surprise, since they themselves were unaware of the extent of their rage. [pp. 50, 51, 53, 58]

But the good news is that even these women were able to benefit from psychotherapy. Passivity was reduced, plans for employment, vocational training, education, and termination of the marriage occurred. However, therapists are warned that

because of the real possibility of escalating violence as a result of the changes in her behavior, it is stressed that the woman should not be pushed to move beyond what she feels are safe boundaries in terms of her acknowledgment of anger or actions to confront her husband. The clinician must assume that her assessment of her own controls, the extent of the danger to herself and children, and her husband's potential for violence are accurate. [p. 61]

Medicine and Battering

As women have entered medicine in large numbers, their influence is being felt at the highest levels of the medical establishment. The June 17, 1992 issue of *JAMA,* the journal of the American Medical Association, is devoted to the role of the physician in treating the victims of violence. Article after article calls for increased attention to domestic violence by physicians in emergency rooms and as part of routine examination and in response to complaints of physical or mental distress by women patients.

In one article (Randall 1992), the president of the American College of Obstetricians and Gynecologists (ACOG), Richard F. Jones, calls for a campaign against domestic violence and announces a four-part program emphasizing both physician and patient education. The issue of domestic violence will now be part of both undergraduate and graduate medical training programs, including special emphasis on the identification of battered women, appropriate interventions, and legal issues. The campaign of ACOG will also encourage physicians to become advocates for resources needed by battered women.

Jones reports that he had no idea how often his patients experienced violence until he changed the questions he asked them: "When I saw a women with black and blue marks in my office, I used to ask her how she got them. This gave her the obvious opportunity to say 'I'm clumsy' or 'I live with a big dog who jumps on me' or 'I take aspirin so I bleed easily.' " About two years ago he began to ask directly: "Have you been hit or harmed any time in the past year? Are you in any danger? [or] Is someone doing this to you?" He says he was "stunned" by the responses. "Whereas, in the past, I would confront a case of battering a few times a year, now I was confronting these cases two or three times a week. I had viewed myself as a reasonably perceptive, reasonably kind and caring physician—and I had missed all this. . . . Surely others have as well" (p. 3131).

The same issue of *JAMA* includes a strong statement by Antonia C. Novello, the surgeon general of the United States:

> Domestic violence is an extensive, pervading, and entrenched problem in the United States. It is an outrage to women and the entire American family.
>
> Health care providers must take an active, vigorous role in identifying this serious recurrent public health problem. This is not a "minor dispute" between spouses or loved ones. It is a violation of our criminal laws and a callous disregard for human life. . . . One essential solution is for physicians to increase their awareness. . . . Finally physicians must step forward and help establish broad-based community coalitions to enhance awareness of domestic violence. We must assume the leadership role that is incumbent on us as professionals and compassionate citizens of this country. [p. 3132]

A report by Sugg and Inue (1992) of their research among primary care physicians describes the barriers to recognition of and intervention in the problems of domestic violence. These include the fear of "opening Pandora's box," close identification with patients of their own socioeconomic background leading to denial, fear of offending, feelings of frustration and inadequacy, loss of control, and the tyranny of the time schedule.

The report of the Council on Scientific Affairs of the AMA includes disturbing figures on battering during pregnancy. The 1985 National Family Violence Survey found that 154 out of every 1,000 pregnant women were assaulted by their mates during the first four months of pregnancy, and 117 per 1,000 were assaulted during the fifth through the ninth months, amounting to 37 percent of obstetric patients across class, race, and educational lines.

The Council report also states that in a review of fifty-two studies with comparison groups, only one of forty-two potential risk markers for women—having witnessed parental violence—was consistently associated with having been battered. They concluded that "the symptoms that most battered women exhibit appear most likely to be sequelae of the violence rather than its antecedents" (p. 3186).

The report of the Council on Ethical and Judicial Affairs reiterates the recommendations of other reports, urging physicians to routinely inquire about abuse as part of the medical history, to consider battering in the differential diagnosis for a number of medical complaints, and to be familiar with community resources. In addition, the report states that physicians have a duty to be aware of societal misconceptions about domestic violence, including the idea that victims are responsible for the abuse.

The Catholic Church and Battering

In September 1992, the nation's Roman Catholic bishops made their first statement on spouse abuse (Bishops denounce abusive husbands, 10/30/92, *New York Times,* p. A16) declaring that nothing in the Bible requires women to submit to abusive husbands or to remain in abusive relationships. It also urges parish priests to provide a safe place for battered women seeking help. In the document the bishops express concern about how biblical passages encouraging wives to be submissive to husbands have been taken out of context to justify spouse abuse, distorting the intent of the biblical text. This surely is progress reflecting the efforts of activist women in the Catholic Church.

The Male Batterer

Walker lists the following characteristics of the male batterer:

> Low self-esteem but believes in male supremacy.
> Believes myths about battering relationships.

Believes in stereotyped masculine sex role in the family; a traditionalist.

Projects blame onto others for his actions.

Paranoid jealousy—accuses wife of having affairs.

Shows marked personality changes.

Uses drinking and wife battering to cope with stress.

Often uses sex as an act of aggression to enhance self-esteem.

Believes his violent behavior should not have negative consequences.

Low frustration tolerance, poor impulse control, explosive temper; external locus of control.

Emotionally dependent on wife and children; a loner.

Family history of domestic violence.

Accepts violence as viable method of problem solving and maintaining the family intact.

As a control mechanism, often abuses or threatens children and pets.

Was physically and/or sexually abused as child or saw "significant other" abused by spouse (usually mother by father).

High degree of job dissatisfaction, under- or unemployment, which leads to feelings of inadequacy.

Maintains close contact with his own family.

Unrealistic expectations of relationship.

Preoccupation with weapons. (See Walker, pp. 36–41.)

Hunt (1977) believes that the major point that must be made about wife abuse is that it is not a problem of a few "sick" individuals. Gelles (1972) points out that many wife beaters cannot be categorized as sick at all, in the usual sense of the word. The problem must be seen in the context of a society that condones and even encourages the use of power, in the form of physical force if necessary, to coerce women and others who are weaker and therefore vulnerable. Our national foreign policy reflects these values.

In contrast to a traditional psychological view of seeing pathology in either the male or the female individual, the feminist view of a "sick" patriarchal society blames the culture. The male therapists who have gotten involved in the treatment of the male batterer tend to follow the feminist view of seeing the source of the problem in the patriarchal culture, that is, the ideal of masculinity and male domination of women. For example, Hamish Sinclair, who runs the men's program at the Marin County Abused Women's Services, treats violent male behavior as a political rather than a clinical problem, not an aberration but an extension of how the culture defines sex roles. As quoted in a *New York Times* article (Gross 1989) he says that

> it has nothing to do with individual experience, neurosis, psychosis or the misuse of anger. It has to do with the fact that we all come out of a patriarchal belief system. We are all trained that we are superior to women and it is our right to punish, discipline or intimidate them. . . . Male behavior falls along a continuum from outright violence to subtle domination, insisting on the last word in arguments and dictating the comings and goings of everyone else in the household. ["Helping men," p. A16]

A men's movement writer, Michael P. McGinnis (1978), also focuses on control, which he considers central to being a man in our culture. A man is taught to control his actions, his behavior, and his emotional self. The primary psychological method used by men to achieve control is denial. Men must continually create defenses against their inner feelings. He believes this constant self-maintenance against inner feelings creates alienation from oneself, a hollow feeling that men are taught to fill with outer, worldly experiences. Self-identity is experienced through others' reflection of behavior, instead of from a sense of emotional self-connectedness; thus a man has a strong dependency upon others to reaffirm his self-concept as meeting the male ideal.

> This puts the male psyche in a very precarious position. The moment a man experiences an unfavorable reflection of who he is, particularly by someone he is intimate with, self-doubt and a lowering of self-esteem occurs. The male feels that somehow he has failed . . . the perceived act of failure becomes internalized as a definition of a man's being—he starts to define himself as a failure.
>
> Not to succeed, achieve or accomplish is experienced by men as a movement away from the rigid, internalized definition of masculinity and it implies a loss of control. It is this perceived loss of control over the situation that I believe to be at the crux of intimate violence. Once a man perceives that he has lost control, his very existential being is in danger and his identity is in danger of being annihilated. Thus control over the situation must be regained at any cost. . . .
>
> I strongly believe that in most cases of wife-abuse, the trigger for a man's violent behavior is his deeply felt fear of loss of control and of identity. The dynamics of trying to live up to the internalized male ideal, coupled with the fear of loss of power and dependency on the spouse is the central dynamic in the battering phenomenon. The withdrawal of care, love or respect in any manifestation is perceived by the dependent male as a threat to his psychological and existential

being. He feels that in order to survive as a man, the frustrating situation
must be brought under control at any and all costs. The physical abuse
of a loved one is such a cost. [unpublished]

A third male writer, Stan Taubman (1986), believes in the validity of
a psychosocial perspective on male violence toward women but states that
to assume patriarchy and not the individual is responsible for the individual's behavior can amount to an apology for violence.

Childhood development, specific trauma, and the dominant culture's
valuation of male dominance might create certain attitudes and tendencies, but the adult individual must be held responsible for managing
these behaviors in a prosocial way. . . . The author views male sex role
acquisition as a process of psychosocial violence against young boys; a
process that creates a lingering sense of shame, powerlessness, self-
alienation, isolation from others, and retaliatory rage, which inhibits
the adult male's capacity for intimacy and mutuality. Coupled with the
culture's apparent legitimation of men's violence toward and domination of women . . . these inhibiting qualities serve to promote and
maintain the high level of exploitation practiced by men in this society.
[p. 13]

Taubman, a social worker, proposes participation of abusive men in
groups and communities that are both confrontational and supportive as
the best means for change. Men need to develop empathy; to learn how to
make requests assertively rather than to make demands aggressively; to
take direction as well as to give it; and to negotiate, compromise, and
accommodate rather than to force compliance when conflict arises.

Allan Regenstrief (1984), a counselor in a San Francisco program for
male batterers, also shares similar views that "compulsive masculinity"
and misogyny are the source of abusiveness. He finds typical defenses to be
denial, minimization, projection, repression, rationalization, identification
with an abusive father (they often regard their father's physical discipline
as having been good for them), dissociation, and displacement. He experiences the major resistance of the men he works with as giving up control
in the relationship and having to learn to negotiate and compromise
around disagreements.

Yet in reading some of the many descriptions of male manipulation
and control of women and physical violence toward them, one is struck by
what appears to be the behavior of a raging maniac. Surely there are
individual diagnostic differences that separate the men who control the
checkbook from those who wield butcher knives. There is a strong
paranoid flavor to the jealousy and possessiveness, and I suspect that many

of these men, as do the women, qualify for a diagnosis of borderline personality disorder.

Edward W. Gondolf, a Pittsburgh sociologist, divides male batterers into two categories: "garden variety," first-time or sporadic offenders; and a more lethal group who are out of reach of group therapy efforts, which he calls "antisocial or even sociopathic batterers"—about 30 percent, who not only resist intervention, but may be further antagonized by it (quoted in Hoffman, 1992, p. 64). He warns women not to be taken in when the man enters counseling, because she may let her guard down and increase the danger to herself. "Counseling is the American way to heal a problem. She'll think, 'If he's trying I should support him' while he's thinking, 'I'll go to the program until I get what I want—my wife back' " (p. 64).

Richard J. Gelles, director of the Family Violence Research Program at the University of Rhode Island, is quoted in the same article as saying that the reason men hit women is "because it works" (p. 64) by breaking down her sense of self-worth and her belief that she can do anything about it. But Ellen Pence, a founder of the Duluth, Minnesota Domestic Abuse Intervention Project (DAIP) in 1982, says that some of the approaches to treatment of the male batterer fail to confront his "hatred of women as well as his desire to dominate them" (p. 64).

There are about 250 programs around the country that are helping some men but that also report some discouraging results. Programs range from 12 weeks to one year and are often court ordered. The program in Duluth is 26 weeks. Since its inception it is estimated that one out of nineteen Duluth men have been through the program and not one Duluth woman died from a domestic homicide. Based on the statistics in the 1970s, there would have been five deaths in this period. But a study in Duluth shows that five years after going through the program and judicial system, fully 40 percent of the men become offenders again, either with the same woman or a new one, and the number of cases that come before the courts in Duluth remains the same, about 450 each year.

Leading a Group for Battered Women

In 1985 I was asked to co-lead a group for battered women. I had no experience in the field but plunged in, doing some reading and counting on my co-leader, Sara Lou D'Ombrain, for her specialized knowledge and experience with battered women. The women had all come to our local battered women's agency for help, but a group outside the agency was necessary to handle the demand. Each member was interviewed by one of the leaders prior to admission to the group, so that we knew something about her background and could rule out psychosis. The group meetings were electric with the intensity of the issues, the emotions of the women,

and the often critical situations they were in. My experience with consciousness-raising groups was very helpful but had not prepared me for the
abundance of trauma in the lives of these women, all living in San
Francisco, mostly white, ages 20 to 60. Most were clerical workers, but
some were college graduates and a few had graduate school education. The
group continued actively for three years, with new members coming in to
replace the women who finished. It was not long before it became clear to
me that being a "battered woman" was the end product of a life of abuse—
physical, psychological, and sexual. These were woman who had never
been protected from predatory men or hostile women as children and
therefore had no sense of a right to protect themselves as adults. Their
sense of entitlement was almost nil. Their pain was less difficult to elicit
than their rage, which had simmered well below the surface for so many
years. The rage, on occasion, was revealed in their angry feelings toward,
and at times abusive treatment of, their own children. The few who could
express anger became the focus of fear and admiration and served as role
models for some of the others. Some never did express anger, but quietly
took action to change their lives. The group was often the first opportunity
these women had to talk about their childhood experiences. It was
riveting, chilling, and at the same time illuminating and thrilling to hear a
woman tell, sometimes for the first time in her life, of incest, psychological
torment, and physical abuse. One woman told of having her stepfather tie
her up regularly and rape her at age 9 and 10, in addition to having a
mother who gave her no love and used her to do all the housework,
isolating her from children her own age. She said she felt like "damaged
goods."

Just as in the consciousness-raising groups, there was the tremendously therapeutic effect of having the attention and encouragement of a
group of women who listened, cared, shared, and respected each other's
experiences and need for dignity. Time and time again a woman would
describe, with minimal affect, terrible treatment from her parents or from
a husband or boyfriend, and the group would rise up in anger in the
woman's defense. The response of the group lent credibility to her
experience and nurtured her soul as she struggled to come to terms with
the impact of the event on her life. As the stories unfolded and as the lack
of self-respect became clearer, it became easier to see the profound
boundary problems these women had and to come to the conclusion that
most of them would be classifiable as borderline personalities. The question of masochism was dwarfed by the ego deficits resulting from the
boundary diffusion from which they suffered. Most of the interpretive
work done by the therapists was on this level.

As the underlying problem of boundary diffusion became clear, and as
some of the initial group members left, we decided to open the group to

anyone with a borderline diagnosis and began to include women from our own private practices. In Chapter 3, I described the positive effect that the group had on one of my patients, Linda, who had had years of individual psychotherapy but who made her greatest changes during her year in the group, when she applied to and was accepted in law school. In the beginning we had encouraged members to be in individual psychotherapy, and as the group expanded, we required it. The intensity of the group experience, especially for those who were revealing secrets of abuse for the first time, required individual time to help the woman deal with the powerful meaning of these events.

In the group, the integration of the cultural, economic, and individual psychological factors in the lives of battered women was accomplished with a combination of feminist and psychoanalytic interpretations. The individual psychodynamics could have been handled in individual therapy, but the value of the group was that the women could see the cultural similarities as they shared their feelings of passivity, helplessness, and dependency on men. The similarities gave the therapists opportunities to point out connections among them and then to relate these connections to the norms and traditions of a society that considers women inferior to men and promotes their dependence on men.

Anger was elicited cautiously by the therapists, but vociferously by group members. As with groups for those with addictions, the value of the group that individual psychotherapy or psychoanalysis cannot provide is that it creates a community of like-minded souls who can understand and empathize and encourage each other. However, because of the boundary diffusion, there were times when what a group member believed was understanding of another woman was really a projection from her own experience. One of the jobs of the therapists was to support a member who was not feeling understood, because in fact she was the recipient of a projection that missed the mark. She may have needed help in separating what in another group member's experience was applicable to her life, and what was different. Being able to say no within a cohesive body such as a woman's group where there is a strong pull for "togetherness" was part of the therapeutic process that led to a greater capacity for differentiation in the members. At times anger flared up in the group, and the members' capacity to disagree and even feel hurt and anger toward another member truly tested their developing ego strength. Keeping the focus on the group rather than on the relationship with the therapist gave more opportunity for testing the capacity for autonomy on a realistic level. The therapists served as facilitators and role models as well as occasionally making interpretations for an individual and on the group process. Here are some examples of both kinds of therapeutic interpretations:

Therapist: Judy, you seem uncomfortable with what Anne just said she thought you were feeling, yet you're nodding your head yes, as if you agreed.

Judy: Well, I guess it isn't the way it happened for me, but I know Anne is trying to be helpful.

Therapist: Anne, you seem hurt and angry that Judy didn't accept your idea. You meant to be helpful, but I think your comment comes from your experience and doesn't really fit for Judy.

Therapist: Cindy, you're describing an experience that sounds terrible for you, yet you're not showing much feeling about it.

Joan: I know exactly what she's going through. You are so frightened when that happens that you just go numb, then you don't know what you're feeling.

Therapist: Cindy, you're being quiet. Do you think Joan is right, that you go numb rather than feel how frightened you are when Jim starts to hit you?

Cindy: (Tentatively) I suppose, I don't know, everything happens so fast that I don't know what I think.

Susan: I know what she means. You can't think about how you're feeling, you're just concentrating on how you can get out alive, trying to save yourself.

Therapist: So it may not be until later, or until you talk about it here in the group that you can let yourself know how terrified you were, when you're in a safe environment.

Therapist: Barbara, I've noticed that you haven't said anything. You've been in the group for several weeks now but we don't know much about you.

Barbara: I've been listening. I like to get to know people before I say anything about myself.

Therapist: Perhaps you need to be sure you can trust the group before you open yourself up to us.

Barbara: Maybe that's it. I do feel good about everyone in the group so far. Maybe next week.

Therapist: Trust is an important issue for you. Based on what you told us the first night you were here, I can imagine that you could never trust your mother or your father to care about your feelings, so it's not surprising you're cautious with us. I hope you can tell us more about yourself next week.

Jeanne: I'm really getting nervous about my job. My boss hasn't been very friendly lately. I'm working so hard and trying to please him but he acts like he just takes it for granted and doesn't ever say anything nice to me.

Therapist: I've noticed how often job problems are similar to problems you have in your relationships with men. Have you noticed how many of the women in the group have trouble feeling good enough about themselves to ask for what they deserve, whether it's from the boss, your parents, or your boyfriends?

Joan: The problem is, I don't know if I deserve anything. I've never done much with my life, I've never had a good relationship, and I'm so worried at my job, I'm always afraid I'll make a mistake and the boss will fire me.

Cindy: Me too. If I could even once feel proud of myself, feel I had done something right, it would make such a difference.

Joan: It's no wonder you never feel like you've done anything right. Your folks were always telling you how stupid and clumsy you were. I have that same problem, but I can really see it now, especially when I hear all of you putting yourselves down and I know it's not true. I think you're all smart, and try hard too, but people don't give women credit for what they know. They just care about you for sex.

Judy: Yeah, you should hear my 11-year-old daughter, already worried about her figure and telling me how ugly she is. She's not beautiful, but she's very sweet looking and it makes me so mad that she already has this low self-image. I guess I know where she got that.

Therapist: Lots of women find it hard to think of themselves as smart and to feel attractive as women too. With all the messages from society telling women they aren't smart or competent, and all the focus on looks, it's not surprising that most of you don't have much self-esteem, especially when you combine that with all the abuse you endured in your families.

Cindy: Sometimes I meet a woman who seems to really feel good about herself and I really envy her. How does she do it?

Judy: Yeah, I have a friend who's really pretty and has a great figure and the guys are always after her. She doesn't take any shit from any of them.

Therapist: Looks help, but I think it goes deeper than that. There isn't one woman in this group who isn't attractive looking; the problem is that nobody ever gave you the feeling that you were loved and special and really cared about. The women who have confidence are the ones who felt that special love and attention that you all missed. It's hard to feel smart and pretty when the most important people in your lives made you feel stupid and ugly and unworthy of love.

Barbara: I guess I'm ready to talk this week. There's something I have to say that is very, very hard to talk about. Well, here goes. My parents were divorced when I was 5, and every summer I would go to visit my father and spend two weeks with him. The summer when I was 12, my father had sex with me. I didn't think I could say no. It was so important to me to have a relationship with him, and to believe he cared about me—I suppose I would have jumped out of a plane if he told me to. It happened several times that summer and then the next summer too. Then he remarried. I never told anyone and felt so ashamed when I went back to my mother's house. When it happened, I thought maybe that meant I was really special to him, that he really liked me, but afterwards I knew he was just using me, that he didn't really love me. He just took advantage of me because I needed his love and approval so badly. It made me feel worthless and awful about myself. When Joe starts to smack me around, I feel he knows what a worthless, terrible person I am. I don't fight back because I feel I deserve bad treatment, after what I did with my father. I hate myself, I hate myself for needing him so much and for letting him do that to me. Sometimes I hate him, too, but I've never said a word to him about it.

Mary: I'm so glad you told us about this. It must have been so hard keeping it a secret all these years. I don't think you should hate yourself at all. After all, you were a child—he shouldn't have done that to you. Now I feel you've really become part of the group, that you trust us, that you could tell us this. That makes me feel good, like now we're your friends.

Joan: Yes, you don't have to be alone with your secret anymore, like I was for so many years before I told my therapist about my uncle feeling me up in bed all the time.

Barbara: All my dad's friends think he's such a great guy. If they only knew.

Therapist: You protect your father and the image of your relationship with him by not telling.

Barbara: Yeah, well probably nobody would believe me anyway, he's so nice to other people. His boss thinks he's the greatest.

Therapist: You keep reenacting the abusive relationship you had with your father by staying with Joe and letting him punish you for the guilt you feel for having sex with your father. You don't think you deserve to be truly loved and respected by a man.

Judy: None of us do. But it's so hard. Sometimes Dale is really nice to me and then I get my hopes up. When he's nice, it's better than it's been with anyone for me. If I leave him I'll be so lonely, and I don't know if I can find anyone better. I'll be alone every night, I'm afraid of getting really depressed, and then I'll probably start eating too much again and get fat. It really scares me.

Jeanne: You could join Weight Watchers. They helped me.

Barbara: Before the incest thing happened, I looked up to my dad so much, I really looked forward to those visits and sometimes he would write me letters. That ruined it for me.

Therapist: That was a terrible loss for you, but you know something, it was a terrible loss for him too. He lost a wonderful daughter, and he can never replace you.

Some women stayed with the group for a year or more and made dramatic changes. Others left after a few weeks or months and we don't know how they did, but they were making decisions for themselves. The women who stayed were able to leave battering relationships. It may be that some of the women who left did so because they felt pressure from the group to leave a relationship when they were not strong enough to make the change or were too ambivalently tied to the man to be objective about him, but they got a taste of another way to live and of the potential for help from other women. The defense mechanism of splitting makes it very difficult for the woman to integrate the good and the bad qualities in the man and make a rational decision that allows action to break the cycle of violence.

An Object Relations Approach to the Phenomenon and Treatment of Battered Women—Irene Gillman

Irene Gillman, co-director of the Center for Psychologically or Physically Abused Persons at Hofstra University in New York, published an article on battered women in 1980 in which she presents her conclusions that these women are not neurotic but borderline, the same conclusion I reached after working with the group. She disagrees with the traditional Freudian view that battered women are neurotic masochists who solve an oedipal conflict by rejecting the male's love and instead provoke his aggression in order to avoid competition with the mother and maintain the mother's love. She finds that these women take far too much physical aggression to warrant calling it "neurotic" behavior, and that they do not have typical neurotic symptoms and defenses. She does not find repression of oedipal conflict in her patients but rather finds the source in preoedipal relations with the mother.

Kernberg (1975) outlines four developmental stages. In the first two stages the images of the self and the other are merged or undifferentiated. In the third, the child has differentiated self from other but has two separate sets of object relations, one good and one bad. In the adult, persistence of this mode of object relatedness results in the defense mechanism called *splitting.* The bad part, or bad mother, is split off from the good part, or good mother, and the bad self is split off from the good self. This is a more primitive mechanism than repression. A good, compliant self-image that is in a positive, loving relation to a warm, giving, good mother image exists separately from a bad self-image in a hateful tie to a depriving or rejecting bad mother image. Defense mechanisms include splitting, projective identification, introjective identification, idealization, omnipotence, and denial. Gillman (1980) states:

> Splitting operates during phase three to reduce the anxiety that the bad image might overwhelm the good if they were allowed to come together. . . . When splitting is used, quite different opposing descriptions of other people by the battered woman are possible, depending on which self-object representation is activated. The woman is unaware of the gross discrepancy in her perceptions of the emotionally significant people in her life. Descriptions by battered women are replete with such contradictory images. For example, "My childhood was completely normal" but "My father beat me with a strap at least once a week." [pp. 348,350]

In phase four, good and bad dyadic relations are joined into a whole object and an integrated self, and the defense mechanism is repression. Gillman believes that a neurotic woman would not take the extreme abuse the borderline woman takes, because the psychic effects of battering would necessarily alter dramatically the woman's attitudes, perceptions, and overall relationship with her husband. Because she cannot deny or split off the self-damaging aspects of the relationship to keep the marriage intact, she is likely to end the marriage or seek therapy. If she cannot get her husband to cooperate in therapy, she is likely to leave him. Gillman refers to the neurotic woman as the "masochistic neurotic" woman. It is not clear why she employs this terminology, unless it is in her effort to differentiate a neurotic woman with a masochistic character from the borderline woman who stays in a battering relationship. However, if a woman is able to leave a man who hits her, why would we describe her as masochistic? She describes the difference as follows:

> The battered woman has two separate and quite distinct dyadic representations: her lovable self in a warm, friendly relation to a good providing husband-mother, and her helpless, worthless self who is in a hateful, destructive relation to a persecuting, damaging husband-mother. When one of these self-object representations is in operation, the other dyadic relation is split off and kept intact and unchanged. After the storm, love can reemerge with the good self-object representation uncontaminated by the bad self-object representation. If not for this splitting process, she would leave him more readily. Splitting preserves the often extended and sometimes loving relationship between husband and wife. [p. 349]

The process may repeat itself with her children. She projects her bad, worthless self onto her child and is cruel to it, feeling justified in acting out the role of her cruel mother. This is different from a mother who can see that her child has good and bad qualities and is ambivalently attached to the child but unlikely to behave sadistically.

> The low self-esteem often seen in battered women is just one part of the battered woman syndrome. Low self-esteem represents an aspect of the bad-self in relation to a persecutory yet guilty mother. When her husband beats her, the battered woman may identify with her own guilty mother. However, at other times, she can assume (via introjective identification) the role of the bad mother and thereby justify her covert aggression toward her husband, who represents the bad-child-self. Thus guilt and low self-esteem can exist side by side with superiority and hostility. [pp. 351–352]

Not surprisingly, this analysis can be applied to the husband, and the man can be diagnosed as borderline as well, thus creating a pathological symbiosis.

> A battered woman will only stay with a man who can assume the role her splitting mechanism demands and into whom she can project her bad parts. Conversely, a battering man could not tolerate a woman who was independent of him, who would assert herself and not assume the guilty role called for by his accusations and attacks. [p. 353]

This view helps to explain the repeated question, often in the form of an accusation, of why the woman does not leave. To do so she would have to stop the splitting, which she fears will destroy the "good object" in the husband, and have no one. That emptiness is a chasm that cannot be crossed until the split objects are replaced by an integrated object. The interim can be terrifying and is only made possible in psychotherapy when the therapist fills that chasm with a steady, reliable, helpful presence.

Gillman never mentions incidents of incest in her paper, a common omission in all psychoanalytically oriented writings until quite recently. Her characterization of the source of the borderline phenomenon in the preoedipal phase, with the entire responsibility for the disorder being placed with the mother, is typical of the "absent father" in so much writing dealing with the preoedipal period. It is as if the father does not even arrive in the house until the child is 4. Of course the father is present and in a very profound way, as recent research has shown. T. Berry Brazelton, the renowned pediatrician, has focused a great deal on the importance of the father in the life of the young child. He has shown that even infants can tell the difference between the father's approach and the mother's, and respond in anticipatory excitement to the father's approach because of his more playful way of relating to his baby.

I believe it unlikely that a woman would be unable to develop past the splitting stage of defense and would marry and stay married to an abusive, borderline husband, if she had a father who was psychologically healthy and not abusive to her. A father who related in a more mature manner and gave loving but nonincestuous care and attention to his daughter would provide an opportunity for her to recreate that attachment with a healthy male. The father could have a corrective function for the child even if the mother were borderline. The obvious question here is: What would a healthy man be doing married to a borderline wife? In some cases this might happen if the woman were exceptionally beautiful, talented, smart, or rich, and he married her for one of these qualities rather than for her pathology. It is most likely that the borderline mother whose abusive relationship with her daughter eventually produces a battered woman is married to a man at her own developmental level who can neither relate to the daughter in any better way nor control his wife's abuse. He may be abusing his wife and/or his children in addition to any cruelty from the mother, who may in fact be taking out her rage at her husband on their children in a classic pecking-order fashion, where the strong hurt the weak. The older siblings may be abusing the younger siblings. Gillman's article never mentions the alcoholic fathers, abusive fathers, incestuous fathers, or abandoning and neglectful fathers such as I have found in the family picture of these women. I am convinced it "takes two" times two to produce the phenomenon of the battered woman; the parents of the woman and the parents of the battering male, as well as the traditional cultural norms of femininity and masculinity.

THE SEXUAL ABUSE OF CHILDREN

Definitions

In discussing incest it is important to define it first. I am going to use the definition proposed by E. Sue Blume in her book *Secret Survivors* (1990), in which incest is not limited to a blood relationship but rather includes any relationship where the child is dependent upon the perpetrator for her/his care and welfare and in which there is an ongoing bond of trust between the child and a caretaker. In the case of siblings or cousins, what distinguishes abuse from sex play is an imbalance of power, usually because of age difference, but not necessarily limited to that. Using this broad definition, depending on the ongoing bond of trust, a perpetrator may be a grandparent, father, mother, stepparent, foster parent, parent's lover, uncle, cousin, sibling, brother-in-law, doctor, dentist, teacher, principal, priest, neighbor, family friend, coach, therapist, nurse, residential care worker, or anyone else in long-term (six months) contact with the child (pp. 2–3).

It is also important to define what constitutes sexual abuse or molestation. The best definition from the point of view of our patients is any inappropriate touching. Cleaning or washing a baby who is still in diapers may involve genital stimulation, but that is appropriate touching. Bathing a young child will include soaping the genital area. Some mothers may linger too long in this activity, and there could be unconscious sexual meaning in the cleansing process. However, there can be sexual abuse even without touching, such as in genital exposure. Butler (1978) gives an example of a daughter whose father never touched her but who still suffers from nightmares and is unable to have satisfying sexual relationships.

> Can you imagine the terror of never knowing, when I would be sitting at the table doing my homework, coming home from school or getting ready for church, when my father would tap me on the shoulder and I would turn to find him grinning nervously, his face all red, standing behind me with an erection? When I would see him like that, he would run back into his room. But I never knew when it would happen, and I still have awful nightmares that my father is going to touch me and I'll turn around and see him like that. And I haven't seen or talked to him in over twenty years! [pp. 66–67]

What about a lascivious look? That can be both stimulating and frightening to a child or adolescent as well. What about a verbal proposition? It is important in work with a particular patient to explore the memory of the mood, the feelings, and whether the look, the words, or the behavior was disturbing and how so. A common experience of women is to be whistled at and ogled by men on the street. Some feminists have called this sexual abuse. This experience is disturbing because most women feel "visually undressed" by it, but I think a significant difference is that it is done in public with no secrecy. The aspect of secrecy is very important in sexual abuse. Even in the case of a gang rape, or a rape at a party, the aspect of secrecy is still there, as opposed to a public display. Verbal harassment of a woman on the street, though unwelcome, is generally not considered "forbidden" because of the male prerogative in this culture and thus is clearly not secretive. In some cultures, such as in socialist China, this is forbidden activity.

Because so much public attention has recently been focused on this issue, some men feel very worried and inhibited around children, claiming they are afraid to be friendly to a neighbor's child for fear of being accused of sexual intent. Can a friendly neighbor hold a child on his lap without it being sexual? Of course, but these concerns illustrate how subtle the distinction sometimes is between affection and sex. What makes it molestation has so much to do with unconscious meanings as well as conscious intent.

Sometimes we have to evaluate what constitutes sexual abuse when it involves physical contact but is not overtly a sexual act. For example, I supervised a therapist who had a woman patient whose physician-father gave her gynecological examinations. This behavior is such a boundary violation between father and daughter that I think it constitutes a sexual violation and therefore can be defined as incest. The key here is how we define *appropriate*.

What about enemas, a very frequent practice in the past, less so now. If a parent administers an enema to a child when an objective party can say there was no medical justification for it, would we consider that a sexual violation? Most likely we would need to know more about it to make a final determination but it certainly can be experienced as cruel and sadistic by the child and may in fact be a form of unconscious sexual sadism on the part of the parent. Perhaps that parent had had enemas administered by his or her parent and is reenacting the experience in the conscious belief that she/he is doing the correct thing. The conscious and unconscious motivation is impossible to know when we are working with our adult patients many years later, but it needs to be attended to in any analysis of feelings of helplessness, vulnerability, and submissiveness to irrational and abusive authority.

Going one step further in the direction from severe to mild, how do we classify spanking? We know that there can be sexual meaning to spanking and that it can be sexually stimulating, because of the occurrence of spanking in adults for whom it is part of sexual arousal. Is spanking ever a reasonable form of teaching a child acceptable behavior? When is it sadistic and perhaps unconsciously sexually motivated? Reconstruction of the incidents will usually help to clarify these questions, and the analysis of the transference will be most useful in determining the degree of sadism experienced by the child and the presence or absence of a sexual component in the adult's behavior.

Sometimes the terms *sexual abuse* and *sexual molestation* are really euphemisms for what is in fact rape. It is important to call a rape a rape when in fact that is what happened, to be clear that force was used. Rape would usually involve penile penetration but could also involve the forced insertion of other objects and could include oral, anal, or genital penetration. Some professionals may prefer the term *abuse* because they find it less disturbing, but the effect is to minimize the brutality of what was actually done to the child.

In the last ten years of my practice I have had female patients who have been sexually violated by a grandfather, a father, a mother, a brother, a family friend, a minister, a neighbor, or a foster father. I have had other patients whose weight problems could be traced to covert seductiveness by the father, where the parents' marital relationship was clearly unhappy and the father turned to his daughter for emotional closeness. (This is also the most common incestlike problem for sons of unhappily married mothers.) I have heard that there are so many women coming to county mental health clinics in California needing help with memories of incest that there is not the staff to see them for more than six sessions. John N. Briere, Ph.D., assistant professor of psychiatry at the University of Southern California, studied women requesting counseling at an outpatient crisis intervention center. Nearly half of them had been sexually abused during childhood. In another study of women in a psychiatric emergency room sample, more than two-thirds had been sexually abused. Incest is being reported at Alcoholics Anonymous and Overeaters Anonymous meetings and in battered-women's groups. Multiple personality disorder specialists are finding that incest experiences are a major source of this disorder.

Freud's Abandonment of the Seduction Theory—Jeffrey Moussaieff Masson

Freud's views on the question of the sexual molestation of children were rarely challenged within psychoanalysis until 1981. Freud published his revolutionary paper "The Aetiology of Hysteria" in 1896; it was received with anger and disbelief. Subsequently he found himself isolated by the Viennese medical community because of the shocking nature of his revelations that at the core of the neurosis of his hysterical female patients was repressed and dissociated sexual abuse by parents or other trusted caretakers. Hysterics, he said, suffer from reminiscences. When a hysteric was able to talk about the traumatic event, the symptoms disappeared through "abreaction." Freud had concluded that the "primal experience" conducive to hysteria dated from before the age of 4. He had become convinced that the persons most often guilty of the sexual abuse of young children, primarily of girls, were their fathers—including his own, although Freud never said this publicly. Although the ambiguous term *seduction* comes into use in Freud's later writings, in this early paper there is no doubt that Freud meant a real sexual act forced on a young child who in no way desired or encouraged it; an act of cruelty and violence, often an actual rape for which she is prepared neither physically nor emotionally yet is too frightened to protest, too weak to defend herself, and too dependent on the care of the adult for her survival to complain (Masson 1984b, pp. 34–35).

> All the strange conditions under which the incongruous pair continue their love relations—on the one hand the adult, who cannot escape his

share in the mutual dependence necessarily entailed by a sexual relationship, and who is at the same time armed with complete authority
and the right to punish, and can exchange the one role for the other to
the uninhibited satisfaction of his whims, and on the other hand the
child, who in his helplessness is at the mercy of this arbitrary use of
power, who is prematurely aroused to every kind of sensibility and
exposed to every sort of disappointment, and whose exercise of the
sexual performances assigned to him is often interrupted by his imper-
fect control of his natural needs—all these grotesque and yet tragic
disparities distinctly mark the later development of the individual and
of his neurosis, with countless permanent effects which deserve to be
traced in the greatest detail. [Freud 1896]

This exquisite description probably still stands as the finest writing on the
subject. Freud was sensitive to the interaction from the position of the
perpetrator as well as the victim. By September 1897, in a letter to Wilhelm
Fliess, Freud was expressing doubts. He later recanted, replacing his
seduction theory with the theory that the stories were in fact fantasies
created out of the oedipal complex. "I was at last obliged to recognize that
these scenes of seduction had never taken place, and that they were only
fantasies which my patients had made up" (p. 36). Masson writes:

The taboo against speaking about fathers seducing their children seems
to have been handed down through the generations of analysts since
Freud. Thus, the editors of *The Origins of Psychoanalysis,* Ernst Kris
and Anna Freud, omitted from the letters several case histories in which
a father seduced a child, thereby depriving posterity of the opportunity
to judge or even become aware of the evidence Freud was finding in his
clinical practice for his belief in the reality of early sexual traumas.
[1984b, p. 47]

At the end of January 1984, Masson's book *The Assault on Truth:
Freud's Suppression of the Seduction Theory* was published amidst much
publicity and fanfare and caused tremendous interest within the psychoanalytically informed community and much concern and distress within
psychoanalytic circles. For example, Masson, himself a psychoanalyst
living in Berkeley, and his book were the subject of a four-part series in the
San Francisco Chronicle the week of 13 February 1984. It included
biographical information on Masson and long quotations from his book, as
well as interviews with local psychoanalysts giving their reactions to the
book. On February 17, 1984, a debate about the book was held on the
UC–Berkeley campus featuring several academic speakers and attended by
hundreds of interested students, faculty, and community people.
    This was not the first time Freud's reversal of his early seduction

theory of neurosis was questioned. Judith Herman, a psychiatrist at Harvard Medical School, had written *Father–Daughter Incest,* published in 1981; and Florence Rush, a social worker, had written "Freud and the Sexual Abuse of Children," published in a feminist journal in 1977. Both authors focused on the reality of the prevalence of sexual abuse of children. However, the Masson book was the first written by a member of the psychoanalytic establishment, and Masson's position as projects director of the Freud Archives had given him access to much previously unpublished correspondence between Freud and his close associates in which Freud expressed the development of his thinking and his inner conflicts about this subject. In fact, much of the correspondence had been suppressed and was opened to Masson as a trusted comrade of the then current inner circle.

In August 1981, the *New York Times* had published a two-part series of articles on new Freud scholarship that questioned some long-accepted understandings about Freud's work and private life revealed in the contents of letters from Freud to Wilhelm Fliess, a Berlin nose and throat specialist with whom Freud carried on a passionate friendship for fifteen years. After the publication of these two articles, Dr. Masson was dismissed from his position by Dr. Kurt R. Eissler, the director of the Archives, and Anna Freud. A fascinating two-part article on Masson and his book, written by Janet Malcolm, was published in *The New Yorker* in December 1983. It described how Masson had won the confidence of Eissler and Miss Freud and how the relationship had collapsed after Masson began to reveal his views. Based on his findings in research at the Freud archives, Masson claimed that Freud had erred in retracting his original theory, which was based on the premise that the stories of incest revealed by his female patients were true. He retracted the seduction theory when he had concluded from his self-analysis that the oedipal phase produced such powerful fantasies of sexuality with the parent of the opposite sex that it was most likely that the stories his patients had been telling him were not fact but fiction, the fiction created in their childhood imagination by their own sexual desires. In the letter to Fliess on September 21, 1897, Freud wrote "surely such widespread perversions against children are not very probable."

Yet Freud did not completely drop the topic. In his "Three Essays on The Theory of Sexuality" (1905), in referring to a second phase of infantile masturbation occurring some time before the fourth year, he writes:

> The reappearance of sexual activity is determined by internal causes and external contingencies, both of which can be guessed in cases of neurotic illness from the form taken by their symptoms and can be discovered with certainty by psycho-analytic investigation. I shall have to speak presently of the internal causes; *great and lasting importance*

> *attaches at this period to the accidental external contingencies.* In the
> foreground we find the effects of seduction, which treats a child as a
> sexual object prematurely and teaches him, in highly emotional circum-
> stances, how to obtain satisfaction from his genital zones, a satisfaction
> which he is then usually obliged to repeat again and again by mastur-
> bation. An influence of this kind may originate either from adults or
> from other children. *I cannot admit that in my paper on 'The
> Aetiology of Hysteria' I exaggerated the frequency or importance of
> that influence,* though I did not then know that persons who remain
> normal may have had the same experiences in their childhood, and
> though I consequently overrated the importance of seduction in com-
> parison with the factors of sexual constitution and development.
> Obviously, seduction is not required in order to arouse a child's sexual
> life; that can also come about spontaneously from internal causes.
>
> *It is an instructive fact that under the influence of seduction
> children can become polymorphously perverse,* and can be led into all
> possible kinds of sexual irregularities. . . . In this respect children
> behave in the same kind of way as an average uncultivated woman in
> whom the same polymorphously perverse disposition persists. . . .
> Prostitutes exploit the same polymorphous, that is infantile, disposition
> for the purposes of their profession. [Freud 1905; italics mine]

It would seem, then, that Freud did not completely retract his theory
of the sexual seduction of children but rather modified it by recognizing
that there are even more cases than come to our attention, because not all
children develop symptoms as a result of their molestation; yet he states he
did not exaggerate the frequency or importance of the occurrence of such
molestation. This important distinction has been overlooked in much of
the criticism of Freud and by many practitioners of psychoanalysis and
psychotherapy. This could be because of individual analysts' resistance to
face these sordid facts rather than Freud's denial of them. For example,
Helene Deutsch never even mentions incest in her two-volume work on
women (1944–1945). She mentions seduction only in relation to playing
with the father, making the sexuality entirely covert and beneficial, using
the example to once again emphasize the normality of female masochism:

> He appears, without being conscious of it, as a seducer, with whose
> help the girl's aggressive instinctual components are transformed into
> masochistic ones. The masochistic ingredient in the relation to the
> father appears in the active games with him, which later assume an
> increasingly erotic character. It is enough to observe the little girl's
> fearful jubilation when the father performs acrobatic tricks with her
> that are often painful when he throws her up in the air, or lets her ride
> "piggy back" on his shoulders. When this seduction on the part of the
> father is lacking, the girl will encounter difficulties in her feminine
> development. [Vol. 1, pp. 252–253]

Freud still stands as most courageous, especially considering that he was the pioneer breaking down walls of ignorance and distortion. I suspect he was wrong when he stated that not all adults who were molested as children show symptoms, and that in fact Freud did not have sufficient experience to recognize certain symptoms such as overeating, sexual promiscuity (this was reserved for uncultivated women, showing his class bias), and disturbances in boundary formation as clues to the possibility of repressed or dissociated sexual molestation.

It would take another seventy-five years before feminists and psychotherapists would make the connection between childhood molestation and the choice of prostitution. Rather than being "uncultivated," we now recognize that many of the women and men who enter prostitution have been victimized and exploited sexually as children and reenact through prostitution both the role of sexual victim and exploiter. Economic factors are involved as well, but often are secondary to the traumatic childhood sexual abuse. A common pattern is that a sexually abused boy or girl either is forced out of the home or runs away from home and is economically destitute. The child becomes drawn into the trade through the attention of a pimp (in the case of girls) and resorts to the only means she knows of getting some loving attention, the sexual use of her body.

The *New York Times* published two extensive articles on the Masson book on January 24, 1984, the week of its publication, and *The Atlantic* published a cover article written by Masson, with long excerpts from the book, in February 1984. Masson accused Freud of a failure of courage, a betrayal of the truth, and stated his conviction that the reversal was a cover-up, an effort to protect his friend Fliess from the bizarre, nearly fatal treatment of his patient Emma Eckstein, as well as an effort to regain acceptability in the Viennese medical world following unbearable scorn and ostracism. Two weeks after he had delivered the paper, in 1896, Freud wrote to Wilhelm Fliess: "I am as isolated as you could wish me to be: the word has been given out to abandon me, and a void is forming around me" (previously expurgated sentence, quoted in Masson 1984a, p. 10).

A book by Marie Balmary (1982) had suggested that Freud's theory of focusing on the child's sexual impulses rather than the parents' could have been an effort to defend his own father's reputation. She points out that Freud's switch came a year after his father's death and suggests that Freud wished to conceal some facts about the sexual life of his thrice-married father, Jakob, and Freud's own illegitimate conception. Masson disclosed a letter to Fliess in which Freud wrote: "Unfortunately, my own father was one of these perverts and is responsible for the hysteria of my brother (all of whose symptoms are identifications) and those of several younger sisters" (Blumenthal 1984, p. 19). Balmary's thesis proved prescient, as Masson's revelations substantiated her views, although sex before marriage is minor compared with incest. Considering how even today the revelation of incest results in such severe denial and shame, we should not be surprised that Freud and his daughter did all they could to deny and conceal evidence he discovered of his own father's incestuous attacks on his brother and sisters. This part of Freud's family history also is revealing of what may have been a significant factor in Freud's heightened intellectual curiosity about childhood sexuality, though he may never have associated his "discoveries" with what must have been some awareness of the incest going on in his own family home.

In a *New York Times* interview (Blumenthal 1984), Masson

> contends that, by doubting the reality of a patient's early memories of trauma, today's psychoanalyst, like Freud, "does violence to the inner life of his patient and is in covert collusion with what made her ill" in the first place. "The silence demanded of the child by the person who violated her (or him) is perpetuated and enforced by the very person to whom she has come for help," he asserts. "Guilt entrenches itself, the uncertainty of one's past deepens and the sense of who one is is undermined." [p. 19]

Reaction to Masson's book varied, and a review of the reviews finds Masson being given some credit for the research he has contributed to an understanding of Freud as an individual and his thinking on this issue but criticized for his exaggeration of the importance and the effect of his own findings. The major issue for psychoanalytic theory is whether real traumatic events matter in the lives of patients, and if so, how much. Perhaps only a small corps of analysts believe actual events do not matter, but Masson was understandably disturbed by hearing of women patients whose analysts did not believe them. It seems quite sensible to me that one needs to evaluate in each case what the actual intensity of the trauma was (the external reality) and explore the internal meaning of the event to the patient, as well as what the long-term effects have been on her/his personality. What are the defenses that have been developed by the patient to protect her from future pain or, on the contrary, what patterns of behavior is she unconsciously engaging in to reenact the trauma in a hopeless attempt to master it? Clearly, sexual abuse is damaging. How damaging depends on what actually was done and the degree of violence, the degree of secrecy, and whether threats of retaliation were involved; the age of the child; the importance of the perpetrator in the child's life; and when and if the child has an opportunity to talk about it with a caring adult.

Sandor Ferenczi

Masson claimed that his research revealed Freud's attempt to suppress opposition to his revised theory when Sandor Ferenczi wrote a paper in

1932, disagreeing with Freud and stating "Even children of very respectable, sincerely puritanical families fall victim to real violence or rape much
more often than one had dared to suppose" (p. 227). In fact, the paper,
entitled "Confusion of Tongues between the Adult and the Child," was
delivered, after some hesitation, in September 1932 at the Twelfth International Psychoanalytic Congress in Weisbaden but was not published in
English until 1949. Ferenczi died of pernicious anemia in 1933. Before his
death, his formerly close relationship with Freud had deteriorated, due to
disagreements regarding technique. According to Jones (1959, vol. 3),
Ferenczi was suffering mental deterioration on account of his illness and
had begun to engage in unorthodox techniques such as kissing, with his
patients, with which, of course, Freud had to disagree. However, the paper
contains some remarkable observations on patients who suffer from
childhood sexual trauma, and statements acknowledging the widespread
occurrence of the sexual abuse of children.

Ferenczi states that there had been an unjust neglect of the effect of
actual traumatic factors in the pathogenesis of the neuroses, and rejects the
theory that they are the sexual phantasies of the child. As evidence of the
prevalence of such incidents he cites confessions of actual assaults on
children made by patients in analysis. He also cites the report of a teacher
who discovered that five of his male students between the ages of 9 and 11
were "living a regular sexual life" (p. 227) with their governesses.

Ferenczi makes a distinction between childhood tenderness and adult
passion, stating that love between a child and an adult may contain some
erotic components for the child but that it remains on the level of
tenderness. A pathological adult mistakes the play of a child for the sexual
desires of a mature adult. Ferenczi writes that the rape results in the child's
being paralyzed by enormous anxiety. Children feel helpless and unable to
protest against the overpowering force and authority of the adult.

> The same anxiety, however, if it reaches a certain maximum, compels
> them to subordinate themselves like automata to the will of the
> aggressor, to divine each one of his desires and to gratify these;
> completely oblivious of themselves they identify themselves with the
> aggressor. [p. 228]

He then shifts from the term *identification* to the concept of *introjection*.

> Through the identification or, let us say, introjection of the aggressor,
> he disappears as part of the external reality, and becomes intra- instead
> of extra-psychic; the intra-psychic is then subjected, in a dream-like
> state as is the traumatic trance, to the primary process . . . the attack as
> a rigid external reality ceases to exist and in the traumatic trance the

child succeeds in maintaining the previous situation of tenderness. [p. 228]

Ferenczi's next step is to propose that the child introjects the guilt feelings of the adult, further confusing the child who feels both innocent and culpable at the same time. He also points out an important additional factor—the relationship with a second adult, often the mother, is not intimate enough for the child to seek help, and the child's tentative attempts to get help are dismissed by the mother as nonsensical. The child then becomes a "mechanical obedient automaton" (p. 228) or becomes defiant, without understanding the reasons for his or her behavior. Ferenczi concludes: "It is hatred that traumatically surprises and frightens the child while being loved by an adult, that changes him from a spontaneously and innocently playing being into a guilty love-automaton imitating the adult anxiously, self effacingly" (p. 230).

On the basis of his conclusion that traditional analytic technique had not been successful in treating these traumatized patients, Ferenczi proposes a modification in technique that became the source of his disagreement with Freud. Ferenczi found that these patients repeated the submissive and compliant stance with the analyst that they had taken with the aggressor.

> . . . the patients have an exceedingly refined sensitivity for the wishes, tendencies, whims, sympathies and antipathies of their analyst, even if the analyst is completely unaware of this sensitivity. Instead of contradicting the analyst or accusing him of errors and blindness, the patients identify themselves with him . . . normally they do not allow themselves to criticize us. [p. 226]

The analyst must try to learn of the painful past from the patient's suppressed or repressed criticism of him or her. Ferenczi uses the term *professional hypocrisy* to describe the suppression by the analyst of difficult and uncomfortable reactions to the patient and proposes that the analyst reveal the source of his discomfort to the patient and discuss it as a fact. Ferenczi claims that this exposure of the analyst's feelings effect a remarkable improvement in the patient's condition, producing confidence in the analyst on the part of the patient. This confidence reflects the contrast between the present and the past. It then allows the patient to "re-experience the past no longer as hallucinatory reproduction but as an objective memory" (p. 227). The traumatized patient is in a trancelike state when reexperiencing the trauma and cannot be reached by the cool, clinical attitude of the analyst. The patient is left feeling like an abandoned child, reenacting the original abandonment of the trauma, and requires sincere sympathy. This departure from neutrality was clearly a source of distress to Freud and is still an issue for today's therapist in the treatment of traumatized patients.

The disturbing element is the traumatized patient's extreme sensitivity to the wishes of the analyst. Thus, a patient who was a victim of child sexual abuse might not bring it up if he or she sensed the analyst's resistance. As the mother had resisted the child's timid attempts to get help, so have, I fear, many analysts. But this also raises the worrisome idea that if the analyst wants to find sexual abuse the patient might offer the analyst a plausible story to meet the analyst's needs.

At this juncture in the history of psychoanalysis, my concern lies less with analysts denying the reality of the sexual abuse of children as revealed by their patients, because of the widespread attention given to the epidemic of child abuse in all its forms; I am more concerned about the multitude of patients who have repressed or dissociated all memory of their abuse and thus require an analyst or therapist who is alert to symptoms and who will seek out information through diagnostically relevant questions and through clues offered in dreams, in the transference, and in acting-out behavior. For male therapists seeing female patients, a countertransference reaction of sexual excitement with the patient is a most important clue. Working with these patients involves a level of commitment, caring, and belief in order to overcome the very powerful resistances to recovery of memory on the part of the patient, and, equally important, the ability to overcome one's own resistance to accepting the reality of acts that are at the same time repulsive and erotically stimulating.

The role of the women's movement in the revelations of abuse—physical, psychological and sexual—of women and children has been paramount in bringing this issue out of the closet of fear and shame and into the light of public and professional recognition. In her review of the Masson book, Judith Herman (1984) wrote:

> The secrecy surrounding the male prerogatives of rape and incest has been so tenaciously guarded that only a social movement of women has been capable of breaking it, and that only very recently (p. 293). . . . The facts of sexual abuse of children are by now so well documented as to be beyond the power of social denial. Too many women have spoken out, and empowered by the women's movement, more victims daily are breaking the silence. But the most important insights of psychoanalysis are in no way incompatible with acceptance of the reality of sexual violence, or any other social reality. It is time for psychoanalysis to free itself from the neurotic re-enactment of its history. [p. 296]

I believe that the role of feminists in asserting the reality of the problem and attributing its suppression to the patriarchal value system, combined with the role of the psychoanalytic method of reaching repressed material through dream interpretation, analysis of the transference, and reenactments in current relationships, enables therapists to confront this problem and help our patients to recover from these damaging events. Here we have a striking example of how the two theories, feminism and psychoanalysis, have worked in combination to enrich both. Masson's disclosures came at a time when women were already actively involved in this work and gave it not a necessary, but a helpful, boost of support.

In 1977 I read an article by Florence Rush in a woman's journal, *Chrysalis*. Rush, a social worker on the staff of a home for delinquent girls, was impressed with the frequency and verifiability of these girls' reports of sexual abuse. She suggested that rather than viewing the reports as fantasy, perhaps it was necessary for the male analysts to view them as fantasy so as to protect the men involved, often men with whom they could identify as husbands, fathers, and men of their own class. I talked with a number of friends about the *Chrysalis* article and was surprised that each one recalled sexual advances made by an adult man when she was a girl. This realization enabled me to raise my consciousness of the possibility of sexual molestation in the lives of my own patients so that after 1977 it was, as Mildred Ash said, one of the things I "thought about" in listening to them. The case of Penelope developed into an example of repressed sexual seduction and rape.

Statistical Evidence of the Prevalence of Seduction in Childhood

As with battering, males are usually the perpetrators and females the victims of sexual abuse. Numerous studies show that about 75 percent of all reported cases are committed by someone the child knows and trusts. When boys are the victims, the perpetrators are most often males. Leidig (1981) reports that of 305 sexual assault cases seen in the emergency room of Denver General Hospital in 1976–1977, 5 cases were male and in each case the perpetrator was male. Rush reports that boys comprise about 10 percent or less of the incest population. Accurate statistics are impossible because so many cases are never reported, yet Robin Lloyd reports nearly three hundred thousand boys working the streets as prostitutes in the U.S. Those familiar with this population believe more than half of these boys were sexually abused in their homes. Justice and Justice (1979) report that a history of sexual abuse is found among many prostitutes, drug addicts, runaways, and prison inmates. Other sources report 90 percent of male and female prostitutes are sexual abuse victims, as are other persons in the sex industry such as strippers and pornography models. Many sources believe that the cases most likely to come to the attention of police and social agencies are from poor and disorganized families, whereas in middle-class and upper-class families the incest or abuse is more likely to remain a secret. Leidig concludes that all evidence now suggests that rape, battering, incest, and other victimizations of women occur across all socioeconomic levels and racial categories at approximately the same rates, but this conclusion cannot be validated because of the significant problem of secrecy. Butler (1978) states:

> Men who are reported as incestuous aggressors seldom have prior criminal records. They have little or no psychiatric history, are not necessarily excessive drinkers, and appear to be of average intelligence and education. Their work histories are steady, and their marital histories primarily monogamous. [p. 79]

In 1967, the Children's Division of the American Humane Association estimated that a minimum of eighty thousand to one hundred thousand children are sexually molested each year. In the majority of these cases the offender is well known to the child, and in about 25 percent of them, a relative. By 1989, a report in the *Comprehensive Textbook of Psychiatry* (V. Sadock) stated that current estimates are that between 12 and 15 million American women have been the subject of "incestuous attention" and that between one hundred thousand and three hundred thousand children are sexually abused each year. One study reports 19 percent of women and 9 percent of men have been molested as children; another study reports 15 percent of women and 6 percent men, with males comprising 94 percent of the abusers. Diana Russell (1986), who studied 970 randomly selected nonpatient women, found 38 percent had been sexually victimized by adults before the age of 18; 16 percent by a family member and the majority by a trusted adult. According to Herman and Hirschman (1981), a constant finding in all existing surveys is the overwhelming predominance of father–daughter incest. Weinberg (1955) found that of 200 court cases in the Chicago area, there were 164 cases of father–daughter incest compared with 2 of mother–son incest. Sadock (1989) reports 75 percent of reported incest cases involve father–daughter relationships. Other surveys produce results of 5 percent father–son incest and 4 percent mother–son incest. Herman and Hirschman conclude that 92 percent of the victims of incest are female and 97 percent of the offenders are male. Kinsey found 6 percent of his female sample reporting sexual approaches by adult relatives. Few of the 12,000 men surveyed reported childhood sexual contact with adult males. In regard to mother–son incest, they quote Kinsey (1948) in his work on the human male as stating that "heterosexual incest occurs more frequently in the thinking of clinicians and social workers than it does in actual performance" (pp. 157–158).

What seems to be most often ignored in the research is mother–daughter incest. In my clinical experience I have treated several women where the patient experienced touching by her mother that didn't feel right and that the patient in retrospect believed was incestuous in terms of the affect even if no direct genital contact occurred. The mother of one of my patients was an alcoholic, and the patient's "icky" feeling about her mother touching her occurred during drinking episodes. One woman in our women's group was both sexually and physically abused by her mother. She was not even allowed her own bed and had to sleep at the foot of her mother's bed each night.

The incidence of incest in the general population is less significant to us than the incidence in a clinical population. The clinician must be able to recognize symptoms of incest and have the emotional capacity to accept the patient and elicit the details. As recently as 1975, a basic American psychiatry textbook estimated the frequency of all forms of incest as one case per million. Only recently has psychiatry faced the grim truth on this subject. In the June 1979 issue of the *American Journal of Psychiatry,* A. Rosenfeld reported that six of eighteen women he treated in a six-month period at a psychiatric clinic reported incest. As state legislatures pass laws requiring teachers, social workers, doctors and others to report suspected cases, the figures increase dramatically. One problem with such estimates is that it is not clear whether "victimized" includes cases not involving direct physical contact, such as flashing, but it is indicative of the change in the last ten years in reporting and recognition of the depth and breadth of the problem.

A Feminist Analysis of Father–Daughter Incest—Judith Herman and Lisa Hirschman

Herman and Hirschman (1981) observe that none of the literature makes any attempt to account for the striking discrepancy between the occurrence of father–daughter and mother–son incest. They suggest that in a patriarchal culture the incest taboo must have a different meaning for the two sexes and may be observed by men and women for different reasons.

> Major theorists in the disciplines of both psychology and anthropology explain the importance of the incest taboo by placing it at the center of an agreement to control warfare among men . . . the first and most important peace treaty. An essential element of the agreement is the concept that women are the possessions of men: the incest taboo represents an agreement as to how women shall be shared . . . agreements among men regarding sexual access to women. . . . Men create rules governing the exchange of women; women do not create rules

governing the exchange of men. Because the taboo is created and enforced by men, we argue that it may also be more easily and frequently violated by men. [p. 209]

Additionally, they point out that men "give away" daughters in marriage to another man, whereas mothers do not give away either daughters or sons. It is also true that fathers do not "give away" sons. For the man, the taboo against his sexual desires for his mother is enforced by his father, but *"there is no punishing father to avenge father–daughter incest"* (p. 209). The boy knows that when he grows up he will have power as a man, whereas the girl learns that she may acquire power only indirectly, as the favorite of a powerful man, by marrying or by having a sexual relationship with a man like her father, a man who has power over her, perhaps her therapist, her boss, her graduate advisor, or her lawyer.

> A patriarchal society, then, most abhors the idea of incest between mother and son, because this is an affront to the father's prerogatives. . . . We believe this understanding of the asymmetrical nature of the incest taboo under patriarchy offers an explanation for the observed difference . . . we might expect violations of the taboo to occur most frequently in families characterized by extreme paternal dominance. This is in fact the case. Incest offenders are frequently described as "family tyrants." . . . We believe that the greater the degree of male supremacy in any culture, the greater the likelihood of father–daughter incest. [pp. 209–210]

They then give the results of a clinical case study of fifteen victims of father–daughter incest, all women in therapy who reported the incest to their therapist after the fact. There were six therapists involved. All the patients were white, and the majority had some college education. Their presenting complaints were depression and social isolation, plus marital problems for those married or separated. The severity of their complaints seemed related to the degree of family disorganization and deprivation in their histories rather than to the incest history per se. Five had been hospitalized, three had been suicidal, and two were addicted to drugs or alcohol. Seven brought up the incest initially, and eight revealed it only after having established a relationship with the therapist, with disclosure for some taking one to three years. In all but two cases the sexual relationship remained a secret. Four fathers were blue-collar workers, two were white-collar workers, six were professionals, and three were of unknown occupation.

The authors conclude that there is convincing evidence that the incest experience was harmful and left long-lasting scars. One of the most frequent complaints was a sense of being different and distant from ordinary people, which was experienced as painful isolation. Most of their relationships were superficial and empty or else extremely conflictual. They feared that they were unable to love, and there was an absence of feeling in sexual relationships. Some expressed negative feelings toward men, but most overvalued men and kept searching for a good father. Half had had affairs during adolescence with older or married men wherein they recreated the sense of specialness, power, and secrecy of the incestuous relationship. The authors make a distinction between rape and seduction and describe their sample as having been seduced.

> Unlike rape, it occurs in the context of a caring relationship. The victim feels overwhelmed by her father's superior power and unable to resist him; she may feel disgust, loathing and shame. But at the same time she often feels that this is the only kind of love she can get, and prefers it to no love at all. . . . What is involved here is not simply an assault, it is a betrayal. [p. 215]

Herman and Hirschman summarize their findings on the group of patients as follows:

> Many victims had severely impaired object relations with both men and women. The overvaluation of men led them into conflictual and often intensely masochistic relationships with men. The victims' devaluation of themselves and their mothers impaired development of supportive friendships with women. Many of the victims also had a well-formed negative identity as witch, bitch, or whore. In adult life they continued to make repeated ineffective attempts to expiate their intense feelings of guilt and shame. . . . They saw themselves as socially "branded" or "marked," . . . as powerful and dangerous to men. . . . These daughters seemed almost uniformly to believe that they had seduced their fathers and therefore could seduce any man. . . . They had experienced some pleasure in the incestuous relationship. . . . This led to intense feelings of shame, degradation and worthlessness . . . and [they] did not feel entitled to care and respect. [pp. 218, 219]

Over half the mothers were partially incapacitated by physical or mental illness or alcoholism and either assumed an invalid role within the home or were periodically absent because of hospitalization. Their oldest daughter often took over the traditional female household duties. Many of the daughters became their fathers' surrogate wives and gained some feeling of value and importance, often feeling responsible for holding the family together. Because they kept the incest secret, they had an extraordinary power that could be used to destroy the family. Another aspect of the role of the patriarchal system in the commission of incest is described as follows:

> What is most striking to us about this family constellation, in which the daughter replaces the mother in her traditional role, is the underlying assumption about that role shared apparently by all the family members. Customarily, a mother and wife in our society is one who nurtures and takes care of children and husband. If, for whatever reasons, the mother is unable to fulfill her ordinary functions, it is apparently assumed that some other female must be found to do it. The eldest daughter is a frequent choice. The father does not assume the wife's maternal role when she is incapacitated. He feels that his first right is to continue to receive the services which his wife formerly provided, sometimes including sexual services. This view of the father's prerogative to be served not only is shared by the fathers and daughters in these families, but is often encouraged by societal attitudes. Fathers who feel abandoned by their wives are not generally expected or taught to assume primary parenting responsibilities. [p. 216]

The authors also deal with the problems for therapists in working with incest victims. They believe male therapists identify with the father and have trouble responding empathically to the woman, denying or excusing his behavior and projecting blame onto the victim. On the other hand, women therapists tend to identify with the victim and may have trouble facing the details of the experience and convey to the women that their secrets are too terrible to hear, reinforcing the shame and isolation of the patient.

The work done by Herman and Hirschman is very valuable as it contributes a feminist analysis to a psychodynamic analysis of incest. I disagree with their conclusion that incest is seduction and not rape. In my experience it is not so easy to make that distinction because what may begin as seduction may end in rape.

I Know Why the Caged Bird Sings—Maya Angelou

Before proceeding to a case example on this point of seduction versus rape, I want to quote from a work of literature, a powerfully written first-person description of a seduction that turned to rape, by Maya Angelou in her book *I Know Why the Caged Bird Sings* (1970). The author, Marguerite (Ritie), and her brother Bailey had been sent to live with their paternal grandmother in the South when they were aged 3 and 4 because their parents divorced. When they were 8 and 9 they were brought back to St. Louis by their father to live with their mother. Angelou describes her relationship with her brother as extremely close and loving. Mother worked evenings in a club and lived with her boyfriend, Mr. Freeman. Angelou says that she suffered from fears and sometimes at night her mother would take her into bed with her and Mr. Freeman.

> One morning [Mother] got out of bed for an early errand, and I fell asleep again. But I awoke to a pressure, a strange feeling on my left leg. . . . It didn't move, and I was too startled to. I turned my head a little to the left to see if Mr. Freeman was awake and gone, but his eyes were open and both hands were above the cover. I knew, as if I had always known, it was his "thing" on my leg.
>
> He said "Just stay right here, Ritie, I ain't gonna hurt you." I wasn't afraid, a little apprehensive, maybe, but not afraid. Of course I knew that lots of people did "it" and they used their "things" to accomplish the deed, but no one I knew had ever done it to anybody. Mr. Freeman pulled me to him, and put his hand between my legs. He didn't hurt but Momma had drilled into my head: "Keep your legs closed, and don't let nobody see your pocketbook."
>
> "Now, I didn't hurt you. Don't get scared." He threw back the blankets and his "thing" stood up like a brown ear of corn. He took my hand and said, "Feel it." It was mushy and squirmy like the inside of a freshly killed chicken. Then he dragged me on top of his chest with his left arm, and his right hand was moving so fast and his heart was beating so hard that I was afraid that he would die. . . .
>
> Finally he was quiet, and then came the nice part. He held me so softly that I wished he wouldn't ever let me go. I felt at home. From the way he was holding me I knew he'd never let me go or let anything bad ever happen to me. This was probably my real father and we had found each other at last. But then he rolled over, leaving me in a wet place and stood up.
>
> "I gotta talk to you, Ritie. Get up. . . . You peed in the bed." He poured water on the wet spot, and it did look like my mattress on many mornings.
>
> Having lived in Southern strictness, I knew when to keep quiet around adults, but I did want to ask him why he said I peed when I was sure he didn't believe that. If he thought I was naughty, would that mean that he would never hold me again? Or admit that he was my father? I had made him ashamed of me.
>
> "Ritie, you love Bailey?" He sat down on the bed and I came close, hoping. "Yes." He was bending down, pulling on his socks, and his back was so large and friendly I wanted to rest my head on it.
>
> "If you ever tell anybody what we did, I'll have to kill Bailey."
>
> What had we done? We? Obviously he didn't mean my peeing in the bed. I didn't understand and didn't dare ask him. It had something to do with his holding me. . . . The thought that he might kill Bailey stunned me. . . .
>
> It was the same old quandary. I had always lived it. There was an army of adults, whose motives and movements I just couldn't under-

stand and who made no effort to understand mine. There was never any question of my disliking Mr. Freeman, I simply didn't understand him either. . . .

I began to feel lonely for Mr. Freeman and the encasement of his big arms. Before, my world had been Bailey, food, Momma, the Store, reading books and Uncle Willie. Now, for the first time, it included physical contact.

I began to wait for Mr. Freeman to come in from the yards, but when he did, he never noticed me, although I put a lot of feeling into "Good evening, Mr. Freeman."

One evening, when I couldn't concentrate on anything, I went over to him and sat quickly on his lap. He had been waiting for Mother again. . . . At first Mr. Freeman sat still, not holding me or anything, then I felt a soft lump under my thigh begin to move. It twitched against me and started to harden. Then he pulled me to his chest. . . . He smelled of coal dust and grease and he was so close I buried my face in his shirt and listened to his heart, it was beating just for me. Only I could hear the thud, only I could feel the jumping on my face. He said, "Sit still, stop squirming." But all the time, he pushed me around on his lap, then suddenly he stood up and I slipped down to the floor. He ran to the bathroom.

For months he stopped speaking to me again. I was hurt and for a time felt lonelier than ever. But then I forgot about him, and even the memory of his holding me precious melted into the general darkness just beyond the great blinkers of childhood. [pp. 60–63]

Up to this point we could all agree that Ritie has been seduced by Mr. Freeman and that she has enjoyed his attention. She is confused and hurt when he ignores her after the intimate moments, a typical occurrence. She is frightened by the threat to kill her beloved brother and is made uncomfortable by having to keep a secret from Bailey, the first time she had ever kept a secret from him. However, this incident is not that different from her other impressions of adults, and she does not seem to be very damaged by it. She seeks out Mr. Freeman's attention again because she has such a hunger for a father, but she clearly wants holding and not sexual contact. She is not, from her vantage point, being seductive. Her next contact with him is quite different. One night her mother does not return home after work. The next morning she is on her way to the library when Mr. Freeman calls to her:

"Ritie." He was sitting in the big chair by the radio. "Ritie, come here." I didn't think about the holding time until I got close to him. His pants were open and his "thing" was standing out of his britches by itself.

"No, sir, Mr. Freeman." I started to back away, I didn't want to touch that mush-hard thing again, and I didn't need him to hold me any more. He grabbed my arm and pulled me between his legs. His face was still and looked kind, but he didn't smile or blink his eyes. Nothing. He did nothing, except reach his left hand around to turn on the radio without even looking at it. Over the noise of music and static, he said, "Now, this ain't gonna hurt you much. You liked it before, didn't you?"

I didn't want to admit that I had in fact liked his holding me or that I had liked his smell or the hard heart-beating, so I said nothing. And his face became like the face of one of those mean natives the Phantom was always having to beat up. His legs were squeezing my waist. "Pull down your drawers."

"We was just playing before." He released me enough to snatch down my bloomers, and then he dragged me closer to him. Turning the radio up loud, too loud, he said, "If you scream, I'm gonna kill you. And if you tell, I'm gonna kill Bailey," I could tell he meant what he said. I couldn't understand why he wanted to kill my brother. Neither of us had done anything to him. And then.

Then there was the pain. A breaking and entering when even the senses are torn apart. The act of rape on an eight-year-old body is a matter of the needle giving because the camel can't. The child gives, because the body can, and the mind of the violator cannot.

I thought I had died—I woke up in a white-walled world and it had to be heaven. But Mr. Freeman was there and he was washing me. [pp. 63–64] (italics added)

Angelou describes how she struggled to go to the library and then struggled home, feeling a burning between her legs.

She went to bed. Her mother thought she must be sick, suspecting the measles. She says "I wasn't sick but the pit of my stomach was on fire." She couldn't eat and had a fever. Mr. Freeman came to her bedside and threatened her again. That night he and her mother fought and he moved out. The next day her mother changed the linen and found the underpants stained red and yellow that she had hidden under her mattress. She was hospitalized and Bailey convinced her to tell him who had raped her. Mr. Freeman was arrested and stood trial. She was put on the witness stand and cross-examined.

"Was that the first time the accused touched you?" The question stopped me. Mr. Freeman had surely done something very wrong, but I was convinced that I had helped him to do it. I didn't want to lie, but the lawyer wouldn't let me think, so I used silence as a retreat.

"Did the accused try to touch you before the time he or rather you say he raped you?"

I couldn't say yes and tell them how he had loved me once for a few minutes and how he had held me close before he thought I had peed in my bed. My uncles would kill me and Grandmother Baxter would stop speaking as she often did when she was angry. And all those people in the court would stone me as they had stoned the harlot in the Bible. And Mother, who thought I was such a good girl, would be so disappointed. But most important, there was Bailey. I had kept a big secret from him.

"Marguerite, answer the question. Did the accused touch you before the occasion on which you claim he raped you?"

Everyone in the court knew that the answer had to be No. Everyone except Mr. Freeman and me. I looked at his heavy face trying to look as if he would have liked me to say No. I said No.

The lie lumped in my throat and I couldn't get air. How I despised the man for making me lie.

Mr. Freeman was given one year and one day, but he never got a chance to do his time. His lawyer (or someone) got him released that very afternoon. [pp. 65–71]

Soon after, a policeman comes to the door and tells her grandmother that Freeman has been found dead. She knows it was her uncles who killed him.

A man was dead because I lied. Where was the balance in that? One lie surely wouldn't be worth a man's life. Bailey could have explained it all to me but I didn't dare ask him. Obviously I had forfeited my place in heaven forever. . . . Even Christ Himself turned His back on Satan. Wouldn't He turn His back on me? I could feel the evilness flowing through my body and waiting, pent up, to rush off my tongue if I tried to open my mouth. I clamped my teeth shut, I'd hold it in. If it escaped, wouldn't it flood the world and all the innocent people? . . .

In those moments I decided that although Bailey loved me he couldn't help. I had sold myself to the Devil and there could be no escape. The only thing I could do was to stop talking to people other than Bailey. Instinctively, or somehow, I knew that because I loved him so much I'd never hurt him, but if I talked to anyone else that person might die too. Just my breath, carrying my words out, might poison people and they'd curl up and die like the black fat slugs that only pretended. I had to stop talking. [pp. 72–73]

What follows is a posttraumatic stress syndrome in which Ritie does not speak. The children are sent back South to their paternal grandmother. Ritie remains in a state of partial dissociation.

Sounds came to me dully, as if people were speaking through their handkerchiefs or with their hands over their mouths. Colors weren't true either, but rather a vague assortment of shaded pastels that indicated not so much color as faded familiarities. People's names escaped me and I began to worry over my sanity. [p. 77]

It is clear that now she has been severely psychologically damaged by the rape, the trial, and its aftermath. Her guilt is enormous because of what she believes is her complicity. She loses her mother again and feels evil, dangerous, and unlovable. She cannot trust herself or any adults. She emotionally isolates herself.

Incest and Resolution of the Oedipal Complex in Girls

Because of the prevalence of this trauma, we need an understanding of how incest affects the resolution of the oedipal complex in girls. I propose the following:

1. The girl's sexuality has been prematurely and inappropriately stimulated, leading to a more highly eroticized connection to, yet a distrust of, men. The severe repression and dissociation involved complicates oedipal resolution and makes it unlikely it can be worked through. If the perpetrator is not the father or a father figure, the fact that the father has failed in his role to protect the girl makes his idealization less likely. If it is the father, the fear of retaliation from the mother and guilt in relation to her intensify the bisexual triangle.

2. The trauma may be acted out in childhood sex play, possibly with younger children, as well as reenacted in adulthood by a choice of inappropriate partners, especially married men and men in positions of parentlike authority such as male psychiatrists and other male psychotherapists, but also doctors, lawyers, and employers. Guilt may result from the acting out, which may be remembered, whereas the incest is repressed.

3. Often, in an effort to protect herself from such self-destructive involvements and from fear of sexual attack by men, the girl may attempt to magically hide her sexuality through overeating, thus providing a protective shield around her female organs and female body shape.

4. The fear of men, combined with anger and a highly sexualized desire for male attention, leads to successive ambivalent involvements with men, which are inevitably unsuccessful. Alcohol and drugs may be used to treat the anxiety, loneliness, and pain of repeated losses.

5. Guilt, shame, self-blame, and a feeling of being "damaged goods" lead to sabotaging of success and low self-esteem. Involvement with men who are narcissistic, irresponsible, and violent is common.

6. Considering these long-term effects, it becomes clear that the notion of the distant father and a lesser need for repression of incestuous desire in girls (the weaker superego theory) than in boys, who are usually considered closer to their mothers than daughters are to fathers, does not apply to these girls. The erotic attachment to the father must be repressed very strongly yet cannot be resolved in a way that enables her to enter adulthood without projecting this highly ambivalent conflict—overstimu-

lated erotic attachment, guilt at intimacy, fear of attack, and a very intense anger (often unconscious) at exploitation—into all future love relationships. A paranoidlike approach–avoidance conflict toward men results. The girl's attachment to her father, or other significant men, cannot be idealized because the boundary of generation has been crossed and trust betrayed and destroyed. In the cases of nonfather incest, the father's image may be preserved but the guilt, shame, anger, and mistrust toward men still applies.

7. Some of the women in the case examples of sexual abuse from my own practice have not had a child. I suspect that the sexual seduction has resulted in ambivalence toward the mother much more intense than in the normal oedipal situation because the mother failed to protect her, and this has interfered with the reproduction of mothering. Abortions are common in this group. We may also hypothesize that there was a damaged relationship with the mother prior to the incest as part of a picture of a highly dysfunctional family. This made the girl more vulnerable to seduction because of her unmet emotional needs in the maternal relationship. This need not be true and is surely not true in all cases. Her bisexual triangle involves intense ambivalence either way she turns, making future relationships with men and closeness to other women very problematic.

8. Some incestuous relationships occur at a very young age, 2 or 3, and then stop. In other cases, incest continues throughout latency until menstruation, which usually brings about its demise. At the time of ending the incest, the perpetrator may turn cold and emotionally abandon the girl because of his own guilt and because she can no longer serve his needs. This can be both a relief and a hurtful rejection, adding to the mistrust of men, fears of abandonment by men, and pathological defenses of denial, splitting and isolation, as well as guilt, shame and chronic depression.

The Sexual Seduction of a Young Girl—A Clinical Illustration

I introduced Penelope in Chapter 1, where I focused on her relationship with her mother. I also described my work with Penelope in Chapter 4 as an example of overeating in relation to both the mother–daughter relationship and to her sexual molestation. Now I want to focus on the sexual seduction and to again illustrate my disagreement with Herman and Hirschman that incest is seduction, not rape. In Penelope's case, as in the work of Maya Angelou, we can see the seduction turn to rape.

It is ironic that the same Freud who proposed that the sexual seduction of children was often only fantasy is also the Freud who discovered repression, the existence of the unconscious, and the theory that dreams reveal material from the unconscious that can be retrieved through his technique of dream interpretation. Remember that prior to

Freud, dreams were, among other things, believed to be predictive of the future. Were it not for my knowledge of dream interpretation, I might never have known that Penelope had been sexually abused as a child by a trusted friend of the family, "F." All of the material we have worked with to uncover her repression of this trauma has come from her dreams, her fantasies, and analysis of the transference—also a contribution of Freud, but one that has been developed extensively by his followers and given a more important place in analytic work.

I do not believe that the reality of actual incest means that the oedipal theory is wrong and should be discarded. Both can be true: that girls have sexual fantasies about their fathers, that this creates an ambivalent tie to their mothers and may lead to guilt and conflict for them, which forces repression of these wishes to replace the mother; *and* that there are cases where the father or brother or a variety of other men have acted out upon their old oedipal fantasies with a young girl, a forbidden sexual object, or have reenacted with a child a sexual molestation from their own childhood which may still be repressed. In fact the two are quite complementary.

With Penelope, oedipal love for her father was very strong, and upon his death when she was only 9, the loss was so painful that it left her bereft and needy and thus very vulnerable to the overtures of a grown man who had been her father's close friend and was a father surrogate. This shows how the two theories, the psychoanalytic theory of oedipal fantasy and the feminist exposure of real sexual molestation, can interact. In fact, one of the most startling revelations of her therapy had to do with her memory of a childhood fantasy of marrying her father. In spite of her being over 40 and never having married, Penelope maintained a sense of confidence that there was a man for her out there. This appeared to be a healthy and positive viewpoint, which I never examined until one day the persistence of this optimism struck me as becoming unrealistic, in that there was no man in the picture and her weight was out of control. I decided to explore the idea, and to both of our surprise it emerged that the man who was waiting for her was her father, waiting in Heaven. As is common, at the time of his death she had been told that he had gone to Heaven and that some day she would join him there. This religious fantasy had become a true personal fantasy for her and unconsciously had remained so for thirty-five years, giving her the assurance and optimism about her future that I had mistakenly believed was a positive attitude. Her realization of the source of this fantasy was a crushing blow, for it eliminated the dream that had been keeping her from feeling forever abandoned by her father. On the other hand, it was a necessary corrective that forced her to face the possibility that if she did not make some changes in her life, she could end up alone permanently.

When Penelope began therapy with me in 1976, her relationships with men were difficult to explain. She often went to bars in mostly black neighborhoods and had sex with men she met there, none of whom were appropriate choices in terms of education or life-style, and who treated her badly. The man she was seeing when I first began to work with her was dealing cocaine. I had assumed that this was a result of her having lost her father and never having grieved his death. My consultant said that the death of her father was not sufficient to explain this behavior, because her recollections were that he was warm and loving. This was my first clue that I should be looking for something else, but I had no idea what to look for.

In 1977, having read Florence Rush's article about her discovery that many of the girls in the home for delinquent girls where she worked had in fact been sexually molested, I had a new idea to think about but still had no indication of sexual abuse in Penelope's case until she spoke of a series of dreams in which she is pursued by rats and other frightening rodents, probably triggered by an actual incidence of mice in her apartment. The dreams led to associations to the husband in the couple who were her parents' best friends, and with whom they exchanged baby-sitting duties. At times, my patient and her sister were left alone in this man's care. He remains, along with his wife, a close friend of her mother, and on the occasion of a visit home she was invited to dinner at his house. She associated the tight squeeze he gave to her hand, a squeeze from which she could not free her hand and felt trapped, to the bite on her wrist in one of her rat dreams. She strongly resisted the implications of these associations, but a later dream pointed the direction more clearly. She is in a swimming pool and looks down to discover that she has a very large penis and she is looking right at it. A moment later she reported to me that as she described seeing the penis, she felt a strong pressure on the back of her neck, which meant to her forced oral copulation.

It would take another thirteen years of work before the realization and acceptance of her sexual molestation would be a certainty for Penelope, and literally hundreds of dreams were analyzed in these thirteen years. The theme of something painful squeezing or biting her hands or wrists was ongoing throughout her dreams, as was the theme of friendly animals, usually rabbits or dogs, changing in her dreams to attacking, biting, frightening animals. We concluded that her hands and wrists must have been held down and immobilized in the course of what later emerged to be a rape of her by F. sometime within the first year after her father's death. The possibility remains that there was also some sexual molestation when she was much younger, during the baby-sitting. It seems likely that a man with the potential for raping a 9-year-old child would have used his voluntary baby-sitting as an opportunity for some kind of sexual stimulation and gratification for himself, but that remains a matter of speculation.

Throughout the thirteen years of this work, I received very little support or encouragement from the field or from other therapists. In fact, my woman's consultation group discouraged me from pursuing the repressed sexual molestation, fearing that my patient might accuse the wrong man because she had had no clear memory for so many years. I nevertheless continued to have faith that we were onto something, but without any help from the psychoanalytic literature or other professionals I felt isolated and had to rely on my own personal experience. I had never been able to bring back an actual memory of molestation either, and so I had had to piece it together as best I could from symptoms, memory traces, screen memories, and dream analysis. Were it not for my own experience, I fear that I would not have had the courage to persist in bringing up the issue whenever I heard it in a dream. Dream after dream involved illicit sexual relations with older, married men, in which sometimes the wife or her mother discovered the sexual liaison. Many other dreams contained violence or the threat of violence, in which dangerous men would threaten her with guns or with rape. In some dreams she was forced to have sex, in others she was able to escape. Several dreams involved men breaking in to the place where she worked and threatening her.

In addition to our work with dreams, I encouraged Penelope to be aware of her sexual fantasies and to report them to me. The sexual fantasies that were the most effective for sexual arousal were of two kinds. In one she is a child, passively accepting sexual stroking and oral sex from an adult man. At times she was able to see F.'s face as the older man. The other fantasy was as an adult in which she is aggressive, sexually arousing an older man who is helplessly attracted to her sexually. I pointed out how the adult fantasy in which she had the power and control over the man, was a role reversal of the child fantasy. The sense of power that a child has as she witnesses the immense emotional and physical reactions of an adult male that she has aroused is very damaging to her sense of proportion. She develops the idea of how exciting and yet dangerous she can be at the same time that she is powerless to control the abuse. The enlarging penis, the fast and heavy breathing, the moment of orgasm are all frightening to a child and at the same time convey what powerful reactions and emotions she can create in this large adult. In many of Penelope's dreams, some phallic-looking object began small, and then enlarged and became big. There were so many of these dreams that it became no longer necessary for me to interpret them; she recognized the disguised penis herself, going from small and flaccid to erect and large.

I appeared in disguised form in many dreams. Once she had a sexual dream about me without disguise. In the dream it is the end of our session and I want a sexual relationship with her. I tell the receptionist to hold calls. (In fact I do not have a receptionist.) I undress from the waist down and expect her to do something to me. She feels trapped and says she doesn't know what to do. Some friends come in. She thinks "saved by the bell." I whisper to her that I'm eager for them to leave. They leave, and I'm in a seductive pose and take out a box with a chain, something to do with sadomasochism. She is horrified and says, "It's a two-way street." I say "Yes." She remembers she is late to get to work and leaves.

I pointed out her fear that I will betray her trust and will sexually exploit her dependence on me. She remembered that in the previous session she had wanted to leave early, was anxious, but I had encouraged her to keep talking. She made a connection to F., wanting his attention. She remembered a later dream. I am on vacation and send her postcards. It has something to do with taking the vacation as a tax deduction. It is fraud, but again she likes the special attention.

The theme of wanting special attention as a factor in the transference, in her relationship to her mother, and as a probable component of her having welcomed attention from F. is one we worked with many times. She welcomed his attention and probably experienced sexual pleasure from his fondling, but as in the dream about me, it was a "two-way street." She had to perform sexual acts for him that were frightening and filled her with guilt and shame. Her worst feelings come from what she calls "cooperat-ing." Why didn't she fight? Why did she go along with it? Her complicity felt so great to her that for years she was terrified of facing the truth and resorted to denial rather than blame herself. Maybe it never happened.

Why didn't she tell anyone? When she finally did tell her mother and sister, her suspicion that had she told her mother she would herself have been blamed is confirmed. Her mother did not believe her, nor did her sister. They were both angry at her for talking about it.

It was not until 1986, when I met Mona Smith, founder of Incest Help, and saw the film *Breaking Silence,* that I had help from within the profession on Penelope's case. *Breaking Silence* is a 1-hour video about incest. Theresa Tollini, its producer and director, told me that she was inspired to make a film on this subject when, in 1980, she met a former policewoman who had left her job because she couldn't stand what happened in her child sex abuse cases. The children were never believed by the judges, the lawyers, or others in the system, and therefore the perpetrators were never prosecuted. Tollini spent four years on the film, two years raising the money and two years directing it. In the film, several incest survivors are interviewed and tell about their experience and how therapy helped them to work it through and to confront the perpetrator. In one case, the woman had no memory of the incest. She was very distressed and unhappy and went into therapy. What brought forth the memory of incest began with her observation that in a journal she kept, she often drew pictures of flowers. She found a photograph taken in her parents' bedroom and was struck by the flowered wallpaper and its similarity to the flowers she drew over and over again. The photo triggered the memory of an incestuous sexual relationship with her father, which had been repressed for years. She remembered that to help herself detach from the incest as it was occurring, she had focused on the flowers in the wallpaper. This encouraged me to believe that although sexual molestation may be severely repressed, it can be remembered with the proper clues. Penelope saw the film when it was shown on our local PBS television station, taped it, and viewed it several times. We both began to wonder about the potential value of using memories of the different houses she had lived in as well as F's. house to help uncover memories of her sexual molestation.

There was a series of dreams in which she is in the basement of a house, which she was able to identify as the house they moved to shortly after her father's death. Various sexual seductions take place in the basement, and in one dream she runs to her mother who is sitting with friends upstairs and tries to tell her of the danger, but her mother dismisses it and goes on talking to friends. Her mother's bedroom was in the basement of that house. In one dream she can see a scene of a river with mountains and canoes in the river. There are skeletons in the canoes, and the scene represents some Indian burial service. She was able to associate that scene to a mural that was on the wall above her mother's bed and to fit some missing pieces of the puzzle: the sex had occurred on her mother's bed in the basement of that house when she was 9 years old.

In spite of the pieces coming together over the years, Penelope remained very ambivalent about pursuing the work, and often weeks or even months would elapse in which she never brought it up. She continually doubted that it had in fact happened, since she had no actual memory, and she had trouble being certain of who the perpetrator was. We were both concerned that she not wrongly accuse F. We reviewed every other man in her life—her father, other friends of the family, her uncles, her grandfather—but what distinguished her memories of F. from the rest was the ever-present feelings of anxiety when she thought of him and the complete absence of anxiety when she remembered her father or any of the other men. At one point when F. was visiting the area and she knew she would see him at a party, Penelope decided to bring up the subject in a confrontation with him. She was extremely anxious about this plan, and we spent weeks preparing for it. She told F. that she was in therapy and that she believed she had been sexually molested as a child and wondered if he knew anything that could be helpful to her. She told him she was not yet certain of who it was but was determined to get to the bottom of it and would like his help. He pretended at first not to know what she was talking about and then said, "Well, you know it couldn't have been your father, he was not the kind of man to do anything like that," but volunteered no other comments, expressions of concern or sympathy, or offers of help. When

Penelope decided she was sure enough of her suspicions, she wrote a letter to F., with copies to her mother and her sister. F. responded by calling her mother and sister, having lunch with them, and denying everything; and apparently they all concluded there was something wrong with Penelope. The shock of betrayal by her mother and sister was very stressful to her, but it helped us to focus on the other component of her vulnerability to seduction. It was not just the loss of her father but the lack of love, care, and protection by her mother and sister that had combined to make the incest (according to Blume's definition) possible. In spite of Penelope's many efforts to enlist their help and sympathy, including showing her mother the *Breaking Silence* video, they both maintained a distance from the subject and never offered sympathy or support. When pressed by her, they stated that she was wrong; that either it had never happened or that it was somebody else. At one point her sister made a great concession. She said, "I believe that you believe it happened."

As I listened month after month to the tales of repeated avoidance, denial, and outright rejection by her mother, I would try to imagine my own daughter coming to me with a similar story and felt such an over-whelming desire to care for her, to help her, and to find the perpetrator, that I knew in my heart that this mother could not love her daughter. Her own narcissistic needs made that impossible. I hated to tell Penelope the truth of what I felt, but I knew that I must, that if I did not I would compound the cover-up and perpetuate the tragedy. I made a very strong statement that her mother was selling her out; that she was more concerned about losing her friendship with F. and his family than she was about Penelope's painful and troubled life. The recognition that her mother could not really love her brought profound pain and grief but was a necessary step in her therapy.

Several weeks after sending the letters, she got a letter from F. saying he had been to see a lawyer and threatening her with legal action if she accused him, referring to the allegation as libel. She was very frightened and I had to reassure her that she had done nothing illegal and that libel involved printing something or saying something in a public forum, not in a personal conversation or letter. His reaction did not appear to me to be that of a caring, concerned, close friend of the family, but rather of someone who had decided that the best defense is a good offense.

Penelope's reaction varied. At times she was furious and at other times frightened of losing her only family if she persisted. My support and the support of friends was crucial. Her participation in my group for abused women was a very important contribution to her breaking silence and receiving care, support and encouragement from other women. She was believed and she was not blamed. Her feelings about her mother fluctuated as she alternated between trying to keep on her mother's good list, and being so angry that she could not bear to speak to her mother and didn't answer the phone. Her relationship with her sister deteriorated badly. But the dreams kept coming and were a constant reminder of her molestation as well as providing additional clues as to what was done to her and the identity of the perpetrator. Sometimes they were minor clues, like a dream with a woman in it who had the same name as F's. wife. The animal dreams in which animals changed back and forth from friendly to dangerous continued, but in addition she had dreams of dangerous men or sexual men with dangerous wives. The animals in her dreams became more overtly dangerous and attacking, such as an alligator and a strange snake-like creature that wrapped itself around her arm, squeezing her painfully, another clue that her hands and arms must have been pinned tightly during the rape.

An experience at a gynecological exam in June 1990 proved very meaningful. She arrived late for a session one morning, explaining that she had drunk too much wine the previous night and had overslept. She had a dream in which she and her mother and sister are walking together and pass a house where children are playing with a dog. The dog is purple. Penelope pets the dog and says, "Oh, isn't that nice, the dog is purple." Two other dogs run out and they too are purple, they are from the same family. All three dogs start biting her hands and she can't get free. She calls to her sister for help and her sister comes back and helps her. Associations to the dream are to a neighbor's dog that she loves to pet and to her sister's dog that she loves. There is also an association to a man at work who has asked her if she is free. She is afraid he will ask her out—he is unattractive and she does not want to go out with him.

Therapist: Was there something last night you were trying not to think about? You drank too much and then you overslept this morning, nearly missing your session.

Patient: It was a beautiful day and I was feeling so good all day. I did have an appointment with the nurse-practitioner at Kaiser, but it was good, my Pap smear was OK and we discussed menopause. But the speculum, I never felt so uncomfortable. I couldn't wait until it came out. The speculum felt like a rape. But why did I dream about hands?

Therapist: Your hand may have been forced to stroke his penis, or your hands may have been held back so you couldn't protect yourself.

Patient: In that dream with my mother and sister we are driving on a twisty road and I'm frightened. That reminds me of the parking garage, it felt dangerous going downhill, down the levels of the garage at Kaiser.

Therapist: That's a connection to the danger you felt after leaving the appointment.

Patient: This explains what happened after the examination. I started talking, telling her about therapy, about being sexually molested, how many years of work it had taken. I said you should know it's worth it so you can tell your other patients. That wasn't why I was telling her. I just couldn't stop talking.

Therapist: You were trying to tell her that you felt as if you'd been sexually abused by the speculum. Then you drank too much wine so as not to think about it, so it came out in the dream of the "nice" dogs biting your hands.

Patient: She said cheerfully, "Well, you're only 47, you have so much of your life ahead of you."

Therapist: The purple dog—dogs aren't purple. You pretended it was nice like in all your dreams where animals start out nice and then change to dangerous.

Patient: Yes, purple could be a penis, the change of colors could be frightening to a child.

Therapist: This dream is tied to the feeling of being sexually molested at your appointment and helps to reconstruct the molestation. He stimulated you and then had you fondle his penis, perhaps making references to petting an animal, then he raped you.

In this example it is clear that I am encouraging the patient's associations to her molestation by making formulations in which I connect the material from the dreams to possible scenarios. One might criticize this approach as a kind of "leading the witness," but this is not a courtroom. In trying to retrieve memories in psychoanalysis or psychotherapy, the role of the therapist is to tie together material and attempt reconstructions. The reconstructions may be elaborated or may change as more material produces new information. Langs (1973) states:

> When a patient reports an acute trauma from any period in his life, and especially from his childhood, the therapist should anticipate that this will be a focal point of therapeutic work. . . . Included in such work will be efforts at reconstruction on the part of both the patient and therapist, the latter fulfilling his responsibilities to fill in important missing (repressed) dimensions reflected in disguised derivative form in the patient's associations. . . . Readiness to offer reconstructions is part of the therapeutic stance of the therapist to the very end. . . . Valid reconstructions are sometimes vital to the progress of psychotherapy. Further, there are, indeed, in the associations of patients in psychotherapy sufficient derivatives of these missing events in the life of the patient to build constructions and sufficient material in the patient's responses to assess crucial intrapsychic changes in the patient. In

essence, then, a therapist should be ready to offer reconstructions where they are needed. They can be an exciting and important intervention in insight psychotherapy. [pp. 534, 537]

In the early years of psychoanalysis, Freud believed that a successful analysis enabled the patient to recover the lost memories of childhood. However, experience proved this was not always possible. By 1937, Freud is more modest: "Quite often we do not succeed in bringing the patient to recollect what has been repressed. Instead of that, if the analysis is carried out correctly, we produce in him an assured conviction that the truth of the reconstruction achieves the same therapeutic result as a recaptured memory" (1937a, pp. 265–266). Clearly, this shift throws into doubt many of the earlier formulations by psychoanalysts of infantile sexuality, including the concept of penis envy; but in some cases of suspected sexual molestation, reconstruction is simply the best we can do.

Another clue to Penelope's childhood molestation was her response to reading material about incest or other sexual abuse of children. When the subject came up in a novel, sometimes unexpectedly, she was terribly ashamed that she became sexually stimulated by it. It reinforced her fears that she was to blame and that she had enjoyed the sexual activity as a child. I emphasized repeatedly that no matter what her degree of interest in the molestor's attention or enjoyment of the sexual stimulation, that the adult is completely responsible for the molestation. *A child cannot seduce an adult.* As the details of what had happened to her emerged and became clearer, she concluded that she had been anally raped, and then it was no longer possible to excuse the perpetrator and blame herself. Dreams of painful penetrations of her skin brought much sobbing in final recognition of the painful and humiliating ordeal F. had forced upon her. When she could finally use the word *rape*, I knew she was on her way to a successful completion of her work with me.

Another confirmation to me of the reality of her rape was her strong emotional reaction to stories on the news about the sexual abuse of children. The Southern California case of the McMartin day-care center abuse was in court during the therapy, and there was a local story, an exposé of child sexual abuse at the day-care center at the Presidio, the Army base located in San Francisco. She would report the stories to me and get very angry and then cry, saying, "Those poor children." When the mother and son in the Southern California case were acquitted, she was furious. It was much easier for her to experience her emotions in relation to the children she could believe were "innocent" than in relation to herself who was so complicit, until the realization that she had been raped.

She never remembered being threatened by F., but her tremendous fear of him and anxiety on the subject even in her forties led me to believe she may well have been threatened. His threatening her with a lawsuit adds to my suspicion that he did. Penelope had certain memories of him that resulted in her awareness of her fear of him. One was that he had a rifle and went hunting. Her mother insisted that Penelope go along with him on a hunting trip even though she remembers being frightened and begging not to go. She also remembers seeing him kill a chicken once by twisting its head off at the neck. As the only adult male of the two closely knit families after her father's death, he had much status and power, and her mother relied on him for help and advice.

Another repetitive theme in her dreams was bowel movements. At first I tried to draw a connection to possible early and severe bowel training, which seemed likely with such a strict mother, but although that may have been true, it did not seem to account for the frequency of the dreams and the degree of anxiety in each dream. When she had a dream that a Volkswagen bus was driven into the back of a house she was in, landing right in the room, I wondered about anal intercourse and suggested this to her. She felt it was a possibility, so we both waited and watched the theme in her dreams.

It is not clear how many times she engaged in mutual fondling and oral sex with him or how many times she was anally raped. She was satisfied to know that it was more than once and did not need to know how many times it was. The difficulty was in the recognition that it was more than once and that she had submitted again after the first time, for which she was very self-critical. I kept reminding her of how powerful this man was and how small she was. She found some pictures of herself at age 9 and tried to identify with herself as a child. She also observed young girls, especially the 9-year-old daughter of a friend, and was so touched by their innocence. I commented that F. had destroyed her innocence, robbing her of her childhood.

The problem of not remembering sexual abuse is mentioned in an article by Oremland (1975) and is applicable to this case. Oremland describes the analysis of a jazz musician in his early twenties. "Tom" was very overweight as an adolescent and was the object of intense teasing at school. He was taunted and scapegoated in gym class, where he had to undress in front of others.

> One time during the height of this fat period, when he was about 14, a group of boys invited him to play with them. Tom was fearful to accept for he knew they had been leaders in the torment. However, he agreed, half hoping that this heralded a change in attitude. They all met after school at a nearby playground. Suddenly they pounced on him, stripped him naked, and ran off with his clothes, yelling, "Look, no balls at all." He was paralyzed with fear, humiliation, and anger. His only thought was a wish that he could disappear. He longed to be dead.

He never, even during the analysis, was able to recover the memory of
how he got home. It was as though his "mind stopped working." [pp.
382–383]

This is an excellent description of dissociation during a sadistic sexual
attack, though not a rape. Wishing he was dead led to his temporarily
destroying his mind to protect himself from a conscious experience of
unbearable fear, humiliation, and anger. This was not depersonalization
(*DSM-III-R,* 300.60), which is defined as "feeling detached from and as if
one is an outside observer of one's mental processes or body, (or), feeling
like an automaton or as if in a dream," during which reality testing remains
intact. In the process of dissociation, the event is psychically removed from
memory. It is not even accessible, as with Oremland's patient, in full-term
psychoanalysis.

It is important to recognize that the phenomenon of not remembering
should neither disqualify the patient from being believed nor serve to
discourage the therapist from pursuing the work, but is in itself a *symptom*
indicative of a severe traumatic experience. Many patients can later recall
"going numb" during the molestation and continue as adults to go numb
during sexual intercourse psychically or through the use of drugs and
alcohol.

To give more detailed reporting of the therapeutic work with Penelope I will describe several successive sessions, including my interventions
and her responses. I did not use a tape recorder, so these are approxima-
tions from notes. I include my own thoughts as well as my statements to
illustrate how psychoanalytic technique is combined with a feminist
consciousness of the reality and the seriousness of the crime of incest.

The following series of dreams occurred three months before the
termination date of January 1991, which had been set at the end of July
1990. The treatment had been going on for about fifteen years and so
required a long period for termination. Other attempts at termination had
failed, but this one looked like it would succeed. The incest dreams often
occurred in cycles and appeared to be efforts to work through some aspect
of the repression, with each successive dream building on previous dreams
until some component of the abuse and its effects on the patient become
clear. This period proved to be very productive, and I wondered if the
approaching termination was a factor.

October 31, 1990

Patient: I had a dream I want to talk about today. I read the article in
the *New York Times.* It was wonderful, but I read it after the dream. But

you had told me about it before the dream and I was planning to read it. [An article in the *New York Times Magazine* of October 21, 1990, entitled "Incest and the Law," about victims being able to sue perpetrators years after the crime.] Dream: I am with a group of people. We are traveling to Southern California for some competition. There is a hotel room. I am with several women who are given instructions and we go off to fulfill the instructions. I see a clock and it says twenty minutes to nine. We have an appointment at nine. [She doesn't mention it, but our appointment time is at twenty minutes to nine that day, a change both in day and time at her request, owing to a temporary conflict with her work schedule.] We pass a big, ugly industrial cinder-block building. Someone says, "Oh, that's the dating service building," it's part of a chain like McDonalds. We comment "What an ugly building." A big black limousine is parked in front of the building. I recalled having passed by it shortly before, going the other way. I knew I had seen it before. The driver smiled pleasantly and said "Good morning, ladies." Some people commented that it was an awful dating service. Then we hear a man's voice saying "Freeze!" It's the limousine driver with a large gun, the barrel of the gun is large. He says "Get in there," motioning us into the dating service building with the gun. I was the only one in the group of women who protested. "You can't do this," I said several times, but each time I said it he clicked the gun, so I stopped. We were herded inside. There is a sense in the dream of people being herded from place to place. I protest again, "We have an appointment at nine o'clock." They staple our hands to something and staple us some-where else too, I don't know where. The stapling is like handcuffs and it hurts. I've had my hands hurt in other dreams. I keep protesting but I'm the only one who does.

Therapist: Are you aware of it hurting on any other part of your body?

Patient: No, just the hands. We're waiting for the president of the company who arrives. He looks like a typical CEO. I realize the reputation of this company isn't very good. Someone comments on this and says, "Yeah, and this isn't going to help it any." We're being let go. I think to myself, "We're going to sue, of course, they can't do this to us" [day residue]. I say this to the group but they are reluctant. One of the group is the mother, she reminds me of that actress who was on the TV series "Soap," I can't remember her name, she was just so lovable, but dim-witted. I just loved her. The group was a family, but not my family, and some other people. There was resistance to suing, they were silent when I brought it up, but they definitely didn't want to. I say, "Then the issue is that there isn't enough money, is that it?" She, the mother, didn't answer. At that point I gave up. I keep repeating, "Look what they did to us, they can't do this to us," and I tick off what they had done: "They stapled our hands, they forced us in here at gunpoint." But they remain silent, they are unwilling. I just give up. This reminds me of my mother, when I was talking to my mother and was ticking off all my symptoms that indicate that I had been molested. The family is enlarged now, I spot my own mother in the group. We're all gathered now for the competition, I think it's a swimming pool, there are bleachers—Have you ever been to a swimming meet? I don't think I have, but I'm pretty sure that's what it is. [The patient recently started swimming for exercise and possible weight control.] I see my mother sitting at some distance from me but I can't make a connection with her. [*Tearfully*] That makes me sad, I didn't feel sad in the dream." [*She stops speaking and cries.*]

Therapist: You're sad because you can't get close to your mother.

Patient: They were supposed to be my family but they weren't. My mother was down quite a ways away. The competition was over and people were going home. I didn't want to go home. I stayed. The mother had a son, he was younger than I am. I ended up with him. I say that I want to stay longer, that I would like to vacation in Southern California for a while. Someone says that it's Sunday already and I realize that I have to get back to work. The family agreed to let me go along with them. I went to their house. The young son sexually stimulated me to the point that I was aching and then he left. I tried to seek a bathroom so I could masturbate to orgasm. Someone was herding us around again. The mother came into the bathroom. I had no privacy. My physical sense of being sexually frustrated was very strong. Then I am supposed to have a bowel movement, we were supposed to do number two, people were being herded into the bathroom. The mother has not been a strong person. She is herded in also. When she interrupted me in the bathroom it was because we were all supposed to have bowel movements, and we did. I had driven to the family home after we left the competition. There were lots of people there. The mother said to her son, "It's your birthday. You don't have to go to church today." That's why he was there. I've had so many dreams related to sexual abuse that involve lots of people nearby, like my mother being in a room nearby. I didn't fear discovery. Remember the first dream I had that located the abuse in the basement and then I went up some back stairs to find my mother and she was sitting with a group of people? In driving to this house I had gotten lost. I had to back up the car. There was this enormous queue of Chinese people. I had to be careful not to hurt anyone. I got to the house and that's when the sexual abuse took place. The son is in his twenties. After the bathroom scene I'm looking at him. He's wrestling with another young man. He is on top of the other man. I notice the other man is naked. They are rolling around and he squashed his penis. The man on the bottom has an orgasm. I can't see it but I know he does. I think to myself, "Oh, the young man on the bottom must be gay." He was so surprised by the orgasm, he just stopped and stiffened. This was supposed to be just play but the young man on the bottom is finding out he is gay. It was supposed to be a playful romp but it became sexually stimulating. I had heard from G. [a close woman friend] another story about Perfect Strings [a dating service they had heard advertised for classical music lovers and for which both had gotten membership applications]. It's funny, I had a creepy feeling about the man I spoke to in two phone calls I made. The man was extremely rude. I showed in my voice I resented it and he got ruder. G. had not had the same problem when she called. She has a friend who responded to the ad and got the same man I did and he was very rude to her. She handled it better than I did. She called KKHI [a local classical music station] and complained that he denied what had been promised in the ad and they made him change the ad. He had advertised it on the radio as being a waltz party but when she called he had said "No, it's not, it's a cocktail party." He just grilled me when I called, he said "You know this organization is not for just anybody, just for classical music lovers." I thought he was just someone hired to take telephone calls but G.'s friend found out from the station that he is the owner. You know, I hate this dream because of the sexual stimulation angle. I resist the idea of my being so stimulated very strongly. I don't want to think about it. It's the most intense physical feeling in the whole dream outside of the stapling of my hands. The whole idea of competition is puzzling—the swimming. I just can't tell you how much pleasure this swimming is giving me. I swim almost every day. I've just been sort of like my sister used to be. On Sunday I had so much planned but I got over to the pool and did my swimming and still managed to meet this man to go to the Forty-niner game with him. He's the owner of a bar I go to, he's not someone I'm interested in. He took BART (Bay Area Rapid Transit) over and I met him and then we joined a group from the bar, they are heavy drinkers but I was just fine! I had one drink on the way over and one drink on the way back and that was it. My sister has been more active than I have, but you know that isn't really true.

Therapist: Has that been her territory?

Patient: I guess so, I went along with it being her territory.

Therapist: You did dance well.

Patient: I can do it, too! I have my bag and I even got goggles, it's wonderful, I can see. I'm launching into it in the way my sister would. I go to this gymnasium, like the gym in the dream—well, no, it's really a fitness center. I walk from the parking lot with all the other people coming there, except they are young and slim, but I feel fine. There is some competitiveness, not there but at the "Y" where I swim on Sunday morning. It's very crowded, you have to keep up in your lane. I can hold my own in the lane I choose, but sometimes someone will run over me. It brings my sister into focus.

Therapist: Did your sister swim?

Patient: Yes, but it wasn't really her sport, she loves skiing. You know what she said when I told her I've started to swim? "That's wonderful, you mean you don't have any trouble breathing, with your asthma and your health?" I don't know where she got that idea. Is she keeping me in the past? She thinks of me as asthmatic, but even when I had asthma attacks, the rest of the time I could do anything. Maybe it has something to do with the competitive aspects of the dream. But no one competed in the dream. Even when we were in the bleachers, gathered there, but the setting was competitive. But nothing happened, that's the important thing. When I talked to my mother about it she said "You loved it so."

Therapist: Did you swim as a child?

Patient: Oh yes, when we moved to L. there was a huge municipal pool outdoors, it was like a lake with sand. I went every day in summer. It was just wonderful! What great summers!

Therapist: Weren't there some sexual incidents with boys at the pool? [I now remember that we had discussed her swimming in the past.]

Patient: The boys were always frightening us. They would jump on us, dunk us, and hold our heads under the water for a long time. I hated that part. Boys were always bothering us in a brutal way. They wanted physical contact and didn't know how else to do it I guess.

Therapist: Might that physical contact have been sexually stimulating to you?

Patient: It must have been, I just remember the frightening part. I wonder about the man in the dream being younger. I wonder why that is. [She has often had dreams of sexual encounters with older men.] Oh, I see that time is up.

Therapist: But there is the inappropriateness of the age difference, even though in this case the man is younger. You have often worried about the reported high incidence of people who have been molested then turning around and molesting younger people.

Patient: But he abused me.

Therapist: Yes, but the dream may be concealing the real perpetrator by making him younger. I'll see you tomorrow.

Discussion.   There is so much left unanalyzed in the dream, and I am not happy with my rushed final remarks. I am glad that we have another session tomorrow. First, I recognize that my having introduced an article for her to read in the previous session seems to have triggered the dream, which took place the previous Thursday night, the day of our last session. This is part of an ongoing ambivalent struggle for her to keep this issue repressed, in which my focus on it serves to pull her in the direction of facing the issue, but not without negative reactions. The wish to please me is always in conflict with her wish to be independent from me, and this ambivalence, mirroring her ambivalent tie to her mother, is continually at play and I continually interpret it. The dream is laden with pregnant material and she has made some good connections, but there is much left that she has not associated to. She has raised the issue of her resistance to the part of the dream in which she experiences such strong feelings of sexual stimulation but then has gone on to another, less uncomfortable issue, competition. In thinking about continuing with the dream the next day, it will certainly be important to return to the topic of her shame at being sexually aroused. This is a familiar topic for us but keeps needing repetition, that the fact she was aroused does not mean she was to blame. She was only a child. But the question of the younger man is also an important one to return to. Could there have been an incident in which she participated in sexually arousing activity with a younger child, a boy, about which she also feels guilty? We have not dealt with this possibility yet, and this dream and her question seems like a good opening. Perhaps this is a source of the rigidity of the repression—like the rigidity of the gay young man in the dream. What about this homosexual incident in the dream? This is a new reference for her. Also, the time of the new therapy hour, twenty to nine, needs to be brought up. What could the meaning be of this new hour appearing in the dream? She was 5 minutes late, having arrived at 8:45, and this needs to be mentioned as well. What could the reference to the young man's birthday mean, and the curious idea that because it is his birthday he need not go to church, thus resulting in her being sexually abused? What about the Chinese people she tries not to harm? She works not far from my home/office, in a middle-class, heavily Chinese part of the city.

The familiar theme of competition with her sister may not need any more mention other than the often-repeated connection to any effort she makes toward weight loss always threatening her sister's position as the one who is prettiest and most attractive to men. This always frightens the patient because she fears her sister's anger, and in the past this has often contributed to her sabotaging any weight loss effort.

As I think further about the dream, I am struck by the fact that I have a son in his twenties and that, some years ago, I was at a shopping center with my son and we happened to meet this patient there. I introduced him to her. This could give a particular meaning to all the references in the dream to her traveling with a family but not her family, a family with a mother and son. Could this be a disguised wish to get close to me, since she can't get close to her own mother, by being sexually connected to my son? The man we suspect of having been her abuser was a close friend of her parents, a member of a family that was close to her family. This should be explored as well. What is the significance of Southern California? We know that she and her mother and sister took a vacation trip to visit good friends (also a family) in Southern California the summer after her father died, and this trip has come up in many dreams. She wondered if this father could have been the abuser, but had ruled it out because when she thought of him she felt no fear, whereas she did feel fear at the thought of F., the suspected abuser.

The references to bowel movements are also frequent in her dreams, and we have wondered if her toilet training was severe, but also if anal penetration may have been part of her sexual abuse. I remember the dreams in which she is attacked from the rear, one in which a van crashes through the back of a house she is in. I wonder if she was subjected to enemas by her mother and think I will ask her about this.

The theme of violence against her by men is common in many of her dreams. The driver with the gun and the stapling of her hands are part of this ongoing theme. What about the knowledge in the dream that she had passed the car before? Is there something of importance here to explore? It is surely worth a try.

With a termination date three months from now, she is ambivalent, fearing the loss of me in her life yet looking forward to independence and the additional money for herself. Are there any references to termination in the dream? I'm not sure, but I'll be listening for it tomorrow.

November 1, 1990

Penelope calls 1 hour before her session to cancel. She feels sick, is not going to work, and will skip the performance tonight. I say that it seems important to continue work on her dream and wonder if she could come in tomorrow. She is very receptive and says that yesterday, being Halloween and the anniversary of her father's death, was very hard for her. She kept remembering the part in the dream where her mother was seated so far away and how sad that was for her. She tells me she called her mother last night to talk about her father's death. I had been aware of the anniversary during the session but had not mentioned it as so much was going on around the issues in the dream. Perhaps I should have brought it up.

November 2, 1990

Patient: I felt awful yesterday, I cried a lot, felt I was losing control. I got my period this morning and I'm feeling somewhat better today.
Therapist: You were afraid you wouldn't be able to stop crying?
Patient: No, just crying feels out of control to me.

The first time she cried in my office was when she spoke of her father's death. She got up and left the session. At the next session she said she couldn't remain, she had never before cried in front of another person. She had never seen her mother cry, even after her father's death.

That image in the dream of my mother being at a distance didn't strike me until I was sitting in your office. Yesterday I was feeling such despair. I called my mother to talk about my father's death. She was desperately trying to comfort me but she doesn't know how, so she just kept talking. She said "Here's some good news," and told me about some friend of hers. Of course how could that help me?

Therapist: She can't tolerate your crying.

Patient: Yes. But I'm still glad I called her. She said it makes her sad to think of all the things in life that my father has missed, that she has gotten to enjoy. I said that what saddens me is all that I have missed by losing him.

Therapist: You were trying to feel a connection to her.

Patient: I actually feel sorry for her, she wants to help but she just isn't able to. I had another dream Wednesday night [the night of our last session]. It was about another mother. She was very beautiful and powerful, very different from the mother in the other dream. I was part of an organization and I kept getting promoted. I was given increasing responsibilities and more roles. It was not a good organization. The woman and her husband ran it. I was a newcomer but I was being promoted rapidly. This reminds me of the orchestra, I've been given new roles, more responsibilities. But I don't believe it's because I play that well, I think it's just because I'm so nice. There was a fairly handsome man who had a position of authority, like the accompanist at the orchestra. My friend B. was there, she said "Look at him, I would love to go out with him." Actually B. and I do look over the new men every year and there was a nice new one whom B. is going out with now, but she only complains about him. In the dream this man comes up to me and runs his hand over my rear and down my leg. I get so sexually stimulated that I groan in pleasure. He says "Ohhhh" and says "Do you want to go to bed with me?" I say yes and we start making plans. I realize that he prefers me to B. He offers me some cocaine and I say "Oh, I used to like that" and then sniff up my nose, to show him I'm hip. Then he forces a very big piece up my nose, it's a huge amount, it's enormous. I think, This is way too much. It's generous of him but he is harming me—it's potentially dangerous. I had to report back to the husband and wife, but the wife had all the power. I had to go into their bedroom to report to them. We were like slaves. I had to be sexually available, like in a harem. Both of the mothers in the two dreams are disasters, one is so weak and the other so powerful. I remembered something from the first dream that I left out when I told you about it. When the son is on top of another young man who is naked and he rolls over him and he ejaculates, I don't see him ejaculate but I know he does, and then he realizes he's gay and gets very stiff, the semen is running down his leg and the young man on top sees it and says "Uuuh" and is revolted by it. I know now that molesters don't prefer one sex to the other, I used to think they did. That's why I was worried about F's. grandson. [The suspected molester took a train trip with his grandson and the patient heard that the grandson was distressed by the trip and said he never wanted to go on a train again. The patient wondered and worried whether F. had molested the grandson.] I had dreams during the day yesterday, I dreamed that I wanted to seduce H. [the husband of a friend], I had such a strong need for sex, I was intensely aroused. He wanted to come to my apartment but in the dream my apartment was like my college dorm, and I only had a single bed. Then I had this terribly strong feeling of having to urinate. I mix up sexual arousal and urination. I had a sense of loss of control. When I woke up I wondered if I had wet my bed. It's like the bowel movements in the other dream, the mother came into the bathroom and we were all supposed to have bowel movements just when I was so sexually stimulated. Sexual stimulation seems to lead to fears of loss of control of urination.

Later, I think that I could have made the connection here to loss of control in crying, which she mentioned at the beginning of the session, but I did not think of it at this point.

I can't stand it when H. tries to touch me, he's always putting his hand on my leg. I just won't be alone in a room with him anymore. J. [H.'s wife] would be so angry with him if she ever knew. She would never leave him but it would create a lot of conflict. I have to protect her from knowing. She would want to protect me.

As I write it up after the session I think of the contrast between being repelled by H. in her conscious life and wanting sex with him in her dream life.

Therapist: That's different from your mother, who has not gotten angry or tried to protect you.
Patient: Yes, there is a difference. When I was living with that black man, Mother said that if I married him she would have to leave R. [her second husband]. She did in fact move out of the house to a friend's when I told her. That was her threat to me, although she didn't make it as a threat, but she was actually telling me how destructive I would be to her.

I said "Mother, I'm not going to marry him!" but I did continue to live with him. There would be terrible conflict if J. found out, I would be destructive to tell her. M. [F.'s wife] is a strong woman but I never was afraid of her. The mothers certainly aren't like you. I was forced to be attached to S., though, the younger brother [in F's. family]. One night we slept in the same room together, I know there was one night, there may have been more.

Therapist: At the end of the session on Wednesday, you wondered about the younger man in your dream.

Patient: You said the age difference was the important thing.

Therapist: I'm wondering, could there have been any sex play between you and S. You've been concerned about whether you could abuse someone younger since you've heard how common that is for those who've been abused.

Patient: I don't think so, I don't remember anything. That would have been before my father died. I don't think we ever spent the night at their house after he died. I used to tell him stories. I made them up and he liked that. He was four years younger than me, so I was 9 when my father died, and he would have been 5. He asked me about rockets once. I didn't know the answer but I made one up. I did have power over him. It's quite possible there was some sex play.

Therapist: In the dream there is a mother and a son and you want to go to their house, you don't want to go home. I have a son and you met him once some years ago. You come to my house for your sessions.

Patient: Yes, I did meet him. My mother is such a distant part of that dream. [*Crying*] She is emotionally inaccessible. I have a better connection with her now, though, from time to time. Now I'm starting to feel afraid of her death. A few years ago the conversation we had the other night would have made me so angry and I would have been miserable about it, but now I can love her with all her shortcomings. When she dies I'll have no sister, no close family.

Therapist: Those feelings are accentuated now because your relationship with me will be ending.

Patient: [*Cries again, puts her head down*] This is the first time in my life I don't want my mother to die. I feel some love for her. I felt so awful yesterday, such aloneness, such desolation. I keep going back to that image in the dream where my mother is at a distance across the gym. [*She starts to cry*] You know, I didn't mention that in that dream she is talking and laughing with other people. In my phone call to her on Halloween she told me that she had never been able to celebrate it but that this year her neighbor's grandchildren were coming over for trick or treat and she was looking forward to it. She loves this neighbor, she is the one she went to Germany with. She was glad she could do that, but what has that to do with my feelings? She just talks about herself. That doesn't help me. In the dream of Wednesday night, I am favored, I have a special status in this organization.

Therapist: That may have been part of what drew you to F., the special attention, the special status, that could have been part of the seduction.

Patient: When I think about F. in that house on Madison Street, I can't imagine him doing me any favors.

Therapist: You could have felt favored in a competition with your sister, like with B. in your dream.

Patient: B. is getting attention from the only available man. I am resentful. This does relate to my sister. He is between us in age. I am ten years older than B. I feel like my sister when she talks about him. These words come to my mind to say but I don't let myself say them, I bite my tongue, hurtful things like my sister would say to me: "Oh, grow up." I feel like lashing out at her but I can hear my sister's voice so I don't.

Therapist: Time is up, but we haven't covered a lot of the material from the first dream. You've had another dream since then. Would you be able to come in again tomorrow? I expect to be here all day working on my book.

The next day is a Saturday, so I feel the need to explain my availability; we never meet on Saturday. I had recently told her of the book to ask her permission for use of her material.

Patient: Oh yes, that would be good. I'm not working, I just want to go swimming, if I'm feeling well. [We agree on a time.]

Therapist: I want to tell you that I did hear from that publisher about the book on incest, and it is the same book that you found at the library.

Patient: Oh, good! So I managed to circumvent my undermining.

Discussion.   I had given her a notice of a new book on incest, *Secret Survivors,* in case she was interested in it; she reads a lot on the subject and sometimes recommends books to me. She had lost the notice and I had commented about her resistance. She then found a new book at the library and brought it to me, but I hadn't thought it was the same book.

Many of my questions about the first dream had never been touched because the material from her phone call to her mother and the new dream took precedence. Clearly, the issue of lack of closeness to her mother was primary for her and she was reacting strongly to it. When she mentioned fearing her mother's death, something she had never raised before, I felt there was a connection to termination and raised it. I attempted, as I had on other occasions, to connect her lack of closeness with her mother to her vulnerability to sexual abuse. The purpose of this is not to blame her mother but to help her not to blame herself, to see herself as sad and lonely and therefore easily exploitable.

November 3, 1990

Patient: I haven't gone swimming yet. My nose is stuffed and I'm waiting to see if it will clear. I took some Sudafed. I was thinking about what you said about you and your son. We didn't go into it, what was there about it that related to the dream?

Therapist: In the dream you want to connect to a mother and son. You go to their house and then you are sexually abused by the son. I was thinking that if we think of the dream in relation to termination, that one way you could have of keeping connected with me would be through a sexual relationship with my son. That way you could be part of my family.

Patient: The thought of termination brings on incredible feelings of sadness. The dreams bring it out. There was not really sexual abuse from the young man, it's just that I was terribly sexually stimulated by him. I don't know what he did, it was the stimulation and the frustration. I went to the bathroom to masturbate but then the mother came in and we were ordered to have bowel movements. She was weak. The abuse in the dream was really being forced at gunpoint into the building. The mother was making it possible for the son to be with me by saying he didn't have to go to church.

Therapist: You mean it was more mutual with the young son?

Patient: Well, it isn't clear, it's more neutral. I just know he is there and I get very sexually excited.

Therapist: What about the other young man finding out he is gay. What ideas do you have about that?

Patient: The most important part of that scene is actually the son's reaction. He was so disgusted when he saw the semen. The incident just happened when he rolled over on the naked man, it wasn't his fault. The disgust is the strongest feeling. When I listened to the tape of this dream again [she started about a year earlier keeping a tape recorder next to her bed and telling the dream into the recorder because she had gotten so frustrated with how much of her dreams she forgot] I remembered how hard it was for me to say the word *semen,* I hesitated and couldn't think of the word. The disgust must be mine. In the early days when I read about child abuse, I was surprised to find that abusers don't care if it's a boy or a girl. I had thought it was either heterosexual or gay. Thinking that helped me to deny that F. could have abused his grandson on the train. I wish I would have gotten a response to my letter. I am glad I wrote it, though. I've thought more about S. [F.'s young son]. There could have been some sex play between us. I was struck by the word *play* in the dream where the two young men are playing, but it becomes sexual.

Therapist: You were probably curious about S. After all, you didn't have a brother. And he may have been curious about you.

There is a pause here and I wait, but nothing more seems to be coming up for her. I decide to change the subject because I want to work on the "splitting" of the two mothers.

You commented yesterday about the two mothers, how different they are from each other: one is weak and one is powerful. You tried to connect them to M. [F.'s wife and her mother's best friend], to your own mother, and to me, but it didn't fit. Yet I think that they can both represent your mother. At times, especially when you were young, she was so very powerful, even more so than normally because of your father's death, and even when you were older a look from her could make you shudder. But now you are starting to see her weaknesses, like what you said about your phone call with her on Halloween: she didn't have the capacity to tolerate your crying and she hasn't had the strength to help you with your sexual abuse or to face the possibility that it was F. and so risk losing her dependency on that family.

Patient: With the second mother, I was the favorite. My recent calls with my mother are re—what's the word—reviving my feeling that I am the favorite. She has been making snide comments about my sister. She thinks our relationship is close again. You know, both of the mothers in the dreams are redheads. My mother was a redhead until she was about 30 and I was a redhead until I was 20. But they were both beautiful and I idolized them, one reminded me of an actress—I still can't think of her name.

Therapist: Children think their mothers are beautiful, and they certainly idolize them. [*Patient nods in agreement*] You know, there are two sides to me too. In some ways I have been a very powerful person in your life and you have talked about being so grateful to me, but in other ways I'm very weak. I can't really change any of the things that are problems for you. You also may feel that you are a favorite of mine.

Patient: I do think the dreams are about termination. [*She starts to cry*] It does feel like death. You both will die soon. When I see my mother in the dream, I can't connect to her, it's as if she is in another world. She is talking to people. You once said something that was so important to me, you used the word *endure,* that I have endured a lot. L. [a friend] said that to me too. There is an oratorio with a line that has "endure" in it and I can't hear it without starting to cry.

Therapist: I know you are looking forward to termination because of the independence and having the money to spend on yourself, to travel or get a nicer apartment, but perhaps you are afraid that you have been able to endure because of your connection with me, and that without that connection you will not be able to endure anymore.

Patient: I can't be your daughter, that fills me with sadness. I feel so grateful to you and overwhelmed by your loss at the same time. Maybe I am afraid of being without you, but not nearly as much as I used to be. Something tells me I'll be all right. I won't be your favorite person anymore. I may end a relationship with a man, or maybe not even have a man, but either way I'll be all right. I'm longing to have that kind of a relationship with a man, the kind of merging I can do. When I came back to the orchestra last night, the director said "It's good to see you back," in front of the whole group. I'm one of his favorites. He has some favorites and some he doesn't like. Once you get on his bad side, you can never get off. B. has commented on that and says I'm one of the favorites. But he is not a real possibility for me to be close to, he keeps everyone at a distance. There isn't anyone with whom I can connect in the deepest way.

Therapist: I think that is part of your ambivalence about me. Your real needs ultimately cannot be met by me. I can't be your mother and I'm not a man. It's hard to be close to your mother because you have to keep so much inside, secret from her: your tears, your sexual excitement, all the natural feelings and needs like urination, and bowel movements have to be secret or only come out when she directs it in the right time and place, like the order to have a bowel movement in the first dream. Semen is another natural part of the body that comes out with strong feelings. Your mother can't tolerate strong feelings—sexual feelings, anger, sadness.

Patient: My mother is a gracious hostess, but ultimately she is limited to being that. When she was describing how she would entertain her neighbor's grandchildren on Halloween, I could just picture her doing that. She told me about that to make me feel better about my father's death. How could that help me! And then the story about going to a brunch for the [local pro football team]. That was supposed to make me feel better! She's so inadequate. She couldn't say how sad for you that you have missed having a father. I think that is a reason I feel guilty. She talks about what my father missed and then I feel selfish for thinking of myself. I bet she focused on what he missed by dying when I was young too, and that made me feel selfish.

Therapist: Your mother is narcissistic. She doesn't recognize that you are a separate person from her. If she has some activities that make her feel better on Halloween, that is supposed to make you feel better, as if you are an extension of her.

Patient: You're absolutely right. Imagine her telling me "I'm going to the _____ brunch." That has nothing to do with me!

Therapist: She can't involve herself in your sexual abuse, to help you, to show concern for you, she wants to be left alone, not bothered by your problems. She doesn't want her relationship with F.'s family disturbed, because she is dependent on them.

Patient: When I read the *New York Times* article I found myself alternating between being glad about the women who can sue and regretting that I'm not in my twenties and that it is too late for me.

Therapist: It's actually three years from the time you discovered the abuse in therapy.

Patient: It's been more than that.

Therapist: It could be that it is three years from the point at which you are certain.

Patient: I felt some relief that I couldn't sue so that I don't have to confront him.

Therapist: Time is up. There are still some parts of the dreams we haven't gotten to, like the twenty minutes to nine, which was the time of your appointment.

Patient: Oh, that's right! I never thought about that. I was thinking nine o'clock in the dream, there was an appointment at nine o'clock.

Discussion. My telling her about the article can become an area of her trying to please me if she thinks I want her to sue. I'll have to listen for this and try to determine what she imagines I want from her to please me— meet my narcissistic needs. We seem to have an answer on the meaning of the gay sex—it is a reference to F., the suspected perpetrator, and her fear that he molested his grandson. I think I missed a point on the powerful mother and the weak mother. I made the connection to her mother and to myself but not to her. She can be powerfully destructive. She could tell her friend that the friend's husband has made sexual advances to her. When she was involved with a black man, her mother said she would have to leave her husband if Penelope married him. She has the power to be the favorite because she can be so nice; the favorite daughter, the favorite patient, the favorite of the conductor, and the favorite in the harem in the dream. I will look for a chance to bring this up.

November 6, 1990

Penelope relates two dreams that she had the previous night. They are both common themes. In the first, she visits some old neighbors and is bitten on the hand by their dog. She does not get sympathy and they do not seem very concerned. She relates this to a real experience some years ago of being bitten on the hand by her cousin's dog. It was at a Christmas party. Her cousin did not apologize or seem sympathetic. She also has a memory from childhood of a bee landing on her hand and her being terrified—she has never been sure whether she was actually stung or was just fearful of being stung. She received no sympathy from her family. The repetitive nature of this theme in dreams and the recalling of these two memories has led me to wonder, and repeat on this day, the similarity of being penetrated in these dreams and memories. In an earlier dream, a snakelike creature wraps himself around her arm and hand and squeezes her hand to the point of being painful. We have wondered if painful pressure may have been applied to her hands during a sexual attack on her, holding her down and preventing her from escaping. When I made this suggestion (reconstruction) some time ago, she reacted strongly, crying, getting angry, and feeling over the next few days a recognition of the painful physical force used in her sexual abuse, both in terms of penetration and in being held down.

A second dream had another very familiar theme. She is on a double date. He is tall, handsome, exciting, and she looks wonderful and thinner. The private room at the restaurant becomes a bedroom. She and her date, a black man, become sexually aroused, and she initiates love making. She realizes she is naked and spends the rest of the dream trying to hide her nakedness, trying to get her fancy dress back on. They find a motel. She goes to a bathroom to masturbate, as in the dream a few nights ago, but is again interrupted by other women coming into the bathroom. The bathroom is awful, communal. Her sister is involved, knows her date, and has arranged it. She frequently dreams of becoming sexually involved with a desirable man and then having to hide it and hide her nakedness, sometimes from her mother. She associates to a phone call from B., a married man she has been having an affair with for several years. He travels in his work and wants to see her whenever he comes to San Francisco. She liked him a lot at first. He is an old high school friend. The past year she had been very ambivalent about seeing him, being sad and angry that he will never leave his wife—he has a family, she has none. She agreed to spend a few days with him, and after hanging up she realized she didn't want to and decided she would lie to get out of it. He had made a reference to how much he enjoyed his young son, and that had irritated her.

November 8, 1990

Patient: A new dream. I had joined an Urban Forest group—it was like an institute, like a cult, it makes me think of the cult in the other dream. It was led by a man. I think I had been intimate with him in some way—it was vague. I was "busted down"—is that the term?—demoted in my job with this group. I was suddenly low on the totem pole. It was like a very

sophisticated computer or technical company. It was outdoors. I realized I
was new—was hired at a low level—but I had had an intimate connection
with the creator. He was a genius, it was all his idea. I was given jobs to do
but didn't know how to do them. There was some tolerance of my
slowness by the other women workers, but some threat. I was left alone. I
went indoors to ask for help from an older woman in the room. I asked if
I should burn a certain area outdoors. She said yes and provided directions.
I set fire to the area but then saw that the flowers were being burned, or
maybe it was a cluster of plants. I raced back inside to tell the woman.
"Should the flowers be burning?" The fire had spread and the other
workers were furious. They knew who had done it. Then they weren't so
tolerant anymore, but I had admitted it. "But I was told to do this," I said,
thinking of the older woman. "I was following her instructions." I was in
agony. How could I have such a low status when the president of the
company is someone I had had a relationship with?

I didn't remember this dream until the end of the day—it kept trying
to break through all day while I was at work. I would keep remembering
parts of it. I didn't record it when I woke up, I didn't want to. I woke up
with a headache and felt depressed. I've been swimming almost every day,
but I'm not eating properly, so I'm not losing any weight. I'm eating candy
bars. I'm not shopping and planning. And I'm still smoking, it's up to about
a half pack a day. I have to set a date for stopping. The dream kept knocking
all day. The first thing I thought of was how recently I talked of F.'s
sleepwalking and his stamping out a fire in his dream state. The flowers
make me think of you, these flowers I love seeing. [I pick fresh flowers
from my garden and have them in a vase each day next to the patient's
chair. She frequently comments on them.] The confusion reminds me of
the confusion of a child—is this right or wrong?—the burning. It's so
difficult to decide. That makes me think of the election. [Tuesday, 6
November had been election day.] There were so many things to decide, it
was hard to know in some of the propositions what was right or wrong.
The fire spread, it was out of control, but I was innocent. I shouldn't be
blamed for it.

I wonder if she has seen the film *Avalon,* in which children set fires,
but I don't interrupt as she continues associating.

There was some threat, I was going to get into trouble, but my
honesty would help me. That reminds me of that phone call with B. Why
did I think I had to lie. I should tell him the truth. He'll think I'm crazy,
changing my mind. In the dream it is supposed to be some intellectual

endeavor, but it was beyond me. I thought, He'll figure it out—he's a genius.

Therapist: This dream is similar to one you had a few weeks ago, in which you were at a party in the large home of a famous man on Lake Street (a street near my home/office) with whom you had a sexual connection, but your status was very unclear to you: were you there as a servant to help with the party, or as a guest, or as his girlfriend? He acknowledged you with glances and at one point put his arm around you, and you felt he was recognizing you as someone he had a special relationship with.

Patient: Yes, that's right, it is like that dream.

Therapist: I think that this dream, like that one, tells us about an aspect of your sexual abuse and that is why you resisted remembering it. It tells us what it was like for you to be at family gatherings with the two families and just be a low-level worker when you had had this special sexual relationship to F. At those events, F. was like the president of the company, I suppose, being the male, the head of the family, and being in the leadership position after your father's death. How confusing it must have been, to have that intimate connection with him and then not to get any recognition or special attention at these social events. You both had to keep it a secret, so he couldn't favor you in any way. [I remember later that I had asked during the previous session about whether she had felt special because of her connection with him, but her response was quite negative, that F. would not have done her any favors.]

Patient: [*Starts to cry, and nods in agreement*] This is another part of the abuse I hadn't thought about, another way I must have suffered—how terrible, it makes me so angry. I thought I had stopped resisting it, but I guess I still am. That's disappointing.

Therapist: How often did the two families get together? Once a week, once a month?

Patient: It was very often in the first year after my father died.

Therapist: I think the part in the dream about the fire is about the sexual abuse, too. Fire is very symbolic of strong feelings out of control. It can have a sexual meaning as an intense feeling. It comes up in songs that way, like "Smoke Gets In Your Eyes" [Therapist quotes lyrics from the song].

Patient: It's funny you should mention that, it's one of my favorite songs. Actually it was my parents' favorite song. Yes, that's really amazing that you should mention that song.

Therapist: Do you remember that song "Light My Fire"?

Patient: Yes, I know that song.

Therapist: I think the dream is about my recommending to you that you read that *New York Times* article. Suing F. would really start a fire that could get out of control. What could be more intense than a legal trial, exposing the abuse before everyone. But I tell you to do it, so you are not to blame. I wonder if you interpreted my telling you about the article as encouragement to sue?

Patient: Not rationally. I wouldn't want to sue, but I suppose I could have.

Therapist: I'm not encouraging you to sue; the important thing, I believe, is for you to get all the pieces of the puzzle together for your own sake, so that you understand what happened to you and how it affected you. I thought you would be interested in seeing the article, though.

Patient: Oh, yes, I really felt good about it. It's late.

We have gone 10 minutes overtime. This is unusual because she is very responsible about stopping at 10 minutes before the hour, but the interchange about what it was like for her at those family gatherings was so intense, we both forgot the time.

Therapist: I also want to mention that you can't help but have noticed that I have been taking notes on your dreams. I wonder if that makes you feel that I'm putting too much pressure on you.

Patient: Oh no, I'm glad to see you taking notes. Someone is paying attention, someone thinks it's important.

Discussion. I don't pursue the ambivalence here, because it is too late to do so. Remember that she had not wanted to remember this dream and had not recorded it, but it kept breaking through. Also, I am curious about the "intellectual endeavor" line in the dream, and the reference to the president being a genius. I referred to it in relating F. to the president in the dream but I wonder if in some sense I too am like a powerful president of a cult group in her fantasy, a genius, in her transference to me of an omnipotent, powerful mother. (She was a member for about a year of a women's group I co-led, in which members worked on incest issues, among other problems.) Then there is my "amazing" reference to the song that was her parents' favorite. I want to pursue the possibility of this connection. Ours, too, is a secret relationship that would be denied in a public situation. Could termination represent being "busted down" from the level of special intimacy to a low level in my "company"? She will lose the special connection with me and had recently acknowledged feeling that she is one of my favorites. The other women workers can represent not only the other women in the two families of her childhood (her mother and sister and F.'s wife and daughter) but also the other women patients I see in my practice and who were in the group. What about my book? Could she be hoping and fearing that my writing of her sexual abuse will start a fire?

I notice my going over the time limit today and offering her a Saturday appointment last week, and wonder how the termination date is affecting me. I feel like we're in the bottom of the ninth with one out. There is not much time left, and there is still much resistance and clearly more incest-related material on which to work. I am feeling some pressure to get the job done by the deadline. How might this affect my work? It makes me ambivalent about her termination as well. I want to see the job done to my satisfaction, but of course I know the job is never done, and she will continue to dream and have memories well past termination. It makes me doubt if the deadline should be adhered to, but I don't want to express any doubt directly so that I don't undermine her confidence and appear to be holding on to her, as her mother has. My doubts are probably being expressed in a greater sense of urgency, and she must be picking this up. If these feelings of mine continue (countertransference), they will have to be addressed sooner or later because they will creep into the interaction.

November 13, 1990

The patient had meant to write just a brief note to her mother, but she wrote more than she had expected to. She told her mother that she is continuing to work very hard in therapy. She wants her mother to know that her terminating does not mean she will drop the issue of the sexual abuse. She noticed having a fantasy that her sister would ask to borrow money from her, and that her mother would also. She knows it doesn't make sense. I comment that she will have extra money when she stops therapy and is worried that she won't be able to keep it for herself. She has had a wish to save money for some traveling. I make the suggestion that perhaps I am a "cult leader" like the one in her dream, and the women's group I led was the cult group. She thinks about it but does not agree. She talks more about the powerful woman and weaker husband in the earlier dream and says she has thought more about her but has trouble placing her. As the discussion ensues, she remembers the woman owner of a dude ranch where she worked as a waitress one summer and believed the dream woman was like her, beautiful and powerful. The patient had worked terribly hard at that job, from morning to night, and remembers how poorly paid she was. In thinking about the group of women workers in the dream, about being a low-level worker compared with the other workers in the dream with the powerful woman, she recalled the factor that she was rising rapidly in the earlier dream but was a low-level worker in the later dream.

I point out the similarity that in each dream she depends on a powerful person whom she tries to please. She comments that the later dream is a very important dream because it actually gives her the final clue she needed that F. was indeed the perpetrator: the workers at the company really do fit the scene of the two families getting together after her father's death, including the position of lowly worker, which she in fact held in relation to her older sister and to F's. older daughter, who teamed with her sister to belittle her. I comment that I can see why she did not want to remember this dream, since it would be so tempting to tell her mother of her new conviction, but then she would be afraid of her mother's withdrawal. She agrees. She makes a reference to the man who gives her cocaine in one of the dreams but describes the scene as his forcing the cocaine into her mouth, and it being too large. In her earlier description of this part of the dream, she had said he put the cocaine in her nose. I was surprised but didn't comment. I should refer back to this difference, which again clearly indicates the likelihood of forced oral copulation.

November 15, 1990

Patient: I had a dream last night that was upsetting to me because it was about crossing boundaries. I was in a session with you telling you about a dream. I realized I was dreaming, so it was complicated, it's a dream within a dream within a dream. I suggested we take a vacation together. I made the arrangements. We were buddies, roommates. I felt awkward. You were the boss, you directed me. I asked, "What shall we do?" and you said horseback riding. I asked where, and you directed me to the place. I made the reservations for us. I worried about having the money but I didn't have to pay in advance. At night I was cold in bed. It was an old-fashioned room, like an English bed and breakfast. I kept looking in cupboards but couldn't find a blanket. You gave me one but it wasn't very warm. You found an afghan that was warm. It reminds me of the ones my grandmother used to make [maternal grandmother].

Therapist: What about your grandmother?

Patient: At least with my grandmother I was always warm and comfortable and felt safe. I just thought of something, maybe I felt safe at my grandmother's cabin because I was away from the molester.

Therapist: The blanket I give you isn't warm enough.

Patient: But it's not like my mother, you provided the warm blanket, you directed me to find it. Then you got out of character. You said, "I'm on vacation now." You gossiped, and said some negative things about people. I was startled, alarmed because I knew in no way were we equals. The next day we were scheduled to go horseback riding, and you said "Let's just hang out," so we did.

Therapist: How did you feel about my canceling the riding plans?

Patient: I was relieved. It's like my sister, she would always be the one to want to do athletic things and I'd force myself to go along with her. We rode back to the city with a bunch of people. There was something significant, but I don't remember it. The professional relationship was no more. I wasn't sure what to do, you were like an older person giving orders. You even had a different voice, not your voice. It was upsetting when I woke up.

Therapist: It sounds like you're concerned about what kind of relationship we will have after you terminate. Have you wondered about that?

Patient: Not consciously. I guess I won't see you. I wonder why I dreamed about my grandmother. It's true that she wasn't any fun, but with her I was always comfortable, warm, and safe. Oh, I just realized, I was looking at the pictures of that summer we spent with my grandparents after my father died. I looked at myself in the pictures and thought *that child was sexually abused.* They had built this wonderful cabin in Wyoming for their retirement and spent summers there. We went there in the winter too, after my father died. I felt safe and protected there. We went horseback riding at my grandparents—I just looked at a picture of my sister and me with our favorite horse.

Therapist: You connected the powerful woman in a recent dream to the owner of a dude ranch where you worked one summer. Did that involve horseback riding?

Patient: Yes, we took the guests on two overnight pack trips. I remember a horse stepped on my foot and it really hurt. One night there was a storm in the middle of the night. The wrangler came up and covered me with a tarp. He was such a nice man. I felt safe with him, he was protective. The cabin was extremely comfortable—what a wonderful place! There was an afghan and a huge fireplace and a loft where my sister and I slept. But in the dream, how uncomfortable I felt. At one point I had to go out and get you something at a store, like a mother ordering a child to do an errand.

Therapist: You wish you could continue a relationship with me after therapy, but then you fear I would be like your sister, mother, or grandmother. People aren't what they are supposed to be; you don't know if you'll be safe or unsafe.

Patient: In the dream I felt uncomfortable, not unsafe. Like my sister and mother abandoning me.

She disagrees with me: *progress.* She always used to agree with whatever I said. She can now feel separate from me, have different ideas, but not be threatened. She feels safe to be separate and still remain connected.

Therapist: You're not sure who you have to depend on after termination. Your grandmother is dead, your sister and you are quite distant, and you can't be honest with your mother about your sexuality or your sexual abuse.

Patient: Yes, but I'm not as concerned about my mother as I used to be. I had another dream. I think it's about your being politically active. I remember I saw you at a political picnic once. I've been thinking that I should get politically active.

Therapist: That would be a way of keeping in contact with me after termination.

Patient: I went to a house for a political meeting [in the dream]. There were dogs, but they were all friendly. It was election day. It was a polling place. Upstairs all the people who had been politically active were sitting around in the front room. They sang a song, like a benediction. There was a woman whose house it was, and I liked her dog. That got me in her good graces. There were familiar faces in the room. There was a bar in the house, and we were celebrating the election. Two men forced themselves on me, kissing me. I didn't want to be kissed. The women were getting angry at me. I try to get back in the group. I'm at another home for a meeting. I'm trying to make a speech, but they won't listen. I feel very guilty about not having been active.

Discussion. The theme of being sexually abused by men recurs in this dream in a mild way except for the significance of the women being angry at her. We have talked about her fears of F.'s wife and her mother and sister finding out and her fear she would be blamed.

November 21, 1990

Patient calls 10 minutes before the starting time of her session to say she has overslept and will be late, as she has just awakened. When she arrives, we agree she will stay 15 minutes over her hour; my next session is one-half hour later and she will be a bit late to a meeting. She is distressed because she ate and drank last night and stayed up late. It was not sensible, since she knew she needed to get up early for our appointment. Why had she just not gone to bed with a book as she should have. We had met the day before (22 November is Thanksgiving), and when she left the session she remembered the mansion in her dream and in a previous dream. She realized that in the earlier dream the mansion was clearly on a corner not far from my home/office and that she always drives past it when she leaves my office. When driving past it yesterday she realized that F.'s family had moved from their small house to a much larger one shortly after her father's death and that the large house could have seemed like a mansion to a 9-year-old girl.

Her mother talked a lot about this new house and how M., F.'s wife, was decorating it in color-coordinated rooms. It also had an intercom, which was very impressive.

(At the end of yesterday's session I had commented that it seemed it was much easier for her to spend her hour talking about termination now than about the sexual abuse. She had described signing up for a rafting trip and was excited about it. It would cost the money she would save from stopping therapy.)

I say that the mansion being on her way from my office could represent the connection to her therapy and therefore to her sexual abuse because she is thinking of what we have spoken about as she drives away. She agrees. I tell her I thought her oversleeping this morning was a resistance to bringing up the material around her connecting the mansion dreams to F. and sexual abuse. She was afraid that with this further confirmation that F. was the perpetrator, it could be even harder to keep this news from her mother. She was in a conflict of wanting to tell her mother and fearing telling her because she was feeling a warmer connection to her mother now and was afraid of her mother's withdrawal, especially when she will be terminating.

She says that the issue of closeness to her mother does not seem so important now as it had been, but that what she is disturbed by is the intense feelings of sexual excitement in the recent dreams as they point to her complicity in the sexual activity; the terrible shame she feels about having cooperated is, she believes, the major component in her resistance now.

The patient's capacity to disagree with me and to assert her own ideas is a vast improvement over the many years when she would always comply with my interpretations. It is wonderful to hear her disagree with my formulations.

I wonder if her mother's being so impressed by F's. new house indicated another aspect of her mother's dependence on this family, that they were of a social status that was higher than her own. I say it may not be a coincidence that her sister had married a man who was so disturbed yet of a very high social status. She responds by pointing out that her mother's second marriage was also to a disturbed man, but one with high professional status. I comment that her sexual excitement probably was a part of the sexual abuse initially, but that when it got painful and frightening it would have been very hard to say no to someone her mother admired so much, the "president of the company." We know she couldn't say no to her mother until recently. She agreed that F. was definitely the president of the company in her dreams, that when the two families were together he was the leader, the only adult male. The dream in the mansion where she is uncertain whether she is the help, a guest, or a special lover indicates how much she enjoyed the special attention and privileged position of being the secret lover of this important and powerful man.

She goes on to say that she had taken out a book of poetry from the library because it had been so well reviewed. The reviewer had said that this is what poetry should be like. When she started reading it, she was surprised to find that the third poem was about sexual abuse, and she had started to cry in reading it. She comments that of course she had not wanted to go to bed with her book last night, because it would have brought up the issue of sexual abuse. I say that she had stayed up watching TV, eating and drinking, all so that she could deny the mansion connection and her fear of her own complicity in the sexual abuse. She then raises a point she had raised a number of times, that is, not knowing whether the abuse had occurred one time or more than once. The importance of this to her is that if it was one time, then she would not feel guilty and ashamed of her own participation, but if it was more than once, then she would be complicit. I say that I think it would have been very hard for a 9-year-old to say no to someone who was such an important figure to her mother, and who had such a big house that her mother admired. It was only recently that she could say no to me, to disagree with me, and she is now an adult in her forties.

Discussion. It is definitely a change for me to extend the hour when Penelope is late. I have never done this before, and it is against the "rules." This was another indication of the pressure I was feeling to achieve a certain progress in relation to the memories of her sexual molestation before the termination of treatment. I also thought that to punish her by depriving her of part of her session for her resistance, which in fact is a symptom of the sexual abuse, did not make much sense, so since I had the time I decided to break the rule in this instance. Some may disagree with this decision.

November 27, 1990

Patient: Last Tuesday night I had a dream that I didn't get in on Wednesday, but I don't know how much I can remember because I didn't listen to it before coming today.

Therapist: Let's see what you do remember, and then when you do listen to it, it will be interesting to see what you have left out.

Patient: I was in a place of business, working for a company. The company president was in his office upstairs. He was on the phone to me making sexually suggestive remarks. It was confusing because my colleagues in the office heard his remarks and were critical of them. But how could they know what he was saying? It reminds me of my mother insisting on hearing my telephone conversations with boyfriends, not letting me have any privacy because of her fear of sexuality. But he was upstairs, how had they heard him? It makes me think that I may have had some phone conversations with F.

This is a big change for her. She is making a connection to her abuser herself, not prompted by my drawing a connection. She is working independently.

The setting was an old house. It reminds me of the beautiful older buildings on my college campus. He was supposed to be an upstanding person but he was making these sexual remarks to me. He was married. The man who is an "upstanding citizen" has come up before. [This is a reference to F. being an upstanding citizen, a churchgoing man of standing.] I am fascinated by what he is saying, very interested. He asks me to get together with him and I agree although I know he is married. My colleagues say "what an awful person, making suggestive remarks." They are disapproving.

This theme has come up many times, the disapproval of other women when she herself may be sexually excited by a man's advances. Her fear of this female disapproval is enormous.

Then the dream skips and I do meet him. I've never met him before. Up walks this man—he looks like a customer at our office who gives me the creeps, but there is something attractive to me about him—like the bums in my old dreams.

Years ago she had a number of dreams in which she would engage in sexual activity and feel sexually attracted to older men who were poorly dressed and whom she classified as bums. This was an example of splitting, in which the real perpetrator was disguised as an unlikely character as opposed to the "upstanding citizen" in her later dreams. At the time of her bum dreams she was having one-night stands with inappropriate men of somewhat unsavory character rather than the middle-class but married men of more recent times.

I despise him although he's never done anything to create that much strong feeling—he's older, sometimes his nose drips. [She is referring to the actual customer who looks like the company president.] My mother would say "Ooooew." This man is as close to F. as anyone in any of my dreams. It was his hair, it is white and worn in a crew cut. F.'s hair was white and he wore it in a crew cut.

Therapist: Then it's the hair that reminds you of F.?

Patient: Not just the hair, a sense I have because it is so very clearly the face of someone I know. I've seen this man for seventeen years. He used to work at one of our offices. Now he comes back and intrudes. He comes back into the office and tells jokes. The staff refers to him as "The Colonel."

Therapist: What was his position when he worked for your office? Was he in authority?

Patient: No, he was in a low position, a clerk. He intrudes and forces himself on us—maybe that's a connection. [*Returning to the dream*] I was so interested in what he had to say. Then I am going upstairs to his office in this old building, after hours. It feels illicit. The most uncomfortable part of the dream was the disapproval of my co-workers. I had to be secretive. That makes me think of a story I heard on the late news last night. Donna O., who was missing from Berkeley, turned up in _____ . The story was presented by the reporter with suspiciousness of her story—it infuriated me.

I have not followed local news much and am not familiar with this story. She seems to be assuming I am, but I prefer not to ask any questions about it and just listen to her reactions to it.

They used words like "odd circumstances." The police are treating it like a kidnapping. She might have been hiding out for a week because she was so fearful after having been sexually abused. I'm so angry [*She gets tearful*], maybe she's been hiding. The women at work this morning were talking about it and were suspicious of her story. Of course the dream was last night. My fear in the dream was of what the women would say about me. I can't truly be a victim either. There is something about this phoning. I bet he did phone me to see if the coast was clear. Maybe I'm afraid to even tell you because you'll be critical. You would have been braver than I was. You wouldn't have let a man abuse you. You would think that I wasn't brave enough to fight back.

By idealizing me she depreciates herself, yet she needs me to be ideal so that she can feel protected by my omnipotence, a vicious circle.

Therapist: This gets to the real problem, that you were sexually so stimulated by it and enjoyed the attention, but you were frightened of the disapproval of other women. I wonder if the women's group I had that you were in could be the co-workers?

Patient: No, I don't think so. Maybe I'm afraid that you'll uncover that I just didn't have enough spine, enough moral—oh, what's that word—turpitude, is that the word? If you might think that, what might the others think? I think I have to be honest with myself that I fear that. Deep down I feel lacking. I am often unable to stand up for myself.

Therapist: Is there a current example of that?

Patient: Yes, I back down a lot with my current supervisor. I am afraid. As I said that, I just thought about my mother—how strongly she would object when she didn't approve of something. With my supervisor we were at loggerheads about a particular item to order. There are two kinds; I preferred one and she the other. She made her argument and I backed down.

Therapist: She's above you, though.

Patient: Yes, but I'm lacking in character. I still suffer after all these years from being too agreeable. It's just so scary to be different, to have a different opinion, to say no, to disagree.

I think to myself, this is straight out of Gilligan. She sacrifices self, dignity, pride, to maintain connection because the connections feel so essential and fragile to her; she can be abandoned by mother, supervisor, therapist, lover, sister, if she disagrees, says no. If the connections are not fragile, this quality need not become pathological for the woman.

Therapist: You now disagree more with me.

Patient: I've been aware of that change. I've always been so afraid of criticism, yours and others. I think I was a weak child and oversexed.

Therapist: You were sexually aroused and it was pleasurable.

Patient: ME! I hear this voice saying ME, sexually aroused at age 9? How can that be? I needed to have something that felt good. The need was so great—the deprivation was so great. I was at brunch with a friend this weekend and I saw a young father holding his baby. He was doing everything to care for the baby. He was just delighted by the baby. I love to watch parents with their children, how kind they are to them. Of course some don't treat their children well.

I think of my father, he would have been delighted with us as babies. But I just can't conjure up a picture of my mother being delighted.

Therapist: There are no grandchildren, so you don't have the opportunity to see how your mother is with a baby.

Patient: That's right, except there were R.'s grandchildren [mother's second husband], but I didn't get to see her with them. But I can't picture my mother playing with a baby.

Therapist: It seems as if you are beginning to have some empathy for yourself as a 9-year-old.

Patient: How deprived I must have felt.

November 28, 1990

Patient: I listened to the tape of that dream, and it was the women's group. You had asked me about that and I had said no, but then on the tape I had said that, that it reminded me of the women's group. They had been critical of B. [her married lover] and had urged me to stop seeing him. They had said I deserved more than that, a man who was truly available for me. But I pursued B. anyway. I felt guilty about it. I've been thinking about B. recently, although he hasn't called. In the dream I have this terrible degraded feeling. I feel awful that I'm sexually attracted to this man because he is disgusting. I wonder why I'm so disgusted by him.

Therapist: Disgust is a complicated feeling.

Patient: Yes, it is!

Therapist: How did you feel about the group's disapproval of B.?

Patient: I was pleased, they were saying I deserved better than that, and I did stop seeing him for a while.

Therapist: How did you imagine I felt about your seeing B.?

Patient: I never felt that you disapproved of him, or that you were critical of me, you just wanted to understand how I felt about him. This man we call the "Colonel" does remind me of F., the crew cut, it's the first dream where the man is actually someone I know. I just hate him, though. When he comes back to the office he tells these terrible jokes. I just keep working and won't pay attention to him. Why do I hate him so much? And yet I now know that I'm also sexually attracted to him, since he was the president of the company in my dream.

Therapist: It's a very strong conflict; you're sexually attracted to him and you are repulsed by him and hate him. If he is a bad man, like the group said in the dream and the real group, but you are sexually excited by him and pursue him, then that makes you bad.

Patient: If he was bad, why didn't I tell my mother? I guess I couldn't because she thought he was so marvelous.

Therapist: You couldn't tell your mother he was bad because she thought he was marvelous and because if he was bad and you were attracted to him and enjoyed his attention, then you were bad too.

Patient: Of course.

Therapist: The conflict of being attracted and being angry is there with B. You were furious when he told you in your last phone call how much he delighted in his son, like the father you saw in the restaurant. You know he won't leave his wife because he adores his son and you're angry because you want his attention.

Patient: He doesn't adore his two daughters, he's told me that. I may have been excited to receive F.'s phone calls.

Therapist: I wonder what it must have been like for you over the years at the many social events with F. and his family. Do you have any memory of feeling uncomfortable with F. before that time we talked about in therapy when he took your hand and held it tightly?

Patient: [*Pause*] I don't know. After we moved we didn't see them very much. I do remember Thanksgiving at their big house. He would say the blessing and his voice would be soft, not like his usual voice. I remember being uncomfortable about that. Perhaps he had a different voice during the sexual abuse too, and that's why his voice made me uncomfortable. But I was 9! How could I have let that happen, it's not like I was only 5.

Therapist: That's the issue of your culpability, which frightens you so much because then you aren't a victim and other women will be angry at you. How old are you now?

Patient: Forty-eight.

Therapist: And you're still afraid to assert yourself with your supervisor. Then you were 9, and you were guilty about enjoying the attention and feeling implicated because of your own sexual excitement.

Patient: It's going to get worse with my supervisor because I'm going to have to start supervising four workers in January and I'm worried about that. And that's our last month, I just realized that, it's part of my anxiety.

Therapist: Your problems with supervising have always been because of your fear of being too harsh, like your mother. You won't be able to improve your problem with supervision until you stop being so harsh with yourself. That "there's no excuse" idea is what makes you so fearful of other people's judgment of you, that they will think there was no excuse for a 9-year-old to be sexually abused. It's that harshness that makes supervision so difficult for you. You get afraid of disappointing anyone because you think they'll be angry at you if you don't decide a conflict between two staff members in their favor. When you can have some empathy for that 9-year-old child, you'll be able to supervise others more easily.

Discussion. This is an interpretation related to her severe superego. "There's no excuse for lateness" was a common remark of her mother's that complicated her work on her sexual abuse. She projects that severity of judgment onto others, and it makes relationships where there is an authority and a subordinate person very stressful for her either way, whether she is the supervisor or the supervisee.

December 4, 1990

A dream. She has adopted a baby. A lesbian couple she knows have in fact just had a baby and many people are very critical of them. Her baby is a beautiful girl, but the baby disappears. A salesman who has arranged for the baby says he will do everything he can to find the baby and bring her back. He comes the next day and has not been able to find the baby. She says to him "But it cost me fifteen thousand dollars!" Her association is that she has been in therapy for fifteen years. Another association is to a friend who has been trying desperately to get pregnant but cannot. She is critical of her friend for trying, as she doesn't think the couple should have a baby. They can't afford it and the husband is 75. Another friend has just had a second baby. She didn't offer the first friend her opinion for fear it would upset her, but when she asked, she told her. She associates the baby with therapy and termination. She has a terrible sense of loss in the dream about losing the baby.

December 11, 1990

Patient: A dream. I find myself lying face down. I've been hurt. I struggle to get up. A friend comes and peers down at me and says "Oh, but look at you, you're badly hurt, you're covered with blood." I look at my chest and there are great globs of blood. It looks somewhat phony, congealed, maybe it's not real. But it's quite frightening. I realize I'm really hurt. I say to a man standing there, "You may as well shoot me." I'm seriously hurt. The bullet goes in the left side of my neck, it penetrates— then stops. It's lodged in there. I'm not dead. I realize *it hasn't killed me.* The dream brings up several things. I fully expected to die. Like in the movies, "Go ahead, finish me off." I had the realization when I woke up that I quite possibly was literally raped. I tried to picture F. and picture my sister. How could he have done it with my sister in the house, if it happened when he was baby-sitting, she would have been there. Or how could she have not known, even if it was when I was 9—the blood. It makes me wonder about an anal rape. When I first had intercourse I bled, so my hymen must have been intact, I don't know. The other thing I realized is the evolution in my dreams. Remember that dream of the van driving into the back of the house? I never thought of it, but you mentioned the possibility of anal rape. I've gone from that image to it being a direct penetration of my body, the bullet penetrating my neck. How could that have happened and yet no one knew?

Therapist: You still have resistance to accepting that such a terrible thing really happened to you. The resistance shows in the dream. You deny that you are badly injured. You try to get up. It takes a friend to tell you you are badly injured, as I have to keep telling you. Then the blood—is it really blood or not?

Patient: My fear of termination is that without you I can slip back into denying. And what if I keep dreaming? I don't know if I can understand the dreams without you.

Therapist: You know, you could read Freud's *Interpretation of Dreams.* It will tell you a lot about understanding your dreams, and the technique of analyzing them.

Discussion.   My reason for this recommendation is to deal with her strong dependence on me, which is still in conflict with her desire for independence. The fear of the separation from me is due to a sense of vulnerability without me, that she will be unprotected. We had talked in that regard about a fear of going home alone to her apartment. She may overeat and drink in her apartment in the evenings because of a fear of being alone. I want to communicate to her that she too can learn to understand dreams, that this is not magical knowledge that only I have, and which keeps her dependent on me.

December 13, 1990

Patient: I realized something about the baby dream—the salesman. B. is a salesman. I don't know why I didn't think of that at first. In the other dream I was lying face down. That means it was an anal rape. That's a message to me how desperate the effect was, I couldn't help but be ruined and damaged. I can remember the feeling in the dream of not wanting to go on, telling him to just shoot me. Actually, I felt that way for a few days last week, like I couldn't go on. The sequence in the dream is backwards—first I see the blood and then I experience the penetration. I suppose dreams can be that way. So many times since our last session I've thought, it seems to me it would be easier to remember the painful part, which would portray me as a victim. Instead, I keep having difficulty with guilt. The clues keep coming up. This dream is so graphic, someone is there, the girl who tells me I'm injured. But how could he have done it in secret? How could someone not notice? It makes me think it must have not happened.

Therapist: You'd rather believe it didn't happen than to think that your mother and sister never protected you enough.

Patient: I keep hearing my sister's voice in me: *Oh, don't be a victim. Pull yourself up by your bootstraps.* You know, when she was taking EST. I'm so clear about her disapproval. *Just take steps in the right direction.* I'm almost afraid because of that judgment.

Therapist: If you did remember, would you then judge them as having neglected you?

Patient: [*Pauses, sighs*] My first thought is I blame them for currently neglecting me.

Therapist: Their current neglect is a clue to their earlier neglect. They both were either too self-involved or else needed to deny and so couldn't see the clues.

Patient: Probably both. On the issue of judging, I wonder in that baby dream, that terrible sense of loss, I wonder if I'm judging you in some way. It was such an overwhelming sense of loss. But my complaint was that it cost me fifteen thousand dollars.

Therapist: In your family you could only feel positive, no ambivalence, it was either good or evil. You can only be grateful to me, not angry. The truth is your therapy is only a partial success, and is a partial failure. You can never have a baby, and you have not married.

Patient: But I don't want to spoil the happiness that I've had about having found you. That was not a mistake, I could have gotten someone I wouldn't have been happy with. I don't want to be critical.

Therapist: It's hard for you to integrate the gratefulness and the disappointment. The truth is, I have very limited power. I didn't have the power to get B. to leave his wife so that you could have a baby with him.

Patient: It makes me think of my mother. She would frighten me by her response. In England when my sister and I argued, she said "You're tearing me apart." And then her response "I just want to be left in peace."

Therapist: It sounds like you were afraid you were damaging her, your negative feelings were very powerful.

Earlier in her therapy we talked about her fears as a child that she was somehow responsible for her father's death, and her guilt about not wanting to look at his body at the funeral home.

This was the first dream in which it's clear to me that there was penetration. [*She cries*] The bullet went inside my body, there's no question about it. That's pretty horrible for a child to experience. [*Cries more*] Just like the end of the world. And to have no one to comfort you. When you're a child and you have to get a shot in the doctor's office, the nurse is there to comfort you. The pain, the invasion, the taking at will—to do that to a child—what a great shock.

Therapist: Especially when it's someone you had trusted.

Patient: I was deeply wounded.

Therapist: Physically and emotionally.

Patient: In the dream it's physical, but I was feeling the lack of a desire to go on. I can't allow myself to dissolve in self-pity. I'll feel like I want to die. I have to go to work! Actually, what I feel is self-loathing. I hate myself for my desire to please. Show a happy face! It's so dishonest! It was a survival technique. That SON OF A BITCH! It's totally his fault! He made me feel that way. It's almost more than I can tolerate when I read about it. What if I kill him? I'm afraid to stop therapy, I might lose control.

This is the first time she has expressed such anger toward anyone in therapy. I am surprised and relieved.

Therapist: Then you are using me to suppress your feelings, like your mother did. I think it's perfectly understandable that you would have fantasies of killing him.

She gets up to leave and seems calmed down, mentioning a date the next month when she can't come at the regular time. This is an amazing session. It is the first time she has been so open in her anger towards F. and the first time she has not turned the blame on herself.

December 18, 1990

Penelope was very distressed on Thursday after our session, realizing she had been raped. She had trouble working, felt like sobbing, finally left work early. Her mother called to tell her about her Christmas plans. She wanted to say something but suppressed it for fear of how angry she was. She just let her mother talk and was pleasant to her. She feels such self-loathing at her dishonesty, her covering up. She's so good at it. She felt the urge to call B. but did not. She called her favorite friend, G., and just started sobbing and telling her. This dream feels so close to the truth of what happened, it's as if she now knows what happened. Then J. called and she told her. At work the next day she had some time with her supervisor with no one else around, and told her. The supervisor got very angry and said "How can they get away with it?" She felt better, but has been very distressed since Thursday. The image of blood splattering on the wall—she keeps going back to that image in the dream and believes the emotion she felt in the dream is in fact how she felt at the time, that it was the end of the world. She has not dreamed since then. She saw friends on Sunday, which helped. She's afraid of losing control. She had seen B. twice last week and still cannot have an orgasm although she trusts him. It's part of her fear of losing control.

Therapist: You're afraid of losing control of your anger when you talk to your mother because you are still so dependent on your mother. Because of your sexual abuse, or rape, you have never been able to marry and have your own family, so you are still dependent on your mother and sister because they are your only family. Then you are afraid of your anger toward them for not giving you any sympathy, and end up feeling self-loathing for not having the courage to tell your mother the truth. It's a vicious cycle.

Patient: [More about B., her fear of her feelings]

Therapist: You have cried with me. You were not able to lose control in that way before, and now you have lost control with G. on the phone. The sky did not fall in. You were too angry Thursday night to let out your anger, but you might be able to do it in a letter to your mother. F. can come later. After all, you have confronted him. Let's focus on the feelings of not having been protected by your mother and sister. It is interesting that your mother couldn't tell how upset you were, how insensitive she was to that.

I put myself in her mother's place and imagine that someone I am very close to and love is talking to me on the telephone, and how I can tell from the sound of her voice what her mood is, regardless of the words.

Patient: But I cover up so well.

Therapist: Nevertheless, a really attentive, sensitive person would know, although it is harder on the telephone because she can't see your face. But at the time of your father's death, there was such grief on everyone's part, it's not acceptable but it is understandable that they were insensitive to you. But why now? You can try working on this issue of your anger and your fear of losing control.

December 20, 1990

She has been very upset since last Thursday and wakes up with a headache each morning. She hasn't had a dream for a week, which is unusual. Has had one fantasy, not a very strong one. She imagines gathering both families together, hers and F.'s, and making them all be quiet and listen to her as she tells them of what he did and the effects it has had on her. He is shamed and isolated, condemned to never see his grandchildren again. He has to live in a five-dollar-a-night hotel. Not jail, because in jail he would be taken care of, given meals. His wife has always taken care of him.

Therapist: The absence of children and grandchildren, no one to take care of him, sounds somewhat like your own life.

She cries, yes. She does plan to write to her mother but hasn't been able to. She will do it after Christmas. Heard from her sister, strange letter, two clippings. No Christmas gift yet. Never got a birthday gift from her. [July]

Therapist: I suggest you start making notes to yourself on ideas for the letter to your mother. You are like a pressure cooker, keeping so much anger inside and getting headaches. Let some of it out by jotting down thoughts and phrases.

Patient: I talked to B. Tuesday night, told him about my fantasy. Wednesday morning I didn't have a headache.

Therapist: Have you thought of telling your mother the fantasy?

Patient: What a good idea. No, I hadn't. I will. I haven't started a letter to F. It makes me so anxious.

Therapist: You still feel intimidated by him.

Patient: G. mentioned the bullet and F.'s guns.

January 6, 1991

Sunday. She writes letters to F., her mother, and her sister.

January 7, 1991

Patient: A dream. You have arranged for Dr. Adler to come for a consultation. You have prepared me by telling me to get prepared to discuss things with him. It was like an assignment you had given me. We wait for him in a small, dark room; there is a dining room table. We are crammed in. You say "We had to move the couches." He is very late, almost a whole session. I ask if you can wait or if you have another patient. When he finally arrives, he is a big, demanding man, self-important. His style is to take over. I am amazed that he is so rude. He is mean and hostile, only wants to satisfy his own appetites. There are some small pies, which he eats, and then demands that you bring him more. He sounds like a child molester. You have some dogs, there is one who has such a sweet face. I petted it and loved it. Dr. Adler sat in the next room on the couch, like a living room. It would be like this house, the dining room opening into the living room.

Therapist: Was he supposed to be a psychiatrist who I was consulting on your case?

Patient: Yes, I suppose the famous Dr. Adler. When it comes time for me to tell him my case, I can't say anything. I haven't prepared and I'm speechless.

Therapist: What does he look like?

Patient: He is tall and has a big belly. He reminds me a little of a customer whom I disliked, but then I got to know him better and he wasn't so bad. He also reminds me of a professor I had in college.

Therapist: A few weeks ago when you suggested anxiety about terminating because of the fear of being unable to analyze your dreams by yourself, I suggested that you could read Freud's *Interpretation of Dreams*. I wonder if you experienced that as my turning you over to a male expert?

Patient: I wondered if there was a connection too. I found an old college book from a psychology class I took that had excerpts from it and looked through the book. I don't know if there was any mention of Adler but there certainly might have been.

Therapist: It seems that Dr. Adler in the dream is an intruder in the privacy between us. I am turning you over to him as if he is an expert who can help you. Did your mother take you to male doctors?

Patient: Actually, my pediatrician was a woman. I didn't like her, she was very stern. I can remember the sound of her feet approaching the room, she had a very strong step. But my mother thought she was wonderful.

Therapist: What about your stepfather, would you have seen him as an intruder?

Patient: Oh absolutely, very much so. I didn't like him at all.

Therapist: It sounds like your mother did not have very good judgment about whom to trust in a man. She put you in a vulnerable position by trusting men who were untrustworthy. That is what I do in the dream.

Patient: Yes, that's true. I couldn't understand why you would consult such a terrible man.

Discussion. The recommendation that she read Freud triggered associations to her perpetrator and her now deceased stepfather, both men her mother trusted, who were authorities in her mother's eyes (the stepfather was a physician) and upon whom the mother was dependent. Her stepfather appeared in a number of her earlier dreams, always in a negative way, and at times with sexual implications. In reality, her mother once told her that the stepfather had threatened her with a gun if she did not have sex with him. The mother sought the help of a marriage counselor, who told her that she had better have sex with him. The sister married a man who later became psychotic. We can never know if there was any psychiatric disturbance in her father since her memories of him are all wonderful, but of course he died before she could make a mature evaluation of him.

She hated F.'s political views. He was a terrible racial bigot. The old fear of her mother's poor judgment gets projected onto me in the dream and reveals her deep doubts about my judgment. The reason behind my recommendation was to encourage independence from me in dream analysis, when she had expressed anxiety about termination. The unexpected reaction brought up another aspect of her relationship to her mother, namely, her mother's poor judgment in choosing men, and pedia-tricians. If the pediatrician had been a sympathetic woman, there might have been a chance for Penelope to confide in her.

This concludes the detailed sessions. She terminated at the end of January. These are the three letters she wrote:

F.,

My memory is beginning to return. I am starting to have real memories of the sexual abuse I suffered as a child, and I now know it was you who abused me. It was you who took the trust I had in you, and shattered my world. I will be angry at you the rest of my life for what you have done to me.

You will now for the rest of your life have to carry around the knowledge that I know it was you. I hope you suffer from this knowledge, and I hope your suffering leads you to seek the help you need, so that you will never ever do this again to any child.

Don't think for one minute that you can threaten me with an attorney. If anyone has the right to seek legal action, it is I. You cannot hurt me anymore. The crime you committed has had terrible effects on me for years, but I am now healing, and going beyond the pain and anguish I have had to endure. I have finally gotten to the bottom of this, as I told you I would, and I can now tolerate real memories of your crime. From now on, the secret is out, and the shame is on you.

Dear Mom,

I have completed and sent the letter to F. It is enclosed. I have taken all that pain and all those years of anguish and put them where they belong . . . back on the perpetrator of the crime of sexually abusing a defenseless, trusting child. With the same kind of hard work and dedication I have exhibited over the past several years, I now have a chance to create for myself a life free of shame and guilt and self-destructive behavior. A life of happiness. I now have a chance to permanently stop smoking, to lose weight and stick to my beloved swimming, all of which I must do to avoid life-threatening illness. My anger since that memory of being anally raped is a powerful anger, and turning it inward or trying to ignore it is more of a danger than ever. Of equal importance is that by allowing myself to be angry (and who wouldn't be?) I no longer have to feel the shame and guilt that are a result of keeping quiet about the crime that was committed against me.

As I asked you before, please let F. know, if he calls you for another "meeting," that you will have to talk to me because I want to be there and I will need to make plane reservations and arrange to get off work.

I am proud that I am able to stand up for myself. I am finished with being nice about this! I am like a mother who has seen her child wounded, and I am outraged on my own behalf. I know that you love me, but I wish you were able to feel outrage on behalf of me, your own child.

I have written to D., also, and sent her a copy of my letter to F. Feel free to share my letter to you with D. if you wish to.

Dear D.,

The purpose of this letter is to share with you the major progress I have made recently through my work in therapy. A few weeks ago I had my first memory of being sexually abused when I was a child. I was raped anally, and I know it was F. who did it. After I got through the shock and pain of that memory, I have gotten very very angry. So often in the past I have turned any anger I experience inward, or attempted to anesthetize it out by smoking, drinking, overeating. I still smoke and overeat, and I am just not willing to go on doing those things. My letter to F., which I enclose, is to put that anger where it belongs, back on the man who committed the unthinkable crime of sexually abusing a defenseless, trusting child. One of the reasons I am sending you a copy of it is that if he asks you and mother to meet with him, I wanted you to have already seen the letter. I would also ask you what I have asked mother, and that is if he does contact you about getting together to discuss me, I want to be there, and I would like you to tell him that.

Further memories of the abuse may come. Whatever comes, the days of being fearful and ashamed are OVER! The days of being powerfully angry are now, and the days of increased good health and a chance for happiness and a family of my own are straight ahead. It will take the same kind of hard work I've put in all these years, but I now know there is hope for a good future.

I've also written mother a letter and sent her a copy of the letter to F. Feel free to share my letter to you with mom if you wish.

Discussion

The concept of insight in psychoanalysis and psychotherapy is hard to define. It can include connecting a memory with a feeling, an old feeling with a current feeling, a historical interaction with a transference interaction, and intellectual awareness with emotional awareness. For Penelope, the connections between F. and me consisted of the feelings of dependency, of awe, of being grateful, and of fearing to say no because of a very strong need to please. In analyzing the transference to me she was able to have the realization of how difficult it would have been for her to say no to F. When she finally had full insight, she described her recognition of this conflict as feeling a "wave of understanding, not memory," and described herself as being "awash with understanding." This is insight into her emotional state as a child without specific memory. She believed that the molestation occurred several times and that it took place after her father's death, after school when she was alone in the house; her mother was working, and her sister, who was supposed to be with her, often neglected her duty, probably out of resentment. F. drove around during the day on his job, which meant he would have been free in the after-school hours to stop by and "look in on her," as she reconstructed it.

She came to appreciate that by cooperating with F. and not reporting him, she was not lacking in character, but rather being "dutiful." She had a moral dilemma: choosing between right and wrong or protecting the family. This is the moral dilemma that child victims of incest face every day in our country. The Carol Gilligan work on moral dilemmas (1982) can help us to understand how a child or a wife might choose to protect the family in order to maintain the emotional connections rather than make the "principled" choice. What scale can possibly appreciate the profound fear in making that choice, and the terrible consequences? What a travesty that young children are forced to deliberate a choice that most adults would be weighted down by, and, as we shall see, often come down on the side of protecting the abuser in order to preserve the family. "Family values" is a term currently popular with politicians. What does one do when family values conflict with moral values? In the case of battered women and children and sexually abused children, physical safety must come before "family values."

Penelope came to see me six months after termination. She had confronted her sister on the phone with the fact that the sister had never spoken to her since receiving the above letters. Her sister had raged at her on the phone, calling her selfish and accusing her of not caring about the family. Her sister's attack against her was a screaming, at times irrational tirade. Penelope had been quite disturbed by the attack but had held her ground. She looked better than I had ever seen her look. She had on a very attractive outfit, had lost 30 pounds, gotten contact lenses and a becoming new hair style. If I had seen her on the street, I would not have recognized her.

The Literature on Child Sexual Abuse

I have already mentioned the Florence Rush article that appeared in 1977. In 1980 Rush published a book, *The Best Kept Secret: Sexual Abuse of Children*. Sandra Butler's book, *Conspiracy of Silence: The Trauma of Incest* appeared in 1978, David Finkelhor's *Sexually Victimized Children* in 1979, and Judith Herman's *Father–Daughter Incest* in 1981. Masson's book was published in 1984, and since then there have been too many to mention. There are first-person accounts by survivors, research reports by psychologists, and clinical books by therapists, such as Alice Miller's *Thou Shalt Not Be Aware: Society's Betrayal of the Child* (1986). The video film

Breaking Silence was released in 1985. In the mid-1980s the subject became a theme on television dramas and in newspaper articles. The exposures of sexual abuse in day-care centers frightened parents across the country. A director of a local private day-care center told me she will not hire any men. Mental health professionals in California were notified that we were all required by law to report suspected cases of child abuse to child protective services. If we failed to do so, we would be charged with violation of the penal code. In 1986 and 1987 we all took a course on child abuse assessment, treatment, and reporting. The principle of confidentiality was not to apply in such cases. Child abuse was to be reported "when one acquires knowledge of or observes facts which give rise to a reasonable suspicion."

The Courage to Heal—Ellen Boss and Laura Davis

In recent years, self-help books for survivors of child sexual abuse began to appear; I started recommending one of them, *The Courage to Heal* (1988), to my patients. The book is a detailed description of the process of remembering and facing sexual abuse, with many examples from the authors' groups. It is painful to read, and most people, including myself, can only take it in small doses. Society has moved from secrecy to sensationalism. The victims have come out of the closet, and clinics are overwhelmed with the numbers of sexually molested adults wanting treatment. Child protective services are flooded with complaints. The progress in ten years is truly gratifying, but the number of sexually molested children is sobering.

The contents of the first half of *The Courage to Heal: A Guide for Women Survivors of Child Sexual Abuse* reveal the authors' approach: The Decision to Heal, The Emergency Stage, Remembering, Believing It Happened, Breaking Silence, Understanding That It Wasn't Your Fault, The Child Within, Trusting Yourself, Grieving and Mourning, Anger—The Backbone of Healing, Disclosures and Confrontations, Forgiveness?, Spirituality, Resolution and Moving On, The Process of Change. The second half talks about self-esteem and gives many clinical examples.

Secret Survivors—E. Sue Blume

Another valuable book is *Secret Survivors* (1990) by Blume, whose definition of incest I used earlier. She describes "post-incest syndrome" and introduces the Incest Survivors' Aftereffects Checklist, which includes thirty-four items that could be symptoms of incest. One of the often overlooked symptoms is self-injury, which serves to dull unmanageable emotions by numbing feelings. Examples of such self-hatred are a child's response to violations against her body by the perpetrator. Like the compulsions of drugs and alcohol, compulsive self-injurers attempt to deny their feelings of pain and anger through the ritualistic behavior involved in the infliction of pain. Louise Kaplan (1991) believes this can be understood as a sexual perversion.

Blume originally thought that the purpose of treatment was to discuss the details of the abuse but shifted her approach to identifying and dealing with its consequences. She states that sexual abuse is the greatest single underlying reason why women seek psychotherapy and that many, or maybe even most, do not know that the abuse occurred or cannot remember what happened. Her estimate is that between 25 and 38 percent of women have been sexually abused but that it could be as high as 50 percent because of the many who have repressed the memory. Incest is a violation of body, boundaries, and trust and is possibly the most crippling experience a child can endure. The basic themes of incest are powerlessness, boundary violation, and the secret. When the father is the abuser, the effect is the most traumatizing because the daughter's emotional and physical survival depend on her acquiescence and, as with other family or friends, trust and love are violated along with boundaries.

The issue of "forgiveness" of the abuser has produced disagreement among those who work in the field. In the twelve-step programs, forgiveness is an important component. However, Blume and also Bass and Davis have reservations. Bass and Davis are clear that forgiveness is quite secondary:

> When talking about the stages in the healing process, the question is inevitably raised: What about forgiveness? The only necessity as far as healing is concerned is forgiving *yourself*. Developing compassion and forgiveness for your abuser, or for the members of your family who did not protect you, is *not* a required part of the healing process. It is not something to hope for or shoot for. It is not the final goal.
>
> Although there is a need for you to come eventually to some resolution—to make peace with your past and move on—whether or not this resolution encompasses forgiveness is a personal matter. You may never reach an attitude of forgiveness, and that's perfectly all right. . . . Giving up anger and pardoning the abuser, restoring a relationship of trust—is not necessary in order to heal from the trauma of being sexually abused as a child. You are not more moral or courageous if you forgive. [pp. 149–150]

Sexuality between Brothers and Sisters

The Sibling Bond—Stephen P. Bank and
Michael D. Kahn

Bank and Kahn (1982), in their book *The Sibling Bond,* describe two types of sibling incest. *Power-oriented incest* is sadistic, exploitive, and coercive, and often involves deliberate physical or mental abuse. *Nurturance-oriented incest* often occurs by mutual consent; contains many elements of erotic pleasure, loyalty, love and compassion; and exists as a welcome island of refuge in an ocean of trouble and despairing family relationships. A common finding in sibling incest is that one of the parents is having an extramarital relationship.

All children are sexually curious and may sexually play with each other, exploring genitals in the "doctor" game. The issue for therapists is when the play becomes something else, either erotic love or exploitative force.

> Brothers and sisters will sometimes seek love, tenderness, and compassion from one another in a larger context of fear and terror. Sexual involvement can become an island of refuge for them in a world where they feel abandoned and without protection. . . . [They are] often driven together by the absence of adult nurturance, and by the basic need for continued contact with what is intimate and familiar. . . . Incest is more likely to occur if there is parental neglect or abandonment, so that brothers and sisters begin to need each other for solace, nurturance, and identity, or as a vehicle to express rage and hurt. [pp. 160, 195]

Freud's (1910) view was that erotic experiences between brother and sister were common and stemmed from repressed lust for a parent. In Freud's "Wolf-Man" case, he describes his patient's seduction by his sister, who was $5\frac{1}{2}$ years old when her brother was $3\frac{1}{4}$. Bank and Kahn believe sibling incest can also develop out of loyalty, caring, and mutual sense of destiny. Sibling incest carries the same burden of secrecy as adult–child incest. Finkelhor (1979), in a survey of college students, found that 13 percent reported sibling sexual activity but that only 12 percent of that group had ever told anyone about it. The younger the child, the more confusion and potentially damaging is the incest experience. The effect on the girls is often a splitting between their public world of appearance and pretense as "good" or "conscientious" and their private world of intense sibling eroticism. As stated by Bank and Kahn:

> These girls developed what has been called a "pseudo identity" or "false self," a mask over the secret, powerful sense of the personal identity they felt when with their brothers. The eroticized self was their core; the pseudo identity, their persona. . . . Sexual experiences between siblings can be thrilling, exciting, and emotionally intense and hence can be used to bring life and feeling into a home that is depressing, cold and deadening. [pp. 177, 186]

Bank and Kahn conclude that the long-term effects of childhood sibling incest are more pronounced and dangerous in women than in men and can adversely affect a woman's functioning in the areas of trust, self-concept and identity, sex, marriage, and work. All the women they saw in psychotherapy were depressed, and there was a high incidence of substance abuse. Those who succeeded in work and marriage did so under a strain and handicap, needing psychotherapy to "get them through," owing to constant feelings of depression, masochism, dissociation, and self-denigration (pp. 192, 194).

It is interesting that Bank and Kahn do not mention brother–brother or sister–sister incest. Tisza (1982) mentions brother–brother incest very briefly. There is no rational basis to believe it does not exist. I was consulting with a therapist who had a woman patient who had been sexually molested by her brother but who also had two older sisters who engaged in sexual activity with each other. She was usually rejected by these sisters, so when she was invited to join them in sexual activity she was very pleased at being included. When they later rejected her she felt forlorn and isolated again. I believe that because we live in a patriarchal society, the issue of sex between women is not taken as seriously as sex that involves men. I pointed out the almost total avoidance of reports of mother–daughter incest and have also never seen reports of sister–sister incest. It is as if there is a tacit understanding that what goes on between women is not significant. This mentality clouds the recognition of female sexual desire *uninitiated* by a male. It is in contrast to the long-held prejudice that had allowed men and the professional community to see girls and women as provocateurs of sexual attacks from men in rape and incest. It is strange, indeed.

Brother–Sister Incest—A Clinical Illustration

I described Carolyn in Chapter 1 as an example of a patient with a psychotic mother. Carolyn's mother died when she was 9, but her brother's repeated rape of her had begun before their mother's death. He was four years older, and his acts definitely fell into the category of sadistic, exploitive sibling incest. The mother's cruel treatment of the brother led him to take out his rage against his younger, vulnerable sister. The father was probably having affairs, a contributing factor that brought a forbidden, erotic quality into the family. Carolyn remembered being close to her brother, admiring him and following him around. He betrayed her trust and admiration by repeatedly raping her orally, anally, and vaginally. He threatened to kill her if she told, and she believed his threats and was terrified. She did have a sense of complicity, however, because after a rape he would always leave a dime on her dresser and she would then go out and buy herself candy. Clearly the neglect of both parents allowed this tragic situation to develop. He was finally sent away to boarding school after he attempted to molest their stepsister, who told her mother.

It is unclear to what extent Carolyn's symptom picture was attributable to the incestuous attacks and how much was related to her disturbed mother and neglectful father. She began using drugs in adolescence and continued to do so until partway through her treatment with me, at about age 40. The drugs served as antidepressant and antianxiety self-medication and dulled her pain. She had sex with men, but in response to my questioning realized that she never had sex without drugs or alcohol. She was also a heavy smoker. She was clearly alienated from society by her traumatic family experiences and engaged in the international drug trade, applying her intelligence to live in a foreign country and purchase and export drugs to the United States. She made a lot of money and was never apprehended. When she began treatment with me, she had a straight job.

One of her complaints in her therapy with me was her relationships with men. She was involved with a man who was an alcoholic and drug user and who supplied her with drugs both for her own use and to sell in San Francisco. I searched for connections to her brother in her description of this man. A clue to that connection was her insistence that she could only be sexually attracted to tall men, at least 6 feet 4 inches. She was tall herself, about 5 feet 9 inches, but I interpreted her need to have the man be so much larger as a reenactment of the sexual relationship with her older brother, who must have been considerably larger than herself. This insight enabled her to reevaluate her current relationship with this man who was unreliable and narcissistic, giving her very little. She was able to end the relationship, break the drug connection (a symbolic dependent tie to her brother), tolerate periods without a man, and demand better treatment from men when she did have involvements. She finally solved her drug dependency problem by speaking to a psychiatrist she knew and trying antidepressant medication, which was very helpful. She could not drink with it and that reduced her drinking habit as well.

I focused on the sexual molestation and my concern about the traumatic effects on her. I connected her use of drugs and alcohol in sex with the incest, a way to block out feelings and associations. This enabled her to face the traumatic impact and the ongoing selfish way her brother continued to relate to her. She was reluctant to break off the relationship with him because his wife and daughter were the only family she had. Because of the accidental death of her only child, a daughter, she could not bear to lose her niece. However, she was able to put a stop to any current rudeness or exploitation and to pursue the issue of her brother's molestation of her with her father. She got closer to her father in the course of therapy. He had had his fifth divorce and by then was growing older and weaker and turned to closeness with Carolyn for some comfort. This suited her needs and the father–daughter bond was finally repaired. He also helped her financially. Ironically, her brother had become a very successful businessman and was a millionaire. He then decided to retire and go to law school! She improved her relationship with her sister-in-law, which assured her access to her niece.

Carolyn is an example of a woman who had not repressed the incest but had repressed the emotional impact with the help of alcohol and drugs. Therapy helped her to recall the affect and connect it to her current relationships with men, her drug use, and her other self-denigrating behavior.

The Perpetrators and the Mothers

Like male batterers, the fathers who commit incest often come from deprived family backgrounds, including economic hardship and institutionalization at an early age. They also report having harsh, authoritarian fathers who left them with feelings of unfulfilled longings for acceptance. They often have experienced physical and/or sexual abuse. They have a wide range of intelligence and are steady workers in blue-collar and white-collar occupations. The most consistent factor is a stereotypically patriarchal dominance in the family, ranging from sociopaths who used family members as objects to, what is most common, men who are overinvested in their families, controlling all aspects of family life as a result of a severe lack of masculine identity and a sense of inadequacy. Most perpetrators have no criminal history and are not psychotic. Some traits of a paranoid flavor are common: hostility, suspiciousness, intellectualized defensive structure, introversion, and projection of blame onto others.

Sandra Butler

Butler (1978), using a feminist analysis, describes the men as "the products of our society's beliefs about maleness" (p. 65). She finds the men hold "rigidly patriarchal values and world views" (p. 73):

> When all else in their lives fails, they have been led to believe that the exercise of the power of their genitals will assure them of their ultimate competence and power. . . . The difference is that these men choose their own children as the sexual objects through whom they attempt to relieve feelings of uncertainty about their manhood. . . . They are victims of male-defined standards of appropriate behavior that leave little room for the acknowledgment of deeply felt and repressed needs for love, acceptance, nurturing and warmth; victims of not being permitted to feel and express the full range of human feelings and of not being taught to understand the strength in admitting weakness. [pp. 65, 77]

Diane Leroi

Leroi (1987) describes her clinical observations of the fathers:

> One of the most common patterns in the incestuous family is the expectation that the child is expected to take care of the parents rather than vice-versa. Within these families the parents compete with each other over who is going to take care of whom, and the loser—the parent who ends up making most of the decisions for the family, taking on most of the responsibility and feeling deprived of love and care— will then turn to the child in an attempt to get the love and care he or she failed to find elsewhere. Since a child cannot fulfill such a demand the child then becomes the brunt of pent up frustration and anger when the parent is under stress. This dynamic is called symbiosis. . . . This destructive game involves both parents competing for the loyalty of their children until everyone is aligned in one camp with the mother and the other camp with the father. . . . The child[ren] so aligned with a dysfunctional father may then be molested in an act of hostility and revenge by the father towards the mother. [personal communication]

Louise J. Kaplan

Kaplan (1991) describes the fathers as "starved for loving affirmation":

> When the dependent, narcissistically wounded women they married begin to show even a spark of independence, these husbands turn in panic to their impressionable daughters. . . . Both father and daughter

felt neglected by the mother, . . . both were hungry for affection. It is not unusual for the daughter to collaborate with her father in a version of the incest scenario that puts the blame on the mother. . . . The wife of an incest father plays the *role* of devoted mother but is more involved in salvaging her self-esteem by maintaining her husband's grandiose narcissism than in ensuring the welfare of her children. She is emotionally oblivious to her children's needs but highly attuned to her husband's emotional requirements. When she turns her admiring eyes away from his and stops baking pies, he regresses to incest.

Almost always the father who sexually abuses his children has been insanely dependent on his pathetically dependent wife from the day they met. What he needed from her was her assurance that she regarded him as a mighty lord, the most important thing in her life, and that she derived all her emotional satisfactions through her relationship with him. . . . Typically what triggers an incest father's regression to incest is an alteration in the structure of his relationship to his wife. The wife's prolonged illness, her death, their separation or divorce, her showing some sparks of independence—losing weight, changing her hair style or mode of dressing, going back to school, spending long hours at a paid job or volunteer work. . . . Another precipitating factor is merely the stress of losing a job or professional prestige. [pp. 439–440]

Kaplan (1991) adds an interesting note on the subject by comparing pedophiles with incest fathers. The incest fathers and other male family members have had primary relationships with adult women and regress under stress to girls. The pedophile, by contrast, is not able to relate to adult women, preferring girls or boys to women. Kaplan says that a new breed of child-molester has emerged in recent years, the *crossover* pedophile-incest father who seeks out divorced or widowed women with children to marry. Such a man is the protagonist of Nabokov's novel *Lolita,* Humbert Humbert, who marries a woman to reach her daughter.

The so-called incest mother has been studied and described in much of the incest literature. Some of it comes close to blaming the mother for the father's crimes, the usual "blame Eve" affliction of the culture that protects men and dares not hold them responsible for their behavior. Instead the mother is perceived by some writers as setting up the father and daughter for incest by withdrawing from her sexual role, or she is seen as partially responsible through her failure to take any action that would prevent or terminate the incest. Of course this would mean abandoning her passive role as wife to a male "head of the household" and reversing the roles by taking on the power of "head of the household." Then she could be seen as "castrating" her husband and causing his feelings of inadequacy and again be blamed for the incest, but with an alternate explanation. Thus she may be held responsible whether she is passive or strong.

The obvious flaw in blaming the mother because she withdrew

sexually from the father is that there are millions of women who actually have been abandoned by their husbands and the fathers of their children, and who never commit incest with their sons. We must look for a more accurate explanation, one that takes into account the reality that the vast majority of perpetrators are male. This is equally true in cases of sexual activity among psychotherapists with patients, where it would be absurd to hold the psychiatrist's wife withdrawing sexually from him as responsible for his having sex with a female patient, an incestlike experience. An affair, yes; incest, no.

Clearly, the mother may bear some responsibility in some cases and may believe herself to be totally helpless and victimized in others. Family dynamics require an examination of the mother and how she functions in the incest, whether the perpetrator be her husband, her son, her brother, or her father. In Penelope's case it was the mother's best friend's husband who served in a role akin to a stepfather after her father's death. There is so little evidence of mother–son incest that there is not much research on it, but I am curious as to whether the father is held accountable for colluding in such cases.

The accusation of collusion on the part of the mother is surely not borne out in a description by Butler of a mother, "Margaret," who suspected that her 5-year-old daughter was being molested by her husband, a leading political figure in a midwestern city. Margaret tried to get help for years and was dismissed wherever she turned. First she confronted her husband, who claimed he was just stroking and playing with the daughter and that Margaret must be "crazy" to be upset about it. She then went to her sister-in-law, who assured her not to worry, that in their family that was considered "natural." Margaret became more and more worried about her daughter, could not sleep, became agitated, and then was hospitalized for six weeks with a "nervous breakdown," which allowed her husband and his family to further discredit her perceptions.

When the father raped his 14-year-old son on a camping trip, the son reported this to his mother, saying that another camper had witnessed the assault; he also reported it to the campground authorities, who minimized it and said not to get "so worked up about it." The mother went for advice to an attorney, who suggested an agreement be drawn up so that the father would financially provide for the boy, who was advised to leave the house.

When Margaret came upon her husband molesting their younger daughter, she turned to his aunt and uncle for help and was assured she was "overreacting" and being too emotional. She then visited her children's school and met with the principal and assistant principal, telling them of the incestuous abuse and asking them for help. She was told that they had no counselors who were trained in "that sort of thing." When Margaret finally went to the chief of police, he told her, "Get yourself a gun and blow the bastard away if he ever comes close to your kids again." She then went to her church and at a meeting of the church deacons disclosed her story and asked for guidance. She had belonged to the church for years, even prior to her marriage, but after an initial reaction of horror and disbelief she was ignored. The next day she was visited by two of the church trustees, who asked her not to attend any further church functions until she had things "straightened out at home." This was followed by a formal letter. When she approached her husband again, he told her she was "sick" and "nuts." Butler met her when she telephoned a crisis center in response to seeing a poster about child abuse.

The notion that the mothers collude may be a displacement of the guilt that society experiences for colluding for so many years in the violence against women and children. The debate over whether sexual abuse is primarily a problem among the poor seems irrelevant. It exists in all classes, and the higher the socioeconomic status of the perpetrator, the more obstacles there will be to the child or the wife being believed and the more likely society will endeavor to protect the male. I know of one case where, when the daughter attempted suicide because of repeated rape by her father, the girl was put in a psychiatric ward and was never accepted back in the home again.

The question of whether the mothers know what is going on is frequently raised, and is not always simple to answer. Knowing or not knowing is probably less significant than the capacity of the mother to prevent the abuse by maintaining her husband's respect, or to put a stop to it when she does know. Not "letting herself know" may be the only way she knows, through denial, of avoiding the painful and conflictual moral dilemma of choosing to protect her daughter versus destroying her family and losing her husband. The mothers in the majority of these families are weakened by physical or mental illness, by economic and emotional dependence on the husband, and by deprivations in their own family of origin which have often left them with significant ego defects.

Margaret H. Myer

In a study conducted by the Family Crisis Program of the Division of Child Psychiatry at the New England Medical Center in Boston, forty-three mothers of female incest victims were evaluated or in treatment. Margaret H. Myer, the social worker coordinating the program, concluded that "not all mothers in incestuous families are alike. They cannot be grouped into any one diagnostic category and they vary markedly not only in their initial response to the revelation of sexual abuse, but in their ability to protect their daughters and maintain the family unit" (1984, p. 3). The researchers were able to divide the forty-three mothers into three basic groups: (1)

those who protected their daughters and rejected their mates, twenty-four mothers (56 percent); (2) those who did nothing, only four; and (3) those who rejected their daughters and protected their mates, fifteen mothers. All of the four mothers who did nothing were diagnosed as borderline personalities with hostile relationships with their own mothers. The children were taken from the home, and the men disappeared to avoid the authorities. Those who rejected their daughters were all described as passive, dependent women, fearful of their domineering, abusive husbands who battered them, and none of them separated from their husbands. None had good relationships with their own mothers and none had much empathy for their children. They protected themselves and their husbands and abandoned their daughters, often as their own mothers had abandoned them.

Myer found that most of the mothers in the study were dependent personalities with a multitude of other diagnoses. Mothers who did nothing or rejected their children were also diagnosed as either borderline personality disorder or narcissistic disorder. She found that 75 percent of the mothers did not know that the incest was going on. The initial reaction of the mother to learning of the incest is denial, which is typical of the grieving process with death or other major loss. The healthier the mother, the sooner she gets over the denial and works through the following stages: guilt, depression, anger, and acceptance. The angrier they are toward the offender and the abuse, the more likely they are to protect their children and become engaged in therapy.

In this study, 65 percent of the 43 mothers were themselves incest victims, and this was true for those who protected their children and those who did not: "They never dealt with their own abuse. It was too painful to face and therefore any signs that their daughter was being abused were ignored. If we consider that most professionals ignore signs of sexual abuse, it is easier to see why these mothers do the same" (p. 4). Myer sees the mothers as needing emotional support, physical help, and economic support, and views the mothers too as victims. She concludes that their inability to prevent the incest should not be construed as collaboration or an inability to protect their daughters in the future.

A common theme in the writing on incest is a "painful estrangement between the mother and her victimized daughter" (Butler, p. 109). Owing to the mother's illness, alcoholism, hospitalizations, or withdrawal, the daughter feels abandoned by her mother and angry at her for leaving the daughter with the household responsibilities. Yet generally the mothers are too afraid of the consequences if they intervene. Like the battered women—and some of them are battered women—they fear the breakup of the family and don't know where to go for help or how they can support their family if they leave their husbands. Additionally, many mothers feel a deep sense of loyalty to their husbands who have provided for them and who may have rescued them from abusive families of origin. The men are usually hardworking and loyal and sometimes the only thing the woman has to keep her out of a life of poverty. In some cases, the husband is an alcoholic and the wife has no choice but to work and be out of the home, leaving the husband with the children. As with the male batterers, sometimes their wives know of their husbands' own abused backgrounds and identify with them. Merging between husband and wife diminishes the mother's capacity for objective judgment.

Until recently, as a result of the women's movement, women were raised to be psychologically and financially dependent on men, and one of the many tragic consequences of that dependency is the vulnerability of the children to abusive fathers because of the mother's lack of enough independent strength to leave her husband. The responsibility for the tragedy of child sexual abuse ultimately lies with a system that encourages women to trust men with their own and their children's health and welfare, but often *does not develop men who are capable or deserving of that trust.*

Diane Leroi (1984) has written a dissertation on the "incest mother." Leroi reviews the current hypotheses about the characteristics of the mothers, which fall into several categories: A background of emotional deprivation; a personality of passivity, dependency, masochism, and chronic depression; an aversion to sexuality or sexual promiscuity; and a mother–daughter relationship characterized by role reversal (the daughter takes the role of wife and mother). She says that the consistency in the findings about the incest mother obscures the deficits that exist in the research: the use of small samples (often fewer than eight subjects); post-incest description of the mother by a daughter, husband, or therapist who was asked to recall her personality dynamics; lack of operational definitions to prevent the use of emotionally and culturally loaded terminology; poorly described procedures used in data collection and analysis; lack of comparison groups; the absence of studies that focus specifically on the mother. Her study attempts to determine whether there are differences in the familial background, personality structure, sexual behavior, and relationships of mothers of molested daughters when compared with mothers whose daughters have not been molested, using personality assessment tools whose reliability and validity are more substantial than clinical descriptions, which rely on unsystematic interviews.

There is a current notion of the mother as an "incest carrier," because at least 20 percent of the mothers are incest victims themselves. Leroi's study involved 125 mothers of molested daughters who were compared with 127 mothers of nonmolested daughters ("comparison mothers"). The incest mothers were divided into two groups; molested incest mothers and nonmolested incest mothers. Of the incest mothers, 43 percent came from homes where the parents were divorced or separated, 15 percent had been placed outside the home in foster care, juvenile centers, and so on. Twenty-eight percent were physically abused, most often by the mother (14) or father (10) or both (9), 34 percent were sexually abused by an uncle or other relative (18), father (10), stepfather (8), and mother's boyfriend or neighbor (8). These figures were significantly higher than for the comparison mothers. Parents were divorced in 45 cases of incest mothers compared with 15 of the nonincest mothers; the mother was separated from her own mother in 26 cases of incest mothers and 4 cases of nonincest mothers; 19 incest mothers had been in juvenile centers or foster homes as compared with 1 nonincest mother; physical abuse was experienced by 35 incest mothers and 9 nonincest mothers; and the sexual abuse figures are 43 for the incest mothers and 9 for the comparison mothers. Additionally, the incest mothers were significantly more critical of their own mothers as more dominating and used more critical adjectives in describing their daughters than did comparison mothers. They had a significantly higher Psychopathic deviate (Pd scale 4) profile on the Minnesota Multiphasic Personality Inventory (MMPI). This includes acting out, impulse-ridden behavior, and a hostile and suspicious personality.

The mothers of molested daughters who were themselves molested described their daughters as significantly more critical and distrustful than did nonmolested incest mothers and comparison mothers. The molested mothers perceived themselves differently from the nonmolested mothers. Rather than attempting to avoid the expression of hostility, independence, and power through overoptimistic conventionality, these mothers present themselves as helplessly dependent, naive, and so inferior as to be subject to self-depreciation in a masochistic way. They will go to great lengths to provoke sympathy, help, and direction from others through helplessness, fearfulness, and suffering, behaving like martyrs who are unable to say no to the demands of others. This leaves them resentful and cynical. The molested incest mother is primarily dependent and her conflicts are more primitive, whereas the nonmolested incest mother is primarily conventional and uses denial to avoid any unpleasant reality.

Leroi believes the most common mistake of the female therapist is to overidentify with the victim and, finding it difficult to contain her sense of outrage, to express anger at the offender that the patient does not share. In contrast, the male therapist's tendency is to identify with the perpetrator, often having difficulty allowing the patient to express anger at the offender. The female therapist may avoid eliciting sexual details, whereas the male therapist may show an excessive interest in them. The male therapist may find himself becoming excited by the victim's account of forbidden sexual activity and runs the risk of becoming sexually involved with the patient, either in fantasy or in reality.

Leroi gives a clinical profile of incest mothers as having difficulties with trust. Poor emotional boundaries result in an exaggerated sense of responsibility, painful identification rather than empathy, difficulties with self-protection, and difficulties with self-esteem. This may result in splitting, being overly aggressive, and avoiding genuine human contact. They convey a sense of being unlovable or unworthy, cannot identify or articulate their needs, and make few if any demands. Abuse, love, and caring are inappropriately fused, and thus they choose abusive mates. They overidealize men and have contempt for women. They are also characterized by self-righteousness; are poor at resolving conflicts, remaining either the aggressor or the victim; and have parenting difficulties owing to confusion about the difference between discipline and abuse and intrusiveness versus caring. Although both groups describe their mothers as actively exhibiting dominant characteristics, incest women describe their mothers as significantly less loving than the mothers of nonincest women. In this regard the figures on physical abuse by the mothers of incest mothers are telling. Fourteen incest mothers were abused by their own mothers as compared with two nonincest mothers, whereas ten incest mothers were physically abused by their fathers compared with seven in the nonincest group. Transference to daughters from the mother's own relationship with her mother is a prominent observation in clinical work with women. It is most difficult to give love, nurturance, and protection to one's daughter when a mother has not received that kind of care from her own mother. Psychotherapy can be very helpful to make the mother aware of her reenactment of her own unhappy relationship with her mother in her attitude toward and treatment of her own daughters. Of the incest mothers who were separated from their own mothers, this occurred at an average age of 7, for an average period of $6\frac{1}{2}$ years. The defensive maneuvers practiced by incest mothers generally involve projection, rationalization, and as described by others, a tendency to remain aloof and appear uninvolved. They have a tendency to act out conflicts, are unreliable, have shallow loyalties, are manipulative, project hostile feelings onto others, and have an exaggerated need for affection and attention. They are sensitive to anything that can be construed as a demand upon them, yet are overly demanding in narcissistic and egocentric ways.

However, the MMPI results showed that the mean scores on depression, dependency and masochism, though significant, are not as wide apart as one might expect. The incest mothers had a mean depression score of 62.63 versus 52.57 for comparison mothers; a mean dependency score of 55.49 versus 44.8 for comparison mothers; and a mean masochism score of 56.36 versus 47.11 for comparison mothers. It seems fair to summarize these figures by saying that all the women had scores of higher than 50 percent for depression and around 50 percent for dependency and masochism, reminding us once again of the serious psychiatric problems faced by most women, even those who are well educated, in the contemporary United States, and reinforcing the importance of a feminist analysis of female development.

Leroi's study found that mothers of molested daughters had a mean level of education of high school graduation, whereas the comparison mothers had an average of completion of four years of college. The incest mothers married and had children younger than did the comparison mothers, and had fewer financial resources with more children than comparison mothers. This leads to Leroi's speculation that less education weakens the incest mother's capacity to be an effective restraining agent against the partner's potential for dysfunctional sexual behavior. The income in the comparison mother families is higher (forty-five thousand dollars compared with twenty-five thousand dollars) but may partially reflect the higher percentage of intact families with two incomes in this group. Her central hypothesis, that the more adequately a mother functions, the less likely that molestation of the daughter will occur, helps to make sense of the college education factor. The figure of nine comparison mothers who had been sexually molested is most significant. Could the factor of education have made the difference? Looking at eight of that original group of nine women, the average length of education is $2\frac{1}{2}$ years of college. The MMPI scores are less indicative of pathology than those of the incest mothers, and the degree of sexual molestation is considerably less. In every case the molestation involved fondling only; in one case there was one instance of fondling, and in three cases the duration was 1 to 6 months. The Psychopathic Deviate (Pd) score appears to be in direct relation to the severity, length, and source of the abuse. A woman who has graduated or at least attended college is more likely to have a higher sense of self-worth, greater self-esteem, and is less likely to be a passive, compliant wife than a non-college-educated woman. If she works, she is more likely to work at a job that brings her more satisfaction, gives her more prestige, and for which she receives higher pay than a high school graduate. It is interesting to note the difference in the self-descriptions of the two groups. Incest mothers describe themselves as significantly more complaining, distrustful, modest, submissive, respectful, trustful, cooperative, supportive, and generous than do comparison mothers. Comparison mothers describe themselves as significantly more domineering, proud, and advising than do incest mothers. Thus we reach the paradoxical conclusion that incest mothers are more traditionally feminine and come closer to the patriarchal ideal of womanhood than nonincest mothers. Considering that the incest fathers are described as domineering tyrants, we can see how well the match fits. We could say that the incest family, as the family of the battering male, is a stereotypic exaggeration of the patriarchal ideal of male supremacy and female modesty.

When Mothers Are Molesters

All researchers have found that a vast majority of child molesters are men, but nonetheless there are some women, and we should be alert to this possibility and learn the characteristics of mothers who sexually abuse their children. In a recent survey, Reinhart (1987) found that 96 percent of the perpetrators in his sample of 189 cases were male. Others have found 3 percent female (DeFrances, 1969). Weinberg (1955) found only 2 cases out of 200 to involve female perpetrators. Some studies suggest that the figures may be higher but incidents are less likely to be reported and are often concealed in the bathing and dressing of the children. Blair and Rita Justice (1979) believe that secretive sexual activity is passed off as child care more easily by mothers. Shrier's retrospective study of male sexual abuse victims (1987) found that among adolescent males who reported sexual victimization as children, 60 percent have been molested by females, a much higher figure than that of other researchers. It is counter to our stereotypes to view women as perpetrators of sexual abuse or to view males as victims of female abusers. Women are supposed to be nurturant and males are supposed to be in control. It is these very stereotypes that make the male victim so ashamed and even less likely than the female victim to report his abuse or even define his sexual activity as abuse. The example of the film *The Last Picture Show,* in which a married woman in her thirties has an affair with a teenage boy, has not been considered sexual abuse of the boy, but according to those who research and treat male victims, is in fact an example of a woman offender exploiting a male victim. Who are these women?

Ruth Mathews

Mathews (1987) classifies the women molesters into three groups:

1. *Exploration/Exploitation.* Typically 16 years old or younger, with victims 6 years or younger; abuse usually occurring during baby-sitting, and may happen only once.

2. *Personality Disordered/Severe Abuse History.* Adolescents or adults, described as self-destructive, depressed, aggressive and poorly adjusted. They themselves have been subjected to severe sexual and physical abuse, usually by a male family member. Their victims may be male but are more often female children between the ages of birth to 10 to whom they are related, including their own children, with whom they reenact their own victimization.

3. *Developmentally Arrested or Regressed.* Married, divorced, or single adults, socially isolated. About 50 percent of these women have sexual abuse histories and are similar to "fixated" pedophiles. Victims between 11 and 16 with whom they have a self-initiated "love affair" (in Bolton, p. 54).

Almost half of the adolescent female offenders and half of the adult female offenders fall within the second category. The predominant number of child female perpetrators (ages 4 to 13) also fall in this category.

In a later report (1990) Mathews, Matthews, and Spelz revise this typology to include the aggressive female rapist, the predisposed, male-coerced, experimenter/exploiter, teacher/lover, accomplice, and psychotic offender types. In approximately 42 percent of the cases of male sexual victimization and 54 percent of the cases of female victimization by females, the female offender was acting in the company of others. Male perpetrators do not report being coerced by females or being an accomplice to a female.

Kathleen Faller

Faller (1988) describes three scenarios in which women may be perpetrators.

1. *Noncustodial Parent.* Abuse occurs during visitation following a separation or divorce that was strongly resisted by the abusing parent. Three factors may contribute: the unstructured situation in which the perpetrator has unsupervised access to the child; the offender being devastated and lonely due to the loss of the spouse and turning to the child for emotional support; and the perpetrator's tremendous anger toward the spouse who initiated the marital breakup, which gets indirectly expressed through the sexual abuse of the child.

2. *Single Parents.* In these cases the parent is the custodial parent. The mothers are likely to be women who have never had a consistent partner, whereas in the cases of fathers, the mother is either dead, has deserted, or is an unfit mother. The oldest child becomes a substitute for the absent parent: a parental child. One form is the case in which the parent and oldest child are both sad and start sleeping together for comfort. Or the older child starts taking over the duties of the absent parent and the sexual abuse evolves gradually. In these cases the sexual relationship is part of an affectionate and nurturant tie and does not involve force. The family is often geographically or socially isolated.

3. *Polymorphous or Polyincestuous Families.* These are cases where there is more than one perpetrator, perhaps father and mother, father and older son, grandfather and father, or father and uncle. There are multiple sexual relationships including father–daughter, father–son, and siblings involved with each other. Sometimes persons outside the family are included. It is often difficult to separate the perpetrators from the victims, as one victim may then abuse another family member. In almost all these cases the male is the instigator and the wife follows her husband's direction, and may not in all cases be a direct molester herself (Finkelhor, 1986).

Mathews, Matthews, and Spelz (1990) find that the most frequent type of female offender reported in adult clinical research populations is the male-coerced female. Many of these women express a belief that they would never have sexually abused another person if not coerced. Many of the male-coerced offenders experienced being beaten, sexually abused, and dominated by their husbands or boyfriends; have extreme feelings of inferiority; and are nonassertive with men. They have a very poorly developed sense of identity and very low ego strength. Although these authors do not use the diagnostic description of borderline disorder, it seems clear that these women do fit that picture. There would be very little chance for them to have developed a mature sense of boundaries when physical and sexual boundaries were traumatically invaded in their own childhood. This is likely to be a larger category than the overtly psychotic women. The psychodynamic understanding can be joined with the cultural stereotype explanation of the weak, dependent, selfless female by appreciating how the borderline patient is less able to forge a positive female identity based on qualities of independence and redefinition of herself apart from the cultural stereotypes. Her pathology dovetails with "femininity" to an exaggerated and unhealthy degree. In these examples of battered women and incest perpetrators, the dangers inherent in the traditional female role are highlighted by the vulnerability of these women to sadistic men. These cases are the extreme, but the pattern exists in marriages where the husband dominates the wife and demands compliance without resorting to physical force as well, relying on his financial power and control to prevail over her wishes on a variety of matters. Examples of the dangers for women who are assertive and headstrong are numerous in film and fiction, such as the famous Bette Davis role in *Jezebel* (1938), in which she loses her fiancé (Henry Fonda) to another woman because of her independent and rebellious behavior.

Charlotte Davis Kasl

Kasl (1990) presents a feminist perspective on female perpetrators of sexual abuse and differs in her view of the prevalence of this problem from Diana

Russell, whose data showed that less than one percent of female abuse survivors are abused by women. Kasl, based on her clinical observation, estimates that 15 to 25 percent of victims of sexual abuse have been abused by women. The highest incidence of people who had been sexually abused by women occurred in male perpetrators. She discusses the problems inherent in these statistics for feminists but urges that the taboo against the recognition of female sexual abusers be broken. She divides sexual abuse, which she says is a catchall phrase, into overt abuse, covert abuse, sexual violation, boundary crossing, and ignorant parenting. The female perpetrator's abuse is often elusive and difficult to define because it does not involve penetration; in fact, in the case of penetration of the mother, aunt, or other older female by a teenage boy, the boy is the victim in spite of his role as penetrator. Walking around the house in a sheer nightgown is a particularly female display that can excite a boy. Bathing a child or giving enemas are other examples of female behavior that can be sexually intrusive and in some cases even sadistic.

> As women, our self-image is challenged when we open our eyes to abuse by other women. It destroys the myths about the innocence of women and thus about ourselves. It may bring to the surface internalized hatred of other women and raise issues about our own sexual fantasies, obsessions, or behaviors.
>
> As the subordinate group in a patriarchal culture, women do not want to give information to men that may be used against them. . . . Another fear is that men will attempt to assuage their guilt and obscure the preponderance of male sexual abuse by saying, "But women do it too." [p. 261]

In a study by Shirley Carlson, reported by Kasl, sixty male perpetrators were in treatment for four years. Over 90 percent of these men reported being victims of overt sexual abuse as children, and of that group 39 percent acknowledged abuse by a female. Much of this abuse was recovered in the course of therapy over the four-year period. Walter Bera (1985) reports on a program for teenage male sex offenders. Of 300 seen over four years, 20 to 25 percent were sexually abused by females, very often teenage baby-sitters. A significant side issue is that 62 percent of these teenage males reported getting the idea for the abuse from pornography!

Selma Kramer

Kramer has written extensively about maternal incest and its treatment. In her recent chapter in Levine's book *Adult Analysis and Childhood Sexual Abuse* (1990) she describes two forms of residue of parental sexual abuse: varieties of physical sensation and disturbances in sexual functioning that she calls "somatic memories," and general and specific learning problems (p. 149). In the case of mother–child incest, Kramer believes the mothers have more serious psychopathology than do the fathers who commit incest.

> The child, who is often the product of an unwanted pregnancy, is considered by the mother to be unrewarding and imperfect, as often turns out to be how the mother felt herself to be perceived and treated by her own mother. . . . The sexual abuse started early as an outgrowth of the mothers' too zealous attention to the hygiene of their children's peritoneal areas. The "cleansing" continued for much too long and was converted by the mothers into masturbation of their children. [p. 150]

In two of her cases, a man and a woman, it was not until adolescence that the patients stopped their mothers when they began to fear that they would reach orgasm. The abuse of a third patient, "Abby," stopped only after the child had been brought to treatment.

> I have come to believe that because the abuse started so early and was perpetrated by their mothers, at a time when they were at the center of their children's universe, the consequences for these children were extensive and severe, leading to the particular disturbance in reality testing that underlies what I have termed "object coercive doubting." [pp. 150–151]

I am interested in how the fathers are portrayed in these descriptions of analyses where the mother is the perpetrator. Is he considered an "incest father"? A feminist analysis would lead us to predict that he is not so portrayed, that in fact he is more likely to be protected than blamed, and the blame squarely placed with the mother. In Kramer's case of "Casey," a 20-year-old young woman, the only reference to the father is one sentence in which he is described as a successful professional tied to his career, who seemed glad that Casey's and her mother's preoccupation with each other made his wife "less burdensome" to him.

In her case of "Donald," an only child of parents who had married late, she describes the mother as tied to her own mother and the father, to his own father. Donald's mother thought him strange-looking from birth, thought he was too large, ugly, and too serious. His father tried to protect him from his mother's carping by spending a great deal of time with him. Donald came for treatment at age 15 complaining of temper outbursts, describing himself as a volcano about to erupt. Kramer diagnosed the mother as a paranoid psychotic; Donald had sensed that such was the case but had trouble acknowledging it. Both parents were sexually stimulating, and one or the other slept in his room from the time he was 7 until he was

14. It was not until the end of the analysis, following a reconstruction by Kramer of the meaning of Donald's delusion that his analyst could see his nose and lips get bigger and smaller as a displacement from his genitals, that Donald revealed that his mother bathed him until he was past 14, including fondling his penis to erection. He found the bathing "exquisitely painful, emotionally shameful, and exciting all at the same time."

Kramer diagnoses the mother as psychotic, and I have no reason to doubt it, but she does not diagnose the father. Yet she says that the father spent many nights sleeping in Donald's room and was tied to his own father. I suggest that this is another example of the father's pathology being minimized, just as in the cases where the father is clearly the perpetrator the mother's pathology is maximized. The father is not described as "colluding" or as an "incest father" in the case of Donald or Casey.

The traditional male powerful, female submissive roles that are so culturally syntonic for us all are reversed in the case of mother and child. The mother has all the power of the care-giving parent with the child, whether male or female, dependent upon her. It is in this situation, which does not often require any aggressive or violent actions on the part of the mother, that women, either on their own or under pressure from a male partner, may become perpetrators of sexual trauma against a helpless child. Those under pressure from males are more likely to be borderline; those acting on their own and whose behavior is aggressive and sadistic are more likely to be psychotic. The others are reenacting sexual violence against themselves and selecting a younger, helpless victim.

Psychoanalysis Rediscovers the Sexual Abuse of Children

Adult Analysis and Childhood Sexual Abuse—
Howard B. Levine

During the 1980s, pressure was building as more and more cases of the sexual and physical abuse of children were reported and more and more authors wrote books describing their research or their work with adults abused as children. (I first reported my work with Penelope in 1984, reading the paper at two conferences and several local clinics and agencies.) Psychoanalysis finally responded in 1990 with the publication of *Adult Analysis and Childhood Sexual Abuse,* edited by Howard B. Levine. Ten psychoanalysts, five of whom are women, describe their treatment of adult patients in whom childhood sexual abuse is uncovered in the analysis. In one shocking case, it was a second analysis; the sexual abuse had never been uncovered in a previous ten-year analysis. Evidently the former analyst had never thought of it and therefore never asked the right questions.

In his introduction, Levine acknowledges that the analytic literature in this area has "barely begun to emerge" and that the book is an attempt to remedy this "oversight." (Oversight is a mild word for a subject of such profound pathology and brutality and one with such devastating effects on the victims; but however belated, the book is excellent.) Here is Levine's position:

> While I do not share Masson's position, I do feel that in making the necessary and useful shift away from the seduction hypothesis toward a more complex theory that encompasses psychic reality and the vicissitudes of fantasies related to infantile sexual and aggressive wishes, Freud inadvertently may have contributed to a tendency in psychoanalysis to downplay the impact of actual traumatic events on the etiology of neurosis. In retrospect, one might imagine that this tendency was abetted by the fascination that the newly discovered intrapsychic domain held for those working within the young field of psychoanalysis and by the need of analysts continually to emphasize and demonstrate to a skeptical and resistant audience of critics the power and effect of unconscious, subjective, infantile forces operating within the psyche. [p. 5]

No doubt this explanation is valid, but is remarkable in that it fails to mention any emotional factors, such as the resistance to facing the very difficult issue of incest on the part of analysts themselves who, after all, are human beings with the same conflict of abhorrence and fascination that lead to denial on the part of professional and lay persons alike. Another factor mentioned by several current authors is that male analysts and therapists identify with the male perpetrator and feel less sympathy for the female victim. This identification leads to a need to protect the perpetrator, rationalize his behavior, and thus deny their fascination with him. Rutter (1989), whom I will discuss later in Chapter 6, gives a detailed description of this phenomenon in describing how male psychiatrists protect each other's sexual misbehavior as well as that of other men.

Levine goes on to remind us that Freud never lost sight of the fact that some patients were sexually traumatized; for example, "Phantasies of being seduced are of particular interest because so often they are not phantasies but real memories" (1917), and "Actual seduction is common enough" (1931), and "The object of sexual seduction may direct her later sexual life so as to provoke entirely similar acts" (1937). Levine states:

> A more contemporary view of the impact of a sexual—or any other— trauma on a child, considers the way in which that trauma is experi- enced in line with current developmental conflicts and issues and how it is responded to by the child and his or her network of supportive

objects. Our focus includes an appreciation of how the trauma became elaborated in fantasy and play, connected with character formation and symptoms (including the regressive reversal of previously obtained levels of development), and contributed to subsequent developmental disturbances; and how the affects and memory traces connected to the trauma underwent repression, distortion, and symbolic elaboration. [p. 10]

The first writer is Brandt F. Steele, a psychiatrist who has been the consultant to the Kempe National Center for Prevention and Treatment of Child Abuse and Neglect in Denver, Colorado, who surveys some of the current literature on sexual abuse. He mentions promiscuity in adolescence and later life as a common sequel to earlier incest. Had I known that in 1976, I would have probably been able to identify Penelope as a victim of sexual abuse much sooner. Burland and Raskin report on the discussion group of psychoanalysts working with adults who experienced sexual abuse in childhood. One of their conclusions is that when abuse occurs before the age of 3, prior to the completion of self–other boundaries, the interference with differentiation tasks can result in severe character pathology, including the possibility of a sexual perversion. The danger for the phallic-oedipal child who is abused is that the child imagines himself or herself to be an active participant and thus develops a burden of guilt and responsibility. There is almost always a strong tendency for fantasy elaborations at the time and later; thus the elements of fact and fantasy can be very difficult for the clinician to differentiate. The group concluded that certain features appear in treatment related to early sexual abuse: unusually intense fears of castration; repetitive and traumatic dreams; a need to distance oneself from others; basic depressive affect; periods of cognitive confusion and dissociative states when repressed memories of the abuse are being uncovered; doubting of one's own associations, inability to differentiate between fantasies and actual memories, and a need to disbelieve one's own thoughts (p. 38). These features were all prominent in the female incest survivors I have treated, except for castration anxiety, unless you use the fear of damage to the internal female organs as an example of castration anxiety.

In most of Levine's cases, memories of the abuse had been repressed and were recalled only during the course of analysis. In those cases where there was recall prior to treatment, aspects of the trauma, especially the more powerful affects, had been repressed. The family pattern was marked by repression and acting out, reinforced by the use of lies, secrets, denials, and handling of complaints with such dismissals as "It's just your imagination" (p. 40). Underlying maternal deprivation was found to be a factor, and this needed to be analyzed first. Memories of the abuse would then surface.

The most likely explanation for this sequence is that the successful analysis and working through of the negative dyadic transference strengthens the working alliance and the positive transference, thereby offering support to the patient's ego and making it possible for the patient to confront the intense and painfully disruptive affects associated with the memories of sexual abuse. [p. 41]

David L. Raphling.   Raphling cites an example of mother–daughter incest, a welcome addition to the literature. He also raises the issue of countertransference problems especially likely with these patients, such as seductive attempts or the special appeal of someone who has been victimized. The patient and the analyst may share the idea that the analyst can replace the abusing parent with an idealized, loving, and caring analyst/ parent. The patient may feel entitled to compensation or reparation, and the analyst needs to explore these wishes and not be drawn in to acting upon them.

Anne E. Bernstein.   Another contributor to this book, Bernstein focuses on the effects of incest on ego development:

My own clinical experience has been that memories of actual childhood seduction can be recalled in analysis. When reports of such memories are accompanied by specific ego deficits, panic states, traumatic dreams or depersonalization, the clinician should be alerted to the possibility that the patient was a victim of actual incest trauma. [p. 66]

She gives two detailed case examples of women who suffered incest trauma and remembered it in the course of long analyses. The memories emerged over time with severe panic and depersonalization. Defenses employed had been vertical splitting or compartmentalization. They had both been taught not to trust their perceptions of reality and to keep secrets. Ruth had experienced maternal deprivation. In the case of Mrs. A., who had trouble with depression and cognitive functioning, her mother was viewed as cold and uncaring and her father, whom she loved very much, had died when she was 12. The first clue to her childhood seduction was revealed in a dream in which her father's head was slowly getting bigger and bigger until it finally burst. Associations to the dream led to panic, depersonalization, and the feeling that she was suddenly blind. "She needed to be blind to the sexual meaning of the dream and was unconscious of this need" (p. 72). Following the dream, she recovered memories of childhood that had been split off, not repressed.

I always knew about that, only, I never thought about it. If I ever wanted to, like when my children were in plays or started a new subject, it just wasn't there. I couldn't think. It wasn't like forgetting. Once in a while, I'd have a flash, the color of a dress I'd worn, but then I couldn't be sure whether it was real or made up. [p. 73]

Another dream followed in which she visualized the details of her childhood bedroom from a strange angle. Bernstein remarked that from her description it must have been early morning and she must have been lying face down with her neck craned up. She answered immediately, "Yes, that's when he used to do it to me," and burst into tears. She then was able to relate the history of her father's forced anal rape of her when she was between 9 and 11 years old. This excellent piece of analytic work was only possible because the analyst, a woman, had the capacity to entertain the idea of the reality of father–daughter incest and to be exquisitely sensitive to the clues in a dream. The distinction between repression and splitting is valuable here as well. Panic followed and when it subsided, Mrs. A. entered a period of severe mourning. It is of special interest that the memory of the incest was triggered by memories of her bedroom in a dream. Recall that this was the case in the example of the flowered wallpaper in the film *Breaking Silence* and in Penelope's dream of a scene of a river and mountains, which she associated to a mural above her mother's bed.

Bernstein emphasizes the point that the introjection of a caring, maternal figure (the analyst) is essential to the recovery of memories of the incest trauma, owing to the earlier maternal deprivation. In my view, this removes the patient from the emotional isolation in which the incest first occurred and makes it feel safe to remember for the first time. The mother appears to contribute to the possibility of incest through her coldness to the daughter, a coldness which is replaced by the analyst's attentive and caring listening and commenting. An analyst who ignores the clues of incest because of his or her denial, need to protect the paternal figure, or ignorance would be repeating the maternal trauma of an uncaring, self-absorbed mother. The analyst's highly attuned perceptiveness is necessary because the patient's own perceptions were denied or distorted to meet the narcissistic needs of her parents. In the course of therapy, you are in fact helping the patient to relive her life through memories in which your perceptions are employed to correct the false or denied perceptions imposed on the patient by her family. We can appreciate that a young girl with a cold mother would turn to her father for love and attention. She is too young to turn to boys her own age until she reaches adolescence. The question that remains to be answered is why in some cases of coldness by a wife, the husband turns to other adult women with whom he has sexual affairs, and why in others he turns to his own daughter(s). The essence of incest still remains this pathological crossing of boundaries on the part of the father in exploitation of his own children.

Susan P. Sherkow.   The next contribution, Sherkow, takes an interesting approach to the problem of diagnosis of actual sexual abuse by comparing the symptoms of child patients in cases of suspected abuse with the disturbances of an adult patient. She lists the following factors in making a diagnosis in children:

> intense sexualized play appearing very early in the course of consultation or treatment, with an emphasis on castration anxiety and fear of loss of object; a distinctive intensity and driven, compulsive quality of this play; preoccupation with one idiosyncratic kind of play to the exclusion of all others; the extremely hostile nature of regression in play, particularly in vicious attacks on dolls; stereotyping of symbolic play, especially phallic and thrusting play; exaggeration of normal curiosity about sexual issues and the genital difference; persistent confessions and retraction; and a preoccupation with fantasy versus reality—"Did I see it or did I make it up?"—sometimes expressed visually as in "I saw it" or "I didn't see it." [p. 95]

The ego function that is primarily disturbed is reality testing. Memories of the abuse are obscured and fantasies become real, partially owing to guilt, and thus self-esteem is significantly impaired. In her adult case, Mr. G., we have the example of the patient with a previous ten-year analysis that dealt with his active homosexuality, which he did renounce, but was left with anxiety, mixed phobias, and repugnant homosexual preoccupations. What he had considered memories in his first analysis, of his parents, grandparents, and aunt and uncle (mother's younger siblings) emerged in the second analysis to be screen memories that protected him from memories of homosexual seduction by his teenaged uncle. Again, the clues emerged through dream analysis with a dream about his uncle's dog sniffing at his penis. A phobia of vomiting was finally explained. Her patient became convinced that his fear of vomiting was a fear (or wish) for fellatio. The fear represented being trapped with the wish to put the penis in his mouth while watching his uncle masturbate but being afraid of gagging on it. The patient said: "I don't know if I gagged because I did put the penis in my mouth or only wished to. I don't know—I guess it doesn't matter" (p. 107).

Like the case examples of molested children, Mr. G. was preoccupied with the question, "Did it happen or did I make it up?" In spite of his being a writer, he used the primitive defenses of projection, physical avoidance, denial, and action instead of words. Over his lifetime Mr. G. had created fantasies, which he took to be real, and which were so convincing that he even had his previous analyst convinced of their validity. Clearly, the therapist should be alert to oral or anal phobias as a possible source of direction for exploring the possibility of molestation. Remember, my first clue of my own molestation was my inability to eat bananas. Apparently many molestations occur in oral and anal forms for both male and female victims. I fully agree with Sherkow's recognition that the best we may be able to do is reconstruct what is "likely" rather than what was "true" (p. 111). Dreams have the advantage of exposing material that would otherwise be unavailable to the conscious mind, but the disadvantage of continuing to obscure the actual events.

Judith N. Huizenga.   Huizenga reports on a case where her patient had remembered the incest, sexual intercourse with her father at age 9, but had split off the affect. Twelve months into her analysis she had a dream in which she hemorrhaged from her vagina and called out to the analyst for some sanitary pads. In the dream, the analyst replied that she could handle this on her own, and, dripping blood, the patient left her office, desperate but knowing that her bleeding was not fatal. During the next hour she associated to the fantasy of being ripped up by a knife in her uterus and wondered if she had bled after intercourse with her father. In spite of knowing of her incest, she had not before been able to connect her feelings of being inadequate as a woman and mother and the belief that her genitals were different from those of other women, to this incest-related fantasy of having her uterus ripped out in the incestuous rape.

This patient, Nancy, had functioned extremely well in school and socially and had married but could not be sexually attracted to her husband. Her first symptoms appeared after her marriage when, following a visit to her parents' home, she had her first panic attacks and nightmares. This led her to psychotherapy, which was helpful, and then later into psychoanalysis, where she recalled the facts of the incest but recited them with no apparent affect. Analysis of her nightmares resulted in the return of the affect whose splitting-off had severely inhibited her ego development, numbed her sexual feelings, and constricted her cognitive field and use of fantasy, play, and symbols, especially in regard to aggression, conflicts, and memories related to the incest. As memory fragments of the incest emerged, she felt numb, guilty, and frightened. Analysis was successful in improving her ego capacity and then her ability to work through the damage caused by the incest. Huizenga remarks metaphorically that psychoanalysis provided the sanitary pad, the bandage for her vaginal wound that she longed for in her dream (p. 134).

Lydia Lisman-Pieczanski.   The other contributors cite further examples of clues in dreams that lead to incest reconstructions. There is a case of maternal incest with a male child reported by Selma Kramer and a report by Lisman-Pieczanski of an incest victim who had a long sexual relationship with her former psychiatrist. The author describes her own countertransference reaction as feelings of deadness, disillusionment, helplessness, and disbelief, emerging with unusual strength (p. 137).

The patient, herself a psychotherapist, explained that after two years of psychotherapy, her psychiatrist had ended the treatment and they began to live together. After three years of living together she decided to leave because he was twenty years older and the relationship seemed to have no future. Her personal and professional life was in a state of complete chaos. After the separation she was unable to work because he had been her sole source of referrals.

After two years of analysis, she reported a dream that revealed sexual molestation by her godfather, a neighbor who was at least fifteen years older. A conversation with her sister revealed that the sister had discovered her almost unconscious after he had tried to penetrate her at the age of $6\frac{1}{2}$. She had completely repressed the memory. He had been an important figure in her family and was idealized. When she was 17, working for him in his office, he made a sexual advance to her and she left the country soon afterwards. The connections to her psychiatrist are clear. Rather than helping her to uncover the incest and to heal from it, he reenacted it with her and compounded the trauma. The reference to her being found "almost unconscious" is significant and is similar to what sounded like a brief unconscious state described by Maya Angelou following the rape of Ritie at age 8: "I thought I had died—I woke up in a white walled world and it had to be heaven. But Mr. Freeman was there and he was washing me" (p. 64). This seems likely to be a bathroom, and Ritie was unconscious as she was taken from the scene of the rape to the bathroom where she "woke up" after passing out from the pain and fear, which had felt like being killed.

In Penelope's final dream in which the rape was revealed, she too thinks she is dying when the "bullet" penetrates her neck. "Go ahead, finish me off," she tells her attacker in the dream. In adolescence, years after her childhood rape, Clare, a patient of mine whom I will describe next, had fantasies of her vagina being ripped by power drills and jackhammers, another way to conceptualize the horrendous attack as it is experienced by a child (age 5, in Clare's case). These four examples may allow us to formulate a significant hypothesis.

The rape of a young girl by a grown man is such a physical trauma, and engenders such intense pain from vaginal or anal tearing combined with the weight and physical thrusting of the man on top of her, that the child's physical pain and emotional terror of what is happening to her may result in her losing consciousness as she believes she is being killed by her attacker.

I was once in a serious car accident, and the other driver had claimed that I had said "What was I thinking?" when I came out of my car, bleeding, but I had not known what I could have meant. In having to think about what had happened for the trial a year later, I was forced by my attorney's questions to remember something that I had completely repressed. I remembered that after the impact and as my car was swerving out of control, I was thinking that I was about to be killed. These terrifying thoughts in the mind of a child could surely contribute to dissociation of the event and an actual brief loss of consciousness. The rape of a child is truly a horrific crime, and the perpetrators are surely sadistic persons.

Julien Bigras.   Bigras found that of the fourteen victims of incest he has seen as adult patients, the incest began at the age of 2 or 3 in more than half the cases. He also found that the traumatic shock in adolescent victims is caused not only by the incest itself but by its interruption after prolonged incestuous contact with their father, when the incest was revealed and the abuser was jailed or thrown out of the home. The daughters then suffered severe posttraumatic stress syndrome manifested in serious behavior disorders such as running away, suicide attempts, depressive states, aggressive and oppositional behaviors, sexual acting-out, and drug addiction (p. 175). He called this "compulsive masochistic reaction" syndrome, based on the girl having been fixated submissively to her father from the first instance of the abuse. Driven by the repetition compulsion, the girl searches for a substitute sadistic partner.

> Acting out or psychosis is the only recourse open to the adolescent incest victim because she frequently cannot symbolize (in fantasy or symptom formation) her unstable or dead inner world. This sadomasochistic fixation, I have come to understand, serves to deny profound maternal deprivation. The loss of the abuser, sometimes the only member of the family with whom the girl has enjoyed some tenderness and degree of care, has left her unshielded before the full desolation of the mother–child relationship. The compulsion to repeat the trauma . . . constitutes the major transference process to be worked through. [p. 175]

Bigras makes the common error, I believe, of referring to one of the mothers as a "more or less conscious accomplice to the incest" (p. 176). His evidence for this is that when she discovered the incest, and he puts discovered in quotation marks, she suggested that her daughter lead her father on so that he would be caught in the act, in order to produce evidence for the court. It is not at all clear to me how this proves that the mother encouraged the incest. It could easily be seen as a clever way to prove her case, perhaps by a mother who was knowledgeable enough to know that children are often not believed in such matters.

I agree with Bigras in his identification of maternal neglect or even hostility as a factor that leaves the girl vulnerable to inappropriate affectionate advances by her father or other men, as I pointed out in the case of Penelope, and I can easily share his personal reaction of anger and frustration at mothers who fail to protect their children, but that is an entirely different matter from charging the mother with "colluding" or being an "accomplice." This is a most important distinction, one which many analysts and researchers have failed to make. We must differentiate between a mentally or physically ill or depressed and ineffectual mother who may be withdrawn or narcissistically unavailable or rejecting of her children, and a mother whose perversity and sadism are so great as to lead her to encourage her husband or other men to rape her son or daughter. Mislabeling them "incest mothers" leaves us in the peculiar position of not knowing what to call the mothers who in fact are perpetrators of incest against their sons or daughters. Between this black or white are shades of gray in which mothers who were themselves incest victims are not able to see signs that abuse is going on because they have denied their own sexual abuse so thoroughly. It seems fair to acknowledge this phenomenon, describe it as "unconsciously motivated tolerance," and understand it as another unfortunate aftermath of incest in which a victim mother, who was herself unprotected as a child, cannot then protect her child. She is so needy and insecure that she protects her husband in order to protect her own security. This needs to be added to the list of symptoms in adulthood resulting from childhood sexual abuse, and just as we don't blame adults for other symptoms of sexual trauma, such as overeating or promiscuity, we should be most cautious in applying the derisive terms *collusion* or *accomplice* to mothers who are themselves incest survivors. If any of these mothers, like so many of the male survivors of sexual abuse, reenact the abuse by molesting their own or others' children, that will be the time to label them incest offenders.

Once the incest is revealed and they are offered treatment, the mothers surely are responsible for getting help for themselves and their children. If at that point they refuse help and deny the abuse, they cannot be allowed to continue as mothers since their failure to protect their children could easily be repeated. Sadly, then, the children need to be removed from the home and placed in safe homes with relatives or in foster care. I believe that the persistence of this issue reveals the anger of both men and women, professionals and lay persons, toward their own mothers, especially the fantasied omnipotence of their own mothers as described by Dinnerstein and elaborated in Chapter 4 of my first book.

Levine does a fine job summing up the book and makes the point that adults abused as children do not exhibit a specific syndrome that is unique to them because of the tremendous variation in the nature and extent of the trauma. What is useful is the presentation of the clinical dilemmas present with this group of patients, whose treatment is often long and stormy and contains periods of distrust and intense negative or erotic transferences.

> From a diagnostic perspective, it may be useful to think of many of these analysands as having a spit-ego organization in which a healthier, neurotic part of the personality alternates with or lies buried beneath a more impulsive, primitive part of the personality. This organization seems to be more pronounced when the childhood sexual abuse was violent or repeated or involved incest with an actual or surrogate parent figure. [p. 198]

Analysis offers an opportunity for healing because "the experience of the analytic situation then becomes the trauma, be it seduction or failure to protect." The quality of the transference can be more like transference psychoses than neurotic transferences (p. 199). As was true in my work with Penelope in the early years, Levine points out that it is not unusual for these patients to "hold to a relationship to the analyst that is marked by a defensive counterdependency and self-sufficiency for very long periods of time" (p. 206).

"Recovery of a Memory of Childhood Trauma from a Dream"—Adrienne Applegarth

A paper by Applegarth (1990), "Recovery of a Memory of Childhood Trauma from a Dream," is an additional contribution to the recent recognition within psychoanalysis of childhood sexual abuse. Applegarth describes her psychotherapy treatment of a patient who had dreams over a several-week period of black, hairy spiders on the ceiling, in danger of falling on her. Her associations were to a black hairy hand and reminded her of a man somehow who would touch her or get on top of her. Spontaneously she wondered whatever had happened to S., a male relative who had been close to her family until she was 5. Her husband was able to check police records and discovered the relative had been arrested when she was 5, but the record had been expunged, and at the request of the family the charge was dropped. This brought forth some memories of her uncle hurting her somehow. "From all this she developed the conviction, which I shared, that she had been molested by S. and had completely forgotten it until this time" (p. 19).

It is most encouraging to have psychoanalysts like those above publishing revelations of actual child sexual abuse. For other therapists and analysts it is important to have confirmation that although absolute memories may remain repressed or dissociated, the patient and analyst can piece together enough parts of the puzzle to be convinced, as Applegarth was, of the reality of molestation as a result of dream analysis, one of Freud's greatest contributions.

Clinical Illustration—a Case of a Partial Memory of Sexual Abuse as a Child in a Foster Home

None of the above examples illustrates the situation with my patient, Clare, who remembered part of her sexual abuse and whose greater awareness of the severity of the abuse did not occur until after fifteen years of psychotherapy. Clare's case is also different because the sexual abuse occurred in a foster home placement. When we started work together she was divorced from a brief, young marriage and living with a man in an unsatisfactory relationship. Clare was introduced in Chapter 6 of my first book as an example of a nonorgasmic woman. Her mother had been hospitalized for psychosis when Clare was 4, and she was placed in a foster home. Clare remembered a few visits with her mother in the hospital but then never saw her again. She then lived with her father and paternal grandparents for a year, until her grandparents moved. Her father placed her in another foster home at age 5 and a third at age 6. At the age of 9 he took her to the San Francisco area with him and a woman friend who had a young son, close to Clare in age. When that relationship broke up, however, Clare was left alone for long hours after school and during school vacations while her father worked. She read a lot, but it was during this period that she remembers starting to pull out her hair, a disorder called trichotillomania, which she has had since that time. She is now in her mid-forties. Her father remarried when she was 12 and then had three boys with his new wife. Clare did a lot of child care while resenting her stepmother and the new babies for taking her father's attention away from her. She has never desired to have children. Her best memory of her stepmother is that she had convinced Clare's father to get her a few dresses. Until that time Clare had only one dress to wear to school. When Clare divorced her first husband, her father was angry and withdrew from her. One Christmas, Clare brought expensive Christmas presents to the whole family and received none herself. She decided to sever her relationship with them and has had no contact in nearly twenty years.

Early in her therapy the sequence of foster homes was reported but the picture was not very clear, especially why she was moved from the second home to the third. Later she revealed that there was some sexual contact with the foster father that she thinks the foster mother suspected, and that this was the reason for the change. I asked her several times over the years what she remembered actually to have happened between herself and the foster father, but she was never able to answer. Her memories in that home are of terrible loneliness, missing her father and grandparents, and standing by the window hoping to see their car come to the house. Her fears of abandonment were so strong that she never wanted to leave the house to go out to play. More recently she remembered that her foster father had come into her room and seen her masturbating and that that had led to his molestation of her. She still could not remember the details but did remember knowing that it was wrong, enjoying his special attention, and believing that this made it less likely that she would be abandoned again.

She did remember knowing that the molestation must be kept a secret and feeling guilty in relation to her foster mother. She also remembers being hospitalized as a child and remembers crying and fearing her father would not come back for her, the way he had left her mother in the hospital.

There were so many problems to work on with Clare that the foster father molestation was not too prominent for many years. She had serious separation anxiety, there were problems with men, problems with jobs, a driving phobia, trying to uncover memories of her mother and the events leading to her mother's hospitalization, and an effort to locate her mother. At my urging, she wrote to the hospital in the city they were from, and from there got a new address of a hospital in England where her mother had been sent at the request of relatives there. Her parents had met in England, where her father had been stationed during World War II. A contact with the hospital in England led to a visit to her mother, a reunion that was valuable but disappointing. Her mother had been given a frontal lobotomy in the first hospital (the mid-1950s) and was extremely dependent and childlike, turning to Clare for mothering. However, the contact resulted in a visit with her aunt in England, her mother's sister, who did give her more information on her mother's family and life history.

The driving phobia was worked through with my interpretations of her fear of her own destructive anger and the possibility of killing someone when she was driving, a fear that had developed when she was a teenager and was driving her three young half-brothers on a winding coastal road. Her hair pulling proved much more difficult, and although we did much work on it and the number of incidents lessened dramatically over the years, it still remains a very distressing symptom to Clare. It leaves her feeling ashamed and out of control.

Clare remarried in 1980 and seemed to have made a much better match than with her previous relationships, but her sex life remained unsatisfactory and she had many fears of being abandoned by her new husband. Any separation from him or from me were anxiety-provoking and often led to hair-pulling incidents. She experienced enormous shame about this symptom and only when she read a newspaper article about the illness did she realize she was one of thousands of women with this affliction, some much worse than her own. She saw a psychiatrist and received a prescription for Prozac. The thought of revealing the symptom to a doctor produced such fears of disgust that we had to work for weeks to prepare her for it, and the disgust itself became a focus that revealed fears of identification with her mother as a crazy woman. The antidepressant was helpful and may have reduced the intensity of the episodes but did not eliminate them entirely.

It was not until I saw that trichotillomania was included in E. Sue Blume's Incest Survivors' Aftereffects Checklist that I thought there might be a connection to the foster father incident. Karen Conterio and Mary Jo Bever report in the Blume book on their 1988 study of self-injurers that 49 percent had been sexually abused and 45 percent had been physically abused, including some overlap. They include "cutting, burning, breaking bones, pinching skin, ingesting, injecting and inserting foreign material, interfering with the healing process of wounds, punching, slapping, picking skin, and pulling hair" (pp. 185–186). Before that we had worked on associations to the loss of her mother and a wish to connect to her mother through an association to electroshock treatment involving the placement of connecting wires to the head; numerous instances of cruelty by her father, including his pulling her hair painfully when he combed it; and anger at various bosses and men in her current life, connecting the suppression of anger with a hair-pulling incident. Thus anger, separation, and identification with and connection to her mother and her sadistic father had been interpreted as causative factors, but sexual abuse had not. We reworked all she could remember about her sexual contact and the aftermath, but she still remained stuck for memory. She did not reveal sexual trauma in her dreams, which were only occasional.

She did, however, make connections among several factors that all related to a terrible fear that if she didn't please a man he would leave her, or in the case of a boss, fire her: her father's abandonment of her to a foster home, her anxiety when her husband went out of town, and her fear of angering her husband by asserting herself in behalf of her goal to stop working and go to college. She could understand how important it must have been to her to please her foster father by acquiescing to his sexual demands, for fear that if she refused she would be moved again to another home. She could understand her transfer to her husband of the fears from these old traumatic events and the vulnerability she must have felt as a 5-year-old girl who had lost her mother, her grandparents, and then her father. She recalled that in the very first foster home at age 4 she cried continually. She also remembered that the parental response was "She'll get over it." With the loss of her mother, she came to depend entirely on her father. This was reinforced by her lack of education, which left her doing secretarial work for male bosses. Her first therapist was a male psychiatrist who later referred her to me, thinking it might be good for her to see a woman.

At about age 40, Clare began to make progress toward her dream to attend college. She had very much wanted to attend college after high school graduation, but her father had not allowed her to use his car to go to school, and in their isolated suburban neighborhood there was no public transportation to the local junior college. Instead she went to work and married, much to her father's relief. Her anxiety about whether she was college material was so great that at first she only audited a few university extension classes, feeling very intimidated by other students who were college graduates. When she felt ready to take courses for credit, she worked hard, received excellent grades, and her exceptional intelligence, in which I had always had full confidence, was confirmed. A very complimentary comment by a literature instructor was the final push she needed. It may not be sheer coincidence that the subject matter was a Kafka story, "The Hunger Artist," about another self-abuser. Her instructor wrote: "This is a stunningly fine paper. Your arguments about the meaning of the hunger artist are complex and lucid. You are articulate to the point of being poetic. Your general observations and conclusions are profound. Very impressive work."

At about this time, Clare had a dream in which she buys her husband a sleek black antique car and then buys herself one. They are side by side and she is very pleased. No doubt this is the kind of dream in which a classical psychoanalyst would see penis envy and interpret it as such. In Clare's case, and at this point in her therapy, I did not see it that way, although it may have been possible to find that element in it as well. I chose not to place the focus there. A car is surely a phallic symbol, but it is also a symbol of success and independence. For someone who had had a driving phobia, the aspect of independence was especially significant. I also saw it in relation to a very meaningful interpretation that a marriage counselor had made to them both, which was that it seemed as though they were in the marriage together for his goals (the husband's) but not for hers. That became Clare's rallying cry in the following months as she tried to convince her husband that going to college was very important to her and should be a goal of their marriage. I therefore interpreted the dream as meaning that she now felt they were in the marriage together for her goals as well as his. She had worked to enable him to start his own business, and now she could stop working for school.

When she cautiously revealed that she would like to get an M.S.W., we worked through all her fears of how I would feel about that. She recalled that when she had told her father of her desire to become a social worker he had discouraged her, telling her she was too emotional. Her basic mistrust of women, which had surfaced before primarily in the form of contempt for and distancing from other women, was revealed more clearly during the period following her revelation of the desire to go into social work. She had a succession of dreams in which I appeared. She recognized as they progressed that they all involved the crossing of boundaries. In the first I visit her in her home and remove my clothes. She assumes it is OK since I seem very comfortable with it. I leave without my dress and she calls after me to take it. A second dream takes place in my office:

Clare: I had another dream about you last night. There were just a couple of images. You were shedding your therapist image and becoming someone else—or an added dimension. You said "This isn't my house, you know," and you started picking up things that made this your office, your briefcase, other personal things. I realized this isn't really your house. Then I remember seeing a guitar in a guitar case. I thought, "Oh, she's a musician," and that added another dimension to you that I hadn't known before. That's all I can recall. The point was that something I had always assumed to be true turns out not to be true. I was surprised, the assumption I had was false. This is the first time I've had a series of dreams, and this is the third dream about you. When you packed up all the stuff to leave, I looked around the room—it really is a room that doesn't have any personality, it takes on the personality of who's in it.

Therapist: In the dream you create more distance between us. If it's not really my house, then there is less intimacy between us. You had said that my office in my home had been a factor in your discomfort about boundaries. But there is also the factor of my having misled you, telling you it's my house and then your finding out it's not. That means you can't trust what I say. That trust is so basic to our relationship.

Clare: I wasn't really thinking of it that way, just that I had made an assumption that turned out to be wrong.

Therapist: What if your dream were true, it was not my house, what would that mean to you? [She is denying the negative implications of my having deceived her, so I am trying another approach.]

Clare: It would mean you had lied to me, manipulated me, wanted to lead me in a certain direction.

Therapist: What were my motives?

Clare: I don't know, I have no choice but to accept what you tell me.

Therapist: What was to be gained by my being manipulative? [Searching for the projections]

Clare: I would dismiss it. It has no bearing on anything. What does it matter?

Therapist: It matters a lot because it means you can't trust me, I'm dishonest, I misled you.

Clare: There are benign manipulations.

Therapist: I think you are excusing me, protecting me.

Clare: That's my calm acceptance, my inability to confront people who need to be confronted.

Therapist: Have there been things to confront me with that you haven't told me about?

Clare: No, not you. It's issues about money. We're running low on money again. I don't know how I can keep paying $400 a month, or $320. In December the property taxes are due, and we have a $6,000 balloon payment due. I'm protecting M. [her husband]. He's not the superstar I thought he was. He has made mistakes in his investments, and we're paying for them now. There are assumptions about money in his family, that the family will take care of each other. I'm not sure if that means me. What if M. dies, this property that he owns with his family, will I be protected? This building that we manage and his brother owns, it's a mess. There is a tenant who is suing us now, claiming the handrail came off and caused her to fall. I think she's just trying to get money.

Therapist: You think she's manipulating.

Clare: It's an awful building. While my car was parked outside, someone siphoned gas from the tank. I think it was one of the tenants.

Therapist: You have a dream about my property. Your concern is whether your interests will be protected by your husband's family if he dies. You don't know whether you own a house or not.

Dream and Session, January 6, 1990

Clare: I had another dream about you. You were distraught, weeping. Someone you cared about very much had died on the East Coast. You were imploring me to go and pick up the body. While we are talking about it, you tell me she is an older woman you cared about very much. She hadn't been properly cared for. They had put her body in the backyard. You want me to go and get the body and bring it back here. I am thinking to myself, will she pay for my plane fare? Is the body in a coffin? What if the body is decomposing? It never becomes clear. [I wonder about her mother-in-law, who is an old woman in the East.]

Therapist: It's another dream about a boundary violation between us.

Clare: I was telling my husband about it and he said "Oh, you're worried about my mother."

Therapist: That was his association to your dream. What was yours?

Clare: We were talking on the phone to her; she has an arm problem, carpal tunnel syndrome. She just got a cortisone shot and the doctor wants to see how that works. She may need surgery. She went to visit my brother-in-law and sister-in-law and they were shocked at how she looked.

Therapist: Where do you come into the plans for your mother-in-law? [I am wondering if there is some question of the mother-in-law coming to live in their home.]

Clare: She has said that she never wants to live with either of her children and she had made plans for her admission to a nursing home a long time ago.

Therapist: In the dream we are connected, we have a social relationship as in the earlier dream where I visit you in your home. I know and care very much about a woman like your mother-in-law. It may be a wish to be connected with me as in your getting an M.S.W. so that we would then be in the same profession.

Clare: In this dream I was reluctant to do what you wanted me to do. I was very concerned about the condition of the body. I thought to myself, *Wait a minute, who's going to pay for this? Why aren't you taking care of this?*

Therapist: Closeness to women for you is ambivalent. You're afraid of getting burdened with responsibility. You decided not to visit your mother in England when you took a trip to Europe. Your stepmother gave you a lot of responsibility for her three babies, work was foisted off on you, you had to do the dirty work. Did you change diapers?

Clare: Oh yes! I had a slight hair-pulling incident, but it was slight.

Therapist: What was going on?

Clare: It was a very busy week. I was helping to run the campaign for mayor. I was being good. There was a 60-year-old district manager at the office and I was aware of myself as a sensible, competent person trying to do a job. The office was chaotic. I was getting what had to be done, done.

Therapist: You haven't told me about the hair-pulling incident itself.

Clare: Well, I was involved outside myself with the campaign, something larger. I have the capacity to give a lot, but the other side is that I can be exploited. This woman was so glad to have my help. She said she could use me again on another campaign.

Therapist: Your competence means you can give a lot, but if you are afraid of abandonment then you are vulnerable to being exploited, as with your stepmother and your foster father. I wonder if you feel I could exploit you by my writing a book in which you are a case example?

Clare: No, not at all. Unless it's a best-seller. [*Laughs*] I can't even tell anybody, no fame or notoriety. In the dream, it was so distasteful—they had just thrown her body in the backyard. You were so outraged by this treatment of a person you loved and respected.

Therapist: How did you feel about it?

Clare: My reaction was focused more on feelings of disgust at having to handle a dead body. I wondered how long the body had been out in the yard, how [decomposed] it was, would pieces come off in my hand? I had no connection to the person, but you did.

Therapist: How had she died?

Clare: Old age, illness, neglect, not an accident and not murder.

Therapist: Some time ago you had a dream about a body in a back-yard, trying to hide it and parts showing. Do you recognize that backyard?

Clare: No, it was unkempt.

Therapist: There's an expression, "not in my backyard," which means not wanting responsibility. Is there anything like that going on for you now?

Clare: I keep thinking about my mother-in-law. She's in a complete state of denial.

Therapist: Perhaps you are feeling ambivalent about how much responsibility to take for your mother-in-law. You did quite a bit for her the last time you were in New York. You're thinking about becoming a social worker. That's taking a lot of responsibility for other people.

Clare: When I see you, it's a reminder to me of how easy it is for me to avoid conflict.

Therapist: You've been in conflict about how long it will take you to get through school.

Clare: I met a friend of my husband's this weekend. She [was in her car, and] said, "Look in the back seat," and there were twins there. I said, "I didn't know there were twins in your family." She said, "There's not, we adopted them." She's a social worker, and she said she got so tired of taking care of other people's abused kids that she decided to take care of her own. They went to Rumania and got these twins there and brought them back. She said she decided this was another way to help the world. I thought, that's another way for me too.

Discussion. In searching for the meaning of the dream, I was trying to make some connection between her mother-in-law and the boundary issue with me, since she had announced her intention to work toward an M.S.W. degree. The other theme is the neglect of the old woman and my exploiting her competence to do a messy job for me. This is connected to the older woman in the campaign headquarters where she cleaned up the mess. Unlike so many cases where there is a difficulty for a woman separating from her mother, this patient was traumatically separated from her mother at age 4 and never replaced her with any other woman until her long-term work with me. Her desire to identify with me, by becoming educated and becoming a social worker, comes into conflict with her resentment at being forced to take care of herself for so much of her life and take care of others. The ambivalence about her own mother, when she finally found her again, and about her mother-in-law, and the recent dreams about me in which I am crossing boundaries, getting close to her but acting inappropriately, show her fear of closeness to a woman. This illustrates the problem with feminist-psychoanalytic theory in clinical work. We cannot assume anything about our patients' relationships, because their early relationships have often been damaged and they have had to construct survival mechanisms. Assuming that the woman patient is able to establish and maintain intimate connections with other women would be a mistake in Clare's case, and in the cases of many patients. This patient has often ended friendships with women when the other woman has shown weakness, dependency, or problems in relationships, because my patient is afraid of being leaned on and is quite disgusted by any masochistic tendencies she sees in women's relationships. She feels little sympathy and wants to withdraw.

In retrospect, another possible interpretation of this dream would be in terms of sexual exploitation. Her having to touch a body that disgusts her could be a representation of the body of the foster father who abused her. Something coming off in her hand might be the experience of his ejaculation on her hand. Might I represent the foster mother who could have foisted off the messy job of dealing sexually with her husband onto Clare, just as her stepmother did with the diapers? There is also the issue of self-disgust about her hair pulling and perhaps disgust about her own mother's mental illness.

Although the first dream of nudity contains a clear example of very inappropriate behavior on my part, and the second dream has me misleading her that this was my own home, Clare had not experienced any impropriety on my part in either dream. Analysis revealed that Clare was made uncomfortable by the prospect of becoming close to me as a social worker, fearing that she was crossing a boundary. She had already felt discomforted by the move of my office to my home after years of its being in a professional building, and then by my asking to read the paper for which she was so highly praised. When I asked her permission to use her case in my book, she was very pleased but was again discomforted by my offering her a copy of a paper I had published, using her as a case example, in order that she have a chance to see how she might appear in the book. She experienced this exchange of writing as having put our relationship "on a different level." These fears of more intimacy between us were expressed in all three dreams, as well as her fear of inappropriate advances I might make toward her. Such dreams are hints of earlier experiences of betrayal of trust with parental figures.

We continued to work through her fears about going to school, as evidenced by her procrastination in signing up for classes. She related the fear to her husband's reaction. It took her a whole week to write a term paper, and she had had to pretty much ignore him for that week. How could she do that in school with so many papers to do? I explored this fear as follows:

> *Therapist:* What's the fear with your husband?
> *Clare:* He won't like it.
> *Therapist:* And if he doesn't like it?
> *Clare:* He'll be angry.
> *Therapist:* And what if he is angry. Are you afraid he'll abandon you?
> *Clare:* No.
> *Therapist:* Your parents both abandoned you. You may have believed it was because you couldn't satisfy them.
> *Clare:* Maybe I am afraid he'll abandon me.

When she had finally signed up for classes and had her husband's acceptance of the plan, though not his enthusiasm for it, she started to talk about being very sexually attracted to a man she had recently met. She found herself having fantasies of having an affair with him. I wondered to myself, Why now? and proceeded to engage her in this exploration.

> *Therapist:* You have finally won your husband's agreement for you to go back to school full time. It seems to me that having an affair now means taking a big risk that you could sabotage your dreams.
> *Clare:* Yes, I have wondered about that.
> *Therapist:* You are letting a man get in the way again, just as your father got in your way the first time you wanted to attend college.
> *Clare:* You think that's what it means?
> *Therapist:* You are making winning the love and attention of a man more important than your own independent dreams and goals.
> *Clare:* Yes, I can see that, this is the first time a man isn't in the way. And after ten years of work in therapy.
> *Therapist:* You're leaving me out, our work together, your identification with me, as your mother was left out.

Discussion. This example shows my feminist values and thus my feminist interpretations. There were several possible interpretations of these illicit sexual fantasies: anger at her husband, competition with the man's wife, an abandonment and betrayal of her husband as she had been abandoned; but I chose to focus on her starting school because of the timing. I decided to stress the self-destructive aspects so as to interrupt what could have been a reenactment of her not being able to get what she wants because of undependable men, and thus remaining dependent on men for her security and leaving herself vulnerable to exploitation. I also stressed her abandonment of me, of our work together, because her going to college was something I had encouraged and I had often assured her of my conviction that she had the intelligence to do it. She had needed not only a willing father/husband to support her but a mother/therapist to encourage her and to be a positive role model.

At this point, her husband was having financial problems, she didn't want to have to work, and she had started school full time, so when she suggested coming every other week (she had come twice a week for many years and then had cut back to once per week), I raised the possibility of termination. An effort to analyze her resistance to termination a year earlier had been met with great anxiety, and this time she reported another hair-pulling episode following my suggestion. It was at this time that Clare brought to my attention a review of the Louise Kaplan book already mentioned, *Female Perversions* (1991). I located the book and read it, finding the sections on delicate cutting and trichotillomania especially applicable to understanding Clare. I had already suggested that she look at the Blume book because of the reference to hair pulling and sexual abuse; and the Kaplan book, interpreting hair pulling as a sexual perversion, further reinforced my interest in pursuing the symptom that remained for her an obstacle to termination as well as a response to thoughts of termination.

For years I had tried to help Clare recall what she was thinking and feeling just before and during her hair-pulling episodes, but to no avail. She didn't know. I now realized that she actually went into a state of depersonalization in which she was aware of herself pulling out her hair but had no control of her behavior. Rather than diagnosing it as an impulse control disorder as it is defined in *DSM-III-R,* or a compulsive disorder as defined by those who recommend medication for it, it seemed that it was more accurate to diagnose her hair pulling as part of a dissociative state and to see it related to the absence of memory of her sexual abuse. The phrase that many victims use, "I just went numb," became clear to me; going numb actually means dissociating. For Clare, hair pulling was part of a dissociative state in which she went numb, just as she numbed her sexual feelings in the intimacy of a marriage, but could feel sexual in her fantasies of men. With this helpful view, I suggested we forget about termination for the present and make a commitment to work on the connection of her symptom to her molestation, but that she would need to come a minimum of once a week.

In a brief digression, I want to note that in the discussion of trichotillomania in the fifth edition of *Comprehensive Textbook of Psychiatry* (Kaplan and Sadock eds., 1989) there is a less than comprehensive discussion of this disorder because in no place is the possibility mentioned of a connection to sexual abuse, thus leaving yet another generation of psychiatrists unaware of the significance of sexual abuse in an uncommon (estimates range from less than 1 percent to as high as 3 percent of the U.S. population) but difficult-to-treat and perplexing disorder.

Shortly after this decision to continue the work on her sexual molestation, Clare reported that a viewing of an interview on the television program "60 Minutes" had brought back to mind some repetitive fantasies that she had had as an adolescent. On the show, three adult sisters, daughters of an FBI investigator, reported to a national audience that their father had sexually abused them as children and that one had later had fantasies of knives cutting her vagina. Clare reported to me that during her adolescent years she had had fantasies of a jackhammer and of a power drill penetrating her vagina. I immediately said that this most likely meant that her sexual abuse had involved vaginal rape. This put a whole new perspective on what had hitherto been viewed by both of us as probably some mutual masturbation with guilt on her part, about the secrecy and badness of what had happened. Remembering the Maya Angelou story, I said it helped to explain why she was moved to another foster home, that her foster mother may have found bloody linen or underpants that had revealed the rape.

I asked about her first sexual experiences, and she replied that she tried to avoid sex, never enjoyed it, and that it was a source of considerable tension in her first marriage. She also revealed that there was very little sex in the long-term live in relationship she was in when she had first come to see me, and in retrospect she thought the man was homosexual but concealing it. Her first enjoyment of sex was in an affair prior to her second marriage, around 1980.

This illustrates the value of having newspaper and television revelations as a means of helping other sexually abused adults to feel less isolated and shameful and to be able to come forth and seek help. It seems clear to me that Clare had concealed these fantasies for all these years because she felt so ashamed of them and fearful that I would find them disgusting, as she found her hair pulling disgusting, and would abandon her. Journalists too have a contribution to make by exposing these secret crimes against children and giving courage to others.

This story is not yet over, but we are both hopeful that we are finally on the right track. It seems most important that therapists who see patients, both male and female, with symptoms of self-mutilation explore the possibility of childhood physical and/or sexual abuse and even rape. Not remembering the acts and only knowing that "something" happened means much work must be done to uncover enough memory to at least attempt a partial reconstruction of the molestation.

6

THERAPIST–PATIENT SEX

Emilia: Let husbands know
Their wives have sense like them: they see and smell,
And have their palates both for sweet and sour,
As husbands have. What is it that they do
When they change us for others? Is it sport?
I think it is; and doth affection breed it?
I think it doth; is't frailty that thus errs?
It is so too. And have not we affections,
Desires for sport, and frailty, as men have?
Then let them use us well: else let them know
The ills we do their ills instruct us to.

—*Othello,* act 4

That the number of men who batter spouses and molest children is overwhelmingly greater than the number of women who do so is reflected in a similar disparity associated with the phenomenon of therapists who have sex with patients. Such occurrences are finally being exposed, again owing to the influence of the women's movement and the increasing assertiveness of women clinicians and women patients in reporting this "best-kept secret" of psychotherapy. Attorneys have played a constructive role as well, by bringing legal action against offending psychiatrists and others. An interesting question is the nature of the reverse problem, that of female therapists having sex with male patients. This group is small and one wonders, as with female perpetrators in cases of incest, whether the women are more mentally disturbed than the men, for whom it is more culturally syntonic to be rapacious toward the opposite sex.

STATISTICS

As with statistics of battering and incest, one cannot know with any certainty whether they represent just a fraction of the crimes or a realistic picture. Many of the statistics on therapist–patient sex are the result of surveys seeking self-reports by therapists, which leaves a serious question of validity because many guilty parties may be reluctant to report even if they are promised confidentiality or if no names are used in the survey. According to Rutter (1989), a consensus figure based on various studies is that "96 percent of sexual exploitation by professionals occurs between a man in power and a woman under his care" (p. 20). Nelson (1982), Diesenhouse (1989), and Goleman (1990) review the research.

In a 1973 survey of 460 physicians, Kardener and associates (1973) found that between 5 and 13 percent had engaged in erotic behavior with patients, but that the figure for psychiatrists was 5 percent. This is consistent with earlier findings reporting that 5.5 percent of male and 0.6 percent of female licensed Ph.D. psychologists reported having sexual intercourse with patients during therapy. An additional 2.6 percent of male psychologists and 0.3 percent of females reported having intercourse within three months after the end of therapy. A 1986 report by Nanette K. Gartrell found that of 1,423 respondents, 7 percent of the men and 3 percent of the women said they had had sexual contact with a patient. However, 65 percent of the psychiatrists said they had seen a patient who reported sexual contact with a previous therapist but only 8 percent had reported the cases to authorities. In a 1986 study by Jacqueline Bouhoutsos (Rutter 1989) of psychotherapists of all professional backgrounds, practicing therapists were asked to report whether they had treated patients who had had a sexual relationship with a previous therapist, and found a rate of 70 percent of therapists reporting at least one patient. Of these, 96 percent were male therapists. This work is particularly valuable because it does not rely on self-reporting as in the Gartrell study. Still left unclear, however, is the estimated number of patients affected.

Gary Schoener (Goleman 1990) conducted 150 interviews with therapists who have admitted having sex with patients. Six distinct types emerged:

1. *The seriously disturbed.* Psychotic or nearly so; may suffer from delusions; though few, each may have as many as 100 victims.

2. *Sociopathic.* Very self-centered, exploitative, and pleasure oriented; they are superb liars and cover their tracks well. Multiple victims.

3. *Impulsive.* Impulse disordered; sex with patients one of several symptoms. One seduced at least 40 patients.

4. *Isolated.* Few personal relationships. Meet their own emotional needs through patients. Frequently sex occurs after two or three years of therapy.

5. *Undergoing personal crisis.* Widowed or divorced, so seeks sexual relationship with a patient who in other circumstances might have been a potential mate. Are contrite and frequently report themselves.

6. *Naive.* Poorly trained, do not understand professional boundaries, become enmeshed in patient's personal lives outside therapy. (p. B21)

Thus, from the point of view of the numbers of patients affected, the number of psychotherapists committing the crime is only part of the story. The number of patients victimized is multiplied many times. The word *crime* is apt. Since 1985, psychotherapists' sex with patients has been made a felony in Wisconsin, Minnesota, North Dakota, Colorado, Florida, Maine and California. Massachusetts and New Mexico are expected to follow.

The main problem with these statistics is that various groups are being reported upon and are not all comparable. Some include just psychologists, some just psychiatrists, and some an unspecified mixture of "therapists." When social workers are included, the number will be brought down because it is primarily a woman's profession. The following optimistic report by Pope in December 1990 therefore, may be misleading:

> The frequency of such contact may be decreasing. While a 1977 survey of psychologists found that 12% of the men and almost 3% of the women admitted such contact, a survey last year of 4,800 psychiatrists, psychologists and social workers found that only 0.9% of the men and 0.2% of the women admitted having had sexual contact with a patient. [Goleman 1990, p. B21]

It is important to distinguish between sexual fantasies and sexual behavior. A 1986 survey of 1,000 psychologists found that 87 percent said that they had at times felt a sexual attraction toward a patient. Even if this figure were 100 percent, it would not be a problem as long as the therapist was aware of the attraction, analyzed the meaning of it for him or herself, watched for ways it might be affecting the treatment, used it as a source of information about the patient's communications, and, most important, had no self-doubts about his or her capacity to refrain from acting upon the fantasies. Pope (Goleman 1990) says that if the therapist fails to acknowledge his or her sexual attraction, the therapy can be affected by an unconscious distancing from the patient, making the patient feel rejected, or by an avoidance of any discussion at all of sex, another serious error.

One of the most significant aspects of therapist–patient sex is that of the women who become sexually involved with a therapist, a very high percentage were incest victims in childhood. Sidney Smith reports that of all the patients he studied who had been sexually exploited by a therapist, "the most startling uniformity in their histories was that all of these women save one had been sexually abused by their fathers." For this reason he believes that what happens when there is sexual abuse by a therapist "resembles incest more than rape" (Nelson 1982, p. 19).

In the following clinical example, we confront the issue of neutrality in psychotherapy. Can and should we be neutral about child sexual abuse, women or children being battered, and therapist–patient sex? Feminist theory rejects the notion of the masochistic woman "asking" to be beaten. Children may be sexually excitable but clearly need protection, just as psychotherapy patients may have sexual feelings toward a therapist and may even be overtly seductive, but need protection from reenacting earlier boundary violations. In the following case, I make clear judgments about the behavior of a patient's former psychiatrist and do not maintain analytic distance or neutrality on this matter. The therapy with Mrs. D. involved the usual analysis of her transference to me and of issues of boundary diffusion, superego severity, narcissistic elements in her relationships, as well as ongoing problems with depression and anxiety. On the issue of sexual abuse I reacted differently, however. I was clear and direct about my personal disapproval while continuing to interpret Mrs. D.'s denial of the ambivalence, destructiveness, and even hostility in the behavior of those she sought to please, but who exploited her vulnerability. She kept her awareness of her real feelings about these violations from herself and maintained with me a facade of acceptance, dismissing any pain or damage to herself.

In the following summary, I focus on the sexual abuse component of her treatment and also include some analytic work on the mother–daughter relationship.

CLINICAL ILLUSTRATION—A PATIENT WHO HAD BEEN SEXUALLY SEDUCED BY HER PSYCHIATRIST

I first met Mrs. D. when she joined the group I was co-leading for battered women. She was articulate, attractive, well dressed, well educated, and seemed almost out of place in our group. Still beautiful at age 48, her entrance into the room was always dramatic. Her clothes and jewelry bespoke good taste with a touch of flamboyance. Her bright colors, voice tones, facial expressions and gestures all contributed to a rapid diagnosis of hysterical character disorder. She told a story of having fled from her second husband after he had beaten her, taking only what she could fit in her car and driving across country to escape. Upon arriving in San Francisco she moved in with an aunt while she tried to get a job and pull her life together. She was in weekly psychotherapy with a male psychiatrist and seemed quite pleased with her work with him. She met him in an overnight stay in a psychiatric hospital shortly after her arrival here, when she had spoken of suicidal thoughts at a psychiatric clinic and was sent under commitment to a hospital for observation. The next morning she convinced him that she could be released, that it was all a mistake, and he offered to see her privately as an outpatient.

Several months after she left the group, I received a call from Mrs. D. telling me that after three years of work her psychiatrist had suddenly announced to her that he was closing his private practice and taking a job in another city and that this was their next-to-last session. She was shocked but thought she would be all right. She wanted him to send me her records in case she needed individual help in the future. I agreed, but never received anything.

Several months later she called and requested individual treatment with me, which began with my questioning her denial of any impropriety in the abrupt way in which her psychiatrist had terminated with her as well as denial of any anger or grief about it. I interpreted her current depression as related to this loss and she gradually came to see that she had concealed her feelings from herself, thereby protecting him.

She described what she called her "dysfunctional" family. Both parents were upper-middle-class alcoholics, and she was the oldest child with two younger brothers. Her father was described as an angry tyrant who was mean and unloving; and her mother was cold, narcissistic, and immature, although well educated. Mrs. D.'s worst childhood memory was of seeing her father knock her mother's teeth out. She too was beaten by both her father and her mother, but was very much identified with her mother and hated her father. Her father died during her attendance in the group and she was very glad to make the decision not to attend his funeral. She had never realized her parents were alcoholics until she attended Adult Children of Alcoholics (ACA) meetings in San Francisco on the recommendation of a friend.

She revealed that when she was 19 and away at college, her mother began divorce proceedings against her father and Mrs. D. made a suicide attempt, was hospitalized briefly, and then moved to her maternal grandmother's. Mother wanted her as a companion on vacations and they double-dated. She was not to reveal that they were mother and daughter. She saw a psychiatrist, began to work, returned to a local college, and eventually completed her master's degree. She married at age 24 had two children, and began divorce proceedings at 39. She had begun seeing psychiatrists at age 9 and had seen a total of fifteen different therapists over the course of her life. She had had several periods of depression and was treated with antidepressant medication.

During the course of her work in the group, Mrs. D. heard several of our members reveal that they had been in incestuous relationships with their fathers. She wondered aloud if that had happened to her, but she had no memory of it. She said it felt like a real possibility to her. Because of evidence of some boundary diffusion, I could not tell whether this was true, or whether she needed to merge with the other group members. Her dramatic style created some doubts in my mind. It was difficult to know whether or not the description of her travails reflected an exaggeration of her complaints. Did she really need to be in hiding from her second husband? Were her parents really both alcoholics, or could this be a need to find some identity and connection via the ACA group? I did not doubt her accounts of both physical and psychological abuse by her father toward both her mother and herself. She felt her father preferred her brothers.

After several months of individual therapy, while speaking of family visits to her grandparents' home when she was a child, she had a memory of playing at her grandparents that triggered another memory when she left my office. She called an hour later to say that while sitting in her car after her session she was struck with the realization that her father had abused her sexually. She came in again that week and I listened with great interest and some skepticism because I knew that incest was also being reported in the ACA groups she was attending. However, I was also aware of my negative countertransference. She reminded me of a narcissistic and manipulative member of my own family, and so I made a special effort to listen fairly and openly.

Her memories were carefully pieced together to produce her conclusion, and as I followed her account I became impressed with the likelihood of its accuracy. I reminded myself that the hysterical personality features she exhibited fit a history of sexual molestation and could in fact be viewed as confirmation, rather than as a cause for suspicion. She remembered that there was a certain toy she liked to play with at her grandparents' home, a set of small colored building blocks that had some green columns she called "ging-gings." As she sat in the car and remembered the ging-gings, she knew that that was the word for her father's penis. She remembered that at the age of 28 months, when her mother was in the hospital after having given birth to her brother, her father had forced his "ging-ging" into her mouth.

Mrs. D. had already felt so much anger toward her father for his abusive verbal and physical attacks on her and her mother that the memory of sexual abuse was the "icing on the cake" of her hatred of him. She vented more anger, told some friends, and joined an Incest Anonymous group. She also went through several weeks of sadness and grieving but noticed a significant change: *she no longer felt suicidal,* a feeling she had experienced on and off most of her life.

A few weeks later she said, rather coyly, "I thought I should tell you that I had sex with my psychiatrist in New York." Whatever small doubt may still have lingered in my mind about the incest was now gone because I immediately realized that she had reenacted the incest with the "help" of her psychiatrist. As she described the relationship, I was amazed at how it exactly reproduced the original experience.

She began therapy with Dr. E.'s wife, a psychologist. She worked with Mrs. E. and liked her. The following year Mrs. D. married and both Dr. E. and Mrs. E. came for dinner to Mrs. D.'s new apartment with her husband a year later, after therapy sessions had stopped. However, two years later Mrs. D. returned for therapy with Mrs. E. and was told that Mrs. E. would like her to see her husband, Dr. E., for an evaluation because she was not clear about the problems. I told Mrs. D. that Mrs. E. was telling her that it took a person with a penis to understand her. I strongly believe that Mrs. E. was unconsciously offering her patient to her husband for his sexual neediness. The patient did meet with Dr. E. and then continued to work with Mrs. E. for a time. When she called Mrs. E. again two years later, Mrs. E. told her that she had cancer and suggested that she see her husband. She then saw Dr. E. off and on over a period of twelve years. The sexual encounters began while Mrs. E. was in the hospital for cancer, and continued on and off along with social visits, telephone calls, lunches, and birthday outings. Paid sessions occurred on and off during these years. At the time of her sessions with me, Mrs. D. was still exchanging birthday calls with Dr. E. and he telephoned her every New Year's Eve. He had attended her daughter's bat mitzvah. Both social and sexual boundaries had been broken repeatedly.

I pointed out that she had had sex with Dr. E., a man in his sixties, while his wife (her former therapist/mother) was in the hospital, just as she had had sex with her father while her own mother had been in the hospital. Mrs. D. was amazed at the connection, which she had never thought of before. However, she considered herself equally responsible for the sex. After all she was an adult, and had been flattered by Dr. E.'s attention. I made it clear that I did not view it that way and considered Dr. E. 100 percent responsible. I told her that it was unethical to take advantage of a patient and that I believed his sexual interest in her had prevented them from ever uncovering her own major problem of incest with her father. This conversation took place just around the time (1990) that the California Department of Consumer Affairs pamphlet *Professional Therapy Never Includes Sex* was distributed, and I gave her a copy. In no uncertain terms it tells patients that the therapist who engages in sex with a patient has committed a crime and explains why this is so. She finally came to realize that she had been denying the exploitation and protecting Dr. E. and then got furious. For her own sake, just to express her feelings, she wrote him a long letter, which she read to me. It was so magnificent that I burst into applause when she finished.

This personal response on my part is surely unconventional, but it would have been hypocritical (Ferenczi 1933) to appear to be neutral. The letter showed how much progress she had made in uncovering her true feelings and being able to express them.

Then the work began: putting together how this experience was one of many whereby she had been harmed and had never let herself know it, with her mother; bosses who had fired her for refusing them sex; or with her previous psychiatrist, who, for reasons about which I can only speculate, perhaps having to do with his own sexual conflicts about her, had failed to give her a chance to terminate with any exploration of her feelings.

At this time she became very depressed and began taking antidepressant medication. She could not look for a job, which she needed to do, because the combination of remembering the incest and then reevaluating the very important relationship that had begun with Dr. E. when she was 25 and he was 63 left her feeling very wounded and in great pain. She had loved and trusted him and been dependent upon him. He had symbolically been the good father she had never had. Her realization that he had abused that trust and had acted illegally and unethically and that she, rather than being an equal participant had again been victimized, brought profound despair. Fortunately she had met and fallen in love with a good man and had his financial and emotional support during this period. But she was in much pain and felt raw.

The following dream occurred during this period: She is peeling a layer of skin off her right breast and nipple. The left breast is intact. She is mutilating herself. The skin is darkened, but underneath the skin is lighter. There is a third nipple growing from the side. The scene shifts and she is at a luncheonette. A man goes outside and there is violence. He returns with his arm ripped off. She had a sense of body parts being lost. To my mind this represents both the fragmentation she was experiencing as her relationship with Dr. E. was psychologically destroyed by our work, and the common side effect of incest, self-mutilation, expressed in the dream rather than in reality, yet giving us a valuable clue to the element of fragmentation involved for self-mutilating patients. The mutilation serves as a defense against fragmentation.

Her associations were to a discussion with her brother. His son had been suspected of sexually abusing his 2-year-old half-sister when he was 12. That son was now visiting his brother, who has two little girls. Mrs. D. got upset, thinking that he might molest his nieces. She went on to talk about the problems she is having finding a job. Work has always been very important to her because it was her way of being independent, free from her family, but she had always had difficulties on jobs because of being a woman in a man's field. She didn't get the promotions she should have gotten, and had to turn away sexual advances from men. She related this to the dream; she had always had to have tough skin. Beneath that tough outer layer there is tender, painful skin. All of our uncovering in therapy has felt like peeling away that outer layer and exposing the tender skin underneath. Note that I did not make a phallic interpretation of the third nipple or a castration interpretation of the ripped arm, both traditional responses. I believed the fragmentation interpretation, a preoedipal view, was the more accurate approach.

In the months that followed, she began to realize how much she had hidden from herself and how she had kept her body and mind separate during sex. As she had warm, loving sex with her fiancé, she was not able to reach orgasm, but was able to really be there with him, both physically and mentally. She was confident she would be able to have orgasms again. She felt safe with him and realized it was the first time she had felt safe with a man. She gradually became aware of her feelings of anger, pain, and love—really aware, she said, whereas before it was as if her feelings had been filtered. Analysis of current interactions with her mother had led to awareness of her denial of her mother's hostility and brought forth feelings of rage toward her mother.

She had been putting off marrying her lover, not feeling able to trust him enough, but as she began to come out of this period of grief and anger, she decided she would marry him. She began to make plans for the wedding and lovingly devoted herself to making every detail just the way she wanted it. Her parents had ruined her first wedding, fighting over everything, so that she and her fiancé had decided to just elope and be rid of them. Her second marriage was very hurried for her and difficult to plan because she was working full time. Now she was not working and could have the wedding she had always wanted. However, she began to present the planning as a terrible burden, was getting annoyed with her fiancé because she was doing all the work, and began to shift back into a former, more masochistic orientation. I sensed a typical neurotic "Don't envy me, I'm really miserable even though you may think I am happy" style. "Believe me, you wouldn't want to be in my place, burdened as I am planning this wedding and honeymoon that my new husband insists on taking me on and paying for everything." She was also planning a prewedding visit to her old home city to introduce her fiancé to all her relatives and friends, and was burdened by having to make arrangements for a big dinner there. After several sessions of hearing her complaining,

I commented, keeping in mind stories Mrs. D. had related to me that indicated much competitiveness on her mother's part:

Therapist: You're suffering when you should be feeling joyful. Is there any reason for you to feel guilty?
Mrs. D.: No, there isn't.
Therapist: Your mother is old and alone. She had an unhappy marriage and she never remarried. Her sons are rejecting her. I wonder if you are afraid of her envy. Your suffering is a way of saying "Don't envy me—you wouldn't want to be in my shoes. I'm under so much pressure."
Mrs. D.: [*Crying*] My father treated her so badly. She stayed married because of the children. She only left him when I went to college.
Therapist: You felt very close to your mother. It's hard for you to feel separate from her now. If she isn't happy, it doesn't feel possible for you to be happy.

This led to her recognition that she had several single women friends who wanted very much to remarry, but who had not met anyone. With these friends she felt uncomfortable about her good fortune, although they seemed genuinely happy for her.

After this interpretation she began to enjoy the planning again. One day Dr. E. telephoned her and she spoke to him very briefly and hung up, saying she was very busy. She became very distressed and her suicidal thoughts returned. He called again and she told him not to call her anymore and hung up. He called and left a message that was friendly on the surface but said something about "her problem." I was concerned about the suicidal thoughts and that the wedding was a big distraction from what was still unfinished for her. She began to express a lot of rage toward him again and wondered about legal action. She wondered if he was still practicing since he was almost 90. It did not seem worth pursuing because he was in New York and by now was so old. I reminded her of the letter she had written. She edited the original letter, now six months old, and sent him a shorter version, nonetheless a very strong and angry statement repeating that he was not to call her again. This stopped the suicidal thoughts, and she proceeded with her wedding plans. It was a long way from her earlier version of the affair, in which she had described herself as feeling favored and flattered. Her later memories of the sexual involvement with him were actually very unpleasant. He was impotent and she had had to perform oral sex on him to try to help him get an erection. She now fully appreciated that he had violated her trust and his own professional duty.

EFFECTS ON THE PATIENT

A number of researchers have reported on the dangerous aftereffects of the sexual contact for the patient. Most agree that it constitutes a trauma and that, occurring as it does in a relationship based on trust and dependency and caring of a vulnerable patient, it constitutes an incestlike experience. Judd Marmor, a psychoanalyst, stated: "Such behavior between a therapist and patient has all the elements of incest on an unconscious psychodynamic level" (*New York Times,* November 23, 1982, p. 19).

In his book *Love's Executioner and Other Tales of Psychotherapy* (1989), Irvin D. Yalom cites an example of an elderly woman patient suffering from severe depression. For the previous eight years she had been obsessed with love for her former therapist, a much younger man with whom she had been in treatment for twenty months. During the treatment her therapist began to socialize and then sexualize their relationship. After several weeks he discontinued, saying "It's not right, and we both know it," yet she suspected he had dropped her for another patient. She had attempted suicide but failed and her depression continued.

Amazingly, there have been therapists who have been open about engaging in sex with patients and have insisted it was for the therapeutic benefit of the patient. One such psychiatrist even presented his position at a professional conference, and another published a book proclaiming his views. However the fact that most of the women chosen for this kind of "therapy" are young and attractive belies the benign assertions of such therapists. It should be clear that sexuality between a psychotherapist and a patient is always wrong and is always the therapist's full responsibility. Trying to rationalize this boundary violation with the complaint that the client was seductive is never a valid excuse. Enid Pine, a psychiatrist, rightly asserts that it is no more reasonable for the therapist to respond sexually to the seductive behavior of a patient than it would be to join a violent patient in smashing windows. Kardener (1973), in comparing therapist–patient sex with incest, says that the trauma of incest is orphaning. The patient who has sex with her psychotherapist loses a parental figure and becomes a psychological orphan.

Research by a California State Psychological Association task force

(Nelson 1982) showed that about 90 percent of 559 patients having sexual relations with therapists were found by succeeding therapists to be suffering ill effects, including inability to trust new therapists or men in general, severe depression, drug abuse, and suicide. Nanette Gartrell (Goleman 1990), a psychiatrist, reports that these patients have trouble trusting anyone, are frightened of being taken advantage of in intimate relationships, and are severely depressed. About 10 percent have problems so severe they need to be hospitalized, and 1 percent commit suicide. Rutter (1989) reports that in his conversations with many victims of therapist or other professional-male exploitation of females, the women were still dealing with discovering how extensively damaging these experiences had been, even after as long as twenty years.

PROTECTING THE CONSUMER IN CALIFORNIA

In April 1990, the California Department of Consumer Affairs published a pamphlet written by Valerie Quinn, *Professional Therapy Never Includes Sex,* which was distributed to every licensed mental health professional in the state. It is an excellent exposition, for patients and therapists, of the illegality, immorality, and unprofessionalism of any sexual contact or sexual misconduct between patient and therapist. It describes the law and reporting options including administrative action, criminal action, civil action, and professional association action. It includes a client Bill of Rights and a good list of warning signs for patients to watch for as clues that sexual abuse or exploitation may follow:

> telling sexual jokes or stories
>
> "making eyes at" or giving seductive looks to the client
>
> discussing the therapist's sex life or relationships
>
> sitting too close or lying next to the client
>
> inviting a client to lunch, dinner, or other social activities
>
> dating
>
> changing any of the office's normal business practices (for example, scheduling late appointments so no one is around, having sessions away from the office, and so on)
>
> confiding in a client (for example, about his or her love life or work problems)
>
> relying on a client for personal and emotional support

giving or receiving significant gifts

providing or using alcohol or drugs during sessions

Signs of misuse of power include:

hiring a client to do work for the therapist, or bartering goods or services to pay for therapy (dual relationship)

any violation of the client's rights as a consumer. [p. 3]

According to a spokeswoman, since the publication of this pamphlet the department has been flooded with complaints. The Board of Behavioral Science Examiners, which includes licensed clinical social workers, licensed marriage and family counselors, and licensed educational psychologists, in May 1991 had 1,000 complaints to handle with a staff of three persons. Although criminal and civil actions have a statute of limitations, two years in the case of criminal and four years in the case of civil, there is no statute of limitations for administrative actions (removing a license), and therefore complaints going back twenty years are currently being reviewed. We may now get a clearer picture of how widespread this practice is and has been. It has been estimated by Pope that in the past only 4 percent of abused patients have brought legal action. The ability of the women's movement to bring about a sense of power in women is turning this issue from a "family secret" into an exposé of great significance, legal and professional.

The California statistics continue to show a vast gender difference. Of the disciplinary actions sustained by the Board of Behavioral Science Examiners for 1984 through 1990, I divided the actions by whether the charge was for a sexual act with a patient or for a nonsexual offense, such as insurance fraud or other white-collar crimes. A third small category was for those who lost their licenses because of criminal convictions, which were all for sexual perversions. Counting this group, which consisted of eight males, the total number of fully licensed male marriage and family counselors, clinical social workers, and educational psychologists charged with sexual abuse of patients added up to fifty-eight males and three females. The figures on the white-collar crimes totalled thirty-eight for the males and twenty-nine for the females, a much narrower margin, yet another example of the unlikelihood of females committing crimes of sexual aggression and violence.

Several professional associations, including the American Psychological Association and the American Psychiatric Association, have recently taken action in writing codes of ethics in regard to the sexual misconduct of therapists. One issue that remains unsettled is that of the ethics of sexual involvement when the therapy relationship has terminated. In a telephone interview with a representative of the Department of Consumer Affairs in Sacramento, California, I was told that a sexual relationship within three years of termination of treatment would be viewed as likely exploitation, but that for beyond three years there is less certainty. Each case would have to be reviewed on the basis of the individual circumstances.

However, in November 1991 the *Journal of the American Psychiatric Association* published an article by Paul Appelbaum, a psychiatrist, and Linda Jorgenson, an attorney, recommending only a one-year waiting period following termination before entering a sexual relationship. They state their goal as an effort to "balance the goals of protecting former patients and avoiding unnecessary interventions into consensual relationships" (p. 1466), and refer to a constitutional right to choose with whom one will associate. They believe that an absolute ban is not essential to protecting former patients but rather propose that a one-year waiting period during which even social contact is prohibited could be followed by the releasing of any constraints on a personal relationship. Their justification rests on their assumption that the likelihood that impaired decisions will be made or adverse effects occur is weaker a year following termination, and that persons' choices should be respected, thus "there are insufficient grounds to warrant an outright ban" (p. 1471).

The authors arrived at the one-year waiting period compromise by studying 100 cases of sexual contact in which only one was begun more than one year after the termination of treatment. In a study of more than 2,000 cases in Minneapolis, fewer than 1 percent involved contact more than one year after termination.

This proposal clearly does not view the therapist–patient relationship as parallel to a parent–child relationship. When a daughter leaves home and becomes independent, we would all agree that the incest taboo against sexual involvement with her father still exists. Appelbaum and Jorgenson also avoid dealing with the reality that any therapist has experienced in her or his practice, of terminating with a patient and then hearing from that patient again anywhere from six months to many years later. In my view, termination, although an achievement at the time, cannot be viewed as permanent. The return for further treatment of a former patient has occurred with sufficient frequency in my experience as to make this a significant oversight in the Appelbaum and Jorgenson proposal. And even if a patient does not return, knowing that you are there and that he or she can return to see you if the need arises becomes part of the ego strength of the former patient that allows for weathering future storms with the knowledge and comfort of your presence, even in absentia. One might argue that another therapist could be sought out and then the balance could tilt in favor of sexual involvement if it is a committed and enduring relationship. What is best for the patient must be the primary consideration in any ethical review of an individual case. Thus a mere sexual attraction would never be sufficient justification for breaking the healing relationship, no matter how many years had passed, unless there was a serious intent on the part of the therapist with the long-term best interests of the patient as his or her major consideration. And who can be objective about that?

Surveys of psychiatrists and psychologists have found that one-third of those responding believed that sex after termination was acceptable. Owing to the difficulty in obtaining consensus among the professionals involved, the legislatures and the courts have been stepping in to fill the void. It is unfortunate that lawsuits and the threat of lawsuits will determine what is ethical in our profession. Because of the difficulty of proving beyond a reasonable doubt that a former patient is still under the influence of a positive transference, four of the seven states that have criminalized sexual contact with current patients have chosen not to criminalize posttermination sexual involvement, although California and Minnesota do so for two years. This article raises many interesting legal questions that should be debated by our profession, such as whether there should be different rules depending on different types of treatment. The major weakness in their proposal is that no mechanism for monitoring the waiting period has been put forth.

A SAMPLE CODE OF ETHICS: SAN FRANCISCO JUNGIAN INSTITUTE

The C. G. Jung Institute of San Francisco, after a ten-year process of internal evaluation following complaints of sexual abuse of patients on the part of one of their leading members, has made a clear decision on this matter in writing a new code of ethics (April 12, 1991).

> It can be argued that in many cases transferences and counter-transferences are never fully resolved. Thus the analytic relationship may endure for the life of the participants. This possibility should be considered whenever an analyst, candidate or other therapist affiliated with the C. G. Jung Institute of San Francisco considers developing a sexual relationship with an ex-patient, no matter how long after termination of the psychotherapeutic relationship. It would be a rare circumstance in which such a relationship between therapist and a former patient could be considered ethical. [p. 2]

The Jung Institute also takes up the issue of "dual relationships," which it says may also be "subject to the conscious or unconscious exploitation of transference feelings (p. 2)," and thus raises "serious ethical questions" and could be the basis of a finding of unethical conduct. Members are also advised to "exercise extraordinary care in allowing a personal or business relationship to develop with a former patient (p. 2)." Also included under this heading are social relationships with family members of current patients, and being a personal analyst to someone and at the same time being his or her designated supervisor. The Institute also takes a clear position on teacher–student sex:

> It is unethical to engage in a sexual relationship with a current student, supervisee, or control analysand. It is a misuse of power and a violation of trust for a person in greater authority to become sexually involved with someone he or she is to evaluate, grade, or promote. [p. 3]

Members are also cautioned about pursuing such relationships after the teaching relationship has ended because of the potential that projections, transferences and feelings about unequal power will continue.

The American Psychological Association amended its code of ethics in 1989 to include a prohibition against teachers having sex with students. Research shows that therapists who abuse patients often had sexual contact with their teachers. Also in 1989, the American Psychiatric Association revised its ethics code to bar teacher–student sex (Diesenhouse 1989). According to Rutter (1989), 20 to 30 percent of female college students have been approached sexually by their professors. Seventeen percent of female graduate students in psychology had become sexually intimate with a professor during their training, and an additional 30 percent rejected advances. Rutter was told by a colleague that at his psychology graduate school it was an open secret, and completely accepted, that nearly every female graduate student was sleeping with her dissertation adviser, yet nobody reported this. Rutter estimates that there are over 1 million women in this country who have been sexually victimized in relationships of trust.

THE RESPONSE OF PSYCHOANALYSIS TO THERAPIST–PATIENT SEX

Freud was always clear about the inadvisability of sex with a patient, but C. G. Jung is said to have had several affairs with women patients. Otto Rank had a long affair with Anais Nin. In the memoirs of Margaret S. Mahler (Stepansky 1988), Mahler describes her analysis with August Aichorn, following her dismissal by Helene Deutsch, and refers to herself as his favorite pupil. She adds, "As our personal relationship blossomed, I became his lover as well," until, after two and a half years they agreed she

should complete her analysis with someone else and decided upon Willi
Hoffer (p. 69).

Phyllis Greenacre

Greenacre (1954) deals openly with the issue in an article titled "The Role
of Transference." She writes that she has heard many times a remark of a
quite eminent analyst that so many analysts overstep the boundaries of the
transference in sexual ways that therefore the best thing to do is to say
nothing about it. Greenacre strongly disagrees and urges discussion of
these possible offenses and emphasizing their dangers to students and
"among ourselves," rather than punishment of the offenders. In regard to
the frequency of sexual relationships between analyst and analysand, either
during the analysis or relatively soon after termination, she states:

> That this is not so infrequent as one would wish to think becomes
> apparent to anyone who does many re-analyses. That its occurrence is
> often denied and the situation rather quickly explained by involved
> analysts as due to a hysterical fantasy on the part of the patient (indeed
> one knows how universal and necessary such fantasies are) is an
> indication of how great is the temptation. . . . The carrying through
> into a relationship in life of the incestuous fantasy of the patient may be
> more grave in its subsequent distortion of the patient's life than any
> actual incestuous seduction in childhood has been. [in Langs 1990, pp.
> 21–23]

Greenacre had the courage to expose the problem, but denies the validity
of punishment, proposing instead discussion among those who have not
yet committed the incestuous betrayal of the patient. The prevention
approach is surely advisable, but protecting the perpetrator only allows
him or her to continue to exploit more patients.

Harold F. Searles

Searles (1975), in his paper "The Patient as Therapist to His Analyst,"
attempts to analyze the problem of the analyst who breaks the incest
boundary with a patient.

> It has long been my impression that a major reason for therapists'
> becoming actually sexually involved with patients is that the therapist's
> therapeutic striving has desublimated to the level at which it operated
> in childhood. He has succumbed to the illusion that a magically curative
> copulation will resolve the patient's illness which tenaciously had

resisted all the more sophisticated psychotherapeutic techniques learned in his adult-life training and practice.

In my clinical experience, the temptation toward such activity is most intense in my work with patients whose childhood histories included the patient's having been involved in a relationship with a parent in which the child sensed the incestuous fulfillment would provide the parent with relief from neurotic or psychotic suffering. . . .

Unacceptable incestuous urges become acceptable to the therapist's superego by clothing themselves in the guise of healing.

In many instances the primitive healing strivings are no less powerful than are the sexual strivings, and the therapeutic strivings can be the most powerful of all in bringing about a tragic deforming of the therapeutic endeavor, predatory sexual behavior by the therapist under the guise of the emancipated healer. A need for therapeutic omnipotence can lead the therapist to seize upon any available, intentionally therapeutic measures, including actual sexual involvement with the patient. . . . one can surmise that the sexual involvement gives unconscious release, as well, to the two participants' murderous urges toward one another. I have worked analytically with only one patient who had had an affair with a previous therapist, and I was not surprised to learn that powerful murderous urges evidently had been at work in both of them in the mutual omnipotent-healer strivings toward one another. . . . [in Langs 1990, pp. 123–124]

Lucia E. Tower

In "Countertransference," a 1956 paper, Tower states that there has been wide disagreement about countertransference among analysts. She quotes Freud's admonitions to the physician to recognize and overcome countertransference in himself (1910). Tower writes:

It is striking that a natural and inevitable phenomenon, so rich in potential for understanding, should have sustained so forbidding a tone toward its existence for forty-five years. I refer to the fact that no analyst has ever been presumed to have been so perfectly analyzed that he no longer has an unconscious, or is without susceptibility to the stirring up of instinctual impulses and defenses against them. . . . At no time is it expected that he will have been perfectly analyzed. In addition, our recommendations for periodic reanalysis of analysts presuppose a large unconscious reservoir of sources for the development of new neurotic responses to emotional pressures from analytic patients upon the analyst's unconscious. [1956, p. 162]

After giving examples of the forbidding nature of writing on the subject, she writes:

Virtually every writer on the subject of countertransference, for example, states unequivocally that no form of erotic reaction to a patient is to be tolerated. This would indicate that temptations in this area are great, and perhaps ubiquitous. . . .

All of these—and similar attitudes—presuppose an ability in the analyst consciously to *control* his own unconscious. Such a supposition is in violation of the basic premise of our science—namely, that human beings are possessed of an unconscious which is *not* subject to conscious control, but which is (fortunately) subject to investigation through the medium of the transference (and presumably also the countertransference) neurosis.

In my experience, virtually all physicians when they gain enough confidence in their analysts, report erotic feelings and impulses toward their patients, but usually do so with a good deal of fear and conflict. [pp. 163, 164]

Nineteen years later, Searles wrote his paper and revealed very strong countertransference reactions of a mixed erotic and aggressive nature toward his patients. In fact, in a description of his work with a hebephrenic man, Searles says he experienced moments of "murderous rage, violent sexual urges, and acute fear" (p. 123). After several years of intensive work, Searles writes, "To my enormous relief I realized that I could now be related to him without having either to kill him or fuck him" (p. 123).

Surely, the Searles paper shows progress in self-revelation, but none of these writers deals with the important issue of what is to be done about an analyst who has had sexual relations with a patient. How is he to be controlled from repeating, a common occurrence? Even if he reenters analysis, it may take years for him (or her) to reach the material that will enable him to develop sufficient impulse control so that the profession can be assured he will not harm another patient. In the meantime, is he to be allowed to continue to practice? Should any disciplinary action be taken against him? If he is contrite, a constructive approach may be possible, but what if, as in some cases, he refuses to admit to responsibility and seeks to project blame onto the woman patient for being seductive, or insists it is only her fantasy? Surely dismissal from the local Institute and the American Psychoanalytic Association, and removal of his license to practice psychiatry would be necessary in such a case.

Person (1983b) reports that in her treatment of male therapists intensely erotically tempted by female patients, two had acted upon the temptation. The two factors that had emerged were an impulse toward self-destruction and a feeling of betrayal by their previous analysts. In each of these cases, the therapist had discovered himself described in a paper published by his former analyst, although in a disguised way, without permission having ever been asked or granted.

> Although neither had reacted negatively at the time of the discovery, in re-analysis each expressed the feeling that he had been "raped." Therapists who act out with patients are often re-enacting problems in their own analyses, much as the parents who abuse their children were themselves abused as children. [p. 201]

Bigras (1990) reports that many of the incest victims he has seen came to him after previous experiences with male therapists or psychoanalysts. They complained of having been severely hurt and repelled by these attempts to find help because of having been sexually abused, in some cases more than once, by the analyst/therapist, which led to their leaving the treatment in crisis, or they had felt traumatized by encounters with cool and remote analysts. In both cases, he says, the patients left treatment in a state of shame and despair. He wondered why they had again chosen a male analyst and suggests that they felt compelled to repeat the same sadomasochistic pattern: "The working through of this compulsion could only begin, I soon realized, by the analyst's changing his attitude and manner of working so as to accept the importance of the real, as well as the transferential, relationship with this type of patient" (p. 194).

One cannot ever know, since some analysts may be cool and remote with every patient, but I wonder if the "cool and remote" attitude with these patients was in fact a defensive maneuver on the part of the analyst to help him control the incestuous pull he found in himself toward the incest victim patient. By maintaining distance he may have hoped to control his impulses, and this process may have been happening without his conscious awareness. As Bigras says, the result was to leave the patient in a state of despair, and the analyst perhaps never dealing with his erotic countertransference.

WOMEN ANALYSTS EXAMINE SEXUAL FEELINGS TOWARD PATIENTS IN WOMEN THERAPISTS

Although I have been aware of feelings of sexual attraction to some male patients, I have never had fears of acting upon the attraction. I have always made careful mental note of the feelings, and in some cases the dreams in which a male patient appears. It has always been very clear in my mind that any such action would be an inexcusable exploitation of the patient and the ruin of our work together. I can no sooner imagine acting sexually on impulses toward a male patient than toward my own son. Rather than looking for the explanation in my own personal background or my personal circumstances at the particular time, it seems more likely that this attitude reflects a gender difference that should be examined. Why can't a man be more like a woman?

I suggest that it is the fact of motherhood—of carrying, birthing, and nursing a baby and then nurturing young children—that makes women so much more sensitive to the vulnerability of children and patients than men are. It is also true that as mothers, women therapists have had years of putting their needs second, or third or fourth, and acting in the best interests of the dependent child. This is ideal training for therapists. What about women analysts or therapists who have never been mothers? It would be interesting to see if nonmothers are more likely to be offenders of this basic law of psychotherapy than mothers, but I do not have such data available to me. Even nonmothers may have a strong maternal identity through their connection to their own mother.

In my mind, the roles of mother and of therapist are parallel. Clearly, for the men who act out sexual impulses with their patients, there are no nurturing, protective feelings engendered in them by the relative weakness and vulnerability of the woman patient; rather that vulnerability stimulates selfish desires. It may be that the best method for reducing father–child incest and therapist–patient incest is to be sure that fathers participate actively in the care of their own infants and hope that caring and compassion for those who are dependent is a by-product, as shown in the research of Diane Ehrensaft (1985) on dual parenting, reviewed in my first book.

Ethel S. Person

Person observed (1983b) that sexuality in the case of female therapists occurs frequently in terms of sexual competitive themes in the analyses of women working with women analysts, both in transference and counter-transference reaction. She cites two examples in which women therapists acted out erotic competition with female patients by becoming erotically involved with the patient's male relatives. Curiously, this factor has not been mentioned by any of the writers about male analysts. Could the sexual abuse of a female patient have some bearing on the male therapist's competitive feelings with her father, husband, or boyfriend, thus making an oedipal triangle? I once had a male patient who knew of my husband and reported a fantasy that my husband was actually observing and listening in on our sessions through a peephole in the wall. He needed a male presence to repeat the triangular aspects of his transference.

She also states that women therapists have no special virtue, in this regard.

> The relative subordination of the patient and authority of the analyst is not congruent with the most predominant type of female sexual fantasies. Yet women do have sexual fantasies about male patients. Because of cultural prohibitions, women therapists are less likely to dwell upon or openly acknowledge such fantasies. [p. 201]

This point seems to me to be a significant factor in understanding the very low incidence of female therapist–male patient sexual activity. It also explains the obvious reverse situation, wherein the female patient is particularly vulnerable to seduction by her male psychiatrist or other therapist because of the flattery to the woman, as in the case of Mrs. D., when a male in authority is attracted to her.

Person also finds that the erotic transference is unusually intense in the analyses of homosexual women by women therapists and difficulty interpreting or managing it often leads to the disruption of treatment.

Herta A. Guttman

Guttman (1984) comments that as women, female therapists have been well trained to censor their sexual feelings and thus suppress their conscious awareness of such feelings. Tower (1936) reports an experience similar to several of my own, when the awareness of sexual attraction was revealed in a dream about the patient. Guttman states, "Acknowledging sexual arousal evokes in female therapists, as in all women, images of the incestuous mother or of the whorish 'other woman.' Female therapists may also react in this way to the male patient's sexuality, pretending that he is not attractive, that he is not attracted . . ." (p. 193). She relates this to a cultural phenomenon in which women are told that it is their fault if a man is attracted to them, that they must have done something to be provocative. She reminds us of Freud's (1915) paper on technique in which he states that the charms of the therapist's person are not the source of these feelings in the patient. Nevertheless, women analysts did not wear miniskirts in 1915. Men's suits do not have the erotic potential of women's clothing and have not changed much. Women do need to be modest and professional in their dress. Perfume, for example, is inappropriate.

Guttman finds that the female therapist is more likely to find acceptable to her the viewing of the male patient in the light of maternal feelings, as either the "needy child" or the "provocative child." Female therapists are likely to be less exhibitionistic, often being overly prudent and avoiding opportunities to facilitate the expression of sexual thoughts and fantasies because they fear seeming to be prurient or brazen. They are less likely to prolong therapy with male than with female patients. In addition, some female therapists may respond to negative male images and be put off by sexist comments or behavior by male patients.

Guttman notes a trend in the psychoanalytic literature on counter-transference, in which she finds that male therapists more often report erotic transference in female patients, whereas female therapists more frequently report their own erotic countertransference. "Female therapists, like all women, are not as committed to preserving the illusion of their power in relationships, therapeutic or otherwise. They may more easily admit the patient's reciprocal power over them" (p. 196).

Christine Rienek, Gail Barton, and Elissa Benedek

In a paper by Rienek, Barton, and Benedek (1981), three women psychiatrists report on their experience in training residents to recognize and understand aspects of sexual countertransference. Fifteen female therapists—psychologists, social workers, and psychiatric residents—were interviewed and reported feelings of attraction to or fear of male patients but that they generally did not receive help from supervisors with these feelings because the supervisors seemed uncomfortable about the issue. Both the therapists and the supervisors were hampered by having been raised in sexually repressive home atmospheres where silence on sexual matters created a taboo between parent and child that was reenacted in many of the relationships between trainees and supervisors.

THE IMBALANCE OF POWER: SEX IN PROFESSIONAL RELATIONSHIPS—PETER RUTTER

Following a personal confrontation with sex in the psychotherapy relationship, Peter Rutter (1989), a Jungian analyst, wrote an important book in which he enlarges the topic to *Sex in the Forbidden Zone: When Men in Power—Therapists, Doctors, Clergy, Teachers and Others—Betray Women's Trust.* Rutter candidly describes his own brush with fantasies of forbidden sex, responding to the seductiveness of a woman patient at a point in his life when he was depressed because of a personal loss. He also tells of his profound disillusionment when he heard of charges that his mentor, a prominent Jungian analyst in San Francisco, had had multiple affairs with patients and trainees. It led him to examine this issue and to produce a book that links together men in positions of trust in many professions, men to whom women turn for medical, legal, spiritual, or academic help, and upon whom these women are dependent for healing, access to the legal system, or career advancement. His approach is analytical but also very complimentary to feminist theory. He appreciates that men are most often the "gatekeepers" for women who are attempting to move into careers and often use this power to sexually exploit the career desires of such women. The key is the female's dependency and the male's skill, knowledge, and power, which connects the sexual abuse of a client by her attorney, a troubled patient by her physician, a parishioner needing guidance by her minister, and a student needing access to information and credentials from her teacher or advisor.

Rutter examines the psychology of the normal male to understand how this happens, and the psychology of the normal female who allows it to happen. His description of normal male psychology vis-à-vis women is brutally frank and describes a predatory attitude that could not be more harshly phrased by a radical feminist. Men who read this book will not be pleased to see themselves portrayed so rapaciously. As a woman, I concluded the book feeling most fortunate to have survived my own psychiatric treatment and training without a traumatic incident, and most grateful to the men who have respected me.

In examining his own feelings about "Dr. Reynolds," his mentor, he acknowledged that he was capable of having powerful fantasies of sexual contact with patients and that he had held on to an idealized version of Reynolds long after he should have. He came upon a "darker dimension of the hidden world of masculine sexual psychology."

> I realized that whenever I thought about his forbidden liaisons, beneath my outrage lurked a secret envy. I wished I could do what he had done. I heard my inner voices rapidly run the gamut from, "Oh, how awful! That terrible man. The deceit. The selfishness" . . . to "How could he do it? How did he carry it off?" How indeed? "What's his secret? If he could do it, why can't I? It's something I've always wished for. Maybe one day I won't have to be so strict about upholding sexual boundaries with my own patients." [p. 10]

He distinguishes sex in the workplace, sexual harassment on the job, from the professional relationship, because although in the former there is economic dependency, there is not a violation of trust. In the case of political leaders, he refers to the notorious case of Gary Hart and Donna Rice, claiming that Rice stands as a cultural symbol of the woman who is sexually used by a powerful man and then cast aside when she is no longer useful. Such a political leader betrays *our* trust, says Rutter, and I agree. When the story broke I was amazed at the pain it caused so many people, and the stories they told of grieving again over memories of personal experiences of betrayal that were aroused by Hart's behavior. As a supporter of Hart, I personally experienced depression and disillusionment. A common reaction seemed to be "Is there no one we can trust?" or a more cynical "What do you expect?"

Rutter states his position as follows:

> Any sexual behavior by a man in power within what I define as the forbidden zone is inherently exploitative of a woman's trust. Because he is the keeper of that trust, it is the man's responsibility, no matter what the level of provocation or apparent consent by the woman, to assure that sexual behavior does not take place. . . . The dynamics of the forbidden zone can render a woman unable to *withhold* consent. [pp. 21, 25]

He repeats Sandra Butler's phrase *conspiracy of silence* to describe the intense resistance within the profession to disclosure of these facts. When Nanette Gartrell proposed a survey of the incidence of sexual exploitation by psychiatrists, the American Psychiatric Association, citing a fear of adverse publicity, refused to provide funds or to allow the survey to take place under the association's auspices, forcing Gartrell to obtain private donations for the study. Is it any wonder that mothers have difficulty turning in their husbands, when psychiatrists can't bear to even have a study of the problem? In trying to understand the lure of forbidden sex for men, Rutter states that men's sexual fantasies grow out of "profound needs for healing and self-validation" (p. 61). Although the exploiting male may have no conscious awareness of it, Rutter believes that most destructive sexual behavior toward women is rooted in this effort to heal a wounded sense of self.

Rutter seeks, through the following analysis, to explain the collusion of male professionals in the exploitive behavior of their colleagues. He believes that although the majority of professional men behave ethically, they maintain a fantasy that some day they may actually have a sexual affair with a woman patient. Hearing about a colleague who has had such an affair encourages this hope and allows the man to receive vicarious gratification. Rutter proposes that in a tribal sense, the men who violate the trusting relationship serve as "designated surrogates who live out these fantasies for the rest of the men in the tribe" (p. 62). This, Rutter believes, explains why colleagues fail to act to prevent such occurrences or punish the offenders. The more occurrences of the violation of the sexual taboo between doctor and patient, the more the atmosphere is infected and the more the resistance is lowered for other men who may be struggling not to act upon sexual fantasies. Acting to prevent such sexual exploitation of women would mean the professional's having to limit his own fantasy life and would remove a source of vicarious pleasure.

This hypothesis is intriguing and appealing and no doubt valid for some men. However, there could be another significant factor. We all grew up in the children's culture where being a "tattletale" was a disgrace. Other words include "snitch" and "fink." This attitude, that the one who exposes misbehavior is also culpable is strongly inculcated and implies that the tattletale is too good and is breaking a code of ethics that involves loyalty to the group, which comes above obedience to the rules of the school or other authority. Could it be that this time-honored childhood hierarchy of values is still honored when psychiatrists fail to "snitch" on another psychiatrist? If this is a factor, one would not have to postulate the hidden desire to exploit women. The failure to report could simply be a component of the fear of being rejected by one's peer group. The tattletale is subject to merciless attack and derogation by the group, and fear of that attack surely is a deterrent. In a case reported on the television program "Frontline" on 12 November 1991, a woman psychiatrist, Martha Gay, who testified against a male psychiatrist, Jason Richter, who was being sued for becoming sexually involved with his patient, Melissa Roberts Henry, became the target of hostility on the part of the Denver psychiatric community and by the American Psychiatric Association, which held the malpractice insurance for Dr. Richter. Ultimately, she had to give up her practice and leave town, whereas the perpetrator, Dr. Richter, continues to practice successfully in Denver. Who would have the courage to defend a patient again, if doing so results in the death of your career?

Rutter describes the masculine myth of the feminine as consisting of three elements: women's deference, women's special powers, and women as dark and destructive, all making relationships in which men have power over women so vulnerable to abusive sexuality. He recognizes the terrible destruction of hope that such an experience engenders in the woman, who was searching for recognition from a man. Like rape and incest victims, she tends to blame herself. A surprising finding by Rutter is that not one of the women interviewed for his book has yet borne a child. Although some were already mothers at the time, they have not conceived again. This confirms my finding that among my patients, some sexually abused women are reluctant to bear children, fearing they do not have enough to give, and that they may not be able to protect the child.

In a chapter on the "wounds of men," Rutter finds the lack of intimacy between fathers and sons a problem leading to an absence of inner resources in men, thus leading them to seek out through sexual contact with women the "life-giving, healing elements that they might have found inside themselves" (pp. 101–102). The woman's need for hope and recognition comes together with the man's need for healing to produce a man who crosses the incestuous boundary and a woman who cannot say no because she needs his recognition so profoundly and hopes that his sexual need for her will heal her pain and give her hope. Her boundary problems combine with his, and both parties betray themselves. The terrible conflict for the woman is the danger of losing the connection with a powerful man versus the danger of allowing a destructive invasion of her boundaries with inevitable devaluation and degradation of herself.

> The result is paralysis—of action, judgment, feeling, and voice. The cultural messages encouraging passivity, the personal wounds from her family that have shown her there is no protective boundary, the hope that someone will treat her differently all come together as an over-whelming flood at the moment the man touches her. This paralysis can last for minutes, hours, days and sometimes years. In the meantime, the man has proceeded with his sexual scenario.
>
> At this point, a woman can completely shut down her feelings, dissociating herself from the body that is acting sexually. This split creates a state called "psychic numbing" . . . a prominent symptom of . . . post-traumatic stress disorder. [pp. 131–132]

Peter Rutter has written a courageous book, and thank goodness a man wrote it. The truths in his book cannot be dismissed as the rantings of an angry woman, a "woman's libber," a castrating, penis-envying misfit. His status commands public attention, and I daresay even Norman Mailer will keep quiet (see Prozan 1992).

SUMMARY: THE SIMILAR ELEMENTS IN THE PHYSICAL AND SEXUAL ABUSE OF WOMEN AND CHILDREN AND THE SEXUAL EXPLOITATION OF FEMALE PATIENTS

We all know the tragedy of women whose earlier traumas are repeated in exploitive relationships, over and over again. These are women who were never raised with pride, dignity, and self-respect. The millions of women who do say no to such overtures are those who were not abused as children and do not tolerate such disrespect of their boundaries. Even women who are therapy patients say no, so it is not just the situation of being a patient but the position of dependence in a woman whose sense of herself is so uncertain, so fragile, and therefore so needy, that provides the vulnerable victim for the male predator. Whether the source of that vulnerability was an early rejection by her mother, sexual or physical abuse by either parent, or a combination of economic, social, and psychological injustice owing to racial, class, and gender discrimination and belittlement, such injured girls become the battered women, the prostitutes, the exploited women, and the desensitized mothers who then raise damaged daughters, perpetuating the cycle of cruelty, violence, pain, and degradation.

We have seen in each of the three groups discussed in Chapter 5 and this chapter—battered women, sexually abused children, and women exploited by their therapists—the same elements:

1. A conspiracy of silence by the community
2. A pact of secrecy between victim and victimizer, enforced by fear
3. Collusion of adults whose own selfish or sadistic impulses prevent recognition and exposure of the problem
4. Betrayal of trust in a relationship in which an innocent requires protection (i.e., soul murder)
5. Disbelief of the victim's story
6. Projection of blame onto the victim for being provocative
7. Violation of physical and psychological boundaries
8. A reenactment in a current relationship of a historical violation of trust
9. Exploitation of the weak by the powerful
10. A profound moral dilemma that pits the survival of one weak person against the survival of another
11. Protection of those in power by those who hope to ascend to power and by those who depend upon that power
12. The important role of professionals in breaking the silence
13. The importance of the law to serve in the place of the failed conscience of the individual.

As the field of physical and sexual abuse has burgeoned, the terminology has changed. We used to refer to victims, and now we say "survivors." We need to take this one step further, and I believe we are ready to do so. I propose "conqueror" as the final stage of healing from abusive relationships. Conquerors should not be limited to the military. These healed adults, men and women, are heroes and heroines of our domestic wars, the family wars from which they have emerged victorious. Incest conquerors will serve as models for others and keep the terrible perpetuation of these crimes from multiplying.

The contributions of feminism to these battles for the innocent have not been just in terms of cultural insights, but in the exposure of internal truths as well, the exposure of all the secrets of all the millions of victims, survivors, and conquerors.

Psychoanalysis has provided the tools and the skills to expose the repressed terrors of patients through sensitive listening to dreams and asking of the right questions. Once again, an integration of feminist and psychoanalytic revelations of the truth, has produced a true revolution in the freeing of adults from years of secrecy and fear and, one hopes, the freeing of future generations from the soul murders that have been all too frequent in the past.

Not to be believed is a painful violation in itself. When a child or a woman is not believed, it is another betrayal of the self of that child or woman. It obliterates one's perceptions, the sense of knowing what one knows. It is an insult to the integrity and honor of the individual. It creates the worst kind of cynicism and leads to anger and withdrawal from the human family. The lies, the cover-ups that abound from the family to the heads of state all contribute to an atmosphere of suspicion and mistrust that destroys all that is good in human relationships.

We must all be courageous in breaking silence and protecting the betrayed. In the words of Elie Wiesel: "Let us remember: what hurts the victim most is not the cruelty of the oppressor, but the silence of the by-stander."

7

CLINICAL ISSUES WITH LESBIAN PATIENTS

Mother was sitting in her green stuffed rocking chair when I walked through the door. "You can turn around and walk right out. I know everything that went on up there, the dean of women called me up. You just turn your ass around and get out."

"Mom, you only know what they told you."

"I know you let your ass run away with your head, that's what I know. A queer, I raised a queer, that's what I know. You're lower than them dirty fruit pickers in the groves, you know that?"

"Mom, you don't understand anything. Why don't you let me tell my side of it?"

"I don't want to hear nothing you can say. You always were a bad one. Go on and get outa here. I don't want you. Why the hell you even bother to come back here?"

. . . I picked up my suitcase by the door and walked out into the cool night air. I had $14.61 in my jeans. That wouldn't get me half to New York City. And that's where I was going. There are so many queers in New York that one more wouldn't rock the boat.

—Rita Mae Brown

STATISTICS AND CATEGORIES

Statistics on the numbers of female homosexuals vary widely, depending on the definition. Kinsey estimated about 12 or 13 percent of women had sexual relations to the point of orgasm with another woman at some time during their adult lives. Hite (1976) reports: "144 women in this study (8 percent) said they preferred sex with women. Another 73 identified themselves as bisexual, and 84 women had had experiences with both men and women but did not answer as to preference, another 9 percent" (p. 395). Many other women said they might be interested in having sexual relations with another woman. Hite promotes a very positive approach to sex between women: "A positive attitude toward our bodies and toward touching ourselves and toward any physical contact that might naturally develop with another woman is essential to self-love and accepting our own bodies as good and beautiful" (p. 416).

In my observation, there are several categories of lesbians based on the age of the awareness of the erotic attraction to other women. For some there was never any doubt, their first love at puberty being another girl. Rita Mae Brown (1973) describes this in her novel *Rubyfruit Jungle*. For others there are some disappointing attachments to boys in adolescence and perhaps in college, but at some still young age, perhaps around 20, they become aware that their feelings for other women are much more powerful than their feelings for men. This is not similar to male homosexuals, who generally do not have sexual relationships with girls during adolescence. The biological factor is important here. Females can have sexual intercourse without being either attracted to or aroused by the male, whereas the male cannot if he is not sexually attracted to the female. Another group marries, bears children, and although they have very close women friends, do not enter into sexual relationships with other women until some point in midlife, after some years of disappointment in their marriages. They may have felt some stirrings toward women when they were younger, but resolved the conflict in favor of marriage at that time.

A fourth group can be described as political lesbians. Their sexual involvement with other women began as part of their intense involvement with the women's movement, which brought them into close working relationships with other women at the same time that a lot of anger was being mobilized against men. The realization of male prejudice against women and the dominant-subordinate tendencies in relationships with men occurred in a supportive female atmosphere of sisterhood. For some, a lesbian relationship became a political act of solidarity with other women who shared the goal of freeing women from patriarchal restraints. In some women's projects there was considerable pressure placed on women not to relate to men, who were considered the enemy, thus making the heterosexual woman a traitor to the cause. Yet not all women actively involved in the women's movement made the switch to lesbianism, or stayed with it, so we would still be interested in the internal reasons in addition to the external ones, for those who did.

A patient of mine fit this category and had maintained a lesbian relationship for nine years, throughout which she never felt true sexual love for her mate but did not have the courage to oppose her. The other woman was a psychotherapist. My patient felt drawn to her psychological knowledge as well as to the community of women working in the women's movement, of which this woman was a part, and found it very difficult to extricate herself from the dependent tie. When she began work with me, she was living with a man who was not really suitable for her. He was a drug dealer and provided her with a lot of money, but most importantly, he had provided her with a baby, which she had longed for and which finally, in her mid-thirties, had propelled her to leave her long-term lesbian relationship. The similarity between the two partners seemed to be the rebellious, antiestablishment aspect to both of their lives, which matched her own family experience of being raised by parents who were in the Communist party.

Still another group can be recognized, namely, women who never have sexual relationships with other women but who exclude men from their lives, perhaps after a divorce. They may live with or maintain a very close attachment to their mother, who is likely to be divorced or widowed; and have close women friends, often other women like themselves who have "given up" on men. Sometimes these women have gay male friends or relate to married couples as friends. This group is to be differentiated from women who still are trying to find male companionship but are not successful. I refer here to women who have truly eliminated sexual relationships with men from their lives and may be possessive of women friends whenever they show interest in a man, disparaging the effort. This group of women are not lesbians but have reverted to exclusivity with women as a result of discouraging tries with men and a growing disgust with the whole process.

Some women in the lesbian community select lesbian therapists, but those who came to me did so with a stated preference for a "straight" therapist because, they said, the lesbian community is like a small town where everyone knows everyone and where you are likely to see your therapist at a party and know women who know her. They preferred the professional distance and anonymity provided by a therapist outside their close-knit community. I have worked with a total of ten lesbian patients over the years and found a variety of diagnoses, life-styles, and psychological issues that make it impossible to categorize them based on their object choice. It could be argued that lesbian patients who come to a heterosexual psychotherapist differ in some way from those who seek out a lesbian therapist.

An additional patient has been in a long-term marriage but had had a brief homosexual relationship in her late twenties, before her marriage, which continued to cause her anxiety although she had full sexual pleasure with her husband. The anxiety took two forms: it was projected onto her daughter with the fear that her daughter would become a lesbian, and it prevented her from having close women friends. She imagined that her husband would find each friend more desirable then herself and run off with her. I have no way of knowing if there was any truth to her fears about her husband, but I do know that this was largely a projection of her own fears of being attracted to a woman and being drawn away from her husband to her. This patient is a severe borderline with many depressive, paranoid, and masochistic features; her homosexual anxiety was only one of many fears that dominated her life. Her dependent transference to me gave her the connection she longed for with a caring older woman, without the fear of a sexual union in which she believed she would become irreparably merged with her partner in a regressive, childlike attachment. Her mother is very domineering, hostile, and paranoid and had infantilized and been severely critical of both my patient (an only child) and her father.

In seven cases the family constellations varied, and these patients' relationships with their parents were neither more nor less difficult than those of most patients who come for treatment. Two had psychotic mothers and were themselves psychotic. Francine, described in Chapter 1, is an example of a psychotic teenager who was raised by a psychotic mother. She improved in seven years of psychotherapy between the ages of 14 and 20, and became a lesbian and part of the homosexual community in San Francisco, which was very helpful to her.

Another example was a long-term patient, Mary Ann, an "illegitimate" baby who had been placed by her mother in a Catholic orphanage for girls run by nuns. When she was 9, her mother married and brought her to live with her and the stepfather. Her memories of her mother were such that I was led to conclude her mother was psychotic. She recalled rages in which her mother would chase her around the house with a broom, hitting her.

When Mary Ann started treatment she was heterosexual, but after two years, in her late twenties, became a lesbian and gradually developed a psychotic transference to me. This switch may have been precipitated by the death of her mother and the subsequent refusal of her stepfather to share any of the small inheritance with her and his breaking off contact with her. After eleven years I had to refer her to another therapist because of her insistence that we get married and her inability to work this through. She had become seriously mentally ill and has not worked in years. She still keeps in touch with me, calling on holidays and at times of crisis, but has been able to maintain a long-term love relationship with another woman. Her intelligence and charm help to sustain her relationships, but her paranoid schizophrenic illness keeps her emotionally fragile.

Other lesbian patients have been capable, of high intelligence, and came for help with issues no different from those of other patients: problems in love relationships, career conflicts, depression, and anxiety. In my work with a lesbian couple, my observation and interpretation of the interactional difficulties was similar to work with heterosexual couples. The only unique issue was that of concealment of the relationship. One woman, a nonpracticing attorney, had "come out" to her family and lived openly with her lover. The other, a physician, kept her homosexuality a secret both at work and from her family, and this situation caused stress between the pair. They maintained two telephones so that the attorney never answered the phone of the physician. The societal factor of prejudice against homosexuals was the main factor that differentiated the lives of these women from that of other women and other couples. The kinds of incompatibilities for which they sought couple treatment included one being more sociable than the other and wanting to "talk things over" more. The less sociable partner became jealous of the friends and many telephone conversations and visits by the more sociable one of the pair. Problems also erupted over the failure to bid high enough for a very desirable home, for which the physician blamed the attorney, who had taken the responsibility for negotiations. Both of these issues are common in heterosexual couples.

The other clearly unique factor is the one of childbearing, a strong urge for some. One of my patients had a very good lesbian relationship, which led to a formal marriage including a religious ceremony and celebration. A year later, after much pressure from her parents, the spouse of my patient announced that she had decided to get a divorce because she wanted children. The phenomenon of lesbian couples having and raising a child together is now a more common occurrence.

An issue commonly discussed and written about in the field is that of boundary diffusion between lesbian women in couples. It has been noted that they start to menstruate at the same time and often share underwear. Surely there is boundary diffusion in many heterosexual relationships, but the gender difference always maintains some boundary. I was once struck by the following scene at a movie theatre. While waiting in line for the film to start I decided to go the ladies' room. Two lesbians standing near us went to the ladies' room too, together. Here is a parting of the ways that heterosexuals take for granted but that does not occur in homosexual couples.

I have observed a difference in society's view of the women who become lesbians from the men who become "gay," which reflects our society's general belittlement of and hostility toward women. Women's movement activists and lesbians are referred to as "man-haters" whereas the males are not referred to as "woman-haters," presumably because that is taken for granted and is not a major source of disapproval. It is their rejection of masculinity, not their rejection of women, that causes the hostility toward gay men in the form of name-calling such as "cocksuckers," "fairies," "queers." In Yiddish the word *faygeleh* is defined as a little bird; a girl's name; a dear little, sweet, helpless, innocent child; and is also the term for a homosexual male, a demeaning but more sympathetic description. In other words, it is their *being like women* that creates the antagonism, not their rejection of women.

CLINICAL ILLUSTRATIONS

Research indicates the lack of sisters in the families of many homosexuals, and the frequency of only children. This may be statistically true, but I have not found this interesting occurrence in many of my lesbian patients. I have noticed that they are often the oldest daughter. It may be that the mother makes her most intense identification and connection with her first daughter. In several of my cases, the patient was one of two sisters of whom one was a lesbian and the other a heterosexual. I think it is interesting to explore two of these examples to see what the differences in the family experience was like for each sister and to appreciate the important role of siblings and other family members in psychological development, a fact often neglected in individual therapy. In comparing the sisters in each pair, we can see how each parent related differently to each daughter and the effects of these differences on the outcome of sexual object choice.

Barbara and Her Sister Joanne

I described Barbara in Chapter 1 as an example of a woman with a mother who was narcissistic, immature, and neglectful. Barbara's mother spent her days shopping and left the housework and child care to hired help. She was very possessive with Barbara, however, and could not tolerate Barbara's fondness for her aunt, her mother's sister, of whom she was very jealous, and who happened to be a psychiatric social worker.

Barbara had been a lesbian since age 18 and had had two long-term relationships with older, masculine women and then, later, a number of casual affairs. She recognized that the masculinity in the women she was attracted to reminded her of her father. Her sexual relationships included mild sadomasochism, which she defended at first against my view of it as problematic. The connection with her mother's having beaten her for masturbation was easily made, and consequently she was able to give up this component both in actual sexual practice and, gradually, in the quality of her relationships. She then fell in love with a woman her own age, and they lived together for two years. She ended the relationship when she became convinced that the woman's immaturity and self-centeredness made for a repetition of her relationship with her mother. She believed she did most of the giving in their relationship.

She made much progress in the seven years of our work together. When she started she was working in secretarial jobs that she found very frustrating. After several years she entered graduate school. She was able to identify with me and with her aunt as women quite different from her mother, women who took their minds and their work seriously. She had had difficulties being alone and would seek out sexual partners to combat the anxiety and depression, but in the course of our work she became able to live alone, be without a sexual partner, and tolerate the anxiety and depression that emerged, using it for exploration in her treatment. She was able to understand the narcissistic and immature nature of her mother's character and how it had affected her, including her fear of succeeding academically because of the distance it would put between herself and her mother, whose main occupation is shopping and decorating herself and her home.

She began therapy with a great deal of hostility toward her father but gradually came to see some of his strong qualities and developed, with some difficulty, a much closer relationship to him and some respect for him. Her younger sister, who had been missing for many years, surfaced near San Francisco about a year before the end of Barbara's treatment and then moved to live near Barbara. The reestablishment of this relationship exposed many earlier problems, for it was soon clear the sister is a low-functioning borderline with no capacity to relate in a mutual way with her. Because of her weakness, she is catered to in some ways by both parents, which made Barbara furious, so that old sibling rivalry issues emerged in full force as she saw her sister being rewarded for weakness and dependency and saw herself as independent and a hard worker who was unrecognized. This was especially difficult for her in the area of attracting men (by now she had become heterosexual), because she saw the sister attracting men continually through her helplessness.

During the course of her treatment with me, she became

dissatisfied with love relationships with women and decided she wanted to try to relate sexually to men. She became impatient with me for being a woman and with all the women friends in her life. The change seemed to occur as a result of her developing a closer relationship with her father and recognizing the severity of her mother's pathology. She came to appreciate some of her father's good qualities and recognized that with all his faults, he was the more mentally healthy parent—worldly, intelligent, and easier to talk to than Mother. Father was proud of her graduate work and praised and encouraged her. He was ambivalent about how much money supporting Barbara in school was costing him and at times was unreliable, making Barbara angry at him all over again. At one point, however, Mother told Barbara that she had just bought herself a ten-thousand-dollar watch and Barbara was able to see that her father's concern that women took advantage of him for his money could have some basis, although it was unfairly being applied to her.

She had two brief sexual relationships with men in her last year of work with me in which she enjoyed the caressing and sex but was very anxious about rejection and disappointed by the men's lack of pursuit. She came to recognize that her idea of herself was that a man could be attracted to her sexually but that she did not have what it takes to get a man to marry her. Her sexual self-image was that of an alluring mistress but not a beloved wife. Her mother behaved more like a mistress than a wife, so Barbara was able to associate this idea with her father's choice of her mother. In being able to connect this with her view of what her father wanted in a woman, she could differentiate from her fantasied connection to her mother, her rejection by her father, and start the process of finding positive qualities in herself that could make her feel valuable to a man. She still feared her aggressiveness and worried that it would get in the way with most men, but this insight helped to dispel some of her pessimism about her chances with men.

Her pessimism related in part to the esteem in which she held her mother's appearance and attractiveness to men. Barbara described her mother as very beautiful and well built. She had been a model before marrying Father, and Barbara could remember that men's heads turned whenever Mother walked by. Mother's hair was dyed blonde and she had had several face lifts by the time Barbara was seeing me. Her wardrobe was vast and Barbara had memories as a child of mother's drawers of scarves, gloves, and other accessories, and shelves of sweaters in every shade and hue. Barbara did not consider herself in Mother's class in terms of appearance. She was actually quite petite and pretty but felt she could only look pretty when she used makeup, whereas Mother was naturally beautiful. I pointed out that the bleached blonde hair was unnatural, but it took several repetitions of this theme before Barbara could recognize how she had overvalued her mother's appearance and depreciated her own. The more Barbara talked about her mother, the more a picture emerged of a severely narcissistic woman with paranoid features.

Barbara was definitely preferred by her mother to Joanne. When Joanne was born, Mother hired a full-time nurse for the baby so that she could continue to pay attention to Barbara. That, in addition to the special relationship Barbara had with her maternal grandmother, one which Joanne did not have, seems to account for the difference in degree of pathology between the two sisters. We can speculate that Father's rather competitive and angry reaction to Barbara's high intelligence and assertiveness resulted in an injury to her trust in men and her hopes of being loved by a man. However, Father did spend time with her. On Mother's insistence, he took the two girls with him every Saturday to sports activities and while he made the rounds of some of his business clients. These Saturdays together involved some good times but were tinged with the forced nature of Mother's demands, which also meant Mother's having additional time away from her children.

Mother's immaturity and self-centeredness combined with her controlling behavior toward Barbara left Barbara seeking true love from a woman, but she was frequently disappointed and believed she always selected narcissistic women who could not meet her emotional needs any better than mother had. The nature of this work, connecting history with current relationships, was no different than it would be with a heterosexual woman, with the focus on the reenactment of pathological connections with parental or sibling figures in current choices of love objects.

I speculated with Barbara, and she believed I may have been right, that the combination of mother's narcissism and exploitive relationship with Father resulted in Father's resenting Barbara's birth because of the attention Mother gave to the new baby, which withdrew attention from him, forming a triangle in which Father felt unappreciated and left out. This apparently did not get repeated when Joanne was born, as Mother did not form the same intense bond with Joanne. Looking back a generation, it is interesting to wonder whether something similar had occurred with the maternal grandmother who had also had two daughters, preferring the first-born daughter, Barbara's aunt, to her (Barbara's) mother, resulting in emotional neglect and lifelong jealousy by Barbara's mother of her own sister and prevention of an attachment by Barbara to her aunt, which was later reenacted in the inhibited transference to me. Another indication that there may be truth to this speculation is the fact that grandmother formed a close attachment to Barbara but not with her sister, Joanne. Grandmother also had a sister who was described by Barbara early in therapy as "eccentric" and exciting. She had lived in France after the war and was involved with her husband in relief work, but later Barbara began to realize that this great-aunt was seriously disturbed. Might grandmother have been a preferred daughter herself? The history of the women in the family, three sets of sisters, was a fascinating component in tracing the variety of Barbara's female role models. She maintained a strong interest in art, her grandmother's field. Her father's brother, her only uncle, was an underworld character who was somewhat frightening to Barbara. Her father often had to bail him out of difficulties.

When Joanne reappeared near San Francisco, Barbara's contact with her brought a reappraisal of the sibling rivalry issues. Joanne was very disturbed and had been collecting welfare and living with a much older woman who had just died. Barbara didn't know if there was anything sexual in that relationship but she had remembered her sister as heterosexual, and Joanne was relating sexually to men and excited about men when they met again. Barbara at this time wanted to relate to men and was very envious of her sister's ability to attract men. She related this to recognition that she had been envious of Joanne's ability to receive more care and affection from their father when they were young because Joanne was passive as a child and Barbara was aggressive. Barbara was very angry as she recalled these memories of father's preference for Joanne, and the anger was rekindled as father began to provide for Joanne financially and accepted her dependency. She felt hopeless, believing that a woman had to be weak and helpless to attract a man. She observed the heterosexual women in her classes and was angry and frustrated when certain women would "dissemble," as she put it, and be treated favorably by the male instructors. A strong feminist analysis of male–female relationships, which was generally accurate, added to her family experience to reinforce her sense of personal hopelessness. It was important that I did not share that hopelessness, although I agreed in a general sense with her feminist analysis. The difference was that I did not believe that all men wanted helpless women, especially not those who had already been married to one. I believed Barbara had enough attractive qualities that if she could work through her mistrustful attitude toward men and have some positive experiences, there was hope for her. Her wish to see a male therapist was another opportunity for this kind of working-through to take place.

Her criticism of my work with her increased as she read more about psychotherapy and increased the frequency of her visits to twice and then three times per week, thus intensifying her dependence on me. This led to many angry accusations of my supposed insensitivity or even cruelty and then further anger at what she felt were my "defensive" responses. She would take a particular phrase I had said out of context and bring it up the following session, distorting its meaning and ignoring the context and all the other components of the session. The paranoid quality became apparent to her after some time, and she was thereby enabled to recognize the paranoid quality in her mother's behavior and accusations against her and father. This transference work, though very difficult, was very helpful in getting a clearer picture of the mother–daughter relationship. It contributed to her impatience with her exclusively female world, including me, and her desire for a male therapist and for sexual intimacy with men.

The story of Barbara and Joanne shows how different the family environment may be for two sisters only two years apart in age. Each parent connected with each daughter differently, resulting in more pathology in Joanne, who made a heterosexual attachment through her special place with father, whereas Barbara, who was mentally healthier and more intelligent, felt more mistrust, disappointment, and anger toward Father and other men. Exploration of all these family dynamics resulted in a rearrangement of loyalties and identifications, leading Barbara to develop a more positive relationship with her father, to feel more identified with his career success, and better able to differentiate from Mother, who was the more pathological parent and had a tighter hold on her emotional life. She was able to identify with me as a career woman who believed that she could be attractive to a man. As Barbara matured and took on the responsibility of graduate school, she won more respect from her father, who was then able to be more complimentary and giving to her, though not without episodes of ambivalence.

Muriel and Her Sister Eileen

Muriel was my patient for a number of years and was heterosexual. Her sister Eileen, five years older, had married and had three children, and then, as part of involvement in the women's movement, became a lesbian. Both had divorced their first husbands, had affairs with other men, and become active in the women's movement, but then Muriel went on to remarry and had two children whereas Eileen became a radical lesbian. When I began to work with Muriel, she told me of her sister's change in sexual orientation but focused more on the ups and downs of her own relationships with men. Gradually, the important influence of her sister in her childhood emerged, and it was clear that this very bright, domineering, and at times cruel older sister had in fact had a very profound and negative effect on Muriel's self-image and had dominated the family system in ways that left Muriel feeling like a second-class citizen. One particularly painful memory involved Eileen, as an adolescent, teasing Muriel by asking her, "How do you know you're a girl, [when] you don't have breasts?" Muriel would remain silent and mortified because in her sexually very repressive household she couldn't possibly say the word *penis*. Ultimately, it may have been her sister's cruelty that kept Muriel from becoming a lesbian because she never wanted to be that vulnerable to a woman again, nor did she have a desire to reverse the roles (turn passive into active) and be cruel to a younger woman. However, the bisexual component was reenacted in the choice of her first husband, a domineering and cruel man who frequently told her she was not sexually attractive.

Muriel had trouble with both parents and at times was angry at each of them, but she was able to maintain an ongoing relationship with them that included some warmth and caring. As the history unraveled, it actually appeared that Eileen was the most toxic factor in the family for her. Memories began to emerge of Eileen's cruelty to her, and eventually Muriel concluded that her sister could never forgive her for being born and intruding on what had been her sister's undisputed territory.

Eileen had identified much more closely with their mother and had blamed Father for Mother's recurrent depressive episodes. By the time Eileen became a lesbian, she refused to talk to Father and held enormous anger toward him and all men. Muriel's continued involvement with men became such an issue of anger for Eileen that it was necessary for Muriel to sever the connection with her. Eileen had consigned the parents and all men and women to categories in a manner that Muriel could not accept or agree with, and when the former little sister stood up to her big sister and defended relating to men, she became linked with the "enemy" and therefore herself an enemy. Muriel gradually was forced to recognize that her sister, whom she had always looked up to, was quite paranoid about men and that it was impossible to have a rational discussion with her on the topic.

Eileen saw their mother as an innocent victim of the father's mistreatment and Father as a sadistic tyrant "like Hitler." She had tried to prevail upon Mother many times to leave Father, but Mother refused. Mother was quite dependent on Father, who had become a successful businessman, and although she was often very critical of him she also admired him, identified with him, and sympathized with him. They were both immigrants from Europe, had come to this country penniless, and had had to make their way in a new culture and learn a new language. Mother had formed a dependent bond with Father similar to the dependent bond she had had with her own mother. She had also formed such a bond with Eileen, and we wondered if Mother had led Eileen to believe she was the favorite, above both Father and Muriel, and then when Eileen made her bid to seduce mother away from Father and failed, she had turned all her wrath against Father, thereby protecting Mother from her rage at her.

Eileen had married a very decent man whom Muriel was extremely fond of, but Eileen kept finding fault with him (much as Mother had always found fault with Father) and divorced him. She had several long-term affairs with other men but they proved to be disappointing. When her children were grown, she began relating to women, asserting that she was the true feminist and insisting that Muriel was something of a counterfeit feminist. As Muriel wondered how this had happened, she heard through a third party that Eileen had said that she, Eileen, had always been Mother's favorite and that Muriel had been Father's favorite. This came as a total surprise because Muriel had never conceptualized the family relationships in that manner at all. She had felt that Eileen, having been an only child for five years, had been the clear favorite of both and that she had never had a chance to compete with Eileen's supremacy in the household. One of Muriel's worst memories was of her wedding day when Mother and Eileen, her matron of honor (she had no brides-maids), were busy preparing themselves and Eileen's children and neither of them offered to help her put on her wedding dress and veil. She didn't even realize that there was anything wrong with this until an aunt of her husband-to-be walked past the hotel room, noticed her alone and struggling to adjust her dress and veil, and with a look of complete shock and disbelief offered to help her.

However, Mother's splitting mechanism worked in Muriel's favor in some circumstances, as Muriel was endowed by Mother with many virtuous attributes, whereas Eileen, although considered the genius and the beauty, was frequently referred to as "lazy," "selfish," and a "fatso." Mother's hostility and competitiveness toward both daughters was symptomatic of her narcissism, which was blended with masochism. Eileen was thus forced by mother's negative characterization of her to feel very competitive with Muriel, who was described as a "saint." Muriel carried the burden of her supposed saintliness into other relationships, although she did rebel from this role as she got older.

Mother was quite open in often telling Muriel how much she had wanted her second child to be a boy. She told her that she had already planned the circumcision party and had bought herself a blue evening dress for the event. One would think that if either was to become a lesbian, Muriel was designated for that role. Yet we reconstructed a family situation in which Mother, who sounded to me like a borderline personality, had created an intense relationship with Eileen with boundary diffusion and coupling that left out both Father and Muriel. In fact it was a reenactment of her own intensely close relationship with her mother, who had lived with her until she died. This left Father and Muriel to pair off at times, and Muriel enjoyed her father's attention. There were elements of overinvolvement and boundary diffusion between Muriel and Mother as well, but Mother's increasingly serious depressions by the time Muriel was an adolescent and Eileen had left home for college put Muriel in a caretaking relationship with her mother, which freed her from the merging that mother encouraged and made a close identification with Mother so frightening that Muriel distanced herself from Mother and her pathology as much as she could.

Father handled Mother's criticism and rejection by having affairs with other women, but he left just enough room in his life for Muriel so that she was able to turn toward Father for attention and affection and enjoyed his company whenever he offered it. She felt deeply hurt and abandoned when she learned of his affairs, experiencing this as a personal betrayal because it meant Father had lied to her. The revelation was a source of trouble in her relationships with men thereafter; however, the closeness between Muriel and her father continued. In her childhood and adolescence he had brought her to his store and taught her to help, making her feel important and valued by him. She worked for him on Saturdays and during summers and took on more responsibility. Not having a son, he urged Muriel to go into the business with him, but she was not interested. However, this special contact with Father appeared to set the stage for a more permanent heterosexual object choice than in Eileen's case.

That Eileen usurped much of Mother's time and attention was a serious loss for Muriel, yet it turned out to be fortunate for her insofar as she did not as strongly identify with Mother, who was very smart but the more pathological of the two parents. Muriel could never accept Eileen's version of reality that Mother was a victim of Father. From Muriel's perspective, Mother had never loved Father as much as he loved her; he had done much to try to please her, including supporting her parents in their home, and Muriel had observed much affection from Father toward Mother and no affection returned. This had led her to feel, as an adult, that Father's affairs were understandable, though not right. She identified with Father when she felt unloved in her first marriage. Her view of their parents' marriage included a recognition of some serious incompatibilities that were a regular source of tension, as well as a lack of real love by Mother for Father no matter what Father tried to do to please her. Mother often expressed to Muriel the view that Father was inferior to her. Eileen's view of Mother as Father's victim gradually evolved into a view of all men as victimizers of women, who are all innocent. In one of Eileen's last visits to Muriel's home, Muriel's 12-year-old son confided in her that "Aunt Eileen makes me feel like killing myself." It was a shocking realization to Muriel of how toxic her sister could be, and she realized she needed to protect her son and herself from this pathology.

As therapy progressed, Muriel began to recognize the subtle ways in which Mother both encouraged marriage yet discouraged attachment to a man at the expense of closeness to Mother. Mother had great respect for her own father, but had had a long separation from him during her childhood when he and the older children emigrated to the United States a number of years ahead of her and her mother. This put Mother, the youngest child, in an extended close attachment to her mother during the frightening years of World War I with her father and older siblings out of the country. Sexual attraction and interest in men was always discouraged, and a severe puritanical attitude was ever-present. Muriel was amazed when she learned from some friends that their mothers actually talked about sex with interest and pleasure. Once, when Mother was visiting Muriel, without asking her daughter's permission she moved her so-called summer clothes to another closet. Muriel was angered by this intrusiveness and told Mother that in San Francisco the weather can be colder in the summer than on some winter days. A few days later she discovered that her two sheer peignoirs had been moved to a closet in her baby's room. When she started to reach for them to take them back to her room, she could feel an invisible hand stopping her and had to force herself against a tremendous internal force to remove the peignoirs. She could not be certain but suspected that this was an old prohibition against masturbation that had been severely imposed by her mother. In fact Muriel did not masturbate until the end of her first year in therapy, at age 30.

Mother became quite depressed and paranoid before Muriel's second marriage and could not attend the wedding. She never accepted her new son-in-law. Father had died by then and Muriel felt Mother did not want to share her with a man, much as Eileen did not want to share either Mother or Muriel with a man. Muriel was determined not to succumb to this pressure from either Mother or Eileen.

Discussion

The story of Muriel and Eileen illustrates how different the family environment may be for two sisters because of the way in which marital discord gets played out in the parent–child relationships. The similarities in these two sister pairs are that in each case the lesbian sister was the older, preferred daughter of a narcissistic and critical mother who was often angry and complaining toward the father but completely financially dependent on him. The heterosexual sister suffered from some neglect by the mother but, perhaps related to that fact, made a stronger attachment to the father than the older sister did. In each case the older sister felt both competitive with and alienated from the father and experienced much anger toward him, although in retrospect it is possible that the father's rejection was actually the result of resentment at some exclusion from the pathologically intense mother–daughter relationship with the first daughter, a reenactment of a boundaryless relationship between the mother and her mother. The second daughter, on account of her more positive connection with father, did not project hostility to men and therefore was more attractive to men, as well as being more attracted to men, thus receiving reinforcement for heterosexual behavior.

The major difference is that in the case of Barbara, the lesbian love attachments began in adolescence, whereas in the case of Eileen they began in midlife after a long marriage and other heterosexual love affairs. The emergence of an attitude of positive regard for lesbianism among some participants in the women's movement appears to be the precipitating source of change for Eileen, yet this cannot be the only explanation in that so many active members of the women's movement never became lesbians, including Muriel. We can speculate that for a woman who had the potential for organizing her paranoid tendencies around a male/female splitting mechanism, the rebellion against second-class citizenship that was the driving force behind the women's movement could have been used as an opportunity to isolate herself from relating to men, thereby avoiding having to confront and do battle with ambivalent feelings of dependence and hostility toward men. Their mother's generation handled these conflicts by remaining financially dependent on men while resenting and belittling them in an adaptation that their daughters found unacceptable with the emergence of feminism and a focus on liberation from such time-honored ambivalent attachments.

The generational difference between Barbara, who was born in the '50s, and Eileen, who was born in the '30s, may account for the different pattern in their lives. Barbara's adolescence occurred as the women's movement developed, providing her with a strong feminist orientation to superimpose on her childhood experience. In the atmosphere of the '40s and '50s, marriage and children were just about the only options for all but a very few women, and apparently Eileen was not one of those lesbians who never feel attracted to men and are homoerotic from puberty. Eileen's switch in her forties and Barbara's switch in her mid-thirties illustrates the frequently mentioned observation of greater variability and flexibility among lesbians as compared with male homosexuals.

THE DYNAMICS OF MERGER IN LESBIAN COUPLES

Studies of lesbian couples have focused on boundary diffusion and the attendant problems. Using Chodorow's analysis of the preoedipal closeness of the mother with her children, the boy and girl differ in their capacity for closeness because the boy must break away from his mother to become a male. The girl can remain close and continue to identify with her mother, which causes lack of synchronicity in heterosexual relationships. A lesbian relationship comes closest to repeating the early mother–daughter intimacy, and some degree of boundary diffusion or merger owing to weaker ego boundaries may result.

Beverly Burch

Burch (1986), a social worker, states that another factor is that owing to the hostile environment of homophobia, lesbians pull together closer for survival. These two factors may inhibit autonomy.

> In the early stages of a relationship, fusion is often pursued. . . . Later in the relationship, if enmeshment replaces the ebb and flow of connection and separation, the two individuals may develop merged identities. Individual differences may be smoothed over so thoroughly that one or both persons abandon whatever parts of the self that do not fit with the other. . . .
>
> Couples come to treatment with symptomatic indications of merger. Loss of sexuality, lack of conflict (or, conversely, constant unresolved fighting), one partner having an affair—all of these suggest the need for greater separateness. . . . Communication patterns in which the two speak as if they were one person . . . when one woman finishes the other's sentences for her, speaks when the other is addressed, assumes she already knows what her partner is thinking, or commonly uses "we" instead of "I" . . . show confusion about their individual feelings or opinions or even identity . . . one or both of the clients is no longer sure what she wants, what she thinks or who she really is. Her personal boundaries have blurred with those of her lover. [pp. 59–60]

Another form of fusion described by Burch is when the two have polarized their feelings: when one is pessimistic, the other is optimistic, when one likes something, the other dislikes it. This represents the inverse of suppressing differences—it is so automatic that real autonomy is impossible. When one is very emotional, the other cannot feel anything. When one is more unhappy with the relationship than the other, she may act out the need for separation by withdrawing, having an affair, being overly critical, or threatening to leave. The other takes the role of crossing the boundary and pursuing the connection. Burch urges a therapeutic approach in which there is discussion and support of differences in feelings, values, and opinions, helping each woman to say no, set personal limits, and accept the limits set by the other. This involves helping the women to tolerate their fears of dissolving the fusion and not making the partner feel guilty for wanting some autonomy.

Burch recognizes that the masculine culture values separateness over connection and is biased in favor of individualism. She urges therapists to keep in mind that "neither separateness nor merger is the desired outcome; movement back and forth between the two is the real goal" (p. 70).

In a later article in *Lesbian Psychologies* (1987), Burch describes "Barriers to Intimacy: Conflicts over Power, Dependency, and Nurturing in Lesbian Relationships," which she sees as the three major issues that must be negotiated in all relationships.

> For many women involvement with another woman is like reclaiming a lost history, an opportunity full of joy promising more fulfilling intimacy. Intimacy becomes a struggle, however, when the threats and injuries of childhood are also reactivated. This triggering of early experience always occurs in adult love affairs, consciously or unconsciously. Because they include such intimate bodily contact, they evoke one's buried primal history. [p. 126]

This quote indicates Burch's psychoanalytic understanding, which she integrates with family-therapy and feminist theory to give an excellent evaluation of the problems likely to be encountered by therapists in working with lesbian couples and suggested therapeutic approaches. Drawing on the work of Dorothy Dinnerstein and Paula Caplan, she describes the fear women have of being engulfed by a woman, of the power of a woman, which can evoke intense feelings of rage, anxiety, and envy. This can cause power struggles in lesbian relationships.

A woman's ambivalent feelings toward her own mother may interfere in the intimacy of the lesbian couple.

> The ambivalence of this identification, simultaneously loving and envying one's mother even while disavowing her, can make an uneasy peace in a lesbian relationship. Each woman has her own conflict of identification as a woman, both her self-love and her self-hate. She may project these contradictions onto her partner; she may keep them deep in her unconscious and cling to the defenses that preserve them there. A relationship with another woman arouses the pain of this conflict as well as an unconscious wish to relive dependency in a more gratifying way. [p. 137]

Issues of dependency and nurturance need to be negotiated in all relationships but are especially a challenge for lesbian couples because the traditional male–female roles are missing and need new solutions based on more reciprocation than is often found in heterosexual couples. Whatever was left unsatisfied by the mother is now sought in the woman lover.

> One of the reasons that Barbara, described above, left her lover of two years was that Jeanne would not cook for her. Barbara's mother had never cooked, she just "opened cans" for dinner or else the family dined out. When Barbara was working and going to graduate school, there were two nights per week when she returned home late after attending a class that involved a long commute home by public transportation. On those nights she hoped Jeanne would have a nice dinner waiting, but she never did. She asked Jeanne to at least shop for dinner on those nights, since Barbara, who loved to cook, shopped and prepared meals on the other evenings. When Barbara returned home late and tired and Jeanne had bought a can of soup, it was the last straw. Barbara was convinced that Jeanne would never provide the nurturance that she hoped for and that she herself willingly gave in the relationship. She asked Jeanne to move out shortly thereafter.

Burch also analyzes problems in lesbian couples with a cultural/feminist analysis.

> When conflicts like the ones I described show up in clinical cases, the presumption is often made that the woman developed psychosexually into a lesbian precisely because she had such pre-genital conflicts. There is a different way to see these problems, however. Women raised in patriarchal culture inevitably have trouble with issues related to sense of self, and, as we have seen, sense of separateness. It does not seem unlikely that most women would encounter some of these conflicts in an intimate relationship with another woman. Further, a woman's capacity for intensity and intimacy is probably heightened in relationship with another woman, who shares a similar capacity. Simply stated, this shared capacity can heighten the problems as well. [p. 140]

Sue Vargo

Vargo (1987) also deals with the issue of merger in lesbian couples in her article "Effects of Women's Socialization" in *Lesbian Psychologies*, and analyzes this problem in relation to women's roles.

If being female has meant attending to others, maintaining a caretaking attitude toward others, and not asserting one's individual needs, as the new literature on women suggests, then two individuals following those rules together may well become involved in a circular process of orienting self toward the other. That two women in a relationship may consider their own and the other's interest in maintaining the relationship could well be the result of successful socializing and not indicative of any individual pathology. Therapeutic work on fusion issues with a lesbian couple will look very different if it is based on an understanding of these dynamics common to women, rather than a hypothesis about the individuals' ego weaknesses or hypotheses about communication patterns in the couple. [p. 165]

She proposes as a goal of therapy that each individual try to balance her needs for intimacy and autonomy between emotional closeness within the relationship and self-actualization in the world. This is very similar to Burch, who proposes a "movement back and forth" between separateness and merger. Vargo uses the Carol Gilligan (1982) work on women's style of conflict resolution in moral dilemmas (discussed in my first book), in which rather than making a principled right/wrong judgment, women attempt to assess the needs and vulnerabilities of the people involved in the conflict and seek the solution that involves the least damage to individuals and their relationship, in order thereby to preserve the relationship, women's highest moral consideration. "One result is that women's individual needs suffer whenever others involved in the conflict are perceived to be more vulnerable or more in need than self" (p. 169).

When lesbian couples have problems in their sexual relationship, Vargo believes it may be a result of a breakdown in the process of conflict resolution rather than from individual pathology around sexuality or around overattachment, overdependence, or inability to express anger or tolerate conflict.

Sarah F. Pearlman

Pearlman (1989), writing on "Distancing and Connectedness: Impact on Couple Formation in Lesbian Relationships," cautions therapists that when an effort is made to change the couple by increasing individuality and separateness and the open communication of needs or negative feelings, the response is often anxiety about the destruction of connectedness and even loss of the relationship.

Lesbian relationships are characterized by two women who each wish the relationship to be central, who display ongoing attentiveness to each other's needs, and willingness to devote time and effort to working out difficulties. In spite of lack of sanction, invisibility, and multiple disruptions, it is this relatedness which distinguishes romantic relationships between women—forging possibilities of extraordinary connectedness, compatibility, and happiness in a disconnected and alienating world. [p. 87]

In spite of all these special features in lesbian couples, it is important to point out how heterosexual marriage promotes the woman's merging her identity with her husband's, such as in taking her husband's name and losing her own identity as a member of her family of origin. Combining income in a joint checking account also merges the couple, and the traditional pattern in which the man supported his wife and she followed him around wherever his job might take him is another example of merger promoted by the nuclear family system. How much the wife's financial dependence affected the degree of psychological merger depends on the individual.

Susan Krieger

A book by Susan Krieger, *The Mirror Dance* (1983), studies the relationships among the women in a primarily lesbian community in the Midwest in which she participated during the '70s. In a review of the book, Barbara Rosenblum (1983) describes the merging tendencies in the community:

> While a lesbian community shares some features with all other human communities, it is also unlike many others because the members are a stigmatized group. Krieger found that the intensity of close bonding that offers profound connectedness at the same time exacts a high degree of conformity from the participants. This constellation causes tensions within the community and occasional anguish within individuals, for individual identity is often overwhelmed and threatened by the demands of the collectivity. Many women are concerned about their perceived loss of privacy and individuality, and they fear merging with others. [p. 8]

Julie Mencher

The Stone Center published a paper by Julie Mencher, a social worker at the Center at Wellesley College, entitled "Intimacy in Lesbian Relationships: A Critical Re-examination of Fusion" (1990). Using the Stone Center's model of female development—which views connection as vital to growth in mutual, authentic relationships—Mencher believes the observation of fusion in lesbian relationships has been wrongly pathologized. She disagrees with the approach of Burch, which is based on the object relations theory of Erikson and Kernberg, and cites the work of Daniel Stern and Jessica Benjamin as presenting a view of fusion and separation more in line with female development and not biased by male development.

> In shifting the emphasis from separation to relationship as the basis for women's self-experience and development, the relational perspective complements Stern's assertion that life begins in a relational template. According to this perspective, for women, "The primary experience of the self is relational; the self is organized and developed in the context of important relationships" (Surrey, 1985). The primary emotional motive for women is to seek a relational process. The goal of development is the increasing ability to build and to enlarge mutually enhancing relationships . . . termed relationship differentiation, a process of differentiation in the embryological sense—in which the individual articulates increasing levels of complexity, fluidity, choice, and satisfaction in her constellation of relationships. . . . Unlike Kernberg and Erikson, who measure healthy adult relationships by the "individualness" of the two selves, the Stone Center theorists mark healthy relationships by the quality of the relational processes. They view mutual engagement, mutual empathy, and mutual empowerment as the fundamental processes of a healthy relationship. A key feature is relational authenticity. [p. 7]

Mencher goes on to say that she is not suggesting that either the heterosexual pattern or the lesbian pattern is better or worse, but that the fused pattern among lesbians is not inherently disturbed and there can exist a full range of possibilities for mutuality, empathy, and authenticity. The actualization of the self and the intense intimacy of a relationship need not be mutually exclusive. ". . . fusion may represent a relational pattern which allows women to express our relational strengths" (pp. 8–9).

In my view, Mencher and perhaps others at the Stone Center do not understand the concept of fusion as it is used in psychiatry as a symptom of borderline pathology and are confusing it with intimacy, reliability, security, and closeness. In my work with borderline patients who truly have boundary diffusion, I have come to understand that there is no way these women can be empathic with another human being. Their interactions with others are distorted by projections, projective identifications, anxiety, and envy; and self-preservation dominates all significant relationships. Earlier I mentioned a borderline patient who had had a lesbian relationship prior to her marriage. One of the ways she handled her own fears of sexual attraction to women was to project these fears onto her daughter. When the daughter developed close relationships with other girls, my patient feared she would become a lesbian. Her relationship with her daughter was so fused that she could not differentiate the daughter from herself and attributed many of her own feelings and adult problems to the girl, projecting that she had or would develop the same problems in intimacy and of depression that my patient has. When Mencher says "empirical data suggest that the prevalence of the relational dynamics that have been called fusion do not necessarily create pathology or dysfunction in lesbian relationships" (p. 4), she is not describing true fusion or merging but a much more benign form of "togetherness" in what may well be mentally healthy individuals. Her empirical data appears to be an in-depth study of six lesbians in three couples who were not in treatment. She describes these relationships as characterized by "fusion" but states that these patterns did not cause the couples any disturbance and that all the women were satisfied. What is being called fusion is described as "intense closeness" and the centrality of the relationship in their lives. The women believed that the intense intimacy fostered self-actualization and risk taking because of the sense of security received. This sounds very similar to the highly beneficial effects of the consciousness-raising group. In contrast, the aggressive and sexual elements that become projected onto the other in true fusion and then become a part of distortion often leading to rage in the relationship are well illustrated by Burch's description of some of the symptoms, such as finishing the other person's sentences for her and having the idea of knowing what the other person is thinking. Rather than enhancing growth within a relationship, this pathology demands a unity that does not allow the other to be different and in which saying no is tantamount to abandonment. For my patient, my going on vacation meant a suicidal nightmare for years, until she very slowly began to realize she could exist in my absence. The image of an umbilical cord is conceptually accurate. Fears of annihilation if the other separates are sometimes handled by alcohol, drugs, or sexual acting out or with suicidal threats or gestures. This phenomenon occurs in heterosexual relationships as well and was described in the section on wife battering (see Chapter 5). Some men are so dependent on their wives that they cannot tolerate separation and will batter or in some cases even murder the wife if she tries to leave. The wife may take him back out of fear, but also because she does not think she can survive emotionally apart from him. These issues are among the most difficult for the therapist to handle correctly, both in evaluating the relationship in terms of the patient's mental health and in interpreting the fusion in the transference. The therapist must be sensitive to the patient's fear, but retain her own boundaries.

Patient: I'm so nervous about your vacation—I can't handle it.
Therapist: What could happen?
Patient: What if I'm desperate and need to talk to you?
Therapist: You can talk to _____ , who is covering for me, or you can wait until I return.

Patient: I feel like I can't survive without you.

Therapist: As if we were connected by an umbilical cord and you rely on me for life.

Patient: I do rely on you to live. What if I feel like killing myself?

Therapist: You can call suicide prevention.

Patient: But they don't know me like you do.

Therapist: I think you're very angry at me for leaving so you're bringing up suicide to try to control me, to make me afraid to leave, and to punish me for leaving you.

Patient: I didn't think I was doing that.

In a couple relationship, homosexual or heterosexual, this quality of needing to be in control of the other person because of a psychological merging, which leads to intense anxiety if the other leaves, can lead to many problems that come from trying to inhibit the other's autonomy. A visit to a friend can become, in the mind of the partner, the beginning of a sexual relationship. It is important to try to differentiate what is dependency and what is projection of unacceptable aggressive and sexual impulses. The issue in the case of lesbians is whether or not fusion is more likely to occur than in heterosexual relationships, and I am not aware of any data that can answer this question authoritatively. That it does occur in lesbian relationships is undoubtedly true. Whether it is more likely to occur in lesbian relationships because there is no gender boundary is uncertain.

LESBIAN PATIENTS AND LESBIAN THERAPISTS: TRANSFERENCE AND COUNTERTRANSFERENCE ISSUES

The January/February 1991 issue of *The Family Therapy Networker* is devoted to articles about homosexuality and is titled "Gays and Lesbians Are Out of the Closet. Are Therapists Still in the Dark?" The editor, Richard Simon, introduces the issue.

> In particular, we've tried to bring to light the subtle shading of homophobia that can undermine the relationship between straight therapists and their gay and lesbian clients. The authors have tried to serve as guides, helping us peer into the shadows where our prejudices and unexamined tribal loyalties lurk. [p. 2]

George Wooley

A statement by George Wooley, now a therapist himself, entitled "Beware the Well-Intentioned Therapist," describes psychotherapy with three different therapists who could not allow him to acknowledge that he was gay.

He says it took forty-five years, two marriages, two divorces, and fifteen years of therapy before he could face it himself. He says his therapists were very helpful on all issues but this one, continually interpreting his sexual impotency with his wives as a symptom of anger toward women but never asking the question "Do you think you might be gay?" although he reported having sexual fantasies about men since age 12.

> All of my therapists were heterosexual, and all had operated on the automatic assumption that everyone is or should be straight. Their heterosexism was a major stumbling block for me. . . . My own fear of being gay was exacerbated by the pressure we all experience to be heterosexual, and it was compounded by the ignorance and fear of my therapists. . . . Until therapists of all professions genuinely and thoughtfully deal with their homophobia, their offices will not be a safe place for me. . . . However well-intentioned they might be, these therapists may be offering fear and confusion, masquerading as healing. [p. 30]

Lauree E. Moss and Rachel Siegel

Moss and Siegel (1984) report that heterosexual therapists may begin from an elitist position, accepting lesbianism as an alternative life-style but being unintentionally condescending. If she is a feminist, she may idealize her lesbian clients or she may deny the differences between herself and her client, being "liberal" and thus invalidating the pain of her client's social/political position, or she may privately interpret the differences as pathological.

On the other hand, there may be problems for lesbian therapists, who may not maintain the usual professional distance with lesbian patients, self-disclosing more than is therapeutic because of regarding the patient as a sister or friend. The erotic feelings that can arise when women work with women are usually more conscious between lesbians, with a mixture of erotic and nurturing feelings in the countertransference.

Before entering therapy with me, Barbara, described earlier, had seen several lesbian therapists. Her last therapist declared that she was in love with Barbara and proposed a sexual relationship. Barbara declined, was not flattered by the offer, and left the treatment. That was what propelled her to seek out a heterosexual therapist who was psychoanalytically oriented, yet a feminist. This crossing of boundaries by a lesbian therapist is a violation of all that psychotherapy stands for as a method of healing in which the therapist uses herself or himself for the patient's health and development. Proposing a sexual relationship is for the therapist's needs and should not occur under any circumstances. If such fantasies develop in a therapist, she or he must get therapeutic help, and if they cannot be brought under control, must refer the patient to another analyst/therapist.

Siegel (1988) reports that in ten years of her work as a heterosexual with lesbian clients, she was able to overcome her fear and ignorance and learn through her own therapy, through literature, with lesbian colleagues, and especially from lesbian clients, by listening carefully and asking for clarification when she felt confused or uninformed, thus learning to overcome the homophobic and heterosexist content of her own professional training.

Eileen Starzecpyzel

Starzecpyzel (1987) recommends working through in therapy the strong ambivalence about the mother, particularly for a lesbian survivor of incest.

> Because of the child's feelings of rejection by her mother, she must deal with a wish to reject, punish and humiliate the mother whom she also needed and loved. This core conflict is reflected in the transference and also in love relationships of the client, which will sabotage her adult life. She feels extremely needy on one hand, and humiliated by what seems to be her "weakness" with lovers (mother) on the other. At the same time, she is intensely enraged by the humiliation of neediness in the face of inadequate response, and she subconsciously wants never to need another woman again.
>
> For many therapists, there is a fear that extreme neediness in a client will become a demand for help so great that they will feel smothered and drained. This countertransference reaction to neediness must be carefully controlled because the therapist must provide a corrective experience for the client who has often been given the message from mother: "You need too much and you are disgusting." . . . [Therapists] must learn eventually to validate their right to give what they can, but not to give beyond their limits. [p. 277]

COMING OUT AS A LESBIAN THERAPIST—
NANETTE GARTRELL

In another Stone Center paper, "Issues in Psychotherapy with Lesbian Women" (1984), Nanette Gartrell, a lesbian psychiatrist, discusses the issue of lesbian therapists "coming out" and her strong view that only an "out" lesbian psychotherapist should treat a lesbian patient. She observes that feminists have focused their writing, thinking, and teaching on power struggles in heterosexual relationships and ignored the egalitarian models in lesbian relationships. She believes this is because feminist theorists have accepted the myth that relationship maturity is possible only through heterosexual union. She quotes Adrienne Rich (1980) in saying that heterosexuality must be recognized as a powerful patriarchal institution that has been "imposed, managed, organized, propagandized, and maintained by force" in order to ensure that women are physically, economically, and emotionally dependent on men. Lesbians are seen as a threat to the institution of compulsory heterosexuality, to the patriarchal exploitation and subjugation of women.

In psychotherapy, the therapist must be skilled at facilitating an exploration of the impact of homophobia on the life of the client. Gartrell sees this as an essential feature in all therapy because it relates to the basic issue of self-image: "Since understanding the personal, economic, social and political ramifications of homophobia is essential in working with clients who are struggling with these issues, I believe that lesbian clients should be treated by 'out' lesbian psychotherapists" (p. 2).

She cites some studies showing that when the therapist and client have the same racial or ethnic background, the commonality of experience produces a more favorable therapeutic outcome. She says that her clinical work with lesbian clients, and the clients' reports of previous treatment experiences with heterosexual therapists, support this finding. The flaw here is that she was seeing only those patients who were dissatisfied with their previous therapist, or else they would not have been there; just as I saw some lesbian patients who were dissatisfied with their work with lesbian therapists.

In seeing lesbian patients for the first time, Gartrell says she provides them with a brief summary of factual information about lesbianism that addresses any negative attitudes, stereotypes, and fears the client may have expressed; she also identifies herself as a lesbian to most clients who are concerned that they might be lesbians and to those who already are. She does not reveal her sexual orientation to women who are frightened of being identified as lesbians and of having contact with other lesbians, because it would frighten them. She believes that identification with a therapist who is lesbian can provide a positive role model, especially for women without family or peer support. She is critical of therapists who question this personal revelation, stating that they reveal their heterosexual status by wearing wedding rings. However, I believe she misses the issue of the patient's projections based on fantasies about the therapist. I have spent years as a therapist being married and nearly as many years being unmarried and have been surprised at how little difference it makes if I wear a wedding ring. I never have personal photographs in my office and I am surprised to hear that the therapists Gartrell knows do. This is a mistake.

Patients have their ideas about me based on their transference needs, which allow them not to see the ring when it is actually there or to imagine a ring is there when it is not. During most of my work with Barbara, described earlier in this chapter, I wore a wedding ring, yet her idea about me was that I was unmarried and devoted completely to my career. We were able to explore this as her fantasy about her own future if she went to graduate school. The danger of the therapist's revealing her status as a lesbian is that she thereby disallows the patient's projections and loses an opportunity to examine their fantasies about her. It is as if she is saying to a patient, "I'm going to set you straight from the beginning so that you don't have a chance to use your imagination in your work with me." This, in my view, is not a good message for the patient to receive. Many of my lesbian patients have imagined that because I was a heterosexual I would not fully accept them. This gave me the chance to explore the meaning of their conviction that I would not accept them or understand them so that we could then use these ideas in learning more about how they felt about other significant people in their lives. If I were a lesbian, I would still allow projections that I was heterosexual so as to receive the projections and all the information they provide about the patient's thought processes. Of course some patients do know of you from some other source, and no doubt Dr. Gartrell is known as a lesbian by some women who come to her; nevertheless, I still believe it is important to allow the patient to raise the issue, in whatever form, or if she does not raise it, to raise it yourself. For example:

Therapist: You have been talking about your fear of revealing your homosexuality to your parents and at work, yet you haven't said anything about your concerns about what I think about it.

Patient: Well, I have wondered. I wonder if you have other lesbian patients, or if you know any women who are lesbians?

Therapist: What are your concerns about that?

Patient: I'd like to know if you've worked with anyone else like me, whether you can understand me.

Therapist: Perhaps you wonder if I can understand you and whether I am critical of you.

Patient: You seem to be nonjudgmental, but I don't know. Do you think of me as a queer, do you want to try to change me? I don't want to change, I just want to feel better about it.

Therapist: You don't know if you can trust me. You're afraid I don't care about what you want, that I think I know what's best for you.

Patient: It's funny you said that, because that's just what I'm afraid of in telling my parents, that they think they know what's best for me and will try to talk me out of it.

Or in another situation:

> *Patient:* I don't know if you can help me. You're straight and you live in a different world.
> *Therapist:* Is there something you think I can't understand?
> *Patient:* Yes, you can't understand what it's like to have to worry about being found out. Besides, you probably think there's something wrong with me for not liking men.
> *Therapist:* What do you imagine I think is wrong with you? [and so on]

One lesbian patient often said: "We have nothing in common."

> *Therapist:* You feel you have nothing in common with your mother, and you are afraid of feeling that terrible distance with me.

The point in these examples is that the fear of not being understood, of being judged and criticized, is certainly not unique to lesbians. It is a fear of many patients who enter therapy, and it can be worked with in the same way as with other patients, by exploring it as a projection from parental figures and as a source of depression, anger, and anxiety, leaving one feeling emotionally isolated and bereft. It can also be a projection of the patient's own judgmental attitudes and criticism of others; in the case of a lesbian, perhaps her criticism of heterosexual women, including the therapist.

Gartrell believes that being a lesbian is essential to, and accelerates, the treatment process. Yet the example she chooses does not involve any treatment but rather education, advice, a reading list, and referral to community resources. This is not psychotherapy but counseling, and therefore none of the issues of working through the transference apply. Like some of the psychoanalysts, Gartrell sees her patient's object choice, her lesbianism, as the major issue of therapy. Heterosexual therapists may have focused on the homosexuality as a disorder and tried to cure it, whereas she focuses on it as a healthy choice albeit with the unfortunate burdens of a homophobic society, but the problem is similar in that the patient is identified by only one issue. Homosexuality, in my view, is not the diagnosis. The patient may be psychotic, borderline, neurotic, or may simply need help with a career choice or in dealing with current relationship problems. The homosexuality may be incidental to some common issue of conflict or, in some cases, to serious pathology. The best therapist is a well-trained, sensitive, experienced clinician who has dealt with his or her own problems in therapy or analysis and has worked through any homosexual or other fears. To insist that only a lesbian therapist can understand another lesbian opens a Pandora's box of categories including race, religion, atheism, political affiliation, social class, national origin, age, and even region of the country. I have often wondered how therapists who have never had children can work with parents and have any way to understand the enormous responsibility being a parent entails and how difficult it is, even when you are well intentioned, to make the right decisions. She is right to point out that those who belong to a racial or ethnic minority, unlike many lesbians, may have close, supportive family members and role models to help them face the larger society's hostility, but she is wrong to assume that no heterosexuals are trustworthy. In truth, the patient will select the therapist she believes is best for her: man or woman, white or black, gay or straight, and we as therapists are not really in a position to tell patients whom they should select or to tell therapists whom they are entitled to see.

The longer you work as a therapist and the more you read, travel, and meet people, the more you bring to your work. Your own life experience may be as enriching as your psychoanalysis. Being in my fifties, I shudder to think of how little I knew as a therapist in my twenties. We all have so much to learn, and the more we learn the wiser and more valuable we are to our patients. Consultation serves to offset for us the gaps in our training and life experience. I saw a number of Catholic patients early in my practice and learned a lot about what it means to be raised as a Catholic; attending Catholic school, going to confession, the difference between a mortal sin and a venial sin. I borrowed a catechism from a Catholic friend and read it through in order to get a sense of what a Catholic child is taught. I learned that my Catholic patients always transferred their experience with and feelings about confession to their sessions with me, and we had to work on that. I learned that for them, a thought can be a sin, not just the deed, which made their thoughts a fearful source of guilt and possible punishment. There was much to correct in order to help them think psychologically rather than in the language of morality, and that is true for many patients.

The importance of objectivity combined with empathy in the therapist has at times led me to think that I might be more effective with patients who are less like me, including men, because of the reduced chance of assuming that I know what they mean when I should be asking what they mean. The risk of merging with your similar patient is as dangerous to true empathy as it is in a love relationship.

Yet Gartrell's discussion of the dilemmas of coming out for both patients and therapists is extremely valuable, and the paper should be read by all therapists who work with homosexual patients in order to increase their sensitivity to this issue. She has found that self-esteem and self-image are enhanced in direct proportion to increasing visibility and openness about one's lesbianism. "The improvement in psychological well-being as one sheds the constraints of secrecy makes exploration of the risks and benefits of coming out mandatory in the treatment of lesbian clients" (p. 6). For example, she saw a third-year medical student who was fearful that coming out would affect her evaluations, which were completely subjective. Coming out would have to wait until the completion of medical school and the selection of a specialty and a metropolitan location that would minimize the dangers.

She discusses the case of the closeted lesbian therapist as a therapist for lesbian patients:

> Because she allows her own fears of homophobia to dictate a life of secrecy, the closeted lesbian therapist may be unable to offer unbiased assistance to lesbian clients who are struggling with the risks of coming out. Some closeted lesbian therapists have been known to counsel lesbian clients against ever coming out. [p. 5]

There is also the risk of the patient finding out through the lesbian network and this threatening the therapeutic alliance because the patient will feel she cannot trust her therapist to be honest.

It is clear, after reading Gartrell's persuasive and sensitive arguments for coming out in spite of the risks, that it must be up to the patient to make the final decision and to choose the time and manner in which she proceeds. In lesbian patients I have worked with, I have thought it best not to attempt to impose my views, which are usually in favor of honesty because of the well-known mental health benefits of honesty Gartrell describes. Only the patient can really know the atmosphere regarding homosexuals in her chosen career, and the patient knows her own family better than I could hope to know them. The therapist can help the patient to differentiate between her own projected homophobia, including her fear and shame, and the reality of the atmosphere in her environment.

I had a lesbian patient who worked for a very large bank on the managerial level. Her assessment was that she should not reveal her sexual orientation, and I felt that her judgment must be respected. After all, what do I know about bankers? She was promoted to vice president, and we will never know if that promotion would have occurred had she revealed her lesbian orientation. One might argue that it would be better to be "out" even if it meant not getting the promotion, but economic security is very important to mental health as well. In this case, the raise enabled her to buy her own house, and that made a tremendous difference in her feelings about herself. She enjoyed setting up the home to be comfortable for herself and inviting friends over for meals in her dining room with a view. It helped bring her out of a social isolation that had been developing because she had no love relationship.

Honesty must be tempered with judgment and with an appreciation of the pain that can sometimes be brought about by honesty. In my view, honesty, though very important, is less important than protecting someone from unnecessary pain, or protecting yourself from danger. This dilemma often faces therapists and patients when dealing in either individual or couple therapy with whether or not to "come out" about extramarital affairs. Here too, one needs to carefully weigh the benefits and the risks, and especially the pain that it can cause the spouse or lover. There are times when even sadism or masochism appears in the guise of honesty. Secrecy is bad, but so is hurting people and sabotaging yourself.

SEXUAL RELATIONSHIPS BETWEEN LESBIAN THERAPISTS AND PATIENTS—LAURA S. BROWN

A chapter in *Lesbianism* (1989) by Laura S. Brown addresses the very important problem of sexual attraction between lesbian patient and therapist. It involves some of the very same issues addressed by Rutter in his book about sexual involvement between male doctors or mentors and female patients or students. "Beyond Thou Shalt Not: Thinking About Ethics in the Lesbian Therapy Community" uses the concepts of power, boundaries, and responsibility and states that it is from a failure to acknowledge and embrace all aspects of power that ethical dilemmas have sprung in the lesbian therapist community. Brown writes that lesbian therapists occupy a special position in the social structure of lesbian communities as leaders, teachers, oracles, and wound healers in much the same way that ministers have functioned in the black community, giving lesbian therapists even greater power than heterosexual therapists. She says she has noticed that the notion that lesbian therapists will probably become sexually involved sometimes with their lesbian clients has been creeping into the literature of lesbian popular culture and has not been censured (p. 15). The idea that if these sexual affairs lead to long-term partnerships and are "true love" they are normal and acceptable indicates that boundary violations have become rationalized and are now difficult to identify as unethical and problematic. "We have felt fuzzy; if it's between two women, is it really that bad?" (pp. 15–16).

Brown believes this fuzziness is due to false dichotomies in which men violate boundaries and women are violated; thus male therapists engage in unethical boundary violations with clients but women therapists do not. Male sexuality is aggressive, whereas women's sexuality is nurturing and enfolding. Power differentials between women are downplayed, whereas power differentials between women and men are exaggerated. If a male therapist hugs and holds female clients, he is sexualizing the relationship, but if a female therapist does so, it is nurturing. Therapists who raise these issues are accused of being judgmental, overly critical, and self-righteous and are thus invalidated as authorities and accused of not being politically correct. These accusations can become an internal problem as well as an external reality, raising self-doubt as to the legitimacy of making judgments about unethical behavior. Brown believes that the best way to confront the problem is for each therapist to own the boundary violator in herself, so to speak. She conceptualizes boundary violations and unethical behavior by therapists along a continuum rather than as one of two polarities. In this way, unethical actions can be seen as less ego alien, something of which at certain times and with certain patients we are all capable.

> . . . a number of life events may serve to move us further down the continuum to violations of increasing gravity and potential for harm if we do not attend in an ongoing way to our position on that continuum. We will also become less confused by the appearance of unethical actions in ethical therapists, because we will no longer be viewing those as mutually exclusive categories. [pp. 20–21]

Brown correctly refuses to be intimidated by charges of being judgmental: "Yes, we are." Therapists need to take the responsibility for defining where the violation of the client's boundaries by the therapist begins to hold the potential for serious harm. This requires a willingness to judge by saying what is clearly unethical and what is just bad therapy.

> It requires that we judge not to condemn, but rather to inform; that our judgment be one that says, not "You are bad," but rather, "Your behavior is highly likely to harm your client, has already harmed you by harming the regard I once had for you." When our judgments are tempered with compassion and self-awareness, they are also likely to be more precise and impactful. [p. 23]

EROTIC TRANSFERENCES OF LESBIAN PATIENTS TO HETEROSEXUAL THERAPISTS—RUTH-JEAN EISENBUD

In a 1982 paper, Eisenbud describes transference and countertransference feelings in work with lesbians from the perspective of a heterosexual analyst. She has observed that attacks on therapists by gay activists can daunt the therapist and make her fear to explore childhood memories and family dynamics.

Under the aggressive attack, the analyst is disarmed and often identifies with the aggressor. . . . Gay liberation's demands for new understanding and new approaches can be valuable if reconsideration is integrated with analytic understanding of unconscious factors, its developmental approach, the profound importance of personal history, and recapitulation in transference. [p. 104]

Eisenbud then discusses the erotic romantic transference with homosexual patients and says striving for sexual bonding should not be invalidated as resistance instead of "giving it the honor, as Freud remarked, all love deserves":

Characteristically, feelings of exclusion and jealousy will be the cue for sexual arousal in therapy. . . . in Lesbian archaic transference, erotic arousal must be understood as primary. If the analyst invalidates the patient's striving for sexual bonding, he or she is responding to the patient's erotic fight for inclusion in much the same way as the patient's mother did in the first place, and as society has continued to respond. . . .

If an erotic struggle against exclusion is not understood as primary in the patient's sexual development, humiliation, hopelessness and deprivation can result. It is denial of sexual aspiration and romantic attachment to the analyst that is truly a resistance, and denial is now reinforced by new exclusion and new narcissistic insult in the patient's life. [pp. 104–105]

Under the heading of Persecutory Transference Feelings, she states that women's sense of injustice can be an authentic reflection of the world and at the same time may be a product of an inner sense of persecution. Envy can only be diminished when the experience of justice grows within the personality and in the therapy.

In treatment, positive, doting transference of primary etiology often occurs preceded by strong, suspicious, programmatic resistance. . . . At first the patient keeps an angry sexual distance from her [the analyst] and makes explicit hostile denials of dependency. In a few months or less, the patient suddenly confesses to a primitive yearning for intimacy with her beloved analyst. [p. 105]

Eisenbud puts forward the hypothesis that sexual arousal may be a function of ego striving and from this new approach understands three possible lesbian erotic transferences: exclusion from the mother, feelings of a double bind, and as a defense against merging.

1. *Exclusion from the mother* involves an overt demand for proof of love, inclusion in the private life of the analyst, and special personal

consideration, which occurs in the context of erotic courtship of the analyst. Analytic limits are bitterly experienced as a recapitulation of mother's exclusion, but positive transference is strong. This fits my patient Mary Ann, described earlier in this chapter as a woman who became a lesbian in the course of treatment, developed a psychotic transference, and insisted that I marry her. I finally had to refer her to another therapist.

2. *Feelings of a double bind* result from a mother who demands that the little girl serve her with romantic love; thus the patient experiences the transference as her being a "good" patient. She courts the analyst, believing she is responding to the analyst's seduction. The analytic deprivation is then experienced as the old hated injustice of being teased, promised, and then denied. A patient of mine, Penelope, never experienced any homosexual attraction to other women, yet I felt that something of this nature had actually taken place in her relationship with her mother at age 9, following her father's death, when Mother attempted to replace Father with Penelope. The strong hold Mother maintained over her did not leave Penelope free to develop open relationships with men, as if that were a betrayal of Mother, yet the mother herself remarried when Penelope went to college. She hated her stepfather and, I believe, felt betrayed by Mother, who had broken the romantic pact between them. Her eating disorder was related at least in part to this double bind. She was always a "good" patient. Frequent interpretation of the transference prevented the development of feelings of injustice.

3. An erotic transference may be *a defense against merging* if projective identification produces a fear of symbiotic death. Eisenbud advises not to disarm the patient in her fight against symbiosis but to allow the active stance of desire and interpret it in the context of individuation. An effort to repress it may result in withdrawal, panic, or violence.

> Interpretation in the context of reconstruction of an early experience restores self to the patient and affective life and movement to the analysis. Understanding of the struggle involved in the origins of self may bring new options and relief from compulsive recapitulation of the past. . . . As her love becomes egosyntonic, understood as active striving, the lesbian woman can have the experience of "free will." "I want to love a woman and I choose to, and I know why." . . .
>
> With new autonomy and acceptance of self, the threats of exclusion and of merging have both become less. Physical expression of mature lesbian love integrates sexuality of many kinds. Cured of transference, the erotic courtship of the analyst analyzed and relinquished, good nurturance of self internalized, an appropriate romantic love can be found. The ego's capacity for sexual arousal organizes, focuses, and defines diverse elements of profound force in human relationships. [pp. 107–108]

CONCLUSION: ISSUES FOR HETEROSEXUAL THERAPISTS WORKING WITH LESBIAN PATIENTS AND THE NEED FOR BOUNDARIES FOR LESBIAN THERAPISTS

Therapy with lesbian patients will vary depending on the diagnosis of the woman, her reasons for entering therapy, and the transference and countertransference issues that develop. As with all patients, class factors (level of education; financial resources) will be influential. Some issues are unique to lesbian patients and couples: the pros and cons of "coming out" to family and at work, which involves the whole internal and external struggle with homophobia; and the question of having children. The issue of whether there is more merging in lesbian couples than in heterosexual or gay male couples and whether that merging is pathological is somewhat controversial but this seems likely to be the case for at least some lesbian pairs. An individual borderline man or woman will have problems with merging in any couple relationship, be it homosexual or heterosexual.

Heterosexual therapists must do much self-examination to provide nonbiased treatment of lesbian patients. By nonbiased I include one's own homosexual fantasies and anxieties, which, if not analyzed, can become part of a pathological countertransference that will distort the relationship through inappropriate projections and harm the treatment. Therapists must be able to differentiate between their own personal views and preferences and what the needs of the lesbian patient are and why she has come for help. Tolerance for a different object choice and perhaps different life-style is essential and does not require that the therapist promote homosexuality but merely accept, without moral judgment, that this is the patient's decision.

For lesbian therapists, the same is true if they are treating heterosexual patients and couples. It appears that in some cases, boundary problems of lesbian therapists with their women patients have caused unfortunate betrayals of the patient's needs and rights to have her therapist remain a neutral but caring observer and analyst. "Sisterhood," a strong value in the feminist movement, does not apply in the therapist–patient relationship, where professional boundaries must be maintained to protect the patient, both in same-sex and opposite-sex relationships.

Neither lesbian nor "straight" therapists should identify their sexual orientation in their treatment of patients but wait for the issue to come up and use the patient's questions and fantasies as a springboard for examining her mental life.

In my view, both heterosexual and homosexual therapists can work with both groups of patients, but only if they have engaged in a thorough self-examination of their own sexual feelings. Acting out of sexual feelings by male or female therapists with women patients, female therapists with male patients, or male therapists with male patients, is always wrong and should not be tolerated under any circumstances. Acting out of one's own moral or religious beliefs about sexuality is also entirely inappropriate in the psychotherapeutic relationship.

Another area of concern is the public behavior of therapists. Involvement in demonstrations, parades, or making public statements is a touchy area but can be compatible with one's role as a therapist if the public speaking or behavior can be seen by the patient as an extension of one's concern about the well-being of children and adults who are in need of public support. Here too, boundaries of what is appropriate for a professional person must be drawn. I once was supervising a gay male psychotherapist who had posed nude in a book of photographs of gay males. One of his patients, a gay male, saw the book and brought it up in therapy. Over the next few months this issue destroyed the treatment and ended a treatment relationship of seven years' duration. The therapist was very resistant to seeing that he had made an error in allowing himself to be a model for this book, and to appreciating the effect it had had on his patient. I finally said, "Can you imagine what it would be like for a male patient of mine if he had seen a nude picture of me in a book? Every time he sat across from me he would be seeing me undressed." He finally seemed to be able to comprehend his poor judgment.

Society's views of sexuality have shifted dramatically, from the Victorian prudery of Freud's time to the sexual freedom of the 1970s. As psychoanalysts and psychotherapists, we are subject, no less than others, to the times and places in which we live. In San Francisco, sexual freedom had been limitless until the AIDS epidemic forced people to use caution. Living as a therapist in times of fads and extremes, especially if one is single, one is called upon to exert discipline, not only within the therapeutic hour but to some extent in one's personal life as well. This is a personal sacrifice that goes with the territory of being a psychotherapist, having chosen to be responsible for other people's mental health. It is a big moral responsibility, but it is rewarded with respect from others, and a sense of internal integrity when it is done conscientiously.

8

THE MIDLIFE WOMAN: LOSS, REBIRTH, AND WISDOM

Successful psychotherapy in the climacterium is made difficult because usually there is little one can offer to the patient as a substitute for the fantasy gratifications.

—Helene Deutsch

The most creative force in the world is the menopausal woman with zest.

—Margaret Mead

When Sleeping Beauty wakes up she is almost fifty years old.

—Maxine Kumin

The years after 30 are the best. Before that, if the guy doesn't call you, you go crazy. After 30, when the phone doesn't ring, you take off your girdle and settle down to watch TV.

—Shelley Winters

MODERN MIDLIFE WOMEN

As women live longer and their health is maintained through proper diet, exercise, and good medical care, the length of midlife can be extended. How do we define midlife? Someone once said that old age begins ten years from your own age. When a person is old depends so much on her individual situation—health, attitude, activity level—that when midlife begins or ends is a very individual matter. Another definition of midlife I have heard is when you are supporting your children in college and a parent in a nursing home. I am going to use the years 40 to 70 as my range for midlife, although other authors, (Rubin 1979) have used 35 to 54. This is based on knowing many people currently in their sixties who are in good health and so vitally involved in their careers that I cannot think of them as "old." Perhaps they will be just as vital in their seventies and eighties. Another categorization is that of the "young old," 55 to 70; the "old," 70 to 85; and the "old old," over 85.

Putting an arbitrary number such as 40 as the beginning of midlife may not seem right to some in their late thirties who still feel "young." It is especially difficult to use a chronological age with women, because a woman at 40 may be in any one of various stages of life. She may be the new mother of a 1- or 2-year-old baby; she may be the divorced mother of two or three teenagers who is going to college herself; she may be an unmarried career woman striving to reach success in her field; she may be in a marriage of twenty years, having entered the work world five or ten years ago when her children were in school, and now feeling competent as a mother and a worker; she may be a recently divorced homemaker with one child in college and another in high school and who is in a quandary about what to do with the rest of her life; or she may be in a first or second marriage with stepchildren and perhaps children of her own from an earlier marriage.

As early as 1927, Eleanor Roosevelt recognized the desirability for women to have an active life. She, at midlife, was a teacher, writer, and public activist. Her husband was Governor of New York State, her children were grown, and she was a grandmother. In an article published in *Success* magazine, she urged mature women to enter politics in order

> to guard against the emptiness and loneliness that enter some women's lives after their children are grown. [Women need to have] lives, interests and personalities of their own apart from their house-holds. . . . And if anyone were to ask me what I want out of life I would say—the opportunity of doing something useful, for in no other way, I am convinced, can true happiness be obtained. [Cook 1992, pp. 381–382]

On her 48th birthday in 1932, Eleanor Roosevelt said "I'm a middle-aged woman. It's good to be middle-aged. Things don't matter so much. You don't take it so hard when things happen to you that you don't like" (p. 462).

A combination of the women's movement and in some cases divorce has had a revolutionary effect on the midlife women I have known. In Chapter 3, I gave the current Department of Labor statistics on the percentages of women in the work force. This included the figure that 76 percent of women aged 35 to 44 were working, and that 58 percent of women worked owing to economic need because they were either single, divorced, separated, widowed, or had a husband who earned less than $15,000. Of college-educated women between 25 and 54, 81 percent are working. In 1970, I was the only woman among my social acquaintances who was working. In 1992, there are only two women among my social acquaintances who are not working. One does beautiful weaving, which is on display in several galleries, and the other does most of the bookkeeping for her husband's law practice. Neither of these women would be included in the statistics as working. Other "nonworking" women in midlife may be caring for an elderly parent, helping a husband or son in business, and helping to raise grandchildren while a daughter or daughter-in-law goes to work. Some women are working and doing all of the above as well. My next-door neighbor, a widow of about 60, works full-time as a travel agent and cooks dinner every Friday, Saturday, and Sunday night for her daughter, son-in-law, and two grandchildren in order to help lighten the load for her daughter who works full time as a nurse. When I commented on how wonderful that was and how hard she was working, her cheerful reply was, "That way I get to see my grandchildren."

Joan, with four children, went back to college in her forties, earned her B.A. and then an M.S.W. She is now a member of a university faculty.

Freda, after raising three children, went to graduate school at age 50 and got an M.A. She works as an art therapist with the elderly.

Gloria, with one child in high school, got a master's degree in anthropology and then went to law school in her forties.

Madlyn, with two children, went to medical school at age 40 and completed a residency, and with her children now grown, works full time as a physician.

Evylyn, after raising three children, got her Ph.D. in sociology in her fifties and is now teaching in college.

Marilyn, after raising two children, got her M.B.A. in her fifties while working full time in a management position.

Myra, with three children, went to school in her mid-thirties and earned a Ph.D. She started working as a psychologist in her forties.

Barbara, with two children, entered college for her B.A. at age 33. At age 37 she received a master's degree and then at 39 went for a Ph.D. in psychology. At 43 she started working as a psychotherapist, and then at age 55 she entered the Psychoanalytic Institute of Northern California for training.

Joan S., with two school-age children, starting taking art courses at age 37 and at age 49 opened an art gallery with a woman friend. She says she has never been happier.

These women were just hitting their stride in their careers at age 55. I am highlighting the lives of women currently in midlife because of the contrast between the lives of many modern women in their fifties and the description of the empty, useless lives of middle-class, midlife women by Helene Deutsch and Simone de Beauvoir. Unfortunately, neither of them spoke of the lives of working-class women, who were unlikely to be idle. An appreciation of how the feminist movement of the sixties and seventies has changed the lives of midlife women must be part of any reckoning of the major contributions that feminism has made to our society. In some ways it is the most profound contribution, because anticipation of an active life of work and independence between 40 and 70 affects decisions made by women between 15 and 40. They can take off ten years between ages 30 and 40 to raise children, knowing that they can return to their careers at 40. They can have children between 20 and 30, knowing that they can return to school between 30 and 40 and start a career then. According to the Department of Labor, the average woman worker who reached age 16 between 1970 and 1980 could expect to spend 29.3 years of her life in the labor force, compared with 39.1 years for a man. That ten-year difference reflects the ten years devoted to child rearing. Clearly, childbearing and mothering is no longer the be-all and end-all of a woman's life.

Yet this view of active midlife women making a valuable contribution to their professions and to their community is in sharp contrast to the traditional view of women at this age and has not penetrated the mass media to any great extent, although older women as experts are appearing more on enlightened news programs such as "MacNeil–Lehrer Newshour." In 1978, Marilyn Block wrote:

> The image of the older woman as an inactive, unhealthy, asexual, and ineffective person has been perpetuated over the years through the transmission of inaccurate information. The cultural denigration of older women is taught through fairy tales and children's picture books. Adult magazines and television programming offer these attitudes through adolescence and young adulthood. Regardless of what profession or status a woman holds, she still sees aging as a negative aspect of

her life. This stems in large part from the negative reception she encounters in the outside world. The myths that have been created about older women have led to the stereotypes that exist in American society today despite the truths that are evident to those who know or have studied older women. . . . While social isolation usually affects widowed older women, cultural isolation is a common occurrence for older women in general. The absence of older women in various forms of the media underscores this isolation. For example, women over the age of sixty are noticeably lacking in American magazine fiction. Television is also guilty of keeping the older woman out of sight. . . . This is further evidence of the lower status that women attain as they age, and the cultural belief that older women are not subjects of interest to a viewing audience. [pp. 13, 15]

The 1971 edition of *Our Bodies, Ourselves* makes no reference to older women and has no section on menopause. It is not too surprising that the young women in the early days of the women's movement were not concerned about aging. By the time of the 1973 edition, this omission was corrected. They (Boston Women's Health Book Collective) write that the popular image of the typical menopausal woman "is negative—she is exhausted, haggard, irritable, bitchy, unsexy, impossible to live with, driving her husband to seek other women's company, irrationally depressed, unwillingly suffering a 'change' that marks the end of her active (re)productive life" (p. 229).

Block describes the effects of these perceptions on the women of this age and on their physicians. Women fear going crazy, losing their husbands, and being discarded. Women who approach their doctor with their concerns are often considered neurotic and treated with tranquilizers. Many women with physical or emotional problems are labeled "menopausal" by their doctors and not given a medical evaluation. Block wrote in 1978, but this problem persists. In a recent (June 1991) news interview, (MacNeil–Lehrer) a midlife woman with heart disease described how she had experienced symptoms she could not understand, such as pain on climbing stairs and fatigue. When she went to her physician, he prescribed tranquilizers. Her symptoms persisted, so she went to another doctor, who also failed to see the signs of heart disease. It was not until her third try that a physician gave her the respect of taking these physical symptoms seriously, diagnosed heart disease, and started treating her for her real problem.

Block points out the discrepancy between the sexual image of women in their forties compared with men in their forties, a "double standard of aging." Women are no longer considered sexually attractive, whereas a man in his forties is still sexually desirable. His status is determined not by his physical youthfulness but by his career achievement and earning power. His status does not diminish until his mid-sixties when he retires, resulting in the social acceptability of men marrying women fifteen to twenty years younger than themselves but not five or more years older. After age 65 or 70 the undesirable older woman image is balanced by the image of the sexually alive but equally undesirable "dirty old man," a twenty-year age differential.

HELENE DEUTSCH AND THE PSYCHOANALYTIC DOUBLE BIND

The negative view of the older woman as the witch of the fairy tale, or the wicked stepmother as in the story of Cinderella, was never helped by psychoanalysis; in fact Deutsch promoted these myths in her very negative description.

In the second volume of her *Psychology of Women—Motherhood* (1945), Deutsch devotes her epilogue to the "climacterium." Just the fact that she calls this section an epilogue reveals her attitude that midlife is really the end of a woman's chances at life. I referred briefly to this epilogue in my first book, using it as an example of Deutsch's very negative view of women's lives as fraught with difficulties, mortifications, struggle, danger, disappointments, protests, renunciations, escapes, resignations, and trauma. She describes the cessation of menstruation as the end of woman's "service to the species," as if reproduction were a woman's only purpose in life and the only way she can contribute to society. The mastering of her psychological reactions to menopause is seen by Deutsch as one of her most "difficult tasks," as a "narcissistic mortification that is difficult to overcome" (p. 457). A "struggle for the preservation of femininity" ensues with a thrust of activity, yet she views the activity as a defense mechanism because of the woman's imminent disappointment and mortification and as a protest, her assertion that she is not merely a servant of the species. She compares the period from ages 40 to 50, the preclimacterium, with prepuberty when the ego is mobilized to achieve a better adjustment to reality as the old values crumble.

> Woman's biologic fate manifests itself in the disappearance of her individual feminine qualities at the same time that her service to the species ceases. As we have said, everything she acquired during puberty is now lost piece by piece; with the lapse of the reproductive service, her beauty vanishes, and usually the warm, vital flow of feminine emotional life as well. . . . This second puberty, just like the first, is marked by all kinds of oddities of conduct and although in an older woman these have a comical external effect, their profound meaning is

rather tragic. . . . The climacterium is known as the "dangerous age," and a certain type of aging woman has become a comical theatrical type. . . . She is suddenly seized by an urge to make her life richer, more active. She feels like a young girl, and, as she says, wants to begin her life all over again. . . . At the age of 50 she is absolutely unready to renounce anything. . . . The suggestibility of women in this life period increases markedly, their judgment fails, and they readily fall victim to evil counselors. . . . Some, again as in puberty, escape into an ascetic mode of life, philanthropic self-sacrifice, or religious devotion.

The active, restless forms of the climacterium as I have described them do not represent exceptions. They are probably just as frequent as the depressive one, which in their external manifestation are more "normal." Almost every woman in the climacterium goes through a shorter or longer phase of depression. While the active women deny the biologic state of affairs, the depressive ones overemphasize it. . . . The frequent depressions . . . contain justified grief in the face of a declining world. [pp. 461–465, 473]

According to Deutsch there is little hope for a woman at midlife. She either overdoes it with her newfound freedom and makes a perfect fool of herself, "ridiculous old women" (p. 474), or else she slips into depression, which may develop into a morbid melancholy. The only group who escape "partial death" with grace are the "feminine women" who enjoy their erotic gifts to the end (p. 474). This is in keeping with her description in Volume 1 (1944) of the erotic woman who is saved from masochistic ruination by her narcissism and sexuality. However the active, so-called masculine woman continues to be punished for her failure to accept her natural passive station in life and, according to Deutsch, has a harder time in menopause than a "feminine-loving" woman. This would seem to be in contradiction to her statement that

in the course of woman's life, masculinity often plays the part of a rock of salvation. This is also true in the climacterium. An intellectual sublimation through a profession protects her against the biologic trauma. This applies to an even greater extent to feminine women who have not staked their feminine qualities on the single card of eroticism and motherliness, but have also invested them in good sublimations. [p. 476]

Yet she warns these women to beware of the danger of "pseudomasculinity," and we are again confronted by Deutsch's constant warnings about stepping out of line—that is, away from passivity, narcissism, and masochism. "Serenity" seems to be the goal for her ideal woman, who must beware of "constant exhaustion" (p. 476).

One wonders what Deutsch would think of all my friends named above, who went to law school, medical school, who earned doctoral and master's degrees in midlife after raising children. Would they be in danger of "pseudomasculinity"? If masculinity means being intelligent, ambitious, and living a life of stimulation and meaning; making a contribution to society along with being a mother, grandmother, and perhaps wife, then I would vote for masculinity, pseudo or real. The flaw, of course, is to have considered all the traits of strength and activity, of a life of challenge in the world outside the home, masculine in the first place. The corollary would be that all the young fathers today who are active in caring for their children are exhibiting "pseudofemininity."

Could Deutsch's views really have been an accurate portrayal of women in the first half of this century, or are we seeing them through the eyes of a woman who has difficulty seeing anything positive in women? How much is Deutsch and how much is reality? She notes the turning of an older woman into a comic character and considers this a realistic picture; I see it as a cruel example of sexism, turning hostility toward a woman who is no longer valued as a sexual object, thus implying that if a man no longer finds her sexually desirable, then she can be made an object of ridicule, as if her only value to the world lies in her sexual desirability to men, a decidedly phallocentric viewpoint. I cannot know what percentage of women in Deutsch's time or even now might actually fit this picture of ludicrousness, but I doubt that Deutsch knew either. She does not say that she is describing particular patients of hers. I especially miss compassion for such a woman in Deutsch's writing, compassion that would come from placing her in the context of the times when women, held to the roles of wife and mother as the only acceptable roles for a woman to be considered feminine, found themselves useless when these functions were lost, an example of what I call the psychoanalytic double bind.

There is more pathology to come as she describes clinging, possessive mothers who try to turn their sons into lovers, a transference from their fathers; keep their daughters from happiness; and interfere with their children's marriages through their jealousy of the daughter-in-law and sexual attraction to the son-in-law. She believes there is a basis in reality for the terrible mother-in-law stereotype, whereas I have always believed it was another example of the depth of sexism. Deutsch takes the worst stereotypes of women proffered by a deeply sexist society and packages them in psychoanalytic vocabulary as if she were presenting the results of truly scientific research.

It is possible to take the view that these tragic examples serve as a warning because they reflect the dangers inherent for a woman in relying solely on the roles of mother and wife for all her fulfillment in her youth. The loss of a husband through death or divorce (perhaps abandonment for a younger woman) and the loss of her children when they depart from home leaves her with no purpose in life. Read this way, Deutsch becomes a treatise for women's liberation, a warning that a woman must develop other aspects of her personality, talents, interests, and desires in order that she not be faced with such a pathetic middle age. The psychoanalytic double bind has called her masculine if she has, however, so psychoanalysis has left women with no choice but this miserable and humiliating middle and late life in order to be considered "feminine."

I am delighted when I see women in their fifties and sixties blossoming and do not put the negative interpretation on it that Deutsch does, that this is a defense mechanism against the reality of their miserable fate. The term *midlife* implies that a woman has half of her life ahead of her and can thrive in this half in a way she could not when she was responsible for young children. Deutsch herself continued to practice and teach through her eighties. At the age of 50, women *should be* "absolutely unready to renounce anything."

Deutsch does allow for a positive view of grandmothers, along with a negative view of some grandmothers she calls "wicked." If there has been a "peaceful reconciliation" between the mother and her children after they have left home, their relationship to her can be very gratifying, though not as intimate and exclusive as before. She quotes from Freud's *Totem and Taboo* (1912) in describing the mother-in-law–son-in-law relationship as truly ambivalent, composed of conflicting feelings of tenderness and hostility.

> Where the psycho-sexual needs of the woman are to be satisfied in marriage and family life, there is always the danger of dissatisfaction through the premature termination of the conjugal relation, and the monotony in the wife's emotional life. The aging mother protects herself against this by living through the lives of her children, by identifying herself with them and making their emotional experiences her own. . . . This emotional identification with the daughter may easily go so far with the mother that she also falls in love with the man her daughter loves, which leads, in extreme cases, to severe forms of neurotic ailments on account of the violent psychic resistance against this emotional predisposition. [in Deutsch, pp. 479–480]

Deutsch describes three types of good grandmothers and seems more generous than in her earlier descriptions of midlife women. The grandmother par excellence "pampers the children, but this pampering when done by the grandmother is an act of wisdom, because she is moved by kindness" (p. 486).

As in Freud's conclusion that women over 30 are not hopeful candidates for psychoanalysis, Deutsch too sees women in midlife as beyond help:

Successful psychotherapy in the climacterium is made difficult because usually there is little one can offer to the patient as a substitute for the fantasy gratifications. There is a large element of real fear behind the neurotic anxiety, for reality has actually become poor in prospects, and resignation without compensation is often the only solution. [p. 477]

I must disagree with this conclusion. I have seen a number of midlife women in my practice and have felt very pleased with the good work we have been able to accomplish together and the positive changes they have made. The presence of "real fears" accompanies all patients, both sexes, at all ages and need not discourage the therapist. Her pessimism may relate to the relatively poorer health condition of women at the time she wrote, but is also largely a matter of attitude and opportunity. Opportunity is at least in part a measure of one's economic status, so the class factor is prominent here. Going back to school may not be possible for women who must fully support themselves unless they are able to get student loans.

OTHER EARLY WRITERS

Therese Benedek

Benedek, like Deutsch, believed that a woman's reaction to menopause was similar to her reactions to puberty and pregnancy. She too focused on the menopause as a time of loss rather than change, according to Notman (1982). In fact it is a time of loss *and* change and new growth potential. However, Benedek did recognize that energy released by the end of the reproductive stage gave women with flexible egos "new impetus for learning and socialization. The manifold interests and productiveness of women after the climacterium, as well as the improvement in their general physical and emotional health, prompts us to regard the climacterium in the psychological sense as a developmental phase" (1950b, pp. 239–240).

Thus, although she shares some of the same perspectives as Deutsch, Benedek differs in being much more optimistic about the possibilities for women's lives in the midlife period. This may be the result of writing in the post–World War II period when women in this country and Europe had gone to work, replacing men who went to war, and developed a pride and confidence in their capabilities. Like Deutsch, she believed that women who had not experienced motherhood and who were less "feminine" had greater problems at this time. This is refuted by Bart's study (1971), which shows women with "high motherliness" scores on psychological scales as more likely to experience depression in midlife. The problem with Bart's work and that of others lies in the failure to differentiate women on the basis of their premenopausal personality or diagnosis.

Simone de Beauvoir

A reading of de Beauvoir's chapter "From Maturity to Old Age" in *The Second Sex* (1952) is very disappointing. The book, touted on its cover as "the classic manifesto of the liberated woman" is, in this chapter, a rewrite of the parallel Helene Deutsch chapter and illustrates the tremendous influence that psychoanalysis had on intellectuals both in Europe and the United States, an influence that had the unfortunate effect of helping to reverse the gains of earlier feminist thinking and plunge women back into an idealized housewife role after World War II and throughout the '50s and '60s. When one reads de Beauvoir after Deutsch, it is clear that de Beauvoir was greatly influenced by Deutsch's view of midlife women and even uses some of the same examples and has a similar tone of contempt for the middle-class, middle-aged woman. One finds words such as "mutilation," "adolescent," "pathetic," "childish," and the same sense of the absurdity of a midlife woman trying to start a new life for herself:

> But in fact there is no question of a real start; she sees in the world no objectives toward which she might reach out in a free and effective manner. Her activity takes an eccentric, incoherent, and fruitless form, because she can compensate only in a symbolic way for the mistakes and failures of the past. [p. 643]

So many of de Beauvoir's statements seem to come so directly from the Deutsch chapter that it almost constitutes plagiarism: "For the woman's restlessness, her illusions, her fervor, are only a defense reaction against the overruling fatality of what has been" (p. 647).

She, like Deutsch, sees midlife women as full of pathologies: "pathological jealousy," "feverish exaltations," "incestuous obsessions," "erotomanias," and as prey for "any and every charlatan." She repeats the references of Deutsch to the relationship to her son and daughter as possessive and disruptive of their marriages. Deutsch and de Beauvoir both also refer to the emergence during this period of homosexual tendencies, which may be directed toward a daughter or a woman friend. Yet one cannot argue with her conclusion that "a mother needs a rare combination of generosity and detachment in order to find enrichment in her children's lives without becoming their tyrant or making them her tormentors" (p. 656).

De Beauvoir finally does differ from Deutsch in her analysis of the fate of middle-aged women owing to the effects of a patriarchal system:

> It is in the autumn and winter of life that woman is freed from her chains; she takes advantage of her age to escape the burdens that weigh

on her; she knows her husband too well to let him intimidate her any longer, she eludes his embraces, at his side she organizes a life of her own—in friendship, indifference or hostility. If his decline is faster than hers, she assumes control of the couple's affairs. She can also permit herself defiance of fashion and of "what people will say"; she is freed from social obligations, dieting, and the care of her beauty. As for her children, they are old enough to get along without her, they are getting married, they are leaving home. Rid of her duties, she finds freedom at last. Unfortunately, in every woman's story recurs the fact we have verified throughout the history of woman: *she finds this freedom at the very time when she can make no use of it.*

    This recurrence is in no wise due to chance: patriarchal society gave all the feminine functions the aspect of a service, and woman escapes slavery only at times when she loses all effectiveness. Toward fifty she is in full possession of her powers; she feels she is rich in experience; that is the age at which men attain the highest positions, the most important posts; as for her, she is put into retirement. She has been taught only to devote herself to someone, and nobody wants her devotion any more. Useless, unjustified, she looks forward to the long, unpromising years she has yet to live, and she mutters: "No one needs me!"

    Here we come upon the sorry tragedy of the aged woman: she realizes she is useless; all her life long the middle-class woman has often had to solve the ridiculous problem of how to kill time. But when the children are grown, the husband a made man or at least settled down, the time must still be killed somehow. Fancywork was invented to mask their horrible idleness; hands embroider, they knit, they are in motion. *This is no real work,* for the object produced is not the end in view; *its importance is trifling,* and to know what to do with it is often a problem. . . . This . . . is hardly an escape, since the mind remains vacant. It is the "absurd amusement" described by Pascal; with the needle or the crochet-hook, woman sadly weaves the very nothingness of her days. Water-colors, music, reading serve in much the same way: the unoccupied woman, in applying herself to such matters, is not trying to extend her grasp on the world, but only to relieve her boredom. [pp. 649–650, 658–659, italics mine]

There is some compassion conveyed for the midlife woman in these excerpts, but there is also contempt for her creativity. Like Deutsch, de Beauvoir wrote before the women's movement and suffers from self-hatred, which is expressed by differentiating herself from other women and viewing other women as inferior to men and to herself. The male-identified woman has not had the many benefits of the consciousness-raising experience in which a woman learns to recognize herself in other women and gain the benefits of the support and encouragement of other women along with a deep respect for women's lives. Even those women whose lives can objectively be seen as parasitic are recognized as attempting an accommodation to the limited roles available to them in a society that has offered them few choices. The recognition that the work women do is demeaned by a phallocentric culture extends to the creative work of cooking, sewing, weaving, knitting, and especially quilt making. Since the rise of the women's movement, quilts have become recognized as a unique art form for women and have been elevated to the status they deserve, including museum shows devoted exclusively to the display of quilts.

The attitude toward men who do no "real work," who are parasites, "playboys," offers an illuminating comparison. The word *playboy* has connotations of a lush life of pleasure and freedom that is coveted and admired. "Aging playboy" does contain some derision, but is not nearly as vehement as the contempt shown in the above quotations. Perhaps there is an element of envy in the working woman's derision of the "lady of leisure."

It is unfortunate for these two highly intelligent and productive women that they did not have the opportunity to develop during a period in which they could feel an affiliation with other women and share the joy and appreciation of the value and beauty in much of women's work. A personal example for me is the thrill I felt upon receiving a hand-crocheted wool lap blanket from my mother-in-law for Christmas. It stayed on my lap through the completion of this book as I sat at my computer in the early hours of each winter morning and through the foggy days of a San Francisco summer as well, providing warmth and the special connection with the work of a woman whose handmade gift meant so much more to me than a store-bought present ever could. I was truly touched by this gift, and its warmth has become a part of the writing of this book for me—a connection between the creative work of women of a previous generation and my own.

Another example that is personally meaningful to me is that of the other grandmother of my two grandchildren, who has handmade quilts for each of her four grandchildren. Helen received her B.A. in science at age 21 and then taught science and physical education in high school and college for seven years while getting a master's degree in physical education. She then worked for the Campfire Girls for seven years, doing organizational work until she married and had children at age 34. At age 44, with three boys in school, she returned to school and got her second master's degree in special education. At age 46 she embarked on her second career, directing a center for developmentally disabled children and adults until she retired at age 64. The beautiful quilts have been used and enjoyed by two families, and one is now hung in the bedroom of my older grandson, who has outgrown his crib.

De Beauvoir goes on to belittle women by quoting from Philip Wylie's *Generation of Vipers,* one of the worst examples of the depreciation of women with no compassion for the straitjacket of choices to which women were consigned. She joins with him in ridiculing women's efforts in charitable and political causes.

> What characterizes most of these organizations, on both continents, is that they are in themselves their own reason for existence; the ends they are supposed to have in view only serve as pretexts. . . . [They] struggle with their rival organizations for prestige: no one must steal their paupers, their sick, their wounded, their orphans; they would rather see them die than yield them to another group. And these ladies are far from wanting a social regime that, in doing away with injustices and abuses, would make their devotion useless; they bless the wars and famines which transform them into benefactresses of humanity. [pp. 659–660]

This harsh judgment is not based on fact. Several women have won the Nobel Peace Prize in recent years: Alva Myrdal of Sweden for her work on disarmament, Mother Theresa of Calcutta for her work with the poor, Mairead Corrigan and Betty Williams of Northern Ireland for their work to try to end the useless killing of the Irish people that has gone on for years between Protestants and Catholics, Daw Aung Saw Suu Kyi of Burma and in 1992, Rigoberta Menchu for her efforts on behalf of the Guatemalan Indians. If we are going to talk about useless, let us point the finger at the world of men who continually engage us all in useless wars of mass destruction that never bring the peace we are promised by the perpetrators of murder in the guise of patriotism. Murder on the highways and streets in this country was finally tackled when a mother of a daughter shamefully killed by a drunk driver with three previous convictions was galvanized into creating a national organization called Mothers Against Drunk Driving, which, through sitting in courtrooms and lobbying legislators, was able to get the laws changed so that drunk driving is now recognized and punished as the crime it has always been, but which had been protected by the predominantly male system of courts and legislatures that looked the other way as drivers, mostly men but sometimes women, killed and maimed us by the thousands and then got away with pleading to reckless driving or got off with only fines when arrested for drunk driving.

As for squabbling for prestige in organizations, that is surely a human frailty, as anyone with organizational experience can testify to, not the preserve of women alone. But Wylie has this to say about the American "mom": "Knowing nothing about medicine, art, science, religion, law, sanitation . . . she seldom has any special interest in *what,* exactly, she is doing as a member of any of these endless organizations, so long as it is *something*" (in de Beauvoir, p. 660). Yet the League of Women Voters has served a most valuable service to us all in providing objective analyses of bills and issues. The viper, I believe, is Wylie himself. "Mom" can't do anything right. When she does work with her hands, she is called mindless, when she reads she is also terrible. According to de Beauvoir: "It is the American woman who is responsible for the degradation of the best-sellers; these books are intended not only merely to entertain, but worse, to entertain idle women in search of escape" (p. 661).

In de Beauvoir's view, "old ladies" are ignorant, incapable, their morality is "abstract," they make no progress, only attack what does exist, and always unite *against* something. Women with true goals are rare.

> As long as woman remains a parasite, she cannot take part effectively in making a better world. . . . Old women take pride in their independence; they begin at last to view the world through their own eyes; they note that they have been duped and deceived all their lives; sane and mistrustful, they often develop a pungent cynicism. . . . In her thinking as in her acts, the highest form of liberty available to the woman parasite is stoical defiance or skeptical irony. At no time of life does she succeed in being at once effective and independent. [pp. 661, 663]

I suppose if one considers useless the women who organized to free the slaves and to obtain the vote and to make contraceptive information available and to end child labor, this statement could stand. It was women, especially, who organized and were active in the antiwar movement during the Vietnam years and today's ecology movement and who are forcing us all to look at the way humanity has been a global parasite, using the planet's resources for taking profit without consideration for the state in which we will leave the earth for later generations. It is difficult to judge how much the condescension of de Beauvoir, like that of Deutsch, is an accurate reflection of some of the middle-class women of twenty to fifty years ago, and how much is their own alienation from the masses of women because of their unusual choices to pursue independent careers, in de Beauvoir's case without marriage or children, in protest of the lot of the married woman in prewar France. Sad to say, the bitterness attributed to the middle-aged woman is not escaped by either of them, regardless of their independence, because in spite of their efforts, their lives as women were damaged by the patriarchal system as have the lives of the women they condemn. Their identification with the male belittlement of women has not served them well in the end, and their examples should remind us of the importance of consciousness raising and a feminism that embraces all women and condemns only those who are truly evil. Imelda Marcos comes to mind.

"The Crisis of Middle Age"—Judd Marmor

A more enlightened view of women at midlife by a psychoanalyst can be found in a short essay by Judd Marmor (1967), "The Crisis of Middle Age." In this essay he speaks of both men and women, using Erikson's term *developmental crisis,* applied to both genders. He does in one line refer to the "gross psychopathologies of menopause" (p. 71) but it is unclear how he conceptualizes psychopathology here, since he goes on to describe normal reactions of both men and women to the crisis of middle age under four categories: somatic, cultural, economic, and psychological. Under psychological he stresses separation loss and the loss of the fantasy hopes of youth as well as existential anxiety, or confrontation with the fact of mortality. He does not set women apart in these problems. "Generally speaking, the weaker the ego-adaptive capacity, the more limited the base of interpersonal relationships, the narrower the foundation of the sense of usefulness and of the interest in the outside world—the more critical will be the impact of the middle-year's stresses" (p. 75).

The four major patterns of response, according to Marmor are (1) denial by escape, (2) denial by overcompensation, (3) decompensation. (anxiety, depression, apathy, or rage), or (4) a state of higher integration. The welcome change in the Marmor essay is his evenhandedness. The man "seeks to refurbish his tarnishing narcissistic self-image by pursuing a chain of sexual conquests," and women may "embark on a desperate search for romance" (p. 75). Women may feel useless and discarded in their forties, but the situation may reverse when the men reach their sixties or seventies and retire and the woman is useful and needed as a grandmother. He is sensitive to the greater cultural pressures on women to look young and beautiful, causing more stress on women in their forties.

INVOLUTIONAL MELANCHOLIA: THE VANISHING DIAGNOSIS

Back in the days when women were seen as mere pawns of biological forces, the diagnosis of involutional melancholia was given to women who suffered depression in midlife, and the syndrome was considered biologically determined by the hormonal changes of menopause. Comparable was the diagnosis of postpartum psychosis. Both of these diagnoses have been eliminated from the nomenclature as of *DSM-III,* though there is still a debate on the question of postpartum psychosis. Some psychiatric researchers report that 10 percent of women experience mild postpartum blues, but severe psychosis occurs in only one or two per thousand deliveries. Other investigators view postpartum psychosis as a variant of major mood disorders and find that a significant portion of sufferers will go on to develop bipolar mood disorders or have recurrent unipolar depressions, and thus do not believe in granting separate diagnostic recognition to postpartum disorders.

In the fourth edition of the *Comprehensive Textbook of Psychiatry* (Kaplan and Sadock, eds., 1985), the following statement is made under the heading "Nonbipolar Depression—Menopause" by Myrna Weissman and Jeffrey Boyd.

> Neither the incidence nor the prevalence of nonbipolar depression shows a tendency to rise in the menopausal years. In fact, the rates tend to fall during those years. Recent research has suggested that menopause does not predispose to depression and that depression occurring in the menopausal period is not a distinct entity in terms of symptom patterns, severity, or absence of precipitants. Thus, eliminating involutional melancholia as a distinct diagnostic entity from *DSM-III* was in keeping with research findings. [p. 767]

Under the heading "Disorders Associated with Female Endocrine Function" by Lynn Reiser and Morton Reiser we find the following:

> Many psychological symptoms have been attributed to the menopause, including anxiety, fatigue, tension, emotional lability, irritability, depression, dizziness and insomnia. There is no general agreement on the relative contribution to those complaints of the psychological and social meanings of the menopause and this developmental era in a woman's life and the relative contribution of physiological changes. . . .
>
> The degree of symptomatology at the menopause seems to be related to the rate of hormone withdrawal; the amount of hormone depletion; a woman's constitutional ability to withstand the over-all aging process, including her over-all health and level of activity; and the psychological meaning of aging for her. Serious, clinically significant psychiatric difficulties may develop during the involutional phase of the life cycle. Women who have experienced prior psychological difficulties, such as low self-esteem and low life satisfaction, are likely to be vulnerable to difficulties during menopause. . . . Epidemiological studies of mental illness showed no increase in symptoms of mental illness or in depression during the menopausal years, and studies of psychological complaints found no greater frequency in menopausal women than in younger women. [pp. 1173–1174]

In the fifth edition (1989), menopause is treated in only one paragraph under "Psychiatry and Reproductive Medicine," authored by Roberta Apfel and Miriam Mazor.

> The significance of menopause has changed over time, with longer life
> expectancy and more social and career options. . . . Contrary to pop-
> ular view, this time is not one of depression for women who have not
> been depressed before. Young women with young children and unsup-
> portive husbands are more likely to become depressed than women
> whose nests are emptying. [p. 1337]

A MODERN VIEW OF MENOPAUSE

Sadja Greenwood's book *Menopause Naturally: Preparing for the Second
Half of Life* (1984) and a book by Paula Doress and Diana Siegal, *Ourselves,
Growing Older: Women Aging with Knowledge and Power* (1988), are two
books with a feminist view of menopause that try to dispel myths of illness
and treat menopause as a natural stage of life. Doress is an original member
of the Boston Women's Health Book Collective and was a coauthor of *Our
Bodies, Ourselves*. She believes that the women who have the most
problems with aging are those who are used to perceiving themselves as
particularly physically attractive, to feeling glamorous, and have no other
identity. These women, she says, are at high risk of becoming depressed.
Both books focus on general health through diet, exercise, social activity,
and a positive approach to sexuality.

Sadja Greenwood

Greenwood (1984) advises her patients to quit smoking, drink only very
moderately, and to cut down on caffeine. She devotes one chapter to how
to cope with hot flashes and one on how to avoid osteoporosis, again
focusing on diet and exercise. She tells of a study in which women at a
nursing home, average age 80, had their bones measured by radiography.
One group of women exercised their arms and legs for 30 minutes three
times a week sitting in their chairs, a second group took extra calcium, and
a control group made no changes in their diet or exercise. Whereas the
control group lost bone calcium during the three years of the study, the
exercise group and the calcium group both gained bone, the exercise group
most of all.

A major issue in her book is a discussion of the pros and cons of taking
estrogen replacement therapy (ERT). She makes the point that ERT does
correct problems of hot flashes, night sweats, and vaginal dryness, but it
does not solve the social and psychological difficulties of the middle years.
She traces the history of the use of ERT:

> In the mid-1970's reports began to appear linking estrogen use in
> post-menopausal women to cancer of the uterus. Women were found

to be about five times more likely to develop this cancer if they used ERT. There was a rapid decline in the prescription of ERT after these reports, and this decline lasted several years. Recently, however, new studies show that the addition of a progestin for ten to fourteen days at the end of each twenty-five day course of estrogen protects women quite effectively against uterine cancer. As this reassuring news became known, doctors began to prescribe post-menopausal hormones again quite liberally. . . .

This alteration of the natural plan for the human body may have both benefits and risks, which need to be uncovered by painstaking study. [pp. 89–90]

The two areas where ERT is most controversial today are cardiovascular disease and breast cancer. Some research claims that ERT causes or worsens these conditions, while other studies show no effects or even benefits. [p. 104]

Greenwood suggests that her readers study her list of advantages and disadvantages of taking ERT and make their own decision. Besides discussing nutrition at length, she also mentions cultural components of aging problems. In China the sixtieth birthday is considered a momentous event, a time when the family gathers to celebrate the status and wisdom of the elder. In societies that have special positions for older women that acknowledge their worth and power, aging is seen as a gain in wisdom, not just a loss of youth, and menopause is not viewed as a negative event but as a time when women rise in social status and enjoy more privileges.

She closes her book with a quote from Millicent Fenwick, who was elected to the U.S. Senate in her seventies and then went to work on world food problems.

I began to know myself in a new way after the children left home and I turned 50. I saw that my life was limited and yet unlimited at the same time. Limited in that I wouldn't live forever. Unlimited in that I could really be myself for the first time in many years. I decided to put my energies into the political work that had always interested me, and within two years I was running for city councilwoman. I feel I can take all my talents in working with and for people and use them in a larger way in politics. I'd like to see a lot more women, especially older women, getting into community leadership. They've got a lot of wisdom to share. [p. 194]

Paula Doress and Diana Siegal

Doress and Siegal (1988) introduce their book as follows:

This book grows out of our conviction that the decades after forty can be rich and fulfilling, a time when we as women can come into our own. . . . We can and do use our added years in ways that please us—learning new skills, traveling, and living out long-delayed dreams. Yet, as survivors, women are also likely to face more of the challenges of aging: chronic health conditions; inadequate income; caregiving responsibilities; lack of care when we need it; and perhaps most devastating of all, the deaths of family members and friends. In this book, we have tried to give equal attention to both the promise and the challenge of the later years. [p. xxi]

A surprising comment in the book is that by the age at which most women need care, the majority of those who had married are widowed, many others have never married, and 25 percent of women over 70 have no living children. Fully half of this book is devoted to understanding, preventing, and managing medical problems likely to confront women as they age. Another section is devoted to living arrangements and relationships in middle and later life, and a third section is on general well-being including eating, exercise, stresses, friendships, and attitudes toward appearance in aging.

So much of the writing on midlife women focuses exclusively on married women with children that a section on single women aging is a welcome addition. The authors cite the work of Barbara Levy Simon, *Never Married Women* (1987), who studied fifty single women aged from 65 through the mid-nineties and found that those women who had never married were as embedded in relationships and social networks as those who were presently, or had been, married. They made many friends through work and in retirement formed new friendships with neighbors or members of organizations to which they belonged. Families, especially siblings, were an important source of relationships. They were used to reaching out for friendship and seemed less likely than married women to go through a midlife crisis. They expressed satisfaction with their lives and their choices. The good adjustment and life satisfaction of many older single women is in contrast to the very negative "old maid" stereotype in society, in which such women are viewed with pity and contempt.

I was a pediatrician for forty-odd years, of which I am proud. But do you know what? At family gatherings and in the old neighborhood they still see me as the one who didn't marry. Not as the first in the family to go to college. Not as one of the first Catholics admitted into the fancy medical school I attended. Not as a well-known physician in Philadelphia. No, just as Sally, "the one who never got married." [B. L. Simon, quoted in Doress and Siegal 1987, p. 140]

One of the great contributions of the women's movement to the lives of women has been the acceptance of combining career and marriage rather than having to choose between them, but those women who are now older often saw no way to do both. Rossi (1965) found that women in science were less likely to be married. Hennig and Jardim (1977) found that half of the executive women they studied had never married and none had children of their own. Simon, Clark, and Galway (1967) found that 50 percent of the women Ph.D.'s were married, whereas 95 percent of male Ph.D.'s were married. These researchers focused on academic and successful women. Educated women do the research and often are more interested in women like themselves. We must keep in mind the difference between "career" for middle- and upper-class women and "job" for working-class women, many of whom marry and work by necessity, not as a choice instead of marriage.

Barbara and Gideon Seaman

A third book, *Women and the Crisis in Sex Hormones* (1977), by Barbara and Gideon Seaman, takes a very dim view of hormones as drugs for women, both as contraceptives and for the treatment of menopausal complaints. They stress a feminist perspective that the problem is largely cultural and decry ads in medical journals that push estrogen for women who are being bothersome to their husbands. They trace in detail the history of the use of ERT: the funding by drug companies, the early detection of the overstimulation of the endometrium by a young gynecologist named Saul Gusberg, his describing the widespread prescribing of ERT as "promiscuous," and the Robert Wilson book *Feminine Forever* (1966), which was written up in *Look* magazine and in *Time,* and resulted in ERT's widespread use. Wilson was finally exposed in an article in the *New England Journal of Medicine* in December 1975, showing the fivefold increase in the incidence of endometrial cancer among ERT users. The Seaman book stops there, because the addition of progestin came after their book was published.

A recent book, *Women of the 14th Moon: Writings on Menopause* (1991), edited by Taylor and Sumrall, contains many essays, poems, and personal writings of women about their feelings and experiences of menopause, including the issue of sexuality after menopause. Many women report a loss of sex drive after menopause, but some have sexual excitement and pleasure that surpasses that of their younger days.

WOMEN AT MIDLIFE—EMPTY NEST OR NEGLECTED SELF?

The role that mothers play in the lives of their children has been studied for years in search of the causes of neurosis and schizophrenia. Feminists have studied the effects on women of having children, and two reports focus on the so-called empty nest syndrome. This term was coined by Sidonie Greunberg, in her book *The Many Lives of Modern Women* (1952).

Pauline Bart

Bart (1971), in her work "Depression in Middle-Aged Women" (also titled "Portnoy's Mother's Complaint"), studied depressed women at the time of first hospitalization in middle age and concluded that role loss was the key factor in their depression. The data for this article were collected in the 1960s for a dissertation completed in 1967. The subjects all complained primarily of their children leaving home and how empty their lives were. She drew a connection between midlife depression in women from ethnic groups that place the greatest importance for the woman on her role as mother, as compared with her role as wife, and concluded that mental breakdown in middle age was more common among these ethnic groups.

In rereading Bart's material, I was struck by the quotes of her women and concluded that rather than the problem being one of role loss, these were in fact women who had suffered from a borderline condition all their adult lives but had been able to maintain a nonpsychotic defense system as long as their children were available to them to project upon and introject from. For example: "I didn't think of myself at all, I was just someone that was there to take care of the needs of my family" (p. 164). Another said, "My son is my husband and my husband is my son" (p. 179). One woman moved from Chicago to Los Angeles with her husband four months after her daughter, son-in-law, and granddaughter did because "my daughter and only child moved here and it was lonesome for her, you know" (p. 171). She said she and her daughter were "inseparable." "She wouldn't buy a pair of stockings without me." However, the daughter had written to the hospital stating that much as she loved her mother, her need to be kept continually busy was destroying the daughter's own private life. This mother obviously had no way of even imagining a private life. Another woman says that she thought the best time for a mother was from infancy until the child was 11 or 12 "because after that they become a little self-centered" (p. 172). We can now translate this to mean that they become independent, or so it is hoped.

This material is important to us as therapists because it shows the interconnections between a feminist–sociological analysis and a psychodynamic analysis. When Bart's work first appeared, it was an important contribution in that it pointed out the potential dangers to women in trying to get all their meaning in life from motherhood. Since then we have had the work of Kernberg (1975) and others, defining clearly the borderline syndrome, and we can now look back at these women patients and fill out the picture of the prepsychotic personality: probably severely obsessive and phobic; splitting off anger so that they cannot experience anger at their children; a depressive-masochistic character; severe repression of sexuality, which kept intimacy from developing with their husbands; and most importantly, a pathological boundary problem that merged them in a symbiotic tie with their children and left them feeling empty upon their children's departure. The distinction here is between opposite ends of a scale: an appropriate sadness when children leave home versus a sense of being an empty woman. In the middle are the majority of women, not borderline but feeling frightened and alone because they never allowed themselves to develop an autonomous identity apart from that of mother and wife.

The external danger to women's autonomy and development has been that society rewards with approval this pathological self-denial as expressed through the so-called devoted mother, devoted daughter, and devoted wife. The internal danger is the guilt and anxiety she feels if she asserts herself, or in the case of more disturbed women, the emptiness and panic they feel in trying to extricate themselves from dependent relationships. Autonomy may unconsciously be equated with destruction, abandonment, and sadistic retaliation.

Lillian Rubin

More recent research on the subject by Rubin, presented in *Women of a Certain Age: The Midlife Search for Self* (1979), revealed a quite different attitude toward the "empty nest" among working-class and middle-class women in the San Francisco Bay Area. Almost all of these women cautiously expressed relief that their children were leaving home so that their responsibilities were lessened and they could have time for themselves. Barbara Artson (1978), a researcher working with Rubin, relabeled the empty nest syndrome the "neglected self" syndrome and feels midlife women suffer from having lost themselves in the process of child rearing and experience an identity crisis when children leave. Rubin, herself a woman who began college in 1963 at age 39 during a second marriage and with a 15-year-old daughter, went on for eight years to obtain a Ph.D.

For this book she interviewed 160 women between the ages of 35 and 54 for a minimum of 3 and maximum of 10 hours each. They all had children in varying stages of leaving the family home. About 80 percent were married, the rest divorced. Almost half worked in paid jobs; of the rest, some were involved in volunteer work and a few were in school. They had all given up earlier jobs to become full-time mothers for usually at least ten years. The median age of the children was 21 years and the median number of children was three. The composition of the sample was 45 percent working class, 24 percent middle-middle class, and 31 percent professional or upper-middle class. Rubin intentionally confined the sample to white women: 54 percent Protestant, 19 percent Catholic, 14 percent Jewish, and 13 percent no religion. She found that for married women, gender transcends class as the major determinant of the quality of their lives. The women felt it was time for their children to leave: "Time, finally, for me. Time to find out who I am and what I want. Time to live for me instead of them. All my life I've been doing for others. Now, before it's too late, it's time for me" (p. 13).

Rubin refutes the work of Bart and other writers in the 1960s in her findings: "It's true that some are sad, some lonely, some are even depressed. It's true also that some are hesitant, some unconfident, and most are frightened as they face an uncertain future. But except for one, none suffers the classical symptoms of the empty-nest syndrome" (p. 15).

The relief was just as clear for the divorced mothers as for the married. A striking fact revealed by Rubin was that although half the women held paid jobs outside the home, not one—including those who worked at high-level professional jobs—described themselves in relation to their work. The women who most often described themselves as competent and capable were those who spent much of their time in volunteer activities in the community. The women were reluctant to think of themselves as powerful, fearing disapproval of their husbands and others. Would this be true for a comparable group of women today, in 1993?

In her afterword, Rubin says that she is grateful to the women's movement, which made the option of returning to school possible for her and supported her efforts. She says she heard such sentiments from many of the women she interviewed, who took courage from the new feminism:

> As much as anything, it was the women's movement that made it possible for me to consider making a serious commitment to a life aside from my family. It isn't that I belonged to anything, or that I considered myself a part of it in any organized way, but it seemed to be surrounding me, and it made all kinds of choices possible that didn't even exist a few years ago. [p. 209]

Here we see illustrated the point I made earlier in this chapter, that the profound effect of the feminist movement has changed the lives of all women, even those not directly involved in it.

Barbara Artson

Artson (1978), like Rubin, studied a group of normal women, not a clinical population, thirty-nine women ranging in age from 40 to 55 who fell into four groups: Homemakers (9); Super Volunteers, or women who spend at least 20 hours a week performing unpaid administrative or executive jobs (9); Late Professionals (13); and Early Professionals (8). All of the women had been married, had children, and were in their late forties. In 1964, when Friedan's *The Feminine Mystique* was published, these women were in their mid-thirties. The Early and Late Professional women sought independent vocational achievement and maintained the traditional roles of wife and mother. The Super Volunteers and Homemakers dedicated themselves to marriage and motherhood; however, the primary focus of the Homemakers was on their role as wife, whereas for the Super Volunteers it was as mother.

The Homemaker group was the most dependent and had symbiotic ties to their own mothers, continuing, as Artson says, "the established mode of vicarious satisfaction through passive attachment to another who leads and dominates" (p. 210). The Super Volunteer's concept of motherhood was a more active one, caring for others rather than being cared for, a role of control and dominance rather than of subservience and continued dependency. The Early Professionals pursued career plans despite objections by parents and relatives and the cultural norms at the time. The Late Professionals put aside early career plans and conformed to traditional expectations.

A crucial find in Dr. Artson's study relates to the empty nest syndrome and contradicts other research that assumes a depressive reaction at the time of the loss of the mothering role. Artson found that Homemakers, Late Professionals, and Super Volunteers experienced no depression, pathologic or otherwise, at the time that children left home; in fact they experienced this change as liberating. Only the Early Professional women showed some signs of depression over the absence of children. Artson believes that what had been labeled by previous researchers as an empty nest syndrome can be better understood as an identity crisis. She suggests that investigators discovered that which they expected to find, a point made in my first book in regard to penis envy. It is curious that work by Deutscher (1968), which described this period in a woman's life as happier and less constraining, was virtually ignored, whereas Bart's work was frequently cited, presumably because it fit the traditional concepts of women's needs, that is, what was biologically determined.

According to Artson, an identity crisis at midlife occurs because women must defer identity consolidation until middle age. During the years of raising a family, the demands of others make it difficult to explore their own needs. Thus motherhood is not conducive to personal growth and identity maturation gets postponed to midlife when it can be more difficult because of having to cope with the signs of physical aging. Yet in my view motherhood does promote personal growth because in the process of raising children many women learn and mature with the responsibility. It is important to distinguish here between two kinds of personal growth: growth that occurs in relationship to others and personal growth that is autonomous. It is the latter that may be inhibited during the years of being a full-time wife and mother because the needs of others are given priority. When children are grown, the woman may have the first real chance to explore her personal needs and interests apart from her connections to family members, and consolidation may occur as a result of increasing self-knowledge and the wisdom of her years of caring for others. The woman may not feel that she is respected in her community because motherhood is not validated in a materialistic culture. She produces no product and earns no income. Yet her life's work is ending in midlife. It is comparable with the crisis some men face at the point of retirement. The Homemaker group experienced this transition most critically and, along with the Super Volunteers, described feelings of desperation and "the need to be something real":

> Implicit was the feeling that the domestic role did not provide them with a meaningful experience upon which to form a positive self-image. They expressed a need to find self-fulfillment and personal enrichment through work. The Homemakers felt that the Feminist Movement depreciated their role, one previously respected. More than the other groups, they felt caught in the interstices of changing social values, cultural pressures and traditional ideals. The Homemakers have little hope that they can find suitable and interesting work which provides gratification, and yet they do not feel saddened at the loss of the mothering role. [pp. 215–216]

The pressure of the feminist movement led to feelings of coercion but not of depression. The explanation for stronger feelings of loss among the Early Professionals appears to be that they had spent less time with their children, and Artson suggests that they are feeling guilty for having had a personally fulfilling life.

> They may need to pay with the coin of guilt as a means of denying the relief expressed by other groups. They need to deny the relief over their children's leaving because they feel guilty about their mothering, and to pay for the pleasure derived from increased opportunities for self-indulgence. . . . The ambivalence is the classic one that leads to depression. [pp. 217–218]

Yet Artson admits that these women continue to function well at home and at work and experience none of the classical symptoms of depression such as weight loss or insomnia. Many used this time to expand their goals, publishing more and attending more professional meetings. They expressed more sadness than the other groups but it seems to me that Artson overstates her case to call this "depression." Mourning should be distinguished from depression. As an "early professional" myself, I felt an enormous sadness when my children left home but not depression. The sadness and some anxiety gradually gave way to an adjustment that offered the rewards of time alone, lessened responsibility and pressure, and an eventual acceptance and gratification at having finished the intense years of mothering and having graduated into being an available mother but not an ever-present one. On the very day I write this paragraph I have made a trip across the city to my son's apartment bringing him groceries and dinner because he had a basketball accident that has left him on crutches. I am pleased to be able to help him out and then to return to my own work.

I believe that the absence of relief observed by Artson can be explained more simply by the fact that the working mother has not "overdosed" on mothering and therefore was less ambivalent about her children. She has always had less time to spend with them and therefore appreciated the time spent with them more. She is saddened to see them go just at the point when their companionship has become the most enjoyable to her, as they become young adults with interesting ideas and her pleasure in their company is reaching its peak. The notion of guilt at this point seems foreign to me. Regret at the loss of the pleasures of mothering by a woman who was never entrapped by mothering seems a more likely explanation. It is not relief when mothering was not experienced as a burden or as a deprivation of one's own desires for development.

Most of the women expressed a commitment to the new wave of feminism. Early Professionals approved of the movement's philosophy and felt that they had gained "retrospective permission" for their early career choices. The Late Professionals supported feminism but in a more qualified way, disowning what they perceived as the movement's excesses. The Super Volunteers were very supportive of the new feminists and looked forward to being able to move into paid employment. Among the Homemakers, self-esteem was the lowest and conflict about the women's movement was the highest. Half were in favor of it although they saw it as coming too late to alter their own lives. The other half held varying views. "Somehow they needed to diminish the Movement's effect upon their own lives in order to quash the fear that their lives' commitment has been invalidated. They understandably felt that the Movement was a threat to the traditional role they had assumed and they fought to preserve it as meaningful" (p. 234).

Yet a consistent characteristic among all four groups was that they all suffered conflict around the issue of self-assertion, wishing they could be more self-assertive yet unable to "turn off their early training." All spoke of the fear of asserting opinions, of refusing a request, of openly disagreeing with others. The primacy of the roles of wife and mother extended across all groups as well, regardless of the rank or status a professional woman had obtained. The career plans of the women were highly sensitive to their perception of their mothers' characteristics and attitudes toward their choices. Interestingly, an early history of trauma may lead to the development of coping mechanisms and the development of a self-concept for autonomous achievement.

In conclusion, Artson finds gains and losses in each of the four choices. By midlife the Early Professional woman has experienced "role strain" and guilt for time spent away from her children. The Homemaker feels cheated as her traditional role wanes and she is without her former function, experiencing a loss of identity. The Late Professional, who performed both roles sequentially, and the Super Volunteer, who performed significant work but without the guilt, appear to "most successfully meet the challenge for personal rewards while appearing obedient to the culture's mandate" (p. 240). They experience losses as well. The Super Volunteer suffers role strain but never receives the recognition, power, and prestige of earning wages. The Late Professional misses opportunities for rising and contributing in her career because of her late start.

For some women there is also time spent away from husbands, and that is usually unacceptable in marriage. There are many role models for men leaving wives in answer to the call of war or career, but not the reverse. Sylvia Earle, an oceanographer and chief scientist of the National Oceanic and Atmospheric Administration, is one of the world's foremost divers. Dr. Earle is the mother of three grown children from her first two marriages. In an interview with Peggy Orenstein (1991), she speaks of the separation from her third husband:

> I was always trying to combine everything, combine science and traditional expectations, and I suppose it never occurred to me that there had to be a choice, or at least it didn't until quite recently. I'm beginning now to think I've had choices thrust upon me. In this case it was on Graham's side. He decided he wanted more than I was able to deliver. But it's repeatedly been my choice to opt for a career as a scientist—if you want to call "being a scientist" a career. A scientist is what I am. It's who and what I am, fundamentally, beyond being a woman, beyond being a wife or beyond being a mother. It's just who I am. [p. 18]

Unlike Rubin and Artson's professionals, Earle does not diminish her professional identity, and perhaps because of that has had three marital breakups. Anthropologist Margaret Mead would be a similar example of this no doubt small but very significant group of women. There is no "free lunch" when it comes to women's choices. The later generation of women who postponed marriage and motherhood have had disappointments too. Some have found themselves unable to get pregnant once their careers have been established, and others have, regrettably, not married. But the success of the women's movement in giving women choices has been revolutionary, and most women have benefited. By limiting her study to middle-class women, Artson has left the question of the effects of the movement on the lives of poor and working-class women still an important unanswered question. It is likely that poor women have not benefited, because their lives have rarely permitted them such choices. Often burdened by unwanted pregnancies and husbands whose earnings are small and unreliable, only in rare cases have they been able to go back to school and complete their development. The battles around abortion, to be dealt with in the following chapter, bear strongly on the future of these women.

Rachel Siegel

Another writer on women in midlife, Siegel (1982) describes her own return to school in midlife. Her turning point was at age 39, when her husband, age 47, suffered a heart attack. At age 44 she had a hysterectomy and her children began leaving home. She continued her volunteer activities, but her depression at feeling the loss of her career as mother felt "like the end of my life." She had wanted to be a psychoanalyst when she was young, but neither she nor anyone else had taken those wishes seriously. She returned to therapy, but that did not help. When she entered graduate school in social work, she "rediscovered my brain and my sense of competence in the world" (p. 97). In her work with women clients less fortunate than herself, Siegel became aware of her privileged position and of the oppression of women. "I began to question the male-centered and male-dominant structure of our society and the male definitions of women's experiences. Becoming a therapist and a feminist was a complicated and confusing process. The inner turmoil was no longer without a purpose, yet still distressing" (p. 97).

She was influenced by her reading of Jean Baker Miller (1976) and recognized herself in Robert Seidenberg's (1972) "trauma of eventlessness." Her self-image changed as she gained confidence in her work and presented her first paper in 1982 at the Women's Institute of the American Orthopsychiatric Association, where she came in contact with other women therapists interested in feminist theory. In Siegel's personalized account we can trace the influence of the women's movement on a woman who eventually came into the mental health field and then made contributions of her own, giving back to the very movement that had given so much to her. This is a common story of nurturance and then replenishment as women spread the word through their writing and the CR groups that we have other choices, especially at midlife, and that women are there to help each other with the changes they need to make to realize their dreams.

CLINICAL ILLUSTRATIONS

As a female psychotherapist or psychoanalyst you are making a statement to all patients about yourself and your view of a woman's place in the world outside her home and family. No matter what degree of neutrality and concealment of your personal life you may adhere to, the fact of your being a career woman is undeniable. How this affects our patients, both male and female, is always of interest and has been explored in several chapters in this book. When working with a midlife woman who has spent her adult life as a housewife, therapists may find that differences in the lives of patient and therapist are especially pronounced and may have both transference and countertransference implications. By the early 1980s, the women's movement had reached the attention of all women in this country, and each one had to deal with it in some way, whether by making life changes or resisting such changes on account of fear or lack of desire to change. Two of my patients at that time represent two responses to the external and internal pressures they were feeling as a result of the changes in their friends and society and in sensing the changed expectations of their own families. One happily married, the other recently divorced, each presented me with challenging countertransference issues.

In my consultation group of women therapists, all of us then in our forties, we saw middle age as an opportunity to rework separation-individuation issues, a residue of earlier life stages. The middle point of life was when many women of our generation were expected to complete certain individuation tasks, in contrast to the current generation of women who are now enabled to complete their identity formation in their twenties. Because marriage and child rearing defined the existence of so many women born in the '30s and before, an identity apart from wife and mother was not generally sought or considered desirable or necessary. The answer to the question Who am I? was "Mrs. Jack Smith," and "Jane and Jim's mother." Thus, for these women, middle age, coming as it did at the height of feminism, offered a second chance for an independent identity. As therapists, we recognized that the woman coming to us at this stage of life could be on the verge of a second career, after "retirement" as a mother. Yet we recognized that she had conflicting values that often made the exploratory process a tug-of-war between her old image of herself as catering to the family, meeting everyone's needs ahead of her own, versus a new feminist image of autonomy and destiny based on a self-esteem that was just emerging and needed nurturance from those she depended upon for support.

For the therapist, it was important to try to maintain a neutral stance while at the same time enabling the woman to take on challenges and overcome both internal and external obstacles. We who participated in the consultation group believed that a feminist analysis of the patient's past choices and her current dilemma was often an appropriate focus of the therapy in addition to a traditional psychodynamic analysis. Our similarity to the patient in age and gender made an empathic response come easily, yet we risked the danger of overidentification and missing what might be major differences between the patient and ourselves in attitude, motivation, and ambition as well as the need for intellectual and social challenge.

The losses of middle age—youth, beauty, children, and perhaps one's husband—could lead to depression and decline or to new opportunity for growth and development. The overused expression *midlife crisis* applies to women in a different way than it does to men, who, like women, may be reacting to a physical decline but are also reacting to whatever disappointments they may be feeling in their work life and the recognition that they must continue to work another twenty years in a job or profession that may have lost its earlier challenge and in which their hopes for achievement may not have been met. Our eagerness to help patients enjoy the satisfaction from work that we do from our own work should not impede recognition of and attention to the meaning of the losses, which can arouse old fears of inadequacy and unlovability. The decline and aging of parents presents another reality at this time of life and may involve responsibility equal to that of child care, a responsibility that most often falls to women. The death of parents can also be both a loss of a meaningful, loving relationship and a freedom of responsibility for care that allows for other possibilities for a woman's energy. As Carol Gilligan's (1982) work illustrates, the ethic of care is so prominent in the morality of women that a woman is not usually able to make a decision about her own life without first evaluating how it will affect all those people with whom she has a caring relationship, and determining whether her own wishes can be justified if anyone else will be hurt.

In addition, our patient may fear for her own marital stability if making changes toward greater independence threatens her husband and she feels the danger of losing him. After years of being catered to, many husbands had little tolerance for the women's movement and especially for the effect it was having on their wives. As husbands left they soon remarried, often women ten or more years younger than themselves, and these examples served as warnings to women who were contemplating greater autonomy within the marriage. To be able to synthesize dreams from the past and the possibilities for the future in a current reality that includes the needs of others is a complex task, and our patients explored a variety of alternatives, hoping not to have to compromise their needs too severely in order to maintain the stability of their home life. The value placed on youth for women serves as a constant reminder that self-assertion may exact a heavy toll, especially for the older woman.

In the cases discussed below, I prefer to think of the dilemma of these two women as an existential crisis. The meaning of their lives had been in their roles as wives and mothers. With their children entering adulthood, this meaning was fading and the crisis they experienced had to do with a true crisis in meaning. Since neither of them was compelled to work because of financial need, they each had the luxury of deciding what to do next at an age when they were far too young to "retire." When a woman's meaning in life has come from her family, the loss of that family creates a vacuum that needs to be filled in a manner that contains a meaningful identity and offers new meaning to her existence. This may be more or less difficult depending on her experience, capabilities, earlier education, and the degree of support available in her environment. For some women, a job is a necessity and therefore serves the meaning and purpose of supporting herself, with the advantage of the independence and pride in that accomplishment. The financially fortunate woman has the advantage of time for school and career development, but because she is not earning her own way, she especially needs to find an occupation for her time and talents that fills the void of meaning left by her children's reaching maturity. She requires a new source of pride and self-esteem, or she may decline into depression, not because of early neurotic complications but because of her current meaningless existence.

As Seligman (1974) recognized, the sense of being in charge of one's life fosters self-esteem, whereas feeling that one is not in charge is associated with depression and a sense of helplessness. An essential component of psychotherapy with women based on a feminist analysis of women's lives is to promote the woman's capacity to take active charge of her life, to make decisions about her future, and to follow through on those decisions toward her goals. This is true in treating women at any age, but especially at those junctures where life-affirming decisions can avert depression whereas passivity can keep a person mired in gloom and a sense of helplessness. It is not menopause that constitutes a partial death, but a masochistic submission to feeling abandoned and useless that can lead a woman to a life empty of meaning and thus partial death. In a 1958 paper that surveys a group of women before the influence of the women's movement, Weiss and Samuelson asked women, "What are the things you do that make you feel useful or important?" They report that "a rather substantial proportion of women in the older age groups said that nothing made them feel useful and important" (in Cox 1981, p. 290). It is with this orientation in mind that I approached my work with Mrs. P. and Mrs. R.

Divorce in Midlife

When I first saw Mrs. P. in 1980, she was a 47-year-old recently divorced mother of four college-aged children. She entered therapy after moving from Europe to San Francisco. A native Californian, she had lived in Europe for many years with her corporate-executive husband. When she learned of his affair with a younger woman, she delayed divorce several years until her last child left home. Her sense of devotion to her children could not allow her to free herself from this demeaning position of betrayed wife until she had fulfilled her motherly duties by keeping the family together while her children were still at home. When her last child left for college, she felt free to try to make a new life for herself with dignity. Her therapy dealt with the following issues: (1) mourning the loss of her marriage, including the expression of anger toward her husband; (2) her devaluation of herself as a woman without a career or a man; and (3) encouragement of a life review, taking into account her upbringing in the '40s and '50s, a time in which women were not expected to have a career and did not prepare themselves for work. The review included looking at all her positive accomplishments in successfully raising four children, and crediting herself for the many contributions she had made to her community through her volunteer work and the great responsibility she had handled successfully in these roles.

Both therapist and patient were close in age and both had been reared in the same Southern California atmosphere of the '50s. Thus positive and negative countertransference issues emerged. I understood the meaning of that atmosphere, with its emphasis on vicarious living through one's husband's status and achievements, and empathized with Mrs. P.'s feelings of abandonment, since I too had lost a husband to divorce. I conveyed to her my understanding of her self-denigration based on her lack of preparation for the life of an independent woman, but reminded her that such had never been expected of her, nor had she ever expected it of herself. I could easily empathize as well with a midlife woman's need to date and with all the anxiety and fear of humiliation as well as the potential for excitement and romance.

However, having always worked, I failed to appreciate the uncertainty and real apprehension Mrs. P. felt about entering the world of work. She had graduated from college and taught school briefly before marriage, but that had been more than twenty years ago. She received spousal support from her husband and had some personal income (she came from a well-to-do family), so work was optional but she wanted to increase her income, and in the atmosphere of San Francisco she recognized that not working was not really respectable in such a career-oriented city. Her children were urging her to develop a new career, and I shared the view that this would be the best thing for her, encouraging her when she expressed an interest in becoming an accountant and began a bookkeeping course. However, she became discouraged with the difficulty of the course and I then realized that I may have inadvertently diminished her self-worth. My encouragement may have been experienced by Mrs. P. as a need to please me, to satisfy my expectations for her, as she had pleased her parents, her husband, and society by conforming to expectations that she marry and have children. The dilemma for the therapist is that there is a delicate line between pushing beyond our patient's psychic capacity, which can result in lower self-esteem, and not expecting enough, thus colluding with a depreciated sense of self. Our own enthusiasm for our professional work and independence must not lead us to devalue or view as neurotic, women who maintain a more traditional life-style.

The case took an unexpected turn when Mrs. P. began suffering from headaches and was diagnosed as having a brain tumor. She was operated on successfully and continued to see me in therapy. What emerged during this period was my recognition of the place of friendship in Mrs. P.'s life. Friends called and wrote from all over the world and some came to visit her. A whole new dimension to her personality and life's course became apparent to me as I viewed this outpouring of love and support from people to whom Mrs. P. had always generously given her friendship over the years. I became aware in a very real way of the importance of connections with other women in the lives of many women who are homemakers and volunteers. I felt a new respect for what apparently had been years of devoted and loyal friendship that she had maintained with people in Europe and the United States who now wanted to extend their help and good wishes to her. I told her that she should be proud of the many warm friendships she had maintained. This was a source of richness in her life that was now bearing fruit in her hour of need. As old friends visited and new friends were made, Mrs. P. no longer felt a need for therapy and terminated with uncertainty about her job possibilities but with greater comfort in her new home and new life. She had children in nearby universities, some family in the area, and was adapting to life in San Francisco. It was an ending of some ambivalence for me because I felt uncertain about her future, but she was starting to get active in some neighborhood affairs and felt satisfied.

An interesting postscript occurred seven or eight years later. I entered a recently opened restaurant that had been highly recommended; a smiling woman handed us our menus and led us to our table. She looked very familiar. At about the same moment, we recognized each other (I had cut my previously long hair and looked quite different) and I asked her if she was Betty P. She said she was and told me she had been working as a hostess in the restaurant and enjoyed her job and the pleasant social atmosphere of the place, which included a grand piano and a large, bright lounge. She looked very well and appeared cheerful and confident. I was delighted by the chance to see how things had turned out, and although she didn't have the income or status of an accountant, she surely was having a better time.

A Woman Faces Her Children Growing Up

Mrs. R. was a 42-year-old woman who came into therapy in 1981 complaining of recent feelings of depression because she didn't know what to do with her life. She was married to a professional man, did not need to work for financial reasons, had two teenage children, and kept very busy. She did volunteer work at her children's school, took dance and art classes, did gardening, visited with family and friends, cooked a gourmet dinner for her family every night, and belonged to a women's writing group. She enjoyed her family and activities very much but felt something was wrong with her—she should be pursuing a career.

Many of her friends were divorcing, going back to school, developing careers, and having love affairs. Her life seemed dull and mundane by comparison. She proclaimed with a touch of humor that she considered herself a "member of a dying species" for remaining married and wondered if she should consider divorce to give her the kick she needed to get out of her comfortable nest. She depreciated herself, referring to herself as a dilettante, and said she should have been born fifty years earlier when her life-style was perfectly acceptable for a woman.

As was typical for women of her class and generation, and like Mrs. P., she had received a good education, taught school for a few years after college, but stopped teaching as soon as she became pregnant. Unlike most women, however, both Mrs. R.'s mother and maternal grandmother were successful writers, resulting in the suspicion that although her mother tolerated her, she was really disapproving of her life as a housewife and mother and would only be pleased if she were to have some professional success. This was all a source of much conflict for Mrs. R., who loved "playing house"—raising her children and providing a warm, nurturant family life—but was filled with self-contempt for being satisfied with so little challenge. She did not know if her dreams of pursuing a career in art were to please her mother—continuing in her pattern of being a dutiful daughter, dutiful student, and dutiful wife and mother— or if this was truly her own wish, which she inhibited because of fears she was not good enough to succeed.

How might a psychoanalytically oriented therapist who is also a feminist approach such a dilemma? The first question we dealt with was that of divorce. She and her husband seemed to genuinely like each other and had a very satisfactory sex life together, so this avenue seemed foolish. She spoke with her husband, and it was clear that she had his full support for whatever she wished to do. A room was cleared in the house to be her work room, a "room of her own." She concluded that her husband was not the obstacle, that the barriers were internal.

She then cut back some of her activities, such as dancing, so as to be able to focus on her art work, and she added a course in graphic design. The next step was to turn down some volunteer work, which made her feel a bit guilty, but with my support she did it. She remained filled with doubt about withdrawing time from her husband and children, so Christmas vacation went by with little of her own work done. I found myself unsure as to what might be the source of this conflict and decided to pursue her self-doubt about her talent and ability, as she often expressed fear that her work might be just mediocre. Two themes emerged. In tracing her history of interest in art, there emerged a picture of Mrs. R. as a "poor little rich girl," alone in her room reading or drawing, with mother and father away, thus exposing the loneliness she had often felt as a child. Mother, who always had several domestic helpers, was pursuing her writing career in a studio away from home and an active society life as well. My patient and her younger brother were left in the care of nursemaids and grandmothers. In addition, her father was gone for several years of military service during World War II. Even after her father's return, evenings were filled with dinner parties and it was the nurse who bathed and fed the children and put them to bed. This was the source of her feelings of not being good enough to be a successful artist. She never felt she was good enough, that is, witty or interesting or charming enough, to deserve her mother's time and attention.

I commented that I could understand why she was such a devoted mother. She wanted to give her children all the love and attention she had missed as a little girl and to create for herself the warm family life which she was denied. Tears ran down her cheeks and she cried silently.

The second theme had to do with her relationship with her mother. After a number of weeks focusing on her feelings about her mother, Mrs. R. summed up our work saying she had come to realize that she really admired her mother and could see her as a product of her time and milieu. She did not feel angry toward her but understood that her mother's expectations and ambitions for her had in fact paralyzed her. She realized that she must proceed to develop in a way that pleased herself, even if it might not satisfy her mother. She must set her own goals and her own pace. She also saw that her life could in this way be both comfortable and challenging. "Why couldn't I have seen that before?" she asked. Now she was not so critical of herself and realized that she could develop into a stronger woman as she grew older, as she suspected her mother had done. At age 42 she was doing the work of separation-individuation from her mother that is so common for women to do in midlife, whereas boys do this in childhood. For Mrs. R., the fear of being "not like mother," with the accompanying fantasies of disapproval, revolved around not having a career, whereas until recently for most women, it was tied to not being a full-time homemaker as Mother was.

In this case, what appeared to be a feminist issue had a psychological source, so the work involved an integration of feminist and psychoanalytic theory. Mrs. R. herself was well aware through her friends and her reading of the changes women were making. The feminist cause was actually the source of disturbance for her because it added yet another element to an internal conflict regarding her identity. Psychotherapy helped her to identify the emotional basis for her attachment to her family and the pleasure she obtained from close family life. Her guilt over being "just a housewife" was put in a sympathetic perspective, and she felt more free to try to work out a life that combined developing her artistic side while maintaining the warm family life she so enjoyed. This was achieved by having work space at home. Having differentiated from her mother, she was enabled to steer her own course, taking on new challenges at her own pace without the paralyzing fear of her mother's disapproval.

It was important that my hopes for her artistic development did not, like her mother's, create a pressure on her that might again paralyze her. As with the case of Mrs. P., it would have been an error for me to assume that because my career had been so gratifying to me, Mrs. R. should follow in my footsteps and combine family and career. Being a dutiful patient is a danger for a woman like Mrs. R., who might have tried to win my approval and again been in conflict about her own needs. In much of the feminist literature, marriage and children are portrayed as a trap for women, an impediment to their autonomous development. In Mrs. R's. case—and I suspect in the case of many other women as well, especially those who did not have a stable family life in childhood—marriage and children actually met her needs for security, and the challenge of a career raised old anxieties about not being good enough. Yet a secure family life with a husband who provided financial and emotional support enabled Mrs. R. to take the risks of testing herself in the competitive world with the knowledge that there was a soft landing place at home if she had disappointments or even failed. Hasn't that been the advantage of marriage for men? Haven't many women worked to support their husbands through school and in the early days of a career? Women shouldn't have to go it alone in the harsh world of business and the professions. They need the support and comfort of a family just as men do, if they can be fortunate to have a husband who encourages them the way so many wives have done for their husbands.

The work with Mrs. R. had some similar features to that with Ruth, discussed in Chapter 1. Ruth was the young musician whose mother was a physician and who grew up feeling she was not special enough to win her mother's full-time attention as her friends did from their mothers. This had led to her anxiety that she could not win and keep the love of a man. In Mrs. R.'s case, her mother's career combined with an active social life led to actual neglect of her emotional needs, although there was nothing actually hostile in her mother's relationship with her. The use of nurses for child care in Mrs. R's. case needs to be seen in the context of the upper-class life-style rather than as a sign of pathology. It is class syntonic. Benign neglect is probably the best way to define it. As I stated in Ruth's case, these patients point to the very important effort required of a career mother to spend quality time with her children, with each child individually, to assure them of their importance to her and her sincere love for them.

One exchange illustrates the way in which therapists may communicate their countertransference to patients when we are unaware of doing so. An analyst's silence or shifting in his/her chair can convey meaning to a patient. In psychotherapy a facial expression or body movement may have meaning to an observant patient. At one point in our work together, Mrs. R. was planning a trip to the East Coast with her husband, where he would be attending professional meetings and she could attend an association meeting of interest to her in the same city. She viewed this as good stimulation for her in a period before she had solidified her identity as an artist. The week before they left, she came in and said she had decided not to attend the meetings after all, that it seemed like more trouble than it was worth. Two weeks later when she returned, she told me that she had in fact changed her mind again and had attended the meetings after encouragement from her friends and because she saw the look on my face when she told me she was not attending. I had not said a word.

Mrs. R.'s career started to take off as she received a contract to illustrate one book and then another. The first book was a big success, and I felt thrilled when I saw it in bookstores. She then branched out to another line of art work but felt some doubts about her ability to succeed. She pursued the work diligently, spending long hours at her drawing board, making commercial contacts, and began to have some success. At this point she felt ready to terminate therapy and did so. About a year later she returned for a few weeks only because she needed help in sorting out some relationship problems that had occurred among a group of women she had done a project with, and which were very disturbing to her. She resolved her conflict and left therapy again, realizing that her initial euphoria over her success had been dampened somewhat by later complications of success, but still very satisfied with her choices and still happily married.

This story has an unusual postscript as well. A number of years later, I bought an item in a gift shop that struck me by its whimsical and clever humor. It wasn't until several days later that I noticed the signature of the artist and saw that it was that of Mrs. R.

A MODERN JUNGIAN VIEW OF MENOPAUSE—JEAN SHINODA BOLEN

Bolen, a Jungian analyst now past menopause, has given considerable thought to the position of the menopausal woman in society from a valuable historical perspective. In a very important statement made at a conference titled "Women's Lives: The Quest for Self," (1991) she considers menopause a time when women develop internal wisdom and describes the "wise woman" or crone archetype. The dictionary definition of *crone* is "an ugly, witchlike, withered, old woman," yet the definition for *crony* is "an intimate friend or companion." I suspect that somewhere in the history of the English language the use of the word *crone* became distorted by sexism and the wisdom component was omitted. Bolen speaks of spirituality in the second part of life and the sacred dimension of menopause. The three female archetypes include the maiden, the mother, and the crone, or wise woman. She recalls the early days of the women's movement and describes the consciousness-raising group as having been a "sacred place" or "sacred circle" in which women defined themselves. She sees the present time, when many of the early participants in the movement are menopausal, as the last wave of the women's movement during which we can reclaim the wise woman archetype for ourselves and define for ourselves what this stage of life means to us. This is a time for thoughtfulness about what we have learned and a time to speak the truth of our lives. After years of being creative through reproduction, we now have a chance to be creative in a different way.

Bolen tells us that in ancient times, people explained pregnancy as the time when a woman retained the menstrual blood to create a baby and menopause as the time when a woman retained the menstrual blood to create wisdom. Midwives attended women not only at the time of birth but also at the time of death, because they were considered wise women. She believes that the Inquisition, that three hundred-year period in history when millions of women were burned for being witches (see Prozan 1992) has left a mark on the psyche of all women since that time. Those burned as witches included midwives, herbalists, eccentric women, and all knowledgeable women. She calls it a women's holocaust. The fear of what happens to a woman who is autonomous, eccentric, and wise remains in our collective psyche and has frightened us from identifying with this archetype of an older woman. The result has been that this image of woman is no longer honored and has been denied us.

In Greek mythology, Hecate, goddess of the earth and the underworld, was the wise woman archetype. When Persephone, daughter of Zeus and Demeter, emerged from the underworld after being raped by Hades, her uncle, Hecate both proceeded and followed her wherever she went, guiding her with her wisdom. Bolen believes that by menopause women are in touch with certain wisdoms, characterized by the theme "After all I have been through, I am still here." The wisdom is the knowledge of humility, the importance of relationship, and the ongoingness of life. Hecate, the goddess of the crossroads, is especially apt as a symbol for midlife women because menopause is a crossroads in a woman's life, with each direction a possible adventure.

Bolen describes the importance of reflection and solitude at this stage of life and refers to the "anguish and joys of solitude." Every creative impulse that you ever had wants to emerge now, and the thought "Maybe it's my turn" is present at a time when, because of the major experiences of one's life with loss, illness, birth, and death, you have something to say. She refers to the "deliciousness" of solitude after a life of caring for others and the importance of protecting and putting a boundary around one's own solitude in order to be able to process the experience of one's own life. She reports that she discovered, when leading groups of women on pilgrimages, that the happiest women of all were those between 60 and 70 who were living alone. It is a radical and subversive notion, she says, to speak of the great joy of solitude and friendship. Choosing freedom over love may be the wisest choice and involves taking risks. She speaks of Georgia O'Keeffe as saying that her success as an artist has not been due to natural genius but to much hard work and risk taking.

She quotes Maxine Kumin, saying "When Sleeping Beauty wakes up she is almost fifty years old." Something happens that jolts her into awakening, and it is an exciting time. Sometimes that jolt may be a death or divorce or her last child leaving home. If we can rid ourselves of the archetypal fear of being burned as witches and reclaim the archetype of the wise woman, there is a freedom to express ourselves: to be outrageous, eccentric, outspoken, autonomous individuals. Bolen recommends that women at menopause make a declaration of independence to be who they are, based on a life filled with both great joy and great sorrow, with the wisdom of knowing that this too shall pass.

THE WOMAN PATIENT—MALKAH T. NOTMAN AND CAROL C. NADELSON

The three-volume work *The Woman Patient: Medical and Psychological Interfaces,* edited by Notman and Nadelson, contains six chapters on midlife women. In Volume 1 (1978), Johanna F. Perlmutter, a gynecologist, reviews the medical aspects of menopause including endocrine changes, vaginal bleeding, vasomotor instability, atrophic changes, osteoporosis, and changes in physique including the growth of facial hair. Yet she stresses that our society, which values youth and does not honor old age, compounds the real changes of aging by societal pressure, fear, diminishing job security, and the degenerating integrity of the family unit.

She states that emotional disturbances have been reported in 10 to 30 percent of women who are menopausal but that these difficulties probably have little to do with the altered hormonal balance; in fact 50 percent of these women have had emotional difficulties in the past. She warns against the use of skin creams containing estrogen, which will not restore the firmness to the skin; what is more, if used in large quantities, the hormones may be absorbed in sufficient quantities to raise systemic estrogen levels and cause vaginal bleeding, mimicking a malignancy and frightening both patient and physician.

A chapter on menopause by Pauline B. Bart and Marylyn Grossman offers a feminist critique of the medical view of women at menopause:

> While there is substantial evidence documenting medical misogyny the topic of menopause does seem especially to elicit such sentiments. This may derive from the conviction of nineteenth-century medical "authorities," such as prominent gynecologist Charles D. Meigs, who described woman as "a moral, a sexual, a germiferous, gestative and parturient creature." . . . Indeed historian Peter Stearns observed that in eighteenth- and nineteenth-century Europe physicians thought women decayed at menopause. [p. 337]

They state that no "substantial changes" in physicians' attitudes have occurred over time and find "pervasive sexism" in current gynecological writing within the traditional male ambience in medical education. At a conference on menopause and aging sponsored by the U.S. Department of Health, Education, and Welfare with no female participant, Johns Hopkins's obstetrician-gynecologist Howard Jones characterized menopausal women as being "a caricature of their younger selves at their emotional worst" (p. 338).

This conference occurred in 1971, and Scully and Bart's review of misogyny in gynecological textbooks was published in 1973. They observe that a few women may "slip through by chance or special privilege" (p. 350). Much has changed in the past twenty years as more and more women have entered medicine, especially the field of gynecology, and younger male physicians have been raised in the more enlightened atmosphere of post-1970 American society and education.

That abuses still occur in medical school and medical practice even for those women who "slipped through" is evidenced by the recent (June 1991) resignation of a Stanford professor of neurosurgery, Dr. Frances Conley, in protest over twenty-five years of being demeaned by male faculty at the Stanford University Medical Center, including being fondled and asked to bed (McCabe 1991). In a letter to *The San Francisco Chronicle* (June 4, 1991) she states she has decided to resign her tenured position in order to rebuild her "personal dignity." She had decided, in Vaclav Havel's terms, to "speak truth to power":

> I can't tell you how many times I have had some doctor run his hand up my leg. Many doctors comment on the size of staff members' breasts. Some women even have their bra straps snapped. [McCabe, p. A21]
>
> Even today, faculty are using slides of *Playboy* centerfolds to "spice up" lectures; sexist comments are frequent and those who are offended are told to be "less sensitive"; unsolicited touching and fondling occur between house staff and students. To complain might affect a performance evaluation.
>
> As a fellow faculty member, I felt I had the right to express an honest difference of opinion but found any deviation from the majority view often was announced prominently as a manifestation of either PMS syndrome or being "on the rag." I find myself unwilling to be called "hon" or "honey" with the same degree of sweet condescension used by this department for all women. [Conley, p. A21]

It may not be a coincidence that Dr. Conley is 50 years old. Her "change of life" involves a profound recognition that her identity as a surgeon had led to a compromise with her identity as a woman for all these years, and she refuses to be demeaned as a woman any longer. Her consciousness had been raised by hearing male and female medical students voice their complaints about the treatment of women at a faculty senate meeting the previous week, asking for greater respect for women. Dr. Conley is an example of a woman who pursued a professional career believing she could rise above the stigma of her gender. Her failure to engage in consciousness raising for herself 20 years ago resulted in her not having the support of the feminist movement to give her the strength to tackle these outrages years ago. We must recognize, however, that had she done so she might never have become a full professor. So, disheartened and discouraged, she sees no alternative but to resign and hope this act of courage and independence will have the political effect that she was not personally able to implement from within a male-dominated and sexist system. By September 1991, Dr. Conley returned to Stanford with promises of change by the administration. Her protest was successful, or so it now seems.

Bart and Grossman take the position that there are no "individual solutions" and that as feminist behavioral scientists they believe that societal problems cannot be dealt with except through the organized efforts of many women working together to structure alternatives for themselves and others. What these alternatives might be is not made clear, but perhaps they are referring to the efforts to create a women's health movement as women demand more knowledge and control over their own bodies.

Volume 2 of Notman and Nadelson's *The Woman Patient* (1982) contains a chapter by Notman called "Midlife Concerns of Women: Implications of the Menopause." She, like the other women physicians I have quoted, distinguishes between the symptoms that are directly related to the hormonal changes of menopause (hot flashes, night sweats, and vaginal dryness) and other symptoms (headaches, dizzy spells, palpitations, sleeplessness, depressions, and weight increase), which are not. She states that depression is more clearly associated with "psychosocial variables" although it does constitute an "important clinical entity" (p. 140).

> Weisman and Klerman concluded that the pattern of relationship between endocrine levels and clinical status is inconsistent and that there is good statistical evidence that menopause does not increase rates of depression. Other authors agree and cite the lack of studies using modern endocrinological methods that have shown correlations between clinical state and endocrine state. [p. 140]

Social class is an important variable, with middle- and upper-class women finding midlife more liberating because they have more alternatives open to them than do women of lower socioeconomic status. Bart and Grossman also cite research showing that cultural factors are important. It makes sense that in those cultures where a woman's status improves at middle age, there is a greater feeling of well-being at menopause. This is more likely to occur in cultures where women maintain a strong tie to their family of origin and kin, where women live in extended families, where there are institutionalized roles of grandmother and mother-in-law, and where the strong mother–child relationship is reciprocal in later life.

It may be that the greatest anxiety occurs in the years just prior to menopause when younger women are concerned with what menopause will be like for them, especially if a mother or other female relative or friend had had a bad time with menopause. Thus postmenopausal women had a more positive view than premenopausal women because they were no longer bothered by the myths and stories from family history.

Notman believes that the life stages of Erik Erikson do not work in the same sequential order for women, for whom an integration of autonomy and care persists through the stages of autonomy, identity, intimacy, and generativity. In this way women may be in different role patterns and phases at different times because of changing combinations of children, work, and marriage. Women's identity and autonomy issues may be resolved only partially in early adult years, then combined with the developmental experiences of motherhood, and then returned to when children are grown. This was illustrated in the cases of Mrs. P. and Mrs. R. and incorporates the work of Gilligan about care in women's hierarchy of values. A factor also involved but not mentioned by Notman would be the longer attachment of girls to their mothers, the Chodorow thesis, which extends into adulthood even if there may be some storminess in adolescence. Mrs. R. was working on psychological separation from her mother at age 42 even though she had left home for college, married, and raised two children. This is not uncommon with women well into their thirties and forties.

An interesting question related to the issue of separation is how a parental divorce might influence the development toward autonomy in both daughters and sons. What is the effect of the custody arrangement on later development? Are children who are raised only by mothers, either single or divorced, more likely to remain attached to the mother? How much does physical proximity reflect psychological dependence, or are they unrelated? Wallerstein (1989) reports that it is common for an older daughter to take a protective role toward her mother at the time of divorce and to help her mother with the care of younger children and with other responsibilities. This might have the effect of prolonging the mother-daughter attachment but in the reverse, with the mother dependent upon the daughter. This can also be true if a mother is ill or depressed. However, the added responsibility can lead to more independence for the daughter and thus greater autonomy later on.

For some midlife women there is no empty nest in that adult children do not always leave home; or if they do, they may return after losing a job or getting a divorce or because it's cheaper and more comfortable. A recent (June 16, 1991) news story *(New York Times)* is headlined "More Young Single Men Clinging to Apron Strings—Recession and Pampering Keep Sons at Home." According to the U.S. Bureau of the Census, the startling statistics are that among single adults between the ages of 25 and 34, a whopping 32 percent of men and 20 percent of women were living with their parents in 1990. The writer reports speculation that with divorce rates rising among parents, mothers who would otherwise be living alone may value the protection and companionship of an adult son, but there are no studies quoted to indicate whether in fact this pattern is occurring more in the cases of divorced mothers than in intact families. Judith Wallerstein (personal communication, June 1991) has found no tendency for adult children to be living at home with a divorced parent in her sample of children of divorce in Marin County, California. However, Marin is an affluent suburb of San Francisco and may not reflect the effects of the current recession as much as other parts of the country. In addition to the singles, there are married children living at home as well. This, combined with the care of grandchildren, makes the empty nest more theory than reality for many midlife women today.

Another chapter, "Marriage and Midlife: the Impact of Social Change" by Nadelson, Polonsky, and Mathews, reports on a number of studies showing that early life problems may be indicative of midlife problems, but that personality changes can and do occur in middle age. Women apparently become more assertive and less restricted or guilty. Men become more contemplative and nurturing, reversing traditional masculine and feminine qualities (Neugarten 1968). Marital satisfaction is reported to be greater for women after children leave home. In some cases the strains related to social changes, such as a wife returning to school or work and attaining increased self-esteem at a time when the husband may be experiencing physical decline can lead to sexual acting out on the part of a husband who fears the loss of sexual vigor. Being abandoned by a husband in a midlife crisis for a younger woman can create quite a midlife crisis for a wife after a long-term marriage. Robert Butler (1985) writes:

> Sexuality in general is a major issue in midlife. Masters and Johnson report, as have Kinsey and others, continuing sexual activity far into old age. Yet, fears and the reality of impotence are a common problem in the middle-aged man. Nothing illustrates the fears surrounding sexual potency more than the controversy over the possibility of men with cardiac disease dying during intercourse. The risk is greater in sedentary men when they are under stress or when intercourse is extramarital, alcohol-involved, after a heavy meal, or in unfamiliar surroundings. The most common cause of impotence in the middle years is not aging, but excessive alcoholic intake; drugs, such as tranquilizers and antidepressants; and stress with fatigue and anxiety. [p. 1949]

A loss of sexuality in a woman's midlife may occur as a result of her husband's impotence because of illness or depression. The common practice of women marrying older men can create another job of caretaking for a middle-aged woman whose older husband becomes ill.

WOMEN IN LITERATURE—CAROLYN HEILBRUN

Heilbrun, a professor of literature, alias Amanda Cross, a detective story writer, has written *Writing a Woman's Life* (1988), a postfeminist version of Virginia Woolf's *A Room of One's Own* that focuses on female characters in fiction, and women writers of fiction, but also on the positive changes in character that occur in women over 50. It might be called "A Life of One's Own." She considers her book a feminist undertaking and defines feminist in the words of Nancy Miller as

> the wish "to articulate a self-consciousness about women's identity both as inherited cultural fact and as process of social construction" and to "protest against the available fiction of female becoming." Women's lives, like women's writing have, in Miller's words, a particularly "vulnerable relation to the culture's central notions of plausibility." It is hard to suppose women can mean or want what we have always been assured they could not possibly mean or want. [p. 18]

Heilbrun finds that the negative use of the term *feminist ideology* has now replaced the earlier criticism of women's words as "shrill" and "strident" as a response to the unacceptability of women's power.

> Although feminists early discovered that the private is the public, women's exercise of power and control, and the admission and expression of anger necessary to that exercise, has until recently been declared unacceptable. . . . Power is the ability to take one's place in whatever discourse is essential to action and the right to have one's part matter. [p. 18]

She believes that when women writers sought female models for self-realization and achievement, they had to find the model in a woman who had died, and found it only with the encouragement of the current feminist movement. She quotes Maxine Kumin: "I began as a poet in the Dark Ages of the fifties with very little sense of who I was—a wife, a daughter, a mother, a college instructor, a swimmer, a horse lover, a hermit—a stewpot of conflicting emotions" (p. 66). Heilbrun goes on to say: "We must recognize what the past suggests: women are well beyond youth when they begin, often unconsciously, to create another story. Not even then do they recognize it as another story" (p. 109). She tells about the history of women writing under pseudonyms, about her own pseudonym, Amanda Cross, and the creation of her character Kate Fansler, a female detective who was a fantasy woman in Heilbrun's imagination, a woman who led a life very unlike her own. Heilbrun is married, has three children, and is a tenured university professor. Kate Fansler is unmarried, has no children, and is "unconstrained by the opinions of others, rich and beautiful" (p. 115). By creating Kate Fansler and her quests she was re-creating herself and adds that for women writers this act of self-creation comes later in life than for male writers. George Eliot and Willa Cather were both 38 when their first fiction was published. "Acting to confront society's expectations for oneself requires either the mad daring of youth, or the colder determination of middle age. Men tend to move on a fairly predictable path to achievement, women transform themselves only after an awakening. And that awakening is identifiable only in hindsight" (p. 118).

Heilbrun says that her character Kate has taught her many things, but mostly about aging. Once beautiful, she is still attractive, but no longer beautiful and not concerned with her looks.

> But most important, she has become braver as she has aged, less interested in the opinions of those she does not cherish, and has come to realize that she has little to lose, little any longer to risk, that age above all, both for those with children and those without them, is the time when there is very little "they" can do for you, very little reason to fear, or hide, or not attempt brave and important things. Lear said, "I will do such things, what they are yet I know not, but they shall be the terrors of the earth." He said this in impotent rage in his old age, but Kate Fansler has taught me to say it in the bravery and power of age. [p. 123]

Virginia Woolf is an example to Heilbrun of a woman writer who found a "new and remarkable" kind of courage when she was 50. She believes this is unique to women, an experience for which there is no male counterpart in our society. At age 50 Woolf wrote *The Years* and *Three Guineas,* both books that "affront the sensibilities of almost all her male critics." In these two books Woolf expresses anger at society's deprivation of women, whereas in *A Room of One's Own,* according to Heilbrun, Woolf "never presses against the bounds of properly charming female behavior" (p. 126). In *Three Guineas* she was finally able to find the courage to "say the unacceptable, an extraordinary release." An earlier chapter in Heilbrun's book opened with a quote by Gloria Steinem. Steinem said that Marilyn Monroe "was a female impersonator; we are all trained to be female impersonators":

> It is perhaps only in old age, certainly past fifty, that women can stop being female impersonators, can grasp the opportunity to reverse their most cherished principles of "femininity." . . . Most often, particularly with the support of other women, the coming of age portends all the freedoms men have always known and women never—mostly the

freedom from fulfilling the needs of others and from being a female
impersonator. [pp. 126, 130]

As in many stories about women, too often young women follow
familiar scripts that promise a happy ending in return for passivity and
premature closure. Those who are privileged—in tenured faculty positions, established psychotherapists and analysts, and our patients who have
succeeded as wives and mothers and even added a career, those with an
assured place and financial security—are "in danger of choosing to stay
right where we are, to undertake each day's routine, and to listen to our
arteries hardening." This was the dilemma Mrs. R. faced. She thought she
needed a divorce to roust her from her comfortable nest. Heilbrun urges
women to "make use of our security, our seniority, to take risks, to make
noise, to be courageous, to become unpopular. . . . The old woman must
be glimpsed through all her disguises which seem to preclude her right to
be called woman. She may well for the first time be woman herself" (p.
131).

Women at 50 are described by Greenwood, Bolen, Artson, Rubin,
Heilbrun, and others as at a true crossroads. As therapists we have an
opportunity, like Hecate, as wise women, to guide them through this new
phase of life, one that may have the promise of growth and development,
of creativity, freedom, and fun. The answer to the question, Is there life
after children? seems to be a definite yes!

THE OLDER WOMAN

The fastest growing group of people in the United States today consists of
women over 85. The organizing of older women has also been an outgrowth of the feminist movement. The Older Women's League, a national
organization, was founded in 1980 to fight discrimination against older
women. Edinburg, in Notman and Nadelson's *The Woman Patient* (1982),
writes about the older woman. For women over 65, widowhood is almost
inevitable; 70 percent of women over 75 are widows, whereas 75 percent
of men over 65 are living with their wives. For men over 65 the remarriage
rate is five times than that of women over 55, and the men remarry faster.
Yet depression is a serious problem for older men and thus for their wives.
White males aged 70 to 74 commit suicide at a rate nearly three times as
high as that of nonwhite men and nearly five times as high as that of all
women the same age. It has often been noted that women handle widowhood better than men handle being widowers, but the financial position of
older women is a major social disgrace. It reveals the cumulative effects of
the lifelong disadvantages of being a woman in a society that depreciates

the value of the labor of women and does not value the extended family or have a dignified role for older women. The philosophical position in the European tradition that places the rights of the individual above the state has been extended in modern America to the family and takes its worst toll on the aging woman living alone (Ness 1991).

According to the 1990 U.S. Census report, 14 percent of women over 65 were living below the poverty line. In 1989 the percentage of elderly women living alone in poverty or near it was 45 percent. For men it was 38 percent. The median income for men 65 and over in 1989 was $13,107, whereas for women it was $7,655. The loss of her husband's pension upon his death has sunk many widows below the poverty line. Having been housewives all their lives, they have no pension of their own. Even those who worked most of their lives received such low pay that combined pension and Social Security payments are too low for a decent standard of living, by American standards.

There are really two categories of older women. In the first group are those who are alert, active, and involved with their family and community, who do volunteer work, travel, and enjoy life with a husband or friends. These elderly are politically organized and have become a strong advocacy group for the preservation of Social Security, Medicare, and other federal programs for older Americans. They may be married or widowed. The other group are those who need care, and it is often the healthy aged who provide care for the ill aged. Women in their sixties and seventies may be caring for a husband, a parent or in-law, an aunt, or a sibling. Other women are in nursing homes, either because there is no family member to care for them or because they require too much care for the family to sustain. As noted by Butler (1989), all the elderly experience multiple losses, and therefore older people expend enormous amounts of emotional and physical energy grieving and resolving grief, adapting to the changes that result from loss, and recovering from the stresses inherent in these crises.

CLINICAL ILLUSTRATION: "C."—MAXWELL GITELSON

There is not much mention of the elderly in the general psychiatric literature. A separate literature has developed, along with a separate field, gerontology. It is hard to find case examples of psychoanalysis or psychotherapy with older women, although there has been some attention to the problems of aging men who experience severe depression. Many therapists have not felt as inspired to work with older people as with younger patients. In a chapter by Gitelson (1965) published in a book edited by Berezin and Cath, *Geriatric Psychiatry,* we find a detailed description of a twice-weekly psychotherapy with a woman of 66 who had formerly been in analysis for two years at age 42. Maxwell Gitelson describes the case as "the survival of the sexual impulse and the capacity for an erotic transference in an elderly woman" (p. 160). (He was younger than his patient, and I would suspect that at a later point in his own life he would not think of 66 as "elderly.") The patient, C., arrived suffering from severe insomnia and depression following the death of her husband six months previously; she immediately asked for electroshock treatment. It was not a happy marriage for her, and she had not been sexually attracted to her husband, participating in sex only to please him. After her earlier analysis was interrupted because her analyst moved to another locale, she had decided to remain in the marriage and make the best of it. Gitelson says: "she immersed herself in her husband's business and in this fashion lived out his life with him" (p. 161). It is remarkable that Gitelson says "his life" rather than "her" life. It is hard to know if this is a reflection of the patient's communications or his own view of the relationship and her demeaned position.

Gitelson describes her involvement in therapy as a "persistent and sustained effort to get at causes," which was in contrast to her analysis of twenty years before, during which she was much more resistant.

> The consequence of her new effort was a persistent, intellectual puzzling about her condition, which introduced a wealth of the kind of material that one ordinarily encounters in an analytic situation. . . . As treatment advanced there was a gradual disappearance of this emotional muting, with a transition from diffidence to friendly rapport and then to a degree of observable warmth. In the end there was explicit transference resentment. [p. 165]

He describes his approach as one in which he refrained from gratuitous supportive intervention and made a technical effort to evoke the positive transference and to make it acceptable. A key feature in her history was a strong erotic love for a man that was never consummated. A contact with this man, owing to which she had experienced strong sexual arousal for the first time in her life, had precipitated her first analysis at age 42.

The patient, C., made significant improvement in the course of her psychotherapy. She achieved a zest for life and only occasional depression. She became active as a grandmother, and pursued lifelong political and social interests. The case is a good example of how much positive change can result from psychotherapy with older women.

TRANSFERENCE AND COUNTERTRANSFERENCE WITH THE OLDER PATIENT

Unfortunately, in the discussion following the lengthy case illustration by Gitelson, Grete L. Bibring states:

> As far as the general concept of the aged person, especially of the aged female, is concerned, this patient represents an exception; and if "average" is used as an equivalent of normal, this patient is abnormal, or deviant. . . . Dr. Gitelson's paper, therefore, contains a challenge to the customary and, as I believe, unrefined, undifferentiated prejudicial consensus on aging. [p. 187]

Yet I wonder why she views C. as an exception, especially as a woman. She goes on to comment that when she had studied older women, she too had observed the same persistence of sexual impulses and fantasies, suggesting that a revision of ideas about the weakening of sexual impulses and erotic fantasies in older women may be necessary. I suspect that just as psychoanalysts have depreciated younger women compared with men, so have they underestimated the intelligence and capacity for insight, of older women and their commitment to working toward change.

Butler (1989) comments on countertransference issues:

> Countertransference issues toward aging persons are serious. It is essential that new attitudes be developed toward the psychiatric evaluation and treatment of older persons and the use of individual psychotherapy. Interactions with aged patients stimulate therapists' fears about their own old age and remind them of conflicts in their relationships with parental figures. Therapists often believe, incorrectly, that nothing useful can be offered because older persons cannot change and that psychodynamic skills are wasted in work with the aged. . . . Time devoted by psychiatrists and other mental health professionals to older patients is disproportionate to their numbers, the severity of their illnesses, and the likelihood of successful treatment. [p. 2018]

Oremland (1991) comments on changing concepts of time:

> Younger patients may see time for psychotherapy as a something taken from them. Older patients endow time with a different meaning; for them, time is something taken from them that can never be replaced. The different view of time between young and old can make psychotherapy more important to the older patient. As a woman in her 60's beginning her second analysis said, "I don't think I have the luxury this time of putting things off for my next analysis." For older psychotherapists, the feeling that something irreplaceable is being taken from them can become a difficult countertransference response to the reluctant or unresponsive patient. [p. 98]

GROUPS FOR THE ELDERLY—MARCIA AMADA

It is also true that some elderly are resistant to psychotherapy because they were raised in an era when it was associated with shame and embarrassment. They may be more likely to accept counseling or a support group. At Rafael Convalescent Hospital in San Rafael, a suburb of San Francisco, a full-time social worker on the staff, Marcia Amada, has a monthly support group for the alert women patients. They talk about their adjustment to the nursing home, feelings of neglect by their family, and the death of other patients. Sometimes members of the group die, and the group meetings are an opportunity to discuss the surviving members' sense of loss and their own fears of dying.

Amada also co-led a support group for widows and widowers with social worker Irving Kermish and two widowed nurses for five years, meeting weekly on Sunday, the loneliest day, on a no-fee basis. Kermish and Amada believed that their group prevented premature institutionalization for the members because of the support provided by the leaders and from members to help each other. In one instance, a member took care of another member's dog while she was in the hospital and did her food shopping for her when she came home. Some of the members were quite emotionally fragile and dependent on the group. When Kermish and Amada decided to end the group after five years, the members moved into facilities that provided more care, but did stay in touch with each other and continued to meet.

Another group Amada has led is for the Alzheimer's Association, in which she meets with the wives of Alzheimer husbands. She commented (personal communication, September 1991) that some of these older women have always depended on their husbands to make all the decisions and handle the finances. Now they have to become strong and independent to take care of their husbands and themselves. The wife herself may be struggling with medical problems and for the first time must bear responsibilities that have been traditionally male as well as provide physical care.

VITAL INVOLVEMENT IN OLD AGE—ERIK AND JOAN ERIKSON

Vital Involvement in Old Age (1986), written by two octogenarians, Erik and Joan Erikson, and a midlife woman, Helen Kivnick, uses Erikson's well-known eight stages of life by way of showing how the mental health of an aging person illustrates the cumulative effect of the psychosocial development preceding this period of life; what they call an epigenetic theory of the stages of human life as completed in old age. Their research involved in-depth interviews with twenty-nine people aged 75 to 95 who were the remaining parents of 248 infants born in Berkeley in 1928 and observed by the Institute of Human Development at the University of California. The Eriksons had available to them the records of the Guidance

Study of the Institute. When the children were 17, in 1945–1946, the parents had been interviewed alone, the focus being the parents' own personal lives and problems. In 1968 the parents of the now 49-year-old children were again interviewed.

The eight stages produce the strengths necessary for a mutual involvement in an ever-increasing social radius, from infancy through adulthood and into old age. The current study was interested in the remaining or new potentials of the last interactions and the vital involvement in the necessary disinvolvements of old age. The goals of the eight stages have been the achievement of hope, will, purpose, competence, fidelity, love, care, and finally, wisdom. The eighth stage involves the achievement of integrity over despair.

> Integrity, we suggested, now is and must be the dominant syntonic disposition, in search of balance with an equally pervasive sense of despair. As for the final strength, wisdom, we have formulated it thus: Wisdom is detached concern with life itself, in the face of death itself. It maintains and learns to convey the integrity of experience, in spite of the decline of bodily and mental functions. [pp. 37–38]

They further extend the eight-stage chart by proposing that each stage has a maladaptive tendency and a malignant tendency. In old age, the maladaptive state would be "presumption" and the malignant state would be "disdain."

> Wisdom, then, probably is truly involved disinvolvement. Otherwise, the remaining involvement is a continuation of care, as it has become focused on procreativity and/or productivity, and/or creativity. But the new affiliation now offered is some kind of grandparenthood . . . which must remain loyal to a defined and planned role for old age within an order of wisdom. [p. 51]

The Eriksons found that a complex process, partly conscious and partly unconscious, goes on in the elderly, in which they attempt to reconcile the earlier psychosocial themes and integrate them in relation to current, old-age development, attempting to make of the entire life cycle a unified whole.

> It is through this last stage that the life cycle weaves back on itself in its entirety, ultimately integrating maturing forms of hope, will, purpose, competence, fidelity, love, and care into a comprehensive sense of wisdom. . . . Those nearing the end of the life cycle find themselves struggling to accept the inalterability of the past and the unknowability of the future, to acknowledge possible mistakes and omissions, and to

balance consequent despair with the sense of overall integrity that is essential to carrying on. [pp. 55–56]

In a letter to the March 1991 conference titled "Women's lives," Joan Erikson wrote that old age is "remarkably interesting." In a beautiful piece of metaphoric writing, she tells the audience that it is not in the least like sliding downhill but much more like plodding up a mountain, the pathway getting narrower and steeper. She writes that you learn to watch your step, keeping as aware as possible of footholds.

> You lighten your backpack as you find so many things are dispensable, in order to free your hands as a safeguard against your upsetting imbalance.
> As you look down on the world you are climbing away from and review the events of the twentieth century, despair is easy: wars, violence. You feel change is imperative. Will we find out in time how to settle disputes without violence and vicious threats? As you continue you must muster enough energy to climb the next stretch to a resting stop where at dusk the stars shine out full of promise and hope.

Her health did not allow her to make the trip from Boston to San Francisco to speak at the conference, but she surely made her presence felt with her words.

CONCLUSION: THE IMPORTANCE OF DIGNITY AND INTEGRITY

In thinking back to Dr. Frances Conley's resignation from her professorship at Stanford, I am struck by her statement that she had everything in her outstanding career but "personal dignity," and that her resignation was in order to rebuild her personal dignity. Integrity, I propose, can only follow from a sense of personal dignity, and Dr. Conley recognized with early wisdom that no matter what professional success she might achieve, success without dignity was leading her to despair.

A number of feminist writers have criticized Erik Erikson's earlier writing for his failure to recognize the special problems for women in proceeding through his stages, which are biased toward autonomy until stages 6 and 7, intimacy and generativity, and especially for his earlier error in stating that women achieve their identity through marriage, whereas men achieve it through work. Women, according to feminist theory, do not achieve their identity through marriage and child rearing. They need a room of their own and time alone to discover who they are and what they can contribute. This may not occur until midlife for a woman who marries and bears children in her twenties. The achievement of integrity for a woman may take the special effort involved in overcoming the sense of inferiority imposed on her by a patriarchal society: the belittlement of her knowledge and work. Thus a very internal self-acceptance and self-appreciation, perhaps in the context of a women's group, is required of a woman in order to integrate the meaning of her life's work of independent pursuits and the caring for others—children, husband, friends, grandchildren, elderly parents. If she entered a male-dominated profession or trade, she has had a very special personal battle to maintain dignity. If she succeeds, she is doubly rewarded; if she fails, no monetary reward can compensate for the loss of dignity and integrity.

Unlike Freud and Deutsch, I believe that midlife can be a most useful time for psychotherapy for women. For those who have never been in therapy, this can finally be a time to focus on themselves and to get insight into the decisions they have made earlier in their lives; a time for a life review, from which they can emerge better able to approach the losses of aging along with the opportunities and the freedoms of aging. Those who have had psychotherapy can use the insights of the past to help them consolidate a new identity as mature women with choices to make for the remaining third of life, a time filled with potential for creative and useful work as well as pleasure.

Margaret Mahler's biographer, Paul E. Stepansky (1988), writes that when Mahler wrote her will she named as the sole residuary legatee of her estate the Grey Panthers Project Fund, with the request that her legacy be used to assist elderly, indigent academicians and scholars in their work. As analysts and feminists age, we will be more attentive to the needs of older citizens, and our attitudes will be affected toward a more positive countertransference with our older patients.

I believe that an integration of the best of feminist theory with the best of psychoanalytic theory can combine to show us the way to help women of all ages to live their own lives as healthy adults and at the same time relate to husbands, children, bosses, lovers, and parents as whole people in reciprocally rewarding relationships without sacrificing their own mental health or destroying the genuine mental health of the male establishment. Men are only demeaning to women who assert themselves in traditionally male territory if they have an irrational fear of female power and thus a need to segregate women into positions where they can be controlled by men. This thinking has kept the sexes apart in a way that has weakened them both, because each has been kept deprived of the other's wisdom.

9

ABORTION: WHO DECIDES?

Six million is the number generally assigned not only to Jews who died under Hitler but to babies who have died under the Supreme Court.
—Patrick Riley, *National Catholic Register*

The life of the law is not logic, but experience.
—Oliver Wendell Holmes

If men risked pregnancy each time they had sexual relations, abortion would be a sacrament.
—Florynce Kennedy, attorney

THE HISTORY OF ABORTION

The history of Western religion sheds light on the changing attitude toward abortion. According to Elaine Pagels (1989), Jesus and his followers had "startlingly different attitudes" toward divorce, procreation, and family from those of the Jews and the pagans within the Roman Empire.

> Many pagans who had been brought up to regard marriage essentially as a social and economic arrangement, homosexual relationships as an expected element of male education, prostitution both male and female

> as both ordinary and legal, and divorce, abortion, contraception and
> exposure of unwanted infants as matters of practical expedience,
> embraced . . . the Christian message, which opposed these practices.
> [p. 10]

Generations of Jewish teachers had warned that pagans thought nothing of pederasty, promiscuity, and incest, yet pagans found circumcision peculiar and barbaric and criticized the Jews for polygamy. Jewish divorce law granted divorce rights to the husband but not to the wife. For "over a millennium Jews had taught that the purpose of marriage, and therefore sexuality, was procreation, thus prostitution, homosexuality, abortion and infanticide were opposed by Jewish law" (p. 12). In Genesis (1:28) God commanded "be fruitful and multiply, and fill the Earth."

Jesus preached against divorce, which was accepted by the Jews. It is of interest that one of the grounds for divorce was if the wife was barren, because of the obligation in marriage to procreate (p. 14). This focus on multiplying was so strong that the practice of taking a younger wife as the first wife reached menopause helped to extend the procreative life of the man and thus provide him with a larger family. Perhaps this practice extends to contemporary life, without the advantage of the large family but with the perceived advantage of a younger woman as a wife for an aging male, to help him with his failing potency.

The world, no longer in need of an expanding population, now suffers from problems of overpopulation. The biblical direction to be fruitful and multiply has been most successful, but to continue to believe that it is a moral imperative to bear as many children as possible is to disregard changing reality. Thus, to understand the current high emotional level of the debate over abortion, we must look beyond the early Jewish and Christian teachings.

On the conscious level, the content of the arguments on abortion are legal, medical, psychiatric, and moral. Like the discourse in analysis and therapy, the meaning is drawn not from the content alone but from the unconscious level as well. In the case of the battles over abortion, I believe the meaning lies in the unconscious fear of the power of mothers and the helplessness of babies. A feminist psychoanalytic view of abortion allows us to see through the various arguments and inconsistencies to the core of the matter: the fear by men and women alike of female power and freedom; of entrusting the power to make the decision to the woman herself. The work by Dinnerstein and Miller on the fear of women, based on the fear of children of their mother's imagined omnipotence, is the way to understand the intensity of the drama on this issue. A woman with the power of life and death over her unborn child is the nightmare of every child become a reality: the wicked witch, the evil stepmother of children's stories comes alive in the image of the evil woman who would "murder" the innocent baby entrusted to her care. It is Hansel and Gretel, Cinderella, Sleeping Beauty, and the Wizard of Oz all rolled up in one. Thus largely male institutions—the church, the courts, the legislatures, and the medical profession—have maintained this power over women, the power to decide whether or not a woman may receive an abortion legally.

In the late 1860s medical societies throughout the United States passed resolutions attacking the prevalence of abortion and birth control and condemned physicians who performed and condoned these illicit practices. Abortions were available in cities and in rural areas from abortionists, and abortifacients could be purchased through the mail. The Michigan Board of Health estimated in 1898 that one-third of all that state's pregnancies ended in abortion, 70 to 80 percent of them secured by prosperous respectable married women. By the 1880s, English medical moralists referred to birth control as the "American sin." Nineteenth-century American women tried to prevent pregnancy and had abortions out of fear of the pain and possible death or injury associated with childbirth, because of economic considerations, and to achieve greater liberty and autonomy (Smith-Rosenberg 1972).

The medical establishment was outraged. In 1871 the American Medical Association's Committee on Criminal Abortion described such women in terms that could hardly qualify as scientific objectivity:

> She becomes unmindful of the course marked out for her by Providence, she overlooks the duties imposed on her by the marriage contract. She yields to the pleasures—but shrinks from the pains and responsibilities of maternity; and, destitute of all delicacy and refinement, resigns herself, body and soul, into the hands of unscrupulous and wicked men. Let not the husband of such a wife flatter himself that he possesses her affection. Nor can she in turn ever merit even the respect of a virtuous husband. She sinks into old age like a withered tree, stripped of its foliage; with the stain of blood upon her soul, she dies without the hand of affection to smooth her pillow. [in Smith-Rosenberg 1972, p. 29]

Family planning was clearly seen as a step toward female emancipation—to new roles and a new autonomy, and the men of the American Medical Association were hostile to such advances in the liberation of women. But for centuries, and still in most of the world, women have not been intimidated by male laws and have taken the power into their own hands, returning the medical role to women who often help each other as they did in the thirteenth through the sixteenth centuries when women were the midwives, wise elders, and herbalists and performed abortions. Unfortunately, this method does not provide the best medical techniques and the advantages of hospital cleanliness. It is women who must bear the burden of the birth and care of the infant and child, and clearly they have made and continue to make their own decisions about their pregnancies. Women in poverty, and with a large family already, know that any more children will be more than their physical and mental health can bear. For middle-class women, the issue is truly more a matter of choice.

Abortion—and I speak of induced abortion rather than spontaneous abortion or miscarriage—is one of those issues where no truly good solution exists. As with divorce when children are involved, the best we can hope for is a balancing of relative harms. Is it more harmful to the mother to abort the fetus than to carry it to term and have it adopted? Is it more harmful to a child to be born unwanted than not to be born at all? Is the mental health of the mother more important than allowing a fetus to develop? All these questions are debated rationally at times, but it is clear that there are irrational components to the debate as well. The irrational side emerges around the issue of who has the power to decide. Is it the church, the legislature, the court, the psychiatrist, or the woman herself? Those who fear leaving the decision up to the woman are in favor of giving that power to the church or the state. Yet on other issues those same people are opposed to power in the hands of the state and favor individualism. Some who favor individualism when it comes to the woman's right to make her own decision favor the power of the state when it comes to other issues such as pornography and the protection of women and children from violence in the home. In the famous Lincoln–Douglas debates, Douglas argued that the government should not take a position on the moral question of slavery. Lincoln said that the government should take a position, and we fought the Civil War based largely on that belief. How one resolves the moral issue is a personal matter, but we would probably all agree that Lincoln was right, that the government did have a moral obligation to end slavery, and that the right of the slave to freedom was greater than the right of the slaveholder to continue to own him—even though he had legally bought him. Is abortion a moral issue that calls for government intervention, or is it a private sexual matter between adults, or between a woman and her own conscience? Our history is replete with instances of government imposing its moral values about sex on individual citizens. It is not surprising that neither feminist nor psychoanalytic theory opposes abortion, because both are predicated on the rights of the individual.

The availability of abortion affects the lives of women from the beginning of the reproductive state at age 12 until menopause at age 50. An unwanted pregnancy can occur in the life of a young adolescent, a late adolescent, an unmarried or divorced woman at any age, a newly married woman who is not ready for children, and a long-term married woman who already has several children. It can happen to a married woman, as it did to a patient of mine, as a result of an extramarital affair or in an unhappy marriage at the point when she is considering a divorce. It can be the result of rape or incest. Gilligan (1982) found that some pregnancies coincided with efforts on the part of the women to end a relationship and served to express ambivalence or as a way of putting the relationship to the ultimate test of commitment, a way of testing truth, thereby making the baby an ally in the search for male support and protection or, if that failed, making the baby a companion victim of male rejection. The various circumstances may provoke more or less sympathy, but that does not change the core question, Who decides?

Since the legalization of abortion in the United States, 1.5 to 1.6 million abortions are performed annually. In 1987, almost 60 percent of abortion patients were under age 25, 82 percent were not married, and half had never given birth. Nearly 69 percent were white, and abortions were most often performed in the first trimester, the median gestational age being 9.2 weeks.

CLINICAL ILLUSTRATION

Abortion needs to be seen as a failure in contraception, and in this sense we as therapists sometimes see how emotional needs and psychological reenactments interfere with the use of contraception and lead to an unwanted pregnancy. Some women have repeated unwanted pregnancies and thus repeated abortions. I have had several patients with this syndrome and have found it difficult in several cases to interpret effectively soon enough to avoid a second abortion, although the patient could easily see and acknowledge how self-destructive her behavior was.

In the case of Melissa, described in Chapter 2, the patient had had four abortions before beginning therapy with me. I made that issue one of the first priorities and discussed contraception with her, expressing my concern about her health. Melissa had lost her mother to alcoholism and her father to death in her midadolescence and had started dating inappropriate men who mistreated her. I interpreted her unwanted pregnancies as attempts to compensate for her guilt in regard to the death of her father, but I also believed that this 22-year-old woman had been so damaged by the disruption of her family that her unwanted pregnancies were an extension of the chaotic life that her mother's drinking and infidelities had created in the household. Melissa was bright and functioning well on her job as a legal secretary, but her love life was always in chaos, as described earlier. She had been using drugs for several years until she attended a drug rehabilitation program as an outpatient, before starting psychotherapy with me. Fortunately, the woman lawyer for whom she worked realized her need and, being a former patient of mine, referred her to me. The use of drugs was partially due to associating with men who were drug users and, I suspect, also a way of dealing with the painful loss of her father and painful disillusionment with her mother. The drugs had helped her to deny the effects of these two traumatic losses but also left her incapable of using contraceptives effectively.

Being in psychotherapy helped Melissa a great deal. After a year and a half she was able to return to college. A stable relationship with a helpful woman therapist provided the transition she needed from her interrupted adolescence into adult womanhood, a transition badly disturbed by her mother's addiction. She had several boyfriends during her two-year therapy with me but never became pregnant. Her increasing sense of worth based on our analysis and reevaluation of her college failure, very negative self-comparison with her older sister, underestimation of her intelligence, and inability to set boundaries with men led to an increased sense of hope and self-confidence. Her improved ego functioning allowed the responsible use of contraceptives.

Melissa's case points up the truth that even with the availability of contraception there will be times in a girl's or woman's life when the chaos and confusion of traumatic events will disable her temporarily and she is at high risk of poor judgment, abandoning herself as she has been abandoned. Abortion may be the best alternative at those times.

In one unusual case, my patient was so determined not to have children that she convinced a doctor to perform a tubal ligation on her when she was only 23. That took care of the contraception problem, but in her late twenties she met and fell in love with a man who wanted a child. They married with the understanding that she would do all she could to reverse the procedure. When she began therapy with me she was very depressed because in spite of several surgical procedures she was not able to conceive. Each month when her menses arrived, she was sent into a depression, and then at each ovulation she got her hopes up again. She and her husband joined a group of infertile couples where they traded information and gave each other support for their frustrations. My patient felt like a fraud because of her earlier surgery, and out of shame and fear of rejection she never told anyone in the group that her problem was self-inflicted.

During the course of her therapy with me, she came to understand how her unhappy childhood and poor relationship with her own parents had led her to reject motherhood. As she was able to sort out the irrational components of her earlier choice, she became more unhappy about her situation. She and her husband decided to try in vitro fertilization despite the expense and the many procedures she would have to endure. The story has a happy ending because she did conceive and deliver a healthy baby and was very happy with motherhood. It is unfortunate that she did not choose therapy before her decision for a tubal ligation and that her health plan so readily granted her request.

The conflicts around motherhood—loss of freedom; interruption of career; demands of a child; and fears of merger, loss of body shape, and the recapitulation of an unhappy childhood with hostile feelings between parents and children—combine to make the abortion decision a clear one for many women. For others there is a sincere wish for a child, but without marriage and with the reality of facing the economic and emotional responsibility for raising a child alone, many women sadly decide that they must abort the pregnancy.

Of all issues, that of abortion has challenged the ideal of "sisterhood" in the feminist movement the most. Here is an issue affecting all women in which women are on both sides, are angry and accusatory of each other, and in which the vision of mutual support and solidarity among women has been most sorely tried. The two sides seem to be irrevocably split about what is best for women and children. The rancor between women on the abortion issue divides women not by class or race (although there are some class factors) but by ideology. Woman as maternal nurturer whose life is meant for motherhood, an ideology often held by religious and conservative women, contrasts with the view that a woman's life is her own; her autonomy and freedom from childbearing are more essential to her being and society than her role and duties as mother. "Pro-life" women oppose feminism and praise the traditional view of women as primarily wives and mothers. Yet the urge for motherhood among feminists sometimes emerges in their thirties or forties and the use of artificial insemination or adoption by single women determined to be mothers is no longer uncommon when marriage is not an option.

Abortion, legal or not, has been used by women for centuries and will continue to be used to terminate pregnancy. In some countries it is a common form of birth control. Psychoanalytic and psychiatric views of abortion can be found in the professional literature, starting with Helene Deutsch.

HELENE DEUTSCH

Deutsch (1945) discusses abortion in the context of the two problems of sterility and compulsive pregnancy. She regards ambivalence about pregnancy as normal:

> What seems most important to me, however, is the fact that there is in almost every pregnant woman a constantly active tendency to interrupt the harmony of the pregnancy state. I have found this tendency repeatedly in both healthy and neurotic individuals. But an excessively strong or abnormal reaction to the physiologic signals that are normal in pregnancy takes place only if additional motives leading to a quantitative increase of the normal response are present. [p. 130]

She recognizes that the legal and religious sanctions may be powerful for some women yet also states that the "secular and religious laws are sometimes used as rationalizations that conceal deeper psychologic motivation against abortion" (p. 179). Speaking personally, she states: "In my view, every woman has the right to achieve motherhood and to renounce motherhood, and every normal woman seems to assume this right emotionally, whether it is legal or not" (p. 179).

Deutsch divides women who become pregnant outside of marriage into three groups, based on their reactions:

1. The "revolutionary" reaction gives the victory to motherliness in its struggle against society, and the woman decides to take all the consequences and assume social responsibility for the child.
2. The woman accepts it as an inescapable personal fate, in the face of which she feels helpless.
3. The third type of reaction—outwardly perhaps the best adjusted to reality—consists in an attempt to eliminate the consequences by abortion. . . .

> An active-aggressive woman may resist social morality and keep the child or, appealing to the idea of equal rights with men and sexual freedom . . . may unhesitatingly eliminate the child. The passive woman will not permit her desire for a child to interfere with the

convention and will eliminate it as a matter of course, under outside pressure. [pp. 180–181]

In describing pregnancy and abortion in married and unmarried women, Deutsch attempts to analyze the psychological reactions and concludes that the reaction to abortion depends upon the motives for it. She believes that a "harmonious-motherly woman," happy with her other children, reacts to the loss rationally, without further emotional complications. The woman who compulsively becomes pregnant reacts to an induced abortion either with severe neurotic symptoms or with an immediately following new conception. "The immediate reaction is often very characteristic: it is a kind of triumph over her own compulsion to be pregnant, which she had defeated by abortion. But shortly afterward a depression or a new pregnancy sets in" (p. 181).

Yet Deutsch believed that even if the woman consciously desires to end a pregnancy, such pregnancies "nevertheless fulfill old wishes" and therefore interruption of them is traumatic. She also recognizes that an unexpected pregnancy itself is an interruption of "an existing psychologic order" but the additional interruption by an abortion also breaks off the "psychologic process that accompanies the biologic events." She concludes that therefore the psychological picture is a complicated one.

An old wish fulfillment is interrupted, the trauma of the conception is only apparently repaired by the abortion, de facto it is complicated by a new trauma. . . . The social conflict alone can be solved and avoided by abortion. . . . The inner attachment, the identification with the child that we consider characteristic of pregnancy, takes place despite the external circumstances. [p. 183]

However, she makes a statement that in my view is incorrect. She says "the subsequent reaction to an abortion may be stronger than that to separation from the child after it is born" (p. 183). It is not clear how she arrives at this conclusion, but in my experience it is quite the opposite. Later I will give two case examples of women patients who had given birth out of wedlock and given up the baby for adoption. That separation, as I will describe, resulted in lifelong pain to these two women, whereas I have never had a case where abortion resulted in any comparably severe emotional reaction by the woman. The difference between knowing what month a baby would have been born, and actually carrying a pregnancy to term, feeling the baby kicking within you, giving birth to it and then being separated, never to see it or know its whereabouts or its condition again, is much more traumatic.

Deutsch expresses her pro-choice sentiments:

The laws and religious injunctions directed against abortion are, as we have mentioned, complicating factors. Incidentally, it is interesting to note that public opinion, common sense, and normal moral judgment support the woman's human right to be a mother or to avoid being a mother by any of the means at her disposal according to her wishes. For apart from the attitude of certain groups influenced by the Catholic church, the normal emotional reaction to abortion is overwhelmingly, in the most varied civilizations, to take the woman's part despite any laws to the contrary. [p. 187]

So in spite of her assertion of the role of masochism and passivity as natural aspects of a woman's psychology, Deutsch, perhaps in recognition of the healthy aspects of her narcissism, defends her right to determine her own destiny. This may come as a surprise to some feminists, but is not surprising if we recognize the commonality between psychoanalytic and feminist theory in recognizing female sexuality as a normal and healthy component of a woman's life.

ABORTION STATISTICS

Many of us are old enough to remember the days when most abortions were illegal, referred to in the literature as criminal abortions. We all knew of cases where a family member, a friend, or friend of a friend obtained an abortion by finding a referral source, often a nurse, who knew of someone who performed illegal abortions. These abortions were risky legally, but more important is that they were risky medically and could endanger a woman's life. Women who had no resources might attempt a self-inflicted abortion; again, it was a woman's network of advice that would tell her what to do to cause an abortion. The wire coat hanger is the terrible symbol of those days. Death could result from unsterile conditions in either self-induced or illegal abortions. One estimate is that even today, because of the unavailability of legal, safe abortions, 200,000 women throughout the world die from illegitimate abortions each year. Women who used to go to Mexico from California for abortions often ended up in San Diego hemorrhaging. Yet in New York City not a single death resulting from a legal abortion has occurred since July 1971, when Planned Parenthood opened clinics making abortion both safe and accessible. Seaman and Seaman (1977) report the estimate that worldwide, there are one to two abortions for every four live births, and that in countries where abortion is illegal, such as in most of Latin America, abortions are almost as frequent as in countries where it is legal. The National Center for Health Statistics reported that in the U.S. from 1958 to 1962 an average of 292 women died each year from abortion. In 1973, when abortion was legalized, the figure dropped to 36, a reduction of 88 percent. In 1977, deaths had dropped to

18. In California, the number of hospital admissions for an infected uterus following an illegal abortion declined from 69 per 1,000 live births in 1967 to 22 per 1,000 in 1969, the year after the passage of a therapeutic abortion law.

According to Braude (1983), the risk of dying from a term pregnancy is seven times greater than that of dying from an abortion. A study of women who died from abortion between 1975 and 1979 showed they were older than women who sought legal abortion and disproportionately black and Hispanic. Over half induced the abortion themselves, then died primarily from infection or air embolism. Financial considerations and a desire to keep the abortion secret were the most frequent motivations (p. 84).

Each year since 1973, women have been obtaining abortions earlier in pregnancy, making the procedure safer for the woman, and less likely to occur before quickening, a frequent definition historically for the start of life. In 1973, less than 40 percent of women obtained them before nine weeks of pregnancy. By 1978, over half were obtained before nine weeks and over nine in ten in the first twelve weeks. In 1978, less than one percent were obtained after twenty weeks (p. 85).

The United States has one of the highest teenage pregnancy rates in the developed world, probably because our moralistic view of sexuality prevents knowledge of contraception from being taught in schools and contraceptive devices from being available to all who need them. About 40 percent of women in their teens become pregnant, and about 20 percent give birth at least once. In 1978, out of 1,142,000 pregnancies of women under 20, 38 percent were aborted, 22 percent were born to unmarried mothers, 17 percent to married mothers, and 10 percent to mothers who married after becoming pregnant (p. 86).

Home remedies to induce abortion include horseback riding; falling down the stairs; inserting foreign bodies such as twigs, roots, metal rods; infusions of soapy water or household disinfectants; and the ingestion of turpentine, bleach, and massive doses of quinine. Some of these deaths may never have been reported as related to abortion, but rather as suicide or poisoning. Herbal methods are used in some parts of the world, such as laminaria, a marine plant, applied to the cervix or inserted into it. Current hospital methods include the insertion of seaweed, an herbal remedy that helps to dilate the cervix.

THERAPEUTIC ABORTION: THE ROLE OF PSYCHIATRY

Prior to *Roe v. Wade,* the 1973 Supreme Court decision legalizing abortion throughout the country, the only way a woman could have a legal abortion in a hospital was by qualifying for a "therapeutic" abortion, done to preserve the life and/or health of the mother. The grounds to qualify differed by state and by hospital and physician as well. According to Nadelson (1978), few abortions were performed for medical reasons because the technical ability to preserve life through pregnancy had improved to the extent that a threat to the woman's life was rare. Therefore the vast number of therapeutic abortions were performed for psychiatric reasons, but guidelines and criteria were vague and poorly defined. In one hospital a woman would be required to have made a suicide attempt to qualify, whereas in another hospital a statement of suicidal intent was judged to be sufficient. There is no question but that a therapeutic abortion performed by a competent physician under sterile conditions was a vast improvement over an illegal and perhaps not sterile or properly done abortion, but this still left many women ineligible and meant all women had to go through psychiatric examinations to qualify. It was the psychiatrist then who decided, not the woman herself, and the psychiatrist was no doubt deeply influenced by his or her own attitude toward abortion, thereby interpreting the guidelines either strictly or liberally.

Harold Rosen: Essays and Clinical Illustrations

A volume of essays entitled *Therapeutic Abortion: Medical, Psychiatric, Legal, Anthropological, and Religious Considerations,* published in 1954 and edited by psychiatrist Harold Rosen, describes in several chapters the attitude of psychiatrists and psychoanalysts at that time in interpreting the law on the mental health risks to the mother from an unwanted pregnancy. It is surprising to learn that rape per se was not considered sufficient grounds for a therapeutic abortion.

May Romm

Psychoanalyst May Romm differentiates women who may want abortions but can be helped to keep the baby with psychotherapy from those who are schizophrenic or manic-depressive and cannot be helped by therapy. "Women with major psychoses . . . if pregnant should be relieved from continuing the gestation, both as a humane measure for themselves and for the sake of human beings who otherwise would be brought into an untenable environment" (p. 209).

In the cases of nonpsychotic women, Romm says the psychiatrist should consider two factors: the danger of irreversible psychological damage to the mother during the pregnancy and the effect on her of the postpartum state. If previous pregnancies have repeatedly precipitated psychotic episodes in spite of dynamic psychotherapy, she recommends seriously considering abortion. She then discusses "pernicious vomiting" as the most severe psychosomatic symptom of pregnancy and recommends dynamic psychotherapy as the treatment of choice for these women in the early stages, while there is still time remaining for a safe abortion to be performed if the psychotherapy fails to alleviate the vomiting. Vomiting is connected in the unconscious with oral impregnation and an attempt to get rid of the fetus orally, according to Romm.

In a very judgmental tone she states that a woman who cannot tolerate pregnancy or is in intense conflict about it or about giving birth is "immature" and "can be labeled as psychopathological," with problems stemming from "unresolved oedipal situations." Clearly she does not accept the notion that a woman can reject a particular pregnancy for reasons that are mature or healthy, or that there are other valid roles for women besides motherhood.

> Receptivity in the feminine sexual role appears as debasing. Competition with the male is at all times at a high pitch. This, in turn, is an interfering factor with tender feeling toward their husbands. These maladjusted women cannot identify with the accomplishments of their husbands; they cannot enjoy the success of their mates. Envy and jealousy of men are rampant. Pregnancy as a challenge of femininity is unacceptable to them. [p. 210]

There are several references to the psychological dangers of abortion leading to depression and guilt. She believes some women seek abortion for sadomasochistic reasons in which case the abortion can be disastrous, even leading to psychosis. This attitude was challenged by later writers and researchers.

W. G. Eliasberg

A chapter by Eliasberg stresses the patient who is unmarried and at risk of suicide. "We feel that with patients with underlying suicidal depressions, the added emotional strain and uncertainties of pregnancy and childbirth frequently constitute much too heavy a risk for them to be compelled to run" (p. 217).

He also gives an example of a married woman who was helped by psychotherapy to understand the irrational components in her fears and to carry her child to term, happily.

Rosen, the editor, wrote a lengthy chapter, "The Emotionally Sick Pregnant Patient: Psychiatric Indications and Contraindications to the Interruption of Pregnancy." He divides women seeking abortion into three groups: The first group consists of patients who can be treated psychother-apeutically so that their pregnancies continue to term. He gives case examples where he used hypnosis as the form of treatment. In the second group are patients who are determined to have an abortion, legally or illegally, and who apparently suffer no untoward emotional aftereffects as a result. A telling example in this category is that of a woman who sought a therapeutic abortion because she had had such a difficult time with her first baby, now 6 years old, that she couldn't bear the thought of going through the sleepless nights again. Her husband did not want another child either, was angry at her for getting pregnant, and she threatened to kill herself if she couldn't get an abortion. The patient reports that she is nervous, irritable and moody, shouting constantly at her daughter and beating her when she knows she shouldn't. Rosen reports the following:

> Her obstetrician, who was phoned, was surprised and indignant be-cause she had seen a psychiatrist. He characterized her as a "spoiled brat," badly "in need of a spanking," and saw no reason why anyone should listen to her complaints. The other psychiatrist, when phoned, stated that she was merely trying to "put on a show" and would carry the child to term if no attention were paid her. [p. 230]

Rosen learned that she received an illegal abortion within a week. He concludes: ". . . in our opinion this attitude intensified her symptoms, increased what can best be characterized as the 'God-awful' urgency of her demands, and helped make even more impossible, at least at the time, any attempt to treat her obvious emotional illness" (p. 231).

This was in the early 1950s. Is it possible that there exist today obstetricians and psychiatrists who treat their women patients with such condescension, disrespect, and hostility? The likely answer is that there are not so many now, but still some. In contemplating a return to the time when woman-hating doctors had the power to decide whether or not a woman should be granted an abortion, we must recoil in horror at a repetition of this poor woman's experience with the medical profession.

A second example in this category is that of an unmarried couple in which the woman insisted upon the abortion. The man would have liked to marry her but realized that this pregnancy outside of marriage could harm both their careers. They both were highly educated, held very responsible jobs, and could be subject to blackmail if the truth were known. He had only recently separated from his wife, and the divorce would not be final for another nine months. The woman was so opposed to the pregnancy that she told the psychiatrist that she would commit suicide and already had a plan; she would take a cruise ship and jump overboard, making it appear to be an accident. She already had purchased her ticket. She did not want to ever marry because she feared domination by a husband, yet she believed that knowledge of her pregnancy would bring disgrace upon him and her parents.

Rosen told the couple that for a woman in her good condition with no history of previous emotional illness, no hospital board would recommend a therapeutic abortion. The couple said they would each commit suicide. He recommended a "vacation" in another city where she could deliver the child and have it adopted, but she wouldn't consider it. Another psychiatrist was found who agreed to evaluate the case, and with two recommendations for abortion her pregnancy was terminated legally.

> The very fact that this girl was single of itself means that a recommendation for the interruption of her pregnancy, at least for psychiatric reasons, would most probably be rejected even if her emotional status had been such that for a married woman the same recommendation might conceivably have been approved. The decision, logically at least, should be determined not by the marital status of the patient, but by her medical and emotional needs. Few physicians, for instance, would withhold anti-luetic treatment from a patient with syphilis merely because that patient happened to be single. [pp. 235–236]

These two examples convey the desperation of women prior to *Roe v. Wade* and the decision-making power of the psychiatrist, which often put the psychiatrist in a position of conflict and discomfort and perhaps even compromised his or her ethical standards. The fact that psychiatrists were not held in high esteem by many physicians added to the distasteful situation for all involved.

Rosen's third group consisted of patients whose pregnancies previously had been interrupted legally or illegally and who later developed emotional disease, which was precipitated by the abortion. Rosen raises the issue of depression following abortion and quotes Helene Deutsch in this regard. Women may turn their anger against their husbands by divorcing them. There are instances of women who had abortions and then miscarried in wanted pregnancies, feeling anxiety and guilt as well as depression. "We at times even see patients who state they wish an abortion, and who, if it be arranged for them, actually do have it but only as a face-saving device for themselves. Underneath it all, they actually desire the pregnancy. We do not believe it possible to over-emphasize this" (p. 241).

Richard L. Jenkins

Jenkins's chapter is entitled "The Significance of Maternal Rejection of Pregnancy for the Future Development of the Child." Jenkins describes different degrees of ambivalence toward a pregnancy. Some women want the baby but are responding to outside pressure for abortion. Others cannot emotionally accept the child and make attempts to abort it, and if they fail, will reject the child at birth and have it adopted. Short of overt rejection are those mothers who keep the child but only halfheartedly love and care for it, and in whom hostile attitudes and behavior are frank and open. Another outcome may be a type of behavior described as overprotection–rejection, in which a protective attitude can actually be transparently hostile and restrictive in place of real maternal behavior. He describes the different problems brought to child guidance clinics and identifies three out of five as being closely related to maternal rejection: the unsocialized aggressive child who displays uninhibited hostile behavior toward others; the overinhibited or overdutiful child with internal conflict, feelings of inferiority, depression, and seclusiveness; and the schizoid child. Jenkins concludes: "It is important that the question of capacity for maternal response and need for emotional support not be overlooked in considering the important problems relating to the question of therapeutic abortion" (p. 275).

Theodore Lidz

Lidz, a psychoanalyst, contributed a chapter entitled "Reflections of a Psychiatrist," in which he states that it is the "very absence of clarity in the law concerning psychiatric indications for therapeutic abortion that has created major difficulties for the psychiatrist" and that forces the psychiatrist to decide "how to judge when this trauma will be less than the burden of the pregnancy or of having the child" (pp. 277, 279). He goes on to write of the problems of guilt and trauma faced by the woman who aborts, sometimes as late as menopause, citing psychoanalytic theory as previous writers have done: "The loss of the fetus not only reactivates the castration concerns, but threatens a basic compensation mechanism which should lead the woman to feel that she has the ability, denied to the male, of producing and nurturing life" (p. 279).

Arthur J. Mandy

In "Reflections of a Gynecologist," Mandy points out that

> the psychiatrist, however, must also assume a portion of the blame for the state of disrepute in which psychiatry is held. From psychiatrists themselves have come statements which frequently tend to discredit psychiatric recommendations. An example in point is the exaggerated and frightening warning of the frequency with which serious depressions may follow induced abortions. To my knowledge, there is no valid support for drawing such general conclusions from limited

data. . . . No attempt has been made to gather data on the thousands of women who have had one or more induced abortions without suffering any ill effects. In an obstetrical practice, one sees little evidence to justify the alarm created by psychiatrists in this regard. . . . It is surprising how often recommendations are rejected for interruption of pregnancy in seriously depressed patients. One patient who was rejected recently inquired in the clinic: "What must I do to prove how desperately ill I am? Must I attempt or actually commit suicide or finally be committed to a mental hospital to prove it to them?" [pp. 291–292]

This example offers the convoluted logic that in order for a woman to get what she needs and wants she must attempt suicide, hardly the kind of reinforcement we would want to encourage for suicidal behavior. In this instance it paid off, as women learned that they had to feign hysteria to get the medical treatment available to them.

He calls for intelligent reform and asks how such an unsatisfactory situation has continued so long without improvement.

How can we explain or defend a policy that is often arbitrary, discriminatory and scientifically unsound? How can we accept a program which guarantees less unbiased consideration for our patients then we can secure for a pedigreed dog from the neighboring veterinarian? And these are but a few of the disturbing questions which deserve and urgently demand our deepest concern. . . . A program, moreover, that persists in denying an open forum for criticism and defense of its operational procedure is deficient in the basic scientific spirit essential to medical progress. . . . A deliberate conspiracy of silence exists within the medical profession. . . . Admonishing physicians for permitting social and economic factors to influence their decisions indicates a blindness toward the modern concept of social medicine. . . . And repeated exhortations to reaffirm ethical and moral principles would be more meaningful, perhaps, if one did not detect beneath this veil of morality a multitude of thinly disguised prejudices. [pp. 294–295]

He refers to Nicholson J. Eastman, professor of obstetrics at Johns Hopkins School of Medicine, who he says has debunked the charge that therapeutic abortion is equivalent to murder. He laments that hypocrisy in medicine whereby a double standard of morality permits a teacher to decry against the criminal abortionist to his students and yet refer patients to him, to rigidly regulate hospital abortion practices and yet appeal for clemency in behalf of a convicted criminal abortionist.

The reason that Mandy finds this hypocrisy so incomprehensible is that he does not have the benefit of a feminist analysis with which to understand the importance to the patriarchal system, as reflected in medicine, to have power and control over women's bodies and lives, in order to allow for the continuation of male domination and female submission. The further analysis I propose is that of the unconscious fear of female power as represented in allowing the woman the right to make her own decision in regard to terminating an unwanted pregnancy. This is the power of the mother over life and death that all infants and small children fear because the mother appears so omnipotent to them and they are so dependent upon her.

IS THERE CONVINCING EVIDENCE OF PSYCHOLOGICAL DAMAGE DUE TO ABORTION?

A number of the writers reviewed above repeat the warning of serious emotional aftereffects for some women following abortion. Nadelson refers to psychological damage as a "myth" that persisted in spite of a 1955 study by N. Ekblad of 479 women who had legal abortions in Sweden for psychiatric reasons. The study showed that 74 percent of the women followed had no regrets or self-reproach, 14 percent experienced some regret, and only 11 percent regretted having had an abortion. Only 1 percent showed emotional consequences, and all had had previous histories of emotional disorders. Ekblad concluded there was little evidence that abortion had serious effects on the mental health of women.

In a 1963 study in the United States, Ekblad's findings were confirmed. Kummer surveyed thirty-two psychiatrists who frequently saw women postabortion and found that 75 percent stated they had never seen severe emotional sequelae; the other 25 percent had rarely seen it. Nadelson (1978) also cites a study by Peck and Marcus in 1966, which found that women who had already been diagnosed as psychologically ill benefited from abortion. The symptoms of depression and anxiety precipitated by the pregnancy were relieved, and new symptoms were mild and self-limited. A study by Simon, Senturia, and Rothman (1967) reported women generally improved following an abortion, and in fact they found an increased risk of neurotic or depressive illness if an unwanted pregnancy was not terminated. Considering that these abortions were done in the years when the procedure was considered criminal and was a matter of intense secrecy and shame, it is quite remarkable that the results show so little negative effect.

The World Health Organization concludes that emotional stress or lack of it is influenced by the following factors:

1. Whether the abortion is illegal or clandestine
2. The length of pregnancy

3. The type of procedure and amount of pain
4. The attitude of the woman's family and friends
5. The attitude of professionals and others involved in the abortion (Seaman and Seaman 1979, p. 299).

In a recent study (1990) reported in *Science,* Adler and colleagues conclude that legal abortion of an unwanted pregnancy in the first trimester does not pose a psychological hazard for most women. They report a study that showed that having negative feelings toward one's partner, making the abortion decision alone, and experiencing opposition from parents were associated with greater emotional distress. According to former Surgeon General C. Everett Koop, testifying before Congress (Committee on Government Operations), severe distress following abortion is "minuscule from a public health perspective" (1989, p. 14). The authors conclude:

> Despite methodological shortcomings of any single study, in the aggregate, research with diverse samples, different measures of response, and different times of assessment have come to similar conclusions. The time of greatest distress is likely to be before the abortion. Severe negative reactions after abortions are rare and can best be understood in the framework of coping with a normal life stress. [p. 43]

In a presentation at Grand Rounds in the Department of Psychiatry at the University of California, San Francisco, Adler (1990), describing a study of postabortion women, reported that of over 200 studies she reviewed, only 20 met the criteria for validity that she imposed on her own work. Since this is currently a matter upon which much public attention is focused, some of the current research is biased by people trying to find what they want to find. She found that abortion is stressful but not traumatic, which fits with my own informal survey based on many women patients I have worked with both before and after abortions. Adler finds that relief is the most common response, 76 percent, and that guilt was evident in 17 percent. Among Catholics, for whom the abortion was considered a sin, a response of greater conflict was evident because they were taking an action discrepant with the social norms of the church, the role expectations for a good Catholic, and internal values—the belief that abortion represents taking a life. Yet even the Catholic women were coping and showed no pathology. She described a study by Zabin (1990) that interviewed women one to two years later, which found that as compared with women who carried the unwanted pregnancy to term and then adoption, the women who had abortions evidenced higher self-esteem, a greater sense of internal control, and lower anxiety, which indicates to her that if you do not have symptoms in the short term, you are not likely to develop them in the long term. Another significant finding reported by Adler was that women who had abortions for medical reasons, such as rubella, were more distressed because they had wanted the pregnancy.

An interesting study described by Adler in 1990, which attempted to test the views of different groups as to the likely severity of the woman's response to her abortion asked five groups to make a prediction: psycho-analytic students, introductory psychology students, people accompa-nying the woman, the woman herself the day before the abortion, and the woman herself the day afterward. The group predicting the most severe response were the psychoanalytic students, based on psychoanalytic the-ory. Thus psychoanalytic students were out of touch with the common realities in women's lives.

Nada L. Stotland (1992), writing in the *Journal of the American Medical Association,* concludes, "Scientific studies indicate that legal abortion results in fewer deleterious sequelae for women compared with other possible outcomes of unwanted pregnancy. There is no evidence of an abortion trauma syndrome" (p. 2079).

THE UNWANTED CHILD

According to current reports, there has been a dramatic increase in the number of children in the child welfare system, and the cities and states are no longer able to care for the growing number of foster children in their care. In 1991, there were 50,000 children in foster care in New York City alone, compared with 20,000 in 1981. The foster home and group home system is severely taxed, and the history of children in foster care is tragic, being moved from home to home with no sense of belonging anywhere. The combination of physical abuse, neglect, and sexual abuse on account of poverty, family breakdown, and drug and alcohol abuse by parents is leaving thousands of children uncared for and abandoned. The situation is getting so desperate that some child welfare workers are calling for the return of the orphanage, in order to provide stability and continuity in the lives of these children. Yet psychiatric and social work theory have led to the abandonment of the orphanage as damaging to children because of the lack of personal relationship with mother and father figures. In times like this, the prospect of more and more unwanted children being brought into society is frightening, unless the government is willing to back up the antiabortion laws with funds, facilities, and training programs to help mothers to care for their children; or to provide safe, secure, and stable substitute families. Those who are working for the return of criminal abortion laws must recognize that a common alternative to abortion is an unwanted child with parents who are not financially, emotionally, or socially able to provide even minimal care.

The crisis is reflected in the District of Columbia which has agreed to allow a private agency to reorganize its foster care system and bring it into compliance with the law. The city may have to double the number of its foster care caseworkers. There are now ninety-five caseworkers overseeing 2,300 children in foster care, along with the thousands more who remain at home under city supervision after the courts have found them to be abused or neglected. The accord resulted from a lawsuit by the American Civil Liberties Union, which resulted in a ruling that the city was violating the constitutional rights of children in the system to be well cared for and was not regularly reviewing its cases. This was the first time that a judge had ruled in a trial that a foster care system was breaking the law. Similar cases have been brought in Connecticut, New York City, Philadelphia, Kansas City, Missouri, and in the states of Kansas, Louisiana, and New Mexico. More than 407,000 children are now in foster care, up from 280,000 in 1986 (Barden 1991). A surprising study on National Public Radio in October 1992, stated that 25 percent of homeless persons had been in foster care as children.

As to the effect on the child who is born unwanted, Adler reports on a follow-up study done in Czechoslovakia of the children of women who had wanted an abortion, which showed that in their twenties, these children had higher unemployment rates, more alcoholism, more school problems, and more depression compared with a control group.

Nadelson comments that far too little attention has been paid to the psychiatric risks to the unwanted child. She describes two Swedish studies that followed up on the children of mothers who had been denied therapeutic abortion. Hook (1963) studied 213 children and found them both physically and mentally impaired. Forssman and Thuwe (1966) observed 120 children for twenty-one years, who were matched with controls born on the same day, of the same sex, born in the same hospital or district. The unwanted children fared worse in almost every way, including a higher incidence of psychiatric disorders, delinquency, criminal behavior, and alcoholism. They were more often receiving public assistance, exempted from military service, and had less schooling than the control group. Nadelson adds that studies of child abuse and neglect "repeat these warnings about the fate of unwanted children" (1978, p. 176).

THE ABORTION DECISION STUDY—CAROL GILLIGAN

Elizabeth Cady Stanton said "self-development is a higher duty than self-sacrifice." In an earlier book (1992) I discussed the issue of women's fear of selfishness as illustrated in Gilligan's work. In Chapter 2 of the present book I described women's fear of selfishness as it is illustrated in clinical work.

Carol Gilligan (1982) studied twenty-nine women ranging in age from 15 to 33 of diverse ethnic background and social class who were referred by abortion and pregnancy counseling services. Of the twenty-nine women, four decided to have the baby, two miscarried, twenty-one chose abortion, and two were in doubt about the decision and could not be reached for follow-up. Each woman was interviewed once at the time of making the decision in the first trimester and then again at the end of the following year. The study focused on the relation between judgment and action. She refers to Kohlberg's (1976) delineation of three views of morality: (1) preconventional judgment is egocentric and derives moral constructs from individual needs; (2) conventional judgment is based on the shared norms and values that sustain relationships, groups, communities, and societies; and (3) postconventional judgment adopts a reflective perspective on societal values and constructs moral principles that are universal in application. Gilligan explains:

> The shift in perspective toward increasingly differentiated, comprehensive, and reflective forms of thought appears in women's responses to both actual and hypothetical dilemmas. But just as the conventions that shape women's moral judgment differ from those that apply to men, so also women's definition of the moral domain diverges from that derived from studies of men. Women's construction of the moral problem as a problem of care and responsibility in relationships rather than as one of rights and rules ties the development of their moral thinking to changes in their understanding of responsibility and relationships, just as the conception of morality as justice ties development to the logic of equality and reciprocity. Thus the logic underlying an ethic of care is a psychological logic of relationships, which contrasts with the formal logic of fairness that informs the justice approach. Women's constructions of the abortion dilemma in particular reveal the existence of a distinct moral language whose evolution traces a sequence of development. This is the language of selfishness and responsibility, which defines the moral problem as one of obligation to exercise care and avoid hurt. The inflicting of hurt is considered selfish and immoral in its reflection of unconcern, while the expression of care is seen as the fulfillment of moral responsibility. [p. 73]

Gilligan describes the three stages of the abortion decision as moving from an initial focus on caring for the self to ensure survival, followed by a transitional phase in which this judgment is criticized as selfish. The woman then moves into the second stage of an awareness of a connection between self and others in which the concept of responsibility and concern for the care of the dependent child is prominent. Then follows a second transition, which is a reconsideration based on the recognition of the inequality between self and other in the previous stage. She must then sort out the confusion between self-sacrifice and care "inherent in the conventions of feminine goodness" (p. 74). In the third stage she focuses on the dynamics of relationships and the tension between selfishness and responsibility. She comes to understand the interconnection between other and self and recognizes the potential for exploitation and hurt if one does not balance the needs of care with the needs of the self.

> Thus a progressively more adequate understanding of the psychology of human relationships—an increasing differentiation of self and other and a growing comprehension of the dynamics of social interaction—informs the development of an ethic of care . . . [which] evolves around a central insight, that self and other are interdependent. [p. 74]

Josie, a 17-year-old in the study, said:

> I started feeling really good about being pregnant instead of feeling really bad. Being pregnant I started feeling like a woman. . . . I was looking at it from my own sort of selfish needs, because I was lonely. Things weren't really going good for me, so I was looking at it that I could have a baby that I could take care of or something that was part of me, and that made me feel good. But I wasn't looking at the realistic side, at the responsibility I would have to take on. I came to this decision that I was going to have an abortion because I realized how much responsibility goes with having a child. Like you have to be there; you can't be out of the house all the time, which is one thing I like to do. And I decided that I have to take on responsibility for myself and I have to work out a lot of things. [pp. 76–77]

Gilligan offers other quotes, often representing the woman's struggle between selfishness and self-sacrifice. In some instances the selfishness would mean keeping the baby, such as in the case of Denise, a 25-year-old who had an abortion against her own wishes because she felt a responsibility for her lover and his wife and children. Other examples involve women becoming pregnant by married men, an important angle to appreciate when we view statistics of the high percentage of abortions among single women. The woman bears the burden of the abortion on behalf of a man who is being unfaithful to his wife and irresponsible about birth control as well.

Gilligan sought to determine how women dealt with the critical moral issue of hurting others in making their decision. The fear of selfishness was a powerful factor, and she found that "when uncertainty about her own worth prevents a woman from claiming equality, self-assertion falls prey to the old criticism of selfishness" (p. 87). One of the women, "Ruth," saw the issue of power in her decision and feared that adult power meant the loss of feminine sensitivity and compassion, a moral problem for her. She believed that to be ambitious means to be power-hungry and insensitive, stomping on others. In describing the steps in the decision for "Sarah," Gilligan concludes:

> The ultimate choice is abortion: "How can you take responsibility for taking a life?" but also how can you bring a child into the world in order to "assuage your guilt"? The "turning point" for Sarah comes in the realization that in this situation there is no way of acting that avoids hurt to others as well as to herself, and in this sense, no choice that is "right." . . . She finds in the constraint of this dilemma the limits of her previous mode of thought. Thus Sarah reconsiders the opposition between selfishness and responsibility, realizing that this opposition fails to represent the truth of the connection between the child and herself. Concluding that there is no formula for whom to exclude and seeing the necessity of including herself, she decides that in her present situation, abortion is the better choice. [p. 118]

HOW THE HIGHEST COURT IN THE LAND TREATS WOMEN: 1872

Many of the rights of women that we now take for granted had to be fought for in the courts. The right to vote comes easily to mind, but there are many others, some only recently won. In an article in *Sisterhood is Powerful* (1970), "Does the Law Oppress Women?", Diane B. Schulder reviews the status of women in the law as of 1920. A married woman could not enter into a contract, buy property, have her own checking account, or keep her own name. She lost all legal identity. In the criminal law, a woman could be arrested for prostitution but the man was breaking no law. In Italy a woman could be jailed for adultery for one year, whereas there was no punishment for her husband for the same act. This law was only reversed in 1968. In the United States, the law permitted a "passion shooting" of a wife by her husband, but not the reverse. It was not illegal for women to be excluded from juries, as they were in the 1968 trial of Benjamin Spock for aiding draft resisters. However, the Supreme Court had decided in 1879 that it was unconstitutional to exclude "Negroes" from state juries.

To get the full flavor of the Supreme Court's attitude toward women who aspired to be lawyers, the following quotation from *Bradwell v. Illinois,* decided in 1872, is instructive. The case involved a married woman from Illinois who attacked the state law that forbade her from practicing law. The Court answered as follows:

The claim that (under the Fourteenth Amendment of the Constitution, which declares that no state shall make or enforce any law which shall abridge the privileges and immunities of citizens of the United States) the statute law of Illinois, or the common law prevailing in that state, can no longer be set up as a barrier against the right of females to pursue any lawful employment for a livelihood (the practice of law included), assumes that it is one of the privileges and immunities of women as citizens to engage in any and every profession, occupation, or employment in civil life.

It certainly cannot be affirmed, as an historical fact, that this has ever been established as one of the fundamental privileges and immunities of the sex. On the contrary, the civil law, as well as nature herself, has always recognized a wide difference in the respective spheres and destinies of man and woman. Man is, or should be, woman's protector and defender. The natural and proper timidity and delicacy which belongs to the female sex evidently unfits it for many of the occupations of civil life. The constitution of the family organization, which is founded in the divine ordinance, as well as in the natural order of things, indicates the domestic sphere as that which properly belongs to the domain and functions of womanhood. The harmony, not to say identity, of interests and views which belong, or should belong, to the family institution is repugnant to the idea of a woman adopting a distinct and independent career from that of her husband. So firmly fixed was this sentiment in the founders of the common law that *it became a maxim of that system of jurisprudence that a woman had no legal existence separate from her husband, who was regarded as her head and representative in the social state;* and, notwithstanding some recent modification of this civil status, many of the special rules of law flowing from and dependent upon this cardinal principle still exist in full force in most states. One of these is, that a married woman is incapable, without her husband's consent, of making contracts which shall be binding on her or him. This very incapacity was one circumstance which the Supreme Court of Illinois deemed important in rendering a married woman incompetent fully to perform the duties and trusts that belong to the office of an attorney and counselor.

It is true that many women are unmarried and not affected by any of the duties, complications, and incapacities arising out of the married state, but these are exceptions to the general rule. *The paramount destiny and mission of woman are to fulfill the noble and benign offices of wife and mother. This is the law of the Creator.* And the rules of civil society must be adapted to the general constitution of things, and cannot be based upon exceptional cases.

. . . In my opinion, in view of the peculiar characteristics, destiny, and mission of woman, it is within the province of the legislature to

ordain what offices, positions, and callings shall be filled and dis-
charged by men, and shall receive the benefit of those energies and
responsibilities, and that decision and firmness which are presumed to
predominate in the sterner sex.

For these reasons I think that the laws of Illinois now complained of
are not obnoxious to the charge of abridging any of the privileges and
immunities of citizens of the United States. [pp. 140–142, italics mine]

Here we see the patriarchal system in full force, judging women not
fit even to enter the profession, let alone sit as a judge. But there is no
modesty on the part of the Court in declaring that they know the "law of
the Creator" deems it that way. Perhaps they have a special line to the
Creator that tells them His *(sic)* views. We also see the attack on women
from both sides; a married woman cannot be a lawyer because she has no
legal rights apart from her husband. An unmarried woman cannot be a
lawyer because the law can make no exceptions—all women should be
wives and mothers, because it is their "destiny" and "mission." The
absurdity of the reasoning in this opinion needs no further elaboration. I
include it here as background to understanding the attitude of the male-
dominated legal profession to the role of women and their exclusion from
all bodies that have power over their lives. Earlier in this chapter I
discussed the power of psychiatrists over women seeking abortion. In my
first book I discussed the power of organized religion, including Judaism. It
is on the subject of abortion that the full force of patriarchal authority,
judgment, and power combine in the form of the church, the law,
medicine, and the legislature to keep women in their place, serving men.

I do not wish to deny that the issue of when life begins is a valid
question that truly disturbs well-meaning people. The point is, Who will
decide when life begins? and furthermore, Whose interests will be served
by the decision? In my first book I described the witch trials of the Middle
Ages. The issue there too was, Who decides who is a witch? and What
interests are served? I propose that the struggle over abortion is a modern-
day witch hunt, with women accused of murdering babies as they were
when they were tried as witches. The idea of murdering babies has other
historical roots associated with persecution, for it was the Jews who were
accused of murdering Christian babies and drinking their blood, as part of
the whipping-up of emotions that led to pogroms in Europe. So far, no one
has been burned at the stake for abortion, but there are thousands of
martyrs who have been killed or permanently sterilized by illegal abortions. And to make the analogy even tighter, it is the power of the Roman
Catholic church that was behind the witch trials, and that institution is,
along with the Mormon church, the most powerful force behind the
antiabortion movement. The Mormon church is decidedly sexist, for years
countenancing the practice of multiple wives. Neither the Roman Catholic

church nor the Mormon church has seen fit to allow women to be priests. It is probably not a coincidence.

ABORTION AND THE U.S. SUPREME COURT—*ROE V. WADE:* LAURENCE H. TRIBE

Tribe (1990) has written an outstanding book, *Abortion: The Clash of Absolutes,* which traces the legal history of abortion and the political history of the movement to legalize it and now to criminalize it again. His sympathy to the feminist cause is clear throughout, yet he does criticize feminists for not showing respect for the views of their adversaries. He supports most of the reasoning behind *Roe v. Wade,* the 1973 Supreme Court decision affirming a qualified right to abortion based on the right to privacy. He poses the question of abortion as a clash of absolutes, of life against liberty.

> No right is more basic than the right to live. And the untimely death of a young child is among life's most awful tragedies. To cause such a death is a great wrong. And if infanticide is wrong, is the destruction of a fetus at eight months of gestation, or at five, any different?
>
> Nothing is more devastating than a life without liberty. A life in which one can be forced into parenthood is just such a life. Rape is among the most profound denials of liberty, and compelling a woman to bear a rapist's child is an assault on her humanity. How different is it to force her to remain pregnant and become a mother just because efforts at birth control accidentally failed? [p. 3]

The book is filled with fascinating historical facts, such as that until the end of the nineteenth century, the Roman Catholic church's position on abortion—similar to that taken by Aristotle and by some rabbinic scholars in the Jewish tradition—held that "animation" was the standard for human life, and that a male fetus "animated" (became infused with a soul) at forty days, while a female one did not become human until eighty days. There is also a well-written political history of the abortion movement in the United States. But for a nonlawyer, the most rewarding part of reading this book is Tribe's clear explanation of the history of the legal questions involved and his analysis of the *Roe* decision and the opposition arguments to it. Unfortunately, the book ends before the recent Supreme Court decision in *Rust v. Sullivan,* which upheld by a 5-to-4 majority federal regulations barring all discussion of abortion with patients in family-planning clinics that receive federal money. The opinion swept away First Amendment and statutory arguments against the regulations, which were adopted by the Reagan administration to replace long-standing rules under which health counselors had been required to inform pregnant women of all their options, including abortion. The chief justice said that although abortion was a "protected right," the government was not constitutionally required to "subsidize" speech about it. An outcry of protest has followed, including a pledge by Governor Pete Wilson of California to find the funds in the state budget to make up for the loss in federal money, but the signal is clear that *Roe v. Wade* is under attack by the Reagan–Bush court and the campaigns of the "pro-life" movement have had their effect. Even the conservative *San Francisco Examiner,* a Hearst newspaper, editorialized in anger on May 26, 1991:

> For most of the two centuries it has been around, the U.S. Supreme Court has been a bastion of property and privilege. It has generally favored the rights of the state over the rights of individuals. It has stood staunchly by the powerful and given short shrift to the powerless. In the long history of the judiciary, the Warren Court was an aberration, 15 years of decisions that took the Bill of Rights seriously and reached for the highest ideals of the law. That era is over. The pendulum has swung back, and the Rehnquist Court is in full control. Heaven help us.
>
> Last week's decision allowing the government to prevent federally aided family planning clinics from giving abortion advice was an appalling move by a court hell-bent to legislate its agenda from the bench. With a wave of its hand, the Court dismissed arguments based on two constitutional rights: the right of women to have an abortion (Roe v. Wade is still the law, after all) and the First Amendment right of doctors to give advice to their patients.
>
> The decision defied logic, law and common sense. It was legal hair-splitting of the most pernicious kind. A pregnant woman in crisis can't be told that abortion is one of her options. It's absurd. Do the justices know what they're saying? Rich women are unaffected. Poor women will be the victims. [p. A14]

Tribe's two chapters on the politics of abortion give ample understanding of how the vast network of Roman Catholic church parishes throughout the country organized and financed the antiabortion movement and were joined by the fundamentalist Protestant churches, whose agenda included the return of prayer to the public schools and the defeat of the Equal Rights Amendment. Those three issues taken together ought to frighten anyone concerned about the future of secularism and the future of women's freedoms in our country.

The era of judicial protection of abortion rights, begun with *Roe* in 1973, ended with the Supreme Court's 1989 decision upholding certain state regulations of abortion in the case of *Webster v. Reproductive Health*

Services, a 5-to-4 decision that foretold the loss of rights to come. Writing in 1990, Tribe still maintains some optimism:

> It is not this book's goal to "prove" to anyone the correctness of any particular position in the abortion debate. It seems doubtful that anything like "proof" is attainable on this subject. Each side can benefit, though, from recognizing the strengths of the other's arguments and the weaknesses of its own. We may then be able to loosen the logjam that the abortion debate has become. And then, perhaps, we will be able, if not to resolve, at least to make our way through the question of abortion. [p. 8]

Tribe illuminates the *Roe* decision by describing the difference between rights that are held by the Supreme Court to be "fundamental" and which can only be abridged by government when demonstrably necessary to achieve a "compelling" objective; and other rights, such as the right to drive a car, which may be abridged by government as part of a rational scheme to achieve some collective good. In *Roe v. Wade,* Justice Blackmun wrote that a woman's right to decide on abortion is a fundamental right, part of a "right to privacy" the Court had recognized in earlier cases: therefore, the government must find a compelling reason to interfere with the exercise of that right. An abridgment of a fundamental right is almost never upheld (Tribe, pp. 10–11). Under *Roe,* the right to abortion is not absolute. The government maintains the right in the third trimester of pregnancy to interfere with the right to choose abortion, in order to protect fetal life unless the abortion is necessary to preserve the life or health of the woman. Justice Lewis Powell later wrote: "We held in *Roe v. Wade* that the right of privacy, grounded in the concept of personal liberty guaranteed by the constitution, encompasses a woman's right to decide whether to terminate her pregnancy" (in Tribe, p. 13).

Roe v. Wade invalidated the existing abortion legislation in every state but New York. Then, in 1976, the Court strengthened the woman's right by ruling in *Planned Parenthood v. Danforth* that neither the father of the unborn child nor the woman's parents have the right to interfere with her decision to have an abortion. In *Thornburgh v. American College of Obstetricians and Gynecologists* in 1986, the Court struck down state laws that it perceived were designed to facilitate public exposure and harassment of women seeking to exercise their constitutional right.

However, in 1977 in *Maher v. Roe,* the Supreme Court upheld a Connecticut regulation that denied state Medicaid funding from being used for "nontherapeutic" abortions and in *Poelker v. Doe,* that a city-owned public hospital was not constitutionally compelled to provide nontherapeutic abortions. The Court in these cases distinguished between *direct* interference and *indirect* deterrence of the abortion choice.

The political result of the *Roe v. Wade* decision was to galvanize the antiabortion movement which began the process of working for antiabortion candidates, such as Ronald Reagan in 1980, who then gave a litmus test for would-be judges on their abortion views. During his two terms in office, Reagan appointed more than half the members of the federal bench and three new Supreme Court justices, replacing three of the members of *Roe v. Wade*'s 7-to-2 majority. As an indication of the intensity of the legal battle that developed over these years, when the Webster case was argued in 1989, a record seventy-eight amicus briefs were filed. The previous record of fifty-eight was held in the Bakke case on affirmative action. A significant sidelight of the Webster decision was the insults made by Justice Scalia to Justice O'Conner, who had dared to disagree with him. He declared that her opinion "cannot be taken seriously," called her view "irrational," and launched several pointed attacks upon her. The first woman ever appointed turned out to be the Jackie Robinson of the Supreme Court.

Tribe regards two tragic episodes in the 1960s as turning points in the attitude of the medical profession toward a favoring of a woman's right to abortion. The first involved the tranquilizer thalidomide, banned in the U.S. but available in Europe, which caused horrendous birth defects when taken by pregnant women. Sherri Finkbine, a mother of four from Arizona, discovered in the course of her fifth pregnancy that she had taken thalidomide her husband had brought back for her from overseas. Her physician scheduled a legal abortion for her, but the hospital refused permission and Finkbine was forced to go to Sweden to obtain an abortion. Between 1962 and 1965 there was an outbreak of rubella, or German measles, in the U.S., and 15,000 babies were born with birth defects, including severe mental retardation. These two cases mobilized physicians who had previously opposed a woman's right to abortion to recognize that there were cases where abortion might be less tragic than childbirth. During the rubella epidemic some doctors did perform abortions in hospitals, and charges were brought against nine San Francisco physicians, deterring others from performing such abortions. However, this case led to the passage of the California Therapeutic Abortion Act. In 1970, Dr. Jane Hodgson became the first physician convicted of performing an abortion in the U.S., a procedure done for a woman who had had German measles. Her conviction was reversed after the *Roe v. Wade* decision. When the rights of doctors were being restricted, they recognized the legitimacy of abortion, limited only by the "sound clinical judgment" of a physician.

Tribe uses the figure of 1,200,000 abortions performed a year in the U.S. by the late 1960s. Of course this figure is impossible to verify. Braude says estimates range from 200,000 to 2 million (p. 84), quoting Cates in

Science magazine, 26 March 1982. Under California's new reform law in 1968, 2,000 abortions were performed legally but an estimated 100,000 were done criminally.

He traces the involvement of the feminist movement to a 1967 national NOW conference, which, after an intense debate, included the "Right of Women to Control their Reproductive Lives" in NOW's Women's Bill of Rights. Lawrence Lader (1973), a leading abortion rights activist, states that "the most puzzling issue in the revolt against abortion laws [was] why women suffered quietly for so long" (p. 30). Yet to any woman who grew up before 1973, the answer is not a puzzlement. The secrecy and the shame were part of the prohibition against female sexuality outside of marriage, the acknowledgment of which could "ruin" a girl's reputation. For a married woman, the rejection of motherhood was equally shameful. Thus the women's movement focused on issues of economic and political freedom to avoid the reputation of being considered "loose women." By the late '60s, the physicians' reform movement combined with the feminist movement to build a repeal movement with the motto that abortion was every woman's right. In 1969, the National Abortion Rights Action League (NARAL) was formed and became the principal national lobbying group for pro-choice activism.

Tribe tells the story of Kate Michelman, now the executive director of NARAL. In 1970, when Michelman was 33, she was the mother of three children and was pregnant with her fourth child when her husband left her for another woman. She had hoped to have six children, but without a husband or resources to support another child, she saw no alternative but to have an abortion: "I had no car. I couldn't get credit because I had no husband and I had three children to feed. . . . I understood at that moment the kinds of choices women have to make and how they affect the very fabric of a woman's life" (p. 134). When she tried to get an abortion, she had to be approved by a hospital review board upon application by her physician and had to prove to an all-male panel that she was unable to mother another child. Her request was granted, but while lying in bed in the hospital she was told that she could not receive the abortion unless her husband, who had abandoned her, would agree to it in writing. She told the hospital they would have to find him, and they did. She had the abortion, and the experience transformed her life:

> I had to go before a panel of four strange men, whose decision was going to impact on the rest of my life, but who would not have to bear the burden of raising four children. I had absolutely no control over my life. Everyone else had control except me, and I had to bear the consequences. It was then I became acutely aware of how desperate the situation is for women. [p. 135]

The Kate Michelman story is a good illustration of four points. First, the lack of power and control a woman had over her own body and her own future before *Roe v. Wade* and the helpless rage this engendered. Second, the vulnerability of women to the whims of men, who not infrequently behave in a selfish and irresponsible manner. Third, it illustrates how a crisis can transform an individual and, in those with sound ego functioning, can in fact produce a developmental leap. She was able to take her anger about this tragedy and convert it into positive political action, organizing other women to fight for abortion rights. Had she not been pregnant at the point her husband left her, we cannot know what her future would have held, but it is unlikely she would have attained a position of national leadership. Fourth, it is Michelman's story, multiplied by thousands of other examples, that has frightened young women who are reluctant to ever be in a similar position of financial and emotional dependence on a man. So many young women insist on having a career before having children, and some postpone having children into their thirties or beyond, when the risk of infertility is higher, before they feel confident enough in their partner and themselves to risk the responsibility of having children.

Tribe comments on her situation:

> Society's willingness to impose on women alone the sacrifice required by laws restricting abortion, unique within the landscape of Anglo-American law, may well reflect a deeply held traditional view of the differences in character between the sexes. While we might not impose selfless and virtuous behavior on a man—because it would be futile, perhaps, but more likely because it would demean his capacity for individual choice and independence—some may find it less of a contradiction to impose such virtue on a woman because of the traditional view of her nature.
>
> But to impose virtue on any person demeans that person's individual worth. [p. 135]

Tribe's point is a deeply meaningful and disturbing one. The law does nothing to stop a father from abandoning a wife and three live children, plus one in utero. He has committed no crime. In the guise of lauding women as virtuous, the court has "protected" her, as we have seen in the case of *Bradwell v. Illinois,* by finding her "unfit for many of the occupations of civil life," thus leaving her entirely dependent upon her husband. Even today, women attorneys are insulted by judges as O'Conner was insulted by Scalia. But what if her husband fails to assume the role of protector? What if he beats her, or gets drunk and spends his paycheck, or runs off with another woman? How does the law protect her then? This concern for protection of the unborn child does not extend to the protection of live children and their welfare. Where is the government's concern about medical care for children, about hunger? Only very recently has there been any protection for physical abuse and neglect of young children. The case against abortion suggests other motives than the protection of the unborn. It takes us back to the mentality in *Bradwell* and the absolute power and authority wielded by the justices then over the independence of women. The concern, I am convinced, is not with the welfare of children, given the infant mortality statistics we have in the U.S.; the concern is truly with the control of female independence. The right to an abortion is a necessary component of that independence, and it threatens the power and authority men have been able to wield over women by keeping them financially dependent. It is insufficient to place the responsibility for this infringement on the rights of women solely on the church, because in France, a largely Catholic country, virtually any pregnant woman can get a legal abortion within the first ten weeks and social security will cover 70 percent of the cost of the nonmedically necessary abortion. The American courts must bear their share.

The two most fascinating chapters in Tribe's book are "Finding Abortion Rights in the Constitution" and "The Equation's Other Side: Does it Matter Whether the Fetus is a Person?" In these chapters he discusses each argument and performs a brilliant legal analysis that reads like a thriller novel. In dealing first with the question of whether *Roe v. Wade* was rightly decided, he enumerates the objections: "judicial restraint," "legislators and not judges should decide," "the right to privacy is not in the Constitution's text"; and goes on to discuss the meaning of the liberty clause, "incorporation" of the Bill of Rights, the question of "unenumerated" rights, deciding which rights are specially protected, whether there is a "right to privacy," whether the presence of a fetus automatically negates the "private" character of the abortion decision, at how specific a level must "rights" be defined, who decides whether to terminate a pregnancy, abortion rights and sex discrimination, the "original understanding" of the framers, whether *Roe* is judicial legislation. Included is a discussion of what is at stake, in which he points out that if women were held not to have a fundamental liberty interest in control over their own bodies, abortion as well as sterilization could not only be *prohibited* by states, they could also be *mandated* by the state.

Equally compelling are his arguments over the legal status of the fetus, in which he reviews the religious, scientific, and constitutional arguments for the personhood of the fetus, the controversial question about when life begins. He quotes Charles A. Gardner, a biologist who states that a person's constitution is not in fact determined by the genetic material, the DNA, to be found in the fertilized ovum. There is not only one "path" for the fertilized egg to travel on its way to full gestation. As cell division proceeds, the pattern of the embryo's progress toward increasing complexity and differentiation depends not just on the genetic information contained in the original forty-six chromosomes, but, significantly, on the pattern of cells and molecules present in the preceding cell division. "The information required to make an eye or a finger does not exist in the fertilized egg. It exists in the positions and interactions of cells and molecules that will be formed only at a later time" (p. 118).

Under his discussion of the question What if a fetus were a person? Tribe uses an example proposed by MIT philosopher Judith Jarvis Thompson in 1971. She asks us to imagine waking up in the morning attached to a famous and accomplished violinist who has a kidney disorder and, unbeknownst to you, has been attached to your circulatory system while you were asleep. If he were detached, he could not survive. After nine months he will be able to live on his own. Thereafter, however, you will feel a lifelong attachment to him, but if you reach over to disconnect him before then, he will surely die. In fact, no law could justly compel you to accept this situation, and you would be within your rights if you cut the umbilical cord, even knowing he would die. Thomson concludes:

> Trying to decide whether an embryo is a person distracts us from the real question of whether the state may force a woman to incubate that embryo, and to serve as its life-support system, against her will. A woman denied the right to decide whether or not to end a pregnancy is not merely being asked to refrain from killing another person but being asked to make an affirmative sacrifice, and a profound one at that, in order to save that person. [p. 130]

Tribe then points out that in Anglo-American law there is no general duty to give of yourself to rescue another. In the famous 1964 case when a woman named Kitty Genovese was murdered in Queens, New York, thirty-eight neighbors watched and listened and did nothing, not even call the police, until it was too late. Although the neighbors' actions seem morally inexcusable, they violated no law, because there is no legal duty to rescue another person. Thousands of children have been beaten and raped, and no one—family members, neighbors, or teachers—although suspecting, has had the duty to report it. A recent California law corrects this in the case of therapists, physicians, and teachers, but not neighbors or family.

Tribe concludes:

> Perhaps the Supreme Court's opinion in Roe, by gratuitously insisting that the fetus cannot be deemed a "person," needlessly insulted and alienated those for whom the view that the fetus is a person represents

> a fundamental article of faith or a bedrock personal commitment. . . .
> The Court could instead have said: Even if the fetus is a person, our
> Constitution forbids compelling a woman to carry it for nine months
> and become a mother. [p. 135]

He adds, "Most Americans who look at the abortion issue see both a fetus *and* a pregnant woman. Too often when activists on either side present their picture of the abortion issue, they leave room for only the fetus *or* the pregnant woman" (p. 136).

Tribe correctly observes that most people feel uncomfortable with abortion but also uncomfortable with abortion being illegal. He urges prevention through the use of contraceptive education and through more help to mothers for prenatal and postnatal care, parental leave, health care for mothers and children, and day care. If we supported mothers through social policy that encouraged alternatives to abortion, the need for abortion would be lessened. European children and mothers are better off than their American counterparts because of the positive efforts of those countries to meet the needs of mothers and children. I personally would take the pro-life forces more seriously if they did anything to make children more welcome in the world. I know of no activity on the part of these groups promoting child or maternal health and welfare following birth, not to mention their pro–capital punishment stand.

The court battles will undoubtedly continue, and another battle is emerging over RU 486, the French abortion pill, which the French government has declared "the moral property of women," but which, owing to pressure from right-to-life groups, is being kept from testing and development in the United States by the threat of consumer boycotts of the pharmaceutical companies, who have been frightened away from applying for FDA approval. One hopes that the sheer allure of profits, if not concern for the health of American women, will overcome the initial fear, but it may take governmental action, as it did in France, to make this easier, safer abortion method available. The RU 486 battle is yet another example of an effort to control women's sexual and reproductive behavior, this time through threats against drug manufacturers.

· ABORTION AND FEMINISM

Gloria Steinem

Once feminists overcame their initial reluctance to be seen on the side of sexual freedom for women, the abortion issue, along with ratification of the Equal Rights Amendment, became a major focus of women's groups.

Gloria Steinem, writing in *Outrageous Acts and Everyday Rebellions* (1983), recalls covering a local abortion hearing for New York.

> In protest of an official hearing that had invited fourteen men and one nun to testify on the liberalization of New York State's anti-abortion laws, a local feminist group had asked women to testify about their real life experiences with illegal abortion. I sat in a church basement listening to women stand before an audience and talk about desperately trying to find someone who would help them, enduring pre-abortion rapes from doctors, being asked to accept sterilization as the price of an abortion, and endangering their lives in an illegal, unsafe medical underground. It was like the "testifying" I had heard in southern churches and civil rights meetings of the earlier sixties: emotional, rock-bottom, personal truths.
>
> Suddenly, I was no longer learning intellectually what was wrong. I knew, I had had an abortion when I was newly out of college, and had told no one. If one in three or four adult women shares this experience, why should each of us be made to feel criminal and alone? How much power would we ever have if we had no power over the fate of our own bodies? [pp. 17–18]

The article that resulted from that meeting, entitled "After Black Power, Women's Liberation," was published in 1969, and in 1970 it won Steinem a Penney-Missouri Journalism Award as one of the first above-ground reports on this wave of feminism, but her male colleagues were disturbed by it and warned her against identifying herself with women's issues. For the first time she began to question the honor of being the only "girl reporter" among men and began the process of consciousness raising that led to her writing more articles about the women's liberation movement and exposing the fact that she herself had had an abortion. She had gone overseas for the abortion in the 1950s after considering suicide and the inducement of a miscarriage through reckless horseback riding (Tribe, p. 40).

Elizabeth Fox-Genovese

Fox-Genovese (1991) raises some interesting and serious questions about the feminist movement's unqualified support of a woman's right to abortion in her book *Feminism Without Illusions: A Critique of Individualism.* In evaluating the impact of the current feminist movement, she focuses on changes in economic realities in women's lives and concludes that with a 50 percent divorce rate for new marriages, the collapse of alimony, and the erosion of child support (in California over 2 billion dollars is owed in uncollected child support payments), "marriage is not a viable career" for women any longer. It may be a rewarding personal relationship, but "it no longer serves as a surrogate career."

> Today, no law, no father, no brother can force a man to support a woman, and the law is not successfully forcing him to support even their children properly.
> Although the substance of feminism constitutes a response to harsh social and economic realities, much of its rhetoric and that of its opposition has focused on problems of sexuality and identity, rather than on problems of livelihood. Sexual freedom, sexual preference, abortion, figure prominently in public consciousness of the implications of feminism. . . . At the extreme, there are women who apparently oppose abortion out of a deep sense that sexual freedom for any woman exacerbates the pervasive threats to the security of married women; others more vaguely plead that if women would only be women, everything would return to normal. . . . There is no point in arguing with those who desperately cling to such illusions, for economic realities foreclose the return to that "normality" for most women. [p. 2]

The threat of abortion to the security of a married woman could make sense if we recognized the reality that the easy availability of abortion protects a married man who has affairs as much as it protects the unmarried woman. He can have his affairs and expect his lover to obtain an abortion if she gets pregnant. It also protects a married woman who has affairs, but many married women do not identify with that predicament and yet are threatened by single women their husbands meet at work.

Fox-Genovese is a professor of history and a director of women's studies at Emory University. She introduces herself as a committed feminist "despite firm opposition to some of its tendencies that I regard as irrational, irresponsible and dangerous" (p. 6). She offers her book as a "defense and explication of feminism" and as a "critique of feminism's complicity in and acceptance of individualism,"

> its contemporary atomized version that replaces the early and glorious recognition of the claims of the individual against the state with the celebration of egoism and the denial or indefensible reduction of the just claims of the community. . . . The political triumph of individualism has led to its hegemony as the theory of human nature and rights, according to which rights, including political sovereignty, are grounded in the individual and can only be infringed upon by the state in extraordinary circumstances. . . . Here I am arguing that individualism actually perverts the idea of the socially obligated and personally responsible freedom that constitutes the only freedom worthy of the name or indeed historically possible.

In our own time individualism, fueled by the capitalist market, threatens to swing the balance between the individual and society—the balance between personal freedom and social order—wholly to the side of the individual. In this process feminism has played an ambiguous and sometimes destructive role. The implementation of women's rights has whittled away at the remaining bastions of corporatism and community—notably the family—even as women, released to the dubious mercies of the public sphere, require new forms of protection from the state. The issues defy easy solution but do suggest that we have reached a period in our history at which we can no longer deceive ourselves that individualism suffices to define our collective purposes as a people and a nation.

This book . . . explores some ways of imagining the claims of society—the collectivity—as prior to the rights of the individual, some ways of imagining and protecting the rights of the individual as social, not private rights. [pp. 7–9]

Fox-Genovese's support for abortion is qualified. She believes that women should be granted the power to choose to have an abortion "under socially determined conditions":

The fight for women's "right" to choice in the matter of abortion is being misguidedly waged in the name of women's absolute right to their own bodies and, ironically, on the grounds of reproduction as a private matter. It qualifies as ironical since so much feminist energy has been devoted to an insistence that familial relations are not private matters, that "the personal is political," and that women cannot, in justice, be excluded from the public business of society. But the fight over abortion is being waged more in the name of women's sexuality than in the name of their reproductive capacities. That confusion alone indicates the extent to which feminism has absorbed aspects of individualism, which to be coherent, it must resolutely oppose. [p. 7]

This argument accurately points out inconsistencies in feminist theory and feminist political positions but does not deal with the all-important question of "who decides" what are the "socially determined conditions" under which a woman may have an abortion. As long as all institutions of authority—religion, medicine, law, legislatures, and the executive branch of government—are male dominated, we have a situation in which what is in the best interests of women and children will be subsumed under male bias toward what is in the best interest of men, maintaining a status quo in which men have power over women's lives. Yet Fox-Genovese's book is must reading for anyone serious about the study of feminist theory.

Carol Gilligan's thesis that women's morality is based on caring, whereas men's morality is based on individual "rights" is applicable here, but as we saw above, the women in her abortion decision study tried to find a mature balance between caring for themselves and caring for others, a balance of rights and responsibilities. That, it seems to me, is the essence of the difficult choices involved, but still leaves both the burden and the freedom of that choice to the individual woman to make. Any other solution places a woman at a critical point in her life, at the mercy of men who take that choice from her, for motives that are so complex and may be so irrational that the risk is too high to tolerate. It is too easy for men of science, who believe they are being "objective," to be unconsciously swayed by gender prejudices, and the same surely applies to men of the law, religion, and government.

In a stinging critique of "sisterhood," Fox-Genovese brings a Marxist analysis of capitalist relations to bear on what she sees as major flaws in the sisterhood ideal in feminist theory. An affirmation of the solidarity and similarity of all women's lives denies the realities of major race and class differences. The enemy has been patriarchy, not capitalism. She sees sisterhood as giving a network of mutual support to middle-class women for their still private battles in the home or on the job. Rather than trying to please socially dominant males, they have gotten strength to compete with these males for middle-class jobs and privileges. The advances of white middle-class women in the economic world have not had any beneficial effect on the lives of poor and black women, she claims; in fact the opposite may result:

> As a myth in its own right, sisterhood has proclaimed the unity of women on the basis of radically different experiences and in the name of feelings that, like the family feelings from which they derive, mask the realities of power and opportunity. Sisterhood in itself has entailed no special political positions, although it has contributed to the rhetoric of every feminist upsurge. Because of its universal appeal, it has periodically supported a pervasive cultural feminism that, at its most mystifying, elaborates a universal ideology which in practice merely eases the passage of some privileged middle-class women into the public sphere. Thus in an irony that few choose to recognize, the gains reaped in the name of sisterhood frequently result in the sharpening of class lines by pushing lower-class and minority women, singly or together with their men, further down the socioeconomic scale. There can, for example, be no doubt that what is increasingly being called the "feminization of poverty" has emerged during the years in which the women's movement has begun to make substantial gains for middle-class women. [p. 22]

Thus the critique of the ideology of sisterhood is based on its failure to consider political and economic realities. Fox-Genovese proposes instead that the "real lesson of the middle-class feminism of the 1960s and 1970s is that the personal is social" (p. 28). Middle-class women recognized their similarities and assumed that their experiences were true for all women, subordinating the experience of less fortunate women and claiming for themselves the right to speak in the name of all women, thus perpetuating the injustices of race and class in American society. There may be some truth to this accusation, but it is not borne out in the literature, where one frequently finds anthologies that include chapters on minority women and poor women and their special needs and burdens. This is true for many of the books used as references in this volume. Yet there is undeniably, as she says, a widening gap in this country between the rich and upper-middle classes, and the poor. Middle-class, well-educated women are reaching toward equality with middle-class, well-educated men but are leaving their "sisters" who are working-class and poor far behind.

> The worst nightmare that serious feminists must face is that in a decade or two the women's movement may be seen as having done the dirty work of capitalism—of having eroded the older communities and bourgeois institutions that blocked the way to a sinister new despotism. And if so, it should not be surprising to find many women, including many middle-class women, looking back to the older, oppressive bourgeois era as a golden age. [p. 31]

Surely the examples I gave in Chapter 8, of women who returned to school and began professional careers in their forties, are all examples of middle-class or upper-middle-class women. Yet it is clear that the right to a safe, legal abortion that feminists fight for, as well as the battle for comparable worth and the ERA, are rights that benefit poor and working-class women just as much as economically advantaged women, perhaps even more, since the latter have always been able to obtain abortions privately, even if it meant leaving the country. The effort by the courts and the government to divide women by class, to separate out the women receiving federal aid by denying them the right to abortions, will surely not work. This divide-and-conquer tactic is so transparent that it merely serves to anger middle-class women, because they understand that it represents a chipping away at a right that they can be the next to lose. I do not think there is any question but that abortion rights are especially important to poor and minority women, for whom more children can mean longer time on welfare and less chance to finish their education and get decent employment.

As an example of her concern that feminism is leading "inexorably to the final erosion of community" in favor of individualism, she cites the current debate about the right of girls under 18 to obtain abortions without the consent of their parents. "This 'progress' has inescapably depended upon the complementary destruction of the rights of community—understood as binding claims upon individuals" (p. 38). Tribe (1990) gives two tragic examples of cases where girls have died because of the parental consent rule. One girl, pregnant by her father, was shot and killed by him when she told him; another killed herself in trying to abort her pregnancy because she loved her parents and didn't want to hurt and disappoint them by telling them. Fox-Genovese accurately points out different streams of thought within feminism, among those who struggle for women's rights as individuals or women's rights as women—that is, whether women need equality with men or protection for their differences from men. But these two goals are complementary and do not have to be antagonistic. Women need both. For example, protection from rapists and batterers is a need for women as women, whereas equal pay for equal work is protection for women as equals. All that is asked is a level playing field. It is not a matter of either/or, as she poses it, of whether to fight for equality or for protection, but of securing both equality and protection, wherever applicable. The Chinese communists, for example, have had no trouble recognizing this. On days that women are menstruating, they are not put to work standing in water planting rice in the fields. On all other days they are. Women's retirement age is three years earlier than men's, in recognition of the physical burden of child rearing and also, I suspect, to leave them available to care for grandchildren.

> Many feminists continue to found some of their most important claims—above all, the right to "reproductive freedom" and abortion—firmly in individual right, even as they ground others—above all, comparable worth—in a repudiation of individualism. And they ground arguments for affirmative action sometimes in one position and sometimes in the other. Either they do not perceive the contradiction or, worse, they cynically assume that others will not perceive it. In either case they serve their cause poorly and insult the intelligence of the American people. [p. 57]

I see her point in regard to affirmative action but not in regard to comparable worth. What does a librarian or social worker with a master's degree being paid less than a street sweeper or an electrician have to do with individual rights? It is pure and simple the devaluation of a category of work that is traditionally women's work. These women have achieved their position by their individual effort, but the community diminishes their value because they are women. This is the core of the problem. When we have left decisions up to the "community," which takes on some mythical qualities of goodness in her argument, women have, to put it bluntly, gotten screwed. The community is in fact a community of a male power structure, which also finds it to its advantage to demean and depreciate minority males. For years the "community" kept black males out of the skilled-trade labor unions.

Fox-Genovese proposes that marriage, although it subjected women to their husbands' authority and at times exposed women to abuse, also offered women protection against the uncertainties of single life, "offered them economic support and a social and personal identity that enhanced their self-respect." She fails to recognize that an identity based on another's whim, that is, an identity that can be lost if one's husband has affairs or leaves, or even dies, is no identity or security at all. Identity must come from internal sources, not from external approval and submission to external authority. The truth is that women find no certain safety or security in either the married life or the single life. They are, if they are heterosexuals, subject to being demeaned and mistreated as women in either role. It is not surprising that some outstanding women have chosen to forgo heterosexuality altogether. One's identity as a lawyer, a social worker, or a writer is surely more certain than one's identity as a wife. She tends to blame feminism for the breakdown of marriage, a historical mistake, I believe. Feminism was an outgrowth of the breakdown of marriage. The new wave of feminism followed the surge of the "playboy" movement away from male responsibility, a breakdown of the responsibility of men to protect wives and children that she recalls as being an advantage of marriage in the past.

Why should women have to choose between a viable identity as an individual and the security and comforts of marriage? Men have never had to make that choice. The equality argument calls for marriage in which both partners have their family worth in loving connection to each other and their children, and their individual worth in whatever contribution they make as workers in their communities. The right to abortion is the right of women to continue to make their contribution in their communities in whatever capacity they make it—as professionals, skilled workers, or volunteers. Having a baby keeps a woman in the entirely personal sphere of her motherly duties with no time or energy for herself or her community.

She cites the feminist insistence that government move into the realm of the family, the personal, in order to protect women from abuse within the family and to protect women in the community against rape, which may be on the rise as a result of women's growing activities out of the home (except in the case of children and female household help, who historically have been the target of rape within the home). Here lies the real dilemma for feminists. How can we claim the right to government intervention on our behalf to protect us from male violence in the family and then deny the government's right to intervene when we wish to terminate a pregnancy, which is seen by some as an act of violence against the unborn? The classic male argument for wife beating is that it is the man's right to beat his wife, that she belongs to him and that the government cannot interfere in his family. The same argument applies to child abuse within the family. How can we insist that marriage is not private, that a husband should be prosecuted for wife beating, that parents can be prosecuted for child abuse and even have their children removed by the state, and then insist that pregnancy is private and abortion is an individual right of the woman? Here we are forced to rely on the scientific argument that says life does not begin until sometime between the twentieth to the twenty-fourth week of pregnancy. The right of the individual woman to make her choice is very clear until "quickening," a demarcation line drawn in *Roe v. Wade* and historically in other societies. At that stage of pregnancy, should it no longer be a matter of the individual right of the woman, but a balancing of rights? After twenty-four weeks, or five and one-half months, should society, in the form of a judge or a panel of doctors, decide whether the danger to the life or health of the mother is severe enough to justify the ending of the life of the fetus? If it is moving, it is alive, as any woman who has been pregnant can tell you—in good circumstances a moment of great rejoicing. But then we are trapped again with the dilemma of the decision-making power resting outside the woman herself and probably with males who may be unsympathetic and even irrationally punitive. This risk is too great to sustain an argument that the "community" will make a wiser decision than will a woman and perhaps her husband, the parents who will be responsible for the child.

It is not too much to ask that a woman who has accidentally become pregnant, or whose circumstances change, as Kate Michelman's did when her husband left her, make her decision and arrange her fully legal abortion without constraints in the first five and one-half months, and the vast majority of abortions do occur in the first trimester. The problem lies for those women who, because of mental retardation or mental illness, are incapable of even knowing that they are pregnant, or if they do know, of making a decision about it. This small percentage of pregnant women may not be capable of identifying their pregnancy or seeking relief from it until much later. Recently, a psychiatrist I know had a case of a woman who delivered a baby and did not know she was pregnant until she went into labor. He had seen her monthly in his office and had not recognized she was pregnant either. Had he not received a call from the obstetrician who delivered the baby, he would not have believed her story of the birth when she came in for her next appointment. Fortunately, in this case, her married sister adopted the baby. But given what the biological psychiatrists are now learning about the sources of schizophrenia and other major mental illness, are these babies adoptable in the general adoption market, or are they destined to go from one foster home to the next, especially if they are not white babies, and perhaps end up in institutions themselves? The notion of a woman's absolute right is predicated on a sane, at least nominally intelligent woman, who is not drug or alcohol addicted. Should the state have the power in reverse, to compel abortion in the case of a cocaine-addicted mother, for example, or is that opening the door to rampant authority in the case of any "undesirables"? Psychiatrists may be needed to make judgments in these special cases.

Only 1/10th of 1 percent of abortions occur in the third trimester and represent special conflicts for even pro-choice feminists because these babies could live if delivered rather than aborted. Another group of women for whom a third-trimester abortion may be a difficult but important choice are those who learn through a sonogram in the sixth or seventh month that the fetus is severely deformed and who may not be willing to take the risk of delivering a baby who lives only briefly after birth, or if it does survive, may need much intensive hospital care and a lifetime of special care at home. As sonograms have become more precise, this special case for abortion has emerged as a new area, never imagined in the past. Currently there are only three physicians in the United States willing to perform third-trimester abortions (Kolata 1992).

Fox-Genovese is a supporter of abortion based on the social conse-quences of its suppression rather than on a thesis of individual right.

> The vast majority of women who seek abortions are still in their teens, unmarried, and poor. They have scant, if any, prospects of providing bare essentials for a child, and the attempt to do so almost invariably destroys their own prospects for education and decent employment. The hard truth is that our society is not prepared to provide adequately for children, and those who oppose abortion are, in general, those least in favor of expanding social and family services. What social good can possibly be served by forcing a young, poor, unwed woman to bear a child she does not want and cannot provide for and for which society is unwilling to provide. The practical case for abortion is formidable. [p. 81]

Yes, but what of the woman who can provide well for a child, is not poor, is intelligent and in good health, and has a lot to offer a child? We cannot get by on the social-consequences argument alone, although this is often an argument used by feminists, which she does not seem to recog-nize. Fox-Genovese says that the opponents of abortion also fail to recognize the issue that it is not the nine months of pregnancy alone that bind the woman to her pregnancy, it is the years of rearing the child that bind the woman for most of her adult life. This leads again to the alternative of adoption, which would divide the responsibility of carrying the pregnancy to term from the responsibility of rearing the child to adulthood. The collectivity, she states, "does have a practical interest in the fate of children and a moral and political interest in the way in which we define and defend the right to life" (pp. 82–83).

Turning to the cultural feminists who take pride in woman's special maternal, caring, and connecting qualities, she says it is not easy to reconcile the "feminist metaphors of motherhood and community with the feminist defense of abortion on the grounds of absolute individual right" (p. 83) and claims that feminists have not come to terms with the contradictions here. This is unfair. Feminists are thoughtful people, for the most part. Every political movement has its radical fringe, but that fringe is not the essence of the movement. She overlooks Gilligan's careful analysis of the abortion decision and minimizes the appreciation of the complexity of this issue that does exist in the minds of most of us, feminist and nonfeminist alike. Relying on the moral argument, she states: "But the difficulty and sacrifice do not constitute a moral, or even a political justification for abortion. They constitute a justification for enhanced medical and educational programs for all children and hence for the acceptance of collective principles" (p. 85).

I agree. In the best of all possible worlds, there might be no need for abortion. However, not only are we not there, we do not even appear to be on the right road. In the meantime we must allow women to choose from among several less-than-ideal alternatives: abortion, keeping the baby as a single or married mother, marrying the father, placing the child in foster care, or adoption.

GIVING UP A BABY FOR ADOPTION—CLINICAL ILLUSTRATIONS

An alternative to abortion that was common twenty and more years ago was adoption. In order to evaluate the effects of abortion on women, it is important to have some comparison with the effects of the alternatives: keeping the baby as a single mother, marrying the father if he is willing, or giving up the baby to a couple who want a baby but are infertile.

In the early '70s, before abortion had been legalized, I saw two women in their mid-twenties, Rebecca and Joanne, who had become pregnant "out of wedlock" and had carried the babies to term, delivered, and given them up for adoption. Rebecca had gotten pregnant at 18, her sophomore year in college and her first time away from home. When she left home, her mother had said, "if you get pregnant, don't come home." The father of the baby was not interested in marrying her or in taking any responsibility. She dropped out of school and waited out the pregnancy in an apartment, collecting financial aid from the Department of Social Services, who arranged for the adoption. Rebecca had not been allowed to see her baby but was told the sex. The well-meaning professionals who decided on what now seems a barbaric practice believed that it would make it harder for the mother to separate from her infant if she had a chance to see it, and that then she might change her mind. Rebecca now recalls that the received wisdom in those years was that you should deliver the baby and then "put it behind you," a naive notion of how the human mind operates when it comes to emotionally significant experiences.

As psychotherapy progressed with these two women, the powerful emotional impact of the experience became clearer. After several years of working with them, I discovered that they each had an anniversary depression every year around the time of the baby's birthday. At first the nature of the depressions was not clear to me, and I had explored them as I ordinarily would without connecting them to the adoptions. When it occurred to me that this could be the genesis I asked what the respective birth dates were, and this interpretation proved to be correct for both women; the depression coincided with the time of the birthday. They both always knew how old the child was and often thought about him, in Joanne's case, and her, in Rebecca's case. Joanne revealed to me after several years in treatment that the major reason she wouldn't marry the man she was living with was that she did not want to change her name. She hoped that some day her son would find her by looking her up under her maiden name and she did not want to miss the chance. I had been attempting to analyze her reasons for not marrying, unusual at the time, but this reason had never occurred to me. Rebecca wrote and published a poem about the adoption during her therapy. Here are the concluding lines:

> They wouldn't let me
> see you. Told me
> it would make it harder
> to let you go.
>
> I signed my name
> three times on the black lines,
> as I talked about
> the weather.
>
> The milk fell from my breasts
> to my lap, nourishing
> nothing.
> Yellow/white tears I thought
> would never dry.

I saw you around every corner.
The thought of you
kicked at my belly
but I suspect not as hard
as I kicked you.

So we will go on collecting our years,
you and I.
Me not knowing your face.
You thinking I didn't
have time to love you.

If only I could see you
one time, I would tell you to be proud that you're a
woman
and be strong.

That we are all
the mothers and daughters
of each other,
and even if I had kept you,
you would not be
mine.
(Reprinted with permission of the author)

Although the many women I have seen who have had abortions both before and in the course of therapy found it a disturbing experience in various ways, I have never seen a woman for whom an abortion has been traumatic. For Joanne and Rebecca, losing their babies was a traumatic experience with sequelae that continue to this day, twenty-five years later. Statistics show that 38 percent of young women who have their baby adopted never have another child. Joanne earned an M.S.W. degree and worked in child welfare. She financially supported the man she lived with and took care of him in some ways as if he were her son. She had her child at age 36. Rebecca worked as a secretary for many years, never returning to college, and then got involved in writing and theater, in which she has been successful. She wrote a play on the issue of adoption. Many women approach her after her performance to tell her of their secrets, either being adopted or having given up a baby for adoption. Occasional follow-up contact with Rebecca has allowed me to follow the course of her ongoing work on the issue of adoption.

Rebecca: Finding her Daughter

Seven years ago, Rebecca called. I had not heard from her in years. She wanted to tell me that she had located her daughter, had met her, and had established a relationship with her with the knowledge and agreement of her adoptive parents. She had looked in the high school yearbook of the town where her daughter had been adopted and had seen a girl who looked just like herself. When she was sure, she called the adoptive parents. To this date, the seven-year relationship has had its ups and downs. In a recent conversation, Rebecca told me that most adopted children and their mothers go through a brief honeymoon period, then the child or the mother—in the case of an adoptee searching for a parent—retreats in what is apparently a need to integrate the new development and to test the mother's commitment by making it very hard for her to sustain the contacts. If the mother passes the test, the relationship can resume and develop. During the retreat phase, her daughter said "You're not my mother." Rebecca needed help from other women who had been through a similar episode to get through it and handle it properly.

Rebecca's daughter, now age 25, has had two abortions. It is common for adopted girls to develop a compulsive pregnancy syndrome. A lifetime of fantasy about the birth mother takes its toll. The children tend to imagine the mother as either gorgeous and famous or a prostitute, but never ordinary. If the mother contacts the child, the mother has prepared herself for the reunion but the child has not. There is often conflict for the child because of loyalty to the adoptive parents and anger toward the mother. The child fears being abandoned by the adoptive parents, as she had been earlier abandoned by the birth mother. In fact, Rebecca's daughter's relationship with her adoptive parents improved as a result of knowing her birth mother. Her self-image improved as well. She said, "Before I knew who I looked like, I thought I was ugly'.'

In thinking back to her pregnancy and the years following, Rebecca believes she was attempting to deny the significance of what happened, and that in fact it constituted a trauma for her with a classic posttraumatic stress syndrome that followed. She recalled my coming back over and over to the adoption "persistently" during her years of therapy and her resistance to facing it, as well as her realizing as the years went by how painful it had been. She recently met someone who had known her during the pregnancy and who said she had never seen anyone so depressed as Rebecca had been. She recalls spending all her time with friends and being "afraid to be alone with my thoughts." She realizes she never was really given a choice about abortion or about keeping the baby. The counselor at the Department of Social Services had given her the "fast shuffle" and steered her in the direction of adoption. She believes she was manipulated. She learned only recently that her daughter was in foster care for nine weeks after birth with twelve other babies and was malnourished when the adoptive parents did claim her. She had been told her baby would go directly to a home with parents who loved her, but the system did not work that effectively. She has recently learned of cases where the babies stayed in foster homes for one year to one year and a half.

In looking back she realizes she was in a total fog and a state of panic at the time of the decision and allowed herself to be "led by the nose" by her social worker. "I lost my daughter," she says, because "I allowed everybody to make my decisions for me." I acted on what "my assumptions were of what people wanted me to do." She remembers being sent to a psychiatrist for an evaluation and being angry about it. He recommended that she not be granted a therapeutic abortion. She now recalls being more afraid of being found to be mentally ill and put in an institution than she was of not being granted an abortion. Because of her mother's warning not to come home, she did not tell her parents until the fifth month, when it was too late for an abortion, and at that time they were in fact supportive. As a result of therapy, the feminist movement, and a very supportive man in her life, Rebecca was able to pursue reuniting with her daughter when her daughter turned 18. She felt the feminist movement helped to "empower" her. In looking back she wonders if she could have kept her baby. Her parents insisted that she not tell her grandmother, whom she deeply loved, because it "would kill her." She now imagines that if she had told her grandmother, she might have encouraged Rebecca to keep her daughter and even have helped raise her. "All in all I probably made the right choice, but it wasn't an empowered choice."

I asked Rebecca how she felt about abortion, and she is strongly in favor of it. I asked if knowing her daughter now was an argument against abortion. She replied, "It could be, but for me it isn't. In fact, some church groups have contacted me to use my play as a pro-life message, but I don't see it that way."

Abortion is another part of women's lives that has remained a secret and shameful experience. One of the contributions of the women's movement was to bring the revelations of the many women (some well known, such as Gloria Steinem) who have had abortions "out of the closet" as part of the movement to legalize abortion. As with rape, incest, breast cancer, and other tragic events in women's lives, the secrecy compounds the problem. Rebecca told me of a surprising conversation she had with her mother recently. Sixteen years after her pregnancy and adoption decision, she told her mother of having had a dream that she had a brother four years older than herself. Her mother reacted with great emotion and told her that four years before Rebecca's birth she had had an abortion because she ended a brief first marriage. She had never told Rebecca's father. At first Rebecca felt sympathetic, and then angry that her mother had never talked to her about that during her own pregnancy. Her mother's response was that she had always been so ashamed, she couldn't tell anyone. Perhaps it was that terrible secret that unconsciously led her mother to give her the warning that she did, which in fact conveyed an expectation of an unwanted pregnancy that Rebecca then acted out.

What becomes clear in reviewing Rebecca's, and then later Joanne's, experience is that abortion is closure on a difficult decision, although it may remain on the woman's mind. Adoption has no closure. The mother always thinks about her child, wondering where the child is, how it is doing, what the adoptive parents are like, and always knows the child's age. Unknown to me at the time, the adoption had in part determined the transference to me in Rebecca's therapy. In our most recent conversation, she remembered how angry she always felt toward me because my private life was secret from her. She wanted to know where I lived, what my house was like, what my life was like. She searched for clues but could not find any. Years later, she told me, she realized that that anger toward me for my life remaining secret was a reflection of her anger about her daughter's life remaining a secret from her. It was an excellent insight, and I added that it could also have been an identification with her daughter's anger that her mother's life remained a secret from her daughter.

This raises the question posed in Chapter 7 about secrecy in the life of the lesbian woman. When is breaking the silence on these subjects that society has such strong prejudices about an asset to the woman's mental health, and when is secrecy a valid self-protective mechanism? Each patient must weigh and attempt to balance this difficult dilemma. Each therapist must come to terms with it as well. It seems clear to me that total secrecy is almost always harmful. The woman must be selective, but must confide in someone in order not to suffer the negative effects of repression and the likelihood of acting out the suffering in compulsive and self-destructive ways.

Joanne: an Adoption that Remains Secret

I had not heard from Joanne for sixteen years after a five-year, twice-weekly psychotherapy from 1970 through 1974. After speaking to Rebecca I was interested in knowing whether Joanne had located her son and, if so, how matters had turned out. I called her, and she agreed to meet with me to talk about it. She did not want to speak on the phone because, she said, the issue was still so emotional for her that she was reluctant to raise it without the opportunity to talk with me in person. She told me on the phone that she has a successful private practice specializing in children, is married, and has a 12-year-old daughter. She said that having her daughter was the best therapy she ever had for the trauma of the adoption.

Our meeting, which was arranged at her home, was a wonderful reunion. We spoke for 3 hours, and I had a chance to learn about her life since the conclusion of therapy. After catching up on the intervening years, we got to the subject of her pregnancy, many of the details of which I had forgotten, and some details she had never told me. Joanne had graduated from college and felt completely lost. She believes she was, at that time and for many years afterward, in almost a "dissociative state." She said "I didn't know who I was or how I felt." She returned home, not knowing what to do with herself. Her older sister had gotten pregnant by a boyfriend earlier, and her parents had reacted with such horror that they would have nothing to do with her and in fact left town for an extended trip. Her sister had married the young man and had the baby, but her parents had not come back to attend the wedding, which was arranged by an aunt. Joanne remembers her mother saying to her "Don't you ever do this to me."

Joanne then returned to her home town in another state to visit family and friends and met a young man she had known in high school there. They went out, and he talked her into having sex with him. He assured her that he had taken a birth control pill for men and she couldn't get pregnant. She remembers thinking to herself that she had never heard of such a pill for men but thought What do I know? and trusted him. As she spoke, I recalled a woman I had seen twenty-five years ago who had an abortion. The man had told her he had had a vasectomy and she believed him. When Joanne returned home and learned she was pregnant, she went to her family doctor, who asked her if she wanted to keep the baby. She now believes he had left an opening for her to say no, and to give her abortion advice, but at the time, being a Catholic, she says she didn't really know about abortion and said she would have the baby. She then went to a friend who was a social worker and who arranged for her to come to San Francisco to a Catholic home for unwed mothers to deliver. She left without telling her family the truth and to this day has never told them. She has never told her husband or her daughter either.

Upon arriving in San Francisco she was placed as a live-in domestic in a private home in Marin County to care for a young girl. The family was not stable; she was expected to sleep in the same bed as the girl, who was a bed wetter; and the mother was an exotic dancer who wore no underwear. Joanne was so unhappy that she complained to the social worker, who arranged a better placement for her in another home in Marin. She worked seven days a week doing child care, received nothing but a small allowance, and although the mother was very nice, she used Joanne as a confidante to tell all her problems to. As Joanne says now, "I had enough problems of my own." I was horrified as she told this story. I had always believed that she had spent those months in the Home, but in fact she only spent the last two weeks of the pregnancy there. I commented that she had been exploited, and she began to cry. She felt so helpless and did not know what else to do or what would happen to her after the birth. It sounded like the classic "madame–housemaid" relationship described in novels about the Old South and the upper classes in this country and in Europe. I was horrified that the Catholic church would treat these young pregnant women that way, turning them into cheap servants for the upper middle class. And of course, the families who received these girls had a free slave who couldn't leave. I said it sounded like she was an indentured servant. Yet, considering that all the blame and responsibility for pregnancy was placed on the girl or woman, this unpaid service might be the church's idea of penance. She believes there was money due her from the Department of Social Services but that the checks went to the agency, not to her. "Isn't that against the law?" I asked, and Joanne, who had worked in child welfare services for many years, shrugged and her face showed an ironic expression. We both fell silent, and I thought about the powerlessness of one pregnant, dependent woman against the power of the Catholic church in partnership with a Department of Social Services only too glad to have the church take care of the problem of pregnant young women for them.

Joanne continued to recall the past. Once a month she went to San Francisco for a medical check-up and to talk to a social worker. She wavered in characterizing her relationship with the social worker, first saying it was good, then retracting and saying it was barely adequate. She delivered the baby but said nothing to me about the delivery itself, and I chose not to press for details. After delivery, contrary to Rebecca's experience, she was allowed to see the baby and was allowed to hold him and diaper him the following two mornings. She then signed the papers permitting adoption and was on her own, with no plans and no help. She had no job and no apartment. Fortunately, she had met another single pregnant woman who worked in a neighboring home and who had a friend with an apartment in San Francisco. The friend let the two mothers stay with her until they could find their own place. During the pregnancy, Joanne had contacted the father, who had offered to marry her, but she decided she didn't want to marry him, considering how he had misled her. He offered her two hundred dollars, which he sent to her, and she used this money to pay first and last month's rent on an apartment, eighty-five dollars in those years, and got a job at the Department of Social Services the first day she applied. That was in May 1965.

She applied to the Graduate School of Social Work at Berkeley, was accepted for September, and applied for and received a grant from Catholic Social Services to enable her to attend school. She told no one in her graduate program of her ordeal. After graduation she owed Catholic Social Services two years of work, which she completed. She said she again felt totally lost when she finished graduate school, and had moved in with her boyfriend to solve her confusion. Having been a college graduate at the time of her pregnancy gave her many advantages. Being very pretty was an advantage as well, as she had no problem finding a man to live with. In some ways we might say this story has a happy ending, but not when we realize that the burden of that secret continues to weigh on Joanne. The terrible secret gives her a sense of being dirty and ashamed, and those feelings do not go away. She said she cannot bear to tell her husband and daughter because of what they will think of her. Her description of these feelings makes her family sound clean and pure and makes her sound bad and evil. I suggested to her that not telling them is her way of keeping them from being contaminated by her soiled past.

I asked if she had ever thought about trying to locate her son, having explained earlier about the experience of Rebecca. She said she could not consider it as long as she was unable to tell her husband and child. How could she locate her son and then tell him that he cannot come to her home, that she is so ashamed of him that he has to be kept a secret? She said that having her daughter had really resolved the adoption trauma for her: "I gave everything that was supposed to go to him, to her, and everything that was supposed to go to her, to her. She fulfilled all my needs."

After an emotional hour of recalling the pregnancy and adoption, I asked Joanne how she felt about abortion. Her response was immediate and strong: "The adoption was a horrendous thing to go through—it's barbaric—I am against it even if the circumstances were ideal. That whole option is not an option, as far as I'm concerned. I would never suggest that to anybody—NEVER. If my own daughter got pregnant I would want her to have an abortion or else I would keep the baby and raise it for her. I would have had an abortion in a minute if it were legal then."

Then Joanne brought up a new subject. She said that she had been wondering whether she had been sexually abused as a child. She has been appalled at how many of her own patients have been sexually abused. She remembers my asking her that question during therapy and that she had said no and wondered why I had asked. She has been in touch with her younger sister, who has been talking to their mother a lot recently because of a family crisis, and the sister suspects that their grandfather had abused Joanne and her older sister when they were small. The grandfather, a prominent attorney in their city and the first man to own a car there, had died when Joanne was 4. According to the family story, he was so fond of his two granddaughters that he took time off from work to be with them, which she can remember. She asked me if I thought that was possible and said that two days before I had called her, she was thinking of calling me to ask me what I thought. She wondered about all those years of confusion, what she now recognizes was like a dissociative state, even when she was in therapy with me, and why she stayed in her first relationship and marriage so long when it was clearly a terrible situation for her, as I had pointed out repeatedly.

On the first and second nights after her sister told her of her suspicions, Joanne had two dreams. She had no memory of the dreams but had written them down and, with my encouragement, went to get the notes. She recognized that it was unusual for her not to remember her dreams, an indication of resistance on this subject. The dreams were quite transparent even to an untrained listener. One involved sexual abuse of a young girl by a 12-year-old boy, in the form of digital penetration of the vagina and anus, followed by bleeding. In the dream, Joanne is protesting, but the others look at her as if her protests were only an indicator that she is sexually repressed. In the next dream, she is in jail with a group of men and asks to be put in with women, but is refused. She is forced to drink some bitter-tasting liquid through a straw.

We both speculated about the possibility of sexual abuse, and as more information came out about the daughters of this grandfather, her two aunts, and her own state of confusion (which she now thinks of as a dissociative state), the picture became clearer. Why would a 23-year-old college graduate believe such a ridiculous story as that a man has taken a birth control pill? And why did she continue to live for sixteen years with a man who took so much from her and gave so little? And then the inexplicable statement that at age 23 she didn't know anything about the possibility of abortion, which led to her being exploited as a servant during her pregnancy. I suggested that allowing herself to be impregnated had been a reenactment of the illicit sexual abuse and exploitation by her grandfather. The many years of dissociation were the result of having split off or repressed that experience, which then permanently affected her emotional life. Interestingly, it did not affect her intellectual capacity to complete graduate school but did determine her choice of child welfare as her social-work specialization. I also stated that her not telling her husband and daughter about the adoption was comparable to her having kept the terrible secret all those years of her sexual molestation, a secret kept at least in part because, like all children, she probably felt complicit and guilty about what had happened. She feels like a criminal, as in the dream where she is in jail. She must have enjoyed her grandfather's special attention; perhaps he had given her gifts, and perhaps in the process of seduction had sexually stimulated her in ways that were pleasurable, before forcing her to orally copulate him. We agreed that she would speak to her older sister, who she says can never discuss anything, and also speak to the one living aunt, his daughter, as well as see what other thoughts or dreams she might have.

The next day we spoke briefly by telephone, and Joanne said that my interpretation that she kept the adoption secret because it meant illicit sex, like the incest with her grandfather, had lifted the need for secrecy from her, and that she now feels free to tell her husband and daughter and to search for her child. This was surely an unexpected outcome of a meeting to discuss a former patient's feelings about adoption as compared with abortion, but further serves to illustrate how an unwanted pregnancy can be unconsciously motivated and not be the result of the woman's "immoral" behavior. It also illustrates how, in cases where the sexual relations may be a reenactment of past "illicit" sex, the sexual molestation of a young girl may lead to sexual acting out in later years that is not under her conscious control. This was certainly true in the case of Penelope.

Discussion

A psychoanalytic understanding of how repression and splitting operate in mental life helps us to understand these examples and takes them out of the realm of moral judgment and into the realm of psychological understanding. The feminist dictum that women should have control over their own bodies and be free to decide falls far short of this psychoanalytic understanding of behavior, because it leaves all these matters on a conscious level and views unwanted pregnancy as an "accident," except in cases of rape or incest. As we saw in the cases of both Rebecca and Joanne, the pregnancies were no accident but reenactments of sexual molestation in Joanne's case, and her own mother's unwanted pregnancy twenty-two years before in Rebecca's case. Rebecca laughingly said that she didn't think she could get pregnant because in the movies it was always the blond, blue-eyed actresses who got pregnant. This irrational idea suggests denial of something deeper operating in her mental state. An integration of the psychoanalytic analysis of "accidental" pregnancy with a feminist understanding of the importance to women of having the opportunity to make their own decisions about the pregnancy leads to the best possible way of handling these unfortunate situations. The woman should be able to choose what she wants to do, based on her balancing of her own self-care and her responsibility to others, and she should have an opportunity for counseling to help her understand how she allowed this to happen to her, so that she doesn't repeat it. Tribe's wise recommendation that the best approach to abortion is education and availability of birth control can only go so far. There will always be women who reenact earlier sexual trauma and who should have the remedy of abortion available when their sexual conflicts have led to a failure of the rational approach of prevention.

The phenomenon of birth mothers finding their children and of adopted children finding their birth mothers is controversial. Some believe it is an invasion of privacy. In a few cases the child or parent is rejected, but in 92 to 95 percent of the cases, the reuniting is a success, despite the difficult "retreat" period. This phenomenon can be used as an argument against abortion and in favor of adoption. Psychotherapists need to be aware of the pain and struggle of the adopted child and of the adoptive and birth parents. One psychiatrist, Arthur D. Sorosky (1978), reports that 4 percent of adults in our country are adopted but that 55 percent of his patients in his child psychiatry practice are adopted. Knowing adults who were adopted but who might have been aborted creates a further dilemma in the battle over the rights to abortion. However, the issue could be extended to include all forms of birth control.

Proponents of so-called open adoption, in which the birth mother is able to meet the adopting parents and stay in contact with the child, believe they have found the most humane solution, yet it is too early to know about the long-term effects on all those involved. A recent book by Lincoln Caplan, *An Open Adoption* (1990), explores the controversy among those in the field. The anti–open adoption group does not believe that people in such a highly charged situation can behave well; the pro group does. Mr. Caplan offers his personal example, wherein both the birth mother and father and the adoptive mother and father all behaved very well. He tells us that from the start, the open adoption plan was shaped by, and has come back to embrace, the cause of the birth mother, but that from the point of view of the adopted child, research now supports the view that being sealed off from one's roots at birth can have devastating effects. According to Caplan's book, 2 percent of the American population are adopted, yet adopted children account for 5 to 15 percent of the patient load in mental health clinics. The syndrome for adopted children is named "genealogical bewilderment," leaving them more likely to suffer from learning disabilities, social dysfunction, and sometimes drug taking and delinquency.

The demand for babies to adopt has so outweighed the supply that couples are forced to seek foreign adoptions. There are two reasons for this phenomenon. One is the increase in legal and safe abortions, the other is that whereas in the 1950s about one in ten couples were infertile, in the mid-1970s that figure had increased to one in six. This is due to later marriage and possibly to drug use, but also to the higher prevalence of premarital sex by women with several male partners, which can cause benign uterine infections that never become apparent but nevertheless result in sterility. Thus the birth control pill, which eliminated the need for a rubber barrier, allowed exposure to damaging organisms and resulted in serious fertility problems for women.

CONCLUSION: EVERYBODY MAKES MISTAKES

In summary, the legal, medical, psychiatric, and religious battle over abortion seems destined to continue in this country. Clearly, the best solution is the prevention of unwanted pregnancy through education in school and home about birth control and the availability of inexpensive birth control pills or other devices. But there will always be accidents. Some men will lie, some women will have too much to drink, and passion or the woman's wish to please will overtake rational considerations. Either partner may be reenacting an earlier trauma—perhaps sexual exploitation or even adoption. Abortion should be available for women who make mistakes, something we all are capable of, even with the best of intentions.

REFERENCES

Adler, N. E. (1990). Grand Rounds, Department of Psychiatry, University of California at San Francisco, September 18.

Adler, N. E., David, H. P., Major, B. N., et al. (1990). Psychological responses after abortion. *Science* 248:41–44.

Allen, J. (1983). Motherhood: the annihilation of women. In *Mothering: Essays in Feminist Theory,* ed. J. Trebilcot, pp. 315–330. Savage, MD: Rowman & Littlefield.

Angelou, M. (1971). *I Know Why the Caged Bird Sings.* New York: Bantam.

Angier, N. (1990). Diet offers tantalizing clues to long life. *The New York Times,* April 17, p. B5, 7.

Apfel, R., and Mazor, M. (1989). Psychiatry and reproductive medicine. In *Comprehensive Textbook of Psychiatry,* vol. 2, ed. H. I. Kaplan, and B. J. Sadock, 5th ed., p. 1337. Baltimore: Williams & Wilkins.

Appelbaum, P. S., and Jorgenson, L. (1991). Psychotherapist–patient sexual contact after termination of treatment: an analysis and a proposal. *Journal of the American Psychiatric Association* 148:1466–1473.

Applegarth, A. (1990). Recovery of a memory of childhood trauma from a dream. *Dialogue* 8:16–21.

———— (1977). Some observations on work inhibitions in women. In *Female Psychology,* ed. H. P. Blum, pp. 251–268. New York: International Universities Press.

Aracana, J. (1979). *Our Mothers' Daughters.* Berkeley, CA: Shameless Hussy Press.

Artson, B. (1978). Mid-life women: homemakers, volunteers, professionals. Unpublished doctoral dissertion. The California School of Professional Psychology, San Francisco.

Balmary, M. (1982). *Freud and the Hidden Fault of the Father.* Baltimore: Johns Hopkins University Press.

Bank, S. P., and Kahn, M. D. (1982). *The Sibling Bond.* New York: Basic Books.

Barden, J. C. (1991). Washington cedes control of foster care system to private agency. *The New York Times,* July 14, p. I16.

Bart, P. (1971). Depression in middle-aged women. In *Women in Sexist Society: Studies in Power and Powerlessness.,* ed. V. Gornick and B. K. Moran, pp. 99–117. New York: Signet, 1972.

Bart, P., and Grossman, M. (1978). Menopause. In *The Woman Patient,* vol. 1., ed. M. T. Notman and C. C. Nadelson, pp. 337–354. New York: Plenum.

Baruch, G., Barnett, R., and Rivers, C. (1983). *Life Prints: New Patterns of Love and Work for Today's Women.* New York: Plume.

Bass, E., and Davis, L. (1988). *The Courage to Heal: A Guide for Women Survivors of Child Sexual Abuse.* New York: Harper and Row.

Benedict, H. (1986). How to recognize a potential batterer. *Glamour.* October, pp. 206–213.

Benedek, T. (1950a). Climacterium: a developmental phase. *Psychoanalytic Quarterly* 19:1–27.

––––– (1950b). The functions of the sexual apparatus and their disturbances. In *Psychosomatic Medicine,* ed. F. Alexander, pp. 239–248. New York: W. W. Norton.

Bera, W. (1985). A preliminary investigation of a typology of adolescent sex offenders and their family systems. Master's thesis, University of Minnesota.

Bernard, J. (1971). The paradox of the happy marriage. In *Women in Sexist Society,* ed. V. Gornick and B. Moran, pp. 145–162. New York: Signet, 1972.

Bernardez, T. (1988). Gender-based countertransference of female therapists in the psychotherapy of women. In *Women, Power, and Therapy: Issues for Women,* ed. M. Braude, pp. 25–58. New York: Haworth.

Bernstein, A. E. (1990). The impact of incest trauma on ego development. In *Adult Analysis and Childhood Sexual Abuse,* ed. H. B. Levine, pp. 65–91. Hillsdale, NJ: Analytic Press.

Bieniek, C., Barton, G., and Benedek, E. (1981). Training female mental health professionals: sexual countertransference issues. *Journal of the American Medical Women's Association* 36:131–139.

Bigras, J. (1990). Psychoanalysis as incestuous repetition: some technical considerations. In *Adult Analysis and Childhood Sexual Abuse,* ed. H. B. Levine, pp. 173–196. Hillsdale, NJ: Analytic Press.

Birnbaum, J. (1975). Life patterns and self-esteem in gifted, family-oriented and career-committed women. In *Women and Achievement: Social and Motivational Analysis,* ed. M. Mednick, S. Tangri, and L. W. Hoffman. New York: Halstead-Wiley.

Bishops denounce abusive husbands. (1992). *The New York Times,* October 30, A16.

Blau DuPlesssis, R. (1978). Washing blood. *Feminist Studies* 2:1–12.

Block, M. (1978). *Uncharted Territory: Issues and Concerns of Women Over 40.* University Park, MD: University of Maryland, Center on Aging.

Blum, H. P. (1977). Masochism, the ego ideal, and the psychology of women. In *Female Psychology,* ed. H. P. Blum, pp. 157–191. New York: International Universities Press.

Blume, E. S. (1990). *Secret Survivors.* New York: Wiley.

Blumenthal, R. (1984). Freud: Secret documents reveal years of strife: evidence points to anguish over the seduction theory. *The New York Times,* January 24, pp. 13, 19.

Bolen, J. S. (1991). Wisdom from within: wise women archetype. Paper presented at "Women's Lives: The Quest for Self" conference, University of California at Berkeley, Extension Division, March 16.

Bolotin, S. (1982). Voices from the post-feminist generation. *The New York Times Magazine,* October 17, pp. 28–31, 103–117.

Bolton, F. G., Morris, L. A., and MacEachron, A. E. (1989). *Males At Risk: The Other Side of Child Sexual Abuse.* Newbury Park, CA: Sage.

Boston Women's Health Book Collective (1971). *Our Bodies, Ourselves.* Boston: New England Free Press.

———— (1973). *Our Bodies, Ourselves—A Book by and for Women.* New York: Simon & Schuster.

Bowen, M. (1972). Toward the differentiation of a self in one's own family. In *Family Interaction: A Dialogue Between Family Researchers and Family Therapists,* ed. J. L. Framo, pp. 111–173. New York: Springer.

Bowlby, J. (1951). *Maternal Care and Mental Health.* New York: Schocken, 1966.

———— (1969). *Attachment and Loss.* Volume 1, *Attachment.* London: Penguin Books, 1971.

Bradwell v. Illinois, 83 U.S. (Wall) 130 (1872), at 140–142.

Braude, M. (1983). The consequences of abortion legislation. In *Women Changing Therapy,* ed. J. H. Robbins and R. J. Siegel, pp. 81–90. New York: Haworth.

Brody, J. E. (1988). Personal health. *The New York Times,* October 20, pp. B6, B8.

———— (1992). Personal health. *The New York Times*, March 18, B6.

Brooks, A. (1989). Experts find extramarital affairs have a profound impact on children. *The New York Times,* March 9, p. B6.

Brown, C. W., Bhrolehain, M. N., and Harris, T. (1975). Social class and psychiatric disturbance among women in an urban population. *Sociology* 9:225–254.

Brown, L. S. (1989). Beyond thou shalt not: thinking about ethics in the lesbian therapy community. In *Lesbianism: Affirming Nontraditional Roles,* ed. E. D. Rothblum and E. Cole, pp. 13–25. New York: Haworth.

Brown, N. O. (1959). *Life Against Death: The Psychoanalytic Meaning of History.* New York: Random House.

Brown, R. M. (1973). *Rubyfruit Jungle.* New York: Bantam, 1977.

Brumberg, J. J. (1991). Review of *Educated in Romance* by D. C. Holland, and M. A. Eisenhart. *The New York Times Book Review,* January 20, p. 29.

Burch, B. (1986). Psychotherapy and the dynamics of merger in lesbian couples. In *Contemporary Perspective on Psychotherapy With Lesbians and Gay Men,* ed. T. S. Stein and C. J. Cohen, pp. 57–71. New York: Plenum.

———— (1987). Barriers to intimacy: conflicts over power, dependency, and nurturing in lesbian relationships. In *Lesbian Psychologies,* ed. Boston Lesbian Psychologies Collective, pp. 126–141. Urbana, IL: University of Illinois Press.

Burland, J. A., and Raskin, R. (1990). The psychoanalysis of adults who were sexually abused in childhood. In *Adult Analysis and Childhood Sexual Abuse,* ed. H. B. Levine, pp. 35–41. Hillsdale, NJ: Analytic Press.

Butler, R. N. (1985). Psychiatry and psychology of the middle-aged. In *Comprehensive Textbook of Psychiatry,* vol. 2, ed. H. I. Kaplan and B. J. Sadock, 4th ed., pp. 1943–1952. Baltimore: Williams & Wilkins.

Butler, R. N. (1989). Psychosocial aspects of aging. In *Comprehensive Textbook of Psychiatry,* vol. 2, ed. H. I. Kaplan and B. J. Sadock, 5th ed., pp. 2014–2019. Baltimore: Williams & Wilkins.

Butler, S. (1978). *Conspiracy of Silence: The Trauma of Incest.* San Francisco: New Glide Publications.

Caplan, L. (1990). *An Open Adoption.* New York: Farrar, Straus & Giroux.

Caplan, P. J. (1983). Between women: lowering the barriers. In *Women Changing Therapy: New Assessments, Values and Strategies in Feminist Therapy,* ed. J. H. Robbins and R. J. Siegel, pp. 51–66. New York: Haworth.

Carmen, E. H. (1982). Wife abuse: culture as destiny. In *The Woman Patient,* vol. 3., ed. M. K. Notman and C. C. Nadelson, pp. 47–64. New York: Plenum.

C. G. Jung Institute of San Francisco (1991). *Code of Ethics for the C. G. Jung Institute of San Francisco.* Pamphlet. San Francisco, CA.

Chernin, K. (1981). *The Obsession: Reflections on the Tyranny of Slenderness.* New York: Harper and Row.

Chodorow, N., and Contratto, S. (1976). The fantasy of the perfect mother. In *Feminism and Psychoanalytic Theory,* pp. 79–96. New Haven: Yale University Press, 1989.

Chodorow, N. (1978). *The Reproduction of Mothering: Psychoanalysis and the Sociology of Gender.* Berkeley, CA: University of California Press.

Committee on Government Operations, U.S. House of Representatives. (1989). The federal role in determining the medical and psychological impact of abortion on women, testimony of C. Everett Koop. 101st Cong., 2nd sess., 11 Dec. H. Rep. 101:392. p. 14.

Conley, F. K. (1991). Woman surgeon charges sexual harassment at work. Open Forum. *San Francisco Chronicle,* June 4, p. A21.

Cook, B. W. (1992). *Eleanor Roosevelt,* vol. 1. New York: Viking.

Cotton, D. W. (1965). *The Case for the Working Mother.* New York: Stein & Day.

Cox, S. (1981). *Female Psychology: The Emerging Self,* 2nd ed. New York: St. Martin's Press.

de Beauvoir, S. (1952). *The Second Sex.* Trans. J. M. Parshley. New York: Vintage, 1974.

Deutsch, H. (1944). *Psychology of Women,* vol. 1. New York: Grune & Stratton.

——— (1945). *Psychology of Women,* vol. 2. *Motherhood.* New York: Grune & Stratton.

Deutscher, I. (1968). The quality of post parental life. In *Middle Age and Aging,* ed. B. L. Newgarten, pp. 263–268. Chicago: University of Chicago Press.

Diagnostic and Statistical Manual on Mental Disorders DSM-III-R (1987). 3rd ed, revised. Washington, DC: American Psychiatric Association.

Diesenhouse, S. (1989). Therapists start to address damage done by therapists. *The New York Times,* August 20, p. E5.

Dinnerstein, D. (1976). *The Mermaid and the Minotaur*. New York: Harper and Row.

Domestic violence is target of a proposed federal law. (1990). *The New York Times,* December 16, p. 22.

Doress, P., Siegal, D., and the Midlife and Older Women Book Project. (1987). *Ourselves, Growing Older: Women Aging With Knowledge and Power*. New York: Simon & Schuster.

Dutton, D., and Painter, S. F. (1981). Traumatic bonding: the development of emotional attachments in battered women and other relationships of intermittent abuse. *Victimology: An International Journal* 6:139–155.

Dworkin, A. (1974). *Woman Hating*. New York: Dutton.

Eastwood, J., Spielvogel, A., and Wile, J. (1990). Countertransference risks when women treat women. *Clinical Social Work Journal* 18:273–280.

Ehrensaft, D. (1985). Dual parenting and the duel of intimacy. In *The Psychosocial Interior of the Family,* ed. G. Handel, 3rd. ed., pp. 323–337. New York: Aldine.

Eichenbaum, L., and Orbach, S. (1983). *Understanding Women*. New York: Basic Books.

Eisenbud, R. J. (1982). Early and later determinants of lesbian choice. *The Psychoanalytic Review* 69:85–109.

Ekblad, N. (1955). Induced abortion on psychiatric grounds. *Acta Psychiatrica Scandinavica Supplementum* 99.

Eliasberg, W. G. (1954). The prenatal psychotic patient. In *Therapeutic Abortion,* ed. H. Rosen, pp. 213–218. New York: Julian Press.

Erikson, E. H. (1959). Identity and life cycle. *Psychological Issues* 1:1 (Monograph No. 1).

Erikson, E. H., Erikson, J., and Kivnick, H. (1986). *Vital Involvement in Old Age*. New York: W. W. Norton.

Erikson, J. (1991). Letter to the audience at the conference, "Women's Lives, The Quest for Self," University of California at Berkeley, Extension Division, March 16.

Faller, K. C. (1988). *Child Sexual Abuse*. New York: Columbia University Press.

Faludi, S. (1991). *Backlash: The Undeclared War Against American Women*. New York: Crown.

Ferenczi, S. (1933). Confusion of tongues between the adult and the child. In *Final Contributions to the Problems and Methods of Psychoanalysis,* pp. 156–167. London: Hogarth Press, 1955.

Finkelhor, D. (1984). *Child Sexual Abuse: New Theory and Research*. New York: The Free Press.

_____ (1986). *A Sourcebook on Child Sexual Abuse*. Beverly Hills, CA: Sage.

Firestone, S. (1970). *The Dialectic of Sex*. New York: William Morrow.

Forssman, H., and Thuwe, I. (1966). One hundred and twenty children born after application for therapeutic abortion refused: their mental health, social adjustment and education level up to the age of 21. *Acta Psychiatrica Scandinavica* 42: 71–88.

Fox-Genovese, E. (1991). *Feminism Without Illusions: A Critique of Individualism*. Chapel Hill, NC: University of North Carolina Press.

Frankel, S. A., and Wise, M. J. A view of delayed parenting: some implications of a new trend. *Psychiatry* 45:3.

Freud, S. (1896). The aetiology of hysteria. *Standard Edition* 3:189–221.

_____ (1905). Three essays on the theory of sexuality. *Standard Edition* 7:125–245.

_____ (1910). The future prospects of psychoanalytic therapy. In *Collected Papers* 2:285–296. London: Hogarth Press, 1946.

_____ (1912). Totem and taboo. In *The Basic Writings of Sigmund Freud,* ed. A. A. Brill, pp. 807–930. New York: Modern Library, 1938.

_____ (1914). On narcissism: an introduction. *Standard Edition* 14:73–102. London: Hogarth Press, 1957.

_____ (1933). Further recommendations on the technique of psychoanalysis: observations on transference-love. In *Collected Papers* 2:377–391, ed. E. Jones. London: Hogarth Press, (1933).

_____ (1917). Mourning and melancholia. *Standard Edition* 14:239–258.

_____ (1933). Femininity. *Standard Edition* 33:112–185.

_____ (1937a). Constructions in analysis. *Standard Edition* 23:257–269.

_____ (1937b). Analysis terminable and interminable. *Standard Edition* 23:209–253.

Friday, N. (1977). *My Mother, My Self.* New York: Dell.

Friedan, B. (1963). *The Feminine Mystique.* New York: Dell, 1974.

Gardner, C. A. (1989). Is an embryo a person? *The Nation,* November 13, p. 557.

Gartrell, N. (1984). Issues in psychotherapy with lesbian women. *Work in Progress* No. 83–04. Wellesley, MA: Wellesley College, The Stone Center.

Gartrell, N., Herman, J., Olarte, S., et al. (1986). Psychiatrist–patient sexual contact: results of a national survey. I: prevalence. *American Journal of Psychiatry* 143:1126–1131.

Gill, M. (1979). Analysis of the transference. *Journal of the American Psychoanalytic Association* 27(Suppl.):263–288.

Gilligan, C. (1982). *In a Different Voice.* Cambridge, MA: Harvard University Press.

Gillman, I. S. (1980). An object-relations approach to the phenomenon and treatment of battered women. *Psychiatry* 43:346–358.

Gimenez, M. E. (1983). Feminism, pronatalism and motherhood. In *Mothering: Essays in Feminist Theory,* ed. J. Trebilcot. Savage, MD: Rowman & Littlefield.

Gitelson, M. (1965). A transference reaction in a sixty-six-year-old woman. In *Geriatric Psychiatry: Grief, Loss, and Emotional Disorders in the Aging Process,* ed. M. A. Berezin and S. H. Cath, pp. 160–186. New York: International Universities Press.

Gleick, E. (1990). When food is a four-letter word. *San Francisco Chronicle,* June 17, *This World,* pp. 12–14.

Goleman, D. (1990). New guidelines issued on patient–therapist sex. *The New York Times,* December 20, p. B21.

Gove, W. R. (1980). Mental illness and psychiatric treatment among women. In *Female Psychology: The Emerging Self,* ed. S. Cox, 2nd ed., pp. 351–363. New York: St. Martin's Press, 1981.

Goz, R. (1973). Women patients and women therapists: some issues that come up in psychotherapy. *International Journal of Psychoanalytic Psychotherapy.* 2:298–319.

Greenacre, P. (1954). The role of transference. In *Classics in Psychoanalytic Technique,* ed. R. Langs, rev. ed. Northvale, NJ: Jason Aronson.

Greenspan, M. (1983). *A New Approach to Women and Therapy.* New York: McGraw-Hill.

———— (1984). The fear of being alone: female psychology and women's work. *Socialist Review* 73:14.

Greenwood, S. (1984). *Menopause Naturally.* San Francisco: Volcano Press.

Greunberg, S. (1952). *The Many Lives of Modern Women.* New York: Doubleday.

Gross, J. (1989). Helping men beat back the urge to violence. *The New York Times,* June 1, pp. A14, 16.

———— (1991). More young single men clinging to apron strings. *The New York Times,* June 16, pp. 1, 10.

Guttman, H. A. (1984). Sexual issues in the transference and countertransference between female therapist and male patient. *Journal of the American Academy of Psychoanalysis* 12:187–197.

Havel, V. (1989). *Vaclav Havel: Living in Truth,* ed. J. Vladislav. Boston: Faber and Faber.

Heilbrun, C. G. (1988). *Writing a Woman's Life.* New York: Ballantine.

Hennig, M., and Jardim, A. (1977). *The Managerial Woman.* New York: Anchor Press/Doubleday.

Herman, J. (1981). *Father–Daughter Incest.* Cambridge, MA: Harvard University Press.

———— (1984). The analyst analyzed. *The Nation,* March 10, pp. 293–296.

Herman, J., and Hirschman, L. (1981). Father–daughter incest. In *Female Psychology,* ed. S. Cox, pp. 206–221. New York: St. Martin's Press.

Hite, S. (1976). *The Hite Report.* New York: Dell.

Hoffman, J. (1992). When men hit women. *The New York Times Magazine,* February 16, pp. 22–27, 64–72.

Hoffman, L., and Nye, F., eds. (1963). *The Employed Mother in America.* Chicago: Rand McNally.

Holiday appeal: abused wife finds help in therapy. *The New York Times,* December 21, 1986, p. 82.

Hook, K. (1963). Refused abortion: a follow-up study of two hundred and forty-nine women whose applications were refused by the national board of health in Sweden. *Acta Psychiatrica Scandinavica Supplementum* 168.

Horney, K. (1934). The overvaluation of love. In *Feminine Psychology,* ed. H. Kelman, pp. 182–213. New York: Norton, 1967.

Huizenga, J. N. (1990). Incest as trauma: a psychoanalytic case. In *Adult Analysis and Childhood Sexual Abuse,* ed. H. B. Levine, pp. 117–135. Hillsdale, NJ: Analytic Press.

Hunt, M. (1977). Men who beat their wives. Cambridge, MA: American Friends Service Committee.

James, C. (1990). Pop view: beneath all that black lace beats the heart of a bimbo. . . . *The New York Times,* December 16, pp. 38, 44.

Jenkins, R. L. (1954). The significance of maternal rejection of pregnancy for the future development of the child. In *Therapeutic Abortion,* ed. H. Rosen, pp. 269–275. New York: Julian Press.

Jones, E. (1959). *The Life and Work of Sigmund Freud,* vol. 3. New York: Basic Books.

Jones, E. E., and Zoppel, C. L. (1982). Impact of client and therapist gender on psychotherapy process and outcome. *Journal of Consulting and Clinical Psychology* 50:259–272.

Justice, B., and Justice, R. (1979). *The Broken Taboo.* New York: Human Sciences Press.

Kaplan, H. I., and Sadock, B. J., eds. (1989). *Comprehensive Textbook of Psychiatry,* vol. 2, 5th ed. Baltimore: Williams & Wilkins.

Kaplan, L. J. (1991). *Female Perversions.* New York: Doubleday.

Kardener, S. R., Fuller, M., and Mensh, I. N. (1973). A survey of physicians' attitudes and practices regarding erotic and nonerotic contact with patients. *American Journal of Psychiatry* 130:1077–1081.

Kasl, C. D. (1990). Female perpetrators of sexual abuse: a feminist view. In *The Sexually Abused Male,* vol. 1, ed. M. Hunter, pp. 259–274. Lexington, MA: Lexington Books.

Kaunitz, P. E. (1977). Sadomasochistic marriages. *Medical Aspects of Human Sexuality* 11(2):66–80.

Keller, E. F. (1985). *Reflections on Gender and Science.* New Haven: Yale University Press.

Kernberg, O. F. (1975). *Borderline Conditions and Pathological Narcissism.* New York: Jason Aronson.

——— (1976). *Object Relations Theory and Clinical Psychoanalysis.* New York: Jason Aronson.

Kinsey, A. C., Pomeroy, W., Martin, C., and Gebhard, P. (1953). *Sexual Behavior in the Human Female.* New York: Pocket Books, 1965.

Kohlberg, L. (1976). Moral stages and moralization: the cognitive-developmental approach. In *Moral Development and Behavior: Theory, Research and Social Issues,* ed. T. Lickoma. New York: Holt, Rinehart and Winston.

Kolata, G. (1992). In late abortions, decisions are painful and options few. *The New York Times,* January 5, pp. 1, 12.

Konner, M. (1990). Mutilated in the name of tradition. *The New York Times Book Review,* April 15, pp. 5–6.

Kramer, S. (1990). Residues of incest. In *Adult Analysis and Childhood Sexual Abuse,* ed. H. B. Levine, pp. 149–170. Hillsdale, NJ: Analytic Press.

Krause, C. (1971). The femininity complex and female therapists. *Journal of Marriage and the Family* 33:476–482.

Krieger, S. (1983). *The Mirror Dance.* Philadelphia: Temple University Press.

Kummer, J. (1963). Post abortion psychiatric illness: a myth? *American Journal of Psychiatry* 119:980–983.

Langs, R. (1973). *The Technique of Psychoanalytic Psychotherapy,* vol. 1. New York: Jason Aronson.

Legislating from the bench (1991). Editorial, *San Francisco Examiner,* May 26, p. A14.

Leidig, M. W. (1981). Violence against women: a feminist-psychological analysis. In

Female Psychology, ed. S. Cox, 2nd ed., pp. 190–205. New York: St. Martin's Press.

Lerner, H. (1988). *Women in Therapy.* Northvale, NJ: Jason Aronson.

Leroi, D. C. (1984). *The silent partner: an investigation of the familial background, personality structure, sexual behavior and relationships of the mothers of incestuous families.* Unpublished dissertation, California School of Professional Psychology, Berkeley, CA.

Lester, E. P. (1982). *The female analyst and the erotized transference.* Paper presented at the meeting of the American Psychoanalytic Association, New York, NY, December.

Levine, H. B., ed. (1990). *Adult Analysis and Childhood Sexual Abuse.* Hillsdale, NJ: Analytic Press.

Levinger, G. (1966). Sources of marital dissatisfaction among applicants for divorce. *American Journal of Orthopsychiatry* 36:804–808.

Levinson, D. J. (1978). *The Seasons of a Man's Life.* New York: Alfred A. Knopf.

Levy, H. S. (1966). *Chinese Footbinding: the History of a Curious Erotic Custom.* New York: W. Rawls.

Lightfoot-Klein, H. (1990). *An Odyssey Into Female Genital Circumcision in Africa.* Binghamton, NY: Haworth Press.

Lisman-Pieczanski, N. (1990). Countertransference in the analysis of an adult who was sexually abused as a child. In *Adult Analysis and Childhood Sexual Abuse,* ed. H. B. Levine, pp. 137–147. Hillsdale, NJ: Analytic Press.

Lloyd, R. (1976). *For Money or Love: Boy Prostitution in America.* New York: Ballantine.

Long, L. and Long, T. (1983). *The Handbook for Latchkey Children and Their Parents.* New York: Arbor House.

MacFarland, K., and Waterman, J., eds. (1986). *Sexual Abuse of Young Children.* New York: Guilford Press.

Maccoby, E. (1958). Effects upon children of their mother's outside employment. In *Work In the Lives of Married Women.* National Manpower Council. New York: Columbia University Press.

Mahler, M., Pine, F., and Bergman, A. (1975). *The Psychological Birth of the Human Infant: Symbiosis and Individuation.* New York: Basic Books.

Malcolm, J. (1983). Annals of scholarship: trouble in the archives. *The New Yorker,* December 5, pp. 59–152 and Dec. 12, pp. 60–119.

Mandy, A. J. (1954). Reflections of a gynecologist. In *Therapeutic Abortion,* ed. H. Rosen, pp. 284–296. New York: Julian Press.

Marmor, J. (1974). The crisis of middle age. In *Psychiatry in Transition,* ed. J. Marmor, pp. 71–76. New York: Brunner/Mazel.

Masson, J. M. (1984a). *The Assault on Truth: Freud's Suppression of the Seduction Theory.* New York: Farrar, Straus & Giroux.

—— (1984b). Freud and the seduction theory. *The Atlantic Monthly,* February, pp. 33–60.

Masters, W. H., and Johnson, V. D. (1970). *Human Sexual Inadequacy.* Boston: Little, Brown.

Mathews, R. (1987). *Preliminary typology of female sex offenders. MN: PHASE and Genesis II for women.* Unpublished.

Mathews, R., Matthews, J., and Spelz, K. (1990). Female sexual offenders. In *The Sexually Abused Male,* vol. 1, ed. M. Hunter, pp. 275–293. Lexington, MA: Lexington Books.

McCabe, M. (1991). Stanford brain surgeon quits over sex harassment. *San Francisco Chronicle,* June 1, p. A1.

McGinnis, M. P. (1978). *On the psychology of men who batter.* Unpublished.

Mencher, J. (1990). Intimacy in lesbian relationships: a critical re-examination of fusion. *Work in Progress,* No. 42. Wellesley, MA: Wellesley College, The Stone Center.

Mering, F. H. Von (1971). Professional and non-professional women as mothers. *The Professional Woman,* ed. A. Theodore, pp. 568–583. Cambridge, MA: Schenkman.

Miller, J. B. (1976). *Toward a New Psychology of Women.* Boston: Beacon Press.

Millett, K. (1979). *The Basement: Meditations on a Human Sacrifice.* New York: Simon & Schuster.

Moss, L. E., and Siegel, R. (1984). Workshop on therapist responses to lesbian clients. Women's Institute, American Orthopsychiatric Association, Toronto, Canada, April.

Myer, M. H. (1984). Research dispels incestuous family myth. *NASW News,* March, pp. 3–4.

Nadelson, C. (1978). The emotional impact of abortion. In *The Woman Patient,* vol. 1, ed. M. T. Notman and C. C. Nadelson, pp. 173–179. New York: Plenum.

Nadelson, C., Polonsky, D. C., and Mathews, M. A. (1982). Marriage and midlife: the impact of social change. In *The Woman Patient,* vol. 2, ed. C. C. Nadelson and M. T. Notman, pp. 145–158. New York: Plenum.

Nelson, B. (1982). Efforts to curb sexually abusive therapists gain. *The New York Times,* November 23, pp. 17, 19.

Ness, C. (1991). A women's woe that's worsening. *San Francisco Examiner,* May 26, pp. A1, 16.

Neugarten, B. (1968). *Middle Age and Aging.* Chicago: University of Chicago Press.

Nix, C. (1986). Police step up attack on domestic violence. *The New York Times,* December 31, p. 12.

Notman, M. T. (1982). Midlife concerns of women: implications of menopause. In *The Woman Patient,* vol. 2, ed. C. C. Nadelson and M. T. Notman, pp. 135–144. New York: Plenum.

Novello, A. C. (1992). From the Surgeon-General, U.S. Public Health Service. *Journal of the American Medical Association* 267:3132.

O'Neill, Jaime M. (1990) End paper, Keeping on. *San Francisco Chronicle, This World,* August 26, p. 20.

Olds, S. W. (1975). *The Mother Who Works Outside the Home.* Child Study Press Wel-Met Inc.: Child Study Association of America. Pamphlet.

Orbach, S. (1978). *Fat is a Feminist Issue.* New York: Paddington.

Oremland, J. D. (1975). An unexpected result of the analysis of a talented musician. *Psychoanalytic Study of the Child* 30:375–407.

_____ (1991). *Interpretation and Interaction: Psychoanalysis or Psychotherapy?* Hillsdale, NJ: Analytic Press.

Orenstein, P. (1991). Champion of the deep. *The New York Times Magazine,* June 23, pp. 15–21, 31.

Pagels, E. (1988). *Adam, Eve, and the Serpent.* New York: Random House.

Pearlman, S. F. (1989). Distancing and connectedness: impact on couple formation in lesbian relationships. In *Lesbians: Affirming Nontraditional Roles,* ed. E. D. Rothblum, and E. Cole, pp. 77–88. New York: Haworth.

Peck, A., and Marcus, H. (1966). Psychiatric sequelae of therapeutic interruption of pregnancy. *Journal of Nervous and Mental Disease* 143:417–425.

Perlmutter, J. F. (1978). A gynecological approach to menopause. In *The Woman Patient,* vol. 1., ed. M. T. Notman and C. C. Nadelson, pp. 323–335. New York: Plenum.

Person, E. (1983a). The influence of values in psychoanalysis: the case of female psychology. *Psychoanalytic Inquiry* 3:623–646.

_____ (1983b). Women in therapy: therapist gender as a variable. *International Review of Psycho-Analysis* 10:193–204.

_____ (1985). *The erotic transference in women and in men: differences and consequences.* Unpublished.

Pittman, F. (1989). *Private Lies.* New York: W. W. Norton.

Pollitt, K. (1986). Why are women psychotherapy's best customers? *The New York Times,* January 9, p. C2.

Pope, K. S., and Bouhoutsos, J. (1986). *Sexual Intimacy between Therapists and Patients.* New York: Praeger.

Popkin, M. K. (1989). Impulse control disorders not elsewhere classified. In *Comprehensive Textbook of Psychiatry,* vol. 2, ed. H. I. Kaplan and B. J. Sadock, 5th ed., pp. 1145–1154. Baltimore: Williams & Wilkins.

Prozan, C. (1992). *Feminist Psychoanalytic Psychotherapy.* Northvale, NJ: Jason Aronson.

Quinn, V. (1990). *Professional Therapy Never Includes Sex.* Department of Consumer Affairs, Sacramento, CA. Pamphlet.

Raphling, D. L. (1990). Technical issues of the opening phase. In *Adult Analysis and Childhood Sexual Abuse,* ed. H. B. Levine, pp. 45–64. Hillsdale, NJ: Analytic Press.

Randall, T. (1992). ACOG renews domestic violence campaign, calls for changes in medical school curricula. *Journal of the American Medical Association* 267:3131.

Regenstreif, A. (1984). *Working through defense mechanisms in male clients who are abusing their spouses.* Unpublished. San Francisco, CA.

Reinhart, M. A. (1987). Sexually abused boys. *Child Abuse and Neglect* 11:229–235.

Reiser, L. W., and Reiser, M. F. (1985). Disorders associated with female endocrine function. In *Comprehensive Textbook of Psychiatry,* ed. H. I. Kaplan and B. J. Sadock, 4th ed., vol. 2, pp. 1173–1175. Baltimore: Williams & Wilkins.

Rich, A. (1976). *Of Woman Born.* New York: Norton.

Ritvo, S. (1977). Adolescent to woman. In *Female Psychology,* ed. H. P. Blum, pp. 127–137. New York: International Universities Press.

Romm, M. E. (1954). Psychoanalytic considerations. In *Therapeutic Abortion,* ed. H. Rosen, pp. 209–212. New York: Julian Press.

Rosen, H. (1954). The emotionally sick pregnant patient: psychiatric indications and contraindications to the interruption of pregnancy. In *Therapeutic Abortion,* ed. H. Rosen, pp. 219–243. New York: Julian Press.

Rosenbaum, M. B. (1979). The changing body image of the adolescent girl. In *Female Adolescent Development,* ed. M. Sugar, pp. 234–252. New York: Brunner/Mazel.

Rosenblum, B. (1983). Book review of *The Mirror Dance* by Susan Krieger. *San Francisco Chronicle,* Sept. 4. Review 8-1-R.

Rosenfeld, A. (1979). Incidence of a history of incest among 18 female psychiatric patients. *American Journal of Psychiatry* 136:791–795.

Rossi, A. S. (1965). Equality between the sexes: an immodest proposal. In *The Woman in America,* ed. R. J. Lifton, pp. 98–143. Boston: Houghton Mifflin.

_____ (1973). Maternalism, sexuality, and the new feminism. In *Contemporary Sexual Behavior,* ed. J. Zubin and J. Money, pp. 145–173. Baltimore: Johns Hopkins University Press.

Roth, G. (1984). *Breaking Free From Compulsive Eating.* New York: New American Library.

_____ (1991). *When Food is Love.* New York: Dutton.

Rubin, L. B. (1979). *Women of a Certain Age: The Midlife Search for Self.* New York: Harper and Row.

Rush, F. (1977). Freud and the sexual abuse of children. *Chrysalis* 1:31–45.

_____ (1980a). *The Best Kept Secret: Sexual Abuse of Children.* Englewood Cliffs, NJ: Prentice Hall.

_____ (1980b). Child pornography. In *Take Back the Night,* ed. L. Lederer, pp. 71–81. New York: William Morrow.

Russell, D. (1986). *The Secret Trauma: Incest in the Lives of Girls and Women.* New York: Basic Books.

Russian Proverbs. (1960). New York: Peter Pauper Press.

Rutter, M. (1972). *Maternal Deprivation Reassessed.* Baltimore: Penguin Books.

Rutter, P. (1989). *Sex in the Forbidden Zone.* Los Angeles: Jeremy P. Tarcher.

Sadock, V. (1989). Rape, spouse abuse, and incest. In *Comprehensive Textbook of Psychiatry,* vol. 1, ed. H. I. Kaplan and B. J. Sadock, 5th ed., pp. 1096–1104. Baltimore: Williams & Wilkins.

Salter, S. (1990). Violence begins at home. *San Francisco Examiner,* May 15, p. A21.

Schafer, R. (1977). Problems in Freud's psychology of women. In *Female Psychology: Contemporary Psychoanalytic Views,* ed. H. P. Blum, pp. 331–360. New York: International Universities Press.

Schaffer, H. R. (1977). *Mothering.* Cambridge, MA: Harvard University Press.

Schulder, D. B. (1970). Does the law oppress women? In *Sisterhood is Powerful,* ed. R. Morgan, pp. 153–175. New York: Random House.

Scully, D., and Bart, P. B. (1973). A funny thing happened on the way to the orifice: women in gynecology textbooks. *American Journal of Sociology* 78:1045–1050.

Seaman, B., and Seaman, G. (1977). *Women and the Crisis in Sex Hormones.* New York: Bantam.

Searles, H. F. (1975). The patient as therapist to his analyst. In *Classics in*

Psychoanalytic Technique, ed. R. Langs, pp. 103–135. Northvale, NJ: Jason Aronson, 1990.

Sears, P. S., and Barbee, A. H. (1977). Career and life satisfactions among Terman's gifted women. In *The Gifted and the Creative: Fifty-Year Perspective,* ed. J. Stanley, W. George, and C. Solano. Baltimore: Johns Hopkins University Press.

Seidenberg, R. (1972). The trauma of eventlessness. In *Psychoanalysis and Women,* ed. J. B. Miller, pp. 350–362. Baltimore: Penguin, 1973.

Seligman, M. E. D. (1974). Depression and learned helplessness. In *The Psychology of Depression: Contemporary Theory and Research,* ed. R. J. Friedman and M. Katz, pp. 83–113. Washington, DC: Winston.

Shainess, N. (1983). Significance of match in sex of analyst and patient. *The American Journal of Psychoanalysis* 43:205–217.

Sherkow, S. P. (1990). Consequences of childhood sexual abuse on the development of ego structure: a comparison of child and adult cases. In *Adult Analysis and Childhood Sexual Abuse,* ed. H. B. Levine, pp. 93–115. Hillsdale, NJ: Analytic Press.

Shreve, A. (1984). The working mother as role model. *The New York Times Magazine,* September 9, pp. 38–43, 50–54.

Siegal, A. E., Stolz, L. M., Hitchcock, E. A., and Adamson, J. (1959). Dependence and independence in the children of working mothers. *Child Development* 30:533–546.

Siegel, R. J. (1983). Change and creativity at midlife. In *Women Changing Therapy,* ed. J. H. Robbins and R. J. Siegel, pp. 95–102. New York: Haworth.

——— (1988). Beyond homophobia: learning to work with lesbian clients. In *Women, Power, and Therapy,* ed. M. Braude, pp. 125–133. New York: Haworth.

Simon, N., Senturia, A., and Rothman, D. (1967). Psychiatric illness following therapeutic abortion. *American Journal of Psychiatry* 14:59–65.

Simon, R. (1991). From the editor. *The Family Therapy Networker,* January/February, p. 2.

Simon, R. G., Clark, S. M., and Galway, K. (1967). The woman Ph.D.: a recent profile. *Social Problems* 15:222–236.

Smith-Rosenberg C., and Rosenberg, C. (1973). The female animal: medical and biological views of woman and her role in nineteenth-century America. *Journal of American History* 60:332–356.

Smith-Rosenberg, C., Rosenberg, C. and Rosenberg, C. (1972). The American sin and other transgressions. *Pennsylvania Gazette,* November, pp. 26–29.

Snell, J. D., Rosenwald, R. J., and Robey, A. (1964). The wife-beater's wife. *Archives of General Psychiatry* 11:107–112.

Sorosky, A. D. (1978). *The Adoption Experience: The Effects of the Sealed Records on Adoptees, Birth Parents and Adoptive Parents.* New York: Anchor Doubleday.

Starzecpyzel, E. (1987). The Persephone complex. In *Lesbian Psychologies,* ed. Boston Lesbian Psychologies Collective, pp. 261–282. Urbana, IL: University of Illinois.

Steele, B. F. (1990). Some sequelae of the sexual maltreatment of children. In *Adult Analysis and Childhood Sexual Abuse,* ed. H. B. Levine, pp. 21–34. Hillsdale, NJ: Analytic Press.

Steinem, G. (1983). *Outrageous Acts and Everyday Rebellions.* New York: Holt, Rinehart & Winston.

_____ (1990) Sex, lies and advertising. *Ms.,* July/August, pp. 18–28.

Stepansky, P. E. (1988). *The Memoirs of Margaret S. Mahler.* New York: The Free Press.

Stotland, N. L. (1992). The myth of the abortion trauma syndrome. *Journal of the American Medical Association* 268:2078–2079.

Sugg, N. K., and Inui, T. (1992). Primary care physicians' response to domestic violence: opening Pandora's box. *Journal of the American Medical Association* 267:3157–3160.

Surrey, J. L. (1984). Eating patterns as a reflection of women's development. *Work in Progress,* No. 83-06. Wellesley, MA: Wellesley College, Stone Center.

Taubman, S. (1986). Beyond the bravado: sex roles and the exploitive male. *Social Work,* January/February, pp. 12–18.

Taylor, D., and Sumrall, A. C. (1991). *Women of the 14th Moon: Writings on Menopause.* Freedom, CA: The Crossing Press.

Terry, D. (1992). Stabbing death at door of justice sends alert on domestic violence. *The New York Times,* March 17, p. A1,7.

Thompson, C. (1938). Notes on the psychoanalytic significance of the choice of analyst. *Psychiatry* 1:205–216.

Thomson, J. J. (1971). A defense of abortion. *Journal of Philosophy and Public Affairs* 1:47.

Ticho, G. R. (1974). Female autonomy and young adult women. In *Female Psychology,* ed. H. P. Blum, pp. 139–156. New York: International Universities Press.

Tisza, V. (1982). Incest. In *The Woman Patient,* vol. 3, ed. M. T. Notman and C. C. Nadelson, pp. 65–82. New York: Plenum.

Tollini, T. (1985).*Breaking Silence.* San Francisco, CA: Future Educational Films.

Tower, L. E. (1956). Countertransference. In *Classics in Psychoanalytic Technique,* ed. R. Langs. Northvale, NJ: Jason Aronson, 1990.

Tribe, L. H. (1990). *Abortion: The Clash of Absolutes.* New York: Norton.

Turkel, A. R. (1976). The impact of feminism on the practice of a woman analyst. *American Journal of Psychoanalysis* 36:119–126.

Turkle, S. (1981). *Psychoanalytic Politics: Freud's French Revolution.* Cambridge, MA: MIT Press.

Vargo, S. (1987). Effects of women's socialization. In *Lesbian Psychologies,* ed. Boston Lesbian Psychologies Collective, pp. 161–173. Urbana, IL: University of Illinois.

Viorst, M. (1991). A reporter at large: the house of Hashem. *The New Yorker,* January 7, pp. 32–52.

Walker, L. (1979). *The Battered Woman.* New York: Harper and Row.

Wallerstein, J. S., and Blakeslee, S. (1989). *Second Chances: Men, Women and Children a Decade after Divorce.* New York: Ticknor & Fields.

Wardell, J. (1985). *Thin Within: How to Eat and Live Like a Thin Person.* New York: Harmony.

Weiss, R. S., and Samuelson, N. M. (1958). Social roles of American women: their contribution to a sense of usefulness and importance. *Journal of Marriage and Family* 20:358–366.

Weissman, M., and Boyd, J. H. (1985). Affective disorders: epidemiology. In *Comprehensive Textbook of Psychiatry,* vol. 1, ed. H. I. Kaplan and B. J. Sadock, 4th ed., pp. 764–769. Baltimore: Williams & Wilkins.

Weissman, M., and Klerman, G. (1977). Sex differences and the epidemiology of depression. *Archives of General Psychiatry* 34:98–111.

Who's dieting and why? (1978). Chicago: A. C. Nielson.

Women's Bureau, U.S. Department of Labor, (1990). *Facts on Working Women,* September, Publication No. 90-2. Washington, DC: U.S. Government Printing Office.

Wooley, G. (1991). Beware the well-intentioned therapist. *The Family Therapy Networker,* January/February, p. 30.

Yalom, I. D. (1989). *Love's Executioner and Other Tales of Psychotherapy.* New York: Basic Books.

CREDITS

The author gratefully acknowledges permission to quote from the following sources:

Excerpts from "Early and Later Determinants of Lesbian Choice," by Ruth-Jean Eisenbud in *Psychoanalytic Review*, vol. 69, no. 1. Copyright © 1982 by the National Psychological Association for Psychoanalysis. Reprinted by permission of Guilford Publications, Inc.

Excerpts from *In a Different Voice*, by Carol Gilligan. Copyright © 1982 by Carol Gilligan. Reprinted by permission of Harvard University Press.

Excerpts from "Gender Based Countertransference of Female Therapists in the Psychotherapy of Women," by Teresa Bernardez, and from "An Integration of Feminist and Psychoanalytic Theory," by Charlotte Prozan in *Woman, Power, and Therapy: Issues for Women*, edited by Marjorie Braude. Copyright © 1988 by Haworth Press. Reprinted by permission of Haworth Press.

Excerpts from *The Courage to Heal*, by Ellen Bass and Laura Davis. Copyright © 1988 by Ellen Bass and Laura Davis. Reprinted by permission of HarperCollins Publishers Inc.

Excerpts from *The Battered Woman*, by Lenore Walker. Copyright © by Lenore E. Walker. Reprinted by permission of HarperCollins Publishers Inc.

Excerpts from "Wife Abuse: Culture as Destiny," by Elaine Carmen, in *The Woman Patient*, vol. 3, edited by M. T. Notman and C. C. Nadelson. Copyright © 1982. Reprinted by permission of Plenum Press.

Excerpts from *Female Perversions*, by Louise Kaplan. Copyright © 1991 by Louise

INDEX